Joseph Jacobs, James Howell

The Familiar Letters of James Howell

Epistolae Ho-Elianae

Joseph Jacobs, James Howell

The Familiar Letters of James Howell
Epistolae Ho-Elianae

ISBN/EAN: 9783744766456

Printed in Europe, USA, Canada, Australia, Japan

Cover: Foto ©Thomas Meinert / pixelio.de

More available books at **www.hansebooks.com**

EPISTOLÆ HO-ELIANÆ

The

Familiar Letters

of

James Howell

Historiographer Royal to Charles II.

EDITED, ANNOTATED, AND INDEXED

BY

JOSEPH JACOBS

CORRESPONDING MEMBER OF THE ROYAL ACADEMY OF HISTORY, MADRID

BOOKS II.–IV., NOTES, INDEX

LONDON : PUBLISHED BY DAVID NUTT IN THE STRAND

MDCCCXCII

Familiar Letters.

BOOK II.

I.

To Master Tho. Adams.

Sir,

 PRAY stir nimbly in the business you imparted to me last, and let it not languish; you know how much it concerns your Credit, and the conveniency of a Friend who deserves so well of you : I fear you will meet with divers obstacles in the way, which, if you cannot remove, you must overcome. A lukewarm irresolute Man did never anything well, every thought entangles him ; therefore you must pursue the point of your Design with heat, and set all wheels a-going : 'Tis a true badge of a generous nature, being once embark'd in a business, to hoise up, and spread every sail, *Main, misen, sprit,* and *top-sail ;* by that means he will sooner arrive at his Port. If the winds be so cross, and that there be such a fate in the thing, that it can take no effect, yet you shall have wherewith to satisfy an honest mind, that you left nothing unattempted to compass it ; for in the conduct of human affairs 'tis a rule, That a good Conscience hath always within doors enough to reward itself, tho' the success fall not out according to the merit of the endeavour.

I

I was, according to your desire, to visit the late new married Couple more than once ; and to tell you true, I never saw such a disparity between two that were made one flesh in all my life : he handsome outwardly, but of odd conditions ; she excellently qualified, but hard-favour'd : so that the one may be compar'd to a cloth of Tissue Doublet, cut upon coarse Canvas ; the other to a Buckram Petticoat lin'd with Sattin. I think *Clotho* had her fingers smutted in snuffing the Candle, when she begun to spin the thread of her life, and *Lachesis* frown'd in twisting it up ; but *Aglaia*, with the rest of the *Graces*, were in a good humour, when they form'd her inner-parts. A blind Man is fittest to hear her sing ; one would take delight to see her dance if mask'd, and it would please you to discourse with her in the dark, for there she is best company, if your imagination can forbear to run upon her face. When you marry, I wish you such an inside of a Wife ; but from such an outward Phisnomy the Lord deliver you, and—Your faithful Friend to serve you,   J. H.

Westm., 25 *Aug.* 1633.

II.

To Mr. B. J.

F. B. The Fangs of a Bear, and the Tusks of a wild Boar, do not bite worse, and make deeper gashes, than a Goose-quill, sometimes ; no, not the Badger himself, who is said to be so tenacious of his bite, that he will not give over his hold till he feels his Teeth meet and the Bone crack. Your quill hath prov'd so to Mr. *Jones ;* but the Pen wherewith you have so gash'd him, it seems, was made rather of a Porcupine than a Goose-quill, it is so keen and firm. You know,

Anser, Apis, Vitulus, Populos & Regna gubernant.

The Goose, the Bee, and the Calf (meaning Wax, Parchment, and the Pen) rule the World ; but, of the three,

the

the Pen is the most predominant. I know you have a com-
manding one, but you must not let it tyrannize in that
manner, as you have done lately. Some give out there was
a hair in't, or that your Ink was too thick with Gall, else it
would not have so bespatter'd and shaken the Reputation of
a Royal Architect; for Reputation, you know, is like a fair
Structure, long time a rearing, but quickly ruin'd. If your
spirit will not let you retract, yet you shall do well to repress
any more Copies of the Satire; for, to deal plainly with you,
you have lost some ground at Court by it; and, as I hear
from a good hand, the King, who hath so great a Judgment
in Poetry (as in all other things else), is not well pleas'd
therewith. Dispense with this freedom of—Your respectful
S. and Servitor, J. H.

Westm., 3 *July* 1635.

III.

To D. C., Esq.

SIR,

I N my last, I writ to you that *Ch. Mor.* was dead (I meant
in a *moral* sense). He is now alive again, for he hath
abjur'd that Club, which was used to knock him in the head
so often, and drown him commonly once a day. I discover
divers symptoms of Regeneration in him, for he rails bitterly against *Bacchus*, and swears there's a Devil in every
berry of his Grape; therefore he resolves hereafter, tho' he
may dabble a little sometimes, he will be never drown'd
again. You know *Kit* hath a poetick fancy, and no unhappy
one, as you find by his Compositions; you know also, that
Poets have large Souls, they have sociable free generous
Spirits, and there are few who use to drink of *Helicon's*
Waters, but they love to mingle it with some of *Lyæus*
Liquor, to heighten their Spirits. There's no Creature that's
kneaded of Clay but hath its Frailties, Extravagancies, and
Excesses, some way or other; for you must not think that
Man can be better out of Paradise than he was within't:
Nemo sine crimine. He that censures the good Fellow,
commonly

commonly makes no conscience of Gluttony, and gormandizing at home; and I believe more Men do dig their Graves with their Teeth than with the Tankard. They who tax others of Vanity and Pride, have commonly that sordid Vice of Covetousness attends them; and he who traduceth others of being a Servant to Ladies, doth baser things. We are no Angels upon Earth, but we are transported with some infirmity or other; and 'twill be so while these frail, flexible humours reign within us : While we have Sluices of warm blood running thro' our Veins, there must be ofttimes some irregular motions in us.

This, as I conceive, is the *Black-bean* which the *Turks' Alchoran* speaks of; when they feign, that *Mahomet* being asleep among the Mountains of the Moon, two Angels descended, and ripping his Breast, they took his Heart and washed it in Snow, and after pull'd out a black Bean, which was the Portion of the Devil; and so replac'd the Heart.

In your next, you shall do well to congratulate his Resurrection, or Regeneration, or rather Emergency from that Course he was plunged in formerly; you know it as well as I; and truly I believe he will grow newer and newer every day. We find that a stumble makes one take firmer footing; and the base Suds which Vice useth to leave behind it, makes Virtue afterwards far more gustful: No Knowledge is like that of Contraries. *Kit* hath now o'ercome himself, therefore I think he will be too hard for the Devil hereafter. I pray hold on your Resolution to be here the next Term, that we may tattle a little of *Tom Thumb*, mine Host of *Andover*, or some such matters. So I am—Your most affectionate Servitor,   J. H.

Westm., 15 *Aug.* 1636.

IV.

To T. D., *Esq.*

SIR,

I HAD yours lately by a safe hand : wherein I find you open to me all the Boxes of your Breast : I perceive you

you are sore hurt, and whereas all other Creatures run away from the Instrument and Hand that wounds them, you seem to make more and more towards both. I confess, such is the nature of *Love*, and which is worse, the nature of Women is such, that like shadows, the more you follow them, the faster they fly from you. Nay, some Females are of that odd humour, that to feed their Pride, they will famish Affection: they will starve those natural Passions, which are owing from them to Man. I confess Coyness becomes some Beauties, if handsomely acted; a Frown upon some Faces penetrates more, and makes deeper Impression than the fawning and soft glances of a mincing Smile: yet if this Coyness and these Frowns savour of Pride, they are odious; and 'tis a Rule, that where this kind of Pride inhabits, Honour sits not long Porter at the Gate. There are some Beauties so strong, that they are Leaguer-proof, they are so barricado'd, that no Battery, no Petard, or any kind of Engine, Sapping, or Mining, can do good upon them. There are others that are tenable a good while, and will endure the brunt of a Siege, but will incline to parley at last; and you know, that Fort and Female which begins to parley is half won: for my part, I think of Beauties as *Philip* King of *Macedon* thought of Cities, there is none so inexpugnable but an Ass laden with Gold may enter into them; you know what the *Spaniard* saith, *Davidas quebrantan peñas: Presents can rend rocks:* Pearls and golden Bullets may do much upon the impregnablest Beauty that is: It must be partly your way. I remember a great Lord of this Land sent a Puppy with a rich Collar of Diamonds to a rare *French* Lady, Madam St. *L.*, that had come over hither with an Ambassador; she took the Dog, but return'd the Collar: I will tell you what effect it wrought afterwards. 'Tis a powerful Sex; they were too strong for the *First*, the *Strongest* and *Wisest* Man that was; they must needs be strong, when *one Hair of a Woman can draw more than a hundred pair of Oxen;* yet for all their strength in point of value, if you will believe the

the *Italian, A Man of Straw is worth a Woman of Gold:*
Therefore if you find the thing perverse, rather than to
undervalue your Sex (your Manhood) retire handsomely;
for there is as much Honour to be won at a handsome
Retreat as at a hot Onset, it being the difficultest piece
of War. By this Retreat you will get a greater Victory
than you are aware of: For thereby you will overcome
yourself, which is the greatest Conquest that can be.
Without seeking abroad, we have Enemies enough within
doors to practise our Valour upon; we have tumultuary and
rebellious Passions, with whole Hosts of Humours within
us: He who can discomfit them is the greatest Captain,
and may defy the Devil. I pray recollect yourself, and
think on this Advice of—Your true and most affectionate
Servitor,   J. H.

  Westm., 4 *Dec.* 1637.

V.

To G. G., *Esq.; at* Rome.

SIR,

I HAVE more thanks to give you than can be folded up
   in this narrow Paper, tho' it were all writ in the closest
kind of Stenography, for the rich and accurate Account
you please to give me of that renown'd City wherein you
now sojourn. I find you have most judiciously pried into
all matters, both civil and clerical, especially the latter, by
observing the Poverty and Penances of the Fryer, the Policy
and Power of the Jesuit, the Pomp of the Prelate and
Cardinal. Had it not been for the two first, I believe the
two last, and that See, had been at a low ebb by this time;
for the Learning, the prudential State, Knowledge, and Aus-
terity of the one, and the venerable Opinion the People have
of the abstemious and rigid condition of the other, 'specially
of the *Mendicants*, seem to make some compensation for the
Lux and Magnificence of the two last: Besides, they are
more beholden to the *Protestant* than they are aware of;
for unless he had risen up about the latter end of this last
                                                          Century

Century of years, which made them more circumspect and
wary of their Ways, Life, and Actions, to what an intolerable high excess that Court had come to by this time you
may easily conjecture. But out of my small Reading I have
observ'd, that no Age, ever since *Gregory the Great,* hath
pass'd, wherein some or other hath not repin'd and murmur'd
at the Pontifical Pomp of that Court: Yet, for my part, I
have been always so charitable, as to think that the Religion
of *Rome,* and the Court of *Rome,* were different Things.
The counterbuff that happen'd 'twixt *Leo* X. and *Francis* I.
of *France* is very remarkable; who being both met at
Bolonia, the King seem'd to give a light touch at the Pope's
Pomp, saying, *'Twas not used to be so in former time. It
may be so,* said *Leo, but it was then when Kings kept Sheep*
(as we read in the Old Testament). *No,* the King reply'd,
I speak of times under the Gospel. Then rejoin'd the Pope,
'Twas then when Kings did visit Hospitals; hinting by those
words at St. *Lewis,* who us'd oft to do so. It is memorable
what is recorded in the Life of *Robert Grosthed,* Bishop of *Lincoln,* who lived in the time of one of the *Leos,* that he fear'd
the same Sin would overthrow *Leo* as overthrew *Lucifer.*

For news hence, I know none of your Friends, but are as
well as you left them, *Hombres y Hembras:* You are fresh
and very frequent in their memory, and mention'd with a
thousand good wishes and benedictions. Among others,
you have a large room in the memory of my Lady *Elizabeth
Cary;* and I do not think all *Rome* can afford you a fairer
Lodging. I pray be cautious of your Carriage under that
Meridian ; it is a searching (inquisitive) Air : You have
two Eyes and two Ears, but one Tongue ; you know my
meaning. This last you must imprison (as Nature hath
already done with a double Fence of Teeth and Lips), or
else she may imprison you, according to our Countryman
Mr. *Hoskin's* Advice, when he was in the *Tower :*

Vincula da linguæ, vel tibi lingua dabit.

Have a care of your of Health, take heed of the Syrens,
of

of excess in Fruit, and be sure to mingle your Wine well with Water. No more now, but that in the large Catalogue of Friends you have left behind here, there's none who is more mindful of you than—Your most affectionate and faithful Servitor,   J. H.

VI.

To Dr. T. P.

SIR,

I HAD yours of the 10th current, wherein you writ me Tidings of our Friend *Tom D.*, and what his desires tend to. In my opinion they are somewhat extravagant. I have read of one, that loving Honey more than ordinary, seem'd to complain against Nature, that she made not a *Bee* as big as a *Bull*, that we might have it in greater plenty; another who was much given to Fruit, wish'd the Pears and Plums were as big as Pumpions. These were but silly vulgar wishes; for if a *Bee* were as big as a *Bull*, it must have a Sting proportionable: and what mischief do you think such things will do, when we can hardly endure the Sting of that small infected Animal, as now it is? And if Pears and Plums were as big as Pumpions, 'twere dangerous walking in an Orchard about the Autumnal Equinoctial, at which time they are in their full maturity, for fear of being knock'd in the head. Nature, the Handmaid of God Almighty, doth nothing but with good advice, if we make researches into the true reason of things: you know what answer the Fox gave the Ape, when he would have borrow'd part of his Tail to cover his Posteriors.

The wishes you writ that *T. D.* lately made, were almost as extravagant in civil matters as the aforemention'd were in natural : for if he were partaker of them, they would draw more inconveniencies upon him than benefit, being nothing sortable either to his disposition or breeding, and for other reasons besides, which I will reserve till my coming up; and I pray let him know so much from me, with my Commendations.

mendations. So I rest—Yours in the perfectest degree of Friendship, J. H.

Westm., 5 *Sept.* 1640.

VII.

To Mr. T. B., Merchant in Sevil.

SIR,

THO' I have my share of infirmities as much as another Man; Yet I like my own nature in one thing, that requitals to me are as sweet as revenges to an *Italian.* I thank my Stars, I find myself far proner to return a courtesy than to resent an Injury: This made me most gladly apprehend the late occasion of serving you (notwithstanding the hard measure I have receiv'd from your Brother), and to make you some returns of those frequent favours I receiv'd from you in *Spain*, I have ta'en away (as you may perceive by the inclosed Papers) the *Weights* that hung to that great business in this Court; it concerns you now to put *Wings* to it in that, and I believe you will quickly obtain, what useth to be first in intention, tho' last in execution, I mean your main end. I heartily wish the thing may be prosperous to you, and that you may take as much pleasure in the fruition of it, as I did in following of it for you, because I love you dearly well, and desire you so much happiness, that you may have nothing but Heaven to wish for: In which desire, I rest—Your constant true Friend to serve you, J. H.

White-Hall, 3 *May* 1633.

VIII.

To Doctor B.

SIR,

WHEREAS upon the large theorical discourse and bandyings of opinions we had lately at *Gresham-College*, you desir'd I should couch in writing what I observ'd abroad of the Extent and Amplitude of the *Christian* Commonwealth, in reference to other Religions; I obtain'd obtain'd leave of myself to put pen to paper, rather to obey you, than oblige you with anything that may add to your Judgment, or enrich that rare Knowledge I find you have already treasur'd up: But I must begin with the fulfilling of your desire in a preambular way, for the Subject admits it.

'Tis a Principle all the Earth over, except among *Atheists*, that *omne verum est à Deo, omne falsum est à Diabolo, & omnis error ab homine: All Truth is from God, all Falshood from the Devil, and all Error from Man.* The last goes always under the Vizard of the first, but the second confronts Truth to the face, and stands in open defiance of her: *Error* and *Sin* are contemporary; when one crept first in at the Foredoor, the other came in at the Postern. This made *Trismegistus*, one of the great Lords of Reason, to give this character of Man, *Homo est imaginatio quædam, & imaginatio est supremum mendacium:* Man is nought else but a kind of imagination, and imagination is the greatest lie. *Error* therefore entring into the World with *Sin* among us poor *Adamites*, may be said to spring from the Tree of Knowledge itself, and from the rotten Kernels of that fatal Apple. This, besides the Infirmities that attend the Body, hath brought in perversity of Will, depravation of Mind, and hath cast a kind of Cloud upon all our Intellectuals, that they cannot discern the true Essence of things with that clearness as the Protoplast our first Parent could, but we are involv'd in a mist, and grope, as it were, ever since in the dark, as if Truth were got into some dungeon; or, as the old *Wizard* said, into some deep Pit, which the shallow Apprehension of Men could not fathom. Hence comes it, that the Earth is rent into so many Religions, and those Religions torn into so many Schisms, and various forms of Devotion; as if the heavenly Majesty were delighted as much in Diversities of Worship as in Diversities of Works.

The first Religion that ever was reduc'd to exact Rules and ritual Observances, was that of the *Hebrews*, the ancient People of God, call'd afterwards *Judaism;* the second *Christianity;*

Christianity; the third *Mahometism,* which is the youngest of all Religions. Touching *Paganism,* and heathenish Idolatry, they scarce deserve the name of Religion: But as to the former three, there is this Analogy between them, that they all agree in the first Person of the Trinity, and all his Attributes. What kind of Religion there was before the Flood, it is in vain to make any Researches, there having been no Monuments at all left (besides that little we find in *Moses* and the *Phœnician* Story) but *Seth's* Pillars, and those so defaced, that nothing was legible upon them; tho' *Josephus* saith, that one was extant in his days; as also the Oak under which *Abraham* feasted God Almighty, which was 2000 years after. The Religion (or Cabal) of the *Hebrews* was transferr'd from the Patriarchs to *Moses,* and from him to the Prophets. It was honour'd with the Appearance and Promulgations of God himself, 'specially the better part of it; I mean the Decalogue containing the Ten Commandments, which being most of them moral, and agreeing with the common Notions of Man, are in force all the World over. The *Jews* at this day are divided into three Sects; the first, which is the greatest, are call'd *Talmudists,* in regard that, besides the holy Scriptures, they embrace the *Talmud,* which is stuff'd with the Traditions of their Rabbins and Cacams. The second receive the Scripture alone; the third the Pentateuch only, *viz.,* the five Books of *Moses;* who are call'd *Samaritans.* Now touching what part of the Earth is possess'd by *Jews,* I cannot find they have any at all peculiar to themselves; but in regard of their murmurings, their frequent Idolatries, Defections, and that they crucify'd the Lord of Life, this once select Nation of God, and the Inhabitants of the Land flowing with Milk and Honey, is become now a scorn'd, squander'd People all the Earth over, being ever since incapable of any Coalition or Reducement into one Body Politick. There where they are most without mixture is *Tiberias* in *Palestine,* which *Amurath* gave *Mendez* the *Jew,* whither, and to *Jerusalem,* upon any conveniency, they

2 B   convey

convey the Bones of their dead Friends from all places to
be re-interr'd. They are to be found in all mercantile
Towns and great Marts, both in *Africk*, *Asia*, and *Europe*,
the Dominions of *England*, of the *Spaniard* and *French*
excepted; and as their Persons, so their Profession is despicable, being, for the most part,· but Brokers everywhere.
Among other places, they are allow'd to be in *Rome* herself
near St. *Peter's* Chair; for they advance Trade wheresoever
they come, with their Banks of Money, and so are permitted
as necessary Evils. But put case the whole Nation of the
Jews now living, were united into one collective body, yet
according to the best conjecture, and exactest computation
that I could hear made by the knowingest Men, they would
not be able to people a Country bigger than the Seventeen
Provinces. Those that are dispersed now in *Christendom*,
and *Turkey*, are the Remnants only of the Tribes of *Judah*
and *Benjamin*, with some *Levites* who return'd from *Babylon*
with *Zerubbabel*. The common opinion is, that the other
ten are utterly lost; but they themselves fancy they are in
India a mighty nation, environ'd with stony Rivers, which
always cease to run their course on their Sabbath; from
whence they expect their *Messias*, who shall in the fulness
of time over-run the World with Fire and Sword, and re-
establish them in a temporal glorious Estate. But this
opinion sways most among the *Oriental Jews*, whereas they of
the *West* attend the coming of their *Messias* from *Portugal*;
which Language is more common among them than any
other. And thus much in brief of the *Jews*, as much as I
could digest and comprehend within the compass of this
Paper-sheet; and let it serve for the accomplishment of the
first part of your desire. In my next I shall give you the
best satisfaction I can concerning the extent of *Christianity*
up and down the Globe of the Earth, which I shall speedily
send; for now that I have undertaken such a Task, my Pen
shall not rest till I have finish'd it. So I am—Your most
affectionate ready Servitor,   J. H.

  Westm, 1 *Aug.* 1635.

                                                        IX.

IX.

To Doctor B.

SIR,

HAVING in my last sent you something touching the State of *Judaism* up and down the world, in this you shall receive what extent *Christianity* hath, which is the second Religion in Succession of Time and Truth : A Religion *that makes not Sense so much subject to Reason, as Reason succumbent to Faith.* There is no Religion so harsh and difficult to Flesh and Blood, in regard of divers mysterious Positions it consists of, as the Incarnation, Resurrection, the Trinity, *&c.*, which, as one said, *are Bones to Philosophy, but Milk to Faith.* There is no Religion so purely spiritual, and abstracted from common natural Ideas and sensual Happiness, as the *Christian :* No Religion that excites man more to the love and practice of Virtue, and hatred of Vice ; or that prescribes greater rewards for the one, and punishments for the other : A Religion that in a most miraculous manner did expand herself, and propagate by simplicity, humbleness, and by a mere passive way of fortitude, growing up like the Palm-tree under the heavy weight of Persecution; for never any Religion had more powerful Opposition by various kinds of Punishments, Oppressions, and Tortures, which have been said to have deck'd her with *Rubies* in her very Cradle ; insomuch, that it is granted by her very Enemies, that the *Christian,* in point of passive Valour, hath exceeded all other Nations upon Earth. And 'tis a thing of wonderment, how at her very first growth she flew over the heads of so many interjacent vast Regions into this remote Isle so soon, that her Rays should shine upon the Crown of a British King first of any ; I mean K. *Lucius,* the true *Proto-Christian* King, in the days of *Eleutherius,* at which time she receiv'd her *Propagation :* But for her *Plantation,* she had it long before, by some of the Apostles themselves. Now, as the Christian Religion hath the purest and most abstracted, the hardest and highest spiritual Notions ;

Notions; so it hath been most subject to differences of
Opinions, and distractions of Conscience; the purer the
Wheat is, the more subject 'tis to Tares, and the most
precious Gems to Flaws. The first Bone that the Devil
flung was into the *Eastern* Churches, then 'twixt the *Greek*
and the *Roman;* but it was rather for Jurisdiction and
Power, than for the Fundamentals of Faith; and lately
'twixt *Rome* and the *North-West* Churches. Now the extent of the *Eastern* Church is larger far than that of the
Roman (excluding *America*), which makes some accuse her
as well of Uncharitableness as of Arrogance, that she
should positively damn so many Millions of *Christian* Souls,
who have the same common Symbol of Faith with her,
because they are not within the close of her Fold.

Of those *Eastern* and *South-East* Churches, there are no
less than eleven Sects, whereof the three principallest are
the *Grecian,* the *Jacobite,* and the *Nestorian,* with whom the
rest have some dependance or conformity; and they acknowledge Canonical Obedience either to the Patriarch
of *Constantinople,* of *Alexandria,* of *Jerusalem,* or *Antioch:*
They concur with the *Western* Reformed Churches, in
divers Positions against *Rome,* as in denial of Purgatory;
in rejecting Extreme Unction; and celebrating the Sacrament under both kinds; in admitting their Clergy to
marry; in abhorring the use of massy Statues, and celebrating their Liturgy in the vulgar Language: Among
these, the *Russe* and the *Habassin* Emperors are the greatest;
but the latter is a *Jew* also, from the Girdle downward; for
he is both *Circumcised* and *Christened,* having receiv'd the
one from *Solomon,* and the other from the Apostle St.
Thomas. They observe other Rites of the Levitical Law;
they have the *Cross* in that esteem, that they imprint the
sign of it upon some part of the Child's Body, when he is
baptized; that day they take the holy Sacrament, they spit
not till after Sun-set: And the Emperor, in his Progress, as
soon as he comes in the sight of a Church, lights off his
Camel, and foots it all along, till he loseth the sight of it.

.   Now

Now touching that proportion of Ground that the *Chris-tians* have on the habitable Earth (which is the main of our Task), I find that all *Europe*, with her adjacent Isles, is peopled with *Christians*, except that ruthful Country of *Lapland*, where Idolaters yet inhabit; towards the *East*, also, that Region which lieth 'twixt *Tanais* and *Boristhenes*, the ancient Country of the *Goths*, is possess'd by *Mahometan Tartars :* But in these Territories which the *Turk* hath 'twixt the *Danube* and the Sea, and 'twixt *Ragusa* and *Buda*, *Christians* are intermix'd with *Mahometans :* Yet in this co-habitation *Christians* are computed to make two third parts, at least. For here, and elsewhere, all the while they pay the *Turk* the quarter of their Increase, and a *Sultany* for every Poll, and speak nothing in derogation of the *Alcoran*, they are permitted to enjoy both their Religion and Lives securely. In *Constantinople* herself, under the *Grand Signior's* Nose, they have 20 Churches ; in *Saloniche* (or *Thessalonica*) 30. There are 150 Churches under the Metropolitan of *Philippi*, as many under him of *Athens*, and he of *Corinth* hath about 100 Suffragan Bishops under him.

But in *Africk* (a thing which cannot be too much lamented), that huge Extent of Land that *Christianity* pos-sess'd of old, 'twixt the *Mediterranean* Sea and the Moun-tain *Atlas*, yea, as far as *Egypt*, with the large Region of *Nubia*, the *Turks* have over-mastered. We read of 200 Bishops met in Synods in those Parts, and in that Province where old *Carthage* stood there were 164 Bishops under one *Metropolitan;* but *Mahometism* hath now overspread all thereabout, only the King of *Spain* hath a few Maritime Towns under *Christian* Subjection, as *Septa, Tangier, Oran*, and others. But thro' all the huge Continent of *Africk*, which is estimated to be thrice bigger than *Europe*, there is not one Region entirely *Christian*, but *Habassia* or *Ethiopia :* Besides, there is in *Egypt* a considerable number of them yet sojourning. Now *Habassia*, according to the Itineraries of the observingst Travellers in those Parts, is thought

thought to be, in respective Magnitude, as big as *Germany*, *Spain*, *France*, and *Italy*, conjunctly; an Estimate which comes nearer Truth than that which some make, by stretching it from one *Tropick* to the other, *viz.*, from the Red Sea to the Western Ocean. There are also divers Isles upon the Coast of *Africk* that are coloniz'd with *Christians*; as the *Madera*, the *Canaries*, *Cape Verd*, and St. *Thomas*; but on the East-side there's none but *Zocotora*.

In *Asia* there's the Empire of *Russia*, that's purely *Christian*, and the Mountain *Libanus* in *Syria*; in other Parts they are mingled with *Mahometans*, who exceed them one day more than another in numbers, especially in those Provinces (the more's the pity) where the Gospel was first preach'd, as *Anatolia*, *Armenia*, *Syria*, *Mesopotamia*, *Palestina*, *Chaldea*, *Assyria*, *Persia*, the North of *Arabia*, and South of *India*. In some of these Parts, I say, 'specially in the four first, *Christians* are thick mix'd with *Mahometans*, as also in *East India*, since the *Portugal's* discovery of the passage by the *Cape of Good Hope*, *Christians* by God's goodness have multiplied in considerable Numbers, as likewise in *Goa*, since it was made an Archbishoprick, and a Court of a Viceroy. They speak also of a *Christian* Church in *Quinsay* in *China*, the greatest of all earthly Cities; but in the Islands thereabouts, call'd the *Philippines*, which, they say, are above 1100 in number, in thirty whereof the *Spaniard* hath taken firm footing, *Christianity* hath made a good progress, as also in *Japonia*. In the North-East part of *Asia*, some 400 years since, *Christianity* had taken deep root under the K. of *Tenduck*, but he was utterly overthrown by *Chingis*, one of his own Vassals, who came thereby to be the first Founder of the *Tartarian* Empire: This King of *Tenduc* was the true *Prester John*, not the *Ethiopian* King of the *Habassines*, as *Scaliger* would have it, whose Opinion is as far distant from truth in this point, as the Southermost part of *Africk* from the N.-E. part of *Asia*, or as a *Jacobite* is from a *Nestorian*. Thus far did *Christianity* find entertainment in the old World; touching the new, I mean *America*, which is conjectur'd

jectur'd to equal well near the other three parts in Magnitude, *Spanish* Authors and Merchants (with whom I have
convers'd) make a Report of a marvellous Growth that *Christianity* hath made in the Kingdoms of *Mexico, Peru, Brasil,*
and *Castilia de loro,* as also in the greater Islands adjoining, as
Hispaniola, Cuba, Portorico, and others ; insomuch, that they
write of one ancient Priest who had christen'd himself 700
Savages, some years after the first discovery : But there are
some, who, seeming to be no Friends to *Spain,* report, that
they did not *baptize* half so many as they *butcher'd.*

Thus have you, as compendiously as an Epistle could
make it, an account of that Extension of Ground which
Christians possess upon Earth. My next shall be one of the
Mahometan, wherein I could wish I had not occasion to be
so large as I must be. So I am, Sir—Your respectful and
humble Servant, J. H.

Westm., 9 *Aug.* 1635.

X.

To Doctor B.

SIR,

M Y two former were of *Iudaism* and *Christianity :* I
come now to the *Mahometans,* the modernest of all
Religions, and the most mischievous, and destructive to the
Church of Christ ; for this fatal Sect hath justled her out of
divers large Regions in *Africk,* in *Tartary,* and other places,
and attenuated their Number in *Asia,* which they do wheresoever they come, having a more politick and pernicious
way to do it than by Fire and Faggot : For they having
understood well that the Dust of Martyrs were the thrivingest
Seeds of *Christianity ;* and observ'd, that there reigns naturally in Mankind, being compos'd all of a lump, and carrying
the same stamp, a general kind of Compassion and Sympathy,
which appears most towards them who lay down their Lives,
and postpone all worldly things for the preservation of their
Consciences (and never any died so but he drew followers
after him), therefore the *Turk* goes a more cunning way to
work :

work : He meddles not with Life and Limb, to prevent the
sense of Compassion, which may arise that way; but he
grinds their Faces with Taxes, and makes them incapable
of any Offices, either of Authority, Profit, or Honour; by
which means he renders them despicable to others, and makes
their Lives irksome to themselves. Yet the *Turks* have a
high Opinion of Christ, *That he was a greater Prophet than*
Moses : *That he was the Son of a Virgin, who conceiv'd by*
the smell of a Rose presented to her by Gabriel *the Angel ;*
they believe he never sinn'd ; nay, in their Alcoran *they term*
him the Breath and Word of God; they punish all that
blaspheme him, and no Jew *is capable to be a* Turk, *but he*
must be first an ABDULA, *a* Christian : He must eat Hog's
Flesh, and do other things for three days, then he is made
a *Mahometan,* but by abjuring of Christ to be a greater
Prophet than *Mahomet.*

It is the *Alfange* that ushers in the Faith of *Mahomet*
everywhere, nor can it grow in any place unless it be
planted and sown with Gunpowder intermix'd ; when
planted, there are divers ways of policy to preserve it :
They have their *Alcoran* in one only Language, which is
the *Arabic,* the Mother-Tongue of their Prophet. 'Tis as
bad as Death for any to raise scruples of the *Alcoran ;* thereupon there is a restraint of the Study of Philosophy, and
other Learning, because the Impostures of it may not be
discern'd. The *Mufti* is in as great Reverence among them
as the *Pope* is among the *Romanists;* for they hold it to be
a true Principle in Divinity, *That no one thing preserves and*
improves Religion more than a venerable, high, pious esteem
of the chiefest Ministers. They have no other Guide or
Law both for Temporal and Church-Affairs than the
Alcoran, which they hold to be the *Rule of civil Justice, as*
well as the divine Charter of their Salvation : so that their
Judges are but Expositors of that only ; nor do they trouble
themselves or puzzle the Plaintiff with any moth-eaten
Records, or Precedents to entangle the business; but they
immediately determine it, according to the fresh Circum-
                                                    stances

stances of the Action, *& secundum allegata & probata,* by Witnesses. They have one extraordinary piece of humanity, to be so tender of the rational Soul as not to put *Christian, Jew, Greek,* or any other, to his Oath; in regard that if, for some advantage of gain, or occasion of inconvenience and punishment, any should forswear himself, they hold the Imposers of the Oath to be accessary to the Damnation of the perjur'd Man. By these and divers other reaches of Policy (besides their Arms), not practis'd elsewhere, they conserve that huge bulk of the *Ottoman* Empire, which extends without interruption (the *Hellespont* only between) in one continued piece of Earth, two and thirty hundred miles, from *Buda* in *Hungary* to a good way into *Persia:* By these means they keep also their Religion from distract-ing Opinions, from every vulgar Fancy and Schisms in their Church, for there's nowhere fewer than here; the difference that is, is only with the *Persian,* and that not in Fundamentals of Faith, but for priority of Government, in matters of Religion. This so universal Conformity in their Religion is ascrib'd as to other politic Institutions, so 'specially to the rigorous Inhibition they have of raising Scruples and Disputes of the *Alcoran* under pain of Death, 'specially among the Laity and common People, whose *Zeal commonly is stronger than their Judgment.*

That part of the world where *Mahomet* hath furthest expanded himself is *Asia;* which, as I said before, exceeds *Afric* in greatness, and much more in People: He hath firm footing in *Persia, Tartary* (upon the latter of which the *Musulman* Empire is entail'd), in *Turcomania* itself, and *Arabia,* four mighty Kingdoms; the last of these was the Nest where that Cockatrice Egg was hatched, which hath diffus'd its Poison so far and near, thro' the Veins of so many Regions; all the southerly Coasts of *Asia* from the *Arabian* Bay to the River *Indus* is infected therewith, the vast Kingdom of *Cambaia* and *Bengula;* and about the South part the Inhabitants of *Malabar* have drank of this Poison: Insomuch, that by no wrong computation it may well be

said,

said, that *Mahometism* hath dispersed itself over almost one half of the huge Continent of *Asia*, besides those multitudes of Isles, 'specially seven, *Maldivia*, and *Ceylon*, the Sea-coast of *Sumatra*, *Java*, *Sunda*, the Ports of *Banda*, *Borneo*, with divers others, whereof there are thousands about *Asia*, who have entertain'd the *Alcoran*. In *Europe*, the *Mahometans* possess all the Region 'twixt *Don* and *Meper*, call'd of old *Tanais* and *Boristhenes*, being about the twentieth part of *Europe*; the King of *Poland* dispenseth with some of them in *Lithuania*. Touching *Greece*, *Macedon*, *Thracia*, *Bulgaria*, *Servia*, *Bosnia*, *Epire*, the greatest part of *Hungary* and *Dalmatia*, altho' they be wholly under *Turks* Obedience, yet *Mahometans* scarce make the third part of the Inhabitants. In *Afric* this Contagion is further spread; it hath intoxicated all the shore of *Ethiopia*, as far as *Mosumbic*, which lieth opposite to the midst of *Madagascar*. 'Tis worse with the firm Land of *Afric* on the North and West Parts; for from the *Mediterranean* Sea to the great River *Niper*, and along the Banks of *Nile*, all *Egypt* and *Barbary*, with *Lybia* and the *Negroes*' Country, are tainted and and tann'd with this black Religion.

The vast Propagation of this unhappy Sect may be ascribed first to the sword, for the *Conscience commonly is apt to follow the Conqueror*: then to the loose Reins it gives to all sensual Liberty, as to have eight Wives, and as many Concubines as one can maintain, with the assurance of Venereal Delights in a far higher degree, to succeed after death to the religious Observers of it, as the fruition of beautiful Damsels, with large rolling Eyes, whose Virginity shall renew after every Act; their Youth shall last always with their Lust, and Love shall be satiated with only one, where it shall remain inalienable. They concur with the *Christian* but only in the acknowledgment of one God, and in his Attributes. With the *Jew* they symbolize in many things more, as in Circumcision, in refraining from Swine's Flesh, in detestation of Images, and somewhat in the Quality of future Happiness; which, as was said before, they

they place in Venereal Pleasure, as the *Jew* doth in Feasting and Banquetings: So that neither of their Laws have Punishment enough to deter Mankind from Wickedness and Vice, nor do they promise adequate Rewards for Virtue and Piety: For in the whole *Alcoran,* and thro' all the Writings of *Moses,* there's not a word of Angelical Joys and Eternity. And herein *Christianity* far excels both these Religions, for she placeth future Happiness in spiritual, everlasting and unconceivable Bliss, abstracted from the fading and faint grossness of Sense. The *Jew* and *Turk* also agree in their opinion of Women, whom they hold to be of an inferior Creation to Man; which makes the one to exclude them from the Mosques, and the other from his Synagogues.

Thus far have I rambled thro' the vast *Ottoman* Empire, and taken a cursory survey of *Mahomet's* Religion. In my next I shall take the best view I can of Pagans and Idolaters, with those who go for Atheists: And in this particular this Earth may be said to be worse than Hell itself, and the kingdom of the Devil, in regard there are no *Atheists* there: For the very damned Souls find and feel in the midst of their tortures that there is a God, by his Justice and Punishments; nay, the Prince of darkness himself, and all the Cacodæmons, by an historical faith, believe there is a God, whereunto the Poet alludes very divinely:

Nullus in Inferno est Atheos, ante fuit.

So I very affectionately kiss your hands, and rest—Your faithful ready Servitor,   J. H.

Westm., 17 *Aug.* 1635.

XI.

To Doctor B.

SIR,

HAVING in my three former Letters wash'd my hands of the *Mahometan* and the *Jew,* and attended *Christianity* up and down the Earth; I come now to the *Pagan Idolater,*

Idolater, or *Heathen,* who (the more to be lamented) make the greatest part of Mankind: *Europe* herself, tho' the Beams of the Cross have shin'd upon her above this sixteen Ages, is not free of them; for they possess, to this day, *Lappia, Corelia, Biarmia, Scrifinnia,* and the North parts of *Finmark;* there are also some shreds of them to be found in divers places of *Lithuania* and *Somogitia,* which make a Region nine hundred Miles in Compass.

But in *Afric* their Number is incredible; for from *Cape Blanc,* the most Westerly Point of *Africk,* all Southward to the *Cape of Good Hope,* and thence turning by the back of *Afric* to the *Cape of Mozambric,* all these Coasts being about the one half of the Circumference of *Africk,* are peopled by *Idolaters,* tho' in some places intermix'd with *Mahometans* and *Christians,* as in the Kingdom of *Congo* and *Angola.* But if we survey the inland Territories of *Afric,* between the River of *Nile* and the West Sea of *Ethiopia,* even all that Country from about the North parallel of ten Degrees to the South parallel of six Degrees, all is held by Idolaters; besides, the Kingdom of *Borneo* and a great part of *Nubia* and *Lybia* continue still in their old Paganism: So that by this Account above one half of that immense Continent of *Afric* is peopled by Idolaters. But in *Asia,* which is far more spacious, and more populous than *Afric, Pagans, Idolaters,* and *Gentiles* swarm in great Numbers; for from the River *Pechora* Eastward to the Ocean, and thence Southward to the *Cape of Cincapura,* and from that Point returning Westward by the South Coasts to the Out-lets of the River *Indus,* all that maritime Tract, which makes a good deal more than half the Circumference of *Asia,* is inhabited by Idolaters; so are the Inland Parts. There are two mighty Mountains that traverse all *Asia, Taurus,* and *Imaus;* the first runs from the West to East, the other from North to South, and so quarter and cut that huge Mass of Earth into equal parts; this side those Mountains, most of the people are *Mahometans;* t'other side, they are all Idolaters. And as on the firm Continent

Paganism

Paganism thus reigns, so in many thousand Islands that lie squander'd in the vast Ocean, on the East and South-East of *Asia*, Idolatry o'erspreads all, except in some few Islands that are possess'd by *Spaniards* and *Arabs*.

Lastly, if one take a survey of *America* (as none hath done yet exactly), which is estimated to be as big as all the old Earth ; Idolaters there possess four parts of five. 'Tis true, some years after the first Navigation thither, they were converted daily in great Multitudes ; but afterwards observing the licentious Lives of the Christians, their greediness of Gold, and their Cruelty, they came not in so fast ; which made an *Indian* answer a *Spanish* Fryar, who was discoursing with him of the Joys of Heaven, and how all *Spaniards* went thither after this Life : *Then*, said the *Pagan*, *I do not desire to go thither, if* Spaniards *be there; I had rather go to Hell, to be free of their Company.* America differs from the rest of the Earth in this, that she hath neither *Jew* nor *Mahometan* in her, but *Christians* and *Gentiles* only. There are, besides all those Religions and People before-mentioned, an irregular confus'd Nation in *Europe*, call'd the *Morduits*, which occupy the middle confines betwixt the *Tartars* and the *Russe*, that are mingled in Rites of Religion, with all those that have been fore-spoken : For from the Privy Members upwards they are *Christians*, in regard they admit of Baptism ; from the Navel downward they are *Mahometans* or *Jews*, for they are circumcis'd : and besides, they are given to the Adoration of heathenish Idols. In *Asia* there are the *Cardi*, which inhabit the mountainous Country about *Mozall*, between *Armenia* and *Mesopotamia* ; and the *Druci* in *Syria*, who are demi-*Mahometans* and *Christians*.

Now concerning *Pagans* and heathenish Idolaters, whereof there are innumerable sorts up and down the surface of the Earth ; in my opinion, those are the excusablest kind who adore the Sun and Moon, with the Host of Heaven. And in *Ireland*, the *Kerns* of the Mountains, with some of the *Scotch* Isles, use a fashion of adoring the new Moon to this very day, praying she would leave them in as good Health

Health as she found them: This is not so gross an Idolatry as that of other Heathens; for the Adoration of those glorious celestial Bodies is more excusable than that of Garlick and Onions with the *Egyptian*, who, some think (with the *Sicyonian*), was the ancientest Idolater upon Earth, which he makes thrice older than we do: For *Diodorus Siculus* reports, that the *Egyptian* had a Religion and Kings 18,000 years since: Yet for matter of Philosophy and Science, he had it from the *Chaldean*, he from the *Gymnosophists* and *Brachmans* of *India*; which Country, as she is the next neighbour to the rising Sun, in reference to this side of the Hemisphere, so the beams of Learning did first enlighten her. *Egypt* was the Nurse of that famous *Hermes Trismagistus*, who having no other scale but that of natural Reason, mounted very high towards Heaven; for he hath very many divine Sayings, whereof I think it not impertinent to insert here a few: First, he saith, *That all human sins are venial with the Gods, impiety excepted.* 2. *That goodness belongs to the Gods, piety to Men, revenge and wickedness to the Devils.* 3. *That the Word is* lucens Dei filius, *the bright Son of God,* &c.

From *Egypt* theorical Knowledge came down the *Nile*, and landed at some of the *Greek* Islands; where, 'twixt the 33d, 34th, and the 35th Century of years after the Creation, there flourished all those renowned Philosophers that sway now in our Schools: *Plato* flew highest in divine notions, for some call him another *Moses speaking* Athenian: In one of his Letters to a Friend of his he writes thus, *When I seriously salute thee, I begin my Letter with one God; when otherwise, with many.* His Scholar *Aristotle* commended himself at his death to the *Being of Beings:* And *Socrates* may be said to be a Martyr for the first Person of the *Trinity.* These great Secretaries of Nature, by studying the vast Volume of the World, came by main strength of reason to the knowledge of one Deity, or *primus motor*, and of his Attributes; they found by undeniable consequences that he was *infinite, eternal, ubiquitary, omni-*
                                                                    potent,

potent, and not capable of a definition: Which made the
Philosopher, being commanded by his King to define God,
to ask the respite of a day to meditate thereon, then two,
then four; at last he ingenuously confess'd, that the more
he thought to dive into this mystery, the more he was
ingulph'd in the speculation of it: For the Quiddity and
Essence of the incomprehensible Creator cannot imprint
any formal conception upon the finite Intellect of the
Creature. To this I might refer the Altar which St. *Paul*
found among the *Greeks* with this Inscription, τῷ ἀγνώστῳ
Θέῳ, *To the unknown God.*

From the *Greek* Isles, Philosophy came to *Italy*, thence
to this Western World among the *Druydes*, whereof those
of this Isle were most celebrated; for we read that the
Gauls (now the *French*) came to *Britany* in great numbers
to be instructed by them. The *Romans* were mighty great
Zealots in their Idolatry, and their best Authors affirm,
that they extended their Monarchy so far and near, by a
particular reverence they had of their Gods (which the
Spaniard seems now to imitate), tho' those Gods of theirs
were made of Men, and of good Fellows at first: Besides,
in the course of their conquest, they adopted any strange
Gods to the society of theirs, and brought them solemnly
to *Rome*; and the reason, one saith, was, that they believed
the more Gods they had, the safer they were, a few being
not sufficient to conserve and protect so great an Empire.
The *Roman Gentiles* had their Altars and Sacrifices, their
Archflamins and Vestal Nuns: And it seems the same
genius reigns still in them; for in the primitive Church,
that which the *Pagans* misliked most in *Christianity* was,
that it had not the face and form of a Religion, in regard it
had no Oblations, Altars, and Images; which may be a good
reason why the Sacrifice of the Mass and other Ceremonies
were first instituted to allure the *Gentiles* to *Christianity*.

But to return a little further to our former Subject: In
the condition that Mankind stands now, if the Globe of
the Earth were divided into thirty parts, 'tis thought that
                                                    Idolaters

Idolaters (with horror I speak it) having, as I said before, the one half of *Asia* and *Africk,* both for the inland Country and maritime Coasts, with four parts of five in *America,* inhabit twenty parts of those Regions that are already found out upon Earth. Besides, in the opinion of the knowing and most inquisitive Mathematicians, there is toward the Southern Clime as much Land yet undiscover'd as may equal in dimension the late new World, in regard, as they hold, there must be of necessity such a portion of Earth to balance the Centre on all sides; and 'tis more than probable that the Inhabitants there must be *Pagans.* Of all kind of Idolaters, those are the horridest who adore the *Devil,* whom they call *Tantara,* who appears often to them, 'specially in a Haraucane, tho' he be not visible to others. In some places they worship both God and the Devil; the one, that he may do them good; the other, that he may do them no hurt: the first they call *Tantum,* the other *Squantum.* 'Twere a presumption beyond that of *Lucifer's,* or *Adam's,* for Man to censure the Justice of the Creator in this particular, why he makes daily such innumerable Vessels of dishonour: It is a wiser and safer course far, to sit down in an humble admiration, and cry out, Oh the profound inscrutable Judgments of God! his ways are past finding out: and so to acknowledge with the divine Philosopher, *Quod oculus vespertilionis ad solem, idem est omnis intellectus humanus ad Deum;* what the Eye of a Bat is to the Sun, the same is all human understanding to Godwards.

Now to draw to a conclusion, touching the respective largeness of Christianity and *Mahometism* upon the Earth, I find the first to exceed, taking the new World with the old, considering the spacious Plantations of the *Spaniard* in *America,* the Colonies the *English* have there in *Virginia, New-England,* and *Caribbee-Islands,* with those of the *French* in *Canada,* and of the *Hollander* in *East-India :* nor do I find that there is any Region purely *Mahometan* without Intermixtures, as Christianity hath many : which makes me to be of a differing opinion to that Gentleman who

who held, that Christianity added little to the general Religion of Mankind.

Now, touching the latitude of Christian Faith in reference to the differing Professors thereof, as in my former I shew'd that the Eastern Churches were more spacious than the *Latin* or *Roman* (excepting the two *Indies*), so they who have fallen off from her in the Western Parts are not so far inferior to her in *Europe* as some would make one believe; which will appear, if we cast them in counterbalance.

Among *Roman* Catholicks, there is the Emperor, and in him the King of *Hungary;* the three Kings of *Spain, France,* and *Poland; Italy;* the Dukes of *Savoy, Bavaria,* and *Lorain;* the three spiritual Electors, with some few more. Touching them who have renounc'd all obedience to *Rome,* there are the three Kings of *Great-Britain, Denmark,* and *Swethland,* the Dukes of *Saxon, Holstein,* and *Wittemberg;* the Marquis of *Brandenberg,* and *Baden,* the Landgrave of *Hesse,* most of the *Hansiatic* Towns, which are eighty-eight in number, some whereof are equal to Republiques; the (almost) seven Provinces the *Hollander* hath; the five Cantons of *Swiss* and *Geneva;* they of *France,* who are reputed the fifth part of the Kingdom; the Prince of *Transylvania;* they of *Hungary,* and of the large Kingdom of *Bohemia,* of the Marquisates of *Lusatia, Moravia,* and the Dukedom of *Silesia;* as also they have the huge Kingdom of *Poland,* wherein Protestants are diffus'd thro' all quarters in great numbers, having in every Province their publick Churches and Congregations orderly severed and bounded with Dioceses, whence are sent some of the chiefest and most principal Men of worth to their General Synods: For altho' there are divers sorts of these *Polonian Protestants,* some embracing the *Waldensian* or the *Bohemic,* others the *Augustan,* and some the *Helvetian* Confession; yet they all concur in opposition to the *Roman* Church; as also they of the *Anglican, Scotican, Gallic, Argentine, Saxonick, Wirtinbergick, Palatin,* and

2 C   *Belgick*

Belgick Confessions. They also harmoniously symbolize in the principal Articles of Faith, and which mainly concern eternal Salvation; as in the infallible Verity and full Sufficiency of the Scriptures, Divine Essence, and Unity of the Everlasting Godhead, the Sacred Trinity of the Three Glorious Persons, the Blessed Incarnation of Christ, the Omnipotent Providence of God, the Absolute Supreme Head of the Church, Christ himself, Justification by Faith thro' his Merits; and touching the nature of lively Faith, Repentance, Regeneration, and Sanctification, the difference between the Law and the Gospel, touching Free-will, Sin, and good Works, the Sacraments, their number, use, and efficacy; the Marks of the Church, the Resurrection, and State of Souls deceased. It may seem a rambling wild speech at first view, of one who said, That to make one a complete Christian, he must have the *works of a Papist, the words of a Puritan, and the faith of a Protestant;* yet this wish, if well expounded, may bear a good sense, which were unfitting for me to give, you being better able to put a gloss upon it yourself.

Thus, learned Sir, have I exercised my Pen, according to my small proportion of knowledge, and conversation with Books, Men, and Maps, to obey your desire : tho' in comparison of your spacious Literature, I have held all this while but a candle to the Sun, yet by the light of this small candle you may see how ready I am to show myself—Your very humble and affectionate Servitor, J. H.

Westm., 25 *Aug.* 1635.

XII.

To Mr. T. W.

SIR,

I AM heartily glad you have prevail'd so far with my Lady your Mother, as to have leave to travel a-while ; and now that you are bound for *France* and *Italy*, let me give you this caution, to take *heed of a speedy Friend in the first,*

first, and of a slow Enemy in the second. The courtesies of an *Italian*, if you make him jealous of you, are dangerous, and so are his Compliments : He will tell you that he kisseth your hand a thousand times over, when he wisheth them both cut off.

The *French* are a free and debonair accostable People, both Men and Women. Among the one, at first entrance, one may have Acquaintance, and at first Acquaintance one may have Entrance; for the other, whereas the old rule was, that there could be no true Friendship without commessation of a bushel of salt, one may have enough there before he eat a spoonful with them. I like that Friendship, *which by soft gentle pauses steals upon the affection, and grows mellow with time*, by reciprocal offices and trials of Love : That Friendship is like to last long, and never to shrink in the wetting.

So, hoping to enjoy you before you go, and to give you a friendly Foy, I rest—Your most affectionate Servitor,

J. H.

Westm., 28 *Feb.* 1634.

XIII.

To Sir Tho. Hawk, *Knight.*

SIR,

I WAS invited yesternight to a solemn Supper, by *B. J.*, where you were deeply remember'd ; there was good company, excellent cheer, choice wines, and jovial welcome : One thing interven'd, which almost spoil'd the relish of the rest, that *B.* began to engross all the discourse, to vapour extremely of himself, and, by vilifying others, to magnify his own *Muse. T. Ca.* buzz'd me in the ear, that tho' *Ben.* had barrell'd up a great deal of knowledge, yet it seems he had not read the *Ethiques*, which, among other precepts of Morality, forbid self-commendation, declaring it to be an ill-favour'd solecism in good manners. It made me think upon the Lady (not very young) who having a good while given her guests neat entertainment, a Capon being

being brought upon the Table, instead of a spoon she took
a mouthful of Claret, and spouted it into the poop of the
hollow bird; such an accident happen'd in this entertainment, you know ———— *Proprio laus sordet in ore;* be a
Man's breath ever so sweet, yet it makes one's praise stink,
if he makes his own mouth the Conduit-pipe of it. But for
my part, I am content to dispense with the *Roman* infirmity
of *B.* now that time hath snowed upon his *pericranium.*
You know *Ovid*, and (your) *Horace* were subject to this
humour, the first bursting out into

Jamq ; opus exegi, quod nec Jovis ira, nec ignis, &c.

The other into

Exegi monumentum ære perennius, &c.

As also *Cicero*, while he forced himself into this Hexameter : *O fortunatam natam, me consule Romam !* There
is another reason that excuseth *B.*, which is, that if one be
allowed to love the natural issue of his Body, why not that
of the Brain, which is of a spiritual and more noble extraction ? I preserve your Manuscripts safe for you till you
return to *London ;* what news the times afford, this Bearer
will impart to you. So I am, Sir—Your very humble and
most faithful Servitor,   J. H.

Westm., 5 *Apr.* 1636.

XIV.

To my Cousin, Mr. I. P., *at* Gravesend.

COUSIN,

G OD send you a good passage to *Holland,* and the world
to your mind when you are there. Now that you
intend to trail a Pike, and make profession of Arms, let
me give you this caveat, that nothing must be more precious
to you than your reputation. As I know you have a spirit
not to receive wrong, so you must be careful not to offer
any, for the one is as base as the other; your pulse will be
quickly felt, and trial made what metal you are made of
after your coming. If you get but once handsomely off,
                                                            you

you are made ever after; for you will be free from all baffles and affronts. *He that hath once got the fame of an early riser, may sleep till noon.* Therefore be wondrous wary of your first comportments; get once a good name, and be very tender of it afterwards, for 'tis like the *Venice-glass, quickly crack'd, never to be mended, patch'd it may be.* To this purpose take along with you this Fable: It happen'd that *Fire, Water,* and *Fame* went to travel together (as you are going now); they consulted, that if they lost one another, how they might be retriev'd and meet again: *Fire* said, Where you see smoke, there you shall find me: *Water* said, Where you see marsh and moorish low Ground, there you shall find me; but *Fame* said, Take heed how you lose me, for if you do, you will run a great hazard never to meet me again, there's no retrieving of me.

It imports you also to conform yourself to your Commanders, and so you may more confidently demand obedience, when you come to command yourself, as I doubt not but you may do in a small time. The *Hoghen Moghen* are very exact in their polemical Government; their pay is sure, tho' small, 4s. *a week being too little a hire,* as one said, *to kill men.* At your return I hope you will give a better account of your doings than he who, being ask'd what exploits he had done in the *Low-Countries,* answer'd, That he had cut off a *Spaniard's* legs: reply being made, that that was no great matter, it had been something if he had cut off his head; *O,* said he, *you must consider his head was off before.* Excuse me that I take my leave of you so pleasantly, but I know you will take anything in good part from him who is so much—Your truly affectionate Cousin,   J. H.

Westm., 3 *Aug.* 1634.

XV.

To Cap. B.

MUCH ENDEARED SIR,

THERE is a true saying, that the Spectator oft-times sees more than the Gamester; I find that you have

a

a very hazardous Game in hand, therefore give it up, and do not vie a farthing upon't. Tho' you be already imbarqued, yet there's time enough to strike sail, and make again to the Port, otherwise 'tis no hard matter to be a Prophet what will become of you; there be so many ill-favour'd Quicksands and Rocks in the way (as I have it from a good hand) that one may easily take a prospect of your Shipwrack if you go on : therefore desist, as you regard your own safety, and the seasonable advice of your

J. H.

Westm., 1 *May* 1635.

XVI.

To Mr. Thomas W., *at his Chambers in the* Temple.

SIR,

YOU have much streigthtned that knot of love which hath been so long tied between us, by those choice Manuscripts you sent me lately, among which I find divers rare pieces; but that which afforded me most entertainment in those Miscellanies, was Dr. *Henry King's* Poems, wherein I find not only heat and strength, but also an exact concinnity and evenness of fancy: they are a choice race of Brothers, and it seems the same Genius diffuseth itself also among the Sisters. It was my hap to be lately where Mrs. *A. K.* was, and having a Paper of Verses in her hand I got it from her; they were an Epitaph, and an Anagram, of her own composure and writing; which took me so far, that the next morning before I was up, my rambling fancy fell upon these Lines:

For the admitting of Mrs. *Ann King* to be the Tenth Muse.

Ladies of Helicon, *do not repine*
I add one more unto your number Nine ;
To make it even, I among you bring
Βάσιλ. A.   *No meaner than the Daughter of a* King :
Anna King.   *Fair* Basil-Anna : *quickly pass your Voice,*
I know Apollo *will approve the choice,*

And

And gladly her install; for I could name
Some of less merit, Goddesses became.

F. C. soars higher and higher every day in pursuance of his *Platonic* Love; but *T. Man* is out with his, you know whom; he is fallen into that averseness to her, that he swears he had rather see a Basilisk than her. This shews, that the sweetest Wines may turn to the tartest vinegar. No more till we meet.—Yours inviolably,   J. H.

Westm., 3 *Feb.* 1637.

XVII.
To the Lord C.

MY LORD,

THERE are two sayings which are father'd upon Secre-
tary *Walsingham* and Secretary *Cecil*, a pair of the best-weigh'd Statesmen this Island hath bred: one was us'd to say at the Council-Table, *My Lords, stay a little, and we shall make an end the sooner;* the other would oft-times speak of himself, *It shall never be said of me, that I will defer till to-morrow what I can do to-day.* At first view these sayings seem'd to clash with one another, and to be dia-metrically opposite; but being rightly understood, they may be very well reconcil'd. Touching the first, 'tis true, *that haste and choler are enemies to all great actions;* for as it is a Principle in Chymistry, that *omnis festinatio est à Diabolo,* all haste comes from Hell, so in the consultations, contriv-ings, and conduct of any business of State, all rashness and precipitation comes from an ill spirit. There cannot be a better Pattern for a grave and considerate way of delibera-tion, than the antient Course of our High Court of Parlia-ment, who, when a Law is to be made, which concerns the welfare of so many thousands of men, after a mature debate and long discussion of the Point beforehand, cause the Bill to be read solemnly three times in the House, ere it be trans-mitted to the Lords; and there also 'tis so many times can-vass'd, and then presented to the Prince: That which must stand for Law, must be long stood upon, because it imposeth

an

an universal obedience, and is like to be everlasting; according to the *Ciceronian* maxim, *Deliberandum est diu quod statuendum est semel.* Such a kind of cunctation, advisedness, and procrastination is allowable also in all Councils of State and War ; for the Day following may be able commonly to be a master to the Day past, such a world of contingencies human actions are subject to. Yet, under favour, I believe this first saying to be meant of matters while they are in agitation, and upon the anvil ; but when they have receiv'd form, and are resolv'd upon, I believe then, nothing is so advantageous as speed. And at this, I am of opinion, the second saying aims at : for when the weights that use to hang to all great businesses are taken away, 'tis good then to put wings upon them, and to take the ball before the bound ; for Expedition is the life of Action, otherwise Time may show his bald *occiput*, and shake his posteriors at them in derision. Among other Nations, the *Spaniard* is observ'd to have much phlegm, and to be most dilatory in his proceedings, yet they who have pried narrowly into the sequel and success of his actions, do find that this gravity, reservedness, and tergiversation of his have turn'd rather to his prejudice than advantage, take one time with another. The two last matrimonial Treaties we had with him continu'd long ; the first, 'twixt *Ferdinand* and *Henry* VII. for *Catherine* of *Arragon* seven years ; that 'twixt King *James* and the now *Philip* IV. for *Mary* of *Austria* lasted eleven years, (and seven and eleven's eighteen) : the first took effect for Pr. *Arthur*, the late miscarry'd for Pr. *Charles*, and the *Spaniard* may thank himself and his own slow pace for it ; for had he mended his pace to perfect the work, I believe his Monarchy had not receiv'd so many ill-favoured shocks since. The late revolt of *Portugal* was foreseen, and might have been prevented, if the *Spaniard* had not been too slow in his purpose to have sent the Duke of *Braganza* out of the way upon some employment, as was projected.

Now will I reconcile the former sayings of those two renown'd Secretaries, with the gallant comparison of *Charles* the

the Emperor (and he was of a more temperate mould than a *Spaniard*, being a *Fleming* born) ; he was us'd to say, that while any great business of State was yet in consultation, we should observe the motion of *Saturn*, which is plumeous, long, and heavy ; but when it is once absolutely resolv'd upon, then we should observe the motion of *Mercury*, the nimblest of all the Planets : *Ubi desinit Saturnus, ibi incipiat Mercurius.* Whereto I will add, that we should imitate the Mulberry, which of all Trees casts out her buds the latest, for she doth it not till all the cold weather be past, and then she is sure they cannot be nipped ; but then she shoots them all out

Quodā cum ⎫
strepitu as ⎬
Pliny saith ⎭

in one night : so tho' she be one way the slowest, she is another way the nimblest of trees.

Thus have I obey'd your Lordship's command in expounding the sense of these two sayings, according to my mean apprehension ; but this exposition relates only to publick affairs and political negotiations, wherein your Lordship is so excellently vers'd. I shall most willingly conform to any other injunctions of your Lordship's, and esteem them always as favours, while I am   J. H.

Westm., 5 *Sept.* 1633.

XVIII.

To Sir I. Browne, *Knight.*

SIR,

ONE would think, that the utter falling off of *Catalonia* and *Portugal* in so short a compass of time should much lessen the *Spaniard*, the People of both these Kingdoms being from subjects become enemies against him, and in actual hostility : without doubt it hath done so, yet not so much as the world imagines. 'Tis true, in point of regal power and divers brave subordinate Commands for his Servants, he is a great deal lessen'd thereby, but tho' he be less powerful, he is not a penny the poorer thereby ; for there

comes

comes not a farthing less every year into his Exchequer, in regard that those Countries were rather a charge than benefit to him; all their Revenue being drunk up in Pensions, and Payments of Officers and Garisons; for if the King of *Spain* had lost all except the *West-Indies,* and all *Spain* except *Castile* herself, it would little diminish his Treasury. Touching *Catalonia* and *Portugal,* 'specially the latter, 'tis true, they were mighty Members of the *Castilian* Monarchy; but I believe they will sooner want *Castile* than *Castile* them, because she fill'd them with Treasure: now that *Barcelona* and *Lisbon* hath shaken hands with *Sevill,* I do not think that either of them hath the tithe of that Treasure they had before; in regard the one was the *Scale* whereby the King of *Spain* sent his Money to *Italy;* the other, because all her *East-India* commodities were barter'd commonly in *Andalusia* and elsewhere for *Bullion.* *Catalonia* is fed with money from *France,* but for *Portugal,* she hath little or none; therefore I do not see how she could support a war long to any purpose if *Castile* were quiet, unless soldiers would be contented to take *Cloves* and *Pepper-corns* for *Patacoons* and *Pistoles.* You know Money is the sinew and soul of War. This makes me think on that blunt answer which Capt. *Talbot* return'd *Henry* VIII. from *Calais,* who having receiv'd special command from the King to erect a new Fort at the Water-gate, and to see the Town well fortify'd, sent him word, *that he could neither fortify nor fiftify without Money.* There is no news at all stirring here now, and I am of the *Italian's* mind that said, *Nulla nuova, buona nuova,* no news, good news. But it were great news to see you here, whence you havebeen an Alien so long to—Your most affectionate friend,　　J. H.

Holborn, 3 *June* 1640.

XIX.

To Captain C. Price.

Cousin,

YOU have put me upon such an odd intricate piece of business, that I think there was never the like of it.

I

I am more puzzled and entangled with it than oft-times I use to be with my Band-strings when I go hastily to bed, and want such a fair female Hand as you have to unty them. I must impute all this to the peevish humour of the people I dealt withal. I find it true now, that one of the greatest tortures that can be in the negotiation of the World is, to have to do with perverse irrational half-witted men, and to be worded to death by nonsense; besides, as much Brain as they have, is as full of scruples as a Burr is of prickles; which is a quality incident to all those that have their heads lightly ballasted, for they are like Buoys in a barr'd Port, weaving perpetually up and down. The Father is scrupulous of the Son, the Son of the Sisters, and all three of me, to whose Award they referr'd the business three several times. It is as hard a task to reconcile the Fanes of *St. Sepulchre's* Steeple, which never look all four upon one point of the Heavens, as to reduce them to any conformity of reason. I never remember to have met with Father and Children, or Children among themselves, of a more differing genius and contrariety of humours; insomuch that there cannot be a more pregnant instance to prove that human Souls come not *ex traduce,* and by seminal production from the parents. For my part, I intend to spend my breath no longer upon them, but to wash my hands quite of the business; and so I would wish you to do, unless you love to walk in a labyrinth of Briars. So, expecting with impatience your return to *London,* I rest— Your most faithful Servitor,   J. H.

Westm., 27 *Apr.* 1632.

XX.

To my Cousin, Mr. I. P., *at* Lincoln's-Inn.

COUSIN,

THE last week you sent me word, that you were so cramp'd with business, that you could not put Pen to Paper: If you write not this week, I shall fear you are

not

not only *cramp'd* but *crippl'd;* at least I shall think you are *cramp'd* in your *affection* rather than your fingers, and that you have forgot how once it was my good fortune to preserve you from drowning, when the *Cramp* took you in *St. John's-Pool* at *Oxford.* The Cramp, as I take it, is a *sudden Convulsion of the Nerves.* For my part, the ligaments and sinews of my love to you have been so strong, that they were never yet subject to such *spasmatical shrinkings and convulsions.* Now, Letters are the very *Nerves* and *Arteries* of Friendship; nay, they are the vital Spirits and Elixir of Love, which in case of distance and long absence would be in hazard to languish, and quite moulder away without them. Among the *Italians* and *Spaniards,* 'tis held one of the greatest solecisms that can be in good manners, not to answer a Letter with like civility; by this they use to distinguish a Gentleman from a Clown; besides, they hold it one of the most vertuous ways to employ time. I am the more covetous of a punctual correspondence with you in this point, because I commonly gain by your Letters; your style is so polite, your expressions so gallant, and your lines interspers'd with such dainty flowers of Poetry and Philosophy. I understand there is a very able Doctor that reads the Anatomy-Lecture this Term; if *Ploydon* will dispense with you, you cannot spend your hours better than to hear him. So I end for this time, being cramp'd for want of more matter, and rest—Your most affectionate loving Cousin,   J. H.

Westm., 3 *July* 1631.

XXI.

To my *Nephew,* J. P., *at* St. John's *in* Oxford.

NEPHEW,

I HAD from you lately two Letters; the last was well freighted with very good stuff, but the other, to deal plainly with you, was not so: There was as much difference between them as 'twixt a *Scotch Pedlar's* Pack in *Poland* and

and the Magazine of an *English* Merchant in *Naples;* the one being usually full of Taffaty, Silks, and Sattins; the other of Callicoes, Thread-ribbands, and such polldavy ware. I perceive you have good commodities to vent, if you take the pains : your trifles and bagatells are ill bestow'd upon me, therefore hereafter I pray let me have of your best sort of Wares. I am glad to find that you have stor'd up so much already : you are in the best Mart in the world to improve them ; which I hope you daily do, and I doubt not when the time of your apprenticeship there is expir'd, but you will find a good market to expose them, for your own and the publick benefit abroad. I have sent you the Philosophy-books you writ to me for ; anything that you want of this kind for the advancement of your studies, do but write, and I shall furnish you. When I was a Student as you are, my practice was to borrow, rather than buy some sort of Books, and to be always punctual in restoring them upon the day assign'd, and in the interim to swallow of them as much as made for my turn. This obliged me to read them thro' with more haste to keep my word, whereas I had not been so careful to peruse them had they been my own books, which I knew were always ready at my dispose. I thank you heartily for your last Letter, in regard I found it smelt of the Lamp ; I pray let your next do so, and the oil and labour shall not be lost which you expend upon—Your assured loving Uncle,   J. H.

Westm., 1 *Aug.* 1633.

XXII.

To Sir Tho. Haw.

SIR,

I THANK you a thousand times for the choice Stanzas you pleas'd to send me lately : I find that you were thoroughly heated, that you were inspir'd with a true Enthusiasm when you compos'd them. And whereas others use to flutter in the lower region, your Muse soars up to the

upper

upper ; and transcending that too, takes her flight among the Celestial Bodies to find a fancy. Your desires, I should do something upon the same Subject, I have obey'd, tho' I fear not satisfied, in the following numbers :

1. *Could I but catch those beamy Rays,*
   Which Phœbus *at high noon displays,*
   I'd set them on a Loom, and frame
   A Scarf for Delia *of the same.*

2. *Could I that wondrous Black come near,*
   Which Cynthia, *when eclips'd, doth wear,*
   Of a new fashion I would trace
   A mask thereof for Delia's *face.*

3. *Could I but reach that green and blue,*
   Which Iris *decks in various hue,*
   From her moist Bow I'd drag them down,
   And make my Delia *a Summer-Gown.*

4. *Could I those whitely Stars go nigh,*
   Which make the Milky-Way *in Sky,*
   I'd poach them, and at Moon-shine dress,
   To make my Delia *a curious mess.*

5. *Thus would I diet, thus attire*
   My Delia *Queen of Hearts and Fire ;*
   She should have everything divine,
   That would befit a Seraphin.
   And 'cause ungirt unbless'd we find,
   One of the Zones *her waist should bind.*

They are of the same cadence as yours, and airable. So I am—Your Servitor,   J. H.

Westm., 5 *Sept.* 1632.

XXIII.

To the R. H. the Lady Elizabeth Digby.

MADAM,

IT is no improper comparison, that a thankful heart is like a box of precious ointment, which keeps the smell long after the thing is spent. Madam (without vanity be it spoken)

spoken), such is my heart to you, and such are your favours to me; the strong aromatick odour they carry'd with them diffus'd itself thro' all the veins of my heart, 'specially thro' the left Ventricle, where the most illustrious Blood lies; so that the perfume of them remains still fresh within me, and is like to do, while that triangle of flesh dilates and shuts itself within my breast: nor doth this perfume stay there, but as all smells naturally tend upwards, it hath ascended to my Brain, and sweeten'd all the cells thereof, 'specially the *Memory*, which may be said to be a Cabinet also to preserve courtesies: for tho' the Heart be the Box of *Love*, the Memory is the Box of Lastingness; the one may be term'd the *Source* whence the motions of gratitude flow, the other the *Cistern* that keeps them.

But your Ladyship will say, these are words only; I confess it, 'tis but a verbal acknowledgment: But, Madam, if I were made happy with an opportunity, you shall quickly find these words turn'd to actions, either to go, to run, or ride upon your Errand. In expectation of such a favourable occasion, I rest, Madam—Your Ladyship's most humble and enchained Servitor, J. H.

Westm., 5 *Aug.* 1640.

XXIV.

To Sir I. B.

NOBLE SIR,

THAT old opinion the *Jew* and *Turk* have of Women, that they are of an inferior Creation to Man, and therefore exclude them, the one from their *Synagogues*, the other from their *Mosques*, is in my judgment not only partial, but profane: for the Image of the Creator shines as clearly in the one as in the other; and I believe there are as many female Saints in Heaven as male, unless you could make me adhere to the opinion that Women must be all masculine before they be capable to be made Angels of. Add hereunto, that there went better and more refined stuff to the Creation of Woman than Man. 'Tis true, 'twas a weak part

part in *Eve* to yield to the seducement of *Satan*; but it was a weaker thing in *Adam* to suffer himself to be tempted by *Eve*, being the weaker vessel.

The ancient Philosophers had a better opinion of that Sex, for they ascrib'd all Sciences to the *Muses*, all Sweetness and Morality to the *Graces*, and prophetic Inspirations to the *Sybils*. In my small revolving of Authors, I find as high examples of Virtue in Women as in Men; I could produce here a whole Regiment of them, but that a Letter is too narrow a field to muster them in. I must confess, there are also counter Instances of this kind: if Queen *Zenobia* was such a precise pattern of continency, that after the act of conception she would know her Husband no more all the time of her pregnancy, till she had been deliver'd; there is another example of a *Roman* Empress, that when she found the Vessel fraughted, would take in all passengers; when the Barn was full, any one might thrash in the haggard, but not till then, for fear the right Father should be discovered by the countenance of the Child. But what need I go far off, to rake the ashes of the dead? there are living examples enough *pro* and *con* of both Sexes; yet Woman being (as I said before) the weaker vessel, her failings are more venial than those of Man; tho' Man, indeed, being more conversant with the world, and meeting more opportunities abroad (and opportunity is the greatest Bawd) of falling into infirmities, as he follows his worldly negotiations, may on the t'other side be judg'd the more excusable.

But you are fitter than I to discourse of this subject, being better vers'd in the theory of Women, having had a most virtuous Lady of your own before, and being now link'd to another. I wish a thousand benedictions may fall upon this your second choice, and that————*tam bona sit quam bona prima fuit.* This option shall be my conclusion for the present, whereunto I add, that I am, in no vulgar degree of Affection—Your most humlbe and faithful Servitor,

J. H.

Westm., 5 *Aug.* 1632.

XXV.

XXV.

To Mr. P. W.

SIR,

THERE are two things which add much to the merit of courtesies, *viz.*, *cheerfulness* and *speed*, and the contraries of these lessen the value of them; that which hangs long 'twixt the fingers, and is done with difficulty and a sullen supercilious look, makes the obligation of the receivers nothing so strong, or the memory of the kindness half so grateful. The best thing the Gods themselves lik'd of in the entertainments they receiv'd of those poor wretches *Baucis* and *Philemon*, was open hearty looks.

> ——*Super omnia vultus,*
> *Accessere boni.*——

A clear unclouded countenance makes a Cottage appear like a Castle, in point of hospitality; but a beetle-brow'd sullen Face makes a Palace as smoaky as an *Irish Hut*. There is a *mode* in giving entertainment, and doing any courtesy else, which trebly binds the receiver to an acknowledgment, and makes the remembrance of it more acceptable. I have known two Lord High Treasurers of *England* of quite contrary humours, one successively after the other; the one, tho' he did the Suitors' business, yet he went murmuring; the other, tho' he did it not, was us'd to dismiss the party with some satisfaction. 'Tis true, money is welcome, tho' it be in a dirty clout, but 'tis far more acceptable if it come in a clean handkerchief.

Sir, you may sit in the chair, and read Lectures of Morality to all Mankind in this point, you have such a dextrous discreet way to handle suitors in that troublesome Office of yours; wherein, as you have already purchas'd much, I wish you all increase of honour and happiness.—— Your humble and obliged Servitor,   J. H.

2 D   XXVI.

XXVI.

To Mr. F. Coll., at Naples.

SIR,

'TIS confess'd I have offended by my over-long Silence, and abus'd our maiden Friendship; I appear before you now in this white sheet, to do penance : I pray in your next to me send an *Absolution.* Absolutions, they say, are as cheap in that Town as Courtesans, whereof 'twas said there were 20,000 on the common list, when I was there : at which time I remember one told me a tale of a *Calabrian* who had ——— a Goat; and having bought an Absolution of his Confessor, he was ask'd by a friend what it cost him : He answer'd, I procur'd it for four Pistoles, and for the other odd one, I think I might have had a dispensation to have married the Beast.

I thank you for the exact relation you sent me of the fearful Earthquakes and Fires which happen'd lately in that Country, and particularly about *Vesuvius.* It seems the huge Giant, who, the Poets say, was hurl'd under the vast Mountain by the Gods for thinking to scale Heaven, had a mind to turn from one side to the other, which he useth to do at the revolution of every hundred years; and stirring his body by that action, he was taken with a fit of the cough, which made the Hill shake, and belch out fire in this hideous manner. But to repay you in the like coin, they send us stranger news from *Lisbon;* for they write of a spick and span-new *Island,* that hath peep'd up out of the *Atlantick Sea,* near the *Terceras,* which never appear'd before since the Creation, and begins to be peopled already : Methinks the K. of *Spain* needs no more Countries, he hath too many already, unless they were better united. All your Friends here are well, and mind you often in Town and Country, as doth—Your true, constant Servitor,   J. H.

Westm., 7 *Apr.* 1629.

XXVII.

XXVII.

To Mr. T. Lucy, *in* Venice.

SIR,

YOUR last you sent me was from *Genoa,* where you write that *gli mariti ingravi dano lor moglie cento miglia lontano;* Husbands get their Wives with child a hundred miles off. 'Tis a great virtue, I confess, but 'tis nothing to what our *East-India* Mariners can do here, because they can do so forty times further : for tho' their Wives be at *Ratcliff,* and they at the *Red-Sea,* tho' they be at *Madagascar,* the *Mogor's* Court, or *Japan,* yet they use to get their Wives' bellies up here about *London;* a strange virtue, at such a huge distance; but I believe the active part is in the Wives, and the Husbands are merely passive: which makes them, among other wares, to bring home with them a sort of precious horns, the powder whereof, could one get some of it, would be of an invaluable virtue. This operation of our *Indian* Mariner at such a distance is more admirable in my judgment than that of the Weapon-salve, the *unguentum armarium;* for that can do no good unless the Surgeon have the instrument and blood; but this is done without both, for the Husband contributes neither of them.

You are now I presume in *Venice;* there also such things are done by proxy; while the Husband is abroad upon the Gallies, there be others that shoot his *Gulf* at home. You are now in a place where you may feed all your senses very cheap; I allow you the pleasing of your Eye, your Ear, your Smell and Taste ; but take heed of being too indulgent of the fifth Sense. The Poets feign, that *Venus* the Goddess of Pleasure, and therefore call'd *Aphrodite,* was ingendred of the froth of the Sea (which makes Fish more salacious commonly than Flesh) ; it is not improbable that she was got and coagulated of that Foam which *Neptune* useth to disgorge upon those pretty Islands whereon that City stands. My Lady *Miller* commends her kindly to you, and

and she desires you to send her a compleat Cupboard of the best Christal Glasses *Murano* can afford by the next shipping; besides she intreats you to send her a pot of the best Mithridate, and so much of Treacle.

All your Friends here are well and jovial. *T. T.* drank your health yesternight, and wish'd you could send him a handsome *Venetian Courtesan* inclos'd in a Letter ; he would willingly be at the charge of the postage, which he thinks would not be much for such a light commodity. Farewell, my dear *Tom*, have a care of your courses, and continue to love him who is—Yours to the Altar,   J. H.

Westm., 15 *Jan.* 1635.

XXVIII.

To Mr. T. Jackson, *at* Madrid.

SIR,

THO' a great Sea severs us now, yet 'tis not all the water of the Ocean can drown the remembrance of you in me, but that it floats and flows daily in my brain. I must confess (for 'tis impossible the Mind of Man should fix itself always upon one object) it hath sometimes its ebbs in me, but 'tis to rise up again with greater force: At the writing hereof 'twas flood, 'twas spring-tide, which swell'd so high, that the thoughts of you overwhelm'd all others within me ; they ingross'd all my Intellectuals for the time.

You write to me fearful news, touching the revolt of the *Catalan* from *Castile*, of the tragical murdering of the Viceroy, and the burning of his house: Those Mountaineers are mad Lads. I fear the sparkles of this fire will fly further, either to *Portugal*, or to *Sicily* and *Italy;* all which Countries, I observ'd, the *Spaniard* holds, *as one would do a Wolf by the ear,* fearing they should run away ever and anon from him.

The news here is, that *Lambeth-House* bears all the sway at *Whitehall*, and the Lord *Deputy* kings it notably in *Ireland*; some that love them best could wish them a little more moderation.

I

I pray buy *Suarez's* Works for me of the last Edition : Mr. *William Pawly*, to whom I desire my most hearty commends may be presented, will see it safely sent by way of *Bilboa*. Your Friends here are all well, as thanks be to God—Your true Friend to serve you,   J. H.

Holborn, 3 *Mar.* 1638.

XXIX.

To Sir Edw. Sa., *Knight.*

SIR EDWARD,

I HAD a shrewd disease hung lately upon me, proceeding, as the Physicians told me, from this long reclused life and close restraint, which had much wasted my spirits and brought me low; when the *Crisis* was past, I began to grow doubtful that I had but a short time to breathe in this elementary world ; my fever still increasing, and finding my soul weary of this muddy mansion, and, methought, more weary of this prison of flesh, than this flesh was of this prison of the *Fleet*. Therefore after some gentle slumbers and unusual dreams, about the dawnings of the day, I had a lucid interval, and I fell thinking how to put my little house in order, and to make my last will. Hereupon my thoughts ran upon *Grunnius Sophista's* last Testament, who having nothing else to dispose of but his body, he bequeathed all the parts thereof, in Legacies, as his skin to the Tanners, his bones to the Dice-makers, his guts to the Musicians, his fingers to the Scriveners, his tongue to his fellow-sophisters (which were the Lawyers of those times), and so forth. As he thus dissected his *body*, so I thought to divide my *mind* into legacies, having, as you know, little of the outward pelf and gifts of fortune to dispose of ; for never any was less beholden to that blind baggage. In the highest degree of theorical Contemplation, I made an entire sacrifice of my soul to her Maker, who by *infusing created her, and by creating infused her* to actuate this small bulk of flesh, with an unshaken confidence

fidence of the redemption of both in my Saviour, and consequently of the salvation of the one and the resurrection
of the other. My Thoughts then reflected upon divers of
my noble Friends, and I fell to proportion to them what
legacies I held most proper. I thought to bequeath to my
Lord of *Cherbery*, and Sir *K. Digby*, that little Philosophy
and Knowledge I have in the Mathematicks; my historical
Observations, and critical Researches I made into Antiquity, I thought to bequeath unto Dr. *Usher*, Lord Primate
of *Ireland*; my Observations abroad, and Inspection into
foreign States, I thought to leave to my Lord *G. D.*; my
Poetry, such as it is, to Mistress *A. K.*, who I know is a
great minion of the Muses; School-languages I thought to
bequeath unto my dear Mother the University of *Oxford*;
my *Spanish* to Sir *Lewis Dives* and Master *Endimion
Porter*; for tho' they are great masters of that language,
yet it may stead them something when they read *la picara
Justina*; my *Italian* to the worthy Company of *Turkey* and
Levantine Merchants, from divers of whom I have receiv'd
many noble favours; my *French* to my most honour'd
Lady, the Lady *Core*, and it may help her something to
understand *Rabelais*; the little smattering I have in the
Dutch, British, and my *English*, I did not esteem worth
the bequeathing: My love I had bequeath'd to be diffused
among all my dear Friends, 'specially those that have stuck
unto me in this my long affliction; my best natural affections betwixt the Lord B. of *Br.*, my Brother *Howell*,
and my three dear Sisters, to be transferr'd by them to
my Cousins their Children. This little sackful of bones, I
thought to bequeath to *Westminster-Abbey*, to be interr'd
in the Cloyster within the South-side of the Garden,
close to the Wall, where I would have desir'd Sir *H. F.*
(my dear Friend) to have inlay'd a small piece of black
Marble, and cause this Motto to have been insculped on it,
Hucusque peregrinus, heic domi; or this, which I would have
left to his Choice, *Hucusque Erraticus, heic Fixus:* And
instead of strewing my grave with *Flowers*, I would have
                                                desir'd

desir'd him to have grafted thereon some little *Tree* of
what sort he pleas'd, that might have taken root downward to my dust, because I have been always naturally
affected to woods and groves, and those kind of vegetables,
insomuch, that if there were any such thing as a *Pythago-
rean* Metempsychosis, I think my soul would transmigrate
into some Tree, when she bids this body farewell.

By these Extravagancies, and odd Chimeras of my Brain,
you may well perceive that I was not well, but distemper'd,
'specially in my intellectuals; according to the *Spanish* proverb, *Siempre desvarios con la calentura;* Fevers have always
their fits of dotage. Among those to whom I had bequeath'd
my dearest Love, you were one, to whom I had intended a
large proportion; and that Love which I would have left
you then in *legacy,* I send you now in this *Letter:* For it
hath pleased God to reprieve me for a longer time to creep
upon this Earth, and to see better days, I hope, when this
black dismal Cloud is dispell'd; but come foul or fair
weather, I shall be, as formerly—Your most constant, faithful Servitor,   J. H.

Fleet, 26 *Mar.* 1643.

XXX.

To the Rt. Hon. the Lady Wichts.

MADAM,

SINCE I was hurl'd among these walls, I had divers fits of
melancholy, and such *turbid intervals* that use to attend
close prisoners, who, for the most part, have no other companions but confus'd troops of wandring Cogitations. Now,
*Melancholy is far more fruitful of thoughts than any other
humour;* for it is like the mud of *Nile,* which, when that
Enigmatical vast River is got again to her former bed,
engendereth divers sorts of new creatures, and some kind of
Monsters. My brain in this Fleet hath been often thus
overwhelm'd, yet I never found it so muddy, nor the region
of my mind so much clouded, as it was lately after notice
had of the sad tidings of Master *Controuler's* death: The
news

news hereof struck such a damp into me, that for some space, methought, the very pulse of my blood and the motions of my heart were at a stand; for I was surpriz'd with such a consternation, that I felt no pulsations in the one, or palpitations in the other. Well, Madam, he was a brave solid wise man, of a noble free disposition, and so great a *controuler* of his passions, that he was always at home within himself; yet I much fear that the sense of these unhappy times made too deep impressions in him.

Truly, Madam, I lov'd and honour'd him in such a perfection, that my heart shall wear a broad black ribband for him while I live: As long as I have a retentive faculty to remember anything, his memory shall be fresh with me.

But the truth is, that if the advantageous exchange which he hath made were well consider'd, no Friend of his should be sorry; for in lieu of a *White-staff* in an earthly Court, he hath got a *Sceptre* of Immortality: He that had been Ambassador at the *Port* to the greatest Monarch upon Earth, where he resided so many years an honour to his King and Country, is now arrived at a far more glorious *Port* than that of *Constantinople;* tho' (as I intimated before) I fear that this boisterous weather hath blown him thither before his time. God Almighty give your Ladyship patience for so great a loss, and comfort in your hopeful Issue: with this prayer I conclude myself, Madam—Your Ladyship's most humble and sorrowful Servant,

J. H.

From the Fleet, 15 *Apr.*

XXXI.

To Mr. E. S., *Counsellor at the* Middle Temple.

Sir,

I HAD yours this morning, and I thank you for the news you send me, that divers of my fellow-sufferers are enlarg'd out of *Lambeth, Winchester, London,* and *Ely-House:* whereunto I may answer you, as the *Cheapside* Porter did one that related Court-news to him, how such a one was

was made Lord *Treasurer,* another *Chancellor* of the *Exchequer,* another was made an *Earl,* another sworn *Privy-Counsellor:* Ay, said he, yet I am but a *Porter* still. So I may say, I am but a *Prisoner* still, notwithstanding the releasement of so many. Mistake me not, as if I repin'd hereby at any one's liberty ; for I could heartily wish that I were the unic Martyr in this kind, that I were the Figure of one with never a Cypher after it, as God wot there are too many : I could wish that as I am the least in value, I were the last in number. A day may come, that a favourable wind may blow, that I may launch also out of this Fleet. In the meantime, and always after, I am—Your true and constant Servitor, J. H.

Fleet, 1 *Feb.* 1645.

XXXII.

To Mr. R. B., *at* Ipswich.

GENTLE SIR,

I VALUE at a high rate the sundry respects you have been pleased to show me ; for as you obliged me before by your visits, so you have much endear'd yourself to me since by your late Letter of the 11th current. Believe it, Sir, the least scruple of your Love is not lost (because I perceive it proceeds from the pure motions of Virtue), but return'd to you in the same full proportion. But what you please to ascribe to me in point of merit, I dare not own ; you look upon me thro' the wrong end of the prospective, or rather thro' a multiplying-glass, which makes the object appear far bigger than it is in real dimensions ; such glasses as Anatomists use in the dissection of Bodies, which can make a Flea look like a Cow, or a Fly as big as a Vulture.

I presume you are constant in your desire to travel ; if you intend it at all, you cannot do it in a better time, there being little comfort, God wot, to breathe *English* Air, as matters are carried. I shall be glad to steed you in anything that may tend to your Advantage ; for to tell you

truly,

truly, I take much contentment in this inchoation of
Friendship, to improve and perfect which, I shall lie cen-
tinell to apprehend all occasions.

If you meet Master *R. Brownrig* in the Country, I pray
present my very kind respects to him ; for I profess myself
to be both his and—Your most affectionate Servitor,

J. H.

Fleet, 15 *Aug.* 1646.

XXXIII.

To Captain C. Price, *Prisoner at* Coventry.

COUSIN,

YOU, whom I held always as my second self in Affection, are now so in Affliction, being in the same
predicament of Sufferance, tho' not in the same *prison* as I.
There is nothing sweetneth Friendship more than participation and identity of danger and durance : The day may
come that we may discourse with comfort of these sad
Times ; for Adversity hath the Advantage of Prosperity
itself in this point, that the commemoration of the one is
oft-times more delightsome than the fruition of the other.
Moreover, Adversity and Prosperity are like Virtue and
Vice ; the two foremost of both which begin with Anxieties
and Pain, but they end comically, in Contentment and
Joy ; the other two quite contrary, they begin with Pleasure, and end in Pain : There's a difference in the last
scene.

I could wish, if there be no hope of a speedy releasement,
you would remove your body hither, and rather than moulder
away in idleness, we will devoutly blow the coal, and try if
we can exalt Gold, and bring it o'er the *helm* in this *Fleet ;*
we will transmute metals, and give a resurrection to mortified Vegetables : To which end, the *green Lyon* and the
Dragon, yea, *Demogorgon* and *Mercury* himself, with all
the Planets, shall attend us, till we come to the *Elixir*,
the true Powder of Projection, which the Vulgar call the
Philosopher's Stone.   If matters hit right, we may thereby

get

get better returns than *Cardigan* silver Mines afford : But
we must not melt ourselves away as *J. Meredith* did, nor
do as your Countryman *Morgan* did.   I know when you
read these lines, you'll say I am grown mad, and that I
have taken *Opium* in lieu of Tobacco: If I be mad, I am
but sick of the Disease of the Times, which reigns more
among the *English*, than the *Sweating-sickness* did some
sixscore years since among them, and only them, both at
home and abroad.

There's a strange Maggot hath got into their brains,
which possesseth them with a kind of Vertigo ; and it
reigns in the Pulpit more than anywhere else, for some of
our Preachmen are grown dog-mad, there's a worm got
into their Tongues, as well as their Heads.

Hodge Powel commends him to you ; he is here under
hatches as well as I ; however, I am still, in fair or foul
weather—Your truly affectionate Cousin to serve you,

J. H.

Fleet, 3 *Jan.* 1643.

XXXIV.

To the Rt. Hon. the Lord of Cherberry.

MY LORD,

G OD send you joy of your new habitation, for I understand your Lordship is remov'd from the *King's-*
street to the *Queen's*.   It may be with this enlargement of
dwelling, your Lordship may need a recruit of Servants.
The bearer hereof hath a desire to devote himself to your
Lordship's Service ; and I find that he hath a concurrence
of such parts that may make him capable of it : He is well
studied in men and books, vers'd in business of all sorts,
and writes a very fair hand : He is well extracted, and hath
divers good friends that are dwellers in the Town, who will
be responsible for him.   Moreover, besides this Letter of
mine, your Lordship will find that he carrieth one in his
countenance ; for an *honest ingenious Look is a good Letter
of recommendation of itself.*   If your Lordship hath not
present

present occasion to employ him, he may be about you a-while like a spare Watch, which your Lordship may wind up at pleasure. So my Aim being to do your Lordship service, as much as him a pleasure, by this recommendation, I rest—Your Lordship's most humble Servant,

J. H.

Fleet, 13 *July* 1646.

XXXV.

To Mr. R. Br.

GENTLE SIR,

YOURS of the 4th current came safely to hand, and I acknowledge with much contentment the fair respects you please to shew me: You may be well assur'd, that the least grain of your Love to me is not lost, but counterbalanc'd with the like in full weight; for altho' I am as frail a piece, and as full of infirmities, as another man, yet I like my own nature in one thing, that I could never endure to be in the Arrear to any for Love; where my *Hand* came short, my *Heart* was bountiful, and helped to make an equal compensation.

I hope you persist in your purpose for foreign Travel, to study a-while the World abroad: It is the way to perfect you, and I have already discover'd such choice ingredients and parts of ingenuity in you, that will quickly make a compleat Gentleman. No more now, but that I am seriously—Yours to dispose of,   J. H.

Fleet, 3 *July* 1646.

XXXVI.

To Sir L. D., *in the* Tower.

SIR,

TO help the passing away of your weary Hours between those disconsolate Walls, I have sent you a King of your own Name to bear you company, *Lewis* XIII., who, tho' dead three years since, may peradventure afford you some entertainment; and I think that dead Men of this

nature

nature are the fittest companions for such that are buried alive, as you and I are. I doubt not but you, who have a Spirit to overcome all things, will overcome the sense of this hard condition, that you may survive these sad times, and see better days. I doubt not, as weak as I am, but I shall be able to do it myself; in which confidence I style myself —Your most obliged and ever faithful Servitor,   J. H.

Fleet, 15 *Feb.* 1646.

My most humble Service to Sir *J. St.* and Sir *H. V.*

XXXVII.

To Master R. B.

GENTLE SIR,

I HAD yours of the 2d current by Master *Bloys,* which obligeth me to send you double thanks, first, for your Letter, then for the choice Hand that brought it me.

When I had gone thro' it, methought your *Lines* were as *Leaves,* or rather so many Branches, among which there sprouted divers sweet Blossoms of ingenuity, which I find may quickly come to a rare maturity. I confess this Clime (as matters go) is untoward to improve such buds of Virtue; but the Times may mend, now that our *King,* with the *Sun,* makes his approach to us more and more: Yet I fear we shall not come yet a good while to our former serenity; therefore it were not amiss, in my judgment, if some foreign Air did blow upon the aforesaid Blossoms, to ripen them under some other Meridian; in the interim, it is the opinion of—Your ever respectful Friend to dispose of,   J. H.

Fleet, 3 *Aug.* 1645.

XXXVIII.

To Mr. G. C., *at* Dublin.

SIR,

THE news of this Week have been like the waves of that boisterous Sea, thro' which this Letter is to pass

over

over to you. Divers reports for Peace have swoln high for
the time, but they suddenly fell low and flat again. Our
Relations here are like a Peal of Bells in windy blustring
weather; sometimes the Sound is strong on this side, sometimes on that side of the Steeple; so our Relations sound
diversly, as the Air of Affection carries them; and sometimes
in a whole volley of News we shall not find one true report.

There was, in a *Dunkirk* Ship, taken some months ago
hard by *Arundel Castle,* among other things, a large Picture
seiz'd upon, and carried to *Westminster-Hall,* and put in
the *Star-Chamber* to be publickly seen: It was the Legend
of *Conanus,* a *British* Prince in the time of *Gratian* the
Emperor, who having married *Ursula,* the King of *Cornwall's*
Daughter, was embark'd with 11,000 Virgins for *Britany*
in *France,* to colonize that part with *Christians;* but being
by distress of Weather beaten upon the *Rhine,* because they
would not yield to the lust of the Infidels, after the example
of *Ursula,* they were all slain, their Bodies were carried to
Colen, where there stands to this day a stately Church
built for them. This is the Story of that Picture; yet the
common People here take *Conanus* for our King, and *Vrsula*
for the Queen, and the Bishop which stands hard by to be
the Pope, and so stare upon it accordingly, notwithstanding
that the Prince there represented hath Sandals on his feet,
after the old fashion, that the Coronets on their heads
resemble those of Dukes and Earls, as also that there are
Rays about them which never use to be applied to living
Persons, with divers other incongruities: Yet it cannot be
beaten out of the belief of thousands here, but that it was
intended to represent our King and Queen; which makes
me conclude with this interjection of wonder, Oh the
ignorance of the common People!—Your faithful Friend
to command,   J. H.

Fleet, 12 *Aug.* 1644.

XXXIX.

XXXIX.

To Master End. Por., at Paris.

SIR,

I MOST affectionately kiss your hands for the account (and candid opinion) you please to give of the History I sent Her Majesty of the late King her Brother's Reign. I return you also a thousand thanks for your comfortable Advice, that having been so long under hatches in this *Fleet*, I should fancy myself to be in a long voyage at Sea: 'Tis true, Opinion can do much, and indeed *she is that great Lady which rules the World.* There is a wise saying in that Country where you sojourn now, that *Ce n'est pas la place mais la pensée qui fait la prison :* 'Tis not the *Place*, but *Opinion*, that makes the Prison; the Conceit is more than the Condition. You go on to prefer my captivity in this *Fleet* to that of a Voyager at Sea, in regard that he is subject to storms and springing of Leaks, to Pirates and Picaroons, with other casualties. You write, I have other Advantages also, to be free from plundering, and other Barbarisms, that reign now abroad. 'Tis true, I am secur'd from all these; yet touching the first, I could be content to expose myself to all those chances, so that this were a *floating Fleet*, that I might breathe free Air, for I have not been suffer'd to stir o'er the threshold of this House this four years. Whereas you say, I have a Book for my companion ; 'tis true, I converse sometimes with dead Men, and what fitter Associates can there be for one that is buried alive (as I am) than dead Men ? And now will I adventure to send you a kind of Epitaph I made of myself this morning, as I was lolling a-bed :

> *Here lies intomb'd a walking thing,*
> *Whom* Fortune *(with the States) did fling*
> *Between these walls. Why ? ask not that,*
> *That* blind Whore *doth she knows not what.*

'Tis a strange World, you'll say, when Men make their
own

own Epitaphs in their Graves; but we that are thus buried
alive have one Advantage above others, that we are like
to have a double Resurrection: I am sure of one; but if
these Times hold, I cannot ascertain myself of the other,
for I may be suffered to rot here, for ought I know; it
being the hard destiny of some in these Times, when they
are once clapp'd up, to be so forgotten, as if there were no
such Men in the World.

I humbly thank you for your *Avisos*; I cannot correspond
with you in that kind as freely as I would; only in the
general I must tell you, that we are come to such a pass,
that the Posie which a young Couple did put upon their
Wedding-ring may fit us in general, which was, *God knows
what will become of us.* But I trust these bad Times will
be recompensed with better; for my part, that which keeps
me alive is your Motto there of the House of *Bourbon*, and
'tis but one word, *L'Sperance.* So I pray God preserve
you, and—Your most faithful humble Servitor,   J. H.

Fleet, 2 Jan. 1646.

XL.

To Master J. H., *at St.* John's *College in* Cambridge.

MASTER HALL,

YOURS of the 13th of this instant came safely, tho'
slowly, to hand; for I had it not till the 20th of the
same, and the next day your *Essays* were brought me. I
entertain'd both with much respect; for I found therein
many choice and ripe Notions, which I hope proceed from
a pregnancy, rather than precocity of spirit in you.

I perceive you have enter'd the Suburbs of *Sparta*
already, and that you are in a fair way to get to the Town
itself: I know you have wherewith to adorn her; nay, you
may in time gain *Athens* herself, with all the Knowledge
she was ever Mistress of, if you go on in your Career with
constancy. I find you have a genius for the most solid and
severest sort of Studies; therefore when you have pass'd
thro'

thro' the Briars of Logick, I could wish you to go strongly
on in the fair fields of Philosophy and the Mathematicks,
which are true Academical Studies, and they will afford
rich matter of application for your inventive spirit to
work upon. By all means understand *Aristotle* in his own
Language, for it is the Language of Learning. Touching
Poetry, History, and other humane Studies, they may serve
you for your recreation, but let them not by any means
allure your affections from the first. I shall delight sometimes to hear of your proceeding; for I profess a great deal
of good-will to you, which makes me rest—Your respectful
Friend to serve you,   J. H.

Fleet, 3 *Dec.*

XLI.

To my B., the L. B. of B., *in* France.

MY GOOD LORD AND BR.,

ALTHO' the sense of my own hard condition be enough
to make me melancholy, yet when I contemplate
yours (as I often do) and compare your kind of *banishment*
with my *imprisonment*, I find the apprehension of the first,
wherein so many have a share, adds a double weight to my
sufferings, tho' but single : Truly these Thoughts to me are
as so many corrosives to one already in a Consumption.
The World cries you up to be an excellent *Divine* and
Philosopher; now is the time for you to make an advantage
of both : Of the first, by calling to mind, that Afflictions
are the proportion of the best *Theophiles;* of the other, by
a well-weigh'd consideration, that Crosses and Troubles are
entail'd upon Mankind as much as any other inheritance.
In this respect I am no *Cadet,* for you know I have had a
double, if not a triple share, and may be rather call'd the
elder Brother ; but οἰστέον καὶ ἐπιστέον, I hope I shall not sink
under the burden, but that we shall be both reserv'd for
better days, 'specially now that the King (with the *Sun* and
the *Spring*) makes his approach more and more towards us
from the North.

2 E   God

God Almighty (the God of our good old Father) still
guard you and guide you, that after so long a separation we
may meet again with comfort, to confer Notes, and recount
Matters past : For adverse Fortune, among other Properties,
hath this for one, that her present pressures are not so irksome, as the remembrance of them being past are delightsome. So I remain—Your most loving Brother,   J. H.

Fleet, 1 *Maii* 1645.

XLII.

To Sir L. Dives, *in the* Tower.

SIR,

AMONG divers other Properties that attend a long Captivity, one is, that it purgeth the Humours, 'specially
it correcteth *Choler*, and attempers it with *Phlegm;* which
you know in *Spanish* is taken for *Patience.* It hath also a
chymical kind of quality, to refine the dross and feculency
of a corrupt Nature, as Fire useth to purify Metals, and
to destroy that *terram adamicam* in them, as the Chymist
calls it; for *Demogorgon* with his Vegetables partakes of
Adam's Malediction, as well as other Creatures, which
makes some of them so foul and imperfect; Nature having
design'd them all for Gold and Silver at first, and 'tis Fire
can only rectify, and reduce them towards such a perfection.
This *Fleet* hath been such a *Furnace* to me, it hath been
a kind of *Perillus Bull;* or rather, to use the *Paracelsian*
phrase, I have been here *in ventre equino,* in this limbeck and
crucible of Affliction. And whereas the Chymist commonly
requires but 150 days *antequam corvus in columbam vertatur,*
before the Crow turns to a Dove; I have been here five
times so many days, and upward. I have been here time
enough in conscience to pass all the degrees and effects of
fire, as distillation, sublimation, mortification, calcination,
solution, descension, dealbation, rubification, and fixation; for
I have been fasten'd to the walls of this Prison any time these
fifty-five months : I have been here long enough, if I were
matter capable thereof, to be made the Philosopher's Stone,

to

to be converted from *Water* to *Powder*, which is the whole *Magistery :* I have been, besides, so long upon the anvil, that methinks I am grown malleable, and hammer-proof ; I am so habituated to hardship. But indeed you that are made of a choicer mould, are fitter to be turn'd into the Elixir, than I who have so much dross and corruption in me, that it will require more pains, and much more expence, to be purg'd and defecated. God send us both patience to bear the brunt of this fiery trial, and grace to turn these decoctions into *aqua vitæ*, to make sovereign Treacle of this Viper. The *Trojan* Prince was forc'd to pass over *Phlegeton*, and pay *Charon* his freight before he could get into the *Elysian* fields : You know the moral, that we must pass thro' Hell to Heaven ; and why not as well thro' a Prison to Paradise ? Such may the *Tower* prove to you, and the *Fleet* to me, who am—Your humble and hearty Servitor, J. H.

From the prison of the Fleet, 23 *Feb.* 1645.

XLIII.

To the Right Honourable the Lord R.

MY LORD,

SURE there is some angry Planet hath lower'd long upon the Catholick King ; and tho' one of his Titles to Pagan Princes be, that he wears the Sun for his Helmet, because it never sets upon all his dominions, in regard some part of them lies on the t'other side of the Hemisphere among the *Antipodes ;* yet methinks that neither that great Star, or any of the rest, are now propitious unto him: They cast, it seems, more benign influxes upon the *Flower-de luce*, which thrives wonderfully ; but how long these favourable Aspects will last, I will not presume to judge. This, among divers others of late, hath been a fatal year to the said King ; for Westward he hath lost *Dunkirk : Dunkirk*, which was the Terror of this part of the World, the Scourge of the occidental Seas, whose Name was grown to be a bugbear for so many years, hath now changed her Master, and thrown

thrown away the *ragged-staff*; doubtless a great exploit it
was to take this Town : But whether this be advantageous
to *Holland* (as I am sure it is not to *England*) time will
shew.   It is more than probable that it may make him
careless at Sea, and in the building and arming of his Ships,
having now no Enemy near him; besides, I believe it
cannot much benefit *Hans* to have the *French* so contiguous
to him : the old saying was, *Ayez le François pour ton amy,
non pas pour ton Voisin :* Have the *Frenchman* for thy Friend,
not for thy Neighbour.

Touching *England*, I believe these distractions of ours
have been one of the greatest advantages that could befall
France; and they happen'd in the most favourable conjuncture of time that might be, else I believe he would never
have as much as attempted *Dunkirk :* for *England*, in true
reason of State, had reason to prevent nothing more, in regard
no one place could have added more to the naval Power of
France; this will make his Sails swell bigger, and I fear
make him claim in time as much Regality in these narrow
Seas as *England* herself.

In *Italy* the *Spaniard* hath also had ill successes at *Piom-
bino* and *Porto-longone :* besides, they write that he hath
lost *il Prete, & il Medico*, the Priest, and the Physician; to
wit, the Pope, and the Duke of *Florence* (the House of
Medici), who appear rather for the *French* than for him.

Add to these disasters, that he hath lost within the revolution of the same year the Prince of *Spain* his unic Son, in
the very flower of his age, being but seventeen years old.
These, with the falling off of *Catalonia* and *Portugal*, with
the death of the Queen not above forty, are heavy losses
to the Catholick King, and must needs much enfeeble the
great bulk of his Monarchy, falling in so short a compass of
time one upon the neck of another: and we are not to enter
into the secret Counsels of God Almighty for a reason.   I
have read 'twas the sensuality of the flesh that drove the
Kings out of *Rome*, the *French* out of *Sicily*, and brought
the *Moors* into *Spain*, where they kept firm footing above

seven

seven hundred years. I could tell you how, not long before her death, the late Queen of *Spain* took off one of her Chapines, and clowted *Olivares* about the noddle with it, because he had accompany'd the King to a Lady of Pleasure; telling him, that he should know, she was Sister to a King of *France*, as well as Wife to a King of *Spain*. For my part, *France* and *Spain* is all one to me in point of affection; I am one of those indifferent Men that would have the Scales of Power in *Europe* kept even: I am also a *Philerenus*, a lover of Peace, and I could wish the *French* were more inclinable to it, now that the *common Enemy* hath invaded the Territories of St. *Mark*. Nor can I but admire that at the same time the *French* should assail *Italy* at one side, when the *Turk* was doing it on the other. But had that great naval Power of *Christians*, which were this summer upon the coasts of *Tuscany*, gone against the *Mahometan* Fleet, which was the same time setting upon *Candy*, they might in all likelihood have achieved a glorious Exploit, and driven the *Turk* into the *Hellespont*. Nor is poor *Christendom* torn thus in pieces by the *German*, *Spaniard*, *French*, and *Swedes*, but our three Kingdoms have also most pitifully scratch'd her face, wasted her spirits, and let out some of her illustrious blood, by our late horrid distractions: Whereby it may be inferr'd, that the Mufti and the Pope seem to thrive in their devotion one way, a chief part of the prayers of the one being, that discord should still continue 'twixt *Christian* Princes; of the other, that division should still increase between the *Protestants*. This poor Island is a woful example thereof.

I hear the Peace 'twixt *Spain* and *Holland* is absolutely concluded by the Plenipotentiary Ministers at *Munster*, who have beat their heads so many years about it: But they write that the *French* and *Swede* do mainly endeavour, and set all the wheels of Policy a-going to puzzle and prevent it. If it take effect, I do not see how the *Hollander* in common honesty can evade it; I hope it will conduce much to an

Universal

Universal Peace, which God grant, for War is *a Fire struck
in the Devil's tinder-box.* No more now, but that I am, my
Lord—Your most humble Servitor,   J. H.

Fleet, 1 *Dec.* 1643.

XLIV.

To Mr. E. O., Counsellor, at Gray's-Inn.

SIR,

THE sad Tidings of my dear Friend Dr. *Prichard's*
Death sunk deep into me; and the more I ruminate
upon't, the more I resent it : But when I contemplate the
Order, and those Adamantine Laws which Nature puts into
such strict execution thro'out this elementary World; when
I consider that up and down this frail Globe of Earth we
are but Strangers and Sojourners at best, being design'd for
an infinitely better Country ; when I think that our egress
out of this life is as natural to us as our ingress (all which
he knew as much as any), these Thoughts in a checking
way turn my Melancholy to a counter-passion ; they beget
another spirit within me. You know that in the disposition
of all sublunary Things, *Nature is God's Handmaid, Fate
his Commissioner, Time his Instrument, and Death his Execu-
tioner.* By the first we have Generation ; by the second
Successes, good or bad ; and the two last bring us to our
End : *Time* with his vast Scythe mows down all Things,
and *Death* sweeps away those Mowings. Well, he was a
rare and a compleat judicious Scholar, as any that I have
known born under our Meridian ; he was both solid and
acute ; nor do I remember to have seen soundness and
quaintness, with such sweet strains of morality, concur so in
any. I should think that he fell sick of the Times, but that
I knew him to be so good a Divine and Philosopher, and to
have studied the Theory of this World so much, that nothing
could take impression in him to hurt himself; therefore I
am content to believe, that his Glass ran out without any
                                                    jogging.

jogging. I know you lov'd him dearly well, which shall make me the more—Your most affectionate Servitor,

J. H.

Fleet, 3 *Aug.*

XLV.

To I. W., *Esq.; in* Gray's-Inn.

GENTLE SIR,

I VALUE at a high rate the fair respects you shew me, by the late ingenious expressions of your Letter; but the merit you ascribe to me in the superlative, might have very well serv'd in the positive, and 'tis well if I deserve in that degree. You writ that you have singular contentment and profit in the perusal of some Things of mine: I am heartily glad they afforded any Entertainment to a Gentleman of so choice a judgment as yourself.

I have a foolish working Brain of mine own, in labour still with something; and I can hardly keep it from *super-fetations,* tho' oft-times it produce a Mouse, in lieu of a Mountain. I must confess its best productions are but homely and hard-favour'd ; yet in regard they appear handsome in your Eyes, I shall like them the better. So I am, Sir—Yours most obliged to serve you,   J. H.

Fleet, 3 *Jan.* 1644.

XLVI.

To Mr. Tho. H.

SIR,

THO' the time abound with Schisms more than ever (the more is our misery), yet, I hope, you will not suffer any to creep into our Friendship; tho' I apprehend some fears thereof by your long silence, and cessation of literal correspondence. You know there is a peculiar Religion attends Friendship; there is, according to the Etymology of the word, a ligation and solemn tie, the rescinding whereof may be truly called a *Schism,* or a *Piacle,* which
is

is more. There belong to this Religion of Friendship certain
due rites, and decent ceremonies, as Visits, Messages, and
Missives. Tho' I am content to believe that you are firm
in the fundamentals, yet I find, under favour, that you have
lately fallen short of performing those exterior offices, as
if the ceremonial Law were quite abrogated with you in
all things. Friendship also allows of Merits, and works of
Supererogation sometimes, to make her capable of Eternity.
You know that Pair which were taken up into Heaven, and
placed among the brightest Stars for their rare constancy
and fidelity one to the other: you know also they are put
among the *fixed* Stars, not the *erratices*, to shew there must
be no inconstancy in love. Navigators steer their course
by them, and they are the best friends in working Seas,
dark nights, and distresses of weather; whence may be
inferr'd, that true friends should shine clearest in adversity,
in cloudy and doubtful times. On my part this ancient
friendship is still pure, orthodox, and incorrupted; and tho'
I have not the opportunity (as you have) to perform all the
rites thereof in regard of this recluse life, yet I shall never
err in the Essentials: I am still yours κτήσει, tho' I cannot
be χρήσει: for *in statu quo nunc*, I am grown useless and
good for nothing, yet in point of possession I am as much
as ever—Your firm inalterable Servitor,   J. H.

Fleet, 7 *Nov.* 1643.

XLVII.

To Mr. S. B., Merchant, at his House in the Old-Jury.

SIR,

I RETURN you those two famous speeches of the late Q.
Elizabeth, with the addition of another from *Baudius*
at an Embassy here from *Holland.* It is with Languages
as 'tis with liquors, which by transfusion use to take wind
from one vessel to another; so things translated into another
tongue lose of their primitive vigour and strength, unless a
paraphrastical Version be permitted; and then the Traduct
may

may exceed the Original; not otherwise, tho' the Version be never so punctual, 'specially in these Orations which are fram'd with such art, that, like *Vitruvius's* Palace, there is no place left to add one stone more without defacing, or to take any out without hazard of destroying the whole Fabrick.

Certainly she was a Princess of a rare endowment for Learning and Languages; she was bless'd with a long Life and triumphant Reign, attended with various sorts of admirable Successes, which will be taken for some Romance a thousand years hence, if the World last so long. She freed the *Scot* from the *French*, and gave her Successor a royal pension to maintain his Court: she help'd to settle the Crown on *Henry the Great's* head: she gave essence to the State of *Holland :* she civiliz'd *Ireland*, and suppress'd divers insurrections there: she preserv'd the dominion of the narrow Seas in greater glory than ever: she maintain'd open War against *Spain*, when *Spain* was in her highest flourish, for divers years together: yet she left a mighty Treasure behind, which shews that she was a notable good housewife. Yet I have read divers censures of her abroad; that she was ingrateful to her Brother of *Spain*, who had been the chiefest instrument, under God, to preserve her from the Block, and had left her all Q. *Mary's* Jewels without diminution; accusing her, that afterwards she should first infringe the Peace with him, by intercepting his treasure in the narrow Seas, by suffering her *Drake* to swim to his *Indies,* and rob him there; by fomenting and supporting his *Belgique* Subjects against him then when he had an Ambassador resident at her Court. But this was the censure of a *Spanish* Author; and *Spain* had little reason to speak well of her. The *French* handle her worse, by terming her, among other contumelies, *l'Haquenée de ses propres vassaux.*

Sir, I must much value the frequent respects you have shewn me, and am very covetous of the improvement of this acquaintance; for I do not remember at home or abroad to have seen in the person of any, a Gentleman and

and a Merchant so equally met as in you: which makes
me style myself—Your most affectionate Friend to serve
you,   J. H.
Fleet, 3 *May* 1645.

XLVIII.

To Dr. D. Featly.

SIR,

I RECEIV'D your Answer to that futilous Pamphlet,
with your desire of my opinion touching it. Truly,
Sir, I must tell you, that never poor Cur was toss'd in a
Blanket as you have toss'd that poor Coxcomb in the
Sheet you pleas'd to send me: For whereas a fillip might
have fell'd him, you have knock'd him down with a kind
of *Herculean* Club, *sans resource.* These Times (more's the
pity) labour with the same disease that *France* did during
the League; as a famous Author hath it, *Prurigo scripturientium erat scabies temporum:* The itching of Scribblers
was the scab of the Time: It is just so now, that any
triobolary Pasquiller, every *tressis agaso*, any sterquilinous
Rascal, is licens'd to throw dirt in the faces of Sovereign
Princes in open printed language. But I hope the Times
will mend, and your *Man* also, if he hath any grace, you
have so well corrected him. So I rest—Yours to serve and
everence you,   J. H.
Fleet, 1 *Aug.* 1644.

XLIX.

To Captain T. L., *in* Westchester.

CAPTAIN,

I COULD wish that I had the same advantage of speed
to send to you at this time as they have in *Alexandria*,
now call'd *Scanderoon*, when upon the arrival of any Ships
in the Bay, or any other important occasion, they use to
send their Letters by Pigeons, train'd up purposely for that
use, to *Aleppo* and other places: Such an airy Messenger,
                                                         such

such a volatile Postilion would I desire now to acquaint you with the sickness of your Mother-in-law, who I believe will be in another world (and I wish it may be Heaven) before this Paper comes to your hands: For the Physicians have forsaken her, and Dr. *Burton* told me 'tis a miracle if she lasts a natural day to an end: Therefore you shall do well to post up as soon as you can, to look to your own affairs, for I believe you will be no more sick of the Mother: Master *Davies* in the meantime told me he will be very careful and circumspect, that you be not wrong'd. I received yours of the 10th current, and return a thousand thanks for the warm and melting sweet expressions you make of your respects to me. All that I can say at present in answer is, that I extremely please myself in loving you; and I like my own affections the better, because they tell me that I am—Your entirely devoted Friend,   J. H.

Westm., 10 *Dec.* 1631.

L.

To my Hon. Friend, Sir C. C.

SIR,

I WAS upon point of going abroad to steal a solitary walk, when yours of the 12th current came to hand. The high researches and choice abstracted notions I found therein seem'd to heighten my spirits, and make my fancy fitter for my intended retirement and meditation: Add hereunto, that the countenance of the weather invited me; for it was a still evening, it was also a clear open sky, not a speck, or the least wrinkle, appear'd in the whole face of Heaven, 'twas such a pure deep azure all the Hemisphere over, that I wonder'd what was become of the three Regions of the Air, with their Meteors. So, having got into a close field, I cast my face upward, and fell to consider what a rare prerogative the optic virtue of the Eye hath, much more the *intuitive* virtue in the Thought, that the one in a moment can reach Heaven, and the other go beyond it: Therefore

sure

sure that Philosopher was but a kind of frantic fool, that
would have pluck'd out both his Eyes, because they were
a hindrance to his speculations. Moreover, I began to contemplate, as I was in this posture, the vast magnitude of the
Universe, and what proportion this poor globe of Earth might
bear with it: For if those numberless bodies which stick in
the vast roof of Heaven, tho' they appear to us but as spangles,
be some of them thousands of times bigger than the Earth,
take the Sea with it to boot, for they both make but one
Sphere, surely the Astronomers had reason to term this
Sphere an indivisible Point, and a thing of no dimension
at all, being compar'd to the whole World. I fell then to
think, that at the second general destruction, it is no more
for God Almighty to fire this Earth than for us to blow up
a small squib, or rather one small grain of Gunpowder. As
I was musing thus, I spied a swarm of Gnats waving up and
down the Air about me, which I knew to be part of the
Universe as well as I: And methought it was a strange
opinion of our *Aristotle* to hold, that the least of those small
insected Ephemerans should be more noble than the Sun,
because it had a sensitive soul in it. I fell to think, that in
the same proportion which those Animalillios bore with
me in point of bigness, the same I held with those glorious
Spirits which are near the Throne of the Almighty. What
then should we think of the magnitude of the Creator himself? Doubtless, 'tis beyond the reach of any human imagination to conceive it: In my private devotions I presume
to compare him to a great Mountain of Light, and my soul
seems to discern some glorious Form therein; but suddenly
as she would fix her eyes upon the Object, her sight is
presently dazled and disgregated with the refulgency and
corruscations thereof.

Walking a little further I spied a young boisterous Bull
breaking over hedge and ditch to a herd of Kine in the next
Pasture; which made me think, that if that fierce, strong
Animal, with others of that kind, knew their own strength,
they would never suffer Man to be their master. Then
looking

looking upon them quietly grazing up and down, I fell to consider that the Flesh which is daily dish'd upon our Tables is but concocted grass, which is recarnified in our stomachs, and transmuted to another flesh. I fell also to think what advantage those innocent Animals had of Man, who, as soon as Nature cast them into the world, find their Meat dress'd, the Cloth laid, and the Table cover'd; they find their Drink brew'd, and the Buttery open, their Beds made, and their Cloaths ready: and tho' Man hath the faculty of Reason to make him a compensation for the want of those advantages, yet this Reason brings with it a thousand perturbations of mind and perplexities of spirit, griping cares and anguishes of thought, which those harmless silly creatures were exempted from. Going on, I came to repose myself upon the trunk of a Tree, and I fell to consider further what advantage that dull *Vegetable* had of those feeding Animals, as not to be so troublesome and beholden to Nature, nor to be subject to starving, to diseases, to the inclemency of the weather, and to be far longer-liv'd. Then I spied a great Stone, and sitting a-while upon't, I fell to weigh in my thoughts that that Stone was in a happier condition, in some respects, than either of those *sensitive* Creatures or *Vegetables* I saw before; in regard that that Stone, which propagates by *assimilation*, as the Philosophers say, needed neither grass nor hay, or any aliment for restauration of nature, nor water to refresh its roots, or the heat of the Sun to attract the moisture upwards, to increase growth, as the other did. As I directed my pace homeward, I spied a Kite soaring high in the Air, and gently gliding up and down the clear Region so far above my head, that I fell to envy the Bird extremely, and repine at his happiness, that he should have a privilege to make a nearer approach to Heaven than I.

    Excuse me that I trouble you thus with these rambling meditations; they are to correspond with you in some part for those accurate fancies of yours lately sent me. So I rest
—Your entire and true Servitor,   J. H.

Holborn, 17 *Mar.* 1639.

                                      LI.

LI.

To *Master Serjeant* D., *at* Lincoln's-Inn.

SIR,

I UNDERSTAND with a deep sense of sorrow of the indisposition of your Son: I fear he hath too much *mind* for his *body*, and that superabounds with fancy, which brings him to these fits of distemper, proceeding from the black humour of Melancholy: Moreover, I have observ'd that he is too much given to his study and self-society, 'specially to converse with dead Men, I mean Books: You know anything in excess is naught. Now, Sir, were I worthy to give you advice, I could wish he were well marry'd, and it may wean him from that bookish and thoughtful humour: Women were created for the comfort of Men, and I have known that to some they have prov'd the best *Helleborum* against Melancholy. As this course may beget new Spirits in him, so it must needs add also to your comfort. I am thus bold with you, because I love the Gentleman dearly well, and honour you, as being—Your humble obliged Servant,   J. H.

West., 13 *June* 1632.

LII.

To my noble Lady, the Lady M. A.

MADAM,

THERE is not anything wherein I take more pleasure than in the accomplishment of your commands; nor had ever any Queen more power o'er her Vassals than you have o'er my Intellectuals. I find by my inclinations, that it is as natural for me to do your will, as it is for fire to fly upward, or anybody else to tend to his center; but touching the last command your Ladyship was pleased to lay upon me (which is the following Hymn), if I answer not the fulness of your expectation, it must be

imputed

imputed to the suddenness of the command, and the short-ness of time.

A Hymn to the Blessed Trinity.

To the First Person.

To thee, dread Sovereign, and dear Lord,
Who out of nought didst me afford
Essence and Life, who mad'st me Man,
And, oh much more, a Christian;
  Lo, from the centre of my heart
  All laud and glory I impart.

Hallelujah.

To the Second.

To thee, blest Saviour, who didst free
My soul from Satan's tyranny,
And mad'st her capable to be
An Angel of the Hierarchy;
  From the same centre I do raise
  All honour and immortal praise.

Hallelujah.

To the Third.

To thee, sweet Spirit, I return
That Love wherewith my Heart doth burn;
And these bless'd notions of my Brain
I now breathe up to thee again;
  O! let them re-descend, and still
  My soul with holy raptures fill.

Hallelujah.

They are of the same measure, cadence, and air as was that Angelical Hymn your Ladyship pleased to touch upon your Instrument; which as it so enchanted me then, that my soul was ready to come out at my ears, so your voice took such impressions in me, that methinks the sound still remains fresh with—Your Ladyship's most devoted Servitor,

J. H.

West., 1 *Apr.* 1637.

LIII.

LIII.

To Master P. W., at Westminster.

SIR,

THE fear of God is the *beginning* of Wisdom, and the *Love* of God is the end of the *Law*; the former saying was spoken by no meaner man than *Solomon*, but the latter hath no meaner Author than our *Saviour* himself. Touching this *Beginning* and this *End*, there is a near relation between them, so near, that the one begets the other; a harsh Mother may bring forth sometimes a mild Daughter: So *Fear* begets *Love*, but it begets *Knowledge* first; for—— *Ignoti nulla cupido*, we cannot love God, unless we know him before: Both *Fear* and *Love* are necessary to bring us to Heaven; the one is the fruit of the *Law*, the other of the *Gospel*; when the clouds of *Fear* are vanish'd, the beams of *Love* then begin to glance upon the heart; and of all the members of the Body, which are in a manner numberless, this is that which God desires, because 'tis the centre of Love, the source of our Affections, and the cistern that holds the most illustrious Blood; and in a sweet and well-devoted harmonious soul, *Cor* is no other than *Camera omnipotentis Regis*, 'tis one of God's Closets; and indeed nothing can fill the heart of Man, whose desires are infinite, but God, who is Infinity itself. *Love* therefore must be a necessary attendant to bring us to him. But besides *Love*, there must be two other guides that are requir'd in this journey, which are *Faith* and *Hope*; now that *Fear* which the *Law* enjoins us, turns to Faith in the *Gospel*, and Knowledge is the scope and subject of both: Yet these last two bring us only toward Heaven, but *Love* goes all along with us to Heaven, and so remains an inseparable sempiternal companion of the soul. *Love* therefore is the most acceptable Sacrifice which we can offer our Creator; and he who doth not study the Theory of it here, is never like to come to the Practice of it hereafter. It

was

was a hyperphysical expression of St. *Austin*, when he fell into this rapture, *That if he were King of Heaven, and God Almighty Bishop of* Hippo, *he would exchange places with him, because he lov'd him so well.* This Vote did so take me, that I have turn'd it to a paraphrastical Hymn, which I send you for your Viol, having observ'd often that you have a harmonious soul within you.

The VOTE.

O God, who can those passions tell
Wherewith my heart to thee doth swell!
I cannot better them declare,
Than by the wish made by that rare
   Aurelian *Bishop, who of old*
   Thy Oracles in Hippo *told.*

If I were Thou, *and thou wert I,*
I would resign the Deity;
Thou shouldst be God, I would be Man:
Is't possible that Love more can?
   O pardon, that my soul hath ta'en
   So high a flight, and grows profane.

For myself, my dear *Phil*, because I love you so dearly well, I will display my very intrinsecals to you in this point: When I examine the motions of my heart, I find that I love my Creator a thousand degrees more than I fear him; methinks I feel the little needle of my Soul touch'd with a kind of magnetical and attractive virtue, that it always moves towards him, as being her *summum bonum*, the true centre of her Happiness. For matter of *Fear*, there's none that I fear more than myself, I mean those frailties which lodge within me, and the extravagancies of my affections and thoughts: In this particular I may say, that I fear myself more than I fear the *Devil*, or *Death*, who is the *King of fears*. God guard us all, and guide us to our last home thro' the briars of this cumbersome Life. In this prayer I rest
—Your most affectionate Servitor,   J. H.

Holborn, 21 *Mar.* 1639.
          2 F   LIV.

LIV.

To the Rt. Hon. the Lord Cliff.

My Lord,

SINCE among other passages of entertainment we had lately at the *Italian* Ordinary (where your Lordship was pleas'd to honour us with your presence) there happen'd a large discourse of *Wines*, and of other *Drinks* that were us'd by several Nations of the Earth, and that your Lordship desir'd me to deliver what I observ'd therein abroad, I am bold now to confirm and amplify in this Letter what I then let drop *extempore* from me, having made a recollection of myself for that purpose.

It is without controversy, that in the nonage of the world men and beasts had but one buttery, which was the Fountain and River ; nor do we read of any Vines or Wines till 200 years after the flood : But now I do not know or hear of any Nation that hath *Water* only for their drink, except the *Japonois*, and they drink it hot too ; but we may say, that what beverage soever we make, either by brewing, by distillation, decoction, percolation, or pressing, it is but *Water* at first : Nay, *Wine* itself is but Water sublim'd, being nothing else but that moisture and sap which is caus'd either by rain or other kind of irrigations about the roots of the Vine, and drawn up to the branches and berries by the virtual attractive heat of the Sun, the bowels of the Earth serving as a Limbeck to that end ; which made the *Italian* Vineyard-man (after a long drought and an extreme hot Summer, which had parch'd up all his grapes) to complain, that *per mancamento d'acqua, bevo dell' acqua, se io havessi acqua, beverei el vino ;* For want of water, I am forc'd to drink water ; if I had water, I would drink wine. It may be also applied to the Miller, when he had no water to drive his Mills.

The Vine doth so abhor cold that it cannot grow beyond the 49th degree to any purpose : Therefore God and Nature hath

hath furnish'd the North-west Nations with other inventions of beverage. In this Island the old drink was *Ale,* noble *Ale;* than which, as I heard a great foreign Doctor affirm, there is no liquor that more increaseth the radical moisture, and preserves the natural heat, which are the two Pillars that support the life of Man : But since *Beer* hath *hopp'd* in among us, *Ale* is thought to be much adulterated, and nothing so good as Sir *John Oldcastle* and *Smug* the Smith was us'd to drink. Besides *Ale* and *Beer,* the natural drink of part of this Isle may be said to be *Metheglin,* *Braggot,* and *Mead,* which differ in strength according to the three degrees of comparison. The first of the three, which is strong in the superlative, if taken immoderately, doth stupify more than any other liquor, and keeps a *humming* in the brain ; which made one say, that he lov'd not *Metheglin,* because he was us'd to speak too much of the *house* he came from, meaning the Hive. Cyder and Perry are also the natural drinks of part of this Isle. But I have read in some old Authors of a famous drink the ancient Nation of the *Picts,* who liv'd 'twixt *Trent* and *Tweed,* and were utterly extinguish'd by the overpowering of the *Scot,* were used to make of decoction of flowers, the receipt whereof they kept as a secret, and a thing sacred to themselves ; so it perish'd with them. These are all the common drinks of this Isle, and of *Ireland* also, where they are more given to Milk, and Strong-waters of all colours : The prime is *Usquebagh,* which cannot be made anywhere in that perfection ; and whereas we drink it here in *Aqua vitæ* measures, it goes down there by beer-glass-fulls, being more natural to the Nation.

In the seventeen Provinces hard by, and all low *Germany,* Beer is the common natural drink, and nothing else ; so is it in *Westphalia,* and all the lower Circuit of *Saxony,* in *Denmark,* *Swethland,* and *Norway.* The *Prusse* hath a Beer as thick as Honey : In the Duke of *Saxe's* Country there is Beer as yellow as Gold, made of Wheat, and it inebriates as soon as Sack. In some parts of *Germany* they use to spice their Beer, which will keep many years ; so that
at

at some Weddings there will be a butt drank out as old as the Bride. *Poland* also is a Beer Country; but in *Russia, Muscovy,* and *Tartary* they use *Mead,* which is the naturallest drink of the Country, being made of the decoction of Water and Honey: This is that which the Ancients call'd *Hydromel.* Mares-milk is a great drink with the *Tartar,* which may be a cause why they are bigger than ordinary; for the Physicians hold, that Milk enlargeth the Bones, Beer strengtheneth the Nerves, and Wine breeds Blood sooner than any other Liquor. The *Turk,* when he hath his Tripe full of Pelaw, or of Mutton and Rice, will go to Nature's Cellar; either to the next Well or River to drink Water, which is his natural common Drink: For *Mahomet* taught them, that there was a Devil in every berry of the grape, and so made a strict inhibition to all his Sect from drinking of Wine, as a thing profane: He had also a reach of policy therein, because they should not be incumber'd with luggage when they went to War, as other Nations do, who are so troubled with the carriage of their Wine and Beverages; yet hath the *Turk* peculiar drinks to himself besides, as *Sherbet* made of juice of Lemon, Sugar, Amber, and other ingredients: He hath also a drink call'd *Cauphe,* which is made of a brown berry, and it may be call'd their clubbing drink between meals, which tho' it be not very gustful to the palate, yet it is very comfortable to the stomach, and good for the sight. But notwithstanding their Prophet's Anathema, thousands of them will venture to drink Wine, and they will make a precedent prayer to their souls to depart from their bodies in the interim, for fear she partake of the same pollution. Nay, the last *Turk* died of excess of Wine, for he had at one time swallow'd three and thirty Okes, which is a measure near upon the bigness of our Quart; and that which brought him to this was, the Company of a *Persian* Lord, that had given him his daughter for a present, and came with him from *Bagdat :* Besides, one accident that happen'd to him was, that he had an Eunuch who was used to be drunk, and whom he had

                                                    commanded

commanded twice upon pain of life to refrain, swearing by *Mahomet,* that he would cause him to be strangled if he found him the third time so; yet the Eunuch still continued in his drunkenness. Hereupon the *Turk* conceiving with himself that there must needs be some extraordinary delight in drunkenness, because this Man preferr'd it before his life, fell to it himself, and so drank himself to death.

In *Asia* there is no Beer drank at all, but Water, Wine, and an incredible variety of other Drinks, made of Dates, dried Raisins, Rice, divers sorts of Nuts, Fruits, and Roots. In the Oriental Countries, as *Cambaia, Calicut, Narsingha,* there is a Drink call'd *Banque,* which is rare and precious; and 'tis the height of entertainment they give their guests before they go to sleep, like that *Nepenthe* which the Poets speak so much of; for it provokes pleasing dreams and delightful phantasies; it will accommodate itself to the humour of the sleeper: As if he be a Soldier, he will dream of Victories and taking of Towns; if he be in love, he will think to enjoy his Mistress; if he be covetous, he will dream of Mountains of gold, *&c.* In the *Moluccas* and *Philippines* there is a curious drink call'd *Tampoy,* made of a kind of Gilliflowers, and another drink call'd *Otraqua,* that comes from a Nut, and is the more general drink. In *China* they have a holy kind of liquor made of such sort of flowers for ratifying and binding of bargains; and having drank thereof, they hold it no less than perjury to break what they promise: As they write of a River in *Bithynia,* whose water hath a peculiar virtue to discover a perjurer; for if he drink thereof, it will persently boil in his stomach, and put him to visible tortures. This makes me think of the River *Styx* among the Poets, which the Gods were use to swear by; and it was the greatest Oath for the performance of anything:

Nubila promissi Styx *mihi testis erit.*

It put me in mind also of that which some write of the River of *Rhine,* for trying the legitimation of a Child being
thrown

thrown in; if he be a bastard he will sink, if otherwise he will not.

In *China* they speak of a Tree call'd *Maguais*, which affords not only good drink, being pierced, but all things else that belong to the subsistence of man: They bore the Trunk with an Awger, and then issueth out sweet potable liquor; 'twixt the rind and the tree there is a Cotton, or hempy kind of Moss, which they wear for their clothing; it bears huge Nuts, which have excellent food in them; it shoots out hard prickles above a fathom long, and those arm them; with the bark they make tents; and the dotard trees serve for firing.

Africa also hath a great diversity of drinks, as having more need of them, being a hotter Country far: In *Guiney*, or the lower *Ethiopia*, there is a famous drink call'd *Mingol*, which issueth out of a tree much like the Palm, being bored: But in the upper *Ethiopia*, or the *Habassins* Country, they drink *Mead* decocted in a different manner. There is also much Wine there. The common drink of *Barbary*, after Water, is that which is made of Dates. But in *Egypt*, in times past, there was beer drank call'd *Zithus* in *Latin*, which was no other than a decoction of Barley and Water; they had also a famous composition (and they use it to this day) called *Chiffi*, made of divers cordials and provocative ingredients, which they throw into water to make it gustful; they use it also for fumigation: But now the general drink of *Egypt* is *Nile* water, which of all water may be said to be the best, insomuch that *Pindar's* words might be more applicable to that than to any other, Ἀριϛὸν μὲν ὕδωρ. It doth not only fertilize and extremely fatten the soil which it covers, but it helps to impregnate barren Women; for there is no place on earth where People increase and multiply faster: 'Tis yellowish and thick, but if one cast a few Almonds into a potful of it, it will become as clear as rock water: It is also in a degree of lukewarmness, as *Martial's* boy:

> *Tolle puer calices tepidique torcumata Nili.*

In

In the new world they have a world of drinks; for there is no root, flower, fruit, or pulse but is reducible to a potable liquor; as in the *Barbado* Island the common drink among the *English* is *Mobbi*, made of Potato roots: In *Mexico* and *Peru*, which is the great Continent of *America*, with other parts, it is prohibited to make Wines under great penalties, for fear of starving of trade: so that all the Wines they have are sent from *Spain*.

Now for the pure Wine Countries; *Greece* with all her Islands, *Italy*, *Spain*, *France*, one part of four of *Germany*, *Hungary*, with divers Countries thereabouts, all the Islands in the *Mediterranean* and *Atlantic* Sea, are Wine Countries.

The most generous Wines of *Spain* grow in the midland parts of the Continent, and St. *Martin* bears the bell, which is near the Court. Now, as in *Spain*, so in all other Wine Countries, one cannot pass a day's Journey but he will find a differing race of Wine: Those kinds that our Merchants carry over are those only that grow upon the Seaside, as *Malagas*, *Sherries*, *Tents*, and *Aligants*: Of this last there's little comes over right, therefore the Vintners make *Tent* (which is a name for all Wines in *Spain*, except white) to supply the place of it. There is a gentle kind of White-wines grows among the Mountains of *Galicia*, but not of body enough to bear the Sea, call'd *Rabidavia*. *Portugal* affords no Wines worth the transporting; they have an odd stone we call *Yef*, which they use to throw into their Wines, which clarifieth it, and makes it more lasting. There's also a drink in *Spain* call'd *Alosha*, which they drink between meals in hot weather, and 'tis a *Hydromel* made of water and honey, much of the taste of our *Mead*. In the Court of *Spain* there's a *German* or two that brews Beer; but for that ancient drink of *Spain* which *Pliny* speaks of, compos'd of flowers, the receipt thereof is utterly lost.

In *Greece* there are no Wines that have bodies enough to bear the Sea for long voyages; some few Muscadells and Malmsies are brought over in small Casks: nor is there

there in *Italy* any Wine transported to *England* but in Bottles, as *Verde*, and others; for the length of the voyage makes them subject to pricking, and so lose colour, by reason of their delicacy.

France participating of the Climes of all the Countries about her, affords Wines of quality accordingly; as towards the *Alpes* and *Italy*, she hath a luscious rich Wine called *Frontiniac:* In the Country of *Provence* towards the *Pyrenees*, and in *Languedoc*, there are Wines concustable with those of *Spain:* one of the prime sort of White-wines is that of *Beaume*, and of Clarets that of *Orleans*, tho' it be interdicted to wine the King's Cellar with it, in respect of the corrosiveness it carries with it. As in *France*, so in all other Wine-Countries, the white is called the *female*, and the Claret or Red-wine is called the *male*, because commonly it hath more sulphur, body, and heat in't. The Wines that our Merchants bring over grow upon the River *Garon* near *Bourdeaux* in *Gascony*, which is the greatest Mart for Wines in all *France;* the *Scot*, because he hath always been an useful Confederate to *France* against *England*, hath (among other privileges) right of pre-emption or first choice of Wines in *Bourdeaux;* he is also permitted to carry his Ordnance to the very Walls of the Town, whereas the *English* are forced to leave them at *Blay*, a good way distant down the River. There is a hard green Wine that grows about *Rochell*, and the Islands thereabouts, which the cunning *Hollander* sometimes uses to fetch; and he hath a trick to put a bag of herbs, or some other infusions into it (as he doth brimstone in *Rhenish*), to give it a whiter tincture and more sweetness; then they reimbark it for *England*, where it passeth for good *Bachrag*, and this is called *stooming* of Wines. In *Normandy* there's little or no Wine at all grows, therefore the common drink of that Country is Cyder, 'specially in low *Normandy:* There are also many Beer-houses in *Paris* and elsewhere; but tho' their barley and water be better than ours, or that of *Germany*, and tho' they have *English* and *Dutch*

Brewers

Brewers among them, yet they cannot make Beer in that perfection.

The prime Wines of *Germany* grow about the *Rhine*, 'specially in the *Psalts* or *Lower-Palatinate* about *Bachrag*, which hath its Etymology from *Bacchi ara*; for in ancient times there was an Altar erected there to the honour of *Bacchus*, in regard of the richness of the Wines. Here, and all *France* over, 'tis held a great part of incivility for Maidens to drink Wine until they are married, as it is in *Spain* for them to wear high shoes or to paint till then. The *German* Mothers, to make their Sons fall into hatred of Wine, do use, when they are little, to put some Owls' Eggs into a cup of *Rhenish*, and sometimes a little living Eel, which twingling in the Wine while the child is drinking, so scares him, that many come to abhor and have an antipathy to Wine all their lives after. From *Bachrag* the first stock of Vines, which grow now in the grand *Canary* Island, were brought, which, with the heat of the Sun and the Soil, is grown now to that height of perfection, that the Wine which they afford is accounted the richest, the most firm, the best bodied and lastingest Wine, and the most defecated from all earthly grossness, of any other whatsoever; it hath little or no sulphur at all in't, and leaves less dregs behind, tho' one drink it to excess. *French* Wines may be said to pickle meat in the stomach; but this is the Wine that digests, and doth not only breed good blood, but it nutrifieth also, being a glutinous substantial liquor. Of this Wine, if of any other, may be verified that merry induction, That good Wine makes good Blood, good Blood causeth good Humours, good Humours cause good Thoughts, good Thoughts bring forth good Works, good Works carry a Man to Heaven; *ergo* good Wine carrieth a Man to Heaven. If this be true, surely more *English* go to Heaven this way than any other, for I think there's more *Canary* brought into *England* than to all the World besides. I think also there is a hundred times more drunk under the name of *Canary* Wine than there is brought in; for
Sherries

Sherries and *Malagas* well mingled pass for *Canaries* in most Taverns, more often than *Canary* itself; else I do not see how 'twere possible for the Vintner to save by it, or to live by his Calling, unless he were permitted sometimes to be a Brewer. When *Sacks* and *Canaries* were brought in first among us, they were us'd to be drank in *Aqua vitæ* measures, and 'twas held fit only for those to drink of them who were us'd to carry their *legs in their hands, their eyes upon their noses,* and an *Almanack in their bones:* But now they go down every one's throat, both young and old, like milk.

The Countries that are freest from excess of drinking are *Spain* and *Italy:* If a Woman can prove her Husband to have been thrice drunk, by the ancient Laws of *Spain* she may plead for a divorce from him. Nor indeed can the *Spaniard,* being hot-brain'd, bear much drink; yet I have heard that *Gondomar* was once too hard for the King of *Denmark* when he was here in *England.* But the *Spanish* Soldiers, that have been in the Wars of *Flanders,* will take theirs cups freely, and the *Italians* also. When I liv'd t'other side the *Alps,* a Gentleman told me a merry Tale of a *Ligurian* Soldier who had got drunk in *Genoa;* and Prince *Doria* going a-horseback to take the round one night, the Soldier took his horse by the bridle, and ask'd what the Price of him was, for he wanted a horse: The Prince seeing in what humour he was, caus'd him to be taken into a house, and put to sleep: In the morning he sent for him, and ask'd him what he would give for his Horse. *Sir,* said the recover'd Soldier, *the Merchant that would have bought him yesternight of your Highness went away betimes in the morning.* The boonest companions for drinking are the *Greeks* and *Germans;* but the *Greek* is the merrier of the two, for he will sing and dance, and kiss his next companion; but the other will drink as deep as he: The *Greek* will drink as many glasses as there be letters in his Mistress's name; the other will drink the number of his years, and tho' he be not apt to break out into *singing,* being not of so airy a constitution,

yet

yet he will drink often musically a health to every one of these six Notes, *Ut, Re, Mi, Fa, Sol, La;* which, with his reason, are all comprehended in this Hexameter:

UT RElevet MIserum FAtum SOLitosque LAbores.

The fewest draughts he drinks are three, the first to quench the thirst past, the second to quench the present thirst, the third to prevent the future. I heard of a company of *Low-Dutchmen* that had drunk so deep, that beginning to stagger, and their heads turning round, they thought verily they were at Sea, and that the upper chamber where they were was a Ship; insomuch that it being foul windy weather, they fell to throwing the stools and other things out of the window, to lighten the Vessel, for fear of suffering shipwreck.

Thus have I sent your Lordship a *dry* discourse upon a *fluent* subject; yet I hope your Lordship will please to take all in good part, because it proceeds from—Your most humble and ready Servitor, J. H.

Westm., 17 *Oct.* 1634.

LV.

To the Right Honourable the Earl R.

My Lord,

YOUR desires have been always to me as commands, and your commands as binding as Acts of Parliament: Nor do I take pleasure to employ head or hand in anything more than in the exact performance of them. Therefore if in this crabbed, difficult task you have been pleas'd to impose upon me about Languages, I come short of your Lordship's expectation, I hope my obedience will apologize for my disability. But whereas your Lordship desires to know what were the original Mother-Tongues of the Countries of *Europe*, and how these modern Speeches that are now in use were first introduced, I may answer hereunto, that it is almost as easy a thing to discover the Source of *Nile,*

Nile, as to find out the Original of some Languages : yet I will attempt it as well as I can ; and I will take my first rise in these Islands of *Great Britain* and *Ireland :* for to be curious and eagle-eyed abroad, and to be blind and ignorant at home (as many of our Travellers are now-a-days), is a curiosity that carrieth with it more of affectation than anything else.

Touching the Isle of *Albion*, or *Great Britany*, the *Cambrian*, or *Cymraecan*, Tongue, commonly call'd *Welsh* (and *Italian* also is so call'd by the *Dutch*), is without controversy the prime maternal Tongue of this Island, and connatural with it; nor could any of the four Conquests that have been made of it by *Roman, Saxon, Dane,* or *Norman* ever extinguish her, but she remains still pure and incorrupt; of which Language there is as exact and methodical a *Grammar*, with as regular precepts, rules, and institutions, both for prose and verse, compil'd by Dr. *David Rice*, as I have read in any Tongue whatsoever. Some of the authentickest Annalists report, that the old *Gauls* (now the *French*) and the *Britons* understood one another; for they came thence very frequently to be instructed here by the *British Druids*, who were the Philosophers and Divines of those times: and this was long before the *Latin* Tongue came this side the *Alps*, or books written; and there is no meaner Man than *Cæsar* himself records this.

This is one of the fourteen *vernacular* and independent Tongues of *Europe*, and she hath divers Dialects : the first is the *Cornish*, the second the *Armoricans*, or the Inhabitants of *Britany* in *France*, whither a Colony was sent over hence in the time of the *Romans*. There was also another Dialect of the *British* Language among the *Picts*, who kept in the North Parts, in *Northumberland, Westmerland, Cumberland*, and some parts beyond *Tweed*, until the whole Nation of the *Scots* poured upon them with such multitudes, that they are utterly extinguish'd, both them and Language. There are some who have been curious in the comparison of Tongues, who believe that the *Irish* is but a dialect of

the

the ancient *British;* and the learnedest of that Nation, in a private discourse I happened to have with him, seem'd to incline to this opinion : but this I can assure your Lordship of, that at my being in that Country I observ'd by a private collection which I made, that a great multitude of their radical words are the same with the *Welsh,* both for sense and sound ; the tone also of both the Nations is consonant : for when first I walk'd up and down *Dublin* Markets, methought verily I was in *Wales;* then I listened unto their speech ; but I found that the *Irish* Tone is a little more querulous and whining than the *British,* which I conjectured with myself proceeded from their often being subjugated by the *English.*   But, my Lord, you would think it strange, that divers pure *Welsh* words should be found in the new-found World in the *West-Indies;* yet it is verify'd by some Navigators, as *Grando* (hark), *Nef* (heaven), *Lluynog* (a fox), *Pengwyn* (a bird with a white head), with sundry others, which are pure *British :* nay, I have read a *Welsh* Epitaph which was found there upon one *Madoc,* a *British* Prince, who four years before the *Norman* Conquest, not agreeing with his brother, then Prince of *South-Wales,* went to try his fortunes at Sea, imbarking himself at *Milford-Haven,* and so tarried on those coasts. This, if well prov'd, might well entitle our Crown to *America,* if first discovery may claim a right to any Country.

The *Romans,* tho' they continu'd here constantly above 300 years, yet they could not do as they did in *France, Spain,* and other Provinces, plant their Language as a mark of Conquest; but the *Saxons* did, coming in far greater numbers under *Hengist* from *Holstein-land* in the lower Circuit of *Saxony;* which People resemble the *English* more than any other Men upon Earth, so that 'tis more than probable that they came first from thence : besides, there is a Town there call'd *Lunden,* and another place named *Angles,* whence it may be presum'd that they took their new denomination here.   Now, the *English,* tho' as *Saxons* (by which name the *Welsh* and *Irish* call them to
this

this day) they and their Language are ancient, yet in reference to this Island they are the modernest Nation in *Europe*,
both for habitation, speech, and denomination; which makes
me smile at Mr. *Fox's* error in the very front of his Epistle
before the Book of Martyrs, where he calls *Constantine*,
the first Christian Emperor, the Son of *Helen* an *English*
Woman; whereas she was purely *British*, and that there
was no such Nation upon earth called *English* at that time,
nor above 100 years after, till *Hengist* invaded this Island,
and settling himself in it, the *Saxons* who came with him
took the appellation of *Englishmen*. Now, the *English*
speech, tho' it be rich, copious, and significant, and that
there be divers Dictionaries of it, yet, under favour, I
cannot call it a regular Language, in regard, tho' often
attempted by some choice Wits, there could never any
Grammar of exact *Syntaxis* be made of it; yet hath she
divers sub-dialects, as the Western and Northern *English*,
but her chiefest is the *Scotic*, which took footing beyond
Tweed about the last Conquest; but the ancient Language
of *Scotland* is *Irish*, which the Mountaineers, and divers
of the Plain, retain to this day. Thus, my Lord, according
to my small model of Observations, have I endeavour'd to
satisfy you in part: I shall in my next go on, for in the
pursuance of any command from your Lordship my mind
is like a stone thrown into a deep water, which never rests
till it goes to the bottom: So for this time, and always, I
rest, my Lord—Your most humble and ready Servitor,

J. H.

Westm., 9 *Aug.* 1630.

LVI.

To the Right Honourable the Earl R.

MY LORD,

IN my last I fulfill'd your Lordship's commands, as far
as my reading and knowledge could extend, to inform
you what were the radical primitive Languages of those
Dominions that belong to the Crown of *Great Britain*,
and

and how the *English,* which is now predominant, enter'd
in first: I will now hoise sail for the *Netherlands,* whose
Language is the same dialect with the *English,* and was so
from the beginning, being both of them derived from the
High-Dutch: The *Danish* also is but a branch of the same
tree, no more is the *Swedish,* and the speech of them of
Norway and *Island.* Now, the *High-Dutch* or *Teutonic*
Tongue is one of the prime and most spacious maternal
Languages of *Europe ;* for besides the vast extent of *Ger-
many* itself, with the Countries and Kingdoms before-men-
tioned, whereof *England* and *Scotland* are two, it was the
Language of the *Goths* and *Vandals,* and continueth yet
of the greatest part of *Poland* and *Hungary,* who have a
Dialect of hers for their vulgar Tongue; yet tho' so many
Dialects and sub-dialects be derived from her, she remains
a strong sinewy Language, pure and incorrupt in her first
centre, towards the heart of *Germany.* Some of her
Writers would make the world believe that she was the
Language spoken in Paradise ; for they produce many
Words and proper names in the Five Books of *Moses*
which fetch their Etymology from her ; as also in *Persia,*
to this day, divers radical words are the same with her, as
Fader, Moeder, Broder, Star : And a *German* Gentleman,
speaking hereof one day to an *Italian,* that she was the
Language of Paradise, *Sure,* said the *Italian* (alluding to
her roughness), *then it was the tongue that God Almighty
chid* Adam *in.   It may be so,* reply'd the *German ; but the
Devil had tempted* Eve *in* Italian *before.* A full-mouth'd
Language she is, and pronounced with that strength, as if
one had bones in his tongue instead of nerves.

Those Countries that border upon *Germany,* as *Bohemia,
Silesia, Poland,* and those vast Countries North-Eastward,
as *Russia* and *Muscovia,* speak the *Sclavonic* Language :
And it is incredible what I have heard some Travellers
report of the vast extent of that Language ; for beside
Sclavonia itself, which properly is *Dalmatia* and *Liburnia,*
it is the vulgar speech of the *Macedonians, Epirots, Bosnians,*
Servians,

Servians, Bulgarians, Moldavians, Rascians, and *Podolians;*
nay, it spreads itself over all the Eastern parts of *Europe*
(*Hungary* and *Wallachia* excepted) as far as *Constantinople,*
and is frequently spoken in the Seraglio among the *Jani-
zaries:* nor doth she rest there, but crossing the *Hellespont,*
divers Nations in *Asia* have her for their popular tongue,
as the *Circassians, Mongrelians,* and *Gazarites* Southward:
neither in *Europe* or *Asia* doth she extend herself further
Northward than to the parallel of forty degrees. But those
Nations which celebrate Divine Service after the *Greek*
Ceremony, and profess obedience to the Patriarch of *Constantinople,* as the *Russ,* the *Muscovite,* the *Moldavian, Ras-
cian, Bosnian, Servian,* and *Bulgarian,* with divers other
Eastern and North-East People that speak *Sclavonic,* have
her in a different character from the *Dalmatian, Croatian,
Istrian, Polonian, Bohemian, Silesian,* and other Nations
towards the West: these last have the *Illyrian* Character,
and the invention of it is attributed to St. *Jerome;* the other
is of *Cyril's* devising, and is call'd the *Servian* Character.
Now, altho' there be above sixty several Nations that have
this vast extended Language for their vulgar speech, yet the
pure primitive *Sclavonic* dialect is spoken only in *Dalmatia,
Croatia, Liburnia,* and the Countries adjacent, where the
ancient *Sclavonians* yet dwell; and they must needs be very
ancient; for there is in a Church in *Prague* an old Charter
yet extant, given them by *Alexander the Great,* which I
thought not amiss to insert here: *We* Alexander the Great,
Son of King Philip, *Founder of the* Grecian *Empire, Conqueror of the* Persians, Medes, *&c., and of the whole World
from East to West, from North to South, Son of great*
Jupiter *by,* &c., *so call'd; to you the noble stock of* Sclavonians,
*and to your Language, because you have been unto us a Help,
true in Faith, and valiant in War, we confirm all that tract of
Earth from the North to the South of* Italy, *from us and our
Successors, to you and your Posterity for ever: And if any
other Nation be found there, let them be your slaves.* Dated
at *Alexandria* the 12th of the Goddess *Minerva,* witness
                                                        Ethra

Ethra and the eleven Princes whom we appoint our Successors. With this rare and one of the ancientest Records in *Europe*, I will put a period to this second account I send your Lordship touching Languages. My next shall be of *Greece, Italy, France,* and *Spain,* and so I shall shake hands with *Europe;* till when, I humbly kiss your hands, and rest, my Lord—Your most obliged Servitor, J. H.

Westm., 2 *of Aug.* 1630.

LVII.

To the Right Honourable the Earl R.

MY LORD,

HAVING in my last rambled through *High* and *Low Germany, Bohemia, Denmark, Poland, Russia,* and those vast North-East Regions, and given your Lordship a touch of their Languages (for 'twas no Treatise I intended at first, but a cursory short literal account), I will now pass to *Greece,* and speak something of that large and learned Language; for 'tis she indeed upon whom the beams of the scientifical Knowledge did first shine in *Europe,* which she afterward diffus'd thro' all the Eastern World.

The *Greek* Tongue was first peculiar to *Hellas* alone, but in tract of time the Kingdom of *Macedon,* and *Epire,* had her; then she arriv'd at the Isles of the *Egean* Sea, which are interjacent, and divide *Asia* and *Europe* that way; then she got into the fifty-three Isles of the *Cyclades* that lie 'twixt *Negropont* and *Candy,* and so got up the *Hellespont* to *Constantinople:* She then crossed over to *Anatolia,* where tho' she prevail'd by introducing multitudes of Colonies, yet she came not to be the sole vulgar speech anywhere there, so far as to extinguish the former Languages. Now *Anatolia* is the most populous part of the whole Earth; for *Strabo* speaks of sixteen several Nations that slept in her bosom, and 'tis thought the twenty-two Languages which *Mithridates,* the great *Polyglot* King of *Pontus,* did speak were all within the circumference of *Anatolia,* in regard his dominions ex-

2 G   tended

tended but a little further. She glided then along the Maritime Coasts of *Thrace*, and passing *Byzantium*, got into the outlets of *Danube*, and beyond her also to *Zaurica*, yea, beyond that to the River *Phasis;* and thence compassing to *Trebizond*, she took footing on all the circumference of the *Euxine* Sea. This was her course from East to North; whence we will return to *Candy*, *Cyprus*, and *Sicily;* thence crossing the *Phare* of *Messina*, she got all along the Maritime Coasts of the *Tyrrhene* Sea to *Calabria:* She rested herself also a great while in *Apulia*. There was a populous Colony of *Greeks* also in *Marseilles* in *France*, and along the Sea-Coasts of *Savoy*. In *Africk* likewise, *Cyrene*, *Alexandria*, and *Egypt*, with divers others, were peopled with *Greeks:* And three causes may be alleged why the *Greek* Tongue did so expand herself: First, it may be imputed to the Conquest of *Alexander the Great*, and the Captains he left behind him for Successors: Then the love the people had to the Sciences, speculative Learning and Civility, whereof the *Greeks* accounted themselves to be the grand Masters, accounting all other Nations *Barbarians* besides themselves. Thirdly, the natural Inclination and Dexterity the *Greeks* had to Commerce, whereto they employ'd themselves more than any other Nation, except the *Phœnician* and *Armenian;* which may be a reason why in all places most commonly they colonized the Maritime parts, for I do not find they did penetrate far into the bowels of any Country, but liv'd on the Sea-side in obvious mercantile Places and accessible Ports.

Now many ages since the *Greek* Tongue is not only impaired, and pitifully degenerated in her purity and eloquence, but extremely decay'd in her amplitude and vulgarness. For first, there is no trace at all left of her in *France* or *Italy*, the *Sclavonic* Tongue hath abolished her in *Epire* and *Macedon*, the *Turkish* hath outed her from most parts of *Anatolia*, and the *Arabian* hath extinguish'd her in *Syria*, *Palestine*, *Egypt*, and sundry other places. Now touching her degeneration from her primitive

suavity

suavity and elegance, it is not altogether so much as the deviation and declension of the *Italian* from the *Latin;* yet it is so far that I could set foot on no place, nor hear of any people, where either the *Attic, Doric, Æolic,* or *Bæotic* ancient *Greek* is vulgarly spoken; only in some places near *Heraclea* in *Anatolia,* and *Peloponnesus* (now called the *Morea),* they speak of some Towns call'd the *Lacocones,* which retain yet, and vulgarly speak, the old *Greek,* but incongruously: Yet tho' they cannot themselves speak according to rules, they understand those that do. Nor is this corruption happen'd to the *Greek* Language, as it useth to happen to others, either by the Law of the Conqueror or Inundation of Strangers; but it is insensibly crept in by their own supine negligence and fantastickness, 'specially by that common fatality and changes which attend time, and all other sublunary things. Nor is this ancient scientifical Language decay'd only, but the Nation of the *Greeks* itself is as it were moulder'd away, and brought in a manner to the same condition, and to as contemptible a pass as the *Jew* is: Insomuch that there cannot be two more pregnant instances of the lubricity and instableness of Mankind than the decay of these two ancient Nations; the one the select people of God, the other the most famous that ever was for Arts, Arms, Civility, and Government: So that in *statu quo nunc,* they who term'd all the world *Barbarians* in comparison of themselves in former times, may be now term'd (more than any other) *Barbarians* themselves, as having quite lost not only all inclination and aspirings to Knowledge and Virtue, but likewise all courage and bravery of mind to recover their ancient Freedom and Honour.

   Thus have you, my Lord, as much of the *Greek* Tongue as I could comprehend within the bounds of a Letter; a Tongue that both for Knowledge, for Commerce, and for Copiousness was the principallest that ever was: In my next I will return nearer home, and give your Lordship account of the *Latin* Tongue, and of her three daughters,
the

the *French, Italian,* and *Spanish.* In the interim you find I am still, my Lord—Your most obedient Servitor,

J. H.

Westm., 25 *Jul.* 1630.

LVIII.

To the Right Honourable the Earl R.

MY LORD,

MY last was a pursuit of my endeavours to comply with your Lordship's desires touching Languages: And I spent more Oil and Labour than ordinary in displaying the *Greek* Tongue, because we are more beholden to her for all Philosophical and Theorick Knowledge, as also for rules of Commerce and commutative Justice, than to any other. I will now proceed to the *Latin* Tongue, which had her source in *Italy,* in *Latium,* call'd now *Campagna di Roma,* and receiv'd her growth with the monstrous increase of the City and Empire. Touching the one, she came from poor mud-walls at Mount *Palatine,* which were scarce a mile about at first, to be afterward fifty miles compass, (as she was in the reign of *Aurelianus*) ; and her Territories, which were hardly a day's journey extent, came by favourable successes, and fortune of War, to be above three thousand in length, from the banks of the *Rhine,* or rather from the shores of this Island to *Euphrates,* and sometimes to the River *Tigris.* With this vast expansion of *Roman* Territories, the Tongue also did spread ; yet I do not find by those researches I have made into Antiquity, that she was vulgarly spoken by any Nation, or in any entire Country, but in *Italy* itself: For notwithstanding that it was the practice of the *Roman* with his Lance to usher in his Laws and Language as marks of Conquest, yet I believe his Tongue never took such firm impression anywhere, as to become the vulgar epidemic speech of any people else ; or that she was able to null and extinguish the native Languages she found in those places where she planted her Standard : Nor can there be a more pregnant instance

hereof

hereof than this Island, for notwithstanding that she remain'd a *Roman* Province 400 years together, yet the *Latin* Tongue could never have the vogue here so far as to abolish the *British* or *Cambrian* Tongue.

'Tis true, that in *France* and *Spain* she made deeper impressions; the reason may be, in regard there were far more *Roman* Colonies planted there: For whereas there were but four in this Isle, there were nine and twenty in *France*, and fifty-seven in *Spain;* and the greatest entertainment the *Latin* Tongue found out of *Italy* herself was in these two Kingdoms: Yet I am of opinion that the pure congruous grammatical *Latin* was never spoken in either of them as a vulgar vernacular Language, common among Women and Children; no nor in all *Italy* itself, except *Latium.* In *Afric*, tho' there were sixty *Roman* Colonies dispers'd upon that Continent, yet the *Latin* Tongue made not such deep impressions there, nor in *Asia* neither; nor is it to be thought that in those Colonies themselves did the common Soldiers speak in that congruity as the *Flamines*, the Judges, the Magistrates, and chief Commanders did. When the *Romans* sent Legions and planted Colonies abroad, 'twas for divers political considerations, partly to secure their new acquests, partly to abate the superfluous numbers and redundancy of Rome. Then by this way they found means to employ and reward Men of worth, and to heighten their minds; for the *Roman* Spirit did rise up and take growth with his good Successes, Conquests, Commands, and Employments.

But the reason that the *Latin* Tongue found not such entertainment in the Oriental parts was, that the *Greek* had forestall'd her, which was of more esteem among them because of the Learning that was couched in her, and that she was more useful for negotiation and traffic; whereunto the *Greeks* were more addicted than any people: Therefore, tho' the *Romans* had an ambition to make those foreign Nations that were under their yoke to *speak* as well as to *do* what pleased them, and that all Orders, Edicts, Letters,

Letters, and the Laws themselves, civil as well as martial, were publish'd and executed in *Latin;* yet I believe this *Latin* was spoken no otherwise among those Nations than the *Spanish* or *Castilian* Tongue is now in the *Netherlands*, in *Sicily, Sardinia, Naples,* the two *Indies,* and other Provincial Countries which are under that King. Nor did the pure *Latin* Tongue continue long at a stand of perfection in *Rome* and *Latium* itself among all sorts of People, but she receiv'd changes and corruption; neither do I believe that she was born a perfect Language at first, but she receiv'd nutriment, and degrees of perfection with Time, which matures, refines, and finisheth all things. The Verses of the *Salii,* compos'd by *Numa Pompilius,* were scarce intelligble by the Flamines and Judges themselves in the wane of the *Roman* Commonwealth, nor the Laws of the *Decemviri.* And if that *Latin* wherein were couch'd the Capitulations of Peace 'twixt *Rome* and *Carthage* a little after the expulsion of the Kings, which are yet extant upon a Pillar in *Rome,* were compar'd to that which was spoken in *Cæsar's* reign 140 years after, at which time the *Latin* Tongue was mounted to the Meridian of her perfection, she would be found as differing as *Spanish* now differeth from the *Latin.* After *Cæsar* and *Cicero's* time the *Latin* Tongue continued in *Rome* and *Italy* in her purity 400 years together, until the *Goths* rush'd into *Italy* first under *Alaric,* then the *Huns* under *Attila,* then the *Vandals* under *Gensericus,* and the *Heruli* under *Odoacer,* who was proclaim'd King of *Italy;* but the *Goths* a little after, under *Theodoric,* thrust out the *Heruli,* which *Theodoric* was by *Zeno* the Emperor formally invested K. of *Italy,* who with his Successor reign'd there peaceably sixty years and upwards: So that in all probability the *Goths* cohabiting so long among the *Italians,* must adulterate their Language, as well as their Women.

The last barbarous people that invaded *Italy,* about the year 570, were the *Lombards,* who having taken firm rooting in the very bowels of the Country above 200 years without
interruption,

interruption, during the reign of twenty Kings, must of necessity alter and deprave the general Speech of the natural Inhabitants: And, among others, one argument may be, that the best and midland part of *Italy* chang'd its name, and took its appellation from these last Invaders, calling itself *Lombardy*, which name it retains to this day. Yet before the intrusions of these wandring and warlike People into *Italy*, there may be a precedent cause of some corruption that might creep into the *Latin* Tongue in point of vulgarity: First, the incredible confluence of Foreigners that came daily far and near, from the coloniz'd Provinces to *Rome;* then the infinite number of Slaves, which surpassed the number of free Citizens, might much impair the purity of the *Latin* Tongue; and, lastly, those inconstancies and humours of novelty, which is naturally inherent in man, who, according to those frail elementary principles and ingredients whereof he is compos'd, is subject to insensible alterations, and apt to receive impressions of any change.

Thus, my Lord, as succinctly as I could digest it into the narrow bounds of an Epistle, I have sent your Lordship this small survey of the *Latin* or first *Roman* Tongue: In my next I shall fall aboard of her three daughters, the *Italian*, the *Spanish*, and the *French*, with a diligent investigation what might be the original native Languages of those Countries from the beginning, before the *Latin* gave them the Law. In the interim I crave a candid Interpretation of what is passed, and of my studiousness in executing your Lordship's Injunctions: So I am, my Lord—Your most humble and obedient servant, J. H.

Westm., 16 *Jul.* 1630.

LIX.

To the Right Honourable the E. R.

MY LORD,

M Y last was a discourse of the *Latin* or primitive *Roman* Tongue, which may be said to be expir'd in the
Market,

Market, tho' living yet in the *Schools;* I mean, she may be said to be defunct in point of vulgarity any time these 1000 years pass'd. Out of her ruin have sprung up the *Italian*, the *Spanish*, and the *French*, whereof I am now to treat; but I think it not improper to make a research first what the radical prime mother-tongues of these Countries were, before the *Roman* Eagle planted her talons on them.

Concerning *Italy*, doubtless there were divers before the *Latin* did spread all over that Country; the *Calabrian* and *Apulian* spoke *Greek*, whereof some reliques are to be found to this day, but it was an *adventitious*, no mother-language to them: 'Tis confess'd that *Latium* itself, and all the Territories about *Rome*, had the *Latin* for its maternal and common first vernacular Tongue; but *Tuscany* and *Liguria* had others quite discrepant, *viz.*, the *Hetruscane* and *Mesapian*, whereof tho' there be some records yet extant, yet there are none alive that can understand them : The *Oscan*, the *Sabin*, and *Tusculan* are thought to be but dialects to these.

Now the *Latin* Tongue, with the coincidence of the *Goths* Language, and other Northern People, who like Waves tumbled off one another, did more in *Italy* than anywhere else; for she utterly abolish'd (upon that part of the Continent) all other maternal Tongues as ancient as herself, and thereby their eldest daughter, the *Italian*, came to be the vulgar universal Tongue to the whole Country. Yet the *Latin* Tongue had not the sole hand in doing this, but the *Goths* and other Septentrional Nations who rush'd into the *Roman* Diction had a share in't, as I said before, and pegg'd in some words, which have been ever since irremovable, not only in the *Italian*, but also in her two younger sisters, the *Spanish* and the *French*, who felt also the fury of those People. Now the *Italian* is the smoothest and softest-running Language that is : For there is not a word, except some few Monosyllables, Conjunctions, and Prepositions, that ends with a Consonant in the whole Language; nor is there any vulgar Speech which hath more sub-dialects in so small a tract of ground, for *Italy* itself affords above eight.

There

There you have the *Roman,* the *Tuscan,* the *Venetian,* the *Milanez,* the *Neapolitan,* the *Calabresse,* the *Genoevais,* the *Piemontez ;* you have the *Corsican, Sicilian,* with divers other neighbouring Islands: And as the cause why from the beginning there were so many differing dialects in the *Greek* Tongue was, because it was slic'd into so many Islands ; so the reason why there be so many sub-dialects in the *Italian* is, the diversity of Governments that the Country is squandered into, there being in *Italy* at this day two Kingdoms, *viz.,* that of *Naples* and *Calabria ;* three Republicks, *viz., Venice, Genoa,* and *Lucca,* and divers other absolute Princes.

Concerning the original Language of *Spain,* it was, without any controversy, the *Bascuence* or *Cantabrian ;* which Tongue and Territory neither *Roman, Goth* (whence this King hath his pedigree, with divers of the Nobles), or *Moore* could ever conquer; tho' they had over-run and taken firm footing in all the rest for many Ages : Therefore as the remnant of the old *Britons* here, so are the *Biscaneers* accounted the ancient'st and unquestionablest Gentry of *Spain ;* insomuch that when any of them is to be dubb'd Knight, there is no need of any scrutiny to be made whether he be clear of the blood of the *Moriscos,* who had mingled and incorporated with the rest of the *Spaniards* about 700 years. And as the *Arcadians* and *Attiques* in *Greece,* for their immemorial antiquity, are said to vaunt of themselves, that the one are Προσέληνοι, before the Moon ; the other αὐτόχθονες, issued of the Earth itself ; so the *Biscayner* hath such like *Rodomontados.*

The *Spanish* or *Castilian* Language hath but few sub-dialects, the *Portugues* is most considerable. Touching the *Catalan* and *Valencian,* they are rather 'dialects of the *French, Gascon,* or *Aquitanian.* The purest dialect of the *Castilian* Tongue is held to be in the Town of *Toledo,* which, above other Cities of *Spain,* hath this privilege, to be Arbitress in the decision of any Controversy that may arise touching the interpretation of any *Castilian* word.

It

It is an infallible rule, to find out the mother and ancientest Tongue of any Country, to go among those who inhabit the barrenest and most mountainous places, which are posts of security and fastness; whereof divers instances could be produc'd : But let the *Biscayner* in *Spain*, the *Welsh* in *Great Britain*, and the Mountaineers in *Epire* serve the turn, who yet retain their ancient unmix'd Mother-Tongues, being extinguish'd in all the Country besides.

Touching *France*, it is not only doubtful, but left yet undecided, what the true genuine *Gallic* Tongue was : Some would have it to be the *German*, some the *Greek*, some the old *British* or *Welsh*; and the last opinion carrieth away with it the most judicious Antiquaries. Now all *Gallia* is not meant by it, but the Country of the *Celtæ* that inhabit the middle part of *France*, who are the true *Gauls*. *Cæsar* and *Tacitus* tell us, that these *Celtæ*, and the old *Britons* (whereof I gave a touch in my first Letter), did mutually understand one another; and some do hold that this Island was tied to *France*, as *Sicily* was to *Calabria*, and *Denmark* to *Germany*, by an Isthmus or neck of land 'twixt *Dover* and *Bullen* : For if one do well observe the rocks of the one, and the cliffs of the other, he will judge them to be one homogeneous piece, and that they were cut and shiver'd asunder by some act of violence.

The *French* or *Gallic* Tongue hath divers dialects; the *Picard*, that of *Jersey* and *Guernsey* (appendixes once to the Dutchy of *Normandy*), the *Provensall*, the *Gascon*, or speech of *Languedoc*, which *Scaliger* would etymologize from *Languedoc*, whereas it comes rather from *Langue de Got*; for the *Saracens* and *Goths*, by their incursions and long stay in *Aquitain*, corrupted the Language of that part of *Gallia*. Touching the *Britan* and they of *Bearn*, the one is a dialect of the *Welsh*, the other of the *Bascuence*. The *Wallon*, who is under the King of *Spain*, and the *Liegois*, is also a dialect of the *French*, which in their own Country they call *Romand*. The *Spaniard* also terms his

Castilian,

Castilian, Roman; whence it may be inferr'd that the first rise and derivation of the *Spanish* and *French* were from the *Roman* Tongue, not from the *Latin:* Which makes me think that the Language of *Rome* might be degenerated, and become a dialect to our own Mother-tongue (the *Latin*) before she brought her Language to *France* or *Spain.*

There is, besides these sub-dialects of the *Italians, Spanish,* and *French,* another speech that hath a great stroke in *Greece* and *Turkey,* call'd *Franco,* which may be said to be compos'd of all the three, and is at this day the greatest Language of Commerce and Negotiation in the *Levant.*

Thus have I given your Lordship the best account I could of the sister-dialects of the *Italian, Spanish,* and *French.* In my next I shall cross the *Mediterranean* to *Africk,* and the *Hellespont* to *Asia,* where I shall observe the generallest Languages of those vast Continents, where such number-less swarms, and differing sorts of Nations, do crawl up and down this earthly Globe; therefore it cannot be expected that I should be so punctual there as in *Europe:* So I am still, my Lord—Your obedient servitor, J. H.

Westm., 7 *Jul.* 1630.

LX.

To the Rt. Hon. the Earl E.

MY LORD,

HAVING, in my former Letters, made a flying progress thro' the *European* world, and taken a view of the several Languages, Dialects, and Sub-dialects whereby People converse with one another, and being now wind-bound for *Africk,* I held it not altogether supervacaneous to take a review of them, and inform your Lordship what Languages are original independent Mother-Tongues of Christendom, and what are Dialects, Derivations, or De-generations from their Originals.

The Mother-Tongues of *Europe* are thirteen, tho' *Scaliger* would have but eleven: There is the *Greek* 1, the *Latin* 2, the

the *Dutch* 3, the *Sclavonian* 4, the *Welsh* or *Cambrian* 5, the *Bascuence* or *Cantabrian* 6, the *Irish* 7, the *Albanian* in the Mountains of *Epire* 8, the *Tartarian* 9, the old *Illyrian* 10, remaining yet in *Liburnia*, the *Jazygian* 11, on the North of *Hungary*, the *Cauchian* 12, in *East-Friezeland*, the *Finnic* 13, which I put last with good reason, because they are the only Heathens of *Europe;* all which were known to be in *Europe* in the time of the *Roman* Empire. There is a learned Antiquary that makes the *Arabic* to be one of the Mother-Tongues of *Europe*, because it was spoken in some of the Mountains of *South Spain;* 'tis true, 'twas spoken for divers hundred years all *Spain* over, after the Conquest of the *Moors;* but yet it could not be called a Mother-Tongue, but an adventitious Tongue, in reference to that part of *Europe.*

And now that I am to pass to *Afric*, which is far bigger than *Europe;* and to *Asia*, which is far bigger than *Afric;* and to *America*, which is thought to be as big as all the three; if *Europe* herself hath so many Mother-Languages, quite discrepant one from the other, besides secondary Tongues and Dialects, which exceed the number of their Mothers, what shall we think of the other three huge Continents in point of differing Languages? Your Lordship knows that there be divers Meridians and Climes in the Heavens, whence influxes of differing qualities fall upon the Inhabitants of the Earth; and as they make men to differ in the ideas and conceptions of the Mind, so in the motion of the Tongue, in the tune and tones of the Voice, they come to differ one from the other. Now all Languages at first were imperfect confus'd Sounds, then came they to be Syllables, then Words, then Speeches and Sentences, which by practice, by tradition, and a kind of natural instinct from Parents to Children, grew to be fix'd. Now, to attempt a survey of all the Languages in the other three Parts of the habitable earth were rather a madness than a presumption; it being a thing of impossibility, and not only above the capacity, but beyond the search of the activest and

knowing'st

knowing'st man upon earth. Let it therefore suffice, while I behold these Nations that read and write from right to left, from the Liver to the Heart, I mean the *Africans* and *Asians*, that I take a short view of the *Arabic* in the one, and the *Hebrew*, or *Syriac*, in the other: for, touching the *Turkish* Language, 'tis but a Dialect of the *Tartarian*, tho' it have receiv'd a late mixture of the *Armenian*, the *Persian*, and *Greek* Tongues, but 'specially of the *Arabic*, which was the Mother-Tongue of their Prophet, and is now the sole Language of their *Alcoran ;* it being strictly inhibited, and held to be a profaneness to translate it to any other ; which, they say, preserves them from the encroachment of Schisms.

Now, the *Arabic* is a Tongue of vast expansion ; for besides the three *Arabias*, it is become the vulgar Speech of *Syria, Mesopotamia, Palestine,* and *Egypt ;* from whence she stretcheth herself to the Strait of *Gibraltar*, thro' all that vast tract of Earth which lieth 'twixt the Mountain *Atlas* and the Mediterranean Sea, which is now call'd *Barbary,* where Christianity and the *Latin* Tongue, with divers famous Bishops, once flourish'd. She is spoken likewise in all the Northern Parts of the *Turkish* Empire, as also in petty *Tartary ;* and she, above all other, hath reason to learn *Arabic,* for she is in hope one day to have the *Crescent*, and the whole *Ottoman* Empire ; it being entail'd on her, in case the present Race should fail, which is now in more danger than ever : in fine, wheresoever the *Mahometan* Religion is profess'd, the *Arabic* is either spoken or taught.

My *last* view shall be of the *first* Language of the Earth, the ancient Language of *Paradise*, the Language wherein God Almighty himself pleas'd to pronounce and publish the Tables of the Law, the Language that had a Benediction promis'd her, because she would not consent to the building of the *Babylonish Tower :* yet this holy Tongue hath had also her Eclipses, and is now degenerated to many Dialects, nor is she spoken purely by any Nation upon earth ; a fate also which has befallen the *Greek* and *Latin*. The most spacious Dialect of the *Hebrew* is the *Syriac*, which had her beginning

beginning in the time of the Captivity of the *Jews* at *Babylon*, while they cohabited and were mingled with the *Chaldeans;* in which tract of seventy years' time, the vulgar sort of *Jews*, neglecting their own maternal Tongue (the *Hebrew*), began to speak the *Chaldee;* but not having the right accent of it, and fashioning that new learned Language to their own innovation of Points, Affixes, and Conjugations, out of that intermixture of *Hebrew* and *Chaldee* resulted a third Language, call'd to this day the *Syriac;* which also, after the time of our Saviour, began to be more adulterated by admission of *Greek, Roman*, and *Arabic*. In this Language is the *Talmud* and *Targum* couch'd; and all their Rabbins, as Rabbi *Jonathan* and Rabbi *Onkelos*, with others, have written in it; insomuch that, as I said before, the antient *Hebrew* had the same fortune that the *Greek* and *Latin* Tongues had, to fall from being naturally spoken anywhere, to lose their general communicableness and vulgarity, and to become only School and Book-Languages.

Thus we see, that as all other sublunary things are subject to corruption and decay, as the potentest Monarchies, the proudest Republiques, the opulentest Cities have their growth, declinings, and periods: As all other elementary Bodies likewise, by reason of the frailty of their Principles, come by insensible degrees to alter and perish, and cannot continue long at a stand of perfection; so the learnedest and more eloquent Languages are not free from this common fatality, but they are liable to those alterations and revolutions, to those fits of inconstancy, and other destructive contingencies, which are unavoidably incident to all earthly things.

Thus, my noble Lord, have I evertated myself, and stretch'd all my sinews; I have put all my small knowledge, observations, and reading, upon the tenter, to satisfy your Lordship's desires touching this subject. If it afford you any contentment, I have hit the white I aim'd at, and hold myself abundantly rewarded for my oil and labour: so I am, My Lord —Your most humble and ever obedient Servitor,   J. H.

Westm., 1 *July* 1630.

LXI.

LXI.

To the Honourable Master Car. Ra.

SIR,

YOURS of the 7th current was brought me, whereby I find that you did put yourself to the penance of perusing some *Epistles* that go imprinted lately in my name : I am bound to you for your pains and patience (for you write you read them all thro'), much more for your candid opinion of them, being right glad that they should give entertainment to such a choice and judicious Gentleman as yourself. But whereas you seem to except against something in one Letter that reflects upon Sir *W. Raleigh's* Voyage to *Guiana*, because I term the Gold Mine he went to discover an *airy* and *supposititious Mine*, and so infer that it toucheth his honour ; truly, Sir, I will deal clearly with you in that point, that I never harbour'd in my brain the least thought to expose to the world anything that might prejudice, much less traduce in the least degree that could be that rare renowned Knight, whose Fame shall contend in longævity with this Island itself, yea, with that great *World* which he *Historiseth* so gallantly. I was a youth about the Town when he undertook that Expedition, and I remember most men suspected that *Mine* then to be but an imaginary politic thing ; but at his return, and missing of the enterprise, these suspicions turn'd in most to real beliefs that 'twas no other. And K. *James*, in that Declaration which he commanded to be printed and publish'd afterwards, touching the circumstances of this action (upon which my Letter is grounded, and which I have still by me), terms it no less: And if we may not give faith to such publick regal Instruments, what shall we credit ? Besides, there goes another printed kind of Remonstrance annex'd to that Declaration, which intimates as much : and there is a worthy Captain in this Town, who was Co-adventurer in that Expedition, who, upon the storming of *St. Thomas*, heard

young

young Mr. *Raleigh* encouraging his Men in these words: *Come on, my noble hearts, this is the Mine we come for ; and they who think there is any other are fools.* Add hereunto, that Sir *Richard Baker*, in his last Historical Collections, intimates so much. Therefore, 'twas far from being any opinion broach'd by myself, or bottom'd upon weak grounds ; for I was careful of nothing more, than that those *Letters* being to breathe open Air, should relate nothing but what should be derived from good fountains. And truly, Sir, touching that Apology of Sir *Walter Raleigh's* you write of, I never saw it, and I am very sorry I did not ; for it had let in more light upon me of the carriage of that great action, and then you might have been assur'd that I would have done that noble Knight all the right that could be.

But, Sir, the several Arguments that you urge in your *Letters* are of that strength, I confess, that they are able to rectify any indifferent man in this point, and induce him to believe that it was no Chimera, but a real Mine ; for you write of divers pieces of Gold brought thence by Sir *Walter* himself and Capt. *Kemys*, and of some Ingots that were found in the Governor's Closet at *St. Thomas's*, with divers Crucibles and other refining Instruments : yet, under favour, that might be, and the benefit not countervail the charge, for the richest Mines that the King of *Spain* hath upon the whole Continent of *America*, which are the Mines of *Potosi*, yield him but six in the hundred, all expences defray'd. You write how K. *James* sent privately to Sir *Walter*, being yet in the *Tower*, to intreat and command him, that he would impart his whole Design to him under his hand, promising upon the word of a King to keep it secret ; which being done accordingly by Sir *Walter Raleigh*, that very original Paper was found in the said *Spanish* Governor's Closet at *St. Thomas's:* whereat, as you have just cause to wonder, and admire the activeness of the *Spanish* Agents about our Court at that time, so I wonder no less at the miscarriage of some of his late Majesty's Ministers, who notwithstanding that he had pass'd his Royal Word to the contrary, yet they did

help

help Count *Gondomar* to that Paper ; so that the reproach lieth more upon the *English* than the *Spanish* Ministers in this particular. Whereas you allege, that the dangerous sickness of Sir *Walter* being arrived near the place, and the death of (that rare Spark of courage) your Brother upon the first landing, with other circumstances, discourag'd Capt. *Kemys* from discovering the Mine, but wou'd reserve it for another time ; I am content to give as much credit to this as any Man can ; as also that Sir *Walter*, if the rest of the Fleet, according to his earnest motion, had gone with him to re-victual in *Virginia* (a Country where he had reason to be welcome unto, being of his own discovery), he had a purpose to return to *Guyana* the Spring following to pursue his first design. I am also very willing to believe that it cost Sir *W. Raleigh* much more to put himself in equipage for that long intended Voyage, than would have paid for his Liberty, if he had gone about to purchase it for reward of Money at home ; tho' I am not ignorant that many of the Co-adventurers made large contributions, and the fortunes of some of them suffer for it at this very day. But altho' *Gondomar*, as my Letter mentions, calls Sir *Walter* Pirate, I for my part am far from thinking so ; because, as you give an unanswerable reason, the plundering of *St. Thomas* was an act done beyond the Equator, where the Articles of Peace 'twixt the two Kings do not extend. Yet, under favour, tho' he broke not the Peace, he was said to break his Patent by exceeding the bounds of his Commission, as the foresaid Declaration relates : For K. *James* had made strong promises to Count *Gondomar*, that this Fleet should commit no outrages upon the K. of *Spain's* Subjects by Land, unless they began first; and I believe that was the main cause of his death, tho' I think if they had proceeded that way against him in a legal course of trial, he might have defended himself well enough.

Whereas you allege, that if that Action had succeeded, and afterwards been well prosecuted, it might have brought *Gondomar's* great Catholic Master to have been begg'd for at the Church-doors by Fryars, as he was once brought in

2 H   the

the latter end of Q. *Elizabeth's* days : I believe it had much damnified him, and interrupted him in the possession of his *West-Indies*, but not brought him, under favour, to so low an ebb. I have observed, that it is an ordinary thing in your popish Countries for Princes to borrow from the Altar, when they are reduc'd to any straits ; for they say, *The Riches of the Church are to serve as Anchors in time of a storm.* Divers of our Kings have done worse, by pawning their Plate and Jewels. Whereas my Letter makes mention that Sir *W. Raleigh* mainly labour'd for his Pardon before he went, but could not compass it ; this is also a passage in the foresaid printed Relation. But I could have wish'd with all my heart he had obtain'd it ; for I believe that neither the transgression of his Commission, nor anything that he did beyond the *Line,* could have shorten'd the line of his Life otherwise ; but in all probability we might have been happy in him to this very day, having such an heroic Heart as he had, and other rare helps, by his great knowledge, for the preservation of health. I believe without any scruple what you write, that Sir *Wm. St. Geon* made an overture to him of procuring his Pardon for £1500, but whether he could have effected it I doubt a little, when he had come to negotiate it really. But I extremely wonder how that old Sentence which had lain dormant above sixteen years against Sir *W. Raleigh* could have been made use of to take off his head afterwards, considering that the Lord Chancellor *Verulam,* as you write, told him positively (as Sir *Walter* was acquainting him with that proffer of Sir *Wm. St. Geon* for a pecuniary Pardon) in these words, *Sir, the knee-timber of your Voyage is Money ; spare your purse in this particular, for upon my life you have a sufficient Pardon for all that is passed already, the King having under his Broad-Seal made you Admiral of your Fleet, and given you power of the Martial Law over your Officers and Soldiers.* One would think that by this royal Patent, which gave him power of life and death over the King's liege People, Sir *W. Raleigh* should become *rectus in curia,* and free from all old convic-
tions.

tions. But, Sir, to tell you the plain truth, Count *Gondomar* at that time had a great stroke in our Court, because there was more than a mere overture of a Match with *Spain*; which makes me apt to believe, that that great wise Knight being such an *Anti-Spaniard*, was made a Sacrifice to advance the matrimonial Treaty. But I must needs wonder, as you justly do, that one and the same Man should be condemned for being a friend to the *Spaniard* (which was the ground of his first Condemnation), and afterwards lose his head for being their enemy by the same Sentence. Touching his return, I must confess I was utterly ignorant that those two noble Earls, *Thomas* of *Arundel* and *William* of *Pembroke*, were engaged for him in this particular; nor doth the printed Relation make any mention of them at all: Therefore I must say, that Envy herself must pronounce that return of his, for the acquitting of his fiduciary Pledges, to be a most noble act; and waving that of K. *Alphonso's Moor*, I may more properly compare it to the act of that famous *Roman* Commander (*Regulus*, as I take it) who, to keep his promise and faith, returned to his enemies where he had been prisoner, tho' he knew he went to an inevitable death. But well did that faithless cunning Knight, who betray'd Sir *W. Raleigh* in his intended escape, being come ashore, fall to that contemptible end, as to die a poor, distracted Beggar in the Isle of *Lundey*, having for a Bag of money falsify'd his Faith, confirm'd by the tie of the holy Sacrament, as you write; as also before the year came about, to be found clipping the same Coin in the King's own house at *White-hall* which he had receiv'd as a reward for his Perfidiousness; for which being condemned to be hang'd, he was driven to sell himself to his shirt, to purchase his Pardon of two Knights.

And now, Sir, let that glorious and gallant Cavalier Sir *W. Raleigh* (*who lived long enough for his own honour, tho' not for his Country*, as it was said of a *Roman* Consul) rest quietly in his grave, and his Virtues live in his Posterity, as I find they do strongly, and very eminently in you. I have
heard

heard his Enemies confess that he was one of the weightiest and wisest Men that this Island ever bred. Mr. *Nath.* Car*penter*, a learned and judicious Author, was not in the wrong when he gave this discreet Character of him : *Who hath not known or read of this Prodigy of Wit and Fortune, Sir* Walter Raleigh, *a Man unfortunate in nothing else but in the greatness of his Wit and Advancement, whose eminent Worth was suc hboth in domestic Policy, foreign Expeditions, and discoveries in Arts and Literature, both practick and contemplative, that it might seem at once to conquer Example and Imitation !*

Now, Sir, hoping to be rectified in your judgment touching my opinion of that illustrious Knight your Father, give me leave to kiss your hands very affectionately for the respectful mention you please to make of my Brother, once your neighbour ; he suffers, good soul, as well as I, tho' in a differing manner. I also much value that favourable censure you give of those rambling Letters of mine, which indeed are nought else than a Legend of the cumbersome Life and various Fortunes of a *Cadet.* But whereas you please to say, *That the World of Learned Men is much beholden to me for them, and that some of them are freighted with many excellent and quaint passages, delivered in a masculine and solid style, adorn'd with much eloquence, and struck with the choicest flowers pick'd from the Muse's Garden:* Whereas you also please to write, that *you admire my great Travels, my strenuous endeavours, at all times and in all places, to accumulate Knowledge, my active laying hold upon all occasions and on every handle that might (with reputation) advantage either my Wit or Fortune:* These high gallant strains of expressions, I confess, transcend my merit, and are a garment too gaudy for me to put on ; yet I will lay it up among my best Reliques, whereof I have divers sent me of this kind. And whereas, in publishing these Epistles at this time, you please to say, *That I have done like* Hezekiah *when he showed his Treasures to the* Babylonians, *that I have discovered my Riches to Thieves, who will bind me fast and share my goods:* To
this

this I answer, that if those innocent Letters (for I know none of them but is such) fall among such Thieves, they will have no great Prize to carry away, it will be but *petty-larceny*. I am already, God wot, bound fast enough, having been a long time coop'd up between these Walls, bereft of all my means of subsistence and employment; nor do I know wherefore I am here, unless it be for my sins: For I bear as upright a heart to my King and Country, I am as conformable and well-affected to the Government of this Land, specially to the High Court of Parliament, as any one whatsoever that breathes Air under this Meridian; I will except none: And for my Religion, I defy any creature 'twixt Heaven and Earth, that will say I am not a true *English* Protestant. I have from Time to Time employ'd divers of my best Friends to get my Liberty, at leastwise leave to go abroad on Bail (for I do not expect, as you please also to believe in your Letter, to be delivered hence, as St. *Peter* was, by miracle), but nothing will yet prevail.

To conclude, I do acknowledge in the highest way of recognition, the free and noble proffer you please to make me of your endeavours to pull me out of this doleful Sepulchre, wherein you say I am entomb'd alive: I am no less obliged to you for the opinion I find you have of my weak abilities, which you *pleased to wish heartily may be no longer eclipsed.* I am not in despair but a day will shine, that may afford me opportunity to improve this good opinion of yours (which I value at a high rate), and let the world know how much I am, Sir—Your real and ready Servitor,   J. H.

Fleet, 5 *May* 1645.

LXII.

To Mr. T. V., at Brussels.

MY DEAR TOM,

WHO would have thought poor *England* had been brought to this pass? Could it ever have enter'd into the imagination of Man, that the Scheme and whole Frame

Frame of so ancient and well-moulded a Government should
be so suddenly struck off the hinges, quite out of joint, and
tumbled into such a horrid Confusion? Who would have
held it possible, that to fly from *Babylon*, we should fall
into such a *Babel?* That to avoid Superstition, some People
should be brought to belch out such a horrid Profaneness,
as to call the Temples of God, the Tabernacles of Satan;
the Lord's Supper, a Two-penny Ordinary; to make the
Communion-Table a Manger, and the Font a Trough to
water their Horses in; to term the white decent Robe of
the Presbyter, the Whore's Smock; the Pipes thro' which
nothing came but Anthems and holy Hymns, the Devil's
Bagpipes; the Liturgy of the Church, tho' extracted most
of it out of the Sacred Text, call'd by some another kind of
Alcoran, by others raw Porridge, by some a Piece forg'd in
Hell? Who would have thought to have seen in *England*
the Churches shut and the Shops open upon *Christmas-day?*
Could any soul have imagined that this Isle would have
produc'd such Monsters as to rejoice at the *Turks'* good
successes against *Christians*, and wish he were in the midst
of *Rome?* Who would have dreamt ten years since, when
Archbishop *Laud* did ride in state thro' *London* streets,
accompanying my Lord of *London* to be sworn Lord High-
Treasurer of *England*, that the Mitre should have now come
to such a scorn, to such a national kind of hatred, as to put
the whole Island in a combustion? Which makes me call
to memory a Saying of the Earl of *Kildare* in *Ireland* in
the Reign of *Henry* VIII., which Earl having a deadly feud
with the Bishop of *Cassiles*, burnt a Church belonging to
that Diocese; and being ask'd upon his examination before
the Lord-Deputy at the Castle of *Dublin*, why he had committed such a horrid Sacrilege as to burn God's Church,
he answer'd, *I had never burnt the Church unless I had
thought the Bishop had been in't.* Lastly, who would have
imagin'd that the Excise would have taken footing here?
A word I remember, in the last Parliament save one, so
odious, that when Sir *D. Carleton*, then Secretary of State,
did

did but name it in the House of Commons, he was like to be sent to the *Tower;* altho' he nam'd it to no ill sense, but to shew what advantage of happiness the People of *England* had o'er other Nations, having neither the *Gabels* of *Italy*, the *Taillies* of *France*, or the *Excise* of *Holland* laid upon them; yet upon this he was suddenly interrupted, and call'd to the Bar. Such a strange metamorphosis poor *England* is now come to; and I am afraid our miseries are not come to their height, but the longest shadows stay till the evening.

The freshest news that I can write to you is, that the *Kentish* Knight of your acquaintance, who I writ in my last had an *apostacy* in his brain, died suddenly this week of an *Imposthume* in his breast, as he was reading a Pamphlet of his own that came from the Press, wherein he shew'd a great mind to be nibbling with my *Trees:* but he only shew'd his Teeth, for he could not bite them to any purpose.

William Ro: is return'd from the Wars, but he is grown lame in one of his Arms, so he hath no mind to bear *Arms* any more; he confesseth himself to be an egregious fool to leave his Mercership and go to be a Musqueteer. It made me think upon the Tale of the *Gallego* in *Spain* who in the Civil Wars against *Arragon*, being in the field he was shot in the forehead, and being carried away to a Tent, the Surgeon searched his wound and found it mortal : so he advised him to send for his Confessor, for he was no man for this world, in regard the brain was touch'd. The Soldier wish'd him to search it again, which he did, and told him that he was hurt in the brain, and could not possibly escape : whereupon the *Gallego* fell into a chafe, and said he lyed ; for he had no brain at all, *porque se tuviera, sesso nunca huiera venido esta guerra;* for if I had had any brain, I would never have come to this War. All your Friends here are well, except the maim'd Soldier, and remember you often, 'specially Sir *J. Brown*, a good gallant Gentleman, who never forgets any who deserv'd to have a place in his memory. Farewell, my dear *Tom*, and God send you
better

better days than we have here; for I wish you as much
happiness as possibly man can have; I wish your mornings
may be good, your noons better, your evenings and nights
best of all; I wish your sorrows may be short, your joys
lasting, and all your desires end in success. Let me hear
once more from you before you remove thence, and tell me
how the squares go in *Flanders.* So I rest—Your entirely
affectionate Servitor,   J. H.

Ficel, 3 *Aug.* 1644.

LXIII.

To His Majesty, at Oxon.

SIR,

I PROSTRATE this Paper at your Majesty's *feet*, hoping
it may find way thence to your *eyes*, and so descend to
your Royal *heart.*

The foreign Minister of State, by whose conveyance this
comes, did lately intimate to me, that among divers Things
which go abroad under my name reflecting upon the Times,
there are some which are not so well taken; your Majesty
being inform'd that they discover a spirit of Indifferency,
and Lukewarmness in the Author. This added much to
the weight of my present suffrances; and exceedingly
imbitter'd the sense of them to me, being no other than a
corrosive to one already in a hectic condition. I must
confess that some of them were more moderate than others ;
yet (most humbly under favour) there were none of them but
displayed the heart of a constant true loyal Subject; and as
divers of those who are most zealous to your Majesty's service
told me, they had the good success to rectify multitudes of
People in their opinion of some Things: Insomuch that I
am not only conscious, but most confident that none of
them could tend to your Majesty's disservice any way
imaginable. Therefore I humbly beseech, that your Majesty
would vouchsafe to conceive of me accordingly, and of one
who by this recluse passive condition hath his share of this

                                                      hideous

hideous storm : Yet he is in assurance, rather than hopes, that tho' divers cross winds have blown, these Times will bring in better at last. There have been divers of your Royal Progenitors who have had as shrewd shocks; and 'tis well known how the next transmarine Kings have been brought to lower ebbs : At this very day he of *Spain* is in a far worse condition, being in the midst of two sorts of People (the *Catalan* and *Portuguese*), who were lately his Vassals, but now have torn his Seals, renounc'd all bonds of Allegiance, and are in actual hostility against him. This great City, I may say, is like a Chess-board chequer'd, inlaid with *white* and *black* spots; tho' I believe the *white* are more in number, and your Majesty's Countenance, by returning to your great Council and your Court at *White-hall*, would quickly turn them all *white.* That Almighty Majesty, who useth to draw light out of darkness, and strength out of weakness, making man's extremity his opportunity, preserve and prosper your Majesty according to the Prayers early and late of your Majesty's most loyal Subject, Servant, and Martyr, HOWEL.

Fleet, 3 *Sept.* 1644.

LXIV.

To E. Benlowes, *Esq. ; upon the receipt of a Table of exquisite* Latin *Poems.*

SIR,

I THANK you in a very high degree for that precious Table of Poems you pleas'd to send me : When I had well view'd them, I thought upon that famous *Table of Proportion* which *Ptolemy* is recorded by *Aristæus* to have sent *Eleazer* to *Hierusalem,* which was counted a stupendous piece of Art, and the wonderment of those Times : What the curiosity of that Table was I have not read, but I believe it consisted in extern mechanical artifice only. The beauty of your Table is of a far more noble extraction, being a pure spiritual work, so that it may be called the Table of your Soul,

Soul, in confirmation of the opinion of that Divine tho'
Pagan Philosopher, the high-wing'd *Plato*, who fancied that
our Souls at the first infusion were as so many Tables, they
were *Abrasæ Tabulæ*, and that all our future knowledge was
but a reminiscence; but under favour, the rich and elaborate
Poems which so loudly echo out your worth and ingenuity
deserve a far more lasting monument to preserve them from
the injury of Time than such a slender board; they deserve
to be engraven in such durable dainty stuff that may be fit
to hang up in the Temple of *Apollo*: Your *Echo* deserves
to dwell in some marble or porphyry Grot, cut about
Parnassus Mount near the source of *Helicon*, rather than
upon such a slight superficies.

I much thank you for your visits, and other fair respects
you shew me; 'specially that you have enlarg'd my quarters
among these melancholy walls by sending me a whole Isle
to walk in, I mean that delicate *purple Island* I receiv'd from
you, where I met with *Apollo* himself and all his daughters,
with other excellent society. I stumble also there often upon
myself, and grow better acquainted with what I have within
me and without me: Insomuch that you could not make
choice of a fitter ground for a Prisoner, as I am, to pass over,
than of that *purple Isle*, that *Isle of Man* you sent me; which,
as the ingenious Author hath made it, is a far more dainty
soil than that *Scarlet* Island which lies near the *Baltic* Sea.

I remain still wind-bound in this Fleet; when the weather
mends, and the wind sits that I may *launch* forth, I will
repay you your visits, and be ready to correspond with you
in the reciprocation of any other offices of Friendship: For
I am, Sir—Your affectionate Servitor,   J. H.

Fleet, 25 Aug. 1645.

LXV.

To my Honourable Lady, the Lady A. Smith.

MADAM,

WHEREAS you were pleas'd lately to ask leave, you
may now take authority to command me: And
did

did I know any of the faculties of my mind or limbs of my body that were not willing to serve you, I would utterly renounce them, they should be no more mine, at least I should not like them near so well; but I shall not be put to that, for I sensibly find that by a natural propensity they are all most ready to obey you, and to stir at the least beck of your commands, as Iron moves towards the Loadstone. Therefore, Madam, if you bid me go, I will run; if you bid me run, I'll fly (if I can), upon your Errand. But I must stay till I can get my heels at liberty from among these Walls; till when, I am, as perfectly as man can be, Madam—Your most obedient humble Servitor, J. H.

Fleet, 5 *May* 1645.

LXVI.

To Master G. Stone.

SIR,

I HEARTILY rejoice with the rest of your Friends, that you are safely return'd from your Travels, specially that you have made so good returns of the Time of your Travel, being, as I understand, come home freighted with Observations and Languages. Your Father tells me that he finds you are so wedded to the *Italian* and *French*, that you utterly neglect the *Latin* Tongue; that's not well. Tho' you have learnt to play at *Baggammon*, you must not forget *Irish*, which is a serious and solid game; but I know you are so discreet in the course and method of your studies, that you will make the Daughters to wait upon their Mother, and love still your old Friend. To truck the *Latin* for any other vulgar Language, is but an ill barter; it is as bad as that which *Glaucus* made with *Diomedes*, when he parted with his golden Arms for brazen ones. The proceed of this Exchange will come far short of any Gentleman's expectation, tho' haply it may prove advantageous to a Merchant, to whom common Languages are more useful. I am big with desire to meet you, and to mingle a day's

discourse

discourse with you, if not two; how you escap'd the claws
of the Inquisition, whereunto I understand you were like to
fall; and of other Traverses of your Peregrination. Farewell,
my precious *Stone*, and believe it, the least grain of those
high respects you please to profess unto me is not lost, but
answer'd with so many Carates. So I rest—Your most
affectionate Servitor,   J. H.

Westm., 30 *Nov.* 1635.

LXVII.

To J. J., *Esq.*

SIR,

I RECEIV'D those sparkles of Piety you pleas'd to send
me in a manuscript; and whereas you favour me with a
desire of my opinion concerning the publishing of them, Sir,
I must confess that I found among them many most fervent
and flexanimous strains of devotion : I found some Prayers
so piercing and powerful, that they are able to invade
Heaven, and take it by violence, if the Heart doth its office
as well as the Tongue. But, Sir, you must give me leave
(and for this leave you shall have authority to deal with me
in such a case) to tell you, that whereas they consist only of
Requests, being all supplicatory Prayers, you should do well
to intersperse among them some eucharistical Ejaculations,
and Doxologies, some oblations of Thankfulness; we should
not be always whining in a puling petitionary way (which
is the Tone of the Time now in fashion) before the gates of
Heaven with our fingers in our eyes, but we should lay our
hands upon our hearts, and break into raptures of Joy and
Praise. A Soul thus elevated is the most pleasing sacrifice
that can be offer'd to God Almighty ; it is the best sort of
incense. *Prayer* causeth the first shower of rain, but *Praise*
brings down the second ; the one fructifieth the Earth, the
other makes the Hills to skip. All Prayers aim at our own
ends and interests, but Praise proceeds from the pure motions
of Love and Gratitude, having no other object but the glory
of

of God. That soul which rightly dischargeth this part of devotion may be said to do the duty of an Angel upon earth. Among other Attributes of God, *Præscience*, or Foreknowledge, is one; for he knows our thoughts, our desires, our wants, long before we propound them. And this is not only one of his Attributes, but Prerogative royal; therefore to use so many iterations, inculcatings, and tautologies, as it is no good manners in moral Philosophy, no more is it in *Divinity;* it argues a pusillanimous and mistrustful soul: Of the two, I had rather be over-long in Praise than Prayer, yet I would be careful it should be free from any Pharisaical babbling. *Prayer* compar'd with Praise, is but a fuliginous smoke issuing from the sense of sin and human infirmities: Praises are the true clear sparkles of Piety, and sooner fly upwards.

Thus have I been free with you in delivering my opinion touching that piece of Devotion you sent me, whereunto I add my humble Thanks to you for the perusal of it; so I am—Your most ready to be commanded,   J. H.

Fleet, 8 *Sept.* 1645.

LXVIII.

To Capt. William Bridges, *in* Amsterdam.

MY NOBLE CAPTAIN,

I HAD yours of the tenth current; and besides your *Avisos,* I must thank you for those rich flourishes wherewith your Letter was embroider'd everywhere. The news under this clime is, that they have mutinied lately in divers places about the *Excise,* a Bird that was first hatch'd there amongst you; here in *London* the Tumult came to that height, that they burnt down to the ground the *Excise-House* in *Smithfield,* but now all is quiet again. God grant our *Excise* here have not the same fortune as yours there, to become perpetual; or as that new Gabell of *Orleans,* which began in the time of the *League,* which continueth to this day, notwithstanding the Cause ceas'd
about

about threescore years since. Touching this, I remember a pleasant tale that is recorded of *Henry the Great,* who some years after Peace was established thro'out all the whole Body of *France,* going to his own Town of *Orleans,* the Citizens petition'd him that His Majesty would be pleased to abolish that new Tax. The King ask'd who had impos'd it upon them; they answer'd Mons. *de la Chatre* (during the Civil Wars of the *League*), who was now dead; the King reply'd, Mons. *de la Chatre vous a ligue, qu'il vous desligue;* Mons. *de la Chatre leagu'd you, let him then unleague you for my part.* Now that we have a kind of Peace, the Gaols are full of Soldiers, and some Gentlemen's Sons of Quality suffer daily. The last week Judge *Rives* condemn'd four in your Country at *Maidstone* Assizes; but he went out of the world before them, tho' they were executed four days after. You know the saying in *France,* that *La guerre fait les latrons, & la paix les amene au gibet :* War makes Thieves, and Peace brings them to the Gallows. I lie still here *in limbo, in limbo innocentium,* tho' not *in limbo infantum;* and I know not upon what Star to cast this misfortune. Others are here for their good *conditions,* but I am here for my good *qualities,* as your Cousin *Fortescue* jeer'd me not long since: I know none I have, unless it be to love you, which I would continue to do, tho' I tugg'd at an Oar in a Galley, much more as I walk in the Galleries of this Fleet. In this resolution I rest—
Your most affectionate Servitor,   J. H.

Fleet, 2 *Sept.* 1645.

LXIX.

To Mr. W. B., *at Grundesburgh.*

GENTLE SIR,

YOURS of the seventh I receiv'd yesternight, and read o'er with no vulgar delight: In the perusal of it methought to have discern'd a gentle strife 'twixt the fair respects you pleas'd to shew me therein, and your ingenuity

in

in expressing them, which should have superiority; so that
I knew not to which of the two I should adjudge the Palm.

If you continue to wrap up our young acquaintance,
which you say is but yet *in fasciis*, in such warm choice
swadlings, it will quickly grow up to maturity; and for
my part I shall not be wanting to contribute that reciprocal
nourishment which is due from me.

Whereas you please to magnify some Pieces of mine, and
that you seem to spy the Muses perching upon my Trees,
I fear 'tis but *deceptio visus*; for they are but Satyrs, or
haply some of the homelier sort of Wood-Nymphs, the
Muses have choicer walks for their recreation.

Sir, I must thank you for the visit you vouchsafed me in
this simple Cell; and whereas you please to call it the
Cabinet that holds the Jewel of our times, you may rather
term it a wicker Casket that keeps a jet Ring, or a horn
Lanthorn that holds a small Taper of coarse Wax. I hope
this Taper shall not extinguish here; and if it may afford
you any light, either from hence or hereafter, I should be
glad to impart it in a plentiful proportion, because I am,
Sir—Your most affectionate Friend to serve you,   J. H.

Fleet, 1 *July.*

LXX.

To I. W. *of* Grays-Inn, *Esq.*

SIR,

I WAS yours before in a high degree of Affection, but
now I am much more yours, since I perus'd that
parcel of choice Epistles you sent me; they discover in you
a knowing and a candid clear soul: For *Familiar Letters
are the Keys of the Mind, they open all the Boxes of one's
Breast, all the cells of the Brain, and truly set forth the
inward Man; nor can the Pencil so lively represent the Face,
as the Pen can do the Fancy.* I much thank you that
you would please to impart them to—Your most faithful
Servitor,   J. H.

Fleet, 1 *Apr.* 1645.

LXXI.

LXXI.

To Capt. T. P., *from* Madrid.

CAPT. DON TOMAS,

COULD I write my Love unto you with a *Ray of the Sun*, as once *Aurelius* the *Roman* Emperor wish'd to a friend of his, you know this clear Horizon of *Spain* could afford me plenty, which cannot be had so constantly all the seasons of the year in your cloudy clime of *England*. *Apollo* with you makes not himself so common, he keeps more State, and doth not show his face and shoot his beams so frequently as he doth here, where 'tis *Sunday* all the year. I thank you a thousand times for what you sent by Mr. *Gresley*, and that you let me know how the pulse of the Times beats with you. I find you cast not your eyes so much southward as you were us'd to do towards us here; and when you look this way, you cast a cloudy countenance, with threatning looks: Which makes me apprehend some fear that it will not be safe for me to be longer under this Meridian. Before I part, I will be careful to send you those things you write for, by some of my Lord Ambassador *Aston's* Gentlemen. I cannot yet get that Grammar which was made for the Constable of *Castile*, who you know was born dumb; wherein an Art is invented to speak with hands only, to carry the Alphabet upon one's joints, and at his fingers' ends: Which may be learn'd without any great difficulty by any mean capacity, and whereby one may discourse and deliver the conceptions of his mind without ever wagging of his tongue, provided there be a reciprocal knowledge and co-understanding of the art 'twixt the parties; and it is a very ingenious piece of invention. I thank you for the copy of Verses you sent me, glancing upon the Times: I was lately perusing some of the *Spanish* Poets here, and lighted upon two Epigrams, or Epitaphs more properly, upon our *Henry* VIII., and upon his Daughter Q. *Elizabeth;* which in requital I thought worth the sending you.

A

A Henrique octavo, Rey de Ingalatierra.

Mas de esta losa fria
Cubre, Henrique, tu valor,
De una Muger el amor,
Y de un Error la porfia ;

Como cupo en tu grandeza,
Dezidme enganado Ingles,
Querer una muger a los pies,
Ser de la yglesia cabesa ?

Pros'd thus in *English,* for I had no time to put it on feet :

O *Henry,* more than this cold Pavement covers thy worth, the love of a Woman and pertinacy of Error ; how could it subsist with thy Greatness, tell me, O cozen'd *Englishman,* to cast thyself at a Woman's feet, and yet to be Head of the Church ? That upon Q. *Elizabeth* was this :

De Isabela, Reyna de Ingalatierra.

Aqui yaze Iesabel,
Aquila nueva Athalia,
Del oro Antartico Harpia,
Del mar incendio cruel :

Aqui el ingenio, mas dino
De loor que ha tenido el suelo,
Si para llegar el cielo
No huuiera errado el camino.

Here lies *Jezabel,* here lies the new *Athalia,* the *Harpy* of the Western Gold, the cruel Firebrand of the Sea : Here lies a Wit the most worthy of fame which the *Earth* had, if to arrive to *Heaven* she had not mist her way.

You cannot blame the *Spaniard* to be satyrical against Q. *Elizabeth ;* for he never speaks of her, but he fetcheth a shrink in the shoulder. Since I have begun, I will go on with as witty an Anagram as I have heard or read, which a Gentleman lately made upon his own name *Tomas,* and a

Nun

Nun called *Maria*, for she was his *devota:* The occasion was, that going one evening to discourse with her at the grate, he wrung her by the hand, and join'd both their names in this Anagram, *To Maria mas*, I would take more: I know I shall not need to expound it to you. Hereunto I will add a strong and deep-fetch'd character, as I think you will confess when you have read it, that one made in this Court of a Courtesan:

> *Eres puta tan artera*
> *Qu'en el vientre de tu madre,*
> *Tu tuuistes de manera*
> *Que te cavalgue el padre.*

To this I will join that which was made of *de Vaca*, husband to *Jusepe de Vaca*, the famous Comedian, who came upon the Stage with a cloke lin'd with black plush, and a great Chain about his neck; whereupon the Duke of *Medina* broke into these witty lines:

> *Con tant felpa en la Capa*
> *Y tanta cadena de oro,*
> *El marido de la* Vaca
> *Que puede ser sino* toro.

The conclusion of this rambling Letter shall be a Rhyme of certain hard throaty words which I was taught lately, and they are accounted the difficultest in all the whole *Castilian* Language; insomuch that he who is able to pronounce them is accounted *Buen Romancista*, a good speaker of *Spanish: Abeja y oueja y piedra que rabeia, pendola tras oreja, y lugar en la ygreia, dessea a su hijo la vieja:* A Bee and a Sheep, a Mill, a Jewel in the Ear, and a place in the Church, the old Woman desires her Son. No more now, but that I am, and will ever be, my noble Captain, in the front of—Your most affectionate Servitors,   J. H.

Madrid, 1 *Aug.* 1622.

LXXII.

LXXII.

To Sir Tho. Luke, *Knight.*

SIR,

HAD you traversed all the world over, 'specially those large Continents and *Christian* Countries which you have so exactly surveyed, and whence you have brought over with you such useful Observations and Languages, you could not have lighted upon a choicer piece of Woman-kind for your Wife ; the Earth could not have afforded a Lady, that by her discretion and sweetness could better quadrate with your dispositions. As I heartily congratulate your happiness in this particular, so I would desire you to know, that I did no ill offices towards the advancement of the work, upon occasion of some discourse with my Lord *George* of *Rutland* not long before at *Hambledon.*

My thoughts are now puzzled about my voyage to the *Baltic* Sea upon the King's service, otherwise I would have ventur'd upon an Epithalamium; for there is matter rich enough to work upon : And now that you had made an end of *wooing,* I could wish you had made an end of *wrangling,* I mean of lawing, 'specially with your Mother, who hath such resolution where she once takes. *Law* is not only a pick-purse, but a Purgatory ; you know the saying they have in *France, Les plaideurs sont les oyseaux, le palais le Champ, les Juges les rets, les Advocats les Rats, les procureurs les souris del estat :* The poor Clients are the Birds, *Westminster-hall* the Field, the Judge the Net, the Lawyers the Rats, the Attornies the Mice of the Commonwealth. I believe this saying was spoken by an angry Client ; for my part, I like his resolution who said he would never use Lawyer nor Physician but upon urgent necessity. I will conclude with this rhyme :

> *Pouvre playdeur,*
> *J'ay gran pitie de ta doleur.*

Your most affectionate Servitor, J. H.

Westm., 1 *May* 1629.

LXXIII.

LXXIII.

To Mr. R. K.

DEAR SIR,

YOU and I are upon a journey, tho' bound for several places, I for *Hamburgh*, you for your last home, as I understand by Dr. *Baskervil*, who tells me, much to my grief, that this hectical disease will not suffer you to be long among us. I know by some experiments which I have had of you, you have such a noble Soul within you, that will not be daunted by those natural apprehensions which Death doth usually carry along with it among vulgar spirits. I do not think that you fear Death as much now, tho' it be to some (φοβερῶν φοβερώτατον), as you did to go into the dark when you were a child; you have had a fair time to prepare yourself. God give you a boon voyage to the Haven you are bound for (which I doubt not will be Heaven), and me the grace to follow, when I have pass'd the boisterous Sea and swelling Billows of this tumultuary Life, wherein I have already shot divers dangerous gulfs, pass'd o'er some quick-sands, rocks, and sundry ill-favour'd reaches, while others sail in the sleeve of fortune. You and I have eaten a great deal of salt together, and spent much oil in the communication of our studies by literal correspondence, and otherwise, both in verse and prose; therefore I will take my last leave of you now in these few stanzas :

1. *Weak crazy Mortal, why dost fear*
   To leave this earthly Hemisphere ?
   Where all delights away do pass,
   Like thy effigies in a Glass.
   Each thing beneath the Moon is frail and fickle,
   Death sweeps away what Time cuts *with his Sickle*

2. *This Life at best is but an Inn,*
   And we the Passengers, wherein
   The cloth is laid to some before
   They peep out of dame Nature's door,

And

And warm Lodgings left: Others there are,
Must trudge to find a Room, and shift for Fare.

3. *This Life's at longest but one Day;*
He who in Youth *posts hence away,*
Leaves us i' th' Morn: *He who hath run*
His race till Manhood, *parts at* Noon:
And who at seventy odd forsakes this Light,
He may be said to take his leave at Night.

4. *One past makes up the Prince and Peasant,*
Tho' one eat Roots, the other Pheasant,
They nothing differ in the stuff,
But both extinguish like a snuff:
Why then, fond Man, should it thy Soul dismay,
To sally out of these gross walls of clay?

And now, my dear Friend, adieu, and live eternally in that world of endless Bliss, where you shall have knowledge as well as all things else commensurate to your desires, where you shall clearly see the real Causes, and perfect Truth of what we argue with that incertitude, and beat our brains about here below: Yet tho' you be gone hence, you shall never die in the memory of—Your   J. H.

Westm., 15 *Aug.* 1630.

LXXIV.

To Sir R. Gr., Knight and Bar.

NOBLE SIR,

I HAD yours upon *Maundy-Thursday* late; and the reason that suspended my Answer till now was, that the season engaged me to sequester my thoughts from my wonted negotiations, to contemplate the great work of Man's *Redemption*, so great, that were it cast in counterbalance with his Creation, it would out-poyze it: For I summon'd all my intellectuals to meditate upon those Passions, upon those Pangs, upon that despicable and most dolorous Death, upon that Cross whereon my Saviour suffer'd, which was the first *Christian* Altar that ever was; and

and I doubt that he will never have benefit of the Sacrifice, who hates the harmless remembrance of the Altar whereon it was offer'd. I applied my Memory to fasten upon't, my Understanding to comprehend it, my Will to embrace it. From these three Faculties, methought I found, by the mediation of the Fancy, some beams of Love gently gliding down from the head to the heart, and inflaming all my Affections. If the human Soul had far more powers than the Philosophers afford her, if she had as many Faculties within the head as there be hairs without, the speculation of this Mystery would find work enough for them all. Truly the more I scrue up my spirits to reach it, the more I am swallowed in a gulf of admiration, and of a thousand imperfect notions; which makes me ever and anon to quarrel with my Soul that she cannot lay hold on her Saviour, much more my Heart, that my purest Affections cannot hug him as much as I would.

They have a custom beyond the Seas (and I could wish it were the worst custom they had) that during the Passion-week, divers of their greatest Princes and Ladies will betake themselves to some Convent or reclus'd House, to wean themselves from all worldly incumbrances, and converse only with Heaven, with performance of some kind of penances all the week long. A worthy Gentleman that came lately from _Italy_ told me that the Count of _Byron_, now Mareschal of _France_, having been long persecuted by Cardinal _Richelieu_, put himself so into a Monastery, and the next day news was brought him of the Cardinal's death; which I believe made him spend the rest of the week with the more devotion in that way. _France_ brags that our Saviour had his face turn'd towards her when he was upon the Cross; there is more cause to think that it was towards this Island, in regard the Rays of _Christianity_ first reverberated upon her, her King being _Christian_ 400 years before him of _France_ (as all Historians concur), not-withstanding that he arrogates to himself the title of the first Son of the Church.

Let

Let this serve for part of my Apology. The day follow-ing my Saviour being in the grave, I had no list to look much abroad, but continued my retiredness: There was another reason also why, because I intended to take the holy Sacrament the *Sunday* ensuing; which is an act of the greatest consolation, and consequence, that possibly a *Christian* can be capable of: It imports him so much, that he is made or marr'd by it; it tends to his damnation or salvation, to help him up to Heaven, or tumble him down headlong to Hell. Therefore it behoves a Man to prepare and recollect himself; to winnow his thoughts from the chaff and tares of the world before-hand. This then took up a good part of that day, to provide myself a wedding-garment, that I might be a fit guest at so precious a Banquet, so precious, that Manna and Angels' food are but coarse viands in comparison of it.

I hope that this Excuse will be of such validity, that it may procure my pardon for not corresponding with you this last week. I am now as freely as formerly—Your most ready and humble Servitor,   J. H.

Fleet, 30 *Apr.* 1647.

LXXV.

To Mr. R. Howard.

SIR,

THERE is a saying that carrieth with it a great deal of caution; *From him whom I trust, God defend me; for from him whom I trust not, I will defend myself.* There be sundry sorts of trusts, but that of a secret is one of the greatest: I trusted *T. P.* with a weighty one, conjuring him that it should not take air and go abroad; which was not done according to the rules and religion of Friendship, but it went out of him the very next day. Tho' the inconveni-ence may be mine, yet the reproach is his; nor would I exchange my Damage for his Disgrace. I would wish you take heed of him, for he is such as the Comic Poet speaks of, *plenus rimarum,* he is full of Chinks, he can hold nothing:
You

You know a secret is too much for one, too little for three, and enough for two; but *Tom* must be none of those two, unless there were a trick to sodder up his mouth : If he had committed a secret to me, and enjoin'd me silence, and I had promis'd it, tho' I had been shut up in *Perillus'* brazen Bull, I should not have bellowed it out. I find it now true, That he who discovers his secrets to another, sells him his Liberty, and becomes his Slave : Well, I shall be warier hereafter, and learn more wit. In the interim, the best satisfaction I can give myself is to expunge him quite *ex albo amicorum*, to raze him out of the catalogue of my *Friends* (tho' I cannot of my *Acquaintance*), where your Name is inserted in great golden Characters. I will endeavour to lose the memory of him, and that my thoughts may never run more upon the fashion of his face, which you know he hath no cause to brag of ; I hate such blateroons :

> *Odi illos ceu claustra Erebi*———

I thought good to give you this little *mot* of advice, because the Times are ticklish, of committing secrets to any, tho' not to—Your most affectionate Friend to serve you,

                                                             J. H.
Fleet, 14 *Feb.* 1647.

LXXVI.

To my Honourable Friend, Mr. E. P., at Paris.

SIR,

L ET me never sally hence from among these disconsolate walls, if the literal correspondence you please to hold so punctually with me be not one of the greatest solaces I have had in this sad condition ; for I find so much salt, such endearments and flourishes, such a gallantry and neatness in your lines, that you may give the law of Lettering to all the world. I had this week a Twin of yours, of the 10th and 15th current ; I am sorry to hear of your *achaques*, and so often indisposition there ; it may be very well (as you say) that the Air of that dirty Town doth not agree with
                                                             you,

you, because you speak *Spanish,* which Language you know is us'd to be breath'd out under a clearer clime; I am sure it agrees not with the sweet breezes of Peace, for 'tis you there that would keep poor *Christendom* in perpetual whirl-winds of Wars; but I fear, that while *France* sets all wheels a-going, and stirs all the *Cacodæmons* of Hell to pull down the House of *Austria,* she may chance at last to pull it upon her own head. I am sorry to understand what they write from *Venice* this week, that there is a discovery made in *Italy,* how *France* had a hand to bring in the *Turk,* to invade the Territories of St. *Mark,* and puzzle the Peace of *Italy.* I want faith to believe it yet, nor can I entertain in my breast any such conceit of the most *Christian King* and *first Son of the Church,* as he terms himself: Yet I pray in your next to pull this thorn out of my thoughts, and tell me whether one may give any credit to this report.

We are now Scot-free, as touching the Northern Army; for our *dear* Brethren have truss'd up their Baggage, and put the *Tweed* 'twixt us and them once again : *Dear* indeed, for they have cost us, first and last, above nineteen hundred thousand pounds Sterling, which amounts to near eight Millions of Crowns with you there. Yet if reports be true, they left behind them more than they lost, if you go to number of Men; which will be a brave race of *Mestizos* hereafter, who may chance meet their Fathers in the Field, and kill them unwittingly; he will be a wise Child that knows his right Father. Here we are like to have four and twenty *Seas* emptied shortly, and some do hope to find abundance of Treasure in the bottom of them, as no doubt they will; but many doubt that it will prove but *aurum Tolosanum* to the finders. God grant that from *Aereans* we turn not to be *Arians:* The Earl of *Strafford* was ac-counted by his very Enemies to have an extraordinary Talent of judgment and parts (tho' they say he wanted *moderation*), and one of the prime Precepts he left his Son upon the Scaffold was, that he should not *meddle with Church-lands, for they would prove a Canker to his Estate.*
Here

Here are started up some great knowing Men lately, that can shew the very track by which our Saviour went to Hell; they will tell you precisely whose Names are written in the Book of Life, whose not. God deliver us from spiritual Pride, which of all sorts is the most dangerous. Here are also notable Star-gazers, who obtrude on the world such confident bold Predictions, and are so familiar with heavenly Bodies, that *Ptolemy* and *Tycho Brahe* were Ninnies to them. We have likewise multitudes of *Witches* among us, for in *Essex* and *Suffolk* there were above two hundred indicted within these two years, and above the one half of them executed: More, I may well say, than ever this Island bred since the Creation, I speak it with horror. God guard us from the Devil, for I think he was never so busy upon any part of the Earth that was enlightned with the beams of *Christianity;* nor do I wonder at it, for there's never a Cross left to fright him away. *Edinburgh*, I hear, is fallen into a relapse of the Plague; the last they had rag'd so violently, that the fortieth Man or Woman lives not of those that dwelt there four years since, but it is all peopled with new faces. *Don* and *Hans*, I hear, are absolutely accorded; nor do I believe that all the Artificers of Policy that you use there can hinder the Peace, tho' they may puzzle it for a while: If it be so, the People which button their doublets upward will be better able to deal with you there.

  Much notice is taken that you go on there too fast in your Acquests; and now that the *Eagle's* wings are pretty well clipp'd, 'tis time to look that your *Flower-de-luce* grow not too rank, and spread too wide. Whereas you desire to know how it fares with your Master, I must tell you, that, like the glorious Sun, he is still in his own Orb, tho' clouded for a time that he cannot shew the beams of Majesty with that lustre he was wont to do: Never did Cavalier woo fair Lady as he woos the Parliament to a Peace; 'tis much the *Head* should so stoop to the *Members.*

  Farewell, my noble Friend, cheer up, and reserve yourself

for

for better days; take our royal Master for your Pattern, who for his longanimity, patience, courage, and constancy is admir'd of all the world, and in a passive way of fortitude hath out-gone all the nine *Worthies*. If the *Cedar* be so weather-beaten, we poor *Shrubs* must not murmur to bear part of the storm. I have had my share, and I know you want not yours: The Stars may change their Aspects, and we may live to see the Sun again in his full Meridian. In the interim come what will, I am—Entirely yours,   J. H.

Fleet, 3 *Feb.* 1646.

LXXVII.

To Sir K. D., *at* Rome.

SIR,

THO' you know well that in the carriage and course of my rambling life I had occasion to be, as the *Dutchman* saith, a *Landloper*, and to see much of the world abroad, yet methinks I have travell'd more since I have been immur'd and martyr'd 'twixt these walls than ever I did before; for I have travell'd the *Isle of Man*, I mean this little World, which I have carried about me and within me so many years: For as the wisest of *Pagan* Philosophers said, that the greatest Learning was the knowledge of one's self, to be his own Geometrician; if one do so, he need not gad abroad to see Fashions, he shall find enough at home, he shall hourly meet with new fancies, new humours, new passions within doors.

This travelling o'er of one's self is one of the paths that leads a Man to Paradise : It is true, that 'tis a dirty and dangerous one, for it is thick set with extravagant Desires, irregular Affections, and Concupiscences, which are but odd Comrades, and oftentimes do lie in Ambush to cut our Throats: There are also some melancholy companions in the way, which are our Thoughts, but they turn many times to be good Fellows, and the best company; which
.   makes

makes me, that among these disconsolate walls I am never less alone than when I am alone; I am oft-times *sole*, but seldom solitary. Some there are who are over-pestered with these companions, and have too much *mind* for their bodies; but I am none of those.

There have been (since you shook Hands with *England*) many strange Things happen'd here, which Posterity must have a strong Faith to believe; but for my part, I wonder not at anything, I have seen such monstrous Things. You know there is nothing that can be casual, there is no success, good or bad, but is contingent to Man sometimes or other; nor are there any Contingencies, present or future, but they have their parallels from time past: For the great Wheel of *Fortune*, upon whose Rim (as the twelve Signs upon the *Zodiack*) all worldly Chances are emboss'd, turns round perpetually; and the Spokes of that Wheel, which point at all human Actions, return exactly to the same place after such a time of Revolution: Which makes me little marvel at any of the strange Traverses of these distracted Times, in regard there hath been the like, or such like formerly. If the *Liturgy* is now suppress'd, the *Missal* and the *Roman Breviary* was us'd so a hundred years since: If *Crosses, Churches, Organs*, and *Fonts* are now battered down, I little wonder at it; for *Chapels, Monasteries, Hermitaries, Nunneries*, and other religious Houses were us'd so in the time of old King *Henry :* If *Bishops* and *Deans* are now in danger to be demolished, I little wonder at it, for *Abbots, Priors*, and the *Pope himself* had that fortune here, an age since. That our King is reduc'd to this pass, I do not wonder much at it; for the first time I travell'd *France, Lewis* XIII. (afterwards a most triumphant King as ever that Country had) in a dangerous civil War was brought to such straits; for he was brought to dispense with part of his Coronation Oath, to remove from his *Court of Justice*, from the *Council-Table*, from his very *Bed-chamber*, his greatest Favourites: He was driven to be content to pay the Expense of the War, to reward those that took Arms

against

against him, and publish a Declaration that the ground of their quarrel was good; which was the same in effect with ours, *viz.*, a discontinuance of the Assembly of the three Estates, and that *Spanish* Counsels did predominate in *France.*

You know better than I, that all Events, good or bad, come from the all-disposing high Deity of Heaven : *If good, he produceth them; if bad, he permits them.* He is the Pilot that sits at the stern, and steers the great Vessel of the World ; and we must not presume to direct him in his course, for he understands the use of the Compass better than we. He commands also the Winds and the Weather, and after a storm he never fails to send us a calm, and to recompense ill Times with better, if we can live to see them; which I pray you may do, whatsoever becomes of—Your still most faithful humble Servitor, J. H.

Fleet, 3 *Mar.* 1646.

LXXVIII.

To Sir K. D., at his House in St. Martin's Lane.

SIR,

THAT Poem which you pleased to approve of so highly in Manuscript is now manumitted, and made free denizen of the World : It hath gone from my Study to the Stall, from the Pen to the Press, and I send one of the maiden Copies herewith to attend you. 'Twas your Judgment, which all the world holds to be sound and sterling, induced me hereunto ; therefore, if there be any, you are to bear your part in the blame.—Your most entirely devoted Servitor, J. H.

Holborn, 3 *Jan.* 1641.

Advertisement

Advertisement to the First Edition of this Book.

A MONG *other Reasons which make the* English *Language of so small extent, and put strangers out of conceit to learn it, one is, That we do not pronounce as we write ; which proceeds from divers superfluous Letters that occur in many of our Words, which adds to the difficulty of the Language.* Therefore the *Author hath taken pains to retrench such redundant unnecessary Letters in this Work* (*tho' the Printer hath not been so careful as he should have been*) *as among multitudes of other words may appear in these few,* done, some, come : *Which tho' we, to whom the speech is connatural, pronounce as monosyllables, yet when strangers come to read them, they are apt to make them dissyllables, as* do-ne, so-me, co-me ; *therefore such an* e *is superfluous.*

Moreover, those words that have the Latin *for their original, the Author prefers that Orthography rather than the* French, *whereby divers letters are spar'd, as* Physic, Logic, Afric, *not* Physique, Logique, Afrique ; Favor, Honor, Labor, *not* Favour, Honour, Labour, *and very many more; as also he omits the* Dutch k *in most words : Here you shall read* peeple, *not* pe-ople, tresure, *not* treasure, toung, *not* tongue, *&c.* Parlement, *not* Parliament, busines, witnes, sicknes, *not* business, witness, sickness ; star, war, far, *not* starre, warre, farre, *and multitudes of such words, wherein the two last Letters may well be spar'd. Here you shall also read* pity, piety, witty, *not* piti-e, pieti-e, witti-e, *as strangers at first sight pronounce them, and abundance of such like words.*

The new Academy of Wits call'd l'Academie de beaux esprits, *which the late Cardinal* Richlieu *founded in* Paris, *is now in hand to reform the* French *Language in this particular, and to weed it of all superfluous Letters ; which makes the* Tongue *differ so much from the* Pen, *that they have expos'd themselves to this contumelious Proverb,* The *Frenchman* doth neither pronounce as he writes, nor speak as he thinks, nor sing as he pricks.

Aristotle *hath a topic Axiom, that* Frustra fit per plura, quod fieri potest per pauciora : *When fewer may serve the turn, more is in vain. And as this rule holds in all things else, so it may be very well observ'd in Orthography.*

Familiar

Familiar Letters,
Of a fresher Date.

BOOK III.

I.

To the Rt. Hon. Edward E. *of* Dorset (*Lord Chamberlain of His Majesty's Household,* &c.), *at* Knowles.

My Lord,

AVING so advantageous a hand as Doctor *S. Turner,* I am bold to send your Lordship a new Tract of *French* Philosophy, call'd *L'usage de Passions,* which is cried up to be a choice piece. It is a moral Discourse of the right use of the *Passions,* the *Conduct* whereof, as it is the principal Employment of *Virtue,* so the *Conquest* of them is the difficultest part of *Valour:* To *know* one's self is much, but to *conquer* one's self is more. We need not pick quarrels and seek enemies without doors, we have too many Inmates at home to exercise our Prowess upon ; and there is no Man, let him have his humours never so well balanc'd, and in subjection to him, but like *Muscovia* Wives, they will oftentimes insult, unless they be check'd : Yet we should make them our *Servants,* not our *Slaves.* Touching the

the occurrences of the Times, since the King was snatch'd
away from the Parliament; the Army, they say, use him
with more civility and freedom; but for the main work of
restoring him, he is yet, as one may say, but *tantaliz'd*,
being brought often within the sight of *London*, and so off
again. There are hopes that something will be done to his
advantage speedily; because the Gregarian Soldiers and gross
of the Army is well affected to him, tho' some of the chiefest
Commanders be still averse.

For foreign News, they say St. *Mark* bears up stoutly
against *Mahomet* both by Land and Sea: In *Dalmatia* he
hath of late shaken him by the Turban ill-favouredly: I could
heartily wish that our Army here were there to help the
Republic, and combat the common Enemy, for then one
might be sure to die in the bed of Honour. The commotions
in *Sicily* are quash'd, but those of *Naples* increase; and 'tis
like to be a more raging and voracious fire than *Vesuvius*, or
any of the sulphureous Mountains about her did ever belch
out. The *Catalan* and *Portuguez* bait the *Spaniard* on both
sides, but the first hath shrewder teeth than the other; and
the *French* and *Hollander* find him work in *Flanders*. And
now, my Lord, to take all Nations in a lump, I think God
Almighty hath a quarrel lately with all Mankind, and given
the reins to the ill Spirit to compass the whole earth; for
within these twelve years there have the strangest Revolutions and horridest Things happen'd not only in *Europe*,
but all the World over, that have befallen mankind, I dare
boldly say, since *Adam* fell, in so short a revolution of time.
There is a kind of popular Planet reigns everywhere: I will
begin with the hottest parts, with *Afric*, where the Emperor
of *Ethiopia* (with two of his Sons) was encounter'd and kill'd
in open field by the Groom of his Camels and Dromedaries,
who have levied an Army out of the dregs of the People
against him, and is like to hold that ancient Empire. In
Asia the *Tartar* broke o'er the four-hundred-mil'd Wall, and
rush'd into the heart of *China*, as far as *Quinzay*, and beleaguer'd the very Palace of the Emperor, who rather than
become

become Captive to the base *Tartar* burnt his Castle, and did make away himself, his thirty Wives and Children. The great *Turk* hath been lately strangled in the *Seraglio*, his own house. The Emperor of *Muscovia* going in a solemn Procession upon the Sabbath-day, the Rabble broke in, knock'd down and cut in pieces divers of his chiefest Counsellors, Favourites, and Officers before his face; and dragging their bodies to the Market-place, their heads were chopp'd off, thrown into Vessels of hot Water, and so set upon Poles to burn more bright before the Court-gate. In *Naples* a common Fruiterer had raised such an Insurrection, that they say above sixty Men have been slain already upon the streets of that City alone. *Catalonia* and *Portugal* have quite revolted from *Spain*. Your Lordship knows what knocks have been 'twixt the Pope and *Parma :* The *Pole* and the *Cossacks* are hard at it, *Venice* wrestleth with the *Turk*, and is like to lose her Maidenhead to him, unless other *Christian* Princes look to it in time. And touching these three Kingdoms, there's none more capable than your Lordship to judge what monstrous Things have happen'd; so that it seems the whole Earth is off the hinges : And (which is the more wonderful) all these prodigious passages have fallen out in less than the compass of twelve years. But now that all the World is together by the ears, the States of *Holland* would be quiet : For Advice is come that the Peace is concluded, and interchangeably ratify'd 'twixt them and *Spain ;* but they defer the publishing of it yet, till they have collected all the Contribution-money for the Army. The *Spaniard* hopes that one day this Peace may tend to his Advantage more than all his Wars have done these fourscore years, relying upon the old Prophecy,

Marte triumphabis, Batavia, Pace *peribis.*

The King of *Denmark* hath buried lately his eldest Son *Christian*, so that he hath now but one living, viz., *Frederick*, who is Archbishop of *Breme*, and is shortly to be King Elect.

2 K My

My Lord, this Letter runs upon Universals, because I know your Lordship hath a publick great Soul and a spacious Understanding, which comprehends the whole World: So in a due posture of humility I kiss your hands, being, my Lord—Your most obedient and most faithful Servitor,   J. H.

Fleet, 20 *Jan.* 1646.

II.

To Mr. En. P., *at* Paris.

SIR,

SINCE we both agreed to truck Intelligence, and that you are contented to barter *French* for *English*, I shall be careful to send you hence from time to time the currentest and most staple stuff I can find, with weight and good measure to boot. I know in that more subtile Air of yours *Tinsel* sometimes passes for *Tissue*, *Venice* Beads for Pearl, and Demicasters for Bevers: But I know you have so discerning a judgment, that you will not suffer yourself to be so cheated; they must rise betimes that can put Tricks upon you, and make you take semblances for realities, probabilities for certainties, or spurious for true things. To hold this literal correspondence, I desire but the parings of your time, that you may have something to do, when you have nothing else to do, while I make a business of it to be punctual in my answers to you. Let our Letters be as Echoes, let them bound back and make mutual repercussions; I know you that breathe upon the Continent have clearer Echoes there; witness that in the *Tuilleries*, specially that at *Charenton* Bridge, which quavers, and renders the voice ten times when 'tis open weather, and it were a virtuous curiosity to try it.

For news, the world is here turn'd upside down, and it hath been long a-going so: You know a good while since we have had leather Caps and bever Shoos; but now the Arms are come to be Legs, for Bishops' Lawn-sleeves are worn for Boot-house tops; the Waist is come to the Knee,

for

for the Points that were used to be about the middle are now dangling there. Boots and Shoos are so long-snouted, that one can hardly kneel in God's House, where all Genuflection and Postures of devotion and decency are quite out of use : The Devil may walk freely up and down the streets of *London* now, for there is not a Cross to fright him anywhere ; and it seems he was never so busy in any Country upon earth, for there have been more Witches arraign'd and executed here, lately, than ever were in this Island since the Creation.

I have no more to communicate to you at this time, and this is too much unless it were better. God Almighty send us patience, you in your Banishment, me in my Captivity, and give us Heaven for our last Country, where Desires turn to Fruition, Doubts to Certitudes, and dark Thoughts to clear Contemplations. Truly, my dear *Don Antonio*, as the times are, I take little contentment to live among the Elements, and (were it my Maker's pleasure) I could willingly, had I quit scores with the World, make my last account with Nature, and return this small skin full of Bones to my common Mother. If I chance to do so before you, I love you so entirely well that my Spirit shall visit you, to bring you some tidings from the other World; and if you precede me, I shall expect the like from you, which you may do without affrighting me, for I know your Spirit will be a *bonus Genius.* So, desiring to know what's become of my Manuscript, I kiss your hands, and rest most passionately—Your most faithful Servitor,   J. H.

Fleet, 20 *Feb.* 1646.

III.

To Master W. B.

SIR,

I HAD yours of the last week, and by reason of some sudden encumbrances I could not correspond with you by that Carrier. As for your desire to know the Pedigree and first Rise of those we call *Presbyterians,* I find that your

motion

motion hath as much of Piety as Curiosity in it; but I must tell you 'tis a Subject fitter for a Treatise than a Letter, yet I will endeavour to satisfy you in some part.

Touching the word Πρεσβύτερος, it is as ancient as *Christianity* itself; and every Churchman compleated in holy Orders was called *Presbyter*, as being the chiefest name of the Function; and so 'tis us'd in all Churches both Eastern and Occidental to this day. We by contraction call him *Priest*, so that all Bishops and Archbishops are Priests, tho' not *vice versâ*. These holy Titles of Bishop and Priest are now grown odious among such poor Sciolists, who scarce know the *Hotie's* of things, because they savor of Antiquity; tho' their *Minister* that officiates in their Church be the same thing as *Priest*, and their *Superintendent* the same thing as *Bishop:* But because they are lovers of novelties, they change old *Greek* words for new *Latin* ones. The first broacher of the Presbyterian Religion, and who made it differ from that of *Rome* and *Luther*, was *Calvin;* who being once banish'd *Geneva*, was revok'd, at which time he no less petulantly than profanely apply'd to himself that Text of the holy Prophet which was meant of Christ, *The Stone which the Builders refused, is made the head-stone of the Corner*, &c. Thus *Geneva* Lake swallow'd up the Episcopal *Sea*, and Church-Lands were made secular, which was the white they levell'd at. This *Geneva* Bird flew thence to *France*, and hatch'd the *Huguenots*, which make about the tenth part of that People: It took wing also to *Bohemia* and *Germany* high and low, as the *Palatinate*, the Land of *Hesse*, and the Confederate Provinces of the States of *Holland*, whence it took flight to *Scotland* and *England*. It took first footing in *Scotland* when K. *James* was a child in his Cradle; but when he came to understand himself, and was manumitted from *Buchanan*, he grew cold in it; and being come to *England*, he utterly disclaimed it, terming it, in a public Speech of his to the Parliament, a *Sect* rather than a *Religion*. To this Sect may be imputed all the Scissures that have happen'd in *Christianity*, with most of the Wars that have

have lacerated poor *Europe* ever since; and it may be called the Source of the civil Distractions that now afflict this poor Island.

Thus have I endeavour'd to fulfil your desires in part; I shall enlarge myself further when I shall be made happy with your conversation here; till when, and always, I rest— Your most affectionate to love and serve you,　　J. H.

Fleet, 29 *Nov.* 1647.

IV.

To Sir J. S., *Knight, at* Rouen.

SIR,

OF all the Blessings that ever dropt down from Heaven upon Man, that of his *Redemption* may be call'd the Blessing paramount; and of all those Comforts and Exercises of Devotion which attend that Blessing, the *Eucharist* or holy Sacrament may claim the prime place. But as there is *Devotion,* so there is *Danger* in't, and that in the highest degree: 'Tis rank poison to some, tho' a most sovereign cordial to others, *ad modum recipientis,* as the Schoolmen say, whether they take *panem Dominum,* as the *Roman Catholic,* or *panem Domini,* as the *Reformed Churches.* The Bee and the Spider suck honey and poison out of one Flower. This, Sir, you have divinely exprest in the Poem you pleas'd to send me upon this Subject: And whereas you seem to woo my Muse to such a Task, something you may see she hath done, in pure obedience only to your commands.

Upon the Holy Sacrament.

I.

Hail holy Sacrament ! .
The World's great Wonderment,
Mysterious Banquet much more rare
Than Manna, *or the Angels' fare ;*
Each Crum, tho' Sinners on thee feed,
Doth Cleopatra's *Pearl exceed.*

Oh

Oh how my Soul *doth hunger, thirst, and pine*
After these Cates so precious, so divine !

II.

She *need not bring her stool*
As some unbidden fool ;
The Master of this heavenly Feast
Invites and woos her for his Guest :
Tho' deaf and lame, forlorn and blind,
Yet welcome here she's sure to find,
So that she bring a Vestment for the day,
And her old tatter'd rags throw quite away.

III.

This is Bethesda's *Pool,*
That can both cleanse and cool
Poor leprous and diseased Souls,
An Angel here keeps and controuls,
Descending gently from the Heavens above,
To stir the waters ; may he also move
My Mind, and rocky *Heart so strike and rend,*
That tears may thence gush out with them to blend.

This Morning-fancy drew on another towards the Evening, as followeth :

As to the Pole the Lilly bends
In a Sea-compass, and still tends
By a magnetic Mystery,
Unto the Arctic point in Sky,
  Whereby the wand'ring Piloteer
  His course in gloomy nights doth steer ;

So the small Needle *of my Heart*
Moves to her Maker, who doth dart
Atoms *of Love, and so attracts*
All my Affections, which like Sparks
  Fly up, and guide my Soul by this
  To the true centre of her Bliss.

As one Taper lightneth another, so were my spirits enlightned

lightned and heated by your late Meditations in this kind; and well fare your Soul with all her faculties for them: I find you have a great care of her, and of the main chance, *Præ quo quisquiliæ cætera.* You shall hear further from me within a few days; in the interim be pleas'd to reserve still in your Thoughts some little room for—Your most entirely affectionate Servitor,   J. H.

Fleet, 10 *of Dec.* 1647.

V.

To Mr. T. W., *at* P. Castle.

MY PRECIOUS TOM,

H E is the happy man who can square his mind to his means, and fit his fancy to his fortune: He who hath a competency to live in the port of a Gentleman, and as he is free from being a Head-Constable, so he cares not for being a Justice of Peace or Sheriff; he who is before-hand with the world, and when he comes to *London* can whet his knife at the Counter-gate, and needs not trudge either to a Lawyer's study or Scrivener's shop, to pay fee or squeeze wax. 'Tis *Conceit* chiefly that gives contentment; and he is happy who *thinks* himself so in any condition, tho' he have not enough to keep the Wolf from the door. *Opinion* is that great Lady which sways the World; and according to the impression she makes in the mind, renders one contented or discontented. Now touching *Opinion,* so various are the intellectuals of human Creatures, that one can hardly find out two who jump pat in one: Witness that Monster in *Scotland* in *James* the Fourth's reign, with two heads one opposite to the other; and having but one bulk of Body thro'out, these two heads would often fall into Altercations *pro* and *con* one with the other, and seldom were they of one opinion, but they would knock one against the other in eager disputes; which shews that the Judgment is seated in the *animal parts,* not in the *vital* which are lodg'd in the Heart.

We

We are still in a turbulent sea of distractions, nor as far as I see is there yet any sight of shore. Mr. *T. M.* hath had a great loss at Sea lately, which I fear will light heavily upon him : When I consider his case, I may say, that as the Philosopher made a question whether the *Mariner* be to be rank'd among the number of the *living* or *dead* (being but four inches distant from drowning, only the thickness of a plank), so 'tis a doubt whether the *Merchant* Adventurer be to be numbred 'twixt the *rich* or the *poor,* his estate being in the mercy of that devouring element the Sea, which hath so good a stomach that he seldom casts up what he hath once swallowed. This City hath bred of late years Men of monstrous strange opinions, that, as all other rich places besides, she may be compar'd to a fat Cheese which is most subject to engender Maggots. God amend all, and me first, who am—Yours most faithfully to serve you,   J. H.

Fleet, this St. Tho. Day.

VI.

To Mr. William Blois.

MY WORTHY ESTEEMED NEPHEW,

I RECEIV'D those rich nuptial favours you appointed me for *Bands* and *Hat,* which I wear with very much contentment and respect, most heartily wishing that this late double condition may multiply new blessings upon you, that it may usher in fair and golden days, according to the colour and substance of your bridal *Riband;* that those days may be perfum'd with delight and pleasure, as the rich scented Gloves I wear for your sake. May such Benedictions attend you both, as the Epithalamiums of *Stella* in *Statius,* and *Julia* in *Catullus,* speak of. I hope also to be marry'd shortly to a Lady whom I have woo'd above these five years, but I have found her coy and dainty hitherto; yet I am now like to get her good-will in part, I mean the Lady *Liberty.*

When you see my *N. Brownrigg,* I pray tell him that I did not think *Suffolk* Waters had such a *Lethean* Quality in them

them as to cause such an *Amnestia* in him of his Friends
here upon the *Thames,* among whom for Reality and Seriousness I may match among the foremost; but I impute it to
some new Task that his Muse might haply impose upon him,
which hath engross'd all his Speculations; I pray present
my cordial kind respects unto him.

So, praying that a thousand Blessings may attend this
Confarreation, I rest, my dear Nephew—Yours most affectionately to love and serve you,   J. H.

Fleet, 20 *March* 1647.

VII.

To Henry Hopkins, *Esq.*

SIR,

TO usher in again old *Janus,* I send you a Parcel of
Indian Perfume which the *Spaniard* calls the *Holy
Herb,* in regard of the various Virtues it hath, but we call
it *Tobacco;* I will not say it grew under the King of *Spain's*
Window, but I am told it was gather'd near his Gold-Mines
of *Potosi* (where they report that in some Places there is
more of that Ore than Earth), therefore it must needs be precious Stuff: If moderately and seasonably taken (as I find
you always do), 'tis good for many Things; it helps Digestion
taken a while after Meat, it makes one void Rheum, break
wind, and keeps the Body open : A Leaf or two being steeped
o'er-night in a little White-wine is a Vomit that never fails
in its Operation : It is a good Companion to one that converseth with dead Men ; for if one hath been poring long
upon a Book, or is toil'd with the Pen, and stupified with
Study, it quickeneth him, and dispels those Clouds that
usually o'erset the Brain.   The Smoke of it is one of the
wholesomest Scents that is, against all contagious Airs, for
it o'er-masters all other Smells, as K. *James,* they say, found
true, when being once a-hunting, a Shower of Rain drove
him into a Pig-sty for Shelter, where he caus'd a Pipe-full
to be taken on purpose: It cannot endure a Spider or a
Flea,

Flea, with such-like Vermin, and if your Hawk be troubled
with any such, being blown into his Feathers, it frees him:
It is good to fortify and preserve the Sight, the Smoke
being let in round about the Balls of the Eyes once a-week,
and frees them from all Rheums, driving them back by way
of Repercussion; being taken backward 'tis excellent good
against the Cholique, and taken into the Stomach, 'twill heat
and cleanse it; for I could instance in a great Lord (my
Lord of *Sunderland*, President of *York*), who told me, that
he taking it downward into his Stomach, it made him cast
up an Imposthume, Bag and all, which had been a long
Time engendring out of a Bruise he had received at Football,
and so preserv'd his Life for many Years.   Now to descend
from the Substance of the Smoke to the Ashes, 'tis well
known the medicinal Virtues thereof are very many; but
they are so common, that I will spare the inserting of them
here: But if one would try a petty Conclusion how much
Smoke there is in a Pound of Tobacco, the Ashes will tell
him: for let a Pound be exactly weigh'd, and the Ashes kept
charily and weigh'd afterwards, what wants of a Pound weight
in the Ashes cannot be deny'd to have been Smoke, which
evaporated into Air.   I have been told that Sir *Walter Raw-
leigh* won a Wager of Queen *Elizabeth* upon this Nicety.

The *Spaniards* and *Irish* take it most in Powder or
Smutchin, and it mightily refreshes the Brain, and I believe there's as much taken this Way in *Ireland* as there is
in Pipes in *England;* one shall commonly see the Serving-
maid upon the Washing-block, and the Swain upon the
Plough-share, when they are tir'd with Labour, take out
their Boxes of Smutchin and draw it into their Nostrils with
a Quill, and it will beget new Spirits in them with a fresh
Vigour to fall to their Work again.   In *Barbary* and other
Parts of *Afric*, 'tis wonderful what a small Pill of Tobacco
will do; for those who use to ride post thro' the sandy Desarts,
where they meet not with anything that's potable or edible,
sometimes three Days together, they use to carry small Balls
or Pills of Tobacco, which being put under the Tongue, it
affords

affords them a perpetual Moisture and takes off the Edge of the Appetite for some Days.

If you desire to read with Pleasure all the Virtues of this modern Herb, you must read Dr. *Thorus's Pætologia,* an accurate Piece couch'd in a strenuous heroic Verse, full of Matter, and continuing its Strength from first to last; insomuch, that for the Bigness it may be compar'd to any Piece of Antiquity, and, in my Opinion, is beyond βωτρακομυομαχία or γαλεωμυομαχία.

So I conclude these rambling Notions, presuming you will accept this small Argument of my great Respects to you: If you want Paper to light your Pipe, this Letter may serve the Turn; and if it be true what the Poets frequently sing, that *Affection is Fire,* you shall need no other than the clear Flames of the Donor's Love to make Ignition, which is comprehended in this Distich:

> Ignis Amor si fit, Tobaccum accendere nostrum,
> Nulla petenda tibi fax nisi Dantis Amor.
>
> *If* Love be Fire, *to light this* Indian *Weed,*
> *The Donor's* Love *of Fire may stand instead.*

So I wish you, as to myself, a most happy new Year; may the Beginning be good, the Middle better, and the End best of all.—Your most faithful and truly affectionate Servitor,

J. H.

Fleet, 1 *Jan.* 1646.

VIII.

To the Rt. Hon. my Lord of D.

MY LORD,

THE subject of this Letter may peradventure seem a *Paradox* to some, but not, I know, to your Lordship, when you have pleased to weigh well the Reasons. *Learning* is a Thing that hath been much cried up and coveted in all Ages, especially in this last Century of Years, by People of all Sorts, tho' never so mean and mechanical: every Man strains his Fortunes to keep his Children at School; the

Cobler

Cobler will clout it till Midnight, the Porter will carry Burdens till his Bones crack again, the Plough-man will pinch both Back and Belly to give his Son *Learning;* and I find that this Ambition reigns nowhere so much as in this Island. But under Favour this Word *Learning* is taken in a narrower Sense among us than among other Nations; we seem to restrain it only to the *Book;* whereas, indeed, any Artisan whatsoever (if he know the Secret and Mystery of his Trade) may be called a learned Man : A good *Mason,* a good *Shoemaker,* that can manage St. *Crispin's* Lance handsomely, a skilful *Yeoman,* a good *Shipwright,* &c., may be all called learned Men ; and indeed the usefullest sort of learned Men ; for without the two first we might go barefoot, and lie abroad as Beasts, having no other Canopy than the wild Air; and without the two last we might starve for Bread, have no Commerce with other Nations, or ever be able to tread upon a *Continent.* These, with such-like dextrous Artisans, may be termed learned Men, and the more behoveful for the Subsistence of a Country, than those *Polymathists* that stand poring all Day in a Corner upon a Moth-eaten Author, and converse only with dead Men. The *Chinese* (who are the next Neighbours to the rising Sun on this Side of the Hemisphere, and consequently the acutest) have a wholesome Piece of Policy, *That the Son is always of the Father's Trade;* and 'tis all the Learning he aims at: which makes them admirable Artisans ; for, besides the Dextrousness and Propensity of the Child, being descended lineally from so many of the same Trade, the Father is more careful to instruct him, and to discover to him all the Mystery thereof. This general Custom or Law keeps their Heads from running at random after Book-learning, and other Vocations. I have read a Tale of *Rob. Grosthead,* Bishop of *Lincoln,* that being come to this Greatness, he had a Brother who was a Husbandman, and expected great matters from him in point of Preferment ; but the Bishop told him that if he wanted Money to mend his Plow or his Cart, or to buy Tacklings for his Horses, with other things belonging to his

Husbandry,

Husbandry, he should not want what was fitting; but *wish'd him to aim no higher, for a Husbandman he found him, and a Husbandman he would leave him.*

The extravagant Humour of our Country is not to be altogether commended, that all Men should aspire to Book-learning: There is not a simpler Animal, and a more super-fluous Member of State, than a mere Scholar, than only a self-pleasing Student; he is——*Telluris inutile pondus.*

The *Goths* forbore to destroy the Libraries of the *Greeks* and *Italians*, because *Books* should keep them still soft, simple, or too cautious in warlike Affairs. *Archimedes*, tho' an excellent Engineer, when *Syracuse* was lost, was found at his Book in his Study, intoxicated with Speculations. Who would not have thought another great learned Philosopher to be a Fool or Frantic, when being in a Bath, he leap'd out naked among the People, and cried, *I have found it ! I have found it !* having hit then upon an extraordinary Conclusion in Geometry? There is a famous Tale of *Thomas Aquinas*, the *Angelical* Doctor, and of *Bonaventure*, the *Seraphical* Doctor, of whom *Alex. Hales* (our Countryman and his Master) reports, that it appeared not in him whether *Adam* had sinned: Both these great Clerks being invited to dinner by the *French* King, of purpose to observe their Humours, and being brought to the Room where the Table was laid, the first fell a eating of Bread as hard as he could drive; at last breaking out of a brown Study, he cried out, *Conclusum est contra Manichæos.* The other fell a-gazing upon the Queen, and the King asking him how he lik'd her, he answer'd, *Oh, Sir, if an earthly Queen be so beautiful, what shall we think of the Queen of Heaven?* The latter was the better Courtier of the two. Hence we may infer that your mere Book Men, your deep Clerks, whom we call the only learned Men, are not always the civilest or the best Moral Men, nor is too great a Number of them convenient for any State, leading a soft sedentary Life, especially those who feed their own fancies only upon the public stock. Therefore it were to be wish'd that there reign'd not among the people

of

of this Land such a general itching after Book-Learning, and
I believe so many *Free-Schools* do rather hurt than good:
nor did the Art of Printing much avail the Christian Commonwealth, but may be said to be well near as fatal as
Gunpowder, which came up in the same Age: For, under
correction, to this may be partly ascrib'd that spiritual Pride,
that variety of Dogmatists, which swarm among us. Add
hereunto, that the excessive number of those who converse
only with Books, and whose profession consists in them, is
such, that one cannot live for another, according to the
dignity of the Calling: A Physician cannot live for the
Physicians, a Lawyer (civil and common) cannot live for
Lawyers, nor a Divine for Divines. Moreover, the Multitudes that profess these three best Vocations, 'specially the
last, make them of far less esteem. There is an odd opinion
among us, that he who is a contemplative Man, a Man who
weds himself to his study, and swallows many books, must
needs be a profound Scholar, and a great learned Man, tho'
in reality he be such a dolt, that he hath neither a retentive
faculty to keep what he hath read, nor wit to make any useful
Application of it in common discourse; what he draws in
lieth upon dead Lees, and never grows fit to be broach'd.
Besides, he may want Judgment in the choice of his Authors,
and knows not how to turn his hand either in weighing or
winnowing the soundest opinions. There are divers who are
cried up for great Clerks who want discretion. Others, tho'
they wade deep into the causes and knowledge of things, yet
they are subject to screw up their wits, and soar so high, that
they lose themselves in their own Speculations; for thinking
to transcend the ordinary pitch of Reason, they come to
involve the common Principles of Philosophy in a Mist; instead of illustrating things, they render them more obscure;
instead of a plainer and shorter way to the Palace of Knowledge, they lead us thro' briery, odd uncouth paths, and so
fall into the fallacy call'd *notum per ignotius.* Some have the
hap to be term'd learned Men, tho' they have gathered up
but the scraps of Knowledge here and there, tho' they be
　　　　　　　　　　　　　　　　　　　　　　　　　　　but

but smatterers, and mere sciolists, scarce knowing the *Hoties* of things; yet, like empty casks, if they can make a Sound, and have a Gift to vent with Confidence what they have suck'd in, they are accounted great Scholars. Among all book-learned Men, except the *Divine,* to whom all learned Men should be Lacqueys, the Philosopher who hath waded thro' all the Mathematics, who hath dived into the secrets of the elementary World, and converseth also with celestial Bodies, may be term'd a learned Man : The critical *Historian* and *Antiquary* may be called also a learned Man, who hath conversed with our Forefathers, and observ'd the carriage and contingencies of matters pass'd, whence he draws instances and cautions for the benefit of the *Times* he lives in : The *Civilian* may be call'd likewise a learned Man, if the revolving of huge Volumes may entitle one so; but touching the Authors of the *Common Law,* which is peculiar only to this Meridian, they *may be all carried in a Wheel-barrow,* as my Countryman Dr. *Gwyn* told Judge *Finch :* The Physician must needs be a learned Man, for he knows himself inward and outward, being well vers'd in *Autology,* in that Lesson *Nosce Teipsum ;* and as *Adrian* VI. said, he is very necessary to a populous Country, for *were it not for the Physician, Men would live so long and grow so thick, that one could not live for the other ; and he makes the Earth cover all his faults.*

But what Dr. *Gwyn* said of the common Law-books, and Pope *Adrian* of the Physician, was spoken, I conceive, in merriment; for my part, I honour those two worthy Professions in a high degree. Lastly, a *Polyglot,* or good *Linguist,* may be also term'd a useful learned Man, 'specially if vers'd in School-Languages.

My Lord, I know none of this Age more capable to sit in the Chair, and censure what is true Learning and what not, than yourself: Therefore in speaking of this subject to your Lordship, I fear to have committed the same Error as *Phormio* did in discoursing of War before *Hannibal.* No more now, but that I am, my Lord—Your most humble and obedient Servant,   J. H.

IX.

IX.

To Doctor J. D.

Sir,

I HAVE many sorts of Civilities to thank you for, but amongst the rest, I thank you a thousand times (twice told) for that delightful fit of Society and conference of Notes we had lately in this little *Fleet-Cabin* of mine upon divers Problems, and upon some which are exploded (and that by those who seem to sway most in the Commonwealth of Learning) for *Paradoxes*, merely by an implicit faith, without diving at all into the Reasons of the Assertors. And whereas you promised a further expression of yourself by way of a discoursive Letter, what you thought of *Copernicus's* opinion touching the movement of the Earth, which hath so stirr'd all our modern wits; and whereof Sir *J. Brown* pleased to oblige himself to do the like touching the Philosopher's Stone, the Powder of Projection, and potable Gold, provided that I would do the same concerning a *peopled Country*, and a species of moving Creatures in the concave of the Moon, which I willingly undertook upon those conditions; To acquit myself of this obligation, and to draw on your Performances the sooner, I have adventured to send you this following Discourse (such as it is) touching the *Lunary* World.

I believe 'tis a Principle, which not many will offer to controvert, that as *Antiquity cannot privilege an Error, so Novelty cannot prejudice Truth*. Now, *Truth* hath her degrees of growing and expanding herself, as all other things have; and as Time begets her, so he doth the obstetricious Office of a Midwife to bring her forth. Many Truths are but Embryos or Problems; nay, some of them seem to be mere Paradoxes at first. The opinion that there were *Antipodes* was exploded when it was first broach'd; it was held absurd and ridiculous, and the thing itself to be as impossible as it was for Men to go upon their heads, with their heels upwards:

upwards: nay, 'twas adjudg'd to be so dangerous a Tenet, that you know well the Bishop's name, who in the primitive Church was by sentence of condemnation sent out of this world without a Head, to go to and dwell among his *Antipodes*, because he first hatch'd and held that opinion. But now our late Navigators, and *East-India* Mariners, who use to cross the Equator and Tropiques so often, will tell you, That it is as gross a paradox to hold there are no *Antipodes*, and that the negative is now as absurd as the affirmative seem'd at first. For Man to walk upon the Ocean when the Surges were at the highest, and to make a heavy dull piece of Wood to swim, nay, fly upon the Water, was held as impossible a thing at first, as it is now thought impossible for Man to fly in the Air : Sails were held then as uncouth as if one should attempt to make himself Wings to mount up to Heaven *à la volée*. Two hundred and odd years ago, he would have been taken for some frantic Fool, that would undertake to batter and blow up a Castle with a few barrels of a small contemptible black Powder.

The great Architect of the World hath been observ'd not to throw down all Gifts and Knowledge to Mankind confusedly at once; but in a regular parsimonious method, to dispense them by certain degrees, periods, and progress of time, leaving Man to make industrious researches and investigations after Truth : *He left the World to the disputations of Men,* as the wisest of Men saith, who in acquisition of natural Truths went from the Hysop to the Cedar. *One Day certifieth another,* and one Age rectifieth another : The Morrow hath more experience than the precedent Day, and is oft-times able to be his School-master; the Grandchild laughs at some things that were done in his Grandsire's days; insomuch that hence it may be inferr'd, that natural human Knowledge is not yet mounted to its Meridian and highest point of elevation. I confess it cannot be denied without gross ingratitude, but we are infinitely obliged to our Forefathers for the Fundamentals of Sciences ; and as the Herald hath a rule, *Mallem cum patribus quam cum fratribus errare,*

2 L   I

I had rather err with my Fathers than Brothers; so it holds in other kinds of Knowledge. But those Times which we term vulgarly the *old World*, were indeed the Youth or Adolescence of it; and tho', if respect be had to the particular and personal Acts of Generation, and to the Relation of Father and Son, they who fore-liv'd and preceded us may be called our Ancestors, yet if you go to the Age of the World in general, and to the true Length and Longevity of things, we are more properly the older Cosmopolites: In this respect the *Cadet* may be term'd more ancient than his elder Brother, because the World was older when he enter'd into it. Moreover, besides *Truth*, *Time* hath also another Daughter, which is *Experience*, who holds in her Hands the great Looking-glass of Wisdom and Knowledge.

But now to the intended task touching an *habitable World, and a Species of living Creatures in the Orb of the Moon, which may bear some analogy with those of this elementary World:* Altho' it be not my purpose to maintain and absolutely assert this Problem, yet I will say this, that whosoever crieth it down for a new *neoterical Opinion,* as divers do, commit a grosser error than the Opinion may be in its own nature: For 'tis almost as ancient as Philosophy herself; I am sure 'tis as old as *Orpheus,* who sings of divers fair Cities and Castles within the Circle of the Moon. Moreover, the profoundest Clerks and most renowned Philosophers in all Ages have affirmed it. Towards the first Age of Learning, among others, *Pythagoras* and *Plato* avouch'd it; the first of whom was pronounc'd the wisest of Men by the Pagan Oracle, as our *Solomon* is by holy Writ. In the middle Age of Learning, *Plutarch* speaks of it; and in these modern times, the most speculative and scientificallest Men, both in *Germany* and *Italy,* seem to adhere to it, subinnuating that not only the Sphere of the Moon is peopled with *Selenites* or Lunary Men, but that likewise every Star in Heaven is a peculiar World of itself, which is coloniz'd and replenish'd with *Astrean* Inhabitants, as the Earth, Sea, and Air are with Elementary, the Body of the Sun not excepted,

who

who hath also his *Solar* Creatures, and they are accounted the most sublime, the most pure, and perfectest of all: The *Elementary* Creatures are held the grossest of all, having more matter than form in them: The *Solar* have more form than matter; the *Selenites,* with other *Astrean* Inhabitants, are of a mix'd nature, and the nearer they approach the Body of the Sun, the more pure and spiritual they are: Were it so, there were some grounds for his speculation who thought that human Souls, be they never so pious and pure, ascend not immediately after the dissolution from the corrupt mass of flesh before the glorious presence of God, presently to behold the *Beatifical Vision,* but first into the Body of the *Moon,* or some other Star, according to their degrees of goodness, and actuate some Bodies there of a purer composition; when they are refined there, they ascend to some higher Star, and so to some higher than that, till at last by these degrees they be made capable to behold the Lustre of that glorious Majesty, in whose sight no impurity can stand. This is illustrated by a comparison, that if one, after he hath been kept close in a dark dungeon a long time, should be taken out, and brought suddenly to look upon the Sun in the Meridian, it would endanger him to be struck stark blind; so no human Soul suddenly sallying out of a dirty prison, as the Body is, would be possibly able to appear before the incomprehensible Majesty of God, or be susceptible of the Brightness of his all-glorious Countenance, unless he be fitted thereunto before-hand by certain degrees, which might be done by passing from one Star to another, which, we are taught, differ one from the other in Glory and Splendor.

Among our modern Authors that would furbish this old Opinion of Lunary Creatures, and plant Colonies in the Orb of the Moon, with the rest of the celestial Bodies, *Gasper Galileo Galilei* is one, who by artificial Prospectives hath brought us to a nearer commerce with Heaven, by drawing it sixteen times nearer Earth than it was before in ocular Appearance, by the Advantage of the said Optic Instrument. Among

Among other Arguments which the Assertors of *Astrean* Inhabitants do produce for proof of this high Point, one is, that it is neither repugnant to *Reason* or *Religion* to think, that the Almighty Fabricator of the Universe, who doth nothing in vain, nor suffers his handmaid Nature to do so, when he created the erratic and fix'd Stars, he did not make those huge immense Bodies, whereof most are bigger than the Earth and Sea, tho' conglobated, to twinkle only, and to be an ornament to the Roof of Heaven; but he plac'd in the Convex of every one of those vast capacious Spheres some living Creatures to glorify his Name, among whom there is in every of them one supereminent, like *Man* upon *Earth*, to be Lord paramount of all the rest. To this haply may allude the old opinion, that there is a peculiar *Intelligence* which guides and governs every Orb in Heaven.

They that would thus colonize the Stars with Inhabitants, do place in the body of the Sun, as was said before, the purest, the most immaterial, and refined intellectual Creatures, whence the Almighty calls those he will have to be immediately about his Person, and to be admitted to the Hierarchy of Angels. This is far dissonant from the opinion of the *Turk*, who holds that the Sun is a great burning Globe design'd for the damned.

They who are transported with this high speculation, that there are Mansions and habitable Conveniencies for Creatures to live within the bodies of the celestial Orbs, seem to tax Man of a high presumption, that he should think all things were created principally for *Him;* that the Sun and Stars are serviceable to him in chief, *viz.,* to measure his days, to distinguish his seasons, to direct him in his Navigations, and pour wholesome Influences upon him.

No doubt they were created to be partly useful and comfortable to him; but to imagine that they are solely and chiefly for him, is a thought that may be said to be above the pride of *Lucifer:* They may be beneficial to him in the generation and increase of all elementary Creatures, and yet have peculiar Inhabitants of their own besides, to concur

cur with the rest of the World in the service of their Creator. 'Tis a fair prerogative for *Man* to be Lord of all terrestrial, aquatick, and airy Creatures; that with his harping Iron he can draw ashore the great Leviathan; that he can make the Camel and huge Dromedary to kneel to him, and take up his burden; that he can make the fierce Bull, tho' ten times stronger than himself, to endure his yoke; that he can fetch down the Eagle from his nest, with such privileges. But let him not presume too far in comparing himself with heavenly Bodies, while he is no other thing than a worm crawling upon the surface of this Earth. Now the Earth is the basest Creature which God hath made, therefore 'tis call'd his *Footstool;* and tho' some take it to be the *Centre,* yet it is the very sediment of the elementary World, as they say the Moon is of the celestial; 'tis the very sink of all corruption and frailty; which made *Trismegist* say, that *Terra non mundus est nequitiæ locus;* the *Earth,* not the *World,* is the seat of wickedness: And tho', 'tis true, she be susceptible of Light, yet the Light terminates only in her Superficies, being not able to enlighten anything else, as the Stars can do.

Thus have I proportioned my short discourse upon this spacious Problem to the size of an Epistle; I reserve the fulness of my Opinion in this point, till I receive yours touching *Copernicus.*

It hath been always my practice, in the search and eventilation of natural Verities, to keep to myself a philosophical freedom, and not to make any one's Opinion so magisterial and binding, but that I might be at Liberty to recede from it upon more pregnant and powerful reasons. For as in theological Tenets 'tis a rule, *Quicquid non descendit a monte Scripturæ, eadem authoritate contemnitur, qua approbatur;* Whatsoever descends not from the mount of holy Scripture, may be by the same Authority rejected as well as received: So in the disquisitions and winnowing of physical Truths, *Quicquid non descendit a monte Rationis,* &c. Whatsoever descends not from the mount of Reason, may be as well rejected as approved of.

So

So, longing after an opportunity to pursue this point by mixture of oral discourse, which hath more elbow-room than a Letter, I rest with all candor and cordial affection—Your faithful Servant,   J. H.

Fleet, this 2 of Nov. 1647.

X.

To the Right Honourable the Lady E. D.

MADAM,

THOSE Rays of Goodness which are diffusedly scatter'd in others, are all concentred in you; which, were they divided into equal portions, were enough to complete a whole Jury of Ladies: This draws you a mixture of Love and Envy, or rather an Admiration, from all who know you, 'specially from me, and that in so high a Degree, that if you would suffer yourself to be adored, you should quickly find me religious in that kind. However, I am bold to send your Ladyship this, as a kind of Homage, or Heriot, or Tribute, or what you please to term it, in regard I am a true Vassal to your Virtues: And if you please to lay any of your Commands upon me, your Will shall be a Law to me, which I will observe with as much Allegiance as any Branch of *Magna Charta ;* they shall be as binding to me as *Lycurgus's* Laws were to the *Spartans;* and to this I subscribe,   J. H.

Fleet, this 10 *of Aug.* 1647.

XI.

To R. B., Esquire, at Grundesburgh.

SIR,

WHEN I o'er-look'd the List of my choicest Friends to insert your Name, I paus'd a-while, and thought it more proper to begin a new collateral File, and put you in the front thereof, where make account you are plac'd. If anything upon Earth partakes of angelick Happiness (in civil Actions) 'tis *Friendship ;* it perfumes the thoughts with such

such sweet Idæas, and the heart with such melting Passions: such are the effects of yours to me, which makes me please myself much in the speculation of it.

I am glad you are so well return'd to your own Family; and touching the Wheelwright you write of, who from a Cart came to be a Captain, it made me think of the perpetual rotations of Fortune, which you know Antiquity seated upon a Wheel in a restless, tho' not violent, Volubility: And truly it was never more verified than now, that those Spokes which were formerly but collateral, and some of them quite underneath, are now coming up apace to the top of the Wheel. I hope there will be no cause to apply to them the old Verse I learn'd at School,

Asperius nihil est humili, cum surgit in altum.

But there is a transcendent over-ruling Providence, who can not only check the rollings of this petty Wheel, and strike a Nail into it that it shall not stir, but stay also when he pleaseth the Motions of those vast Spheres of Heaven, where the Stars are always stirring, as likewise the whirlings of the *Primum Mobile* itself, which the Astronomers say draws all the World after it in a rapid Revolution. That Divine Providence vouchsafe to check the Motion of that malevolent Planet, which hath so long lowr'd upon poor *England,* and send us better days. So, saluting you with no vulgar Respects, I rest, my dear Nephew—Yours most affectionately to serve you,   J. H.

Fleet, this 26 *of July* 1646.

XII.

To Mr. En. P., *at* Paris.

SIR,

THAT which the Plots of the Jesuits in their dark Cells, and the Policy of the greatest Roman Catholic Princes have driven at these many Years, is now done to their hands, which was to divide and break the Strength of these three Kingdoms, because they held it to be too great

a

a Glory and Power to be in one *Heretical* Prince's Hands
(as they esteemed the King of *Great Britain*), because he
was in a Capacity to be Umpire, if not Arbiter of this Part
of the World, as many of our Kings have been.

You write thence, that in regard of the sad Condition
of our Queen, their Country-woman, they are sensible of
our Calamities; but I believe, 'tis the *Populace* only, who
see no farther than the Rind of Things: your Cabinet-Council rather rejoiceth at it, who, or I am much deceiv'd, contributed much in the Time of the late *sanguine* Cardinal to
set afoot these Distractions, beginning first with *Scotland,*
who, you know, hath always serv'd that Nation for a Brand
to set *England* a-fire for the Advancement of their own
Ends. I am afraid we have seen our best Days; we knew
not when we were well: so that the *Italian* Saying may be
well apply'd to poor *England, I was well, I would be better,
I took Physic and died.* No more now, but that I rest still
—Yours entirely to serve you,   J. H.
Fleet, 20 *Jan.* 1647.

XIII.

To John Wroth, *Esq., at* Petherton-Park.

Sir,

I HAD two of yours lately, one in *Italian,* the other in
French (which were answer'd in the same Dialect), and
as I read them with singular Delight, so I must tell you, they
struck an admiration into me, that in so short a Revolution
of Time you should come to be so great a Master of those
Languages both for the *Pen* and *Parley.* I have known
divers, and those of pregnant and ripe Capacities, who had
spent more Oil and Time in those Countries, yet could they
not arrive to that *double* Perfection which you have; for if
they got one, they were commonly defective in the other.
Therefore I may say, that you have not *Spartam nactus,*
which was but a petty Republic, *sed Italiam & Galliam nactus
es, has orna; you have got all* Italy *and* France, *adorn these.*

Nor is it *Language* that you have only brought home
with

with you; but I find that you have studied the *Men* and
the *Manners* of those Nations you have convers'd withal:
Neither have you courted only all their fair Cities, Castles,
Houses of Pleasure, and other Places of Curiosity, but you
have pried into the very Mysteries of their Government, as
I find by those choice Manuscripts and Observations you
have brought with you. In all these Things you have been
so curious, as if the Soul of your great Uncle, who was employed Ambassador in the *Imperial* Court, and who held
correspondence with the greatest Men of *Christendom* in
their own Language, had transmigrated into you.

The freshest News here is, that those Heart-burnings and
Fires of Civil Commotions which you left behind you in
France, cover'd over with thin Ashes for the Time, are
broken out again; and I believe they will be never quite
extinguish'd till there be a Peace or Truce with *Spain,* for till
then there is no Hope of Abatement of Taxes. And 'tis fear'd
the *Spanish* will out-weary the *French* at last in fighting; for
the *Earth* herself, I mean his Mines of *Mexico* and *Peru,*
afford him a constant and yearly Treasure to support his
Armies; whereas the *French* King digs his Treasure out of
the Bowels and vital Spirits of his own Subjects.

I pray let me hear from you by the next Opportunity, for
I shall hold my Time well employ'd to correspond with a
Gentleman of such choice and gallant Parts: In which De-
sires I rest—Your most affectionate and faithful Servitor,

J. H.

29 Aug. 1649.

XIV.

To Mr. W. B.

HOW glad was I, my choice and precious Nephew, to
receive yours of the 24th current; wherein I was
sorry, tho' satisfied in point of Belief, to find the ill Fortune
of Interception which befell my last unto yon.

Touching the Condition of Things here, you shall understand,

stand, that our Miseries lengthen with our Days; for tho' the Sun and the Spring advance nearer us, yet our Times are not grown a whit the more comfortable. I am afraid this City hath fool'd herself into a Slavery; the Army, tho' forbidden to come within ten Miles of her, by Order of Parliament, quarters now in the Bowels of her; they threaten to break her Percullies, Posts, and Chains, to make her pervious upon all occasions: they have secur'd also the *Tower*, with Addition of Strength for themselves: besides a Famine doth insensibly creep upon us, and the *Mint* is starv'd for want of Bullion; *Trade*, which was ever the Sinew of this Island, doth visibly decay, and the *Insurance* of Ships is risen from two to ten in the Hundred: Our Gold is ingrossed in private Hands, or gone beyond Sea to travel without License; and much I believe of it is return'd to the Earth (whence it first came) to be buried where our late Nephews may chance to find it a thousand Years hence, if the World lasts so long; so that the exchanging of white Earth into red (I mean Silver into Gold) is now above six in the Hundred: and all these, with many more, are the dismal Effects and Concomitants of a Civil War. 'Tis true, we have had many such *black* Days in *England* in former Ages; but those, parallel'd to the present, are as a shadow of a *Mountain* compar'd to the Eclipse of the *Moon*. My Prayers early and late are, that God Almighty would please not to turn away his Face quite, but cheer us again with the Light of his Countenance. And I am well assured you will join with me in the same Orison to Heaven's Gate; in which Confidence I rest—Yours most affectionately to serve you,   J. H.

Fleet, 10 *of Dec.* 1647.

XV.

To Sir K. D., *at* Paris.

SIR,

NOW that you are return'd, and fix'd a-while in *France*, an old Servant of yours takes leave to kiss your Hands,

Hands, and salute you in an intense Degree of Heat and Height of Passion. 'Tis well you shook hands with this infortunate Isle when you did, and got your liberty by such a Royal Mediation as the Queen's Regents; for had you staid, you would have taken but little comfort in your Life, in regard that ever since there have been the fearfullest Distractions here that ever happen'd upon any Part of the Earth: a belluin Kind of Immanity never rang'd so among Men, insomuch, that the whole Country might have taken its appellation from the smallest Part thereof, and be called the *Isle of Dogs;* for all Humanity, common Honesty, and that Mansuetude, with other moral Civilities which should distinguish the rational Creature from other Animals, have been lost here a good while. Nay, besides this *Cynical,* there is a kind of *Wolvish* Humour hath seiz'd upon most of this People, a true *Lycanthropy,* they so worry and seek to devour one another; so that the wild *Arab* and fiercest *Tartar* may be call'd civil Men in comparison of us: therefore he is the happiest who is furthest off from this woful Island. The King is straitened of that Liberty he formerly had in the *Isle of Wight,* and as far as I can see, may make up the Number of *Nebuchadnezzar's* Years before he be restor'd: the Parliament persists in their first Propositions; and will go nothing less. This is all I have to send at this time, only I will adjoin the true Respects of—Your most faithful humble Servitor, J. H.

Fleet, this 5 of May 1647.

XVI.

To Mr. W. Blois, *in* Suffolk.

SIR,

YOURS of the 17th current came safely to hand, and I kiss your Hands for it; you mention there two others that came not, which made me condole the Loss of such Jewels, for I esteem all your Letters for being the precious Effects of your Love, which I value at a high Rate, and

please

please myself much in the Contemplation of it, as also in the Continuance of this Letter-Correspondence, which is perform'd on your Part with such ingenious Expressions, and embroidered still with new Flourishes of Invention. I am still under hold in this fatal *Fleet;* and like one in a Tempest at Sea, who hath been often near the Shore, yet is still toss'd back by contrary Winds, so I have had frequent Hopes of Freedom, but some cross Accident or other always intervened; insomuch that I am now in Half-despair of an absolute Release till a general Gaol-delivery: yet notwithstanding this outward Captivity, I have inward Liberty still, I thank God for it.

The greatest News is, that between twenty and thirty thousand well-arm'd *Scots* have been utterly routed, rifled, and all taken prisoners, by less than 8000 *English.* I must confess 'twas a great Exploit, whereof I am not sorry, in regard that the *English* have regain'd hereby the Honour which they had lost abroad of late Years in the Opinion of the World, ever since the Pacification at *Berwick,* and divers Traverses of War since. What *Hamilton's* Design was, is a Mystery; most think that he intended no Good either to King or Parliament. So, with my daily more and more endeared Affections to you, I rest—Yours ever to love and serve you,   J. H.

Fleet, 7 *May* 1647.

XVII.

To *Mr.* R. Baron, *at* Paris.

GENTLE SIR,

I RECEIV'D and presently ran over your *Cyprian Academy* with much Greediness, and no vulgar Delight; and, Sir, I hold myself much honour'd for the Dedication you have been pleas'd to make thereof to me, for it deserv'd a far higher Patronage. Truly, I must tell you without any Compliment, that I have seldom met with such an ingenious mixture of Prose and Verse, interwoven with such varieties

of

of Fancy and charming strains of amorous Passions, which have made all the Ladies of the Land in love with you. If you begin already to court the Muses so handsomely, and have got such footing on *Parnassus*, you may in time be Lord of the whole Hill; and those nice Girls, because *Apollo* is now grown unwieldy and old, may make choice of you to officiate in his room, and preside over them.

I much thank you for the punctual Narration you pleas'd to send me of those Commotions in *Paris*; I believe *France* will never be in perfect repose while a *Spaniard* sits at the Stern, and an *Italian* steers the Rudder. In my opinion *Mazarine* should do wisely, now that he hath feather'd his nest so well, to truss up his Baggage, and make over the *Alps* to his own Country, lest the same fate betide him as did the Marquis of *Ancre* his Compatriot. I am glad the Treaty goes on 'twixt *Spain* and *France*; for nothing can portend a greater good to *Christendom* than a Conjunction of those two great Luminaries; which if it please God to bring about, I hope the Stars will change their Aspects, and we shall see better days.

I send here inclosed a second Bill of Exchange, in case the first I sent you in my last hath miscarry'd: So, my dear Nephew, I embrace you with both my Arms, and rest— Yours most entirely to love and serve you, while   J. H.

Fleet, 20 *June* 1647.

XVIII.

To *Mr.* Tho. More, *at* York.

SIR,

I HAVE often partak'd of that pleasure which *Letters* use to carry along with them; but I do not remember to have found a greater proportion of delight than yours afford me. Your last of the 4th current came to safe hand, wherein methought each line, each word, each syllable breath'd out the Passions of a clear and candid Soul, of a virtuous and gentle Spirit. Truly, Sir, as I might perceive by

by your ingenuous and pathetical expressions therein, that
you were transported with the heat of true Affection towards
me in the *writing*, so was I in the *reading*, which wrought
upon me with such an Energy that a kind of extasy possess'd me for the time.   I pray, Sir, go on in this correspondence, and you shall find that your lines will not be ill
bestow'd upon me; for I love and respect you dearly well :
Nor is this Love grounded upon vulgar Principles, but
upon those extraordinary parts of Virtue and Worth which
I have discover'd in you, and such a Love is the most
permanent, as you shall find in—Your most affectionate
Uncle,   J. H.

Fleet, 1 *of Sep.* 1647.

XIX.

To Mr. W. B., 3° Maii.

SIR,

YOUR last Lines to me were as delightful as the *Season*,
they were as sweet as Flowers in *May ;* nay, they were
far more fragrant than those fading Vegetables, they did cast
a greater suavity than the *Arabian* Spices use to do in the
Grand Cairo, where when the Wind is Southward, they say
the Air is as sweet as a perfum'd *Spanish* Glove.   The Air
of this City is not so, specially in the heart of the City, in
and about *Paul's* Church, where Horse-dung is a yard deep ;
insomuch that to cleanse it would be as hard a task as it
was for *Hercules* to cleanse the *Augean* Stable, by drawing
a great River thro' it, which was accounted one of his twelve
Labours.   But it was a bitter taunt of the *Italian*, who passing by *Paul's* Church, and seeing it full of horses, *Now I
perceive* (said he) *that in* England *Men and Beasts serve God
alike.*   No more now, but that I am—Your most faithful
Servant,   J. H.

XX.

XX.

To Sir Paul Pindar, *Kt., upon the Version of an* Italian *Piece into* English, *call'd* St. Paul's Progress upon Earth ; *a new and a notable kind of Satire.*

SIR,

ST. *PAUL* having descended lately to view *Italy* and other places, as you may trace him in the following Discourse, he would not take wing back to Heaven before he had given *you* a special visit, who have so well deserv'd of his Church here, the goodliest pile of Stones in the *Christian* World of that kind.

Of all the Men of our times, you are one of the greatest examples of Piety and constant Integrity, which discovers a noble Soul to dwell within you, and that you are very conversant with Heaven ; so that methinks I see St. *Paul* saluting and solacing you in these black times, assuring you that those pious works of Charity you have done and daily do (and that in such a manner, *that the left hand knows not what the right doth*) will be as a triumphant Chariot to carry you one day up to Heaven, to partake of the same Beatitude with him.   Sir, among those that truly honour you, I am one, and have been so since I first knew you ; therefore as a small testimony hereof, I send you this fresh Fancy compos'd by a noble Personage in *Italian,* of which Language you are so great a Master.

For the first part of the Discourse, which consists of a Dialogue 'twixt the two first Persons of the Holy *Trinity,* there are examples of that kind in some of the most ancient Fathers, as *Apollinarius* and *Nazianzen;* and lately *Grotius* hath the like in his Tragedy of *Christ's Passion :* Which may serve to free it from all exceptions.   So I most affectionately kiss your hands, and am, Sir—Your very humble and ready Servant,   J. H.

Fleet, 25 *Martii* 1646.

XXI.

XXI.

To Sir Paul Neale, *Kt., upon the same Subject.*

SIR,

S T. *PAUL* cannot reascend to Heaven before he gives
you also a salute; my Lord, your Father, having been
a Star of the greatest magnitude in the Firmament of the
Church. If you please to observe the manner of his late
progress upon earth, which you may do by the guidance of
this discourse, you shall discover many things which are not
vulgar, by a curious mixture of Church and State-Affairs :
You shall feel herein the pulse of *Italy*, and how it beats at
this time since the beginning of these late Wars 'twixt the
Pope and the Duke of *Parma*, with the grounds, procedure,
and success of the said War ; together with the Interest and
Grievances, the Pretences and Quarrels that most Princes
there have with *Rome.*

I must confess, my Genius hath often prompted me that
I was never cut out for a Translator, there being a kind of
servility therein : For it must needs be somewhat tedious
to one that hath any free-born thoughts within him, and
genuine conceptions of his own (whereof I have some, tho'
shallow ones) to enchain himself to a verbal servitude, and
the sense of another.   Moreover, *Translations* are but as
turn-coated things at best, 'specially among Languages that
have Advantages one of the other, as the *Italian* hath of the
English, which may be said to differ one from the other as
Silk doth from *Cloth*, the common wear of both Countries
where they are spoken.   And as *Cloth* is the more substantial,
so the *English* Tongue, by reason 'tis so knotted with consonants, is the stronger and the more sinewy of the two:
But *Silk* is more smooth and slick, and so is the *Italian*
Tongue, compared to the *English*.   Or I may say, *Translations* are like the wrong side of a *Turkey* Carpet, which
useth to be full of thrums and knots, and nothing so even
as the right side : Or one may say (as I spake elsewhere), that
Translations

Translations are like Wines ta'en off the lees, and poured into other vessels, that must needs lose somewhat of their first strength and briskness, which in the pouring, or passage rather, evaporates into Air.

Moreover, touching Translations, it is to be observ'd, that every Language hath certain Idioms, Proverbs, and peculiar Expressions of its own, which are not rendible in any other, but paraphrastically; therefore he overacts the office of an Interpreter who doth enslave himself too strictly to Words or Phrases. I have heard of an excess among Limners, call'd too much to the Life, which happens when one aims at Similitude more than Skill: So in version of Languages, one may be so over-punctual in words, that he may mar the matter. The greatest fidelity that can be expected in a Translator, is to keep still a-foot and entire the true genuine sense of the Author, with the main design he drives at: And this was the principal thing which was observ'd in this Version.

Furthermore, let it not be thought strange that there are some *Italian* words made free denizons of *England* in this discourse; for by such means our Language hath grown from time to time to be copious, and still grows more rich, by adopting, or naturalizing rather, the choicest foreign words of other Nations; as a Nosegay is nothing else but a tuft of flowers gather'd from divers beds.

Touching this present Version of *Italian* into *English*, I may say, 'tis a thing I did when I had nothing to do: 'Twas to find something whereby to pass away the slow hours of this sad condition of Captivity.

I pray be pleas'd to take this as a small Argument of the great respects I owe you for the sundry rare and high Virtues I have discover'd in you, as also for the obligations I have to your noble Lady, whose hands I humbly kiss, wishing you both, as the Season invites me, a good new Year (for it begins but now in *Law*) as also a holy *Lent*, and a healthful Spring.—Your most obliged and ready Servitor, J. H.

Fleet, 25 *Martij*.

2 M   XXII.

XXII.

To Dr. W. Turner.

SIR,

I RETURN you my most thankful Acknowledgments for that Collection, or *farrago* of Prophecies, as you call them (and that very properly, in regard there is a mixture of good and bad), you pleas'd to send me lately; 'specially that of *Nostredamus,* which I shall be very chary to preserve for you. I could requite you with divers Predictions more, and of some of the *British Bards,* which were they translated into *English* would transform the World to wonder.

They sing of a *Red* Parliament and *White* King, of a race of People which should be called *Pengruns,* of the fall of the Church, and divers other things which glance upon these times. But I am none of those that afford much faith to rambling Prophecies, which (as was said elsewhere) are like so many odd grains sown in the vast field of *Time,* whereof not one in a thousand comes up to grow again, and appear above ground. But that I may correspond with you in some part for the like courtesy, I send you these following prophetic Verses of *Whitehall,* which were made above twenty years ago to my knowledge, upon a Book call'd *Balaam's Ass,* that consisted of some Invectives against K. *James* and the Court *in statu quo tunc:* It was compos'd by one Mr. *Williams,* a Counsellor of the *Temple,* but a *Roman* Catholic, who was hang'd, drawn, and quarter'd at *Charing-Cross* for it; and I believe there be hundreds that have Copies of these Verses ever since that time about Town yet living. They were these:

> *Some seven years since Christ rid to Court,*
> *And there he left his Ass:*
> *The Courtiers kick'd him out of doors,*
> *Because they had no* grass.*   * grace.
> *The Ass went mourning up and down,*
> *And thus I heard him bray,*

If

If that they could not give me grass,
They might have given me hay ;
But sixteen hundred forty three,
Whosoe'er shall see that day,
Will nothing find within that Court,
But only grass and hay, &c.

Which was found to happen true in *Whitehall*, till the Soldiers coming to quarter there, trampled it down.

Truly, Sir, I find all things conspire to make strange mutations in this miserable Island ; I fear we shall fall from under the *Scepter* to be under the *Sword :* And since we speak of Prophecies, I am afraid among others that which was made since the Reformation will be verified, *The Church-man was, the Lawyer is, the Soldier shall be.* Welcome be the will of God, who transvolves Kingdoms and tumbles down Monarchies as Mole-hills at his pleasure. So I rest, my dear Doctor—Your most faithful Servant, J. H.

Fleet, 9 *Aug.* 1648.

XXIII.

To the Hon. Sir Edward Spencer, *Kt., at his House near* Branceford.

SIR,

WE are not so bare of intelligence between these walls, but we can hear of your doings in *Branceford :* That so general applause whereby you were cried up Knight of the Shire for *Middlesex,* sounded round about us upon *London* Streets, and echo'd in every corner of the Town ; nor do I mingle speech with any, tho' half affected to you, but highly approve of and congratulate the Election, being glad that a Gentleman of such extraordinary parts and probity, as also of such a mature judgment, should be chosen to serve the Public.

I return you the Manuscript you lent me of *Dæmonology,* but the Author thereof and I are *two* in point of opinion that way ; for he seems to be on the negative part, and truly he writes as much as can be produc'd for his purpose. But

But there are some men that are of a mere negative genius, like *Johannes ad oppositum*, who will deny, or at least cross and puzzle anything, tho' never so clear in itself, with their *but, yet, if*, &c.; they will flap the lye in *Truth's* teeth, tho' she visibly stand before their face without any vizard: Such perverse cross-grain'd spirits are not to be dealt withal by arguments, but palpable proofs; as if one should deny that the fire burns, or that he hath a nose on his face; there is no way to deal with him, but to pull him by the tip of the one, and put his finger into the other. I will not say that this Gentleman is so perverse; but to deny there are any Witches, to deny that there are not ill Spirits which seduce, tamper, and converse in divers shapes with human Creatures, and impel them to actions of malice; I say, that he who denies there are such busy Spirits, and such poor passive Creatures upon whom they work, which commonly are call'd Witches; I say again, that he who denies there are such Spirits, shews that he himself hath a Spirit of Contradiction in him, opposing the current and consentient Opinion of all Antiquity. We read that both *Jews* and *Romans*, with all other Nations of *Christendom*, and our Ancestors here in *England*, enacted Laws against Witches; sure they were not so silly as to waste their brains in making Laws against Chimeras, against *non-entia*, or such as *Plato's Kteritismata's* were. The *Judicial* Law is apparent in the holy Codex, *Thou shalt not suffer a Witch to live*: The *Roman* Law, which the *Decemviri* made, is yet extant in the twelve Tables, *Qui fruges incantassent, pœnis danto:* They who shall inchant the fruit of the Earth, let them be punish'd. The *Imperial* Law is known by every Civilian; *Hi cum hostes naturæ sint, supplicio afficiantur:* These, meaning Witches, because they are enemies to Nature, let them be punish'd. And the Acts of Parliament in *England* are against those *that invoke ill Spirits, that take up any dead man, woman, or child, to take the skin or bone of any dead body, to employ it to Sorcery or Charm, whereby any one is lam'd or made to pine away,* &c., *such shall be guilty*

*guilty of flat Felony, and not capable of Clergy or Sanc-
tuary,* &c.

What a multitude of examples are there in good authentic
Authors of divers kinds of Fascinations, Incantations, Pre-
stigiations, of Philtres, Spells, Charms, Sorceries, Characters, and such like ; as also of Magic, Necromancy, and
Divinations ? Surely the *Witch* of *Endor* is no fable ; the
burning of *Joan d'Arc* the Maid of *Orleans* in *Rouen,* and
of the Marchioness of *d'Ancre* of late years in *Paris,* are
no fables : The execution of *Nostredamus* for a kind of
Witch, some fourscore years since, is but a modern story,
who among other things foretold, *Le Senat de Londres tuera
son Roy,* The Senate of *London* shall kill their King. The
best historians have it upon record, how *Charlemain's* Mistress enchanted him with a Ring, which as long as she
had about her, he would not suffer her dead Carcase to be
carry'd out of his chamber to be buried ; and a Bishop taking
it out of her mouth, the Emperor grew to be as much bewitch'd with the Bishop ; but he being cloy'd with his excess
of favour, threw it into a Pond, where the Emperor's chiefest
pleasure was to walk till his dying day. The story tells us,
how the *Waldenses* in *France* were by solemn Arrest of Parliament accus'd and condemn'd of *Witchcraft.* The *Malteses*
took St. *Paul* for a *Witch.* St. *Augustin* speaks of Women
who could turn Men to Horses, and make them carry their
burdens : *Danæus* writes of an inchanted Staff, which the
Devil, Summoner-like, was us'd to deliver some Market-
women to ride upon. In some of the Northern Countries,
'tis as ordinary to buy and sell *Winds* as it is to do *Wines*
in other parts ; and hereof I could instance in some examples
of my own knowledge. Every one knows what *Olaus
Magnus* writes of *Erich's* (King of *Sweethland's*) corner'd
Cap, who could make the Wind shift to any point of the
Compass, according as he turn'd it about.

Touching Diviners of things to come, which is held a
species of *Witchcraft,* we may read they were frequent among
the *Romans ;* yea, they had Colleges for their Augurs and
Aruspices,

Aruspices, who us'd to make their Predictions sometimes by
Fire, sometimes by flying of Fowls, sometimes by inspection
into the Entrails of Beasts, or invoking the dead, but most
frequently by consulting with the Oracles, to whom all
Nations hath recourse except the *Jews.* But you will say,
that since *Christianity* display'd her Banner, the *Cross* hath
scar'd away the Devil and struck the Oracles dumb: As
Plutarch reports a notable passage of *Thamus,* an *Italian* Pilot,
who a little after the birth of Christ, sailing along the Coasts
of *Calabria* in a still silent night, all his Passengers being
asleep, an airy cold Voice came to his ears, saying, *Thamus,*
Thamus, Thamus, The great God Pan *is dead,* who was the
chiefest Oracle of that Country. Yet tho' the Light of
the Gospel chas'd away those great Owls, there be some
Bats and little Night-birds that fly still abroad, I mean petty
Spirits, that by secret pactions, which are made always without witness, enable Men and Women to do evil. In such
compacts beyond the Seas, the Party must *first renounce*
Christ, and the extended Woman, meaning the blessed Virgin ;
he must contemn the Sacrament, tread on the Cross, spit at the
Host, &c. There is a famous story of such a Paction, which
Fryar *Louis* made some half a hundred years ago with the
Devil in *Marseilles,* who appeared to him in shape of a Goat,
and promis'd him the enjoyment of any Woman whom he
fancied, with other Pleasures, for 41 years ; but the Devil
being too cunning for him, put the figure of 1 before,
and made it 14 years in the Contract (which is to be
seen to this day, with the Devil's claw to it), at which time
the Fryar was detected for Witchcraft, and burnt ; and all
those Children whom he had christned during that term of
fourteen years were re-baptiz'd : The Gentlewomen whom
he had abus'd put themselves into a Nunnery by themselves. Hereunto may be added the great rich Widow that
was burn'd in *Lions,* because 'twas prov'd the Devil had lain
with her ; as also the History of Lieutenant *Jaquette,* which
stands upon record with the former : But if I should insert
them here at large, it would make this Letter swell too much.
                                                                    But

But we need not cross the Sea for examples of this kind; we have too too many (God wot) at home. King *James* a great while was loth to believe there were Witches; but that which happen'd to my Lord *Francis* of *Rutland's* Children convinc'd him, who were bewitch'd by an old Woman that was servant at *Belvoir-Castle;* but being displeas'd, she contracted with the Devil (who convers'd with her in form of a Cat, whom she call'd *Rutterkin)* to make away those Children, out of mere malignity and thirst of revenge.

But since the beginning of these unnatural Wars, there may be a cloud of Witnesses produc'd for the proof of this black Tenet: For within the compass of two years, near upon three hundred Witches were arraign'd, and the major part executed in *Essex* and *Suffolk* only. *Scotland* swarms with them now more than ever, and Persons of good Quality executed daily.

Thus, Sir, have I huddled together a few Arguments touching this Subject; because in my last communication with you, methought I found you somewhat unsatisfied, and staggering in your opinion touching the affirmative part of this Thesis, the discussing whereof is far fitter for an elaborate large Treatise than a loose Letter.

Touching the new Commonwealth you intend to establish, now that you have assign'd me my part among so many choice Legislators: Something I shall do to comply with your *Desires,* which shall be always to me as Commands, and your Commands as Laws; because I love and honour you in a very high degree for those gallant free-born thoughts and sundry parts of virtue which I have discerned in you: Which makes me entitle myself—Your most humble and affectionate faithful Servant, J. H.

Fleet, 20 *Feb.* 1647.

XXIV.

XXIV.

To *Sir* William Boswel, *at the* Hague.

SIR,

THAT black Tragedy which was lately acted here, as it hath fill'd most hearts among us with consternation and horror, so I believe it hath been no less resented abroad. For my own particular, the more I ruminate upon it, the more it astonisheth my imagination, and shaketh all the cells of my Brain; so that sometimes I struggle with my Faith, and have much ado to believe it yet. I shall give over wondring at anything hereafter, nothing shall seem strange unto me; only I will attend with patience how *England* will thrive, now that she is let blood in the *Basilical* Vein, and cur'd, as they say, of the *King's-Evil.*

I had one of yours by Mr. *Jacob Boeue*, and I much thank you for the Account you please to give me of what I sent you by his conveyance. *Holland* may now be proud, for there is a younger Commonwealth in *Christendom* than herself. No more now but that I always rest, Sir—Your most humble Servitor,   J. H.

Fleet, 20 *Mar.* 1648.

XXV.

To *Mr.* W. B., *at* Grundsburgh.

SIR,

NEVER credit me, if *Liberty* itself be as dear to me as your *Letters,* they come so full of choice and learned applications, with such free unforc'd strains of ingenuity; insomuch that when I peruse them, methinks they cast such a kind of fragrancy, that I cannot more aptly compare them than to the Flowers which are now in their prime season, *viz.,* to Roses in *June.* I had two of them lately, which methought were like Quivers full of barb'd Arrows pointed with gold, that penetrated my breast.

> —*Tali quis nollet ab ictu*
> *Ridendo tremulas mortis non ire sub umbras?*

Your

Your expressions were like those *Mucrones* and *Melliti Globuli*, which you so ingeniously apply mine unto; but these Arrows of yours, tho' they have hit me, they have not hurt me, they had no killing quality, but they were rather as so many cordials; for you know Gold is restorative. I am suddenly surpriz'd by an unexpected occasion, therefore I must abruptly break off with you for this time: I will only add, my most dear Nephew, that I rest—Yours entirely to love and serve you,   J. H.

June 3, 1648.

XXVI.

To R. K., Esq., at St. Giles's.

SIR,

DIFFERENCE in *Opinion*, no more than a differing *Complexion*, can be cause enough for me to *hate* any. A differing *Fancy* is no more to me than a differing *Face*. If another hath a *fair* Countenance, tho' mine be *black;* or if I have a *fair* Opinion, tho' another have a *hard-favour'd* one, yet it shall not break that common league of Humanity which should be betwixt rational creatures, provided he corresponds with me in the general offices of Morality and civil uprightness: This may admit him to my acquaintance and conversation, tho' I never concur with him in *opinion:* He bears the Image of *Adam*, and the Image of the Almighty, as well as I; he had *God* for his *Father*, tho' he hath not the same *Church* for his *Mother*. The omniscient *Creator*, as he is only *Kardiognostic*, so he is the sole Lord of the whole inward Man: It is he who reigns o'er the faculties of the soul, and the affections of the Heart: 'Tis he who regulates the Will, and rectifies all obliquities in the Understanding by special illuminations, and oftentimes reconciles Men as opposite in *Opinions*, as *Meridians* and *Parallels* are in point of extension, whereof the one draws from East to West, the other from North to South.

Some of the Pagan Philosophers, 'specially *Themistius*, who

who was Prætor of *Byzantium*, maintain'd an opinion, that as the pulchritude and preservation of the World consisted in varieties and dissimilitudes (as also in eccentric and contrary motions), that as it was replenish'd with such numberless sorts of several Species, and that the *Individuals* of those Species differ'd so much one from the other, 'specially *Mankind*, amongst whom one shall hardly find two in ten thousand that hath exactly (tho' Twins) the same tone of Voice, similitude of Face, or ideas of Mind; therefore, the *God of Nature* ordain'd from the beginning, that he should be worshipped in various and sundry forms of Adorations, which nevertheless like so many Lines should tend all to the same Centre. But *Christian* Religion prescribes another *Rule*, viz., that there is but *una via, una veritas*, there is but one true way to Heaven, and that but a narrow one; whereas there be huge large roads that lead to Hell.

God Almighty guide us in the first, and guard us from the second, as also from all cross and uncouth by-paths, which use to lead such giddy brains that follow them to a confus'd labyrinth of Errors; where being entangled, the Devil, as they stand gaping for new Lights to lead them out, takes his advantage to seize on them for their *spiritual Pride*, and *insobriety* in the search of more Knowledge.—Your most faithful Servant, J. H.

28 *July* 1648.

Familiar

Familiar Letters.

BOOK IV.

I.

To Sir James Crofts, *Knight, near* Lempster.

SIR,

PISTLES, or (according to the word in use) *Familiar Letters,* may be call'd the *larum Bells of Love :* I hope *this* will prove so to you, and have power to awaken you out of that silence wherein you have slept so long ; yet I would not have this *larum* make any harsh obstreperous sound, but gently summon you to our former correspondence. Your returns to me shall be more than *larum Bells,* they shall be like *silver Trumpets* to rouze up my spirits, and make me take *pen* in hand to meet you more than half-way in the old field of Friendship.

It is recorded of *Galen,* one of Nature's *Cabinet-Clerks,* that when he slept his *Siesta* (as the *Spaniard* calls it) or afternoon sleep, to avoid excess that way, he us'd to sit in such a posture, that having a gold Ball in his hand, and a copper Vessel underneath, as soon as his *Senses* were shut, and the *Phantasy* began to work, the Ball would fall down,

the

the noise whereof would awake him, and draw the Spring-lock back again to set the outward Senses at liberty. I have seen in *Italy* a Finger-ring, which in the boss thereof had a Watch; and there was such a Trick of Art in it, that it might be so wound up, that it would make a small Pin to prick him who wore it, at such an hour as he pleas'd in the night. Let the *Pen* between us have the virtue of that *Pin:* But the *Pen* hath a thousand virtues more. You know that *Anser, Apis, Vitulus,* the Goose, the Bee, and the Calf, do rule the World; the one affording Parchment, the other two Sealing-Wax, and Quills to write withal. You know also how the *gaggling* of Geese did once preserve the Capitol from being surpriz'd by my Countryman *Brennus,* which was the first foreign Force that *Rome* felt. But the *Goose-quill* doth daily greater things, it conserves Empires (and the feathers of it get Kingdoms, witness what Exploits the *English* perform'd by it in *France*), the Quill being the chiefest instrument of Intelligence, and the Ambassador's prime Tool: Nay, the *Quill* is the *useful'st* thing which preserves that noble Virtue *Friendship,* which else would perish among Men for want of practice.

I shall make no more sallies out of *London* this Summer, therefore your Letters may be sure where to find me: Matters are still involv'd here in a strange confusion, but the Stars may let down milder influences; therefore chear up, and reprieve yourself against better times, for the World would be irksome to me if you were out of it. Hap what will, you shall be sure to find me—Your ready and real Servant,   J. H.

II.

To *Mr.* T. Morgan.

Sir,

I RECEIV'D two of yours upon *Tuesday* last, one to your Brother, the other to me; but the Superscriptions were mistaken, which makes me think on that famous Civilian Doctor *Dale,* who being employ'd to *Flanders* by Q. *Elizabeth,*

beth, sent in a Packet to the Secretary of State two Lettters, one to the *Queen,* the other to his *Wife ;* but that which was meant for the *Queen* was superscrib'd, *To his dear Wife ;* and that for his Wife, *To her most excellent Majesty :* So that the *Queen* having open'd his Letter, she found it beginning with *Sweet Heart,* and afterwards with my *Dear,* and *Dear Love,* with such expressions, acquainting her with the state of his body, and that he began to want money. You may easily guess what motions of mirth this Mistake rais'd, but the Doctor by this *oversight* (or *cunningness* rather) got a supply of money. This perchance may be your policy, to endorse me your Brother, thereby to endear me the more to you : But you needed not to have done that, for the name *Friend* goes sometimes further than *Brother ;* and there be more examples of *Friends* that did sacrifice their lives for one another than of *Brothers ;* which the Writer doth think he should do for you, if the case requir'd. But since I am fallen upon Dr. *Dale,* who was a witty kind of Drole, I will tell you instead of news (for there is little *good* stirring now) two other facetious Tales of his ; and Familiar *Tales* may become *Familiar Letters* well enough : When Q. *Elizabeth* did first propose to him that foreign employment to *Flanders,* among other encouragements she told him, that he should have 20*s. per diem* for his expences : Then, Madam, *said he,* I will spend 19*s.* a-day. What will you do with the odd shilling? *the Queen reply'd.* I will reserve that for my *Kate,* and for *Tom* and *Dick;* meaning his Wife and Children. This induc'd the Queen to enlarge his Allowance. But this that comes last is the best of all, and may be call'd the superlative of the three, which was, when at the overture of the Treaty the other Ambassadors came to propose in what Language they should treat, the *Spanish* Ambassador answer'd, that the *French* was the most proper, because his Mistress entitled herself *Queen of France :* Nay, then, *said Dr.* Dale, let us treat in *Hebrew,* for your Master calls himself King of *Jerusalem.*

I perform'd the civilities you enjoin'd me to your Friends here,

here, who return you the like centuplicated, and so doth—
Your entire Friend,   J. H.
May 12.

III.

To the Right Honourable the Lady E. D.

MADAM,

THERE is a *French* saying, that Courtesies and *Favours*
are like *Flowers*, which are sweet only while they are
fresh, but afterwards they quickly fade and wither. I cannot
deny but your favours to me might be compar'd to some
kind of *Flowers* (and they would make a thick *Posie*), but
they should be to the flower call'd *Life everlasting;* or that
pretty Vermilion *Flower* which grows at the foot of the
Mountain *Ætna* in *Sicily,* which never loses anything of its
first colour and scent. Those favours you did me thirty years
ago, in the lifetime of your incomparable Brother Mr. *R.
Altham* (who left us in the *flower* of his age), methinks are
as fresh to me as if they were done yesterday.

Nor were it any danger to compare Courtesies done to
me to other *Flowers,* as I use them; for I distil them in the
limbeck of my Memory, and so turn them to *Essences.*

But, Madam, I honour you not so much for Favours, as
for that precious brood of Virtues, which shine in you with
that brightness, but 'specially for those high motions whereby
your Soul soars up so often towards Heaven: Insomuch,
Madam, that if it were safe to call any Mortal a *Saint,* you
should have that title from me, and I would be one of your
chiefest *Votaries;* howsoever, I may without any *superstition*
subscribe myself—Your truly devoted Servant,   J. H.
April 8.

IV.

To my Lord Marquis of Hartford.

MY LORD,

I RECEIV'D your Lordship's of the 11th current, with
the Commands it carried, whereof I shall give an account

count in my next. Foreign Parts afford not much matter
of intelligence, it being now the dead of Winter, and the
season unfit for Action : But we need not go abroad for
news, there is store enough at home. We see daily mighty
things, and they are marvellous in our eyes; but the greatest
marvel is, that nothing should now be marvell'd at, for we
are so habituated to wonders, that they are grown familiar
unto us.

Poor *England* may be said to be like a Ship toss'd up
and down the surges of a turbulent Sea, having lost her old
Pilot ; and God knows when she can get into safe harbour
again : Yet doubtless this Tempest, according to the usual
operations of Nature, and the succession of mundane effects
by contrary agents, will turn at last into a calm, tho' many
who are yet in their nonage may not live to see it. · Your
Lordship knows that the κόσμος, this fair frame of the
Universe, came out of a *Chaos*, an indigested Lump; and
that this elementary World was made of millions of Ingredients repugnant to themselves in nature; and the whole
is still preserved by the reluctancy and restless combatings
of these Principles. We see how the Shipwright doth make
use of knee-timber, and other cross-grain'd pieces as well as
of streight and even, for framing a goodly Vessel to ride on
Neptune's back. The Printer useth many contrary Characters in his Art, to put forth a fair Volume; as *d* is a *p*
revers'd, and *n* is a *u* turn'd upward, with other differing
Letters, which yet concur all to the perfection of the whole
Work. There go many and various dissonant Tones to
make an harmonious Consort; this put me in mind of an
excellent passage which a noble speculative Knight (Sir *P.
Herbert*) hath in his late *Conceptions* to his Son : How a
holy *Anchorite* being in a Wilderness, among other contemplations, he fell to admire the method of Providence, how
out of Causes which seem *bad* to us he produceth oftentimes
good Effects ; how he suffers virtuous, loyal, and religious
Men to be oppress'd, and others to prosper. As he was
transported with these Ideas, a goodly young Man appear'd
to

to him, and told him, *Father, I know your thoughts are distracted, and I am sent to quiet them; therefore if you will accompany me a few days, you shall return very well satisfied of those doubts that now encumber your mind.* So going along with him, they were to pass over a deep River, whereon there was a narrow bridge; and meeting there with another Passenger, the young Man justled him into the Water, and so drowned him. The old *Anchorite* being much astonished hereat, would have left him; but his Guide said, *Father, be not amaz'd, because I shall give you good reasons for what I do, and you shall see stranger things than this before you and I part; but at last I shall settle your judgment, and put your mind in full repose.* So going that night to lodge in an Inn where there was a crew of *Banditti* and debauch'd Ruffians, the young Man struck into their company, and revell'd with them till the morning, while the *Anchorite* spent most of the night in numbring his Beads; but as soon as they were departed thence, they met with some Officers who went to apprehend that crew of *Banditti* they had left behind them. The next day they came to a Gentleman's house which was a fair Palace, where they receiv'd all the courteous hospitality which could be; but in the morning as they parted there was a Child in a cradle, which was the only Son of the Gentleman; and the young Man spying his opportunity, strangled the Child, and so got away. The third day they came to another Inn, where the Man of the house treated them with all the civility that could be, and *gratis;* yet the young Man imbezzl'd a Silver Goblet, and carried it away in his pocket, which still increas'd the Amazement of the *Anchorite.* The fourth day in the evening they came to lodge at another Inn, where the Host was very sullen, and uncivil to him, exacting much more than the value of what they had spent; yet at parting, the young Man bestowed upon him the Silver Goblet he had stolen from that Host who had used them so kindly. The fifth day they made towards a great rich Town; but some miles before they came at it, they met with a Merchant at the close of the

day,

day, who had a great charge of money about him; and asking the next passage to the Town, the young Man put him in a clean contrary way. The *Anchorite* and his Guide being come to the Town, at the gate they spied a Devil, who lay as it were centinel, but he was asleep: They found also both Men and Women at sundry kinds of sports, some dancing, others singing, with divers sorts of revellings. They went afterwards to a Convent of *Capuchins*, where, about the gate, they found legions of Devils laying siege to that Monastery, yet they got in and lodged there that night. Being awaked the next morning, the young Man came to that Cell where the *Anchorite* was lodg'd, and told him, *I know your heart is full of horror, and your head full of confusion, astonishments, and doubts, for what you have seen since the first time of our association. But know, I am an Angel sent from Heaven to rectify your judgment, as also to correct a little your curiosity in the researches of the ways and acts of Providence too far; for tho' separately they seem strange to the shallow apprehension of Man, yet conjunctly they all tend to produce good effects.*

That Man which I tumbled into the River was an act of Providence; for he was going upon a most mischievous design that would have damnified not only his own soul, but destroyed the Party against whom it·was intended;·therefore I prevented it.

The cause why I convers'd all night with that Crew of Rogues, was also an act of Providence, for they intended to go a-robbing all that night; but I kept them there purposely till the next morning, that the hand of Justice might seize upon them.

Touching the kind Host from whom I took the Silver Goblet, and the clownish or knavish Host to whom I gave it, let this demonstrate to you, that good Men are liable to crosses and losses, whereof bad Men oftentimes reap the benefit: but it commonly produceth patience *in the one, and* pride *in the other.*

Concerning that noble Gentleman whose Child I strangled
2 N *after*

*after so courteous entertainment, know that that also was an
act of Providence, for the Gentleman was so indulgent and
doting on that Child, that it lessen'd his love to Heaven; so I
took away the cause.*

*Touching the Merchant whom I misguided in his way, it
was likewise an act of Providence, for had he gone the direct
way to this Town, he had been robb'd, and his throat cut,
therefore I preserv'd him by that deviation.*

*Now, concerning this great luxurious City, whereas we
spied but one Devil who lay asleep without the gate, there
being so many about this poor Convent, you must consider, that*
Lucifer *being already assur'd of that riotous Town by cor-
rupting their manners every day more and more, he needs but
one single Centinel to secure it: But for this holy Place of
retirement, this Monastery inhabited by so many devout Souls,
who spend their whole lives in acts of mortification, as exercises of Piety and Penance, he hath brought so many legions
to beleaguer them; yet he can do no good upon them, for they
bear up against him most undauntedly, maugre all his infernal power and stratagems.* So the young Man, or divine
Messenger, suddenly disappear'd and vanish'd; yet leaving
his Fellow-traveller in good hands.

My Lord, I crave your pardon for this extravagancy,
and the tediousness thereof; but I hope the sublimity of
the Matter will make some compensation, which, if I am
not deceived, will well suit with your genius; for I know
your Contemplations to be as high as your Condition, and
as much above the Vulgar. This figurative story shews
that the ways of Providence are inscrutable, his intention
and method of operation not conformable oftentimes to
human judgment, the Plummet and Line whereof is infinitely too short to fathom the depth of his Designs; therefore let us acquiesce in an humble admiration, and with this
confidence, that all things co-operate to the best at last, as
they relate to his glory, and the general good of his Creatures, tho' sometimes they appear to us by uncouth circumstances and cross mediums.

                                                      So

So in a due distance and posture of humility I kiss your Lordship's hands, as being, my most highly honoured Lord —Your thrice-obedient and obliged Servitor,

J. H.

V.

To Richard Baker, *Esq.*

SIR,

NOW that *Lent* and the *Spring* do make their approach, in my opinion *Fasting* would conduce much to the advantage of Soul and Body. Tho'' our second Institution of observing *Lent* aim'd at civil respects, as to preserve the brood of Cattle, and advance the profession of Fishermen, yet it concurs with the first Institution, *viz.*, a true spiritual End, which was to subdue the *Flesh;* and that being brought under, our other two spiritual Enemies, the *World* and the *Devil*, are the sooner overcome. The Naturalists observe, that morning-spittle kills *Dragons*, so *fasting* helps to destroy the *Devil*, provided it be accompanied with other acts of devotion. To fast for one day only from about nine in the morning to four in the afternoon, is but a mock-fast. The *Turks* do more than so in their *Rami-rams* and *Beirams;* and the *Jew* also, for he fasts from the dawn in the morning till the stars be up in the night, as you observe in the devout and delicate Poem you pleas'd to communicate to me lately. I was so taken with the subject, that I presently lighted my Candle at your torch, and fell into these Stanzas:

1. *Now* Lent *is come, let us refrain*
   From carnal *Creatures, quick, or slain ;*
   Let's fast, and macerate the Flesh,
   Impound, and keep it in distress,

2. *For forty days, and then we shall*
   Have a Replevin *from the thrall,*
   By that bless'd Prince, who for this fast
   Will give us Angels' food at last.

3. *But*

3. *But to abstain from Beef, Hog, Goose,*
   And let our Appetites go loose
   To Lobsters, Crabs, Prawns, or such Fish,
   We do not fast, but feast in this.

4. *Not to let down Lamb, Kid, or Veal*
   Hen, Plover, Turkey-cock, or Teal,
   And eat Botargo, Caviar,
   Anchovies, Oysters, and like fare ;

5. *Or to forbear from Flesh, Fowl, Fish,*
   And eat Potatoes in a dish
   Done o'er with Amber, or a mess
   Of Ringo's in a Spanish *dress :*

6. *Or to refrain from each hot thing*
   Which Water, Earth, or Air doth bring,
   And lose a hundred pound at Gleek,
   Or be a Saint when we should sleep.

7. *Or to leave play with all high dishes,*
   And feed our thoughts with wanton wishes,
   Making the Soul, like a light Wench,
   Wear patches of Concupiscence :

8. *This is not to keep* Lent *a-right,*
   But play the juggling Hypocrite :
He truly Lent *observes, who makes the inward Man*
To fast, as well as make the outward feed on bran.

The *French* Reformists have an odd way of keeping *Lent,* for I have seen the walls of their Temples turn'd to shambles, and Flesh hanging upon them on *Lent-Sundays;* insomuch that he who doth not know their practice would take their Churches to be Synagogues of *Jews,* and that the bloody *Levitical* Sacrifices were offer'd there.

And now that my thoughts are in *France,* a witty passage of *Henry the Great* comes into my mind, who being himself in the field, sent to the old Count of *Soissons* to accompany him with what forces he could make. The Count answer'd, That he was grown decrepit and crazy ; besides, his Estate was so, being much exhausted in the former Wars, and all

that

that he could do now for His Majesty was to pray for him :
Doth my Cousin of *Soissons,* said the King, answer me so ?
They say, *That* Prayer *without* Fasting *hath nothing of that
efficacy, as when they are join'd. Ventre de St. Gris,* By
the belly of St. *Gris,* I will make him *fast,* as well as *pray ;*
for I will not pay him a penny of his ten thousand Crowns
Pension, which he hath yearly, for these respects.

The Christian Church hath a longer and more solemn
way of fasting than any other Religion, take *Lent* and
Ember-weeks together. In some Churches the Christian
useth the old way of mortification, by sackcloth and ashes,
to this day; which makes me think on a facetious tale of
a *Turkish* Ambassador in *Venice,* who being return'd to
Constantinople, and ask'd what he had observ'd most remarkable in that so rare a City, he answer'd, that among
other things the Christian hath a kind of *Ashes,* which
thrown upon the head doth perfectly cure madness; for in
Venice I saw the People go up and down the streets (said
he) in ugly antique strange disguises, as being in the eye of
human reason stark mad ; but the next day (meaning *Ash-
Wednesday*) they are suddenly cur'd of that madness by a
sort of ashes which they cast upon their heads.

If the said Ambassador were here among us, he would
think our modern Gallants were also all mad, or subject to
be mad, because they *ashe* and powder their Pericraniums
all the year long. So, wishing you Meditations suitable
to the season, and good Thoughts which are best when
they are the offsprings of good Actions, I rest—Your ready
and real Friend, J. H.

Ash-Wednesday, 1654.

VI.

To Mr. R. Manwayring.

MY DEAR DICK,

IF you are as well when you read this as I was when I
wrote it, we are both well; I am certain of the one,
but

but anxious of the other, in regard of your so long silence; I pray, at the return of this Post, let your *Pen* pull out this *Thorn* that hath got into my thoughts, and let me have often room in yours, for you know I am your perfect Friend,   J. H.

VII.

To *Sir* Edward Spencer, *Knight.*

SIR,

I FIND by your last of the first current, that your thoughts are much busied in forming your new Commonwealth; and whereas the Province that is allotted to me is to treat of a right way to govern the *Female Sex*, I hold my lot to be fallen upon a fair ground, and I will endeavour to husband it accordingly. I find also that for the establishment of this new *Republic*, you have cull'd out the choicest Wits in all Faculties; therefore I account it an honour that you have put me in the List, tho' the least of them.

In every species of Government, and indeed among all Societies of Mankind (*Reclus'd* Orders, and other *Regulars* excepted), there must be a special care had of the *Female* kind; for nothing can conduce more to the propagation and perpetuity of a Republic, than the well managing of that gentle and useful Sex: for tho' they be accounted the weaker vessels, yet are they those in whom the whole Mass of Mankind is moulded; therefore they must not be us'd like Saffron-bags, or Verde-bottles, which are thrown into some by-corner when the Wine and Spice are taken out of them.

It was an opinion truly befitting a *Jew* to hold, That *Woman* is of an inferior creation to *Man*, being made only for Multiplication and Pleasure; therefore hath she no admittance into the body of the Synagogue. Such another opinion was that of the *Pagan* Poet, who stutter'd out this verse, that there are but two good hours of any Woman: Τὴν μίαν ἐν θαλάμῳ, τὴν μίαν ἐν θανατῳ: *Unam in thalamo, alteram in tumulo;* One hour in Bed, the other in the Grave.

Grave. Moreover, I hold also that of the Orator to be a wild extravagant speech, when he said, That if *Women were not conterranean and mingled with Men, Angels would descend and dwell among us.* But a far wilder speech was that of the *Dog-Philosopher,* who term'd Women *necessary Evils.* Of this *Cynical* Sect, it seems, was he who would needs make *Orcus* to be the Anagram of *Uxor,* by contracting *c s* into an *x, Uxor & Orcus—idem.*

Yet I confess, that among this Sex, as among Men, there are some good, some bad, some virtuous, some vicious, and some of an indifferent nature, in whom Virtue makes a compensation for Vice. If there was an Empress in *Rome* so cunning in her lust, that she would take in no passenger until the vessel was frieghted (for fear the resemblance of the Child might discover the true Father), there was a *Zenobia* in *Asia* who would not suffer her Husband to know her carnally any longer, when once she found herself quick. If there were a Queen of *France* that poison'd her King, there was a Queen in *England* who, when her Husband had been shot with an envenom'd Arrow in the Holy Land, suck'd out the Poison with her own mouth, when none else would do it. If the Lady *Barbara,* wife to *Sigismond* the Emperor, being advis'd by her ghostly Father after his death to live like a *Turtle,* having lost such a *Mate* that the World had not the like, made this wanton answer, *Father, since you would have me to lead the life of a Bird, why not of a Sparrow, as well as of a Turtle ?* which she did afterwards ; I say, if there were such a Lady *Barbara,* there was the Lady *Beatrix,* who, after *Henry* her Emperor's death, lived after like a *Dove,* and immur'd herself in a Monastic Cell. But what shall I say of Q. *Artemisia,* who had an Urnful of her Husband *Mausolus's* Ashes in her closet, whereof she would take down a dram every morning nex her heart, saying that her Body was the fittest place to be a Sepulchre to her dear Husband, notwithstanding that she had erected such a Tomb for the rest of his Body, that to this day is one of the wonders of the World ?

                                        Moreover,

Moreover, it cannot be deny'd but some Females are of a high and harsh nature; witness those two that of our greatest Clerks for Law and Learning (Lord *B.* and *C.*) did meet withal, one of whom was said to have brought back her Husband to his horn-book again : As also *Moses* and *Socrates's* Wives, who were *Zipporah* and *Xantippe :* you may guess at the humour of one in the holy Code ; and for *Xantippe,* among many instances which might be produc'd, let this serve for one. After she had scolded her Husband one day out of doors, as the poor man was going out, she whipp'd up into an upper loft, and threw a piss-pot full upon his Sconce, which made the patient *Philosopher* (or *Foolosopher*) to break into this speech for the venting of his passion, *I thought after so much thunder we should have rain.* To this may be added my neighbour *Strowd's* Wife in *Westminster,* who once ringing him a peal as she was basting his roast (for he was a Cook) after he had newly come from the Tavern upon *Sunday* Evening ; she grew hotter and hotter against him, having Hell and the Devil in her mouth, to whom she often bequeath'd him. The staring Husband having heard her a great while with silence, at last answer'd, I prithee, sweet-heart, do not talk so much to me of the *Devil,* because I know he will do me no hurt, for I have married his *Kinswoman.* I know there are many that wear horns, and ride daily upon Coltstaves ; but this proceeds not so often from the fault of the Female, as the silliness of the Husband who knows not how to *manage* a wife.

But a thousand such instances are not able to make me a *Misogenes,* a Female-foe ; therefore towards the policying and perpetuating of this your new Republic, there must be some special rules for regulating of Marriage : for a Wife is the best or the worst fortune that can betide a man thro'out the whole train of his life. *Plato's Promiscuus Concubitus,* or Copulation, is more proper for Beasts than rational Creatures. That incestuous custom they have in *China,* that one should marry his own Sister, and in default of one, the next akin,

I

I utterly dislike : Nor do I approve of that goatish latitude of Lust which the *Alcoran* allows, for one Man to have eight Wives, and as many Concubines as he can well maintain ; nor of another branch of their Law, that a man should marry after such an age under pain of mortal sin (for then what would become of me?) No, I would have every man left at liberty in this point, for there are men enough besides to people the Earth.

But that opinion of a poor shallow-brain'd Puppy, who upon any cause of disaffection would have men to have a privilege to change their Wives, or to repudiate them, deserves to be hiss'd at rather than confuted; for nothing can tend more to usher in all confusion and beggary thro'out the World : Therefore that Wiseacre deserves of all other to wear a toting horn. In this Republic one Man should be contented with one Wife, and he may have work enough to do with her ; but whereas in other Commonwealths Men use to wear invisible horns, it would be a wholesome constitution, that they who upon too much jealousy and restraint, or ill usage of their Wives, or indeed not knowing how to use and *man* them aright (which is one of the prime points of masculine discretion), as also they who according to that barbarous custom in *Russia* do use to beat their Wives duly once a week ; but specially they who in their absence coop them up, and secure their bodies with locks : I say, it would be a very fitting Ordinance in this new-moulded Commonwealth, that all such who impel their Wives by these means to change their Riders, should wear plain visible horns, that Passengers may beware of them as they go along, and give warning to others ―― *Cornu ferit ille, Caveto.* For indeed nothing doth incite the mass of blood, and muster up libidinous thoughts, more than diffidence and restraint.

Moreover, in coupling Women by way of Matrimony, it would be a good Law, and consentaneous to Reason, if out of all Dowries exceeding £100 there should be *two* out of every *Cent.* deducted, and put into a common Treasury for putting off hard-favour'd and poor Maids.

Touching

Touching Virginity and the Vestal Fire, I could wish 'twere the worst custom the *Roman* Church had, when gentle Souls, to endear themselves the more to their Creator, do immure their Bodies within perpetual bounds of Chastity, dieting themselves and using austerities accordingly; whereby, bidding a farewel, and dying to the World, they bury themselves alive, as it were, and so pass their time in constant exercises of Piety and Penance night and day, or in some other employments of Virtue, holding Idleness to be a mortal sin. Were this cloyster'd course of Life merely spontaneous and unforced, I could well be contented that it were practis'd in your new Republic.

But there are other kind of Cloysters in some Commonwealths, and among those who are accounted the wisest and best policied, which Cloysters are of a clean contrary nature to the former: these they call the Courtesan Cloysters. And as in others, some Females shut up themselves to keep the sacred fire of Pudicity and Continence, so in these latter there are some of the handsom'st sorts of Females who are conniv'd at to quench the flames of irregular Lust, lest they should break into the lawful married bed. 'Tis true, Nature hath pour'd more active and hotter blood into the Veins of some Men, wherein there are stronger appetites and motions; which motions were not given by Nature to be a torment to Man, but to be turn'd into Delight, Health, and Propagation. Therefore they to whom the gift of Continence is deny'd, and have not the conveniency to have *debita vasa*, and lawful Coolers of their own by way of Wedlock, use to extinguish their fires in these Venerean Cloysters, rather than abuse their neighbours' Wives, and break into other men's inclosures. But whether such a custom may be conniv'd at in this your Republic, and that such a *Common* may be allow'd to them who have no *Inclosures* of their own, I leave to wiser Legislators than myself to determine, 'specially in South-East hot Countries where Venerean *Titillation* (which *Scaliger* held to be a fix'd outward sense, but ridiculously) is in a stronger degree; I say, I leave others to judge whether such

such a Rendezvous be to be conniv'd at in hotter Climes, where both Air and Food, and the blood of the Grape do all concur to make one more libidinous.   But it is a vulgar error to think that the heat of the Clime is the cause of Lust: it proceeds rather from adust Choler and Melancholy that predominate, which humours carry with them a salt and sharp itching quality.

The dull *Hollander* (with other North-West Nations, whose blood may he said to be as butter-milk in the veins) is not so frequently subject to such fits of Lust, therefore he hath no such Cloysters or Houses for Ladies of pleasure : Witness the tale of *Hans Boobikin*, a rich Boor's Son, whom his Father had sent abroad a *Fryaring*, that is, shroving in our Language ; and so put him in an equipage accordingly, having a new Sword and Scarf, with a gold Hatband, and money in his Purse to visit handsome Ladies : but *Hans* not knowing where to go else, went to his Grandmother's house, where he fell a courting and feasting of her.   But his Father questioning him at his return where he had been a *Fryaring*, and he answering that he had been at his Grandmother's ; the Boor reply'd, God's Sacrament ! I hope thou hast not lain with my Mother : Yes, *said* Boobikin, *Why should not I lie with your Mother, as you have lain with mine ?*

Thus in conformity to your desires, and the task impos'd upon me, have I scribbled out this piece of Drollery, which is the way, as I take it, that your design drives at ; I reserve some things till I see what others have done in the several Provinces they have undertaken towards the settlement of your new Republic.   So, with a thousand thanks for your last hospitable favours, I rest, as I have reason, and as you know me to be—Your own true Servant,   J. H.

Lond. 24 *Jan.*

VIII.

VIII.

To Mr. T. V., Barrister, at his Chambers in the Temple.

COUSIN TOM,

I DID not think it was in the power of Passion to have wrought upon you with that violence; for I do not remember to have known any (of so season'd a judgment as you are) lost so far after so frail a thing as a Female. But you will say, *Hercules* himself stoop'd hitherto; 'tis true he did, as appears by this Distich:

> Lenam *non potuit, potuit superare* Leænam;
> *Quem* Fera *non potuit vincere, vicit* Hera.

The saying also of the old Comic Poet makes for you, when he said, *Qui in amorem cecidit, pejùs agit quam si saxo saliat;* To be Tormented with Love, is worse than to dance upon hot stones. Therefore partly out of a sense of your suffering, as well as upon the seriousness of your request, but specially understanding that the Gentlewoman hath Parts and Portion accordingly, I have done what you desir'd me in these lines, which tho' plain, short, and sudden, yet they display the manner how you were surpriz'd, and the depth of your Passion.

To Mrs. E. B.

> Apelles, *Prince of Painters, did*
> *All others in that Art exceed;*
> *But you surpass him, for He took*
> *Some* pains *and* time *to draw a Look;*
> *You in a trice and* moment's *space*
> *Have pourtray'd in my Heart your Face.*

I wish this Hexastic may have power to strike her as deep as I find her Eyes struck you. The *Spaniard* saith, there are four things requir'd in a Woer, *viz.*, to be *Savo, Secreto, Solo,* and *Sollicito;* that is, to be Sollicitous, Secret, Sole, and Sage. Observe these rules, and she may make herself your *Client,* and so employ you to open her Case, and

and recover her portion, which I hear is in Hucksters' hands.

So, my dear Cousin, I heartily wish you the accomplishment of your desires, and rest upon all occasions—At your dispose, J. H.

IX.

To Sir R. Williams, *Knight.*

SIR,

I AM one among many who much rejoice at the fortunate Windfall that happen'd lately, which hath so fairly rais'd and recruited your fortunes. It is commonly seen, that *Ubi est multum Phantasiæ* (viz., *ingenii*) *ibi est parum Fortunæ; & ubi est multum Fortunæ, ibi est parum Phantasiæ.* Where there is much of *Fancy*, there is little of *Fortune ;* and where there's much of *Fortune*, there's little of *Fancy.* It seems that Recorder *Fleetwood* reflected upon one part of this saying, when in his speech to the *Londoners*, among other passages whereby he sooth'd and stroak'd them, he said, *When I consider your Wit, I admire your Wealth.* But touching the *Latin* saying, it is quite evinc'd in you, for you have *Fancy* and *Fortune* (now) in abundance : And a strong argument may be drawn, that *Fortune* is not *blind*, by her carriage to you, for she saw well enough what she did, when she smil'd so lately upon you.

Now, he is the really rich man who can make true use of his riches ; he makes not *Nummum* his *Numen*, Money his God, but makes himself *Dominum Nummi*, but becomes Master of his Penny. The first is the arrantest beggar and slave that is ; nay, he is worse than the *Arcadian* Ass, who, while he carrieth Gold on his back, eats thistles : He is baser than that sordid *Italian* Stationer, who would not allow himself brown Paper enough to wipe his *Posteriors.*

Now, it is observ'd to be the nature of Covetousness, that when all other sins grow old, *Covetousness* in some sordid souls grows younger and younger; hence I believe sprung the City-Proverb, That *the Son is happy whose Father went*

to

to the Devil. Yet I like the saying *Tom Waters* hath often in his mouth, *I had rather leave when I die than lack while I live.* But why do I speak of these things to you, who have so noble a Soul, and so much above the vulgar?

Your Friend Mr. *Watts* is still troubled with coughing, and truly I believe he is not to be long among us; for, as the *Turk* hath it, *A dry Cough is the Trumpeter of Death:* He presents his most affectionate respects to you, and so doth, my most noble Knight—Your ever obliged Servitor,

J. H.

X.

To Sir R. Cary, *Knight.*

Sir,

I HAD yours of the 20th current on St. *Thomas's* Eve, which was most welcome to me; and (to make a *seasonable* comparison) yours are like *Christmas,* they come but once a year; yet I made very good cheer with your last, specially with that Seraphic Hymn which came inclosed therewith to usher in his holy Tyde: and to correspond with you in some measure that way, I have return'd you another of the same subject. For, as I have observ'd, two Lutes being tun'd alike, if one of them be play'd upon, the other, tho' being a good way distant, will sound of itself, and keep symphony with the first that's play'd upon (which, whether it proceeds from the mere motion of the Air, or the emanation of Atoms, I will not undertake to determine;) so the sound of your Muse hath *scrued* up mine to the same key and tune in these Ternaries :

Upon the Nativity of our Saviour.

1. *Wonder of Wonders,* Earth *and* Sky,
   Time mingleth *with* Eternity,
   And Matter *with* Immensity.

2. *The* Sun *becomes an* Atom *and a* Star,
   Turns to a Candle, *to light Kings from far*
   To see a spectacle so wondrous rare.

A

3. *A* Virgin *bears a Son, that* Son *doth bear
A* World *of* Sin, *acquitting Man's arrear,
Since guilty* Adam *Fig-tree leaves did wear.*

4. *A Majesty both infinite and just
Offended was ; therefore the Offering must
Be such, to expiate frail flesh and dust.*

5. *When no such Victim could be found
Thro'out the whole expansive Round
Of Heaven, of Air, of Sea, or Ground ;*

6. *The Prince of Life himself descends.
To make* Astræa *full amends,
And human Souls from Hell defends.*

7. *Was ever such a Love as this,
That th' eternal Heir of Bliss
Should stoop to such a low abyss ?*

The Muse, confounded with the Mystery according to the subject matter, ends with a question of Admiration.

So wishing you, as heartily as to myself (according to the instant season, and the old compliment of *England*), a merry *Christmas,* and consequently a happy New-Year, I subscribe myself—Your entirely devoted Servant,

J. H.

St. Innocents-Day, 1654.

XI.

To J. Sutton, *Esq.*

SIR,

WHEREAS you desire my opinion of the late History translated by Mr. *Wad:* of the Civil Wars of *Spain,* in the beginning of *Charles* the Emperor's Reign, I cannot choose but tell you, that it is a faithful and pure maiden Story, never blown upon before in any Language but in *Spanish,* therefore very worthy your perusal: for among those various kind of studies that your contemplative Soul delights in, I hold History to be the most fitting to your Quality.

Now,

Now, among those sundry advantages which accrue to a Reader of History, one is, that no modern Accident can seem strange to him, much less astonish him : He will leave off wondring at anything, in regard he may remember to have read of the same, or much like the same, that happen'd in former times ; therefore he doth not stand staring like a Child at every unusual spectacle, like that simple *American*, who, the first time he saw a *Spaniard* on horseback, thought the Man and the Beast to be but one Creature, and that the Horse did chew the rings of his bit, and eat them.

Now, indeed, not to be an *Historian*, that is, not to know what foreign Nations and our Forefathers did, *Hoc est semper esse Puer*, as *Cicero* hath it, this is still to be a Child who gazeth at everything. Whence may be inferr'd, there is no Knowledge that ripeneth the Judgment, and puts one out of his nonage, sooner than History.

If I had not formerly read the *Barons'* Wars in *England*, I had more admir'd that of the *Leaguers* in *France :* He who had read the near upon fourscore years Wars in *Low Germany*, I believe never wonder'd at the late thirty years Wars in *High Germany*. I had wonder'd more that *Richard* of *Bourdeaux* was knock'd down with Halbards, had I not read formerly that *Edward* of *Caernarvon* was made away by a hot Iron thrust up his Fundament. It was strange that *Murat* the great *Ottoman* Emperor should be lately strangled in his own Court at *Constantinople ;* yet considering that *Osman* his Predecessor had been knock'd down by one of his ordinary slaves not many years before, it was not strange at all. The Blazing-Star in *Virgo* thirty-four years since, did not seem strange to him, who had read of that which appear'd in *Cassiopeia* and other Constellations some years before. Hence may be inferr'd, That *History* is the great Looking-glass thro' which we may behold with ancestral eyes, not only the various Actions of Ages past, and the odd Accidents that attend time, but also discern the different humours of Men, and feel the pulse of former times.
                                                                This

This History will display the very intrinsecals of the *Castilian*, who goes for the prime *Spaniard;* and make the opinion a Paradox, which cries him up to be so constant to his Principles, so loyal to his Prince, and so conformable to Government: For it will discover as much levity and tumultuary passions in him as in other Nations.

Among divers other examples which could be produc'd out of this story, I will instance in one: When *Juan de Padillia,* an infamous fellow, and of base Extraction, was made General of the People, among others there was a Priest, that being a great Zealot for him, us'd to pray publickly in the Church, *Let us pray for the holy Commonalty, and His Majesty* Don Juan de Padillia, *and for the Lady* Donna Maria Pachecho *his Wife,* &c. But a little after some of *Juan de Padillia's* Soldiers having quarter'd in his house, and pitifully plunder'd him, the next *Sunday* the same Priest said in the Church, *Beloved Christians, you know how* Juan de Padillia *passing this way, some of his Brigade were billeted in my House; truly they have not left me one Chicken, they have drunk up a whole barrel of Wine, devour'd my Bacon, and taken away my* Catalina, *my Maid* Kate ; *I charge you therefore pray no more for him.* Divers such traverses as these may be read in that Story ; which may be the reason why it was suppress'd in *Spain,* that it should not cross the Seas, or clamber o'er the *Pyreneans* to acquaint other Nations with their foolery and baseness : yet Mr. *Simon Digby,* a Gentleman of much worth, got a Copy, which he brought over with him, out of which this Translation is deriv'd ; tho' I must tell you, by the bye, that some passages were commanded to be omitted, because they had too near an analogy with our Times.

So in a serious way of true Friendship, I profess myself—
Your most affectionate Servitor,   J. H.

London, 15 *Jan.*

XII.

To the Lord Marquis of Dorchester.

MY LORD,

THERE is a sentence that carrieth a high sense with it, *viz., Ingenia Principum fata Temporum,* The fancy of the Prince is the fate of the Times; so in point of Peace or War, Oppression or Justice, Virtue or Vice, Profaneness or Devotion : for *Regis ad exemplum.* But there is another saying, which is as true, *viz., Genius plebis est fatum Principis,* The happiness of the Prince depends upon the humour of the People. There cannot be a more pregnant example hereof, than in that successful and long-liv'd Queen, Q. *Elizabeth,* who having come, as it were, from the *Scaffold* to the *Throne,* enjoy'd a wonderful Calm (excepting some short gusts of Insurrection that happen'd in the beginning) for near upon forty-five years together. But this, my Lord, may be imputed to the temper of the People, who had had a *boisterous* King not long before, with so many revolutions in Religion, and a *Minor* King afterward, which made them to be govern'd by their Fellow-subjects. And the Fire and Faggot being frequent among them in Q. *Mary's* days, the humours of the common People were pretty well spent, and so were willing to conform to any Government, that might preserve them and their Estates in quietness. Yet in the Reign of that so popular and well-belov'd Queen there were many Traverses, which trench'd as much if not more upon the Privileges of Parliament, and the Liberties of the People, than any that happen'd in the Reign of the two last Kings; yet it was not their fate to be so *popular.* Touching the first, *viz., Parliament;* in one of hers, there was a motion made in the House of Commons, that there should be a Lecture in the morning some days of the week before they sat, whereunto the House was very inclinable : The Queen hearing of it, sent them a Message, that she much wonder'd at their rashness, that they should offer to introduce such an Innovation.

Another

Another Parliament would have proposed ways for the regulation of her Court; but she sent them another such Message, That she wondred, that being call'd by her thither to consult of publick Affairs, they should intermeddle with the government of her ordinary Family, and to think her to be so ill an Housewife, as not to be able to look to her own House herself.

In another Parliament there was a motion made, that the Queen should entail the Succession of the Crown, and declare her next Heir: but *Wentworth,* who proposed it, was committed to the *Tower,* where he breath'd his last; and *Bromley* upon a less occasion was clapp'd in the *Fleet.*

Another time the House petitioning that the Lords might join in private Committees with the Commoners, she utterly rejected it. You know how *Stubbs* and *Page* had their hands cut off with a Butcher's Knife and a Mallet, because they writ against the Match with the Duke of *Anjou;* and *Penry* was hang'd at *Tyburn,* tho' *Alured,* who writ a bitter Invective against the late *Spanish* Match, was but confin'd for a short time: how Sir *John Heywood* was shut up in the *Tower,* for an Epistle Dedicatory to the Earl of *Essex,* &c.

Touching her Favourites, what a Monster of a Man was *Leicester,* who first brought the Art of poisoning into *England!* How many of her Maids of Honour did receive claps at Court? Add hereunto, that Privy-Seals were common in her days, and *pressing* of Men more frequent, especially for *Ireland,* where they were sent in handfuls, rather to *continue* a War (by the cunning of the Officers) than to *conclude* it. The three Fleets she sent against the *Spaniard* did hardly make the Benefit of the Voyages to countervail the Charge. How poorly did the *English* Garrison quit *Havre-de-Grace?* and how were we baffled for the Arrears that were due to *England* (by Article) for the Forces sent into *France?* For Buildings, with all kind of Braveries else that use to make a Nation happy, as Riches and Commerce, inward and outward, it was not the twentieth part so much in the best of
her

her days (as appears by the Custom-House Books) as it was in the Reign of her Successors.

Touching the Religion of the Court, she seldom came to Sermon but in *Lent-time,* nor did there use to be any Sermon upon *Sundays,* unless they were Festivals : Whereas the succeeding Kings had duly two every morning, one for the Houshold, the other for themselves, where they were always present, as also at private Prayers in the Closet; yet it was not their fortune to gain so much upon the affections of City, or Country. Therefore, my Lord, the felicity of Q. *Elizabeth* may be much imputed to the rare temper and moderation of Men's minds in those days ; for the Purse of the common People, and *Londoners,* did beat nothing so high as it did afterwards when they grew pamper'd with so long peace and plenty. Add hereunto, that neither *Hans, Jocky,* or *John Calvin* had taken such footing here as they did get afterwards, whose humour is to pry and peep with a kind of malice into the carriage of the Court and mysteries of State, as also to malign Nobility, with the Wealth and Solemnities of the Church.

My Lord, it is far from my meaning hereby to let drop the least Aspersion upon the Tomb of that rare renowned Queen; but it is only to observe the differing temper both of Time and People. The fame of some Princes is like the *Rose,* which, as we find by experience, smells sweeter after 'tis pluck'd : the memory of others is like the *Tulip* and *Poppy,* which make a gay shew and fair flourish while they stand upon the stalk, but being cut down they give an ill-favour'd scent. It was the happiness of that great long-liv'd Queen to cast a pleasing odour among her People both while she stood, and after she was cut off by the common stroke of Mortality; and the older the World grows, the fresher her Fame will be. Yet she is little beholden to any foreign Writers, unless it be the *Hollanders;* and good reason they had to speak well of her, for she was the chiefest Instrument, who, tho' with the expence of much *English Blood* and *Bullion,* rais'd them to a Republic, by casting that fatal
bone

bone for the *Spaniard* to gnaw upon, which shook his teeth so ill-favour'dly for fourscore years together. Other Writers speak bitterly of her for her carriage to her Sister the Queen of *Scots;* for her ingratitude to her Brother *Philip* of *Spain;* for giving advice, by her Ambassador with the *Great Turk,* to expel the *Jesuits,* who had got a College in *Pera;* as also that her Secretary *Walsingham* should project the poisoning of the Waters of *Douay;* and lastly, how she suffer'd the Festival of the Nativity of the *Virgin Mary* in *September* to be turn'd to the celebration of her own Birth-day, *&c.* But these stains are cast upon her by her Enemies; and the Aspersions of an Enemy use to be like the *dirt* of Oysters, which doth rather *cleanse* than *contaminate.*

Thus, my Lord, have I pointed at some Remarks, to shew how various and discrepant the humours of a Nation may be, and the genius of the Times, from what it was; which doubtless must proceed from a high all-disposing Power: A Speculation that may become the greatest, and *knowing'st* spirits, among whom your Lordship doth shine as a Star of the first magnitude; for your *House* may be call'd a true Academy, and your *Head* the Capitol of Knowledge, or rather an *Exchequer,* wherein there is a *Treasure* enough to give *Pensions* to all the Wits of the Time. With these thoughts I rest, my most highly honour'd Lord—Your very obedient and ever obliged Servant, J. H.

Lond., this 15 of Aug.

XIII.

To Mr. R. Floyd.

COUSIN FLOYD,

THE first part of Wisdom is to *give* good Counsel, the second to *take* it, and the third to *follow* it. Tho' you be young, yet you may be already capable of the two latter parts of Wisdom, and it is the only way to attain the first: Therefore I wish you to follow the good Counsel of your Uncle *J.,* for I know him to be a very discreet well-weigh'd Gentleman; and I can judge something of Men,

for

for I have studied many: Therefore if you *steer* by his compass in this great business you have undertaken, you need not fear *shipwreck.* This is the Advice of—Your truly affectionate Cousin,   J. H.

Lond., 6 *Apr.*

XIV.

To my Reverend and Learned Countryman, Mr. R. Jones.

SIR,

IT is, among many other, one of my imperfections, that I am not vers'd in my *maternal Tongue* so exactly as I should be: The Reason is, that *Languages* and *Words* (which are the chief creatures of Man, and the keys of Knowledge) may be said to stick in the memory like nails or pegs in a Wainscoat-door, which useth to thrust out one another oftentimes. Yet the old *British* is not so driven out of mine (for the Cask savours still of the Liquor it first took in) but I can say something of this elaborate and ingenious Piece of yours, which you please to communicate to me so early: I cannot compare it more properly than to a basket of Posies gather'd in the best Garden of Flowers, the sacred Scriptures, and bound up with such Art, that every Flower directs us where his bed may be found. Whence I infer, that this Work will much conduce to the Advancement of Βιβλιοσοφία, or Scripture-knowledge, and consequently to the public good. It will also tend to the honour of our whole Country, and to your own particular repute: Therefore I wish you good success, to make this Child of your Brain free denizen of the World.   J. H.

London, 17 *Sept.*

XV.

To J. S., *Esq., at* White-Fryers.

SIR,

THIS new piece of Philosophy comes to usher in the new Year to you, dropt from the brain of the subtilest
Spirits

Spirits of *France*, and the great Personage (the Duke of *Espernon*), tho' *heterodoxal*, and cross-grain'd to the old Philosophers. Among divers other Tenets, he holds that *Privatio* is unworthy to be one of the three Principles of natural Things, and would put *Love* in the place of it. But you know, Sir, that among other infirmities which Nature hath entail'd upon Man while he gropes here for Truth among the Elements, discrepancy of Notions, and desire of Novelty, are none of the least.

Now, touching this critical Tract, there's not any more capable to censure it than yourself, whose Judgment is known to be so sound and *magisterial :* Let the pettiness of the *Gift* be supplied by the pregnancy of the *Will*, which swells with mountains of Desires to serve you, and to shew in Action, as well as in Words, how ready I would be—At your disposing,   J. H.

Lond., 2 *Jan.*

XVI.

To the Earl of Lindsey, *Great Chamberlain of* England, *at* Ricot.

MY LORD,

I MOST humbly thank your Lordship for the noble Present you commanded to be sent me from *Grimsthorp*, where, without disparagement to any, I may say you live as much like a Prince as any *Grandee* in *Christendom*. Among those many heroik Parts (which appear'd so much in that tough Battel of *Keinton*, where having all your Officers kill'd, yet you kept the Field, and preserv'd your wounded Father from the fury of the Soldier, and from death for the time; as also for being the inseparable *Cubicular* Companion the King took comfort in in the height of his troubles), I say, among other high parts to speak you *noble*, you are cried up, my Lord, to be an excellent *Horseman*, *Huntsman*, *Forester*. This makes me bold to make your Lordship the Judge of a small Discourse, which, upon a critical dispute touching the *Vocal Forest* that goes abroad
in

in my name, was impos'd upon me, to satisfy them who thought I knew something more than ordinary what belong'd to a true Forest.

There be three places for Venery, or Venatical Pleasure, in *England,* viz., a *Forest,* a *Chase,* and a *Park;* they all three agree in one thing, which is, that they are habitations for wild Beasts: The two first lie open, the last inclos'd: The *Forest* is the most noble of all, for it is a *Franchise* of so princely a tenure, that, according to our Laws, none but the King can have a *Forest;* if he chance to pass one over to a Subject, 'tis no more *Forest,* but *Frank-chace.* More-over, a *Forest* hath the Pre-eminence of the other two, in *Laws,* in *Officers,* in *Courts,* and *kinds* of Beasts. If any offend in a *Chase* or *Park,* he is punishable by the *Common Law* of the Land: But a *Forest* hath Laws of her own, to take cognizance of all trespasses; she hath also her peculiar Officers, as *Foresters, Verderers, Regarders, Agisters,* &c., whereas a *Chase* or *Park* hath only *Keepers* and *Wood-wards.* A *Forest* hath her Court of Attachments, *Swainmote-Court,* where matters are as pleadable and determinable as at *Westminster-Hall.* Lastly, they differ something in the species of Beasts: The *Hart,* the *Hind,* the *Boar,* the *Wolf,* are *Forest-Beasts;* the *Buck,* the *Doe,* the *Fox,* the *Matron,* the *Roe,* are Beasts belonging to a *Chase* and *Park.*

The greatest Forester, they say, that ever was in *England* was King *Canutus* the *Dane,* and after him St. *Edward;* at which time *Liber Rufus,* the Red-book for Forest-Laws, was made; whereof one of the *Laws* was, *Omnis homo abstineat à Venariis meis super pœnam Vitæ:* Let every one refrain from my places of hunting, upon pain of death.

Henry Fitz-Empresse (viz., the Second) did coafforest much Land, which continu'd all his Reign, tho' much complain'd of: But in King *John's* time most of the Nobles and Gentry met in the great Meadow 'twixt *Windsor* and *Stanes,* to petition the King that he would disafforest some, which he promised to do, but death prevented him. But in *Henry* III.'s Time, the *Charta de Foresta* (together with *Magna Charta*) were

were establish'd; so that there was much Land disafforested, which hath been call'd *Pourlieus* ever since, whereof there were appointed *Rangers*, &c.

Among other innocent Animals which have suffer'd by these Wars, the poor *Deer* have felt the fury thereof as much as any; nay, the very *Vegetables* have endur'd the brunt of it: Insomuch that it is not improperly said, That *England* of late is full of *New Lights*, her *Woods* being cut down, and so much destroy'd in most places. So, craving your Lordship's pardon for this rambling piece of paper, I rest, my most highly honour'd Lord—Your obedient and ever obliged Servant,   J. H.

Lond., 3 *Aug.*

XVII.

To Mr. E. Field, *at* Orleans.

SIR,

IN your last you write to me, that you are settled for a while in *Orleans*, the loveliest City upon the *Loire*, and the best School for gaining pure Language; for as the *Attique* dialect in *Greece*, so the *Aurelian* in *France* doth bear the bell: But I must tell you, tho' you live now upon a brave River, which divides *France* well near in two parts, yet she is held the drunkenest River in *Christendom*, for she swallows thirty-two other Rivers, which she disgorgeth all into the Sea at *Nantes;* she may be call'd a more drunken River than *Ebro* in *Spain*, which takes her name from *Ebrio*, according to the proverb there, *Me llamo Ebro porque de todas aguas bevo*, I call myself *Ebro* because I drink of all waters.

Moreover, tho' you sojourn now in one of the plentiful'st Continents upon Earth, yet I believe you will find the People, I mean the Peasants, nowhere poorer and more slavish; which convinceth two Errors, one of *Aristotle*, who affirms that the Country of *Gallia*, tho' bordering upon *Spain*, hath no *Asses:* If he were living now, he would avouch the greatest part of the Inhabitants to be all *Asses*, they lie under

under such an intolerable burden of taxes. The second Error is, That *France* is held to be the freest Country upon Earth to all People; for if a Slave comes once to breathe *French* Air, he is free *ipso facto*, if we may believe *Bodin;* it being a fundamental Law of *France, Servi peregrini, ut primum Galliæ fines penetraverint, liberi sunto;* Let Stranger-slaves, as soon as they shall penetrate the borders of *France*, be free. I know not what privilege *Strangers* may claim; but for the native French themselves, I hold them to be under the greatest servitude of any other Nation. There is another Law in *France*, which inhibits *Women* to rule; but what benefit doth accrue by this Law all the while that Women are Regent, and govern those who do rule? which hath been exemplify'd in three Queen-Mothers together. The *Huguenots* have long since voted the first two to Hell, to increase the number of the Furies; and the *Spaniard* hath voted the third thither to make up the half-dozen, for continuing a more violent War against her now only Brother, and with more eagerness than her Husband did.

So I wish you all happiness in your Peregrination, advising you to take heed of that turbid humour of Melancholy, which they say you are too prone to. For, take this for a *rule*, that he who makes much of *Melancholy* will never be rid of a troublesome Companion. So I rest, gentle Sir —Your most affectionate Servant, J. H.

Lond., 3 *May.*

XVIII.

To the Lady E., *Countess Dowager of* Sunderland.

MADAM,

I AM bold to send your La. to the Country a new *Venice* Looking-glass, wherein you may behold that admir'd Maiden-City in her true complexion, together with her Government and Policy, for she is famous all the world over. Therefore, if at your hours of leisure you please to

cast

cast your eyes upon this Glass, I doubt not but it will afford you some objects of entertainment.

Moreover, your Ladyship may discern thro' this Glass the motions, and the very heart of the Author, how he continueth still, and resolves so to do, in what condition soever he be, Madam—Your most constant and dutiful Servant,

J. H.

London, 15 *June.*

XIX.

To the Rt. Hon. the Earl of Clare.

MY LORD,

A MONG those high Parts that go to make up a *Grandee,* which I find concentred in your Lordship, one is the exact knowledge you have of many Languages, not in a superficial vapouring way, as some of our Gallants have now-a-days, but in a most exact manner both in point of *Practice* and *Theory.* This induced me to give your Lordship an account of a task that was impos'd lately upon me by an emergent occasion, touching the *Original,* the *Growth,* the *Changes,* and present *Consistence* of the *French* Language, which I hope may afford your Lordship some entertainment.

There is nothing so incident to all sublunary things as corruptions and changes: Nor is it to be wonder'd at, considering that the Elements themselves, which are the Principles or primitive Ingredients whereof they be compounded, are naturally so qualified. It were as easy a thing for the Spectator's eye to fasten a firm shape upon a running Cloud, or to cut out a garment that but a few days together might fit the Moon (who, by privilege of her situation and neighbourhood, predominates more over us than any other Celestial body), as to find stability in anything here below.

Nor is this common frailty, or *fatality* rather, incident only to the grosser sort of Elementary Creatures, but *Mankind,* upon whom it pleas'd the Almighty to imprint his own Image, and make him, as it were, Lord Paramount of this

this lower World, is subject to the same lubricity of Mutation : Neither is his *Body* and *Blood* only liable thereunto, but the *Ideas of his Mind,* and interior operations of his Soul, *Religion* herself, with the notions of Holiness, and the formality of saving Faith not excepted ; nay, the very faculty of *Reason* (as we find it too true by late experience) is subject to the same instableness.

But to come to our present purpose, among other privileges which are peculiar to mankind, as Emanations flowing from the Intellect, *Language* is none of the least. And Languages are subject to the same fits of inconstancy and alteration as much as anything else, 'specially the *French* Language : Nor can it seem strange to those who know the airy volatile humour of that Nation, that their Speech should partake somewhat of the disposition of their Spirit ; but will rather wonder it hath receiv'd no oftner change, 'specially considering what outward Causes did also concur thereunto ; as, that their Kings should make *six* several Voyages to conquer or conserve what was got in the *Holy Land ;* considering also how long the *English,* being a People of another Speech, kept firm footing in the heart of *France :* Add hereunto the *Wars* and *Weddings* they had with their Neighbours, which, by the long sojourn of their Armies in other Countries caus'd by the first, and the foreign Courtiers that came in with the second, might introduce a frequent alteration. For Languages are like Laws or Coins, which commonly receive some change at every shift of Princes : or as slow Rivers, by insensible alluvions, take in and let out the Waters that feed them, yet are they said to have the same beds ; so *Languages,* by a regardless adoption of some new words, and manumission of old, do often vary, yet the whole bulk of the Speech keeps entire.

Touching the true ancient and genuine Language of the *Gauls,* some would have it to be a dialect of the *Dutch,* others of the *Greek,* and some of the *British* or *Welsh.* Concerning this last opinion, there be many reasons to fortify it, which are not altogether to be slighted.

The

The first is, That the antient *Gauls* us'd to come frequently to be instructed here by the *British Druids,* who were the Divines and Philosophers of those times; which they would not probably have done, unless by mutual communication they had understood one another in some vulgar Language: for this was before the *Greek* or *Latin* came this side the *Alps,* or that any Books were written; and there are no meaner Men than *Tacitus,* and *Cæsar* himself, who record this.

The second reason is, That there want not good Geographers, who hold that this Island was tied to *Gallia* at first (as some say *Sicily* was to *Calabria,* and *Denmark* to *Germany*) by an *Isthmus* or neck of land, from *Calais* to *Dover;* for if one do well observe the quality of the Cliffs on both shores, his eyes will judge that they were but one homogeneal piece of earth at first, and that they were slented and shiver'd asunder by some act of violence, as the impetuous waves of the Sea.

The third reason is, That before the *Romans* conquer'd the *Gauls,* the Country was call'd *Wallia,* which the *Romans* call'd *Gallia,* turning *W* into *G,* as they did elsewhere: yet the *Walloon* keeps his radical Letter to this day.

The fourth reason is, That there be divers old *Gaulick* words yet remaining in the *French* which are pure *British,* both for sense and pronunciation; as *Havre,* a Haven, which is the same in *Welsh, derechef,* again; *Putaine,* a Whore; *Airain,* brass money; *Prou,* an interjection of stopping or driving of a beast: but 'specially, when one speaks any old word in *French* that cannot be understood, they say, *Il parle Baragouin,* which is to this day in *Welsh, White-Bread.*

Lastly, *Pausanias* saith, That *Mark,* in the *Celtik* old *French* Tongue, signifieth a Horse; and it signifieth the same in *Welsh.*

But tho' it be disputable whether the *British, Greek,* or *Dutch* was the original Language of the *Gauls,* certain it is that it was the *Walloon;* but I confine myself to *Gallia*

Gallia Celtica, which, when the *Roman* Eagle had fastened his talons there, and planted twenty-three Legions up and down the Country, he did in tract of time utterly extinguish : It being the ordinary ambition of *Rome,* wheresoever she prevail'd, to bring in her *Language* and *Laws* also with the *Lance,* which she could not do in *Spain,* or this Island, because they had posts and places of Fastness to retire to, as *Biscay* and *Wales,* where Nature hath cast up those Mountains as propugnacles of defence ; therefore the very aboriginal Languages of both Countries remain there to this day. Now, *France* being a passable and plain pervious Continent, the *Romans* quickly diffus'd and rooted themselves in every part thereof, and so co-planted their Language, which in a short revolution of time came to be call'd *Romand.* But when the *Franconians,* a People of *Germany,* came afterwards to invade and possess *Gallia,* both Speech and People were call'd *French* ever after, which is near 1300 years since.

Now, as all other things have their degrees of growing, so *Languages* have before they attain a perfection. We find that the *Latin* herself in the times of the *Sabines* was but rude ; afterwards under *Ennius* and *Cato the Censor* it was refin'd in twelve Tables ; but in *Cæsar, Cicero,* and *Sallust's* time it came to the highest pitch of purity ; and so dainty were the *Romans* of their Language then, that they would not suffer any exotic or strange word to be enfranchis'd among them, or enter into any of their *Diplomata,* and publick Instruments of Command or Justice. The word *Emblema* having got into one, it was thrust out by an express *Edict* of the Senate ; but *Monopolium* had with much ado leave to stay in, yet not without a large Preface and Apology. A little after, the *Latin* Tongue in the vulgarity thereof began to degenerate and decline very much ; out of which degeneration sprang up the *Italian, Spanish,* and *French.*

Now, the *French* Language being set thus upon a *Latin* stock, hath receiv'd since sundry habitudes, yet retaining to
                                                                                this

this day some *Latin* words entire, as *animal, cadaver, tribunal, non, plus, qui, os,* with a number of others.

Chilperic, one of the first race of *French* Kings, commanded by publick Edict, that the four *Greek* Letters Θ X Φ Ψ should be added to the *French* Alphabet to make the Language more masculine and strenuous; but afterwards it was not long observ'd.

Nor is it a worthless observation, that Languages use to comply with the Humour, and to display much the Inclination of a People. The *French* Nation is quick and spriteful, so is his Pronunciation; the *Spaniard* is slow and grave, so is his Pronunciation: For the *Spanish* and *French* Languages being but branches of the *Latin* Tree, the one may be call'd *Latin* shorten'd, and the other *Latin* drawn out at length; as, *Corpus, Tempus, Caput,* &c., are monosyllables in *French,* as *Corps, Temps, Caps,* or *Chef;* whereas the *Spaniard* doth add to them, as *Cuerpo, Tiempo, Cabeca.* And indeed of any other the *Spaniard* affects long words, for he makes some thrice as long as they are in *French;* as of *levement* arising, he makes *levantamiento;* of *Pensee,* a thought, he makes *Pensamiento;* of *Compliment,* he makes *Complimiento.* Besides, the *Spaniard* doth use to pause so in his pronunciation, that his *Tongue* seldom foreruns his *Wit,* and his brain may very well raise and superfœte a second thought before the first be utter'd. Yet is not the *French* so hasty in his utterance as he seems to be; for his quickness or volubility proceeds partly from that concatenation he useth among his syllables, by linking the syllable of the precedent word with the last of the following; so that sometimes a whole Sentence is made in a manner but one Word : and he who will speak the *French* roundly and well must observe this Rule.

The *French* Language began first to be polish'd, and arrive at that delicacy she is now come to, in the midst of the Reign of *Philip de Valois. Marot* did something under *Francis* I. (which King was a Restorer of *Learning* in general, as well as of *Language*); but *Ronsard* did more
under

under *Henry* II.   Since these Kings there is little difference
in the context of Speech, but only in the choice of words
and softness of Pronunciation, proceeding from such wanton
Spirits that did miniardize and make the Language more
dainty and feminine.

But to shew what changes the *French* have receiv'd from
what it was, I will produce these few instances in verse and
prose, which I found in some antient Authors: The first
shall be of a Gentlewoman that translated *Æsop's* Fables
many hundred years since out of *English* into *French*
where she concludes:

> *Au finement de cest' Escuit*
> *Qu'en Romans ay tourné & dit ;*
> *Me nommaray par remembrance,*
> *Marie ay nom je suis de France ;*
> *Per l'amour de Conte de Guillaume*
> *Le plus vaillant de ce Royaume,*
> *M'entremis de ce livre faire*
> *Et de l'Anglois en Roman traire,*
> *Esope appelle l'on cil Livre,*
> *Qu'on translata & fit Escrivre ;*
> *De Griec en Latin le tourna,*
> *Et le Roy Alvret qui l'ama,*
> *Le translata puis en Angloiz,*
> *Et je l'ay tourné en François.*

Out of the *Roman de la Rose* I will produce this Example:

> *Quand ta bouche toucha la moye,*
> *Ce fut dont au Cœur j'eus joye ;*
> *Sire juge, donnes sentence*
> *Par moy, Car la pucelle est moye.*

Two of the most antient and approved'st Authors in
France are *Geoffrey de Villardouin*, Marshal of *Campagne*,
and *Hugues de Bersy*, a Monk of *Clugny*, in the Reign of
Philippe Auguste, above 500 years since : from them I will
borrow these two ensuing Examples ; the first from the
Marshal, upon a *Croisada* to the *Holy Land*.

Seachiex

Scachiex que l'an 1188 *ans apres l'incarnation al temps Innocent* 3. *Apostoille de Rome, & Philippe Roy de France, & Richard Roy d'Engleterre, eut un Saint homme en France, qui et nom Folque de Nuilly, & il ere prestre, & tenoit le paroichre de la ville & ce Folque commença a parler de Biex, & nostre sire fit manits miracles par luy,* &c.

Hugues de Bersy, who made the *Guiot* Bible so much spoken of in *France,* begins thus in verse:

> *D'oun siecle puant & horrible*
> *M estuet commencer une Bible,*
> *Per poindre, & per aiguillonner*
> *Et per bons exemples donner,*
> *Ce n'est une Bible bisongere*
> *Mais fine, & voire en droituriere*
> *Mironer est a toutis gens.*

If one would compare the *English* that was spoken in those times, which is about 560 years since, with the present, he should find a greater alteration.

But to know how much the *Modern French* differs from the *Ancient,* let him read our Common Law, which was held good *French* in *William the Conqueror's* time.

Furthermore, among other observations, I find that there are some single words antiquated in the *French,* which seem to be more significant than those that are come in their places; as, *Maratre, Paratre, Filatre, Serourge,* a Step-mother, a Step-father, a Son or Daughter-in-law, a Sister-in-law, which now they express in two words, *Belle mere, Beau pere, Belle sœur.* Moreover, I find there are some words now in *French* which are turn'd to a counter-sense; as, we use the *Dutch* word *crank,* in *English,* to be *well-dispos'd,* which in the Original signifieth to be *sick.* So in *French, Cocu* is taken for one whose wife is light, and hath made him a passive *Cuckold;* whereas clean contrary, *Cocu,* which is the Cuckow, doth use to lay her eggs in another Bird's nest. This word *pleiger* is also to drink after one is drunk to; whereas the first true sense of the word was, that if the party drunk to was not dispos'd to drink himself, he

2 P   would

would put another for a pledge to do it for him, else the party who began would take it ill. Besides, this word *Abry*, deriv'd from the Latin *Apricus*, is taken in *French* for a close place or shelter, whereas in the Original it signifieth an open free Sunshine. They now term in *French* a free boon Companion, *Roger bon temps;* whereas the Original is, *Rouge bon temps,* reddish and fair weather: They use also in *France,* when one hath a good bargain, to say, *Il a joue a boule rue,* whereas the Original is, *A bonne vue.* A Beacon or Watch-Tower is call'd *Beffroy,* whereas the true word is *L'effroy:* A travelling Warrant is call'd *Pasport,* whereas the Original is *Passe per tout.* When one is grown hoarse, they use to say, *Il a veu le loup,* he hath seen the Wolf; whereas that effect of hoarseness is wrought in whom the Wolf hath seen first, according to *Pliny* and the Poet, ——*Lupi illum videre priores.* There is one saying or proverb which is observable, whereby *France* doth confess herself to be still indebted to *England,* which is, when one hath paid all his Creditors, he useth to say, *j'ay paye tous mes Anglois;* so that in this, and other phrases, *Anglois* is taken for *Greancier* or Creditor. And I persume it had its Foundation from this, That when the *French* were bound by Treaty at *Bretigny* to pay *England* so much for the ransom of King *John,* then prisoner, the contribution lay so heavy upon the People, that for many years they could not make up the Sum. The occasion might be seconded in *Henry* VIII'.s time at the surrendry of *Bullen,* and upon other Treaties; as also in Q. *Elizabeth's* Reign, besides the Moneys which she had disburs'd herself to put the Crown on *Henry* IV.'s Head: which makes me think on a passage that is recorded in *Pasquier,* that happen'd when the Duke of *Anjou,* under pretence of wooing the Queen, came over into *England,* who being brought to her presence, she told him, He was come in good time to remain a pledge for the Monies that *France* ow'd her Father, and other of her Progenitors; whereunto the Duke answer'd, That he *was come not only to be a Pledge, but her close Prisoner.*

There

There be two other sayings in *French*, which tho' they be obsolete, yet are they worthy the knowledge; the first is, *Il a perdu ses cheveux*, he hath lost his *hair*, meaning his *honour :* For in the first race of Kings there was a Law, call'd *La loy de la Cheveleure*, whereby it was lawful for the *Noblesse* only to wear long hair, and if any of them had committed some foul and ignoble Act, they us'd to be condemn'd to have their long hair to be cut off as a mark of ignominy; and it was as much as if he had been *fleuerdelix'd*, viz., burnt on the back or hand, or branded in the face.

The other Proverb is, *Il a quitté sa ceinture*, he hath given up his girdle; which intimated as much as if he had become bankrupt, or had all his Estate forfeited : It being the ancient Law of *France*, that when any upon some offence had that penalty of confiscation inflicted upon him, he us'd before the Tribunal of Justice to give up his *Girdle*, implying thereby, that the *Girdle* held everything that belong'd to a man's Estate, as his budget of Money and Writings, the keys of his House, with his Sword, Dagger, and Gloves, *&c.*

I will add hereunto another Proverb which had been quite lost, had not our Order of the Garter preserv'd it, which is, *Hony soit qui mal y pense ;* this we *English, Ill to him that thinks ill :* Tho' the true sense be, *Let him be berayed who thinks any ill ;* being a Metaphor taken from a child that hath beray'd his clouts : And I dare say, there's not one of a hundred in *France* who understands this word now-a-days.

Furthermore, I find in the *French* Language, that the same fate hath attended some *French* words, as usually attends *Men*, among whom, some rise to perferment, others fall to decay and an undervalue. I will instance in a few : The word *Maistre* was a word of high esteem in former times among the *French*, and appliable to Noblemen, and others in high Office only; but now 'tis fallen from the *Baron* to the *Boor*, from the Count to the Cobler, or any other mean Artisan ; as *Maistre Jean le Savetier*, Mr. *John* the Cobler ; *Maistre Jaquet le Cabaretier*, Mr. *Jammy* the Tapster.

Sire,

Sire was also appropriate only to the King : But now, adding a name after it, 'tis appliable to any mean Man, upon the Endorsement of a Letter or otherwise : But this word *Sovereign* hath rais'd itself to that pitch of greatness, that it is applied now only to the King, whereas in times past the President of any Court, any Bailiff or Seneschal, was used to be so call'd *Sovereign.*

Mareshal likewise was at first the name of a Smith, Farrier, or one that dress'd Horses ; but it is climb'd by degrees to that height, that the chiefest Commanders of the Gend-armery and Militia of *France* are come to be call'd *Marshals,* which about a hundred years since were but two in all, whereas now they are twelve.

This Title *Majesty* hath no great Antiquity in *France,* for it began in *Henry* II.'s time. And indeed the style of *France* at first, as well as of other Countries, was to *Tutoyer,* that is, to *Thou* any person that one spake unto, tho' never so high : But when the *Commonwealth* of *Rome* turn'd to an *Empire,* and so much Power came into one man's hand, then, in regard he was able to confer Honour and Offices, the Courtiers began to magnify him, and treat him in the plural number by *You,* and by degrees to deify him by trans-cending Titles ; as we read in *Symmachus,* in his Epistles to the Emperor *Theodosius,* and to *Valentinian,* where his style to them is, *Vestra æternitas, vestrum numen, vestra perennitas, vestra clementia :* So that *You* in the plural number, with other Compliments and Titles, seem to have their first rise with the Western Monarchy, which afterwards by degrees descended upon particular persons.

The *French* Tongue hath divers Dialects, *viz.,* the *Picardy,* that of *Jersey* and *Guernsey,* appendixes once of *Normandy ;* the *Provençal,* the *Gascon* or the speech of *Languedoc,* which *Scaliger* would etymologize from *Langue d'oc,* whereas it comes from *Langue de Got,* in regard the *Goths* and *Saracens,* who by their incursions and long stay in *Aquitain* first cor-rupted the speech of *Gallia :* The *Walloon* is another dialect, which is under the K. of *Spain :* They also of *Liege* have

a

a dialect of the *French,* which among themselves they call *Romand* to this day.

Touching the modern *French* that's spoken now in the King's Court, the Court of Parliament, and in the Universities of *France,* there had been lately a great competition which was the best; but by the learnedst, and most indifferent persons, it was adjudg'd that the Style of the King's Court was the purest and most elegant, because the other two did smell, the one of *Pedantry,* the other of *Chiquanery.* And the late Prince of *Conde,* with the D. of *Orleans* that now is, were us'd to have a *Censor* in their Houses, that if any of their Family spoke any word that savour'd of the Palace or the Schools, he should incur the penalty of an Amercement.

The late Cardinal *Richlieu* made it part of his glory to advance *Learning,* and the *French Language.* Among other Monuments he erected an University where the Sciences should be read and disputed in *French* for the ease of his Countrymen, whereby they might presently fall to the *matter,* and not spend time to study *words* only.

Thus have I presum'd to send your Lordship a rambling discourse of the *French* Language, past and present; humbly expecting to be corrected when you shall please to have perused it. So I subscribe myself—Your Lordship's thrice obedient Servant,   J. H.

Lond., 1 *Oct.*

XX.

To Dr. Weames.

SIR,

I RETURN you many thanks for the Additionals you pleas'd to communicate to me, in continuance of Sir *Philip Sidney's Arcadia;* and I admir'd it the more, because it was the composition of so young a Spirit: Which makes me tell you, without any compliment, that you are Father to a Daughter that *Europe* hath not many of her equals; therefore all those gentle Souls that pretend to Virtue should

cherish

cherish her. I have herewith sent you a few lines that relate to the Work, according to your desire.

To Mrs. *A. W.*

If a Male *Soul by transmigration can*
Pass to a Female, *and her Spirits* Man,
Then, sure, some sparks *of* Sidney's *Soul have flown*
Into your breast, which may in time be blown
To flames ; *for 'tis the course of* Enthean Fire,
To kindle by degrees, and brains inspire.
As Buds do Blossoms turn to Fruit,
So Wits *ask time to ripen and recruit :*
But yours gives time the start, and all may see
In this smooth piece of early Poesy,
Which, like Sparks of one Flame, may well aspire,
If Phœbus *please, to a* Sidneyan *Fire.*

So, with my very affectionate respects to yourself, and to your choice Family, I rest—Your ready and real Servant,

J. H.

London, 9 *Nov.*

XXI.

To the incomparable Lady, the Lady M. Cary.

MADAM,

I HAVE discover'd so much of Divinity in you, that he who would find your equal, must keep one in the other World. I might play the *Oracle*, and more truly pronounce you the wisest of Women, than he did *Pythagoras* the wisest of Men : For questionless, that *He* or *She* are the wisest of all human Creatures who are careful of preserving the noblest part of them, I mean the *Soul.* They who prink, and pamper the *Body*, and neglect the *Soul*, are like one who, having a Nightingale in his House, is more fond of the wicker *Cage* than of the *Bird :* Or rather, like one who hath a Pearl of an invaluable Price, and esteems the poor Box that holds it more than the Jewel. The *Rational Soul* is the *Breath* of God Almighty, she is his

very

very *Image:* Therefore who taints his Soul, may he said to throw dirt in God's face, and make his breath stink. The *Soul* is a spark of Immortality, she is a divine Light, and the body is but a socket of Clay that holds it. In some this Light goes out with an ill-favour'd stench; but others have a *Save-all* to preserve it from making any snuff at all. Of this number, Madam, you are one that shines clearest in this Horizon, which makes me so much—Your Ladyship's truly devoted Servant,   J. H.
London, 3 *Nov.*

XXII.
To the Lord Bishop of Ro., *at* Knolls.

MY LORD,

THE Christian Philosopher tells us, That *a good Conscience is a perpetual Feast:* And the Pagan Philosopher hath a saying, That *a virtuous Man is always drunk.* Both these sayings aim at one sense, *viz.,* That an upright, discreet Man is always full of good notions, and good motions; his Soul is always in tune, and the Faculties thereof never jarring: He values this World as it is, a vale of trouble and a valley of tears, full of encumbrances and revolutions; and stands arm'd against all events: *Si fractus illabatur Orbis.*

While you read this, you have your own character; for I know none more capable both for the practical part, as well as the theory, to give precepts of Patience, and prescribe rules of Morality and Prudence to all Mankind. Your Mind is like a Stone-bridge over a rapid River, which tho' the waters beneath be perpetually working, roaring, and bubling, yet the Bridge never stirs; *Pons manet immotus:*—— so among those monstrous mutations and traverses that have lately happen'd, you are still the same.

Mens immota manet——

I receiv'd your last under the covert of Sir *John Sackvil,* to whom I present my affectionate Service, with a thousand Thanks

Thanks for that seasonable Present he pleas'd to send me,
which will find me and my friends some employment; so,
desiring your *benediction*, I conclude, and subscribe myself,
my Lord—Your truly devoted Servant,   J. H.
London, 7 *Dec.*

XXIII.

To Sir W. Mason, *Knight.*

SIR,

I PRESENT you with the second part of the *Vocal
Forest;* but before you make an entrance into the
last *Walk* thereof, be pleas'd to take this short caution
along with you, which tends to rectify such who I hear are
over-rash and critical in their censure of what is there contain'd, not penetrating the main design of the Author in
that allegorical Discourse, nor in the quality of the Times,
or the prudential Cautions, and Indifferences that an historical Piece expos'd to public view should require, which
may make them perchance to shoot their *Bolts* at random,
and with wry looks at those *Trees.* Therefore let the discerning Surveyor, as he crosseth this last *Walk*, take a
short Advertisement beforehand; that whatsoever he meets
therein glancing on the *Oak*, consists of imperfect suggestions, foreign criticisms, and presumptions, *&c.* Now every
petty Sciolist in the Laws of Reason can tell that presumptions were never taken yet for proofs, but for left-handed
arguments, approaching rather the nature of cavillations
than consequences.

Moreover, Apologues, Parables, and Metaphors, tho'
press'd never so hard, have not the strength to demonstrate,
or positively assert any Thesis: For as in *Theology*, the
highest of Sciences, it is a receiv'd principle, *Scriptura para-
bolica non est argumentativa;* so this Maxim holds good in
all other Composures and Arts. 'Tis granted, that in the
Walks of this *Forest* there be some free and home expressions drawing somewhat nearer to the nature of *Satyrs*, for
otherwise it had been a vain superfluous curiosity to have

                                                    ,spent

spent so much oil and labour in shrouding *Realities* under Disguises, unless the Author had promis'd himself beforehand a greater latitude and scope of liberty to pry into some miscarriages and solecisms of State; as also to question and perstring some sorts of Actors, especially the *Cardanian* and *Classican*, who, as the whole World can witness, were the first Raisers of those hideous Tempests which pour'd down in so many showers of blood upon unfortunate *Druina*, and all her coafforested Territories.

Now touching that which is spoken of the Oak in the last *Walk*, if any intemperate *Basilean* take exceptions thereat, let him know, that, as 'twas said before, most of them are but traducements and pretensions; yet it is a human principle (and will ever be so to the world's end), that there never was yet any Prince (except one), nor will there ever be any hereafter, but had his frailties; and these frailties in Kings are like stains in the purest Scarlet, which are more visible: What are but *motes* in others are as *beams* in them, because that being mounted so high, they are more expos'd to the eye of the World. And if the Historian points haply at some of those *motes* in the *Royal Oak*, he makes good what he promised in the Entrance of the *Forest*, that he would endeavour to make a constant grain of *evenness* and *impartiality* to pass through the whole bulk of that *Arborical* Discourse.

We read that there being a high feud 'twixt *Cicero* and *Vatinius*, who had crooked bow-legs, *Vatinius* having the advantage of pleading first, took occasion to give a touch himself of his natural imperfection that way, that he might *tollere ansam*, that he might by way of prevention cut off the advantages and intention which *Cicero* might have had to asperse him in that particular: The Application hereof is easy and obvious.

But if the sober-minded Reader observe well what is spoken elsewhere of the *Oak* throughout the body and series of the story, he will easily conclude, that 'twas far from the design of the Author, out of any self or sinister ends, to let

any

any *sour droppings* fall from these *Trees* to hurt the *Oak*. And give me leave to tell you, That he who hath but as much wit as may suffice to preserve him from being begg'd for a *Fool*, will judge so.

Lastly, they who know anything of the Laws of History do well know, that Verity and Indifference are two of the prime virtues that are requisite in a *Chronicler*. The same Answer may serve to stop their mouths, who would say something, if they could tell what, against my *Survey of the Signory of* Venice, and dedicated to the Parliament of *England*, as if the Author had chang'd his principles, and were affected to *Republiques;* whereas there's not a syllable therein but what makes for *Monarchy:* Therefore I rather pity than repine at such poor Critiques, with the shallowness of their Judgments.

Thus much I thought good to intimate to you, not that I mistrust your own censure, which I know to be candid and clear, but that if there be occasion you may vindicate —Your truly affectionate Servant,   J. H.

Lond., 4 *Apr.*

XXIV.

To the Right Honourable the La. E. Savage, *afterwards Countess* Rivers.

EXCELLENT LADY,

AMONG those multitudes that claim a share in the loss of so precious a Lord, mine is not the least. O how willingly could I have measur'd with my feet, and perform'd a pilgrimage over all those large Continents wherein I have travell'd, to have repriev'd him! Truly, Madam, I shall mourn for him while I have a heart beating in my breast; and tho' time may mitigate the sense of grief, yet his *Memory* shall be to me, like his Worth and Virtues, everlasting. But it is not so much to be lamented that he hath left us (it being so infinitely to his advantage), as that he hath left behind so few like him.

I confess, Madam, this is the weightiest cross that possibly could

could come to exercise your patience; but I know your Ladyship to be both *pious* and *prudent* in the highest degree: Let the one preserve you from excess of sorrow, which may prove *irreligious* to Heaven; and the other keep you from being injurious to yourself, and to that goodly brave Issue of his, which may serve as so many living Copies of the Original.

God Almighty comfort your Ladyship; so prayeth, Madam —Your most humble and sorrowful Servant,   J. H.

London, 2 *Feb.*

XXV.

To the Right Honourable John *Lord* Sa.

MY LORD,

I SHOULD be much wanting to myself, if I did not congratulate your lately descended Honours: But truly, my Lord, this Congratulation is like a Vapour exhal'd from a Soil overwhelm'd with a sudden inundation; such is the state of my mind at this time, it being o'ercast with a thick Fog of grief for the death of your incomparable Father.

I pray from the centre of my Heart that you may inherit his high Worth and Virtues, as you do all things else; and I doubt it not, having discover'd in your nature so many pregnancies and sparkles of innated Honour. So I rest in quality of—Your Lordship's most humble Servant,

J. H.

London, 10 *Dec.*

XXVI.

To Mr. J. Wilson.

SIR,

I RECEIV'D yours of the 10th current, and I have many thanks to give you, that you so quaintly acquaint me how variously the pulse of the Pulpiteers beat in your Town. Touching ours here (by way of correspondence with you), I'll tell you of one whom I heard lately; for dropping casually into a Church in *Thames-street,* I fell upon a

Winter-

Winter-Preacher, who spoke of nothing but of the fire and flames of Hell; so that if a *Scythian* or *Greenlander*, who are habituated to such extreme cold, had heard and understood him, he would have thought he had preach'd of *Paradise.* His mouth methought did fume with the Lake of Brimstone, with the infernal Torments, and the thundrings of the Law, not a syllable of the Gospel: So I concluded him to be one of those who use to preach the *Law* in the *Church*, and the *Gospel* in their *Chambers*, where they make some female Hearts melt into *pieces.* He repeated his text once, but God knows how far it was from the subject of his Preachment; he had also hot and fiery incitements to War, and to swim in blood for the *Cause.* But after he had run away from his Text so long, the Spirit led him into a wilderness of Prayer, and there I left him.

God amend all, and begin with me, who am—Your assured Friend to serve you,   J. H.

London, 5 *July.*

XXVII.

To Sir E. S.

SIR,

IN the various courses of my wandring life, I have had occasion to spend some part of my time in literal correspondences with divers; but I never remember that I pleas'd myself more in paying these civilities to any than to yourself: For when I undertake this task, I find that my *Head*, my *Hand*, and my *Heart* go all so willingly about it. The *Invention* of the one, the *graphical Office* of the other, and the *Affections* of the last, are so ready to obey me in performing the work; work do I call it? 'Tis rather a sport, my Pen and Paper are as a *Chess-board*, or as your *Instruments* of *Music* are to you, when you would recreate your harmonious Soul. Whence this proceeds I know not, unless it be from a charming kind of virtue that your Letters carry with them to work upon my spirits, which are so full of facete and familiar friendly strains, and so punctual in

answering

answering every part of mine, that you may give the Law of Epistolizing to all Mankind.

Touching your Poet-Laureat *Skelton*, I found him at last (as I told you before) skulking in *Duck-lane*, pitifully tatter'd and torn ; and, as the times are, I do not think it worth the labour and cost to put him in better cloaths, for the Genius of the Age is quite another thing : yet there be some Lines of his, which I think will never be out of date for their quaint sense : and with these I will close this Letter, and salute you, as he did his Friend, with these options :

> *Salve plus decies quam sunt momenta dierum,*
> *Quot species generum, quot res, quot nomina rerum,*
> *Quot pratis flores, quot sunt & in orbe colores,*
> *Quot pisces, quot aves, quot sunt & in æquore naves,*
> *Quot volucrum pennæ, quot sunt tormenta gehennæ,*
> *Quot cæli stellæ, quot sunt miracula Thomæ :*
> *Quot sunt virtutes, tantas tibi mitto salutes.*

These were the wishes in time of yore of *Jo. Skelton*, but now they are of—Your   J. H.

London, 4 Aug.

XXVIII.

To R. Davis, *Esq.*

SIR,

DID your Letters know how truly welcome they are to me, they would make more haste, and not loiter so long in the way ; for I did not receive yours of the 2nd of *June* till the 1st of *July* ; which is time enough to have travell'd not only a hundred *English*, but so many *Helvetian* miles, that are five times bigger ; for in some places they contain forty furlongs, whereas ours have but eight, unless it be in *Wales*, where they are allow'd better measure, or in the North Parts, where there is a wea-bit to every mile. But that yours should be a whole month in making scarce 100 *English* miles (for the distance between us is no more)

is

is strange to me, unless you purposely sent it by *John Long*
the Carrier. I know, being so near *Lemster's-Ore*, that you
dwell in a gentle Soil, which is good for Cheese as well as
for *Cloth;* therefore if you send me a good one, I shall return my Cousin your Wife something from hence that may
be equivalent: If you neglect me, I shall think that *Wales*
is relapsed into her first barbarisms; for *Strabo* makes it one
of his arguments to prove the *Britons* barbarous, because
they had not the Art of making *Cheese* till the *Romans*
came: But I believe you will preserve them from this im-
putation again. I know you can want no good grass
thereabouts, which, as they say here, grows so fast in some
of your fields, that if one should put his Horse there over
night, he should not find him again the next morning. So,
with my very respectful commends to yourself, and to the
partner of your Couch and Cares, I rest, my dear Cousin—
Yours always to dispose of,   J. H.

Lond., 5 *July*.

XXIX.

To W. Roberts, *Esq.*

SIR,

THE *Dominical* Prayer, and the *Apostolical* Creed,
(whereof there was such a hot dispute in our last
Conversation) are two Acts tending to the same Object of
devotion; yet they differ in this, that we conclude *all* in
the first, and *ourselves* only in the second: One may *beg*
for another, but he must *believe* for himself, there is no
Man can believe by a Deputy. The Articles of the Creed
are as the twelve Signs in the Zodiak of *Faith*, which make
way for the *Sun of Righteousness* to pass through the centre
of our Hearts, as a Gentleman doth wittily compare them.
But what offence the *Lord's-Prayer* or the *Creed* have
committed (together with the *Ten Commandments*) as to
be as it were banished the Church of late years, I know
not; considering that the whole office of a Christian may
be said to be comprehended in them: For the last prescribes

us

us what we should do, the second what we should believe, the third how and what we should pray for. Of all the Hereticks that I ever heard of, I never read of any who bore Analogy with these.

Touching other Opinions, they are but old fancies newly furbish'd. There were *Adamites* in former times, and *Rebaptizers :* There were *Iconoclastæ*, destroyers of Images; but I never read of *Stauroclastæ*, destroyers of Crosses: There were also *Agoniclitæ*, who held it a superstition to bow the knee; besides, there were those who stumbled at the Resurrection, as too many do now : There were *Aereans* also who malign'd *Bishops* and the *Hierarchy* of the Church, but we read those *Aerians* turn'd *Arians*, and *Atheists* at last. The greatest *Greek* and *Latin* Fathers inveigh against those *Aerians* more bitterly than against any other: *Chrysostom* saith, *Heretiques who have learnt of the Devil not to give due honour to Bishops;* and *Epiphanius* saith, *It is the voice of a Devil, rather than of a Christian, that there is no difference 'twixt a Bishop and a Presbyter,* &c.

Good Lord, what fiery clashings we have had lately for a *Cap* and a *Surplice !* What an Ocean of human blood was spilt for Ceremonies only, and outward Formalities, for the bare position of a *Table !* But as we find the ruffling Winds to be commonly in Cemeteries, and about Churches, so the eagerest and most sanguinary Wars are about Religion ; and there is a great deal of weight in that distich of *Prudentius :*

> *Sic mores produnt animum, & mihi credite semper,*
> *Junctus cum falso est dogmate cædis amor.*

Let the *Turk* spread his *Alcoran* by the Sword, but let Christianity expand herself still by a passive Fortitude, wherein she always gloried.

We live in a strange Age, when every one is in love with his own *Fancy*, as *Narcissus* was with his *Face :* And this is true *spiritual Pride*, the usherer-in of all Confusions. The Lord deliver us from it, and grant we may possess our Souls with

with patience, till the great Wheel of Providence turn up
another spoke that may point at Peace and Unanimity
among poor mortals. In these hopes I rest—Yours entirely,   J. H.
London, 5 *Jan.*

XXX.

To Howel Gwyn, *Esq.*

MY MUCH ENDEARED COUSIN,

I SEND you herewith, according to your desires, the
British or *Welsh* Epitaph (for the *Saxons* gave us that
new name, calling us *Welshmen* or *Strangers* in our own
Country), which Epitaph was found in the *West-Indies*
upon Prince *Madoc* near upon 600 years since:

> Madoc *wif mw y die wedd*
> *Jawn genan* Owen Gwyneth,
> *Ni funnum dir fy enridd oedd,*
> *Ni da mowr ondy moroedd.*

Which is *English'd* thus in Mr. *Herbert's* Travels:

> Madoc *ap* Owen *was I call'd,*
> *Strong, tall, and comely, not inthrall'd*
> *With home-bred pleasure, but for Fame*
> *Thro' Land and Sea I sought the same.*

This *British* Prince *Madoc* (as many Authors make mention) made two Voyages thither, and in the last left his
bones there, upon which this Epitaph lay. There be other
pregnant remarks that the *British* were there, for there is
a Promontory not far from *Mexico* call'd *Cape Britain;*
there is a creek call'd *Gyndwor,* which is in *Welsh, White-
water;* with other words, as you shall find in Mr. *Herbert*
and others: They had also the sign of the *Cross* in reverence
among them.

And now that I am upon *British* Observations, I will
tell you something of this name *Howel,* which is your *first,*
and my *second* name: Passing lately by the Cloysters of the
Abbey

Abbey at *Westminster*, I stept up to the Library that Archbishop *Williams* erected there, and I lighted upon a *French*
Historian, *Bertrane a Argentre*, Lord of *Forges*, who was
President of the Court of Parliament in *Renes*, the chief
Town of *Little Britany* in *France*, call'd *Armorica*, which is
a pure *Welsh* word, and signifies a Country bordering upon
the Sea, as that doth, and was first coloniz'd by the *Britons*
of this Island in the reign of *Theodosius* the Emperor,
An. 387, whose Language they yet preserve in their radical
words: In that Historian I found that there were four Kings
of that Country of the name *Howel*, viz., *Howel* the First,
Howel the Second, *Howel* the Great (who bore up so stoutly
against *Ætius* the famous *Roman* General), and *Howel* the
Fourth, that were all Kings of *Armorica*, or the *Lesser*
Britany, which continued a Kingdom till the year 874, at
which time the Title was chang'd to a *Duchy*, but *Sovereign*
of itself, till it was reduc'd to the *French* Crown by *Francis*
I. There are many Families of Quality of that name to
this day in *France:* And one of them desired to be acquainted
with me, by the mediation of Mons. *Augier*, who was there
Agent for *England.* Touching the Castle of good K. *Howel*
hard by you, and other ancient places of that name, you
know them better than I; but the best Title which *England*
hath to *Wales* is by *that Castle*, as a great Antiquary told
me. So in a true bond of Friendship, as well as of Blood,
I rest—Your most affectionate Cousin,   J. H.

London, 8 *Oct.*

XXXI.

To *Mr*. W. Price, *at* Oxon.

MP PRECIOUS NEPHEW,

THERE could hardly better news be brought to me, than
to understand that you are so great a Student, and
that having pass'd through the briars of *Logic*, you fall so
close to *Philosophy:* Yet I do not like your method in one
thing, that you are so fond of new Authors, and neglect the

2 Q   old,

old, as I hear you do. It is the ingrateful Genius of this Age, that if any Sciolist can find a hole in an old Author's coat, he will endeavour to make it much more wide, thinking to make himself somebody thereby; I am none of those; but touching the Ancients, I hold this to be a good moral Rule, *Laudandum quod bene, ignoscendum quod aliter dixerunt:* The older an Author is, commonly the more solid he is, and the greater teller of Truth. This makes me think on a *Spanish* Captain, who being invited to a Fish-dinner, and coming late, he sat at the lower end of the Table where the small Fish lay, the great ones being at the upper end; thereupon he took one of the little Fish and held it to his Ear: His comrades ask'd him what he meant by that; he answer'd in a sad tone, *Some thirty years since my Father passing from* Spain *to* Barbary, *was cast away in a Storm, and I am asking this little Fish whether he could tell any tidings of his body; he answers me, that he is too young to tell me anything, but those old Fish at your end of the table may say something to it:* So by that trick of drollery he got his share of them. The application is easy, therefore I advise you not to neglect old Authors; for tho' we be come as it were to the Meridian of Truth, yet there be many *Neoterical* Commentators and self-conceited Writers, that eclipse her in many things, and go from *obscurum* to *obscurius.*

Give me leave to tell you, Cousin, that your Kindred and Friends, with all the world besides, expect much from you in regard of the pregnancy of your Spirit, and those Advantages you have of others, being now at the source of all Knowledge. I was told of a Countryman, who coming to *Oxford*, and being at the Towns-end, stood listning to a flock of Geese and a few Dogs that were hard by; being ask'd the Reason, he answer'd, that *he thought the Geese about* Oxford *did gaggle* Greek, *and the Dogs barked in* Latin. If some in the world think so much of those irrational poor creatures that take in University Air, what will your Friends in the Country expect from you, who have the Instruments of Reason in such a perfection, and so well strung with a

tenacious

tenacious Memory, a quick Understanding, and rich Invention? All which I have discover'd in you, and doubt not but you will employ them to the comfort of your Friends, your own credit, and the particular contentment of—Your truly affectionate Uncle,   J. H.

Lond. 3 *Feb.*

XXXII.

To Sir K. D., *in* Paris.

SIR,

I HAD been guilty of such an offence, whereof I should never have absolved myself, if I had omitted so handsome an opportunity to quicken my old Devotions to you. Among those multitudes here who resent your hard condition and the protractions of your Business, there is none who is more sensible that so gallant and sublime a Soul (so much renowned throughout the World) should meet with such harsh traverses of Fortune. For myself, I am like an Almanack out of date, I am grown an unprofitable thing, and good for nothing as the times run ; yet in your business I shall play the Whetstone, which tho' it be a dull thing of itself, and cannot cut, yet it can make other bodies to cut : So shall I quicken those who have the managing of your business, and power to do you good, whensoever I meet them. So I rest—Your thirty years Servant,   J. H.

Lond., 2 *Sept.*

XXXIII.

To Mr. R. Lee, *in* Antwerp.

SIR,

AN *Acre* of *Performance* is worth the whole *Land of Promise*; besides, as the *Italian* hath it, *Deeds are Men, and Words Women.* You pleas'd to promise me, when you shook hands with *England,* to barter Letters with me ; but whereas I writ to you a good while since by Mr. *Simons,* I have not received a syllable from you ever since.

The Times here frown more and more upon the Cavaliers,

liers, yet their minds are buoy'd up still with strong hopes; some of them being lately in company of such whom the Times favour, and reporting some comfortable news on the Royalists' side, one of the other answer'd, *Thus you Cavaliers still fool yourselves, and build always Castles in the Air:* Thereupon a sudden reply was made, *Where will you have us to build them else, for you have taken all our Lands from us?* I know what you will say when your read this: *A pox on those true Jests.*

This Tale puts me in mind of another: There was a Gentleman lately, who was offer'd by the Parliament a parcel of *Church* or *Crown-Lands,* equal to his Arrears; and asking counsel of a Friend of his which he should take, he answer'd, *Crown-Lands by all means, for if you take* them, *you run a hazard only to be* hang'd; *but if you take* Church-Land, *you are sure to be* damn'd. Whereunto the other made him a shrewd reply, *Sir, I'll tell you a Tale:* There was an old Usurer not far from *London,* who had train'd up a Dog of his to bring his meat after him in a Hand-basket, so that in time the Shag-dog was so well bred, that his Master us'd to send him by himself to *Smithfield* Shambles with a basket in his mouth, and a note in the bottom thereof to his Butcher, who accordingly would put in what joint of meat he writ for, and the Dog would carry it handsomely home. It happen'd one day, that as the Dog was carrying a good Shoulder of Mutton home to his Master, he was set upon by a Company of other huge Dogs, who snatch'd away the basket, and fell to the Mutton: The other Dog measuring his own single strength, and finding he was too weak to redeem his Master's Mutton, said within himself (as we read the like of *Chrysippus's* Dog), Nay, since there is no remedy, you shall be hang'd before you have all; I will have also my share, and so fell a eating amongst them. *I need not,* said he, *make the application to you, 'tis too obvious, therefore I intend to have my share also of the* Church-Lands.

In that large List of Friends you have left behind you here, I am one who is very sensible that you have thus banish'd yourself;

yourself; it is the high Will of Heaven that matters should be thus. Therefore *Quod divinitus accidit* humiliter, *quod ab hominibus* viriliter *ferendum;* we must manfully bear what comes from Men, and humbly what comes from above. The *Pagan* Philosopher tells us, *Quod divinitus contingit, homo a se nulla arte dispellet;* there is no fence against that which comes from Heaven, whose Decrees are irreversible.

Your Friends in *Fleet-street* are all well, both long-coats and short-coats, and so is—Your inalterable Friend to love and serve you, J. H.

Lond., 9 *Nov.*

XXXIV.

To Sir J. Tho., Knight.

SIR,

THERE is no Request of yours but is equivalent to a Command with me; and whereas you crave my thoughts touching a late History published by one Mr. *Wilson*, which relates the Life of K. *James*, tho' I know for many years your own judgment to be strong and clear enough of itself, yet to comply with your desires, and to oblige you that way another time to me, I will deliver you my opinion.

I cannot deny but the thing is a painful Piece, and proceeds after a handsome method, in drawing on the series and thread of the Story; but it is easily discernible, that a partial *Presbyterian* Vein goes constantly throughout the whole Work, and you know it is the Genius of that People to pry more than they should into the Courts and Comportments of Princes, and take any occasion to traduce and bespatter them: So doth this Writer, who endeavours all along (among other things) to make the world believe that K. *James* and his *Son* after him were inclin'd to *Popery*, and to bring it into *England;* whereas I dare avouch, that neither of them entertain'd the least thought that way, they had as much design to bring in *Prester-John* as the *Pope*, or *Mahomet* as soon as the *Mass*. This Conceit made the Writer to be subject to many Mistakes and Misrepresensations, sentations, which so short a circuit as a *Letter* cannot comprehend.

Yet I will instance in one gross mistake he hath in relating a passage which concerns Sir *Elias Hicks*, a worthy Knight, and a Fellow-servant of yours and mine. And he doth not only misrepresent the business, but he foully asperseth him with the terms of *unworthiness* and *infamy*. The truth of that passage is as followeth, and I had it from very good hands.

In the year 1621, the *French* King making a general War against them of the *Religion*, beleaguer'd *Montauban* in Person, while the Duke of *Espernon* block'd up *Rochel*. The King having lain a good while before the Town, a cunning report was rais'd that *Rochel* was surrender'd; this report being blown into *Montauban*, must needs dishearten them of *Rochel*, being the prime and tenablest propugnacle they had: Mr. *Hicks* happen'd to be then in *Rochel*, being commended by Sir *George Goring* to the Marquis *de la Force*, who was one of them that commanded in chief, and treated Mr. *Hicks* with much civility, so far as that he took him to be one of his domestic Attendants. The *Rochellers* had sent two or three special Envoys to *Montauban* to acquaint them with their good condition, but it seems they all miscarried; and the Marquis being troubled in his thoughts one day, Mr. *Hicks* told him, that by God's favour he would undertake and perform the service to *Montauban:* Hereupon he was put accordingly in equipage; so after ten days' journey he came to a place call'd *Moysak*, where my Lord of *Doncaster*, afterwards Earl of *Carlisle*, was in quality of Ambassador from *England*, to observe the *French* King's proceedings, and to mediate a Peace 'twixt him and the Protestants. At his first Arrival thither, it was his good hap to meet casually with Mr. *Peregrin Fairfax*, one of the Lord Ambassador's retinue, who had been a former Comrade of his: Among other Civilities he brought Mr. *Hicks* to wait upon the Ambassador, to whom he had credential Letters from the Assembly of *Rochel*, acquainting his Lordship with the good state they were in; Mr. *Hicks* told him besides, that he was

engag'd

engag'd to go to *Montauban* as an Envoy from *Rochel,* to give them true information how matters stood. The Ambassador replied, That it was too great a trust to be put upon so young shoulders: So Mr. *Hicks* being upon going to the *French* Army which lay before *Montauban,* Mr. *Fairfax* would needs accompany him thither to see the Trenches and Works; being come thither, they met with one Mr. *Tho. Webb,* that belong'd to the Marshal St. *Gerand,* who lodg'd them both in his own Hut that night; and having shew'd them the Batteries and Trenches the day after, Mr. *Hicks* took notice of one place which lay most open for his design, resolving with himself to pass that way to the Town. He had told *Fairfax* of his purpose before, who discovering it to *Webb, Webb* ask'd him whether he came thither to be hang'd ; for divers were us'd so a little before. The next day *Hicks* taking his leave of *Webb,* desir'd *Fairfax* to stay behind ; which he refusing, did ride along with him to the place which *Hicks* had pointed out the day before for his design, and there *Fairfax* left him : So having got betwixt the *Corps de Gard* and the Town, he put spurs to his horse, and waving his pistol above his head, got in, being pursu'd almost to the Walls of the Town by the King's Party. Being enter'd, old Marshal *de la Force,* who was then in *Montauban,* having heard his relations of *Rochel,* fell on his neck and wept, saying, That he would give 1000 Crowns he were as safely got back to *Rochel* as he came thither : And having stay'd there three weeks, he, in a sallie that the Town made one Evening, got clear through the Leaguer before *Montauban,* as he had formerly done before that of the Duke of *Espernon,* and so recover'd *Rochel* again. But to return to Mr. *Fairfax;* after he had parted with Mr. *Hicks,* he was taken prisoner, and threaten'd the rack; but whether out of the Apprehension thereof, or otherwise, he died a little after of a Fever at *Moysac;* tho' 'tis true that the Gazettes in *Paris* do publish that he died of the torture, with the *French* Mercury since.

    Mr. *Hicks* being return'd to *London,* was question'd by
                                                          Sir

Sir *Ferdinando Fairfax* for his Brother's death: Thereupon Mr. *Webb* being also come back to *London*, who was upon the very place where these things happen'd in *France*, Mr. *Hicks* brought him along with him to Sir *Ferdinand's* Lodgings, who did positively affirm that Mr. *Hicks* had communicated his design to Mr. *Peregrin Fairfax* (and that he reveal'd it first to him); so he did fairly vindicate Mr. *Hicks*, wherewith Sir *Ferdinand* remain'd fully satisfied, and all his Kindred.

Whosoever will observe the carriage and circumstance of this Action, will needs confess that Mr. *Hicks* (now Sir *Elias Hicks*) did comport himself like a worthy Gentleman from the beginning to the end thereof: The design was generous, the conduct of it discreet, and the conclusion very prosperous, in regard it preserv'd both *Montauban* and *Rochel* for that time from the fury of the Enemy; for the King rais'd his siege a little after from before the one, and *Espernon* from before the other. Therefore it cannot be deny'd but that the said Writer (who so largely intitles his Book the *History of Great Britain*, tho' it be but the *particular* Reign of K. *James* only) was very much to blame for branding so well a deserving Gentleman with *infamy* and *unworthiness*, which are the words he pleaseth to bestow upon him; and I think he would willingly recant and retract his rash censure were he now living, but Death *press'd* him away before the *Press* had done with his Book, whereof he may be said to have dy'd in Child-bed.

So presenting herewith unto you my hearty respects and love, endear'd and strengthen'd by so long a tract of time, I rest—Your faithful true Servant,　　J. H.

Lond., 9 *Nov.*

XXXV.

To Mr. R. Lewis, *in* Amsterdam.

Cousin,

I FOUND yours of the first of *February* in the *Post-house*, as I casually had other business there, else it had miscarry'd;

carry'd ; I pray be more careful of your directions hereafter. I much thank you for the aviso's you sent me how matters pass thereabouts : Methinks that *Amsterdam* begins to smell rank of a *Hans* Town, as if she would be independent and paramount over the rest of the Confederate Provinces ; she hath some reason in one respect, because *Holland* contributes three parts of five, and *Amsterdam* herself near upon the one moiety of those three parts, to maintain the Land and Naval Forces of the *States-General.* That *Town* likewise, as I hear, begins to compare with *Venice,* but let her stay there a while ; yet she may in some kind do it, for their situation and beginning have been alike, being both indented with *Waters,* and both *Fisher-Towns* at first.

But I wonder at one news you write me, that *Amsterdam* should fall on repairing and beautifying Churches, whereas the news here is clean contrary ; for while you *adorn* your Churches there, we *destroy* them here.   Among other, poor *Paul's* looks like a great Skeleton, so pitifully handled, that you may tell her ribs thro' her skin ; her body looks like the Hulk of a huge *Portugal Carake,* that having cross'd the Line twelve times, and made three Voyages into the *East-Indies,* lies rotting upon the Strand.   Truly I think not *Turk* or *Tartar,* or any Creature except the *Devil* himself, would have us'd *Paul's* in that manner : You know that once a *Stable* was made a *Temple,* but now a *Temple* is become a *Stable* among us.   *Proh superi ! quantum mortalia pectora Cæcæ Noctis habent.*——

There are strange *Heteroclites* in Religion now-a-days ; among whom, some of them may be said to endeavour the exalting of the Kingdom of Christ, in lifting it upon *Belzebub's* back, by bringing in so much *Profaneness* to avoid *Superstition.*   God deliver us from *Atheism,* for we are within one step of it ; and touching *Judaism,* some corners of our City smell as rank of it as yours doth there.

I pray be punctual in your returns hereafter ; for, as you say well and wittily, Letters may be said to be the *chiefest Organs* (tho' they have but *Paper-pipes) through which*
Friendship

Friendship doth use to breathe and operate. For my part, I
shall not be wanting to set those *Organs* a working for the
often conveyance of my best Affections unto you. Sir *T.
Williams*, with his choice Lady, *blow* over through the same
Pipe their kind respects unto you, and so do divers of your
Friends besides ; but 'specially, my dear Cousin—Yours,

J. H.

Lond., 3 *Jan.*

XXXVI.

To J. Anderson, *Esq.*

SIR,

YOU have been often at me (tho' I know you to be a
Protestant so in *grain*, that all the Water of the *Tyber*
is not able to make you change colour) that I should impart
to you in *Writing* what I observ'd commendable and discom-
mendable in the *Roman* Church, because I had eaten my
Bread often in those Countries where that Religion is profess'd and practis'd in the greatest height. Touching the
second part of your request, I need not say anything to it ;
for there be Authors enough in our Church to inform you
about the Positions and Tenets wherein we differ, and for
which we blame them. Concerning the *first* part, I will
give you a short intimation what I noted to be praise-worthy
and imitable in point of practice.

The *Government* of the *Roman* Church is admirable, being
moulded with as much Policy as the Wit of Man can reach
unto ; and there must be *Civil* Policy as well as *Ecclesiastical* us'd to keep such a world of People of several Nations
and Humours in one *Religion :* Tho' at first when the *Church*
extended but to one *Chamber,* then to one *House,* after to
one *Parish,* then to one *Province,* such Policy was not so
requisite. For the *Church* of Christ may be compar'd to
his *Person* in point of degrees of growing ; and as that
Coat which serv'd him in his *Childhood,* could not fit him
in his *Youth,* nor that of his *Youth* when he was come to
his *Manhood,* no more would the same *Government* (which

compar'd

compar'd to the Fundamentals of Faith, that are still the
same, are but as outward *garments*) fit all *Ages* of the Church,
in regard of those millions of Accidents that used to attend
Time, and the mutable humours of Men. Insomuch that it
was a wholesome caution of an ancient Father, *Distinguas
inter tempora, & concordabis cum Scriptura.* This Government is like a great Fabric rear'd up with such exact rules
of Art and Architecture, that the Foundation, the Roof,
Sides, and Angles, with all the other parts, have such a
dependence of mutual support by a rare contignation, concinnity, and intendings one in the other, that if you take
out but *one* Stone, it hazards the downfall of the *whole*
Edifice. This makes me think that the Church of *Rome*
would be content to part with, and rectify some things, if
it might not endanger the Ruin of the whole; which puts
the World in despair of an *Oecumenical* Council again.

The *Uniformity* of this *Fabric* is also to be admir'd,
which is such as if it were but one entire continued homogeneous Piece: For put case a *Spaniard* should go to *Poland,*
and a *Pole* should travel to the furthest part of *Spain,*
whereas all other objects may seem ne'er so strange to them
in point of *Lodging, Language,* and *Diet,* tho' the Complexion and Faces, the Behaviour, Garb, and Garments of
Men, Women, and Children, be differing, together with
the very Air and Clime of the place; tho' all things seem
strange unto them, and so somewhat uncouth and comfort- ·
less; yet when they go to God's House in either Country,
they may say they are there at home: For nothing differs there
either in *Language, Worship, Service,* or *Ceremony;* which
must needs be an unspeakable comfort to either of them.

Thirdly, It must needs be a commendable thing that
they keep their Churches so cleanly and amiable, for the
Dwellings of the Lord of Hosts should be so: To which
end your greatest Ladies will rise before day sometimes in
their Night-clothes to fall a sweeping some part of the
Church, and decking it with flowers, as I heard Count
Gondomar's Wife us'd to do here at *Ely-House* Chapel;
besides,

besides, they keep them in constant repair, so that if but a quarry of glass chance to be broken, or the least stone be out of square, 'tis presently mended. Moreover, their Churches stand wide open early and late, inviting, as it were, all Comers; so that a poor troubled soul may have Access thither at all hours to breathe out the Pantings of his Heart, and Ejaculations of his Soul either in Prayer or Praise: Nor is there any exception of persons in their Churches, for the *Cobler* will kneel with the *Count*, and the *Laundress* gig by geoul with her *Lady;* there being no *Pews* there to cause pride and envy, contentions and quarrels, which are so rife in our Churches.

The comely prostrations of the body, with genuflection, and other Acts of Humility in time of divine Service, are very exemplary : Add hereunto, that the Reverence they shew to the holy Function of the Church is wonderful; Princes and Queens will not disdain to kiss a Capuchin's Sleeve, or the Surplice of a Priest. Besides, I have seen the greatest and beautifull'st young Ladies go to Hospitals, where they not only dress, but lick the sores of the sick.

Furthermore, the conformity of *Seculars*, and resignment of their Judgments to the Governors of the Church, are remarkable. There are not such *Scepticks* and Cavillers there, as in other places; they humbly believe that *Lazarus* was three days in the grave, without questioning where his Soul was all the while; nor will they expostulate how a Man who was born blind from his Nativity, should presently know the shapes of Trees, whereunto he thought the first Men he ever saw were like, after he receiv'd sight. Add hereunto, that they esteem for Church-preferments most commonly a Man of a pious good disposition, of a meek spirit, and godly life, more than a *Learned* Man, that is either a great Linguist, Antiquary, or Philosopher; and the first is advanced sooner than the latter.

Lastly, They think nothing too good or too much for God's *House*, or for his *Ministers;* no Place too sweet, no Buildings too stately for them, being of the best Profession.

The

The most curious Artists will employ the best of their Skill to compose Hymns and Anthems for God's House, *&c.*

But methinks I hear you say, that you acknowledge all this to be commendable, were it not that it is accompanied with an odd opinion that they think to *merit* thereby, accounting them Works of *Supererogation.*

Truly, Sir, I have discours'd with the greatest Magnifiers of meritorious Works, and the chiefest of them made me this Comparison, that the Blood of Christ is like a great Vessel of Wine, and all the Merits of Men, whether active or passive, were it possible, must be put into that great Vessel, and so must needs be made Wine; not that the Water hath any inherent Virtue of itself, to make itself so, but as it receives it from the *Wine.*

It is reported of *Cosmo de Medici,* that having built a goodly Church, with a Monastery thereunto annex'd, and two Hospitals, with other Monuments of Piety, and endow'd 'em with large Revenues; as one did much magnify him for these extraordinary Works, for which doubtless he merited a high reward in Heaven, he answer'd, *'Tis true, I employ'd much Treasure that way, yet when I look over my Ledger-Book of Accounts, I do not find that God Almighty is indebted to me one Penny, but I am still in the arrear to him.*

Add hereunto the sundry ways of mortification they have by frequent long fastings, and macerations of the flesh by their retiredness, their abandoning the World, and sequestrations from all mundane Affairs; their notable humility in the distribution of their Alms, which they do not use to hurl away in a kind of scorn as others do, but by putting it gently into the beggar's hand.

Some shallow-pated *Puritan,* in reading this, will shoot his bolt, and presently cry me up to have a *Pope* in my belly; but you know me otherwise, and there's none knows my intrinsecals better than you. We are come to such times, that if any would maintain those Decencies, and humble Postures, those Solemnities and Rites which should be practis'd in the holy House of God (and *Holiness* becomes his

his House for ever), nay, if one passing through a Church should put off his hat, there is a giddy and malignant race of People (for indeed they are the true *Malignants*) who will give out that he is running post to *Rome;* notwithstanding that the Religion establish'd by the Laws of *England* did ever allow of them ever since the *Reformation* began, yet you know how few have run thither   Nay, the *Lutherans,* who use far more Ceremonies symbolizing with those of *Rome,* than the *English Protestants* ever did, keep still their distance, and are as far from her now as they were at first.

England had *lately* (tho' *to me* it seems a *great while* since) the Face and Form, the Government and Gravity, the Constitutions and Comeliness of a *Church;* for she had *something* to keep herself *handsome;* she had wherewith to be *hospitable,* and do *Deeds* of *Charity,* to build *Alms-houses, Free-schools,* and *Colleges,* which had been very few in this Island, had there been no *Church-Benefactors:* She had brave degrees of Promotion to incite industry, and certainly the conceit of Honour is a great encouragement to Virtue: Now, if all Professions have steps of Rising, why should *Divinity,* the best of all Professions, be without them? The *Apprentice* doth not think it much to wipe his Master's shoes, and sweep the gutters, because he hopes one day to be an *Alderman:* The *common Soldier* carrieth hopes in his Knapsack, to be one day a *Captain* or *Colonel:* The *Student* in the Inns of Courts turns over *Ploydon* with more alacrity, and tugs with that crabbed study of the Law, because he hopes one day to be a *Judge:* So the *Scholar* thought his labour sweet, because he was buoy'd up with hopes that he might be one day a *Bishop, Dean,* or *Canon.* This comely subordination of Degrees we once had, and we had a *visible* conspicuous Church, to whom all other *Reformists* gave the upper hand; but now she may be said to have crept into *corners,* and fallen to such a contempt, that she dares scarce shew her face. Add hereunto what various kinds of confusions she is involved in; so that it may be not improperly

said,

said, while she thought to run away so eagerly from *Babylon*, she is fallen into a *Babel* of all Opinions: Insomuch that they who came lately from *Italy* say, how *Rome* gives out, that when Religion is lost in *England*, she will be glad to come to *Rome* again to find one out, and that she danceth all this while in a circle.

Thus have I endeavour'd to satisfy your Importunity as far as a sheet of paper could reach, to give you a touch what may be not only allowable but laudable, and consequently imitable in the *Roman* Church; for

————*Fas est & ab Hoste doceri.*

But I desire you would expound all with the *same sense* wherewith I know you *abound;* otherwise I would not be so free with you upon this ticklish subject: Yet I have cause to question your *Judgment* in one thing, because you magnify so much my *talent* in your last. Alas, Sir, a small *Handkerchief* is enough to hold mine, whereas a large *Table-Cloth* can hardly contain that rich *Talent* which I find God and Nature hath *intrusted* you withal. In which opinion I rest always—Your ready and real Servant, J. H.

Lond., 3 *July*.

XXXVII.

To Doctor Harvey, *at St.* Lawrence Poultney.

SIR,

I REMEMBER well you pleas'd not only to pass a favourable censure, but give a high character of the first part of *Dodona's Grove;* which makes this *Second* to come and wait on you, which, I dare say, for variety of fancy, is nothing inferior to the first. It continueth an historical Account of the Occurrences of the Times in an allegorical way, under the shadow of *Trees;* and I believe it omits not any material passage which happen'd as far as it goes. If you please to spend some of the parings of your time, and fetch a walk in this *Grove,* you may haply find therein some recreation: And if it be true what the Ancients write of

some

some Trees, that they are *fatidical,* these come to foretell, at leastwise to wish you, as the season invites me, a good New-year, according to the *Italian* compliment, *Buon principio, miglior mezzo, ed ottimo fine.* With these wishes of happiness in all the three degrees of comparison, I rest—Your devoted Servant,   J. H.

Lond., 2 *Jan.*

XXXVIII.

To R. Bowyer, *Esq.*

SIR,

I RECEIV'D yours of the tenth current, where I made a new Discovery, finding therein one Argument of your Friendship, which you never urg'd before; for you give me a touch of my failings in point of literal correspondence with you. To this give me leave to answer, That he who hath glass-windows of his own, should take care how he throws stones at those of his Neighbours. We have both of us our failings that way, witness else yours of the last of *May,* to mine of the first of *March* before; but it is never over-late to mend: Therefore I begin, and do penance in this white sheet for what is past; I hope you will do the like, and so we may absolve one another without a ghostly Father.

The *French* and *Spaniard* are still at it like two Cocks of the game, both of them pitifully bloodied; and 'tis thought they will never leave, till they peck out one another's eyes. They are daily seeking new Alliances to fortify themselves, and the quarrel is still so hot, that they would make a league with *Lucifer* to destroy one another.

For home news, the freshest is, that whereas in former times there were complaints that *Churchmen* were *Justices of Peace,* now the clean contrary way, *Justices of the Peace* are become *Churchmen;* for by a new *Act* of that *Thing* in *Westminster* call'd a *Parliament,* the power of giving in Marriage is pass'd over to them, which is an *Ecclesiastical Rite* everywhere else throughout the World.

A

A Cavalier coming lately to a Bookseller's shop, desir'd to buy this *Matrimonial Act,* with the rest of that holy Parliament, but he would have them all bound in Calf's Leather, bought out of Mr *Barbone's* Shop in *Fleet-street.*

The soldiers have a great spleen to the Lawyers, insomuch that they threaten to hang up their *Gowns* among the *Scots Colours* in *Westminster-hall;* but their chiefest aim is at the regulation of the *Chancery,* for they would have the same Tribunal to have the power of *Justice* and *Equity,* as the same Apothecary's shop can afford us *Purges* and *Cordials.* So with my kind and cordial respects unto you, I rest—Your entire and truly affectionate Servant, J. H.

Lond., 9 *Nov.*

XXXIX.

To Mr. J. B., at his House in St. Nicholas Lane.

SIR,

WHEN I exchang'd speeches with you last, I found (yet more by your *discourse* than *countenance*) that your spirits were towards a kind of ebb, by reason of the interruption and stop which these confused Times have put to all mercantile Negotiations both at home and abroad. Truly Sir, when after a serious recollection I had ruminated upon what had dropp'd from you then, I extremely wonder'd, which I should not have done at another; in regard since the first time I had the advantage of your Friendship, I discover'd that you were naturally of generous and freeborn thoughts. I have found also, that by a rare industry you have stor'd up a rich stock of Philosophy, and other parts of Prudence; which induc'd me to think that no worldly Revolution, or any cross-winds, tho' never so violent, no not a *Hurricane* could trouble the *Calm* of your Mind. Therefore to deal freely with you, you are not the same Man I took you for.

I confess 'tis a passive Age, and the stoutness of the prudent'st and most philosophical Men were never put to

2 R   such

such a trial. I thank God, the School of Affliction hath brought me to such a habit of Patience, it hath caus'd in me such symptoms of Mortification, that I can value this World as it is. It is but a vale of Troubles, and we who are in it are like so many Ants trudging up and down about a Mole-hill. Nay, at best we are but as so many Pilgrims, or Passengers travelling on still towards another Country : 'Tis true, that some do find the way thither more smooth and fair; they find it flowry, and tread upon Camomile all along : Such may be said to have their Paradise here, or to sail still in Fortune's sleeve, and to have the wind in the poop all the while, not knowing what a storm means; yet both the *Divine* and *Philosopher* do rank these among the most unfortunate of men. Others there are who in their journey to their last home do meet with rocks and craggs, with ill-favour'd sloughs and bogs, and divers deep and dirty passages. For my part I have already pass'd through many such, and must expect to meet with more : Therefore you also by your various Adventures, and Negotiations in the world, must not think to escape them; you must make account to meet with encumbrances and disasters, with mischances and crosses. Now 'twas a brave generous saying of a great *Armenian* Merchant, who having understood how a Vessel of his was cast away, wherein there was laden a rich Cargazon upon his sole Account, he struck his hand on his breast, and said, *My Heart, I thank God, is still afloat, my Spirits shall not sink with the Ship, nor go an Inch lower.*

But why do I write to you of Patience and Courage? In doing this, I do no otherwise than *Phormio* did, when he discours'd of War before *Hannibal :* I know you have Prudence enough to cheer up and instruct yourself; only let me tell you, that you superabound with *fancy,* you have more of *mind* than of *body,* and that sometimes you overcharge the *Imagination,* by musing too much upon the odd traverses of the *World:* Therefore I pray rouse up your Spirits, and reserve yourself for better times, that I may long enjoy the sweetness of your Friendship; for the Elements
ments

ments are the more pleasing to me, because you live with me amongst them. So God send you such tranquillity of thoughts as I wish.—Your true Friend, J. H.

5 *April.*

XL.

To Major J. Walker, *in* Coventry.

SIR,

I HEARTILY congratulate your return to *England,* and that you so safely cross'd the *Scythian Vale;* for so old *Gildas* calls the *Irish* Seas, in regard they are so boisterous and rough. I understand you have been in sundry hot and hazardous encounters, because of those many scars and cuts you wear about you; and as *Tom Dawson* told me, it was no less than a miracle that none of them were mortal, being eleven in all. It makes me think on a witty compliment that Captain *Miller* put upon the *Persian* Ambassador when he was here, who showing him many Wounds that he had receiv'd in the Wars against the *Turk,* the Captain said, That his *Lordship's skin after his death would yield little money, because it had so many holes in it.*

I find the same Fate hangs o'er the *Irish,* as befell the old *Britons* here; for as they were hemm'd in among the *Welsh* Mountains, so the *Irish* are like now to be all kennell'd in *Connaught.* We see daily strange revolutions, and God knows what the issue will be at last; howsoever, let us live and love one another, in which resolution I rest—Entirely yours, J. H.

2 *May.*

XLI.

To Mr. T. C., *at his House upon* Tower-hill.

SIR,

TO inaugurate a good and jovial New-year to you, I send you a morning's draught, *viz.,* a Bottle of *Metheglin.* Neither Sir *John Barly-corn* or *Bacchus* had anything to do with it, but it is the pure juice of the *Bee,* the laborious *Bee,*

Bee, and King of Insects. The *Druids* and old *British Bards* were wont to take a carouse hereof before they enter'd into their Speculations; and if you do so when your Fancy labours with anything, it will do you no hurt, and I know your *fancy* to be very good.

But this Drink always carries a kind of state with it, for it must be attended with a brown toast; nor will it admit but of one good draught, and that in the morning; if more, it will keep a humming in the head, and so speak too much of the House it comes from, I mean the Hive, as I gave a caution elsewhere: And because the bottle might make more haste, I have made it go upon these poetick feet:

J. H. T. C. *Salutem, & annum Platonicum.*

Non Vitis, *sed* Apis *succum tibi mitto bibendum,*
Quem legimus Bardos *olim potasse* Britannos.
Qualibet in bacca Vitis Megera *latescit,*
Qualibet in gutta Mellis Aglaia *nitet.*

The juice of Bees, *not* Bacchus, *here behold,*
Which British Bards *were wont to quaff of old ;*
The Berries *of the* Grape *with* Furies *swell,*
But in the Honeycomb the Graces *dwell.*

This alludes to a saying which the *Turks* have, that there lurks a devil in every berry of the Vine. So I wish you as cordially as to myself an auspicious and joyful New-year, because you know I am—Your truly affectionate Servitor,

J. H.

XLII.

To Sir E. S.

SIR,

AT my return to *London*, I found two of yours that lay in bank for me, which were as welcome to me as the New-year, and as pleasing as if two Pendants of *Orient Pearl* had been sent to a *French* Lady: But your Lines, methought, did cast a greater lustre than any such *Muscle-beads;* for they display'd the whiteness of a comely and

knowing

knowing Soul, which reflecting upon my Faculties did much enlighten them with the choice notions I found therein.

I thank you for the Absolution you send me for what's past, and for your other Invitation: But I have observ'd a civility they use in *Italy* and *Spain,* not to visit a sick person too often, for fear of putting him to waste his spirits by talk, which they say spends much of the inward man. But when you have recover'd yourself, as I hope you will do with the season, I shall return to kiss your hands, and your feet also, could I ease you of that podagrical pain which afflicts you.

I send you a thousand thanks for your kind Acceptance of that small New-year's Gift I sent, and that you concur with divers others in a good opinion of it. So I rest—Your own true Servant,   J. H.

Lond., 18 *Feb.*

XLIII.

To the truly honoured the Lady Sibylla Brown, *at her House near* Sherburn.

MADAM,

WHEN I had the Happiness to wait upon you at your being in *London,* there was a Dispute rais'd about the ten *Sibyls* by one, who, your Ladyship knows, is no great Friend to *Antiquity;* and I was glad to apprehend this opportunity to perform the promise you drew from me then, to vent something upon this subject for your Ladyship's satisfaction.

Madam, in these peevish times, which may be call'd the *Rust* of the *Iron* Age, there is a race of cross-grain'd People, who are malevolent to all Antiquity. If they read an old Author, it is to quarrel with him, and find some hole in his coat; they slight the Fathers of the primitive Times, and prefer *John Calvin,* or a *Casaubon* before them all. Among other tenets of the first times, they hold the ten *Sibyls* to be fictitious and fabulous, and no better than *Urganda,* or the Lady of the Lake, or such doting beldams. They stick not to term their Predictions of Christ to be mere Mock-Oracles,

Oracles, and odd arrepititious frantick Extravagancies. They cry out, that they were forg'd and obtruded on the World by some officious Christians, to procure credit and countenance to their Religion among the *Pagans*.

For my part, Madam, I am none of this incredulous perverse race of men; but what the current and concurrent testimonies of the primitive Times do hold forth, I give credit thereto without any scruple.

Now touching the Works of the *Sibyls*, they were in high request among the Fathers of the first four Centuries, insomuch that they us'd to urge their Prophecies for the Conversion of *Pagans*, who therefore call'd the *Christians Sibyllianists*, nor did they hold it a word of reproach. They were all Virgins, and for reward of their chastity, 'twas thought they had the gift of Prophecy; not by any endowment of Nature, or inherent human Quality, or ordinary Ideas in the Soul, but by pure divine Inspirations, not depending on second Causes in sight. They spake not like the ambiguous *Pagan* Oracles in riddles, but so clearly, that they sometimes go beyond the *Jewish* Prophets; they were call'd *Siobulæ*, that is, of the Counsels of God; *Sios*, in the *Eolic* Dialect, being *Deus*. They were preferr'd before all the *Chaldean* Wizards, before the *Bacides*, *Branchidæ*, and others; as also before *Tyresias*, *Manto*, *Matis*, or *Cassandra*, &c.

Nor did the *Christians* only value them at that height, but the most learned among the *Ethniks* did so, as *Varro*, *Livy*, and *Cicero;* the first being the greatest *Antiquary*, the second the greatest *Historian*, and the third the greatest *Orator*, that ever *Rome* had; who speak so much of that famous *Acrostick* that one of them made of the Name of our Saviour, which sure could not be the work of a *Christian*, as some would maliciously obtrude, it being so long before the Incarnation.

But for the better discharge of my engagement to your Ladyship, I will rank all the ten before you, with some of their most signal Predictions.

The *Sibyls* were ten in number, whereof there were five born in *Europe*, to wit, *Sibylla Delphica, Cumæa, Samia,*

Cumana,

Cumana, and *Tyburtina;* the rest were born in *Asia* and *Africa.*

The first was a *Persian* call'd *Samberthe,* who plainly foretold many hundred years before, in these Words, *The Womb of the Virgin shall be the Salvation of the Gentiles,* &c.

The second was *Sibylla Lybica,* who among other Prophecies hath this, *The day shall come that Men shall see the King of all living things, and a Virgin Lady of the World shall hold him in her lap.*

The third was *Delphica,* who saith, *A Prophet shall be born of a Virgin.*

The fourth was *Sibylla Cumæa,* born in *Campania* in *Italy,* who hath these words, that *God shall be born of a Virgin, and converse with sinners.*

The fifth was the famous *Erythræa,* born at *Babylon,* who compos'd that famous *Acrostick* which St. *Augustine* took so much pains to translate into *Latin.* Which begins, *The Earth shall sweat signs of Judgment, from Heaven shall come a King who shall reign for ever,* viz., *in human Flesh, to the end that by his presence he may judge the world. A River of Fire and Brimstone shall fall from Heaven, the Sun and Stars shall lose their light, the Firmament shall be dissolv'd, and the Moon shall be darken'd; a Trumpet shall sound from Heaven in woful and terrible manner: And the opening of Earth shall discover confused and dark Hell; and before the Judge shall come every King,* &c.

The sixth was *Sibylla Samia,* who saith, *He being rich, shall be born of a poor Maid: The Creatures of the Earth shall adore him, and praise him for ever.*

The seventh was *Cumana,* who saith, *That he should come from Heaven, and reign here in poverty; he should rule in silence, and be born of a Virgin.*

The eighth was *Sibylla Hellespontica,* who foretells plainly that *A Woman shall descend of the* Jews, call'd Mary, *and of her shall be born the Son of God, and that without carnal copulation,* &c.

The ninth was *Phrygia,* who saith, *The highest shall come*
                                                                from

from Heaven, and shall confirm the Counsel in Heaven; and a Virgin shall be shew'd in the Vallies of the Desarts, &c.

The tenth was *Tiburtina,* born near *Tyber,* who saith, *The invisible Word shall be born of a Virgin, he shall converse with sinners, and shall of them be despis'd,* &c.

Moreover, St. *Austin* reciteth these Prophecies following of the *Sibyls: Then he shall be taken by the wicked hands of Infidels, and they shall give him buffets on his face, they shall spit upon him with their foul and accursed mouths, he shall turn unto them his shoulders, suffering them to be whipp'd : He also shall be crown'd with thorns; they shall give him gall to eat and vinegar to drink : Then the veil of the Temple shall rend, and at mid-day it shall be dark night,* &c.

Lactantius relateth these Prophecies of theirs, *He shall raise the dead, the impotent and lame shall go, the deaf shall hear, the blind shall see, and the dumb speak,* &c.

In fine, out of the works of the *Sibyls* may be deduced a good part of the Miracles and Sufferings of Christ; therefore for my part I will not cavil with Antiquity, or traduce the primitive Church, but I think I may believe without danger, that those *Sibyls* might be select instruments to announce the dispensations of Heaven to Mankind. Nor do I see how they do the Church of God any good service or advantage at all, who question the truth of their Writings (as also *Trismegistus* his *Pymandra,* and *Aristæus,* &c), which have been handed over to posterity as incontroulable truths for so many Ages.

Thus, Madam, have I done something of that task you impos'd upon me touching the *ten Sibyls;* whereunto I may well add your Ladyship for the eleventh : For among other things I remember you foretold confidently that the *Scottish* Kirk would destroy the *English* Church ; and that if the *Hierarchy* went down, *Monarchy* would not be of long continuance.

Your Ladyship I remember foretold also, how those unhappy Separatists the Puritans would bring all things at last into a confusion, who since are call'd Presbyterians, or Jews
of

of the *New Testament;* and they not improperly may be
call'd so, for they sympathize much with that Nation in a
revengeful sanguinary humour and thirsting after blood.   I
could produce a cloud of examples, but let two suffice.

There liv'd a few years before the *Long Parliament* near
Clun-Castle in *Wales,* a good old Widow that had two sons
grown to Men's estate, who having taken the holy Sacrament on a first *Sunday* in the month, at their return home
they enter'd into a dispute touching their manner of receiving it.   The eldest Brother, who was an orthodox Protestant
(with the Mother) held it was very fitting, it being the
highest act of devotion, that it should be taken in the
humblest posture that could be, upon the knees; the other,
being a Puritan, oppos'd it, and the dispute grew high, but
it ended without much heat.   The next day being both
come home to dinner from their business abroad, the eldest
Brother, as it was his custom, took a nap upon a cushion at
the end of the table, that he might be more fresh for labour.
The Puritan Brother, call'd *Enoch Evans,* spying his opportunity, fetch'd an axe, which he had provided it seems on
purpose, and stealing softly to the table, he chopp'd off his
Brother's head :   The old Mother hearing a noise, came suddenly from the next room, and there found the body and
head of her ·eldest Son both asunder, and reaking in hot
Blood :   *O Villain!* cried she, *hast thou murder'd thy Brother?*
Yes, quoth he, *and you shall after him;* and so striking her
down, he dragg'd her body to the threshold of the door, and
there chopp'd off her head also, and put them both in a bag :
But thinking to fly, he was apprehended and brought before
the next Justice of Peace, who chanced to be Sir *Robert*
Howard; so the Murderer the Assizes after was condemn'd,
and the Law could but only hang him, tho' he had committed
Matricide and *Fratricide.*

I will fetch another example of their cruelty from *Scotland.*
The late Marquis of *Montrose,* being betray'd by a Lord in
whose house he lay, was brought prisoner of War to *Edin-*
burgh; there the common Hangman met him at the Towns-
end,

end, and first pull'd off his hat, then he forc'd him up to a
Cart, and hurried him like a condemn'd person, tho' he had
not yet been arraign'd, much less convicted, through the
great street, and brought him before the Parliament; where
being presently condemn'd, he was posted away to the
Gallows, which was above thirty Foot high. There his hand
was cut off first, then he was lifted up by pullies to the top,
and then hang'd in the most ignominious manner that could
be. Being taken down, his head was chopp'd off, and nail'd
to the high Cross; his arms, thighs, and legs, were sent to
be set up in several places, and the rest of his body was
thrown away, and depriv'd of Christian burial. Thus was
this Nobleman us'd, tho' one of the ancient'st Peers of *Scotland,* and esteem'd the greatest honour of that Country both
at home and abroad. Add hereunto the mortal cruelty they
us'd to their young King, with whom they would not treat
unless he first acknowledg'd his Father to be a Tyrant, and
his Mother an Idolatress, *&c.*

So I most humbly kiss your hands, and rest always,
Madam—Your Ladyship's most faithfully devoted Ser-
vant,   J. H.
London, 30 *Aug.*

XLIV.

To Sir. L. D., *in* Paris.

NOBLE KNIGHT,

YOURS of the 22d current came to safe hand; but what
you please to attribute therein to my Letters, may be
more properly applied to yours in point of intrinsic value:
For by this correspondence with you, I do as our *East-India*
Merchants use to do, I venture beads and other bagatels,
out of the proceed whereof I have pearl and other oriental
jewels return'd me in yours.

Concerning the posture of things here, we are still involv'd
in a cloud of Confusion, 'specially touching Church-matters:
A race of odd crack-brain'd Schismatiques do croak in every
corner; but, poor things, they rather want a Physician to

cure

cure them of their madness, than a Divine to confute them of their errors. Such is the height of their spiritual pride, that they make it nothing to interpret every tittle of the *Apocalypse;* they make a shallow rivulet of it, that one may pass over and scarce wet his ankles; whereas the greatest Doctors of the Church compar'd it to a deep Ford wherein an Elephant might swim. They think they are of the Cabinet-Council of God, and not only know his Attributes, but his Essence: Which made me lately break out upon my pillow into these metrical Speculations:

1. *If of the smallest Stars in Sky*
   We know not the Dimensity;
   If those bright Sparks which them compose,
   The highest mortal Wits do pose,
      How then, poor shallow Man, can'st thou
      The Maker *of these* Glories *know?*

2. *If we know not the* Air *we draw,*
   Nor what keeps Winds *and* Waves *in awe;*
   If our small skulls cannot contain
   The flux *and* saltness *of the Main;*
      If scarce a Cause we ken below,
      How can we the Supernal *know?*

3. *If it be a mysterious thing*
   Why Steel *should to the* Loadstone *cling;*
   If we know not why Jett *should draw,*
   And with such kisses hug a Straw;
      If none can truly yet reveal
      How sympathetic Powders heal:

4. *If we scarce know the* Earth *we tread,*
   Or half the Simples *there are bred,*
   With Minerals, *and thousand things*
   Which for Man's health and food she brings;
      If Nature's *so obscure, then how*
      Can we the God *of Nature know?*

5. *What the* Bat's *eye is to the* Sun,
   Or of a Gloworm *to the* Moon,

The

The same is Human *Intellect,*
If on our Maker *we reflect,*
Whose Magnitude is so immense,
That it transcends both Soul and Sense.

6. *Poor purblind Man, then sit thee still,*
Let wonderment thy Temples fill ;
Keep a due distance, do not pry
Too near, lest like the silly Fly,
While she the wanton with the flames doth play,
First fries her Wings, then fools her Life away.

There are many things under serious debate in Parliament, whereof the results may be call'd yet but the imperfect productions of a grand Committee ; they may in time come to the maturity of Votes, and so of Acts.

You write that you have the *German Diet,* which goes forth in my name ; and you say, that *you never had more matter for your money.* I had valued it the more ever since, in regard that you please to set such a rate upon't : For I know your opinion is current and *Sterling.* I shall shortly by *T. B.* send you a new History of *Naples,* which also did cost me a great deal of oil and labour.

Sir, if there be anything imaginable wherein I may steed or serve you here, you well know what interest and power you may claim both in the Affections of my Heart, and the Faculties of my Soul. I pray be pleas'd to present the humblest of my service to the noble Earl your Brother, and preserve still in your good opinion—Your truly obliged Servant,   J. H.

XLV.

To Sir E. S., Knight.

SIR,

NOW that the *Sun* and the *Spring* advance daily towards us more and more, I hope your health will keep pace with them ; and that the all-searching beams of the first will dissipate that fretful humour, which hath confin'd you so long to your Chamber, and barr'd you of the use of your

true

true supporters. But tho' your Toes be slugs, yet your Temples are nimble enough, as I find by your last of the 12th current; which makes me think on a speech of *Severus* the Emperor, who having lain sick a long time of the *Gout* at *York,* and one of his Nobles telling him that he wonder'd much how he could rule so vast an Empire, being so lame and unwieldy, the Emperor answer'd, that *He rul'd the Empire with his Brain not with his Feet:* So it may be said of you, that you rule the same way the whole State of that Microcosm of yours, for every Man is a little World of himself.

Moreover, I find that the same kind of spirit doth govern your Body as governs the great World, I mean the celestial Bodies: For as the motions whereby they are regulated are musical, if we may believe *Pythagoras,* whom the Tripod pronounc'd the wisest Man; so a true harmonious Spirit seems to govern you, in regard you are so naturally inclin'd to the ravishing Art of Musick.

Your Friends here are well, and wish you were so too: For my part, I do not only wish it, but pray it may be so; for my Life is the sweeter in yours, and I please myself much in being—Your truly faithful Servant, J. H.

1 *Martii.*

XLVI.

To Mr. Sam. Bon, *at his House in the* Old Jury.

SIR,

I RECEIV'D that choice parcel of Tobacco your Servant brought me, for which I send you as many returns of gratitude, as there were grains therein, which were many (and cut all methinks with a Diamond cut), but too few to express my acknowledgment. I had also therewith your most ingenious Letter, which I valued far more: The other was but a potential Fire, only reducible to smoke; but your Letter did sparkle with actual Fire, for methought there were pure flames of Love and Gentleness waving in every line. The Poets do frequently compare Affection to Fire;

therefore

therefore whensoever I take any of this *Varina*, I will imagine that I light my Pipe always at the Flames of your Love.

I also highly thank you for the *Italian* Manuscripts you sent me of the late Revolutions in *Naples*, which will infinitely advantage me in exposing to the World that Stupendous piece of Story. I am in the arrear to you for sundry courtesies more, which shall make me ever entitle myself—
Your truly thankful Friend and Servant,   J. H.
Holborn, 3 *June.*

XLVII.

To W. Sands, *Esq.*

SIR,

THE Calamaties and Confusions which the late Wars did bring upon us were many and manifold, yet *England* may be said to have gain'd one Advantage by it ; for whereas before she was like an Animal that knew not his own strength, she is now better acquainted with herself, for her Power and Wealth did never appear more both by Land and Sea. This makes *France* to cringe to her so much. This makes *Spain* to purchase Peace of her with his *Italian* Patacoons : This makes the *Hollander* to dash his colours, and veil his bonnet so low unto her : This makes the *Italian* Princes, and all other States that have anything to do with the Sea, to court her so much. Indeed, touching the Emperor, and the *Mediterranean* Princes of *Germany*, whom she cannot reach with her Cannons, they care not much for her.

Nor indeed was the true Art of governing *England* known till now ; the Sword is the surest sway over all People, who ought to be cudgell'd rather than cajol'd to obedience, if upon a glut of plenty and peace they should forget it. There is not such a windy wavering thing in the world as the common People ; they *are got by an Apple, and lost for a Pear ;* the Elements themselves are not more inconstant : So that it is the worst solecism in Government for a Prince to depend merely upon their Affections. Riches and long
Rest

Rest make them insolent and wanton : It was not *Tarquin's* wantonness so much as the People's, that ejected Kings in *Rome;* it was the People's Concupiscence, as much as Don *Rodrigo's* Lust, that brought the *Moors* into *Spain,* &c.

Touching the Wealth of *England,* it never also appear'd so much by public Erogations and Taxes, which the Long Parliament rais'd : Insomuch, that it may be said the last King was beaten by his own Image more than anything else. Add hereunto, that the World stands in Admiration of the capacity and docibleness of the *English,* that Persons of ordinary Breeding, Extraction, and Callings, should become Statesmen and Soldiers, Commanders and Counsellors, both in the Art of War and Mysteries of State, and know the use of the Compass in so short a tract of time.

I have many thanks to give you for the *Spanish* Discourse you pleas'd to send me; at our next conjuncture I shall give you an Account of it : in the interim I pray let me have still a small corner in your thoughts, while you possess a large room in mine, and ever shall while   JAM. HOWEL.

XLVIII.

To the R. H. the E. of S.

MY LORD,

SINCE my last, that which is the greatest Subject of our discourses and hopes here, is the Issue of our Treaty with the *Dutch :* It is a piece that hath been a good while on the Anvil, but it is not hammer'd yet to any shape. The Parliament likewise hath many things in debate, which may be call'd yet but Embryo's, in time they may be hatch'd into Acts.

The Pope, they write, hath been of late dangerously sick, but hath been cur'd in a strange way by a young *Padua* Doctor, who having kill'd a lusty young Mule, clapp'd the Patient's Body naked in the Paunch thereof; by which gentle fomentation he recover'd him of the Tumours he had in his Knees and elsewhere.

Donna *Olympia* sways most, and hath the highest ascendant

dant over him; so that a Gentleman writes to me from *Rome*, that among other Pasquils this was one, *Papa magis amat* Olympiam *quam* Olympum. He writes of another, That the Bread being not long since grown scant, and made coarser than ordinary by reason of the Tax that his Holiness laid upon Corn, there was a Pasquil fix'd upon a corner-stone of his Palace, *Beatissime Pater, fac ut hi lapides fiant panes;* O blessed Father, grant that these Stones be made Bread. But it was an odd Character that our Country-man Dr. *B.* gave lately of him, who being turn'd *Roman* Catholic, and expecting a Pension, and having one day attended his Holiness a long time about it, he at last broke away suddenly; a Friend of his asking, why? he replied, It is to no purpose for me to stay longer, for I know he will give me nothing, because I find by his Physiognomy that he hath a negative Face. 'Tis true, he is one of the hard-favoured'st Popes that sat in the Chair a great while; so that some call him *L'Huomo de tre pele,* The Man with three Hairs; for he hath no more Beard upon his Chin.

St. *Mark* is still tugging with the great *Turk*, and hath bang'd him ill-favouredly this Summer in *Dalmatia* by Land, and before the *Dardanelli* by Sea.

Whereas your Lordship writes for my *Lustra Ludovici*, or the History of the last *French* King and his Cardinal, I shall ere long serve your Lordship with one of a new Edition, and with some Enlargements. I humbly thank your Lordship for the favourable, and indeed too high a character you please to give of my *Survey of Venice;* yet there are some who would detract from it, and (which I believe your Lordship will something wonder at) they are Cavaliers, but the shallowest and silliest sort of them; and such may well deserve the epithet of *Malignants.* So I humbly kiss your hands in quality of—Your Lordship's most obedient and ever obliged Servant, J. H.

XLIX.

XLIX.

To the R. H. the Earl Rivers, at his House in Queen-street.

MY LORD,

THE least command of yours is enough to set all my Intellectuals on work; therefore I have done something, as your Lordship shall find herewith, relating to that gallant Piece call'd *The Gallery of Ladies*, which my Lord Marquis of *Winchester* (your Brother) hath set forth.

Upon the glorious Work of the Lord Marquis of
Winchester.

1. *THE World of Ladies must be honour'd much,*
   That so sublime a Personage, that such
   A noble Peer, and Pen, should thus display
   Their Virtues, and expose them to the day.

2. *His Praises are like those coruscant Beams*
   Which Phœbus *on high Rocks of Crystal streams:*
   The Matter and the Agent grace each other,
   So Danae *did when* Jove *made her a Mother.*

3. *Queens, Countesses and Ladies, go unlock*
   Your Cabinets, draw forth your richest stock
   Of Jewels, and his Coronet adorn
   With Rubies, Pearl, and Saphires yet unworn.

4. *Rise early, gather Flowers now i' th' Spring,*
   Twist wreaths of Laurel, and fresh Garlands bring
   To crown the Temples of this high-born Peer,
   And make him your Apollo *all the year:*
   And when his Soul shall leave this earthly Mine,
   Then offer sacrifice unto his Shrine.

I send also the *Elegy* upon the late Earl of *Dorset*, which your Lordship spake of so much when I waited on you last; and I believe your Lordship will find therein every Inch of that noble Peer characteris'd inwardly and outwardly.

2 S   An

An ELEGY upon the most accomplish'd and heroick Lord, *Edward* Earl of *Dorset,* Lord-Chamberlain to his late Majesty of *Great Britain,* and Knight of the most Noble Order of the Garter, *&c.*

Alluding to
{
The Quality of the Times.
His admired Perfections.
His goodly Person.
His ancient Pedigree.
His Coat of Arms crested with a Star.
The Condition of Mortality.
The Author's Passion, closing with an Epitaph.
}

LORDS have been long declining (we well know)
    And making their last Testament ; but now
They are defunct, they are extinguish'd all,
And never like to rise by this Lord's fall :
A Lord whose Intellectuals alone
Might make a House of Peers, and prop a Throne,
Had not so dire a Fate hung o'er the Crown,
That Privilege Prerogative should drown.
    Where-e'er he sat, he sway'd, and Courts did awe,
Gave Bishops Gospel, and the Judges Law,
With such exalted reasons, which did flow
So clear and strong, that made *Astrea* bow
To his Opinion ; for where he did side,
Advantag'd more than half the Bench beside.
    But is great *Sackville* dead ? Do we him lack,
And will not all the Elements wear black ?
Whereof he was compos'd, a perfect Man,
As ever Nature in one frame did span :
Such high-born Thoughts, a Soul so large and free,
So clear a Judgment, and vast Memory,
So princely, hospitable, and brave Mind,
We must not think in haste on earth to find,
Unless the Times would turn to Gold again,
And Nature get new strength in forming Men.
    His Person with it such a State did bring,
That made a Court as if he had been King.

No

No wonder, since he was so near a-kin
To *Norfolk's* Duke, and the great Maiden-Queen.
He Courage had enough by conqu'ring one,
To have confounded that whole Nation :
Those Parts which single do in some appear,
Were all concentred here in one bright Sphere.
  For Brain, Tongue, Spirit, Heart, and Personage,
To mould up such a Lord will ask an Age.
But how durst pale white-liver'd Death seize on
So dauntless and heroic a Champion ?
Yes, to die once is that uncancell'd debt
Which Nature claims, and raiseth by Eschet
On all Mankind, by an old Statute past
Primo Adami, which will always last
Without Repeal ; nor can a second Lease
Be had of Life when the first Term doth cease.
Mount noble Soul, among the Stars take place,
And make a new one of so bright a Race :
May *Jove* out-shine, that *Venus* still may be
In a benign Conjunction with Thee,
To check that Planet which on Lords hath lour'd,
And such malign Influxes lately pour'd.
Be now a Star thyself, for those which here
Did on thy Crest, and upper Robes appear :
For thy Director take that Star, we read,
Which to thy Saviour's Birth three Kings did lead.

A Corollary.

*T**HUS have I blubber'd out some Tears and Verse*
      On this renowned Heroe, and his Herse ;
And could my Eyes have dropt down Pearls upon't
In lieu of Tears, God knows, I would have don't :
But Tears are real, Pearls for their Emblems go,
The first are fitter to express my Woe.
Let this small Mite suffice, until I may
A larger tribute to his Ashes pay ;
    In the meantime this Epitaph *shall shut,*
    And to my Elegy *a period put.*

HERE

*H*ERE *lies a* Grandee *by Birth, Parts, and Mind,*
    Who hardly left his Parallel behind.
Here lies the Man of Men, *who should have been*
An Emperor, *had* Fate *or* Fortune *seen.*

          Totus in lachrymas solutus, sic
                 singultivit, *J. H.*

   So I most humbly kiss your Lordship's hands, and rest
in the highest degree of service and affection, ever most
ready—At your Lordship's command,   J. H.

Lond., 20 *Dec.*

L.

To T. Harris, *Esq.*

SIR,

*Y*OURS of *Dec.* 10. I had the 2d of this *January*, and I
    account it a good Augury that it came so seasonably
to usher in the New-year, and to cheer up my thoughts,
which your Letters have a virtue to do always whensoever
they come, they are so full of quaint and copious quick
expressions. When the *Spaniards* at their first Coalition
in the *West-Indies* did begin to mingle with the *Americans,*
that silly People thought that those little white Papers and
Letters which the *Spaniards* us'd to send one to another,
were certain kind of Conjurers or Spirits that us'd to go up
and down to tell tales, and make discoveries. Among other
examples, I remember to have read one of an *Indian* Boy
sent from a *Mexico* Merchant to a Captain, with a Basket
of Figs and a Letter. The Boy in the way did eat some of
them, and the Captain, after he had read the Letter, ask'd
him what became of the rest? Whereat the Boy stood all
astonish'd; and being sent with another Basket a little after
to the same party, his maw began to yern again after some
of the Figs, but he first took the Letter and clapt it under a
great stone hard by, upon which he sat while he was eating,
thinking thereby that the Spirit in the Letter could not
discover him, *&c.* Whether your Letters be Spirits or no,
I will not dispute, but I am sure they beget new Spirits in
                                 me

me; and *quod efficit tale illud ipsum est magis tale;* if I am possess'd with *melancholy,* they raise a Spirit of *mirth* in me; if my thoughts are contracted with *Sadness,* they presently dilate them into *Joy, &c.,* as if they had some subtil invisible *Atoms* whereby they operate; which is now an old Philosophy newly furbish'd, and much cried up, that all natural Actions and Motions are perform'd by emission of certain Atoms, whereof there is a constant effluvium from all elementary bodies, and are of divers shapes, some angular, others cyclindrical, some spherical; which Atoms are still hovering up and down, and never rest till they meet with some pores proportionable and cognate to their figures, where they acquiesce. By the expiration of such Atoms the Dog finds the scent as he hunts, the Pestilence infects, the Loadstone attracts Iron, the *Sympathetick* Powder or *Zaphyrian* Salt calcined by *Apollinean* heat, operating in *July* or *August* till it come to a lunary complexion; I say, by the virtue and intervention of such Atoms, 'tis found that this said Powder heals at a distance, without topical applications to the place affected. They who are of this opinion, hold that all sublunary Bodies operate thus by Atoms, as the heavenly Bodies do by their Influences. Now it is more visible in the Loadstone than any other Body; for by help of artificial Glasses a kind of mist hath been discern'd to expire out of it, as Dr. *Highmore* doth acutely, and so much like a Philosopher, observe. For my part, I think it more congruous to Reason, and to the course of Nature, that all Actions and Motions should be thus perform'd by such little atomical Bodies, than by Accidents and Qualities, which are but notional things, having only an imaginary subsistence, and no essence of themselves at all, but as they inhere in some other. If this Philosophy be true, it were no great absurdity to think that your Letters have a kind of atomical energy which operates upon my Spirits, as I formerly told you.

The Times continue still untoward and troublesome; therefore now, that you and I carry above a hundred years upon our backs, and that those few grains of Sand which

remain

remain in the brittle glasses of our lives are still running out, it is time, my dear *Tom,* for us to think on that which of all future things is the most certain, I mean our last removal, and emigration hence to another World : 'Tis time to think on that little hole of earth which shall hold us at last. The time was, that you and I had all the fair Continent of *Europe* before us to range in; we have been since confin'd to an Island, and now *Lincoln* holds you, and *London* me : We must expect the day that sickness will confine us to our Chambers, then to our Beds, and so to our Graves, the dark silent Grave, which will put a period to our pilgrimage in this World. And observable it is, what method Nature doth use in contracting our liberty thus by degrees, as a worthy Gentleman observes.

But tho' this small bagful of Bones be so confin'd, yet the noblest part of us may be said to be then set at liberty, when having shaken off this slough of flesh, she mounts up to her true Country, the Country of Eternity; where one moment of Joy is more than if we enjoy'd all the pleasures of this World a million of years here among the Elements.

But till our Threads are spun up, let us continue to enjoy ourselves as well as we can; let those grains I spoke of before run gently by their own motion, without jogging the glass by any perturbation of mind, or musing too much upon the Times.

Man's life is nimble and swift enough of itself, without the help of a Spur, or any violent motion : Therefore he spoke like a true Philosopher, who excepted against the title of a Book call'd *De statu vitæ,* for he should rather have entitled it *De cursu vitæ;* for this Life is still upon the speed.

You and I have luckily met abroad under many Meridians; when our course is run here, I hope we shall meet in a Region that is above the wheel of Time : And it may be in the concave of some Star, if those glorious Lamps are habitable. Howsoever, my Genius prompts me, that when I part hence I shall not downwards ; for I had always soar-

ing

ing thoughts being but a Boy, at which time I had a mighty desire to be a Bird, that I might fly towards the Sky.

So my long-endeared Friend, and Fellow-Traveller, I rest —Yours verily and invariably,   J. H.

Holborn, 10 *Jan.*

To the Sagacious Reader.

U T clavis portam, sic pandit Epistola pectus ;
Clauditur Hæc cera, clauditur Illa sera.

As *Keys* do open Chests,
So *Letters* open Breasts

T E Λ O Σ.

Gloria Lausq ; Deo Sæculorum in sæcula sunto.

A DOXOLOGICAL Chronogram including this present year MDCLV. and hath numeral Letters enough to extend to the year Nineteen hundred twenty seven, if it please God this World should last so long.

SUPPLEMENT.

—•—

LETTERS, &c, OF AND ABOUT HOWELL

NOT PREVIOUSLY COLLECTED.

Mainly from Unpublished Sources.

I.

To Lord Conway.

(Pub. Rec. Off. Stat. Pap. Dom. Chas. I. xix. No. 100.)

Right hon^ble
&
my very good Lo :
There is a partie that hath lately hanted the Court who
may be fufpected to come for no good. his father was an
englifh Minifter & chaplaine to Sr Charles Cornwallyes & afterward an officer to ye Inquifition in ye Court of Spaine where
he obtained a penfion for himfelf, his wief & children.
This man (a bufie pragmaticall fellowe) comes from Bruffells
& hath dependencye on Gondamar.
Yo^r lo : may pleafe to comand that he be brought before yo^u by
thefe bearers who tell me wilbe employed by yor lo : in ocafions
of this nature So I moft humbly take my leaue & will euer liue
Yo^r lo : moft faithfull
Servant
Ja Howell

The partie's name is
James Wadefworth.

Middle Temple
this Thurfday

(*Endorsed*).

(*Endorsed*).

[Seal, a double headed bird, salient.]

Januarii 1625
Mr. Howell
Giuinge infomaſoñ of
a fuſpecſted pſon one
Wadſworth.

To yᵉ right hon^{ble} my
very good Lo : yᵉ lord
Conway principall Secreatary
to his Matie
    att Court

II.

THE EARL OF SUNDERLAND TO LORD VISC. WENTWORTH.
(Stafford *Letters*, i. p. 48.)

My very good Lord

I underſtand your Lordſhip hath beſtowed the next Attorney's Place in Reverſion at York upon James Howell, my Secretary, I muſt thank you for it, and the rather becauſe he hath deſervingly and faithfully ſerved me in that Place, wherin I hear your Lordſhip hath ſucceeded me. I wiſh you much Happineſs in it, & reſt very faithfully

Your Lordſhip's Friend
E. SUNDERLAND.

Sᵀ MARTIN'S LANE
Dec. 15. 1628.

III.

TO THE LORD VISC^T WENTWORTH, LORD PRESIDENT OF THE NORTH.
(Stafford *Letters*, i. p. 50.)

My ever honoured good Lord,

Herewith I ſend your Lordſhip the inſtrument you pleaſed to paſs unto me for the reverſion of the next Attorney's place in York, for which, by your Lordſhip's appointment, Mr Radcliffe hath given me ſatiſfaction. I was always and ſhall ever continue ſo ſenſible of ſo free and noble a favour, that in the whole courſe of my life I ſhall endeavour to make Expreſſions of my Thankful-neſs, and how much I am,

My Lord
Your Lordſhip's
Moſt true and humble ſervant.
JA. HOWELL.

Sᵀ MARTIN'S LANE
May 5. 1629.

IV.

IV.

LEGATIO COMITIS LEICESTRIÆ IN DANIAM 1632.

(Bodl. MS. Rawl. C. 354.)

Diarium et fidelis relacio Legacionis Illuſtiſſimi Comitis Ley-ceſt[r]encis ad Chriſtianum quartum Regem Daniæ, etc. Jacobo Howell Oratore.

Deſignatus fuit Legatus extraordinarius ad Chriſtianum quartum Regem Daniæ et alios principes Danica ſtirpe oriundos, Regi-æque Magnæ Brittaniæ Maieſtati materno ſanguine coniunctos, Robertus Sydneius Comes Leyceſtriæ, vt luctum ageret pro morte Reginæ *Sophiæ* Frederici ſecundi vxoris, Regum, Magnæ Brittaniæ, Daniæque Matris et Auxœ : et de alijs arduis maximique ponderis negotijs tractaret.

Regia Magnæ Brittanniæ Maieſtas ſe declarabat 6° Aprilis 1632 ſed retroſpiciens quatuor integros menſes in mandatis dedit (regij in dictum Comitem fauoris gratiâ) vt litteræ priuati ſigilli inchoarent 6° Decembris proxime præcædentis, ex quo die con-ſignatæ fuerunt dicto Comiti octo libræ pro quotidiano ſalario, vſque dum ad regiam perſonam reuerteretur.

Vale dixit Regiæ Maieſtati in ædibus *Oatlandiæ* 16° Auguſti, ciuus, pro more oſculatis manibus cum primarijs generoſum qui eum in hac legatione concomitabantur, et duabus mille libris anticipatis, cum teſſeris numarijs Philippo Burlemachi firmatis in Hamburgho recipiendis, ad iter ſeſe accinxit ; Ab ædibus ſuis in Penſhurſt diſceſſit 14° Septembris cum quibuſdam domeſticis famulis verſus Roſſam, vbi integer ſuus comitatus ex numero circiter 55 perſonarum conſiſtens, inter quas plurimi erant genero-ſiſſima proſapia oriundi (quorum primarius fuit Phillippus Baro de Liſle dicti Comitis primogenitus) excellentiæ ſuæ præſtolabantur.

A dicta vrbe tribus currubus et numeroſo equorum Cohorte vehebatur ad *Margetts* vbi marium Admirallus *Penington* (hoc enim titulo tunc temporis fungebatur) in regia Naue *Conuertina* dictum Dom. Legatum expectabat.

Qua Naue, vento Noto-Zephiro ſtrenuè afflante, tridui ſpacio appulit in flumine Alvis et pedem ſigens *Glucstadio* dimorabatur ibi 4' diebus, Deinde conductus fuit a Gubernatore dicti loci regijs currubus et 50 ad minimum apertis vehiculis ad Rendeſ-burgum in terra Holſatica vbi Rex Comitijs interfuit. Hoſpitium Dom. Legato deſignatum fuit in ædibus cuiuſdam Juriſperiti, et reliquis ſui Comitatus in alijs domibus, vbi ſpacio integræ heb-domadis ſumptu Regio epulabatur, 50 circiter Regijs famulis ad inſeruiendum conſtitutis.

Princeps

Princeps Fredericus fecundus regijs Daniæ filius Coadiutor Epifcopatûs Bremenfis, poftridie decoro generoforum agmine ftipatus dictum Dominum Legatum inuifit, et die fequente Det lief Ranzouius nobilium Holfatiæ primarius et ditiffimus. 7° die poft appulfum fuam in dicto loco, admiffus fuit Dominus Legatus ad Arcem Regis, magno generofum Aulicorum numero, et 50 ex proprio Comitatu pullatis veftibus et atratis penulis fub longis decoro agmine fuam perfonam circumeuntibus. Deductus ad præfentiam regiam D. Jacobus Howell (qui erat a fecretis dicto Domino Legato) oracionem quandam encomiafticam inchoauit in laudem defunctæ Reginæ, qua ad finem perducta et literis credentialibus a domino legato regijs manibus oblatis, ad Chriftianum 5um Regis primogenitum electum Daniæ principem, fefe vertit cum fimili Oratione, et deinde ad Fredericum dicti Regis filium fecundum (ambo enim prope Regem circumftabant); Hoc peracto refponfum fuit dictis Orationibus a Doctore Doorne Jurifperito, et regis [sic] apertis vlnis Dominum Legatum amplectente, et manus primarijs fui Comitatûs ad ofculandum porrigente, reductus fuit eodem Comitatu ad Hofpitium fuum.

Poftridie poftulauit Dominus Legatus (condignas agendo grã pro regio fauore) vt prop[r]ia quadra fe aleret et famuli Regis manumitterentur quod (vnoquoque eorum qui inferuierant ample et magnus fice renumerato) conceffum fuit. Poftero die aliam obtinuit audientiam Dominus Legatus, quâ propofitiones in paginis fubfequentibus infertas folemni modo Regijs manibus exhibuit, quibus proximo die refponfum fuit, Rege prima luce verfum Gluckftadium comigrato, Cui triduo poftea Reduci dictus dominus Legatus alias tradidit propofitiones, quibus etiam fubito refponfum fuit, a quibufdam confiliarijs ad hoc ex induftria defignatis, vt in paginis fubfequentibus conftat.

Poftremò, definitiua Regis Daniæ ad dictas propofitiones habita Refolutione, poftulauit Dominus legatus colloquium cum ante memoratis Confiliarijs, quod concessum fuit, et in quodam angulo Ecclefiæ Cathedralis conuenientis, omnia ea quæ a Domino Legato prius fuerant propofita, cum fingulis Regis Daniæ refponfis perlecta, difcuffa ac euentilata ffuerunt, In quo colloquio Dictus Dominus Legatus in fauorem Reginæ Bohemiæ multa Inftructiones fuas excedentia) prop[r]ium honorem patrimoniaque tangentia ad conciliandam auitam hæreditariam portionem propofuit, quibus Durus Auunculus furdas præbuit aures.

Triduo poftea vocatus fuit Dominus Legatus ad epulandum regiâ menfa cum fuo comitatu, vbi liberis pro more, compotationibus vfque ad vefperum protractum fuit prandium. Poftero die Rex ante lucano tempore Gluckftadium tendit iter, Dominufque Legatus ad Gottorpium Frederici Ducis Holfatiæ, (Regis

Danorum

Danorum Nepotis ex forore) Arcem, et inde ad Hufem, ad Auguftam Duciffam viduam Holfatiæ Danorum Regis fororem, proficifcitur, Quibus in locis intra muros Arcium hofpitatus, comiter receptus, et magnificè epulatus eft.

Illinc ad Hamburghum fefe contulit vbi a fenatoribus dictæ Ciuitatis et Anglis Mercatoribus honorificè tractatus fuit; Et ROBERTUM ANSTRUTHERUM ex aula Cæfareâ nuperrimè Reducem legatum, conueniens, eum fecum perduxit cum dicto Admirallo Penington, et regia Naue Conuertina, in Angliam, et ventis minime fauentibus, poft velificationem dierum appulit dictus dominus Legatus apud Margatts, 3° die Decembris inde vere die fubito vectus fuit ad Aulam vbi ad regias manus ofculandas fubitò admiffus, exactiffimam reddebat rationem vniuersæ legationis, fumma cum Regiæ Maieftatis fatiffactione, et indelebili fuipfius honore.

V.

To SIR F. WINDEBANK.

(Pub. Rec. Off. Dom. Chas. I. ccxlv. No. 33.)

Right hon^ble

The packett to Orleans was fafely fent, but j well hoped to haue had ere nowe fome newes from thence, confidering the ftrictnes of frequent correfpondence we agreed vpon at the time of our feparation; from other places there came pofts this week, as Bruxells & Holland, the one brings newes that ye treaty being nowe vtterly diffolud, the ftates Army is in the field againe, & had a defigne to make fudden incurfions vp and downe Brabant & plunder the Countrey before them, but ye enemies army gathering into a head, & ye Boores rifing vp p'uented them. It feemes ther is fome defigne on both fides, for ther was lately a Bidday by ye one and a Bead-day by the other folemnly enioynd. The Spaniards fortifie apace ye Ifle of St. Stephen & Arfen wch they haue lately taken, being both vpon the Maze, to block vp all approches that way towards Maeftricht & make it ripe for a next yeares fiege, for they haue ben mafters of ye field a good while, but now that ye Hollander hath had fome recreuts & thefe new addicōns of forces from Germany & a late fupply of 200^m crowns from France, he hath bruffled vp his feat here againe & is vpon the offenfiue.

From Germany aduife comes, that ye d. of Friedland hath made more deep inrodes into Saxony & taken Lipfick & Holk is before Erford.

The Duke of Feria hath croft the Hills and is come to Alfatia,

Alfatia, to affift y° Lorainer, & relieve Nancy (as the Frencs did Cafal) fome fay y° King is already before y° towne, but tis thought he may throw [his cap at it, as Charles y° Emperour did when he was forc'd to burne his tente, & fly by Torchlight ; the Dukes fifter was lately come thither but gott out difguifed & came in mans habitt to Luxembourg whence fhe was brought to Bruxells. Our Turky Marchants are like to fuffer much by a fight y' happened lately in y° Archiepielago twixt 2 Englifh fhipps of Alderman Freemans, who contrary to y° Capitulacoñs of peace betweene vs & the great Turk taking in a cargazon of corne for Italie & pceiuing] the 7 Gallies of Rhodes to make towards them, by way of preuention fearing to be furprif'd, they lett fly at them, funk y° generall & flew y° Bafha with diuers others, y° 6 gallies y' remaind went & gaue aduife to y° great fleet hard-by confifting of 80 gallies more who (as they yearly do) were come to leuy, & cary home y° Turks tribut from Greece & other parts adjacent, & in a dead calme made way to y° 2 fhippes deuiding themfelfs into 4 fquadrons. The fhipps having betweene them 140 men, & nere vpon 50 peeces of Ordinance refifted manfully (p'ferring death before flauery) & funk 6 of y° gallies, killed 2000 Turks, & fought till they were reduced to that extremity y' fetting fyre to both y° fhipps thofe wch remaind being not many leapt unto y° fea & fo were taken vp prifoners but y° great fleet of gallies is fo tottered & torne that they haue loft this yeares voyage & returnd to the Port (confantinople) empty. The Confulls and Marchants feare fome barbarifme wilbe offered vpon their perfons, or at leaft fome fearfull auenia vpon their goods, this is Alderman Freemans relacion. The Lo ; denbigh is returned from y° great Mogor full of jewells. So with my very humble obferuance j reft ready

Att yor Lo : comandm^ts
JAMES HOWELL.

WESTMINSTER, this 28 of
Aug: 1633.

(Endorsed).

28 Aug. 1633
Mr. Howell rec. at
To the right hon^ble S^r   Bags Efs. 4 Sept.
Francis Windebank
Knight principall Secretary
of State, & one of his Maties
moft hon^ble priuy Counfell
this

VI.

VI.

DR. T. HOWELL TO SIR F. WINDEBANK.

(Pub. Rec. Off. Dom. Chas. I. cccxiii. No. 2.)

Honorable S[r]

I am truly forry and afham'd to heare that my brother hath Lately broken in vpon you, foe farre beyond y[e] bounds of common modefty. Wether I have not longe groan'd vnd[r] the weight of fome iealous thoughts, and accordingly complain'd, leaft happily he might be troublefome to y[r] Hono[r] and I alfo might fuffer with him, befide this euidence, I am fure Dr. Turner will teftify wth me w[ch] put me divers tim's vpon a purpofe to cleare my felfe. But fince it is nowe growne foe high, leaft any mif-prifion fhould fettle, as touching me, I am forc't thus to addreffe my felfe to y[r] Hono[r] for my owne iuftificaōn. yf eu[r] therefore I have found any fauo[r] in y[r] fight (not that I knowe any iuft caufe for it faue only y[r] owne goodnes) Let me humbly befeech you, fince he fayles meerely by the Card and compaffe of his owne Genius, that his actions may not any way reflect upon me, but that each of vs w[th]out any relacōn to other, may ftand or fall in y[r] opinion, according to y[e] refultance of his pticular deeds, and the quality of his owne fingle conu'faōn. for then, I am confident for my owne pt, that I fhall doe nothinge to deferve y[r] iuft difpleafure, though I doe not flatter myfelfe, that by any ftrength or merit of mine I can winne vpon y[r] fauo[r] faue only in this, that (as zealoufly as any oth[r]) I doe & will eu[r] wifh y[e] continuance & enlargem[t] of all profpity both to y[r] Hono[r] & all yours, & fhall moft gladly embrace any oportunity that you fhall vouchfafe to giue, or I can take, to expreffe my felfe

Y[r] Hono[rs] affectionate and
humble fervant
THO: HOWELL.

WALBROOKE 2 ffebr. 1635.

(*Endorsed*).

To the Honorable S[r] Francis
Windebanke, principall Secretary
of State to his Ma[ty]
p'fent thefe.

2 Feb. 1635
D. Howell.
[Seal, a bird with
wings extended.]

VII.

VII.

MR. HOWELL TO THE LORD DEPUTY.
(Stafford *Letters*, i. 488).

My moſt honoured good Lord,

The late coming of the Prince Palatine is the greateſt news here at preſent, he ſtaid windbound five weeks at Fluſhing, having launched out twice and been beaten back. About Dover, the three Hollands' Men-of-War, which tranſported him, paſſing by ſome of the King's Ships my Lord of Lindſey had left in the Downs, Sir John Pennington giving a volley of ſhot, one of the Cannons having a Bullet in it grazed over the Ship where the Palſgrave was, & killed four of his Train, for which the Gunner is like to ſuffer. There are various opinions of the reaſon of his coming, that which ſounds beſt is, that he is come to endear him-ſelf to his Uncle, & follicite his own Buſineſs, & know what to truſt to, to advance the Treaty of the Match with Poland, and do ſome good offices for the Hollanders who are brought to a low ebb, the ſtream having turned extreamly againſt them this Summer; though in the Indies it hath run as much with them, having made themſelves ſole Maſters of the Staple & Trade of Sugars in Braſil (though nobody is the better for it but them-ſelves) whither the Spaniard hath a great Fleet going or gone from Liſbon.

From Germany there is late advice that the ſquandered Rem-nants of Swedes, which were towards the Baltick Sea, made head under Bannier, and have given a ſmart blow to the Duke of Saxe.

The French ſhuffle yet well enough upon the Frontiers of Germany & Lorrain. The Queen-Mother is a dying in Ghent in Flanders in a religious Convent. The French Cardinal bears up ſtill, though Hatred and Danger increaſe daily. The Cardinal Ginetti, the Pope's Legate de Latere, is not yet come to Conſtance. I believe it will be the Spring before he come. Now that the Peace is concluded betwixt the Pole and the Swede by the Inter-vention of the Kings of England and France, the Parliament ſits in Poland about the Match with the young Lady Elizabeth : Mr. Gordon went thither hence, from whom there is news daily ex-pected. The *Ban & Arriere Ban* in France is diſmiſſed for this Winter, & ſome diſbanded themſelves, of whom ſome received exemplary Puniſhment. The Siege is ſtill continued by Crequy before Valencia upon the Territories of Milan.

For home matters, there hath been much grief at Court lately for the Loſs of two noble Lords, the Lord of St Albans and my

Lord

Lord Savage, efpecially the latter. There are two or three Houfes fhut up in Greenwich, though there died none but out of one. The Bufinefs betwixt Sir And. Pell and Sir James Bagge was determined lately in the Star Chamber, & I never heard a Caufe fo equally canvaffed, of the eighteen Judges nine fined him & the other quitted him, & my Lord Keeper's odd Voice carried it; but I hear that it will prove no cenfure, the redundant Voice being to be for Mercy and not Juftice. They fay my Lord Bifhop of Lincoln's Pardon is ready to pafs the great feal with a perfect Redintegration into the King's Favour, Abolition of all old Matters, & my Lord Cottington had a great hand in it. The four youngeft Prebends of Weftminfter have eagerly banded them-felves againft him lately divers ways.

There is a Lottery afoot for bringing in frefh waters by Aquæ-ducts into the Covent Garden (where the new Town is almoft finifhed) & White Hall. There have been lately new Impofitions fet upon Wines and Linnen Cloth & other Commodities, which is thought will enhance his Majefty's Cuftoms £80,000 a year. The Levy of the Ship money in Towns & Country is done, & the Money almoft come in: there is a Computation made, it will amount to two Subfidies & an half. There is nought elfe worth the Advertifement, therefore I muft humbly take my Leave, refting ever

Your Lordfhip's
truly devoted Servant
Jam. HOWELL.

WESTMINSTER
Nov. 28. 1635.

VIII.

HOWELL'S APPOINTMENT AS CLERK OF COUNCIL.
(Privy Council Minutes.)

Att the Court att Nottingham the 30th of Auguft 1642.

Prefent

Lord Keeper	Lo. Vifc. Savile
Lo. D. of Richmond	M' Comptroler
Lo. g. Chamberlaine	M' Secr Nicholas

This day James Howell Efq' was by his Ma^{ts} command fworne clark of the Counfell in extraordinary.

2 T

XI.

IX.

To my Honored and Known Friend, Sir I. C. Knight.

(12 Tr. pp. 169–71.)

Sir,

Among many other Barbarifmes which like an impetuous Torrent have lately rufh'd in upon us, the interception and opening of Letters is none of the leaft, For it hath quite bereft all ingenious Spirits of that correfpondency and fweet communication of fancy which hath bin alwaies efteemed the beft fuel of affection and the very marrow of friendfhip. And truly, in my judgment, this cuftom may be termed not only a *Barbarifme*, but the bafeft kind of *Burglary* than can be, 'tis a plundering of the very brain, as is fpoken in another place.

We are reduced here to that fervile condition, or rather to fuch a height of flavery, that we have nothing left which may entitle us free Rationall creatures; the *thought* it felf cannot fay 'tis free, much lefs the *tongue* or *pen*. Which makes me impart unto you the traverfes of thefe turbulent times under the following fables. I know you are an exquifite Aftronomer. I know the deep infpection you have in all parts of Philofophy, I know you are a good Herald, and I have found in your Library fundry books of Architecture and Comments upon *Vitruvius*. The unfolding of thefe Apologues will put you to it in all thefe, and will require your fecond, if not your third thoughts, and when you have concocted them well, I believe (elfe I am much deceived in your Genius) they will afford you fome entertainment and do the errand upon which they are fent, which is, to communicate unto you the moft material paffages of this long'd-for Parlement, and of thefe fad confufions which have fo unhing'd, diftorted, traverf'd. tumbled and diflocated all things, that England may be termed now, in comparifon of what it was, no other than an *Anagram of a Kingdom*. One thing I promife you, in the perufal of thefe Parables. that you fhall find no gingles in them, the common dialect and difeafe of thefe times. So I leave you to the gard and guidance

Of God and Vertu who do ftill advance
Their Favorite, maugre the Frownes of Chance

Your conftant fervitor
J. H.

X.

X.

To Sir K. Digby.

(*Twelve Treatifes*, p. 194.)

Sir, I long to receive your opinion of thefe rambling pieces of fancy, you may peradventure, have more, when the times are open; furely the wind will not hold ftill in this unlucky hole, for it is too violent to laft. It begins (thanks be to God) to fift already, and amongft thofe multitudes, who expect the change, I am one that lyeth at the *Cape of Good Hope*, though a long time under hatches (in the *Fleet*). Howfoever, though all the winds in the compafs fhall blufter upon me; nay though a *Haraucana* fhould rage, I am arm'd and refolv'd to bear the brunt, to welcome the Will of God, and poffeffe my foul with patience.

If you defire a further intimation of things, I refer you to a Difcourfe of mine call'd *The Tru Informer*, who will give you no vulgar fatiffaction. *So I am*

> *Yours, as at firft, inalterable*
> *J. H.*

XI.

Dedication to Vol. II. of Letters.

To His Highnes James Duke of York; A Star of the greateft Magnitude in the Conftellation of Charles-Wayn.

Sir,

This Book was engendred in a Cloud, born a Captive, and bred up in the dark fhades of Melancholy: He is a true *Benoni* the fon of forrow, nay, which is a thing of wonderment, He was begot in the Grave by one who hath been buried quick any time thefe five and fifty months: Such is the hard condition of the Author, wherein he is like to continue, untill fome good Angell roll off the ftone, and raife him up, for *Prifoners* are capable of a double Refurrection: my *Faith* afcertains me of one but my *fears* make me doubtfull of the other, for, as far as I fee yet, I may be made to moulder away fo long among thefe walls, till

I

I be carried hence with my feet forward : Welcom be the will
of God and the Decrees of Heaven.

>   Your Highneffes, moft
>   humble and moft
>   obedient Servit^r
>   JAMES HOWELL.

From the Prifon
of the Fleet
this *May* day
1647.

XII.

To JOHN SELDEN.
Brit. Mus. *Harl.* 7003 f. 374.

S^r

The principall aym of this fmal prefent is to bring you thanks
for the plefure & profit j haue receaud from yor Works wherwith you haue enrichd the whole Comon Wealth of Lerning, &
wherin may be difcoverd fuch a fullnes & vniverfality of knowledg that it may well be fayed Quod Seldenus nefcit, nemo fcit,
And this was a kind of character that fome of the renownedft
men beyond the feas gaue of you in fom difcourfe j mingled
with them : Moreouer thefe fmall peeces (wch j fhalbe bold to
pourfue with a vifit) com to introduce mee to yor knowledg not
you to mine, for it were an Ignorance beyond Barbarifm not to
know you : May you pleafe when (having nothing elf to do) you
haue caft yor eys vpon them to throw them into fom corner of
the loweft fhelf that ftands in yor library wher it wilbe an honor
for them to be found herafter, & if thefe bee admitted j haue more
to follow. So hoping that this obligation will not be held an
intrufion j reft

(*Endorsed.*)   S^r
For the moft Honored   Yo^r moft humble & ready
John Selden Efq^r   fervit^r
   this.   JAM. HOWELL.

XIII.

XIII.

To THE COUNCIL OF STATE.
(Brit. Mus. Add. 32,093, f. 370).

It is humbly offerd to ye Confideration
of
The Right Honble ye Counfell of State

That, Wheras vpon this Change of Government, & devolution of Intereſt from kingly power to a Comõn Wealth ther may happen fom queſtion touching the primitiue and Inalienable Right that Great Britain claymes to the Souuerainty of her own feas as hath allready appeerd by the late claſh that broke out twixt vs & Holland (which may well be fayed to be a Comon Wealth of England's Creation;) It were expedient, humbly under favor, that a new Treatife be compiled for the vindication, and continuance of this Right notwithſtanding this Change; And if the State be pleafed to impofe fo honorable a comand vpon y^r Subfcriber Hee will employ his beſt abilities to perform it; In which Tretife not only all the learned Reafons & Authorities of Mr. Selden ſhalbe produced, but the Truth of the Thing ſhalbe reinforcd and afferted by further arguments, Examples and Evidences; And it were requiſit that this fayed Treatife ſhold go publiſhed in French as well as Engliſh, French being the moſt comunicable language of Comerce among thofe nations whom the knowledg herof doth moſt concern, and fo may much avayle to difperfe the truth, & fatiffie the world in this point

JAM HOWELL.

(*Endorsed.*)
Mr. Howell
dominion Sea.

XIV.

To JUDGE RUMSEY.
(*Organon Salutis*, Pref.)

To his Highly eſteemed Friend and Compatriot Judge *Rumfey*, upon his *Provang*, or rare peĉtoral Inſtrument and his rare experiments of Cophie and Tobacco.

Sir,
    Since I knew the World, I have known divers forts of *Inſtruments:* The firſt that I was acquainted withall, was *Ariſtotles Organon*

Organon, or Inftrument at *Oxford:* Another was the great happy Inftrument at *Munfter:* The third was the *Inftrument* which was made after the diffolution of the late *long Parliament; That* in *Oxford* was *Inftrumentum Logicæ*, The Inftrument of Logick; That in *Munfter* was *Inftrumentum Pacis*, The Inftrument of Peace; The laft was *Inftrumentum Politicum*, The Inftrument of Policy. Now your Inftrument is moft properly called *The Inftrument of Health*, and may take place among the reft. Without controverfie, it was an Invention very happily lighted upon, and obligeth all mankinde to give you thanks: For he who finds out any thing conducing to humane health, is the beft Cofmopolite, the beft among the Citizens of the World; health being the moft precious Jewel of Nature, without which we cannot difcharge our duties to God or Man. But indeed there's no perfection of health in this life, when we converfe with the Elements; the beft is a valitudi-nary kinde of difpofition; and this proceeds from the perpetual conflict of the humors within us for predomination; which were they equally ballanced, and in peace *Methufelah's* yeers would be but a fhort life among us. Now this Combate and malignity of the Humors arifeth from the ftomach; which like a boyling pot on the fire, is ftill boyling within us, and hath much froth; whence, if the concoction be not very good, there are il-favoured fumes, and fuliginous evaporations that afcend into the head; where being diftill'd they defcend into Catarrhes and Defluxions, fome-times upon the Optiques, and that may be called the Gout in the Eyes; if they fall upon the Teeth, it may be call'd the Gout in the Mouth; if into the Hands 'tis *Chiragra;* if in the Hip, *Sciatica;* if in the Knees, *Gonagra;* if in the Feet, *Podogra.* Now, Sir, *Your Inftrument* ferves to take away the grounds of thefe Dif-tempers, by rummaging and fcouring the ftomach, and make it expectorate that froth, or phlegmy ftuffe which lodgeth there, and that in a more gentle manner than any Drugge. 'Tis true that *Rhubarbe* is good againft Choler, *Agarick* againft Phlegme, and *Hellebore* againft Melancholy, but they ufe to ftir the humours fo violently by their naufeoufnes, that their operation is a fickneffe of it felf all the while: Your Inftrument caufeth no fuch thing, nor leaves any lurking dreggs behinde, as *Druggs* ufe to do.

Touching *Coffee*, I concurre with them in opinion, who hold it to be that black broth which was uf'd of old in *Lacedemon*, whereof the Poets fing; Surely it muft needs be falutiferous, becaufe fo many fagacious, and the wittieft fort of Nations ufe it fo much; as they who have converfed with *Shaftres* and *Turbants* doe well know. But befides the exficcant quality it hath to dry up the crudities of the ftomach, as alfo to comfort the Brain, to fortifie the fight with its fteem & prevent Dropfies, Gouts, the

Scurvie

Scurvie, together with the fpleen, and Hypochondriacal winds (all of which it doth without any violence or diſtemper at all) I ſay, beſides all theſe qualities, 'tis found already, that this *Coffee* drink both cauſed a greater Sobriety among the Nations: for whereas formerly Apprentices & Clerks with others uſed to take their mornings draught in Ale, Beer, or Wine, which by the dizzines they cauſe in the Brain, make many unfit for buſineſs, they uſe now to play the Good-fellows in this *wakeful* and civil drink: Therefore that worthy Gentleman, Mr. *Mudiford*, who introduced the practice hereof firſt to *London*, deſerves much refpect of the whole Nation.

Concerning *Tobacco* which the *Spaniards* call *la Yerva santa*, the holy herb, in regard of the ſundry virtues it hath: without doubt 'tis alſo a wholſom vegetal, if rightly applyed and ſeaſonably taken; it helps concoction, makes one void Rheume, break winde, and keeps the body open: A leaf or two ſteeped in white Wine, or Beer over night, is a Vomit that never fails; It is a good companion to ſedentary men, and ſtudents, when they are ſtupified by long reading or writing, by diſſipating thoſe Vapours which uſe to o're-cloud the Brain: The ſmoak of it is paſſing good againſt all contagious airs; In ſo much, that if one takes two or three puffs in the morning, before he goes abroad, there's no infectious air can faſten upon him; for it keeps out all other ſents, according to the Axiome, *Intus exiſtens prohibet alienum.*

But, Sir, I find you have made other experiments of theſe two ſimples, which though not ſo guſtfull, conduce much to humane health: And touching your *Provang*, or Whale-bone Inſtrument, let me tell you, that it hath purchaſed much repute abroad among Forreiners; In ſo much, that ſome, in imitation of yours, have found a way to make ſuch an Inſtrument in ductible Gold, and you know what a Cordial Gold is. I have been told of another kinde of new Inſtrument that will conveniently reach from the mouth, to let in the ſmoak of Tobacco at the fundament, and it hath done much good. Certainly, there are in Natures Cabinet many boxes yet undiſcovered, there are divers myſteries and Magnalia's yet unknown; there be ſundry effects which ſhe would produce, but ſhe wants the hand of Art to co-operate, as it were by the hand of Mid-wifery: the World muſt needs confeſs that you have done her a great good Office herein.

So with my heartly kinde refpects unto you, wiſhing that ſome happy occaſion were offered, whereby I might be *Inſtrumental* unto you, I reſt, Worthy Sir,

Your moſt affectionate
Friend and Companion,
JAMES HOWELL.

XV.

XV.

To Sir Edward Walker.
(Autograph collection of Mr. A. Morrison.)

S'

Now that a correfpondence may bee kept with more freedom and that neither writer or letter run fo much danger of fhippwrack j thought it not amiffe to give you this invitation in that kind; Touching affairs here, fince the late Diffolution of the Parlement the counfell of State carry all the Sway finoothly before them, & Monk profeffeth ftill an exact & conftant obedience to the Civill power. The Anababtifts have fhewd their teeth lately, but they are kept from biting, for a great ftore of armes were taken away lately from them; Generall Monk fticks ftill clofe to the Citty of London who made a privat ouverture lately to the counfell of State, how Trade was lamentably delayed, And the Mint ftarvd, and that ther was no way to feed the one and advance the other without a peace with Spaine, wch was impoffible to bee done but by calling in king Charles. Tis thought certainly ther wilbe a a Houfe of Peers the next Parlement wch will infallibly begin 25° of Aprill ftylo loci; The new militia is upon fettling in the countrey, and divers Lords, knights & others of good principles are chofen Comiffioners among whom the Earle of Oxford is chief for Effex, Dorfett for Suffex, Rivers for Chefhire, etc.

If I knew that this letter would come fafely to Hand, I wold bee more large which upon yo' anfwer to this I fhalbe in my next.

I pray Sir fend mee word whither my Lo: of Briftoll bee return'd to Bruxells fo I moft affectionatly kiffe yo' hands & if ther bee any thing imaginable wherin I may ferve you here you know what power you haue to comand

Much honored Sir
Yo' very humble & ready
Servant
JAM. HOWELL.

LONDON, *this 23rd of March*, 1659.

From Mr. Lee a Lawyers Houfe ag' the Pye Inne in Fetter Lane where I fhalbe ready to receave yo' addreffes & comands.

(*Endorfed*).
For the much Honored
S' Edward Walker
Knight at the Englifh
Court in Bruxells.

XVI.

XVI.

A letter of Advice confifting all of Proverbs (running in one congruous and concurrent fenfe) to one that was Towards Marriage, *Lexicon Tetraglotton.*

Sir,

Although I am none of thofe that love to have an Oare in every ones Boat, Or fuch a bufie body as deferves to be hitt in the teeth, that I fhould keep my breath to cool my pottage, yet, you and I having eaten a peck of falt together, and having a hint that you are upon a bufinefs that will either make or mar you, for a man's beft fortune or his worft's, a Wife, I would wifh you to look before you leap, and make more than two words to a bargain.

'Tis true that Marriages are made in Heaven, it is alfo true that Marriage and hanging goeth by Deftiny ; But if you are difpofed to marry, marry a fhrew rather than a fheep, for a Fool is fulfome, yet ye run a rifk alfo in the other, for a fhrew may fo tye your nofe to the Grindftone, that the gray Mare will prove the better Horfe ; Befides, there is another old fayed Saw, that every one knows how to tame a fhrew but he that hath her ; If it be your Fortune to meet with fuch a one, fhe may chance put you to the charge of buying a long fpoon, for he muft have a long fpoon who will eat with the Devill.

Moreover, if you needs muft marry, do not fetch your wife from *Dunmow*, for fo you may bring home two fides of a Sow, Nor from *Weftminfter*, for he who goeth to *Weftminfter* for a Wife, to *Pauls* for a Man, and to *Smithfield* for a Horfe, may have a Jade to his Horfe, a Knave to his Man, and a Wagg-tail to his Wife.

But if you needs muft marry let her rather be little than bigg, for of two evils the leaft is to be chofen, yet there is another hazard in that alfo, for a little pott is foon hott, and as fhe will be little and lowd, if you give her an inch fhe will take an ell, fhe will alwayes have a *Rowland* for your *Oliver*, and two words for one, fuch a Wife though fhe be as tender as a Parfons Lemman, yet fhe may prove a wolf in Lambs fkinn, Inftead of a Rofe you will have a Burr ; If you meet with fuch a one, you may be put to anfwer as he was who having a damnable fcold to his Wife, and being afked by Sir *Tho: Badger* who recommended her unto him ? he fayed an old Courtier, Sir ; *what Courtier ?* fayed Sir *Tho:* 'Twas the Devill, Sir.

Furthermore take heed of two hanfome a Wife, for then fhe is likely not to be all your own, and fo fhe may bring you to your

Horn-book

Horn-book again, or rather make you Horn-madd, and then you
have brought your Hoggs to a fair Market.

But by all means, be wary of too coftly and lavifhing a Wife,
for fo you may quickly turn a Noble to nine pence, and come
home by broken Croffe, fhe will in a fhort time make hunger to
dropp out at your nofe, fhe will thwitten a Mill-poft to a pudding-
prick, the Goofe will drink as deep as the Gander, and then,
When all is gone and nothing left, what waits the Dagger with
the dudgeon heft? The Wolf will be then ftill at your door, and
the black Ox will tread on your toe, your Neighbours will make
mowes at you, and fay, you are as wife as *Walthams* Calf, who
went nine miles to fuck a Bull and came home more thirfty than
when he went.

You muft alfo be wary how you marry one that hath caft her
Rider, left you fall into a Quagmire wherein another was loft, I
mean a Widdow, for fo you will be fubjeét to hav a Deaths head
putt often in your Difh; Touching the complexion of your Wife,
the *Spaniard* holdeth black to be the wholefomeft, for He hath
a Proverb, *Muger negra trementina en ella*, A black woman hath
Turpentine in her, the *Frenchman* is for the broun, when he faith,
Fille brunette gaye & nette, A broun Laffe is gay and cleanly,
But they both will tell you, that touching a red-haired and
bearded woman, falute them a hundred paces off.

Laftly, take heed by all means of doting fo far upon any one
Female, as to marry her for meer Affeétion; 'Tis true, that one
hair of a woman will draw more than a hundred yoake of Oxen,
yet meer Affeétion is but blind Reafon, and there are more
Mayds than Malkin; 'Tis true that in love ther's no lack, yet it
is as true, that nothing hath no favour, and there muft be Suet as
as well as Oatmeal to make a Pudding; In this cafe it is better
to buy a Quart of Milk by the penny than keep a Cow, and to
follow the Italian Proverb, *videlicet*, Commend the Sea, but keep
thy felf afhoar, Commend the Hills, but keep thy felf on the
Plains, Commend a wedded Life but keep thy felf a Batchelor;
According to another wife Proverb, He who marrieth doth well,
but he who marrieth not, doth better; Wherunto attendeth a third,
That next to a fingle Life, a married Life is beft; I will conclude
with that of the *Italian*, Honeft men ufe to marry but Wife men not.

When you read this, I know you will be apt to fay, that a
Fools Bolt is foon fhott, or crie out, Witt whither wilt thou? yet,
though I am none of the feven Sages, I can look as farr into a
Milftone as another, and you know that the ftander by feeth
more then the Gamefter.

What I write is the Language of a Friend, and could I fteed
you herein I would do it with as good a will as ever I came from

                                                    School

School, for I am yours as much as any Wife can be, or rather, that I may conclude with the old *Roman* Proverb, I am Yours, *Usque ad Aras*

Yours to the Altar

J. H.

XVII.

To Charles II.

(Pub. Rec. Off. Dom. Chas. II. i. No. 116.)

To the Kings moſt exᵗ Maᵗⁱᵉ

The humble petᵒⁿ of James Howell Eſqʳ

Sheweth, That hauing bin by his late Maᵗⁱᵉˢ imediat comand ſworne one of the Clerks of his Privy Counſell about 18 yeers ſince, And coming to London a little after vpon his Maᵗⁱᵉˢ affairs, he was comitted one of the firſt priſoners in the Fleet where he lay above 8 yeers, & continued vnder bayle 7 years after during which time hee was plunderd 3 feverall times to his vtter vndoing.

Hee humbly prays yoʳ Maᵗʸ wold pleaſe to comand that he may be confirmd in the ſayed place, Or that yoʳ Maᵗʸ would be graciouſly pleaſed to haue him in yoʳ Royall thoughts ſome other way for a Liuelihood

And Hee ſhall pray euʳ

JAM HOWELL.

(Enclosure.)

The Caſe truly ſtated

When the Court was at York j was comanded by my Lord of Briſtol to attend the King one morning in his Bedchamber, when his Maᵗʸ told me, *That he wold giue orders to ſweare me Clerk of the Counſell in Secr: Nicholas his place, but he was ptly engaged to Sʳ Jo: Jacob, & if he had it not, j ſhold haue it prefently, howfoeuʳ ſᵈ his Maᵗʸ, j will giue order you ſhalbe ſworne now, & yᵗ firſt place that falls you ſhalbe ſure of it*, Vpon wᶜʰ words j had yᵉ honor to Kiſſe his hand, ſo his Maᵗʸ Himſelf gaue comand to Sʳ Dudley Carleton to ſweare me, wᶜʰ was done accordingly before divers privy Counſellors.

Sʳ Jo: Jacob keeping ſtill in theſe Parts quitted his deſigne that way, & j coming a little after to London, & being vpon point of returning prcſently to Court, j was app'rhended & comitted priſoner prifoner to ye Fleet vnder ye notion of a dangerous perfon by ye Long Parlement where j lay clofe aboue 8 years notwithftanding my often petitioning for my enlargement, & continued 7 years after vnder good bayl to be forth coming within fo many howers during wch traverfes j was plunderd 3 times.

The time y^t j was fworn ther were but 3 Clerks of the Counfell viz. Sr Tho: Mewtis, Sr Dud; Carlton, & Sr Rich: Brown wherof ye 2 firft died a while after during my imprifonment, yet fince, ther haue bin three Clerks gott over my head ett^s

JAM. HOWELL.

XVIII.

To CHARLES II.

(Pub. Rec. Off. Dom. Chas. II. xvii. No. 6.)

To the Kings moft ex^t Matie
    The humble pet^{on} of James Howell Efq^r
    Clerk of the Counfell to his late Maiefty
        of ever bleffed Memory
Sheweth, That wheras yor Ma^{ty} is gracioufly pleafed for the Regula-
tion & aduancement of Trade to award a Royall Comiffion to fome of the knowingft Marchants, & others whom yor Ma^{ty} fhall pleafe to nominat for the intent aforefayed And wheras yor pet^r hath bin verfd & employd by their late Maties in affaires of that nature to Spaine, Germany, & Denmark
        He prayeth, yor Matie wold pleafe to comand that He may ferve yor Matie in quality of an Affiftant & Secretary to the fayed Comiffion, & He fhall employ his beft endevours to acquit himfelf to his duty therein
                    And duly pray ett^s.

XIX.

To LORD CLARENDON.

(Dom. Chas. II., xxxix., No. 52).

My Lord,
    Yo^r lo^{pp} having bin pleafd to promife mee the contribution of yor favour, j take this great boldnes to defire, yor lo^{pp} wold pleafe to move his Matie that j may attend the la: Infanta (who comes to be our Queen) in quality of Her Tutor for Languages :
                                                            For

For having the Spanifh Toung (with the Portuguez dialeél) As allfo yᵉ Italian & French both for the Praélice and Theory fo farr that j have publifhed a Great Diélionary with Grañars to all the Three dedicated to the King at his firfl coming (for which his Maᵗˡᵉ promifed to fett a mark of his favor vpon me) of which Diélionary j was not wanting to prefent yoʳ loᵖᵖ with one, Having allfo a compendious choice method of Inflruélion I hope j fhalbe thought par negotio, which in all humblenes is left to confideration by

Yoʳ loᵖᵖˢ mofl obedient
and ready fervant
JAM HOWELL.

(*Endorsed.*)
R. 11° July 1661
Mʳ Jam : Howell
to be Tutor for Languages

To my Lo : Chancelor   to yᵉ Queen.

XX.

GRANT TO HOWELL.

(Pub. Rec. Off. Signet Office Docket, Feb. 1661.)

Warrant to the Excheqʳ to pay to James Howell Efqʳ yᵉ fumm of 200ˡˡ as of his maᵗⁱˢ free guift wᵗʰ out accᵗ. Subfcʳ by Mʳ Berd by warrant under his maᵗᵉ Sign manuall ut fupra.

XXI.

JAMES HOWELL'S WILL.
(Somerfet Houfe I. Carr. 323.)

London j4° 8ᵇᵘˢ j666.

[Iacob' Howell.]   In The name of God Amen. y Iames Howell of the Parifh of Sᵗ Andrews in Holborn Efquire : being fickly in body but well in mind and memory doe make this my lafl will and teflament. Aboue all I bequeath my foule to him that gaue it my eternall God and maker. I Defire my body may be carried decently in a herfe : And buried in the Middle Temple Church as privately as can be Att the ffoote of the next great Piller This fide the little Quier where I have direéted Mʳ Marfhall to fett up a large Black Marble with a Braffe Piéture of

mine

mine in the Middle with my Armes and a Latin Epitaph. Touching my worldly goods I bequeath vnto my brother Howell Howell
Twenty ffive pounds To my fifter Gwin fforty fhillings to buy her
a Ring And fforty fhillings to my fifter Roberta Ap-Rice I bequeath
vnto my niece Elizabeth Banifter Twenty pounds and my filver
watch with my beft Cloak and fuite I bequeath vnto my Nephew
Arthur Howell ffour pounds and my light coloured Coate with my
Montero Capp I bequeath vnto my Nephew George at Oxon
fforty fhillings my feale of Armes my Standifh and Privat Clafped
Prayer booke I bequeath Mrs. Leigh my Landlady Tenn pounds
for her felfe and towards the Portion of her daughter Edith. Item
I bequeath ffoure pounds to one Strafford a Heelmaker by Somerfet
Houfe. Of this my will I make my nephew Henry Howell fole
Executor and Adminiftrator not doubting but he will fee the pre-
mifes performed accordingly Witnefs my hand and feale

JAM: HOWELL

In the prefence of J. Lowe /

Memorandum that I leave Mr. Playford the Sexton of the
Temple Church twenty fhillings to buy him a Ring / Mr. Brife of
Old-ftreete ffoure pounds to be fpeedily paid / Item to Mr. Matthew
Pinder an old Jacobus to buy him a Ring / All the reft of my
worldly goods [I] leave to my p'fent Executo' Except Thirty pounds
in a white Bagg which is defigned for a Tomb wherein I defire
my Executor to be very carefull / Iam: Howell / In the p'fenfe of
I. Lowe.

[Proved by Henry Howell 18 Feb. 1666–7.]

SUPPLEMENT II.

DOCUMENTS, &c., OF AND ABOUT HOWELL.

Mostly from Unprinted Sources.

XXII.

HOWELL AND THE POWDER OF SYMPATHY.

(Sir K. Digby. *A Late Difcourfe . . . touching the cure of Wounds by the Powder of Sympathy. . . . Rendered . . . by R. White. Second edition.* 1658, p. 6–11.)

Mr *James Howell* (well known in France for his publick works, and particularly his *Dendrologia*, tranflated into French by *Monfieur Baudoin*), coming, by chance, as two of his beft friends were fighting a duel, he did his endeavour to part them, and putting himfelf between them, feized with his left hand vpon the hilt of the fword of one of the Combatants, while with his right hand he laid hold of the blade of the other, they being tranfported with fury one againft the other, ftrugled to rid themfelves of the hindrance their friend made that they fhould not kill one another; and one of them roughly drawing the blade of his fword, cuts to the very bone the nerves and mufcles of Mr. *Howel's* hand; and then the other difengaging his hilts, gave a crofs blow on his adverfaries head which glanced towards his friend, who, heaving vp his fore hand to fave the blow, he was wounded on the back of his hand, as he had been before within. . . . They bound up his hand with one of his garters to clofe the veines which were cut and bled abundantly. They brought him home and fent for a Surgeon. But this being heard at Court, the King fent one of his own Surgeons, for his Majefty much affeéted the faid Mr *Howel.*

It was my chance to be lodged hard by him; and four or five

days after, as I was making myfelf ready, he came to my Houfe and prayed me to view his wounds, for I vnderftand, faid he, that you haue extraordinary remedies vpon fuch occafions, and my Surgeons apprehend fome fear that it may grow to a Gangrene, and fo the hand muft be cut off. . . . I told him that I would willingly ferve him, but if haply he knew the manner how I could cure him, without touching or feeing him, it may be he would not expofe himfelf to my manner of curing, becaufe he would think it peradventure either ineffectual or fuperftitious; he replyed, That the wonderfull things which many have related vnto me of your way of curing, makes me nothing doubt at all of its efficacy; and all that I have to fay vnto you is comprehended in the *Spanifh* Proverb, *Hagafa el milagro y hagala Mahoma*, Let the miracle be done, though Mahomet do it.

I afked him for anything that had the blood vpon it, fo he prefently fent for his Garter wherewith his hand was firft bound : and having called for a Bafon of water, as if I would wafh my hands, I took a handfull of Powder of Vitriol, which I had in my ftudy, and prefently diffolved it. As foon as the bloody garter was brought me, I put it in the Bafon, obferving in the interim what Mr *Howel* did, who ftood talking with a Gentleman in a corner of my Chamber, not regarding at all what I was doing : but he ftarted fuddenly, as if he had found fome ftrange alteration in himfelf; I afked him what he ailed ? I know not what ailes me, but I find that I feel no more pain, methinks that a pleafing kind of frefhneffe, as it were a wet cold Napkin did fpread over my hand, which hath taken away the inflamation that tormented me before. I replyed, fince that you feel already fo good an effect of my medicament, I advife you to caft away all your playfters, onely keep the wound clean and in a moderate temper twixt heat and cold. This was prefently reported to the Duke of *Buckingham*, and a little while after to the King, who were both very curious to know the circumftance of the bufineffe, which was that after dinner I took the Garter out of the water and put it to dry before a great fire ; it was fcarce dry, but Mr *Howel's* fervant came running that his mafter felt as much burning as ever he had done if not more, for the heat was fuch as if his hand were betwixt coals of fire : I anfwered . . . I know the reafon of this new accident . . . Therevpon he went, and at the inftant I did put again the garter into the water : therevpon he found his Mafter without any pain at all. To be brief, there was no fenfe of pain afterward ; but within five or fix dayes the wounds were cicatrized, and entirely healed.

XXIII.

XXIII.

JAMES HOWELL TO SECRETARY NICHOLAS.

(*Record Office, S.P. Dom. Chas. I.*, v. ccxx. 70).

S^r

My lord of Leicefter being nominated Embaffad^r extraordinary for Denmark intends to embarque himfelf at North yarmouth, therefore his lo^p defires y^t Captaine Pennington who is appointed to tranfport him thither in ye Convertine fhold be at that port with all conuenient fpeed, and in the interim that one of the whelps fhold come to Tilbury to take in his furniture and ordinary fort of Servants, and to go about to the great fhipp, and to attend him to the Sound where his lo^{pp} intends, god willing, to land; yo^u may pleafe to gett a warrant for Cap. Pennington to this effect, fo I reft

Yo^r very affecoñate
Seruant
JA: HOWELL.

WESM^r *this*
15 *of July* 1632.

(*Endorsed*).

To my worthy
good frend Edward
Nicholas efq^r at his
houfe in
Weftm^r this

[*in Nicholas' script*]
16° July 1632
Mr Howell to me
about a fhipp for
· · my lo: of Leifter.

XXIV.

JAMES HOWELL TO CAPT. PENNINGTON.

(*Rec. Off. S.P. Dom. Charles I.*, ccxxi. 34).

S^r

My lo: of Leicefter being appointed Embaffad^r extraordinary for Denmark it hath pleafed his Matie to nominat yo^u to tranfport him thither, my lord was very glad at the election, and willd me to intimate fo much vnto yo^u with his kind commends. He intends to land at Elfinore for w^h place he doubts not but yo^u will make choyce of an expert pylot, when yo^u have landed my lo: embaffad^r Weston in France, he defires yo^u wold make all the conuenient fpeed yo^u can to Tilbury where he intends to embarque the greateft number of his traine wch in all will come to about

about 50 : and his furniture ; he hoped to haue had one of ye whelps to go along wth him, but they being employed elfewife he muft make ye bolder with ye Kings fhipp. When yo^u haue taken in his furniture & Seruants at Tilbury, he defires yo^u wold [make] about for North yarmouth, where his lo: purpofes to embarque himfelf, & make prouifion for his extraordinaries. Mr Nicholas told me y^t he hath allready fent yo^u a warrant from ye Lords Com^{rs} to this effect and for a pylot. Therefore I will trouble yo^u no further at this time

Yo^r humble feruant
JA: HOWELL.

WESTM^r *this*
25 of July
1632.

(*Endorsed*).

To my much
honored friend Captaine
Pennington aboard his
Maties fhipp royall the
Conuertine this

[*In Pennington's script*]
A lett^r from M^r
Howell ye E of
Leifters Secretary
25th July 1632.

XXV.

JAMES HOWELL TO CAPTAIN PENNINGTON.

(*Rec. Off. S.P. Dom. Chas. I.*, ccxxii. 59).

Much honored S^r

In my laft j acquainted yo^u with fome ocafions of delaye, as yo^u well knowe employments of this nature are comonly fubiect vnto, that haue fomewhat retarded my lord embaffad^{rs} proceedings for his intended voyage but, god willing, againft Saturday next or Munday at furtheft the hoy wilbe ready to carry my lords feruants & furniture to yo^u. My lord purpofed to haue fent his fleward to yarmouth before, to make prouifion for frefh victualls, but vnderftanding how Sr Henry Vane & others haue bin accomodated by yo^u, his lo^{pp} hath purpofe to know whither conueniently & wthout trouble yo^u can do the like courtefie for him, for wch he will haue a confideracoñ in fuch a degree of noblenes that fhall giue yo^u euery way contentment. his lo^{pp} will haue at his owne table, befide himfelf, fome 8. or 9. befides of feruingmen, footmen, and cokes, ther fhalbe fent in the hoy a buck or two baked in pies, & 4. or 5. of ye faireft chines of beefe pickled, & fome wine. S^r I defire to know fpeedily by this bearer, whither my lord fhall relye
vpon

vpon yo^u for this or no. I. prefume my lords voyage wilbe at an end at Hamborough. So in haft I ceafe & reft

Yo^{rs} to ferue yo^u
JA. HOWELL.

29° *of Aug.*
1632.

(*Endorsed*).

To my much honored
frend Captaine Pennington
aboard his Maties Shipp_j
royall at Margett-road
the Conuertine
This

[*In Pennington's script*]
1632
A lett^r from Mr. Ja.
Howell y^e
29 Auguft 1632.

XXVI.

JAMES HOWELL TO CAPTAIN PENNINGTON.

(*Rec. Off. S.P. Dom. Chas. I.*, ccxxii. 10).

Much honored S^r

Yo^{rs} of the 30th of the laft was deliuered me by the fame meffenger j fent, I comunicated ye particulars thereof to my lord embaffad^r and his lo^{pp} is nowe refolued to go for the Elve & no further; and to embarque himfelf with his whole traine at Margett, & herein (as formerly for not coming to Tilbury by reafon of the flatts) he approues of yor aduife & intends, god willing, to followe it.

Ther are fome addicoñs made to the Embaffage wch is the reafon of this delay, & truly my lord thinks ye time tedious that he is not aboard of yo^u, to morrowe we lade the Hoy, fo that j hope fhe wilbe with yo^u on Saturday, & vpon Wenefday following or Thurfday at fartheft my lord, god willing, intends to be at Margett with his whole trayne; in the interim if yo^u pleafe to comaund yor feruants (nowe that it is a fett voyage) to make a competent prouifion for my lords table, and his company of whofe number j acquainted yo^u in my laft, my lord will efteeme it a very fpeciall fauour. So vntill my next wch fhalbe by the hoy, I kiffe yor hands and reft

Yo^{rs} to ferue yo^u
JA HOWELL.

I am fory my laft
except one mifcarried,
for j trufted to M^r
Nicholas his conueyance.

WESTM^r *this*
5 *of* 7^{ber} 1632.

(*Endorsed*).

(Endorsed).

To my moſt honored frend
Captaine Pennington aboard
his Maᵗⁱᵉˢ ſhipp the
Conuertine in Margett
Road this
with ſpeed.

[*In Pennington's script*]
A lettʳ from Mʳ
Howell yᵉ 7 7ʰᵉʳ
1632.

XXVII.

ADMIRAL PENNINGTON'S LOG.

(*Hiſt. MSS. Comm.* 10. iv. 278–9.)

[1632] Sept. 12. Wee received my Lord of Leiſter's baggage and
ſome of his ſervants.

13. Wee weyed . . . and flood in as neere Margett as wee could,
where my Lord Ambaſſador imbarked himſelf—about 8 a
clock—with all his trayne, at which inſtant wee ſtood of
to ſea.

16. About noone we made the Flye.

17. About 7 a clock in the morninge wee had ſight of Holbike
Land [Heligoland]. . . . About one a clock in the after-
noone wee were as high as the firſt boye goinge into the
Elve, where wee anchored.

18. Wee came to an anchor ſome 2 leagues ſhort of Browne-
ſbottle [Brunſbüttel]. This afternoone my Lord Ambaſſador's Secretary [Howell] went aſhore, my Lord goinge
likewiſe in our Pinnace, but his Lordſhip returned aboard
again before night, and in the eveninge our boats went
up to Loxtoad [Glückſtadt] with ſome of his gentlemen.

19. In the forenoone wee ſhipt all my Lord's trunkes and baggage
and ſome of his ſervantes in a hoye, and about 11 a clock
my Lord and the reſt of his followers left our ſhipp and
went in our long-boat and pinnace to Luxtoad, wee pre-
ſently ſetting ſayle with the wind SE. and by S. and ſtood
up as high as Flyborough, where we anchored.

Oct. 30. Wee weyed and fell downe ſome 2 leagues below
Brownſbottle.

Nov. 1. Wee weyed and fell downe over the flattes as lowe as
Roſe Beacon, when we anchored . . . that wee might be
in redyneſs to ſett ſayle when my Lord Ambaſſador ſhould
come aboard.

13

13. Some of my Lord Ambaffador's fervants came aboard with his prouifions and baggage.

21. The Earle of Lifter, Lord Ambaffador extra to the Kinge of Denmarke, and Sir Robert Anftruther, Lord Ambaffador to the Emperor, came aboard with all their trayne.

22. We weyed and fett fayle from before Rixkbottle

29. Anchored in Margett Roads.

30. We landed the Earle of Leifter . . . and Sir Robert An ftruther . . . with fome of their trayne in fafty at Margett, and at 2 in the afternoone wee fhipt all their baggage in 2 fmall barkes for London, the reft of their followers going about with it.

XXVIII.

JAMES HOWELL TO SIR JOHN COKE.

(Earl Cowper MSS. ii. 176. *Hift. MSS. Com.*)

I prefume Sir J. North hath before now been with your Honour about a manufcript of mine which contains fome fmall prints of my obfervations abroad by way of hiftorical difcourfe, couched under a difguife.

There are many things that redound much to the honour of our King and State, and all is truth and *res geftæ.* I humbly crave a favourable conftruction, and attend your perufal.

Feb. 20, 1637[-8], London.

Endorfed. Jam Howell to Sir J. Coke, Knight, His Majefty's Principal Secretary of State, at Newmarket.

XXIX.

THE HOUSE OF COMMONS AND THE HOWELLS.

(*Commons Journals*, ii. 478, 486, 850.)

Die Lunæ 14° *Martii* 1641.

Refolved vpon the Queftion, That Doctor Howell fhall be forthwith fent for, as a Delinquent, by the Serjeant at Arms attending on this Houfe for fpeaking very dangerous words, &c.

Die

Die Sabbati 19° *Martii* 1641.

Doctor *Howell* who was formerly fent for as a Delinquent, for Words that were informed on *Monday* laft to be fpoken by him, was called to the Bar: and did then with ferious Proteftation & Affervations, abfolutely deny the Words.

Refolved that Dr Howell fhall be now difcharged from any further Reftraint.

Die Lunæ 14 *Novembris* 1642.

Refolved that Mr *James Howell* be forthwith committed to the Fleet, there to remain during the Pleafure of the Houfe.

XXX.

PRYNNE ON HOWELL.

(*A Moderate Apology*, pp. 1–3, 5).

Being then publikely taxed by Mafter *James Howell*, though in a modeft candid manner, in his *Preheminence and Pedegree of Parliaments, Pag.* 10, 11, &c. (newly printed), as criminall of offering him very hard meafure, nay of doing him apparent wrong, in ftiling him in a Book entituled, *The Popifh Royal Favourite*, p. 42, NO FRIEND TO PARLIAMENT, AND A MALIGNANT; *a charaƈter which* (he faith) *he deferves not, and difdaines ;* I fhall give both himfelf and the world this briefe account of thefe harfh expreffions, not any wayes to traduce this learned gentleman (whofe excellent parts I highly honour), but to acquit my felfe from pretended guilt, of *a malicious* or *groundleffe Calumny.*

The title of a *Malignant,* fince the late deplorable differences betweene his *Majefty* and the Parliament, is growne into fuch common and univerfall ufe, that none but *Neuters* and *Ambo-dexters* (if they) either doe or can evade it. The *Cavaliers* and *Royalifts* on the one fide, the two Houfes of Parliament and their adherents on the other fide, both in their Difcourfes and Writings ftile all fuch who are oppofite or are not profeffedly cordiall to either of them, MALIGNANTS; a truth fo experimentally evident as needs no demonftration. It was Mr. *Howells difafter* among others (as himfelf engenoufly confeffeth, pag. 13) *to fall fo heavily under the difpleafure of the higheft court of Parliament ;* that he was upon fome informations given in againft him by its authority and direƈtion *apprehended and committed to the Fleet (where he has continued prifoner fundry months, and yet remains) his papers feifed, his Letters intercepted,* for this caufe efpecially (as I was credibly informed from fome Members of Parliament, who had the

the perufall of his Papers) that he had been in armes againft the Parliament and was a *dangerous* MALIGNANT, MUCH DESAF-FECTED TO THE PRESENT PARLIAMENT, *who by reafon of his abilities and acquaintances with Malignants might probably do much mifchief, and very ill offices againft the Parliament, if not reftrained.*

Receiving therefore fuch a *Charaćter* of his unknown perfon and difpofition, from fo good authority, and meeting with fundry fatyrical paffages in his *Vocal Foreft,* and in his *Parley between Patricius and Peregrine* againft this and former Parliaments (dif-covering a more than ordinary malignity in him againft fuch Affemblies;) having occafion to tranfcribe fome paffages out of him, touching the Kings voyage into *Spain,* and fome occurences during his abode there, (to fatiffie *Malignants, and Oppofites to the Prefent Parliaments proceedings*) in some Letters and Comple-ments then paffed bytween the Pope and King: I imagined with my felf that I could not probably fo clearly convince, and refolve them in this particular by any printed authorities whatfoever as by this of *Mr. Howels,* reputed one of that party by the Parlia-ment, and moft who knew; and that other Malignant Readers unacquainted with his perfon or inclination, might take notice of him, as one addićted to the Kings Party (without any thought to injure or defame the Gentleman more then any other of the Kings adherents) I ufed thefe expreffions of him : *Now that fuch Letters really paffed between the King and Pope during his abode in Spain, appears not only by divers ancient printed copies of them in fundry languages, but is alfo thus expreffly attefted by* Mr. James Howell (*an attendant upon his Majefty in that expedition*), No FRIEND TO PARLIAMENTS, BUT A MALIGNANT NOW IN CUSTODY, *in his Vocall Forreft, &c.* If Mr. *Howell* be fo great a Royalift, as this Book of his proclaims, and moft repute him ; I prefume he will efteeme it no Calumny, nor difhonour in this age to be ftiled *No friend to Parliament, but a Malignant ;* this being the chief ground of his prefent *Dures* in the *Fleet,* and that title wherein moft *Cavaliers* now Glory : But if his imprifonment hath made him, *as much a friend and as reall an affećtionate humble fervant and votary to the Parliament as poffibly I can be, and that he will live and die with thefe affećtions about him* as he now pro-feffeth in print, I fhall rejoyce at his converfion, and readily retraćt my cenfure of him upon his reconciliation to this Parlia-ment ; and his *Retraćtation* of thefe Anti-Parliamentary Paffages in his *Vocall Forreft,* that have given great offence (which he feems tacitly to confefs, pag. 18).

When this Gentleman, I fay, fhall have fully recanted thefe bitter paffages againft a former Parliament, with all his violent
Invećtives

Invectives in his late *Difcourfe* or *Parley between Patricius and Peregrine* upon their landing in *France, touching the Civill Warres of England and Ireland*, fuppreffed at the Preffe ; the moft *Malignant invective fatyr* I have hitherto met with, againft the Soveraign Jurifdiction of all our Parliaments, and the proceedings of the prefent Parliament, againft which (as I was credibly informed) he had taken up offenfive armes, being in the battle of *Edge hill*, I fhall cordially retract my cenfure of him, till then I muft appeal to his own confcience and the world, whether I have flandered or mifreported him in the leaft degree.

XXXI.

THE STATIONER TO THE READER.

(Epiftolæ Ho-Elianæ, 2nd ed. 1650.)

It pleaf'd the Author to fend me thefe enfuing *Letters* as a fupplement to the greater Volume of *Epiftolæ Ho-Elianæ*, wher they could not be inferted then, becaufe moft of his papers, whence divirs of thefe letters are deriv'd, were under fequeftration : And thus much I had in Commiffion to deliver.

HUMPHREY MOSELEY.

XXXII.

DEDICATION TO SELDEN

In a copy of " Dodona's Grove."

Wood, *Athenæ*, ed. Bliss, iii. 745 *n.*

Ex dono Authoris D. Johanni Selden Anglorum Trefmegifto, Viro, fi quis Mortalium, Omnifcio ad ornamentum Patriæ et Reipub. Literariæ Salutem nato, In cœlo fcientiarum ftellæ primæ magnitudinis, Reftitutori Temporum Scriptorumque hujus faeculi facile principi, Opufculum hoc, Honoris ergo, mittitur archivis fuis reponendum, pygmæum munus voluntatis gigantecæ 3° non. Maii, 1652.

XXXIII.

Contemporary Notices of Howell's Works.

A. DODONA'S GROVE.

(Wood, Athenæ, iii. 745.)

Much cried up and taken in the hands of curious people at its firft publication.

(Digby,

(Digby, *Late Difcourfe*, p. 6.)

Mr. *James Howell* (well known in France for his public works, and particularly his *Dendrologia*).

B.   PATRICIUS AND PEREGRINE.

(Prynne, *Modeft Apology*, p. 5.)

Supprefied at the prefie ; the moft *Malignant inveɛlive Satyr* I have hitherto met with againft the Soveraign Jurifdiɛtion of all our Parliaments.

(Wood, *Athenæ*, iii. 476.)

Written by the author in the prifon call'd the Fleet, prefently after Edghill battel, being the firft book that came forth for the vindication of his Majefty.

C.   SOME SOBER INSPECTIONS.

(Hist. MSS. Com. v. 177.)

Sir W. Dugdale to Sir R. Lewifham, Oct. 9, 1655.

You will receive by the carrier two little books . . . the other a difcourfe [by], James Howell, called "Some fober infpeɛtions into the paffages of the late Parliament," wherein cogging up [the] Proteɛtor (for to him he dedicates it) with fome fuperlative language for deftroying that monfter (as he calls it) [he] hath taken the boldnefs to fpeak more truth, barefaced, than any man that hath wrote fince they fate ; nor doth he [sp]are the Scot and Prefbyterian.   Read it through, I pray you, on my recommend ation, though in fome things he do commit little miftakes, and in others he doth blunder a little.

Sir R. L'Eftrange, *A Modeft Plea*, p. 32.

SOBER INSPECTIONS ?   Why there was one I. H. that dedicated a difcourfe under this Title, *To his Highnefs the L: Proteɛtor* when he would have made himfelf *King*, wherein he compares OLIVER CROMWELL to CHARLES MARTEL. . . . The Book indeed does mightily cry up the Royal Prerogative.

D.

D. S.P.Q.V.

Sir R. L'Eſtrange, *l.c.* p. 34.

The ſaid James Howell, *Eſq.*, in his *Survey of Venice*, dedicated to the Supreme Authority *of the Nation, the Parliament of England* in 1651, is clearly for a Commonwealth.

E. Lexicon Tetraglotton.

(Worthington's *Diary*, ed. Crossley, Chet. Soc. p. 349.)

Aug. 1661. Mr Howel, in his late Dictionary of Four Languages, hath an Appendix of Proverbs eſpecially of the Old Sayings of the Welſh. This Appendix or Second part of the work would ſell well if it were not printed with the Dictionary, which is not ſo deſirable.

F. Poems.

(Inſcription in Brit. Mus. Copy.)

Given me by Mr. James Howell the firſt of March 1663 at yᶜ Roſe in Chriſt's Alley.

F. Williams.

G. Discourse of the Empire.

(Newcome's *Diary* (Chetham Soc.), p. 136.)

Friday Oct. 31 [1662] Was after at Matthew Greaves about an houre, went to prayer wᵗʰ yᵐ, and after read Howell about yᶜ German Empire.

H. Sober Inspections.

L'Eſtrange, *l.c.* p. 36.

The very title ſpeaks the Author no Phyſician ; and he that ſtands condemned to read the Text, may ſwear he is no conjurer.

XXXIV.

L'Estrange on Howell.

(Notes upon Mr. Howell.)

If he that wrote the Caveat to the Cavaliers had been of the Gentlemen's Counſel, that penn'd the Cordial, he ſhould
never

never have difowned the *Author*, and after that, have defended the matter of it. If it was *Well* done why was it *difclaim'd*; if *Ill* why is it *juftified.* . . . The thing itfelf might have been fpared; but then fo *folemnly* to *difclaim* it is not *pro dignitate Hiftorio-graphi Regii.* . . .

Firft to fob the poor *Cavaliers* with a *Cordial* like a *whipp'd Poffet*, that's all *Froth;* and then to mend the matter by a fad Tale that wears a Title to give a Horfe a *Vomit:* This is not kindly done.

.   .   .   .

The Author of the *Infpections* sayes indeed very acutely; *There are more* J. H.'s *than one*——and fo fay I, there may be more James Howells too. . . . .
I knew at firft who wrote the *Cordial*; but truly I had no Ambition to meafure Pens with Mr. *Howell*, . . . No fooner was the *Infpections* publick, but my Stationer comes to me by Mr. *Howell's* Order with a *fleeveleffe ftory how ingenious a piece that fame Cordial was; how much His Majefty was pleafed with it:* with great Additions too, in favour of the perfon that compofed it. . . . .
Upon *Thurfday* and *Friday* laft out comes another miferable Paper done by the fame hand and in juftification of the former, which I muft needs take notice of, for divers Reafons, whereof (I fwear) the Author and the Thing itfelf are none.

XXXV.

⸘   R. LOVEDAY TO HOWELL.

(Loveday's *Perfuafive Secretary*, 1659, p. 46.)

LETTER XXV.

To Mr. H.

Knowing how highly I value your fociety you cannot chufe but think me much difpleafed with thofe cafual impediments that kept us fo long afunder; but repining never made Fortune leffe peevifh : but fince you are there give me leave to hufband the incommodity of your abfence, by intreating fuch courtefies, as could we change places, I fhould with much alacrity perform for your felf. My firft requeft then is that if you latch any news that may prove a Cordial to our dying hopes, you will not grudge to fend it me as a friendly aid that may help to put fome fad
thoughts

thoughts to flight. My next is the profecution of a former defire that you would inquire of *M.* or any other Bookfeller that is likely to inform you, if there be any new French book of an indifferent volume that is worth the Tranflating, and not enterprifed by any other; if there be, let me defire you would fend it me down, with *Cotgraves* Dictionary of the laft edition; and for what you difpurfe, I fhall appoint you where you fhall receive it in London with fome quantity befides which I fhall defire you to fend me. You may well think me unable for fuch an undertaking, but my worft fucceffe will beftow a trebble benefit, becaufe I fhall make it ferve to beguile melancholy, check idlenefs, and better my knowledge in the Language; for the Book I am indifferent whether it be Romance, Effay, Treatife, Hiftory, or Divinity, fo it be worth the rendering in our Language. You may either fend them by *G. F.*, who lies at . . . and comes neereft to *Haughton*, or by *B.*, that comes to *Nottingham*, and lies at the *U.* . . . or by your own *Lincolnfhire*-Carrier. Let me beg to hear from you by your next moft pregnant opportunity, and I fhall be induftrious to let you fee you have not fown thefe favours in a barren Soil, by conferring them upon one that will ever be ftudious to love and ferve you.

R. L.

XXXVI.

T. Forde to Howell.

(Forde, Fam. Letters, p. 85.)

To Mr. J. H.

Sir,

    Having hitherto waited with filence, to hear of your receit of my Letter, and finding none, makes me fearful that it mifcarried in the *delivery;* and I am not ignorant or infenfible of the many *abortives* of the Carriers *Midwifery.* But I hope your candor is fufficient to difpel all clouds of fufpition that might feem to eclipfe my realitie, or to think that I am fo much foe to my felf as not to defire, or at leaft not to endeavour the gainful commerce of your letters. I am not ignorant that all kind of Learning hath been wrapt up in *Letters.* And I affure you, Sir, I fhall, in the enjoyment of yours, think myfelf little lefs honoured, than I do *Lucillius* by Seneca's. Nor fhall I be a little proud, that I may be any wayes (though but occafionally) inftrumental to you to

exercife

exercife your excellencie in this way: Neither do I altogether
doubt of the pardon of my rude fcribling, becaufe I am

Sir *(without compliment)*

your very humble Servant

T. F.

XXXVII.

HOWELL'S APPLICATION FOR POST OF

HISTORIOGRAPHER GENERALL.

(Cam. Univ. Lib. Oo. viii. 47, No. 111.)

A Memorial concerning the appointment of a Minifter of State,
qualified with the title of Hiftoriographer Generall.

It is humbly offered to Confideration,

That among thofe who are obferved to be the prudentft & beft
policed nations ther is a Minifter of State appointed & qualified
with the title of Hiftoriographer Generall, whofe office is to digeft
in Writing and to tranfmitt to pofterity the Actions and Counfells
of that State, As alfo to vindicat them from all erroneous relations,
traducements, and falfities which they who take all things vpon
truft, and outward appeerances not founding the depths of things
do ufe to obtrude vnto the world.

1. This minifter is prefumed to be an Artift this way, who will
difdain to make of his Hiftory a meer Diary, by huddling together
a confufed heap of Materialls, but will take pains to polifh and
reare them up to a Structure with all its due proportions.

2. One who will obferve the method of prouidence in the dif-
penfation of his judgments, making refearches into the caufes of
them which feldom com together, but many yeers & fometimes a
whole Century with a long train of contingencies intervene twixt
ye Judgment & the Caufe.

3. This Minifter is known to be one who hath had pratique
with the world abroad, who is verfd in languages, and in Modern
Stories as well as Ancient.

4. This Minifter among other priuiledges is allowed to enter
into the Archives upon all occafions to fee and fearch any Record
new or old.

6. This Minifter is allowed a liberall allowance out of the
public ftock, or fom confiderable comendam is appropriated to
his office, wherby he may be made fitt to conuerfe at home, &
correfpond

correfpond abroad with the beſt fort of men & furniſh himſelf with the choiceſt Authors.

Sir Henry Wootton, beſides the prouoſtſhip of Eaton, had a penſion of 500ᵗʰ· per an: allowed him for to compile the Engliſh Hiſtory as appeers by the patent and dockett, but death prevented him.

JAMES HOWELL.

XXXVIII.

PAYNE FISHER'S ENCOMIUM.

(Howell's *Poems*, Introdn.)

De Ornatissimo,
Viroq; omnifariàm pererudito
Acris, & Ignei Ingenii,
Polyglotto ad Prodigium usq;
Dom. JACOBO HOWELL *Maridunensi*,
Tam ex Majorum *ceris*, quam sui Ipsius
Meritis Armigero, &c.

SIc Phoebi Delubra patent, sic tota Recessus
Pandit Cyrrha suos, funditq; oracula prægnans
Anglia, Cambriacæ & Cortina remugiit aulæ.
Nempe novum Æonidum Proles Montaccola fortem
Ostendit, sacrasq; aperit Tritonidis arces
Howelli Generosa Domus, Celeberrimæ Gentis
Hoeliae, Patriiq; decus memorabile fundi.
Tolle Coronatas Stirps Maridunia cristas,
Howellumq; Tuum ventura in sæcula jactes
Indigenis peperisse plagis, quâ monstrat Avitos
Insignis Fortuna lares, seriesq; vetusta
Sanguinis à longo volventis flumina Rivo ;
Ad Cujus gavisi olim Cristalla sedere
Grandævi Druides, patulisq; studere sub umbris
Ornorum Bardi, & nemorum se condere lustris.
Unde patet, nec vana fides, genus esse Jacobi
De serie Druidum, suffusaq; pectora dudum
Enthea primævis spirasse oracula cunis.

Ergo

Ergo Credulitas Majorum vana facessat,
Nec sibi Primores cunctos vetus arroget ævum ;
Creta Panomphæum quid progenuisse Tonantem
Intumet ? aut veteres sic altercantur, Homerus
Quâ fuerat de sede satus ? Quid culta superbit
Scaligero Verona suo ? Quid Mantua foelix
Virgilio præcone tumes ? En Cambria *nobis*
Mantua, deq; suis Vates educitur oris
Moeonio nil Vate minor, Cunabula cujus
Circum, tot Charitum croceis Examina turmis
Mellifluos fecere favos, ea gratia Scriptis
Aurea, libratoq; sedet sub carmine nervus,
Et gravitas fictæ non affectata loquelæ.
Scilicet à Teneris docti vestigia Secli
Usq; sequi Tibi *cura fuit ; veterumq; labores*
Volvere limatos, avidisq; Heliconida labris
Exhaustis Vacuare cadis. (a) Harlæus *honoris*
Primitias insignis habet, Qui Numine dextro
Tam Tibi, quam celebri Fratri *primordia jecit*
Urbs Quem (b) Bristoliæ *dudum dignata Tiarâ est*
Præsulis, *& sacram vel adhuc reminiscitur umbram.*
O felix Howelle *nimis novisse Magistrum*
Harlæum *cujus Gens* Herefordia *stirpem*
Jactet, & ingentem tollat per sæcula famam !
Illius *auspiciis solidis, epheba Juventus*
Pieriis afflata modis, quum nobile Flacci
Ante oculos saltabat Epos, & Plectra Lucani
Pharsalico concinna chely. Tum mite Terenti
Ingenium, & stricto servorum scommata socco,
Plautinosq; sales potâsti impubibus annis
Helluo Græcorum Laticum. Mox Sydere verso
Ipse novum moliris iter, quâ Dulce Lycæum
Oxoniæ *plenos reserat sitientibus amnes.*
Heic Jesu *sacrata* Domus *Te amplectitur ulnis*
Admissum geminis, & diæ pocula Lucis
Castalio cum lacte dabat. Sub sensibus haustos
Tum logicos primum gryphos, artesq; loquendi
Digeris, & solide formâ methodoq; locatis,
Venturæ Vigil instauras fundamina Famæ.
Inde Sophistæo *magis inspirata Susurro*
Mens Tua, Te Socium *nullo opponente creavit*
Collegi veneranda Cohors. Nec sistitur ingens

(a) Eruditissimus Dom. Harley Scholae, Hereford. Archididascalus.
(b) Frater nostri Jacobi qui Episcop. Bristoliensis moriebatur.

II.   2 X   *Impetus,*

Impetus, humanæ qui supra nubila vitæ
Gestit, & aprico foelix feriatur olympo.
Ergo Philosophiæ sublimia culmina scandens
Occultas reseras sedes, ubi Scrinia mundi
Naturæq; Arcana habitant: ubi cernitur omnis
Quid Divina velit, vel suaserit Ethnica Virtus.
Quicquid Socratico manavit ab ordine; quicquid
Clara Cleantheæ praescripsit Turba Lucernæ;
Quicquid Erycthracis Cynicorum Secta studebat
Gymnasiis; quicquid dixit, tacuitq; loquendo
Pythagoras Howelle *Tuum est, Qui abstrusa latebris*
Eruis ingenio, Rerumq; oracula pandens,
Concipis immensos dilato pectore mundos.
   Nec Tua Fama Domi, Patriisque morabitur antris,
Vecta per extremum nonis Juvenilibus orbem,
Et regum consueta Aulis, interq; potentes
Europæ Dominos porrectas sumere laurus.
Te Juvenem cognovit Iber; *Te celsa* Philippi
Regia Catholici *Madriti vidit* Agentem
Principis Adventu Caroli, *stupuitq; loquentem,*
Tractantemq; diu alterni Molimina Sceptri.
Inde Revertentem Borealis Syderis Atlas
Ille Comes Præses, *Te* Sunderlandius *imis*
Secretis admisit amans, & Tanta Scientem,
Callentemq; foras, propriis præfecit habenis.
   Nec Patrio requiescis agro, sed cærula suloans (sic)
Cymbrica, *ad ingentem* Danorum *stebiliis Aulam*
Mitteris Orator, *Reginæ busta* Sophiæ
Exequiasq; dolens, Tua circum Rostra Licestro
Legato, *& Danûm Procerum stipante Corona*
Quæ Regio in terris nostro non nota Jacobo?
Quem pede diffusi penetrantem viscera Regni
Teutonides *videre sui; Quem* Gallia *dudum*
Cum Batavo, *&* Veneti, *&* Siculi, *& stupuere* Pelasgi;
Romaq; *tot linguas uno sub corde prementem*
Mirati, Poterantq; levi discrimine, cuncti
Indigenam dixisse suum. *Tunc Patria dignum*
Te Palmis censebat ovans, quum ad Tecta Senatus
Prisca ciebat amans, & ter successibus æquis
Ad sua delecti Te Parlamenta *Sedentem.*
Nec Patriæ cessabat amor, sed honoribus urgens
Continuis, credebat adhuc se parva dedisse
Ni meritis majora daret: sic nobilis audis
Clericus *Augusti* Caroli *qua jungeris imis*
Consiliis Tu Scriba *cluens, Regniq; labores*

                               Multiplices,

Multiplices, Aulæq; vices Atlantis ad instar
Collibras, Patrioq; humeros Supponis Olympo.
Hæc pro Te dudum dignissima, Patria fecit,
Pro Patriâ nec parva facis, facilive rependis
Officio, quæ fecit amor: Communia Testor
Commoda, & attritis operosa volumina proelis
Non uno numeranda Die. Te muta movente
Organa, (c) Vocales *fudere oracula* Sylvae,
Et Trunci didicere loqui, Dodonea Quercus,
Frondiferi Regina chori Tibi Brachia pandens
Tollit ad astra comas, foliisq; Superbior exit
A folis *famosa tuis, Quibus, Illa fatetur*
Se Tibi debendam, contextaq; Serta *dicandam*
Civica, *Romuleis nil inferiora Triumphis.*

Utq; doces Sylvas, & tardo stipite Truncos
Humanos simulare sonos, sic (d) Bruta Ferarum
Guttura conformans, nostræ Vernacula linguæ
Distinctasq; doces haurire, & reddere voces.
Exemplum dabit illud opus sublime, Priori
Vix dispar, ubi gliscit amor Pietasq; Parenti
Sceptrifero ; *& Fidei Mortales* Publica *ductim*
De Brutis Documenta *bibant, trepidentq; Rebelles*
Excandescentem *Britonum irritare* Leonem.

Nec cessat Tua mira manus, celerive remissas
Indulges calamo ferias, quia vana perosus
Otia, victuris lætare laboribus, unam
Vix perdens sine luce diem, Testabitur orbi
Grandius Illud Opus (e) *Bis Bino Idiomate coctum*
Utile Principibus, Populoq; Orientis et Euri
Orbis, & à toto divisis orbe Britannis,
Heic veluti speculo Criticismata cuncta loquelæ
Cantabricæ discernit Iber ; Syrene Jacobo
Ausonios modulante sonos, de finibus exit
Italus allectus propriis; Gallusq; Garumnam
Atq; Ararim rapido referens sermone, Britanglos
Advolat, alternæ miscens commercia linguæ.
(f) *Hisce voluminibus* Nomenclatura *stupendi*
Subjunctum est Opus ingenii (g) *Proverbia Gentis*
A tenebris memoranda trahens, formasq; loquendi

: (c) Dendrologia.
(d) Therologia.
(e) Opus aliud elucubratissimum, cui titulus Lexicon Tetraglotton.
(f) Aliud volumen non minoris molis quam emolumenti.
(g) Aliud volumen, Pentaglotton, Proverbiorum.

Priscorum

Priscorum Britonum, *Quorum venerabile semen*
Cambria *servat adhuc, primosq; à sedibus actos*
Commemorabit avos : *Tua* Cambria *clare* Jacobe
Cui *Superum Ductu Tu post tot secla renascens*
Adderis Exemplar, dum sic virtutibus amplis
Instauras Patriam, & virtutes dotibus aequas.
Egregie nasci laus est ; sed gloria major
Pro Pratriâ *nasci, & primus* Chronista *creari*
Regis ab Historiis.   *Et quis dubitaverit amens*
Te Titulis minus ire Tuis, Oneriveq; lacertos
Impariles, qui tanta manu Monumenta levâsti¦
Pressaq; vix binis portanda Volumina Rhedis.
Lector avet majora ?   Domi quod scripseris olim
Contempletur opus, plorandaq ; damna (h) Senatus
Praelongi *numeret, cunctasq; ab origine causas*
Pendeat, & nostri recolat Commenta Jacobi.
Si ulteriora petit ?   Peregré succinctus ad oras
Longinquas eat, & Te (i) *Directore, viarum*
Prœscius, Europœ varias adremiget urbes,
Conductusq; Tuo formet vestigia Filo.
   Hoc Filo conductus, aquis scopulisq; sedentem
Europœ Dominam (k) *Venetum mirabitur urbem :*
Celsaq; Parthenopis (l) *Regalia culmina cernet*
In Chartis Majora Tuis.   Tunc versus ad oras
Austriacas veterum Imperium venerabitur ingens
(m) *Teutonidum, & senio certantia vasta Viennae*
Moenia Pannonico toties ditata Tributo.
Inde pedem fessum relegens, per Regna feretur
Gallica, & Hoelios *agnoscet ritè labores*
Liligerœ Septem tractantes lustra Tiarœ,
Translatiq; Polo (n) Ludovici *Busta, Suiq;*
Armandi *parvo non designata papyro.*
   Sed quid ego gracili calamo, vel carmine curto
Hoelianas *vanus comprehendere chartas*
Molior, Herculeos quum tot recitare labores
Herculeus labor alter erit ?   Testabitur Anglis
Urbs vetus Heroum (o) *Trinobantia gloria Civûm*

(h) Sobriæ ejus inspectiones in actiones longi Parliamenti.
(i) Directiones peregre proficiscentibus.
(k) Historia ejus Voluminosa Venetum.
(l) Par etiam Neopolitanorum.
(m) Aliud etiam volumen de Imperio Germano.
(n) Aliud exquisitum volumen de vita Ludovici Galliæ xiii.
(o) Aliud nobile volumen cui titulus Londinopolis.

Ingenio

Ingenio ditata Tuo. Testabitur orbi
Cultius Illud opus quo splendet (p) *Epistola crebra*
Flexanimo concinna stylo, quo Faedera belli
Et passim Momenta Togæ, Faciesq; nitenti
Cernitur Europæ Speculo, & velamine dempto
Obvia Summorum pateant, Penetralia Regum.
   Tantis Posteritas cumulabit honoribus, olim
Vulgatos Howelle *libros. Tantumq;* labori
Debebit Gens nostra Novo, *stirps aurea Cujus,*
Formaq; Primævas *nil postponenda* Sorores
Apello Charites, afflataq; cælitus Æstro
Pectora, fatidicum fibris spirantia Phoebum.
A Jove Principium sumens nam Pagina prima
Sacra Sapit, gratoq; fluunt condita lepore
Caetera Mellifluos *redolentia carmina* Flores
Laurigeroq; novas Tibi contextura corollas.
Inde per humanæ raptus spectacula scaenae
Quam parvas habitura moras Mortalia monstras,
Indignoque licet depressus Carcere, Mentis
Remigio super astra volas, Supremaq; versans,
Discis ab immenso quam discrepat angulus Orbe,
Et circumfusi quam curta Scientia Mundi
Æterno *collata* Deo. *Tumet inde Papyrus*
Laudibus Heroum, & Carolum *Te Vate salutat,*
Augurioq; pio jamdudum rite potitis
Induperatoris *summos promittit honores*
Quum procul Austriacæ volucres, succumbere Gallo
Gaudebunt, Gallusq; Anglo parere Leoni.
   Heic etiam Octavi *nitidum sine bile Character*
Pingitur Henrici, *Quod latius Acta loquetur*
Et Genium, quam Windsorii *monumenta superbi*
Majorum constructa manu (r) Sacvillia *Pubes*
Dorsigenis *prælustris honos, caput eruet umbris*
Auspiciis Howelle *Tuis. His* (s) Marchio *grandis*
Pierpontiadum Durotrigumq; *cacumen*
Tollitur, & Celsae Katharinae *stemmata dudum*
Tremoliâ *deducta Domu. Proh celse columna*
Henrice *armorum, & sublimibus Artibus : ingens*
Pro Sedi Coryphae *Tui! Quos Fulguris instar*
Antevolas, patrioq; creas Miracula Mundo.

(p) Aliud opus usus omnifarii, cui titulus Epistolæ Hoellianae.
(r) Nobillissimus ille nuper Edoardus Dorcestriae Comes.
(s) Illustrissimus Henricus Marchio Durotrigum ; Comes de Kingston, &c.,
& Katharinae filiae comitis de Derby.

Hunc

Hunc *Chartis* Howelle *sonas*, Cui *gloria vastis*
Digna voluminibus, gravidoq; canenda Cothurno ;
Illi dumq; litas laudes, aliisq: sub isto
Codice, diffuso spargis Tua nomina mundo
Lataq; non propriis claudi Praeconia Chartis.

Sic raptim cecinit,

P. PISCATOR.

XXXIX.

TABLE OF EDITIO PRINCEPS.

(With additions of 2nd edition in square brackets.)

Thefe *Letters*, for their principall fubject, contain a Relation of thofe Paffages of *State* that happen'd a good part of King *James* His Raign, and of His M^aties^ now Regnant : As alfo of fuch *Outlandifh* Occurrences that had reference to this KINGDOM :

[*Viz. of*
The Wars of *Germany* and the Tranfactions of the Treaties about reftoring the *Palatinat*, with the Houfe of *Auftria* and *Sweden*.
The Treaty and Traverfes of the Match with *Spain*.
The Treaty of the Match with *France*.
An exact furvey of the *Netherlands*.
Another of *Spain, Italy, France*, and of moft Countreys in *Europe*, with their chief Cities and Governments.
Of the *Hans* Towns and of the famous quarrel 'twixt Queen Elizabeth and them.
Divers Letters of the Extent of Chriftianity, and of other Religions upon Earth.
Divers Letters of the Languages up and down the Earth.
Accounts of fundry Embaffies from *England* to other States.
Some pieces of Poetry wherwith the Profe goes interwoven.
Divers new opinions in Philofophy defcanted upon.
Paffages of former Parlements, and of this prefent, &c.]

Wherin ther goes along a Legend of the *Authors* life, and of his feverall employments, with an account of his Forren *Travells* and *Negotiations ;* wherin he had occafion to make his addreffe to thefe Perfonages, and Perfons underwritten.

Letters

Letters to Noblemen.

[*To His Late Maiefty*]
To the Duke of Buckingham
[*To the Marqueffe of* Hartford]
To the Marq. of Dorchefter]
[*To the Erl of* Lindfey *great Chamberlain of* England]
[*To the Erl of* Southampton]
To the Erl of Cumberland
[*To the Erl of* Dorfet]
To the Erl of Rutland
To the Erl of Leicefter
To the Erl of Sunderland
To the Erl of Briftol
To the Erl Rivers
To the Erl of Strafford
[*To the Erl of* Clare]
To the Erl of Carberry.

To the Lord Vicount Conway, *Secr.*
To the L. Vicount Savage
To the L. Herbert *of Cherberry*
To the L. Cottington
To the L. Mohun
To the L. Digby.

To the Lady Marchioneffe of Winchefter
To the La. Scroope.
To the Counteffe of Sunderland
To the La. Cornwallis.
To the La. Digby.

To Bifhop Ufher, *Lord Primat of Ireland*
To B. Field
To B. Duppa
To the B. of London
[*To the B. of* Rochefter]
To B. Howell.

To Knights, Doctors, Efquires, Gentlemen, and Marchants.

To Sir Robert Manfell
To Sir James Crofts
To Sir John North
To Sir Kenelme Digby

To Sir Peter Wichts
To Sir Sackvill Trever
To Sir Sackvill Crow
To Sir Arthur Ingram

To

To *Sir* Thomas Lake
To *Sir* Eubule Theloall
To *Sir* Alexander Ratcliff
To *Sir* Edward Savage
To *Sir* John Smith
To *Sir* William Saint-Geon
To *Sir* Thomas Savage
To *Sir* Francis Cottington
To *Sir* Robert Napier
To *Sir* Philip Manwayring
To *Sir* Bevis Theloall.

To *Doctor* Manfell
To *Dr.* Howell
To *Dr.* Prichard
To *Dr.* Wicham.
[*To Dr.* J. Day.]

To *Master Alderman* Clethero
To *Mr. Alderman* Moulfon
To *the Town of Richmond.*

To *my Father Mr.* Tho. Howell
To *Mr.* R. Altham
To *Mr.* Daniell Caldwall
To *Captain* Francis Bacon
To Ben Johnfon
To *Mr. End. and Cap.* Thomas
   Porter
To *Mr.* Simon Digby

To *Mr.* Walfingham Grelley
To *Mr.* Thomas Gwyn
[*To Mr.* John Wroth]
[*To Mr.* William Blois]
[*To Mr.* Howell Gwyn]
[*To Mr.* Robert Baron]
[*To Mr.* Thomas More]
To *Mr.* John Savage
To *Mr.* Hugh Penry
To *Mr.* Chriflopher Jones
To *Mr.* R. Brown
To *Mr.* William Martin
To *Cap.* Nicholas Leat
[*To Mr.* R. Brownrigg]
To *Mr.* John Batty
To *Mr.* William Saint-Geon
To *Mr.* Philip Warrik
To *Mr.* Thomas Hammon
To *Mr.* James Howard
To *Mr.* Ed. Noy
To *Mr.* William Auflin
To *Mr.* Rowland Gwyn
To *Mr.* William Vaughan
To *Mr.* Arthur Hopton
To *Mr.* Thomas Jones
To *Mistris* Caldwall
To *Mistris* Frances Metcalf
To *Mr.* J. Price
To *Captain* Ol. Saint-Geon,

With divers others.

XL.

HOWELL'S ELECTION AT JESUS.

(Minute books, Jesus Coll. Oxon.)

4 April 1623.

Prefent.   Eubule Thelwall, *Principa'.*
          Thomas Prichard, *Vice Pr.*
          Maurice Merick } *fellows*
          Robert Lloyd   }
agreed to proceed to election of eight fellows and ten fcholars.

                             The

The Statute of the realm having been read, and the Statutes of the College concerning election of fellows and fcholars.

        Roger Phillips
        Rowland Cheadle
        Roger Prichard
        Thomas Lloyd
        James Howells, Sen.
        James Howells, Jun.
        Hugh Penry
        and Henry Bould,
        were elected fellows.

The Principal then pronounced thefe elected fellows.

And then, the oaths of allegiance and fupremacy having been taken, and the oath of obedience to the College Statutes having been taken,

        Roger Phillips
        Rowland Cheadle
        Roger Prichard
        Thomas Lloyd
        James Howells, Junior
        Hugh Penry
        and Henry Bould.
        Admitted April 4, 1623.

Notes

NOTES.

INTRODUCTION.

IN the following Notes I have mainly attempted to identify persons, check dates, trace sources, and explain allusions. I have not devoted much attention to parallel passages, except those occurring in Howell's own works. I have endeavoured not to explain the obvious, the commentator's chief sin, yet I trust I have dealt with all the difficulties, even if I have had to confess, much against my will, that they are for me insoluble, by placing them among the Queries of p. 808. All this as regards the subject-matter: for rare or curious words I refer the reader to the Index, where, for the most part, short definitions are attached to words likely to cause a halt to the reader. Limits of space have often obliged me to give rather sources where full information can be sought for. These will be generally known in most cases under the somewhat abbreviated form I have given. The Domestic Series of State Papers I quote by *S.P.* and the date, which enables the reader to find the volume easily enough, and is less likely to be misprinted, while conveying useful information in itself. Gard. *per se* refers to the cabinet edition of Prof. Gardiner's *History of England*, in 10 vols., but at times I used the separate sections, and quote these as Gard. *Sp. M.* ("Spanish Match"), &c., or *l. c.* The various Series of *Notes and Queries* are distinguished by a prefixed numeral: thus 5 *N. and Q.* vii. 32, means *Notes and Queries*, 5th series, vol. vii. p. 32. I have ventured to throw in the second series of the Fairfax Papers with the first, and call them *Fairf. Pap.* iii. and iv. The dates which are not authenticated with a reference are for the most part from Woodward and Cates' admirable *Encyclopædia of Chronology;* Details of Peerages from Nicholas' *Historic Peerage.* D.N.B. = *Dictionary of National Biography.* References obtained from the notes of the late Mr. Henry King, now in the possession of Mr. C. H. Firth, or from Mr. Firth himself, are marked with their initials. Anything I have been able to add comes for the most part after the initials. I have checked the Notes with the Index and *vice versâ*, but have shrunk from checking the 1001 references to other books.

P. 1.]

P. 1.] TITLE-PAGE, of edition of 1737. For earlier forms see Bibliographical List, Nos. 14, 21, 33, 49.
his late Majesty, Chas. I.

P. 3.] DEDICATION *To his Majesty*, Chas. I. This was in the ED. PR. of 1645, at a time when it argued some moral boldness for a prisoner in the Fleet to express so openly his Royalist proclivities.
Credential Letters, those given to Ambassadors. *Cf.* p. 14.

P. 5.] THE VOTE. This was originally published separately. See Bibl. List, No. 2.
Cal. Jan. 1641, 1 Jan. 1642. In O.S. the year began 25 March.
rare Hillyard, Nicholas Hilliard (1547–1619), goldsmith, carver and painter to Q. Elizabeth. It is curious to see him coupled with Michelangelo and Titian. Charles I.'s love of the Fine Arts is well known, and has been effectively utilised by Mr. Shorthouse, *John Inglesant*, p. 49. *Cf.* Donne's *Storme*, " And a Hand or Eye by Hilliard drawne is worth an history."

P. 6.] *Moreno.* The Rimmel of Madrid, who is referred to on p. 170 as perfuming pockets and gloves for Capt. Porter.
amber, i.e., ambergris, the original meaning of "amber" as applied to the aromatic product of the whale.

P. 7.] *The Sophy*, the Shah of Persia. See on p. 338.
Vocal Forest, his "Dendrologia." See Bibl. List, No. 1.
Arhetine. " Her Mat^tie Queen of England." Key to "Dendrologia."
Great Henry, Henry IV., Henrietta Maria's father.
Loire, the Po and Rhine. French, Latin, and Dutch versions of the "Dendrologia." For the first see Bibl. List, Nos. 2, 41 ; the others were never printed, if they were made, though there were Dutch and Latin versions of H.'s *England's Teares* (B. L., Nos. 17, 30).

P. 8.] *Black Prince*, Chas. II., then Prince of Wales. A reference to the Dedicatory poem of the *Instructions for Forreine Travell*, ed. Arber, p. 8.
Cantabrian waves. St. George's Channel.
Scylla and Charybdis. See pp. 62, 63. *Ætna*, p. 63.
Cosmopolitan. Cf. "a pure Cadet, a true Cosmopolite," p. 373. See also p. 500.
huge Inn. Cf. Epictetus, *Disc.* c. xxiii. *ad fin.*, and Mr. Payn's *Midway Inn. Cf. contra* Browne, *Rel. Med.* ii. § 11, "For the world I count it not an Inn but an Hospital."

. 9] *false glasses.* Telescopes, "opticks," as J. H. calls them, p. 331.
Good Hope's Cape. Cf. "I am one that lyeth at the Cape of Good Hope, though a long time under hatches."—J. H., Pref. to *Parables*.

P. 10.] *Sanguine*, a reference to the four Temperaments.
Luce, fleur-de-lys.

P. 11.] *the great Mogor*, the Portuguese form (*o grão Mogor*) of "the grand Mogul." *Cf.* Camoens x. 66, and Sir R. Burton's translation (Yule, *Hobson-Jobson*, s.v.), *cf.* p. 13, l. 15.
in the North, the war with Scotland.
Frog Vapours, qy. "fog"; the misprint, if such, is in the original. But the same expression is used in *Lustra Lud.*, p. 20, and probably refers to showers of sleet, called "frog" in Scotch.
great year of Plato. When everything returns again to its original state. *Timæus*, 39. *Cf.* Cic. De Nat. Deor., ii. 20, and J. Adams' *Plato's Number*, 1891.

P. 12.]

P. 12.] *To the Knowing Reader.* Prefixed to ED. PR. Also prefixed to Nimmo's Selections from *British Letter-Writers.*
Mogor. See note on p. 11.
Knez, as in ED. PR. From the Russian *Knyas*, a prince.
Prester John, used here for the King of Abyssinia. See note on a reference to Livy, v. 47.
twice prevented. In ED. PR. a side-note gives an off-hand reference to Livy. Dr. Gow suggests that the second occasion may be that referred to, Pliny, N. H. 10, 22, 36, § 81, or Plut. *Camillus.*

P. 13.] *fiery Pile.* "Gunpowder Plot" side-note in ED. PR.
Eagle's Letter. A letter to Lord Monteagle revealed the plot (*Gard.*, i. 248).
Antonine. Howell seems to split up M. Aurelius Antoninus into two personages. No letters of any other Antonine are known.

P. 14.] *Aurelius by his Letters.* He means the *Libro Aureo* of Guevara, which are written in letter form and under the name of Marcus Aurelius. Guevara's book was often translated into English, and is said to have given rise to Euphuism. See my edition of North's *Bidpai.*
Administers in some: this should read "administers. In sum," as in ED. PR.

BOOK I.

This includes all the letters contained in the *editio princeps* of 1645, with the addition of the letter prefixed to the first section, which was first inserted in the second edition of 1650. *The dates were added in the second edition.*
The FIRST SECTION contains 44 letters ranging from the beginning of 1619 to the end of 1621 (with the prefatory letter dated 1625), and gives an account of Howell's first travels abroad to the Low Countries (v.-xii.), France (xiii.-xxi.), Spain (xxii.-xxv.), Italy (xxvi.-xlii.), and France again (xliii., xliv.).

P. 17.] LETTER L—This letter was added in the second edition. It is quoted in Scoones' *English Letters*, No. lv. p. 71, also in Nimmo's *British Letter-Writers*, p. 23.
To Sir J. S. Probably the Sir John Smith of I. ii. 13. p. 113. Other letters to Sir J. S., Kt., occur in I. iv. 19. p. 234, and I. v. 13. p. 264. In the last place Sir J. S. is spoken of as living near Harwich in 1628. There were two John Smiths knighted in the reign of James I., one of Kent, knighted 11 May 1603 (Metcalfe, *A Book of Knights*, p. 140), and one of Essex, knighted in 1605 (*ib.*, p. 156). The former is *our* John Smith, as we know from the reference to Leeds Castle, co. Kent, of which an elaborate description has been given by C. W. Martin, *History of Leeds Castle*, 1869. *Cf.* p. 156. Sir John died 1632. *Cf.* Nicholl's *Prog. Jas. I.*, iii. 252 n.; Hasted, *Kent*, ii. 73, and Herbert, *Autob.* 78 n.
The ancients. Dr. Gow compares Cic. *Epp. ad Fam.*, ix. 21, 1.
Hungerlin, a short fur coat introduced from Hungary, whence the name.

P. 18.] *Narratory, Objurgatory.* These adjectives show that Howell had in mind Day's *Complete Letter-Writer*, the Table of Contents of which is filled with adjectives in *-ory.* I have reprinted the Table in my edition of Day's *Daphnis and Chloe*, p. xxviii.
Bartholomew ware, cheap and nasty, like things sold at Bartholomew Fair.

Echo,

Echo, a reference to *Vox et præterea nihil*, though the Greek original refers to the nightingale.

Balzac, Jean Louis Guez de Balzac (1594-1655). His *Lettres*, almost the first of their kind, written for the writing's sake (Saintsbury, *Short Hist. Fr. Lit.*, p. 354), appeared for the first time in 1624, the year before the date of this letter. They were translated into English by Sir R. Baker, 1655, and a passage is quoted in the *Spectator*, No. 355.

P. 19.] *Urinals.* On this practice of physicians or "waterologers" see a curious note of Rimbault in his edition of Sir T. Overbury's *Works*, p. 302. *Cf. Shakespeare's Jest Book*, ed. Oesterley, pp. 14-16.

LETTER II.—This was the opening letter of the first edition. Consequently all the letters of the first section in the remaining editions differ by one in the numeration.

To my Father. Thomas Howell, curate of Cefn-bryn, co. Brecon, 1576-83 (Th. Jones, *History of Brecknockshire*, ii. 279), minister of Abernant, in Caermarthenshire (Ath. Ox. iii. 744). He died in 1632, as we know from I. vi. 7. p. 306.

choice methodical school. Hereford Free School. I. i. 31. p. 71.

learned (tho' lashing) master, named Harley, as we learn from the Latin verses prefixed to Howell's *Poems.* See Suppt. II. p. 689.

to Oxford to be graduated. J. H. matriculated at Jesus, 16 June 1610, ætat. 16, and took his B.A. Dec. 17, 1613, ætat. 20. See Introd., p. xxvi.

Sir Robert Mansell, Treasurer of the Navy (*Gard.*, ii. 187), and uncle to Dr. F. Mansell, the Principal of J. H.'s college, Jesus, who probably recommended him to the Admiral. On him, see note on I. i. 28.

Lord of Pembroke. William Herbert, third Earl (1580-1630), the W. H., "onlie begetter" of Shakespeare's *Sonnets.* He was Chancellor of Oxford University in 1619, the year in which this letter purports to be written.

Patent of making Glass with Pit-coal. References to this Patent, held by Sir R. Mansell, *S.P.*, 2 Feb. 1611, 17 Nov. 1613, 12 Oct. 1614, 23 May 1615 (proclamation prohibiting all glass-making unless with coal), 1 June 1615, 4 May 1618, 10 Dec. 1618 (Sir R. Mansell has acquired *sole rights*).

P. 20.] *Workmen from Italy*, Venetians, some of whom are mentioned pp. 56, 65. Another, Vescellini, is named in Brit. Mus. Add. MS. 12, 496.

Chief materials, baryllia, from Spain. See I. i. 65. p. 60.

Glass house in Broad St. Cf. G. T. Clark, *Carmarthen Worthies*, p. 18, also Stow-Strype, iii. 112, and a paper in *Journ. Arch. Instit.*, dealing with remains of the glass found a few years ago. Pinners Hall stood on the site.

Captain Francis Bacon. He is mentioned as acting for Sir R. Mansell in his absence, *S.P.*, 10 Jan. 1619.

Sir George Villiers, James I.'s celebrated favourite, frequently mentioned in these letters. He was created Viscount Villiers and Baron Whaddon, 27 Aug. 1616, so that this passage could not have been written in 1619.

The Earl of Somerset, Robert Carr (c. 1585-1645), also a favourite of James I.: through his intrigue with the Countess of Essex, he became implicated in the poisoning of Overbury, and found guilty of murder, 25 May 1616. He was respited, but kept in the Tower till 1622, and not definitely pardoned till 1625 (ch. xx. of Mr. Gardiner's *History* deals with "The Fall of Somerset"). What *the Lease of 90 years for his Life* refers to, I have been unable to ascertain.

his Articulate Lady, Lady Frances Howard, Countess of Essex (b. 1593), became enamoured of Somerset, and procured a divorce from the Earl of Essex in 1613, on grounds of special impotence (ch. xvi. of Mr. Gardiner's *History*

History deals with "The Essex Divorce "). She plotted the murder of Sir Thomas Overbury, was tried and found guilty of it in 1616, and pardoned July 13, 1616 (*Gard.*, vi. 361).

Coke, the Lord Chief-Justice. Edward Coke (1552–1633) conducted the Overbury case, but was discharged from the office of Lord Chief-Justice, 15 Nov. 1616.

poisoning of Overbury. Sir Thomas Overbury (1581-16 Sept. 1613), as a friend of Somerset, dissuaded him from marrying the Countess of Essex, and thus earned her hatred. She caused him to be poisoned in the Tower. The murder became known three years later, and the minor criminals executed. The trial is fully described in the interesting volume of A. Amos, *The Great Oyer of Poisoning,* 1846, and more briefly in E. F. Rimbault's Introduction to *The Works of Sir Thomas Overbury,* 1856.

the Prerogative kept them from the Pot. James pardoned the Countess almost at once, July 13, 1616, and respited Somerset about the same time.

Mistress Turner, Anne Turner, "a doctor of physic's widow, whom prodigality and looseness had brought low." She was the chief instrument in procuring the poison.

the first inventress of yellow starch. Coke, in passing judgment, referred to this, and ordered that she should wear a yellow-starched ruffle at her execution, as did the hangman also. Rimbault, *l.c.* p. xxxvii. Thackeray is fond of referring to the fact, which he doubtless got from his favourite Howell.

P. 21.] *Sir Gervas Elways, Lieut. of the Tower.* Sir Jervis Elves, Sir Gervas Elwes, Sir Jervis Yelvis, Sir Gervase Helwys (the name is written in all these ways, the latter is the form used by Mr. Gardiner, ii. 179 *seq.*), had been appointed to supersede Sir William Wood, for the very purpose of assisting in the murder.

Lord (William) of Pembroke, vide *supra,* on p. 19.

Broad Street, London, 1 *March* 1618. The ED. PR. has no date : this was inserted in the second edition. From the following letters, it is clear that O.S. is used, and that the year was 1619. This makes the disparity between the date of the letter and of the events mentioned still more striking. Howell's father was dead at the time of publication, and he may therefore have come into possession of his own letters to him, but the paragraph beginning "Touching the News of the Time" must have been interpolated, even if the whole letter is not a fabrication.

LETTER III.—*Dr. Francis Mansell,* third son of Sir F. Mansell of Muddlescomb, co. Caermarthen, Howell's county, so that they probably knew one another "at home." Mansell was three times Principal of Jesus, 1620–1, 1630–48, 1660–65, dying in the last-mentioned year, ætat. 80 Anthony à Wood, *Hist. Coll. Oxon.*, pp. 577–9, p. 585 (epitaph). He was still Principal when this letter was published with his name. A privately printed Life was published by L. Jenkyns, 1859 (C.H.F.).

P. 22.] *Glass house, Venetians.* See notes in I. i. 2, p. 20.

School-language, language of the "Schools," Latin, in which language alone the disputations could be held by which degrees could be obtained. C. Wordsworth, *Schola Academicæ,* c. ii.

Gravesend, then, as now, the port for embarking on voyages to Holland or Germany. *Cf.* p. 101, and W. B. Rye, *England as seen by Foreigners,* n. 7.

warrant to travel. A similar warrant to travel for three years provided he does not go to Rome is given to T. Westrop. Harl. MS. 286, f. 290. *Cf.* Mayor's *Lives of Ferrar,* p. 191-2.

Rome,

Rome. Notwithstanding this, we find J. II. at Rome, pp. 81-5. The object of the prohibition was to prevent conversion to Roman Catholicism.

St. Omers, where there was a Jesuit college much frequented by Roman Catholic lads and frequented by youthful converts. *Cf.* p. 326, and Mullinger, *Univ. Cam.,* ii. p. 261.

London, 20 *March* 1618. The ED. PR. has a truncated date, "London *this*," which seems to vouch for the authenticity of the present letter. ,

LETTER IV.—*Sir James Crofts, Kt.,* generally spelt Croft, grandson of the elder Sir James Croft, Controller of Queen Elizabeth's household, of whom an interesting account in *Retrosp. Rev.,* 2nd ser., pp. 469-98. The Sir James here mentioned was a pensioner or member of Queen Elizabeth's bodyguard (Herb. Cherb. *Autob.,* p. 82, and Mr. Lee's note), and died in London, 9 Aug. 1649. *Ret. Rev.,* i. p. 495.

St. Osith, now spelt St. Osyth, co. Essex, at the mouth of R. Colne. J. II. spent some time there afterwards (p. 109). Earl Rivers had a seat there.

P. 23.] *return of Sir Walter Raleigh from his Mine of Gold in Guiana.* Mr. Gardiner devotes ch. xxv. of his history to "Raleigh's Last Voyage." From this it appears that Raleigh's ship, the "Destiny," did not cast anchor in Plymouth Sound till the first week of June (*Gard.,* iii. 131), three months before the alleged date of this letter. Mr. Edwards' *Life of Raleigh,* i. 649, gives the date 21 June 1618.

thirteen ships more. They are enumerated in E. Edwards' *Life of Raleigh,* i. 599.

Count Gondomar (1567-1626), the well-known Spanish ambassador at James I.'s Court. See genealogy and characterisation of him in Edwards, *l. c.* i. 569 *seq.* He is the Black Knight of Middleton's *Game of Chess.* There is a good portrait of him in Mr. Lee's *Lord Herbert of Cherbury.*

Pirates, Pirates, Pirates. Mr. Edwards gives the story (i. 646) as "one of the best known of our Court anecdotes :" he quotes Gondomar's exclamation in Spanish, "Piratas, Piratas, Piratas." Mr. Gardiner does the same (iii. 131), though he declares that there is no other authority for the story than Howell, who gives the words in English ("Pyrats, Pyrats, Pyrats," ED. PR. sect. i. p. 6). It is, however, given in the Spanish form in H.'s treatise on Ambassadors (Bibl. List, No. 68). Also, Mr. Firth reminds me, in Finetti's Remains, edited by H. (B. L. 50).

till he hath his head off his shoulders; this sounds like a *vaticinium post eventum.*

P. 24.] *Santo Thoma,* San Thomé at the mouth of the Orinoco. Between Raleigh's visits the town was moved to the east, near the spot where he expected to find the gold-mine (see map in *Gard.,* iii. 44, and *ib.* p. 121). Capt. Keymis and young Walter Raleigh attacked and burnt it.

Plate Galeons, the Spanish ships which brought the yearly tribute of gold from America to Spain.

Captain Kemish, a misprint (in ED. PR.) of Capt. Keymis, the second in command in Raleigh's expedition, who was the only man who had seen the mine. He led the attack on San Thomé, and on his return to Sir W. Raleigh, after the death of young Raleigh, was received badly by him, and committed suicide.

Convertine. H. was himself a passenger in this ship. See *infra,* pp. 651, 677, 678.

Alphonso, King of Naples. This well-known story has been told of many kings, *e.g.,* Charles of Burgundy and Louis XI. in *Quentin Durward,* of Francis I. and Chas. V. in Bacon's *Apophthegms,* § 200, ed. Spedding. It is probable that Scott got the idea from Howell, who may have got it from Melchior, *Floresta Española,* I. iii. 1.

P. 25.] *London,* 28 *March* 1618. The date is obviously incorrect, even if the letter

letter is authentic ; the year even in O.S. would be 1619. For a defence of the statements in this letter see II. 62. p. 479 *seq.* H. there states that his relation is founded on a proclamation of King James which is printed in the Harl. Misc. vol. iii., see on p. 479. This fixes the inauthenticity of the present letter, especially as H. could not have been in London in 1618.

LETTER V.—*To my Brother*, Thomas Howell (1588-1646), eldest brother of our Howell, entered Jesus 1604 (*Ath. Ox.* 804), took his B.A. 20 Feb. 1609, same day as Fr. Mansell (Clark's *Registers Univ. Oxf.* ii. 285), and proceeded D.D. 1630, became Rector of West Horsley, co. Surrey, and of St. Stephen's, Walbrook (*Ath. Ox. l. c.*), installed Canon of Windsor 26 Nov. 1636 (*Le Neve*, iii. 401), enthroned Bishop of Bristol 12 April 1645, died next year, and was buried in the Cathedral (*Le Neve*, i. 216). His letter about his brother James, given in Suppt. I. p. 655, will sufficiently indicate his time-serving character. His sermons, "like the waters of Siloah, did run softly gliding on," says Fuller, *Worthies*, ii. 575.

P. 26.] *Copernicus his Opinion.* Copernicus' great book, *De revolutionibus orbium cælestium*, appeared in the month of his death, May 1543, but did not win universal acceptance for over a century. Bacon, as is well known, refused to accept the theory (*cf.* Fowler's edition of the *Novum Organum*, Introd., pp. 30-36), and Milton in his *Paradise Lost* retained the Ptolemaic system as more suitable for poetic purpose (Masson in Milton's *Poetical Works*, lib. ed., i. 89-97).
Philosophical Problem. *Cf.* De Morgan, "Old Arguments against the Motion of the Earth." Comp. Brit. Alm. for 1836, and *infra*, i. p. 528 *seq.*
Dike-Grave. Dutch, *Dijkgraaf*, superintendant of the Dikes.
Duke of Alva (1508-83), the governor of the Netherlands who brought about their independence.

P. 27.] *till I come to the Hague.* This promised letter was either not sent or is not included. In either case this is a natural touch which vouches for the authenticity of the present letter.
Captain Bacon, referred to in I. i. 2, p. 20.
1 April 1617. This is clearly a mistake (of the original) for 1619.

LETTER VI.—*Dan. Caldwell*, elsewhere spelt Caldwall, was son of Lawrence Caldwall of Battersea, and held manors at Shreves and Wythefeld, co. Essex. He died 13 Nov. 1634. See Morant, *Essex*, i. 220, ii. 219.
in Oxford. I have been unable to find Caldwall's college either in Anthony à Wood or the *Registers* recently issued by the Oxf. Hist. Society.
was I matriculated. See Introd. p. xxvi.
in the Temple. Caldwall was a member of the Middle Temple (Morant, *Essex*, ii. 219).

P. 28.] *Letters have a strong operation.* *Cf.* with this passage Howell's *Instructions for Forraine Travell* (ed. Arber, p. 28). "Letters which by a Spirituall kind of power do enamour and mingle Soules more sweetly than any embraces." *Cf.* Donne to Wotton, "Sir, more than kisses, Letters mingle souls."
embraces. *Cf.* passage just quoted from *For. Trav.*
Tom Bowyer of St. John's, Oxon., took his degree 17 March 1613, and his M.A. in 1616, having spent the intermediate time in foreign Universities. Clark, *Registers*, iii. 319.
Jack Toldervy. He is probably the Jack T. referred to in similar terms p. 275.
Fleece in Cornhill. "Capt. Cuttle and Curtis and Mootham and I, went to the

the Fleece Tavern to drink," Pepys, 8 Feb. 1661. *Cf.* L'Estrange, *Visions of Quevedo*, p. 137 (H. K). But these quotations (from Cunningham) refer probably to the Fleece in Covent Garden. H. refers to the Fleece in Corn-hill (Wheatley-Cunningham ii. 51).

P. 29.] LETTER VII.—*English Brownists church.* The sect of Brownists or Separatists was founded by Robert Brown (1550–1630), who resided for some time in Holland (*cf.* Masson, *Life of Milton*, ii. 538–42), *cf.* Mayor, *Lives of Ferrar*, p. 182, for his similar experiences at Amsterdam.
Synagogue of Jews. The *Bet Jacob* (House of Jacob) in Amsterdam, the first public synagogue allowed in North Europe for centuries. *Cf.* De Castro, *de Synagoge der portug. israel. Gemeente te Amsterdam*, 1875. *Cf.* Graetz, *Gesch. d. Juden*, ix. 593–5. Evelyn visited it 19th Aug. 1641.
Jew of the Tribe of Aaron. This must be a mistake : the Jews with whom Broughton had a dispute were R. Elias, R. Abraham Rauben, and R. David Ferrar, none of them a Cohen or descendant of Aaron. The chief Cohen in Amsterdam at the time was Jacob Cohen Lobats (Graetz, *l. c.* x. p. 5).
Broughton, Hugh (1549–1612), one of the greatest Hebrew scholars of his day. See full and interesting biography in D.N. B.
Bills of Mortality commenced in London 1592, and were issued regularly from 1603. The weekly deaths would fix the population at 60,000 for Amster-dam, 300,000 for London. Howell, however, calculates the population of London and suburbs at 1,500,000 (*Londinopolis*, p. 403, where there is a similar comparison between London and Amsterdam).
Excises, should be Accises, as in ED. PR. J. H. refers to this later, p. 486.

P. 31.] LETTER VIII.—*Dr. Tho. Prichard*, matriculated 19 June 1610, ætat. 19 (Clark, *Reg.*, 317), Vice-Principal of Jesus 1621 (Wood., *Hist.* 574), was tutor at Worcester House (*infra* 131), and died while J. H. was in the Fleet (p. 438) some time between 1645–9.
Leyden University, founded 1575, was a frequent resort of English students, Sir Thomas Browne, *e.g.*, taking his medical degree there. The Index Society has published a list of them.
Franeker University was founded 1585, and suspended by Napoleon, 1811.
Nations. The students were classified by nationality, a custom borrowed from Paris. *Cf.* Mullinger, *Univ. Camb.* i. 78–9.

P. 32.] *New Inn to Christ's Church*, the smallest to the greatest Oxford College.
Almshouses on Tower-hill, built 1593 by the Merchant Taylors (Stow's *Survey* ed. Thoms, 48).
Sutton's Hospital, the Charterhouse endorsed by Thomas Sutton, 1613. *Cf.* *Gard.* ii. 14. Sutton is said to have been the original of Jonson's *Volpone*.
Oppidanes, lived in lodgings and not in college as on the English system. The Eton boys are still called Oppidans.
Habits, cap and gown. *Cf.* Wordsworth, *Univ. Life*, 454–67, and *infra*, p. 71.
Cicero. Probably, says Dr. Gow, a bad reminiscence of *De Fato*, iv. (7), where the contrary is expressly stated.
Heinsius (1580–1655), classical scholar, secretary of the Synod of Dort.
Grotius, Hugo (1583–1645), the founder of International Law. Just at this time he was imprisoned (May 1619–Mar. 1621).
Arminius, Jacob Hermannsen (1560–1609). His name would be just then prominent owing to his views being condemned at the Synod of Dort which closed 29 May 1619. This anecdote is quoted (doubtless from H.) by Forde, *Apoph.* 88.

Baudius,

Baudius, Dominic, of Leyden (1561–1613), historiographer and Latin poet. *Cf. infra.*
Crassos transire Dies. Persius, v. 60.

P. 33.] LETTER IX.—*Mr. Richard Altham*, second son of Sir James Altham, Baron of the Exchequer, and half-brother of the Sir James mentioned pp. 34, 182. Howell went abroad with him, p. 112. On his family, many of whom are mentioned in the *Letters*, see Morant's *Essex*, i. 24, ii. 60, and *Visit. of Essex* (Harl. Soc.), i. 539. A short genealogy, *infra*, on p. 353. Altham died 1623 : an affecting reference to his death, I. vi. 45.
Gray's Inn. Altham entered the Inn 2 Feb. 1615 (J. Foster, *Register of Admissions*, p. 9).
Plowden, Edmund (1517–84), whose *Commentaries*, 1571, contained "leading cases."
Jack Chaundler. Referred to Worthington, *Diary*, 364.
Littleton on Tenures, Eng. edition, 1539. The celebrated commentary of Coke on Littleton did not appear till 1628. D'Ewes, *Autob.* i. 178, 181, made use of the French edition.
Baron your Father. Sir James Altham, Baron of the Exchequer, 1607, had recently died, 21 Feb. 1617 (Foss., *Biog. of Eng. Judges*, vi. p. 50).

P. 34.] *Sophisters*, name given to second year men at the Universities. *Cf.* P. Fisher's poem *infra*, p. 689, three lines from bottom.

LETTER X.—*Sir James Crofts.* See *supra* on I. i. 4, p. 22. The reference to grey hairs at the end of the letter would indicate that it is the earlier Sir James who is addressed.
Prince Maurice (1567–1625) became Stadholder of the United Provinces on death of his father, 1584 ; Prince of Orange on death of his brother, 1618. His death is referred to p. 228.

P. 35.] *ride the great Horse*, as at tournaments or in warfare. On this see Herbert of Cherbury's *Autob.*, p. 68, and Mr. Lee's elaborate note.
dines about twelve. Dinner beginning at eleven is mentioned p. 295.
Bohemians. Gard. c. xxix. deals with "The Bohemian Revolution."
elected King the Emperor, Ferdinand II., King of Hungary, elected Emperor 28 Aug. 1619.
Ortelius (1527–98), the standard geographer of the time. He is mentioned again, *Fov. Tr.* 21. His Letters have been published by Mr. Hessels *Epistolæ Orteliana* (Cantabrig, 1887).
3 June 1619. The reference to the elected Emperor shows that this letter is at least antedated, even if the paragraph beginning "There are great stirs" is not an interpolation.

P. 36.] LETTER XI.—*Captain Francis Bacon. Cf. supra*, note on I. i. 2. p. 20.
Glass-House in Broad-street, where Howell had himself been (*supra*, p. 20).
Middleburgh, the English staple had probably been removed in 1614, in connection with the scheme of Alderman Cockain (*Gard.* ii. 386).
departure of the English Garison from the cautionary towns (*ib.* 382–4).
cautionary towns. For a further account see *infra*, p. 119.
Sir Ralph Winwood (1564–1617), one of the most important diplomatists of the time.
Lord Caroon, Caron, the Dutch ambassador at St. James's (*Gard.* ii. 382).
Earl of Suffolk, Thomas Howard (1553–1626), Lord High Treasurer, 1614–18.

P. 37.] *Lady Elizabeth*, James I.'s daughter, married to the "Palsgrave" (Elector Palatine) 14 Feb. 1613.
Sig. Antonio Miotti, referred to again p. 65.
Sir Robert Mansell, see I. i. 28, p. 65.

LETTER XII.—*Sir James Crofts.* *Cf.* notes on I. i, 4, p. 22.

P. 38.] *Citadel.* "To see the *Citadell of Antwerp*" is reckoned one of the advantages of travel in Howell's *Instructions*, p. 71.
Tumults in Bohemia, see *supra*, p. 35.
Great Council at Prague. This refers to what is known as the defrenestation, 1618, in which Martinitz and Slawata were hurled from the window. *Gard.* iii. 270 (C.II.F.).
Sir James Altham, Richard's half-brother. His death referred to, 182.
Bishopsgate-street. The home of the Althams was "The Abbot of Waltham's House" in the parish of St. Mary at Hill, Billingsgate Ward. See on this an elaborate paper by C. R. Corner, *Archæologia*, xxxvi. 400–17.
5 July 1619. Clearly postdated, if the letter is authentic, but it would be natural for H. to be better informed on such subjects if he was writing from abroad.

LETTER XIII.—*Dr. Tho. Prichard.* See on I. i. 8, p. 31.
infirma species (should be "infima species" as in ED. PR.), a logical term indicating the smallest class to which an object belongs.
Predicament, the arrangement of classes in order of extension.

P. 39.] *Fresh-man*, the University term for an undergraduate in his first year. This is an early use of the word.
Queen-Mother (late Regent), Maria de Medici, married to Henry IV. 10 Dec. 1600, and Regent of France, 14 May 1610 to 2 Oct. 1614.
Marquis of Ancre. See fuller accounts on I. i. 19, p. 51.
Sir Eubule Theloall or Thelwall. See on II. 6.
Jesus College new Walls, probably the Hall which was built "about the year 1617" (Anthony à Wood, *Hist. Coll. Oxf.* p. 580).
my Countryman Owen. John Owen († 1622) of Carnarvonshire, author of some *Epigrammata* which ran through six editions, 1607–33, and were reprinted in Paris as late as 1794.
Anagram. J. H. was fond of this learned trifling. See Index s.v.

LETTER XIV.—*Dan. Caldwall.* See on I. i.

P. 40.] *Kid-skin gloves*, usual as presents to patrons. Thorold Rogers, *Prices*, v. 716-9. *Cf.* the custom of presenting gloves to judges.
Royal Exchange, built by Gresham after that of Antwerp. Vide *infra*, p. 122.
white worsted stockings, I vastly suspect—however, this is a natural touch which vouches for the authenticity of this letter.
Vacandary, doubtless the "Nicholas Vacandary born in France," mentioned as living in Aldgate Ward, on 7 Sept. 1618, in *Lists of Foreign Protestants* (Camd. Soc. 1862, p. 62).
our Brother Sergeant. There is no Caldwall among the list of Serjeants in Pulling's *Order of the Coif*, 1884, or in Foss' list for Jas. I., vi. 29.
Battersay, where Caldwall's father lived. Morant, *Essex*, i. 220.

LETTER XV.—*To my Father.* See on I. i. 2.

P. 41.] *the great Church*, the Cathedral of Notre Dame. Evelyn gives a similar account under date 18 Jan. 1644.

greatest

greatest Bell of Christendom, called Georges d'Amboise after the Cardinal of
that name ; it was melted down at the Revolution.
St. Oen, Church of St. Ouen, finer even than the Cathedral.
Wardships, qy. wardmotes, courts held in each ward of a city?

P. 42.] *Sequena*, misprint for "Sequana" as in ED. PR.
My last to you. This is a natural touch which seems to vouch for the
authenticity of this letter. The reference would be to the letter from
Amsterdam, I. i. 7, *supra*, p. 28.
Sir Robert Mansel. See on I. i. 28.
Law-businesses, a further reference to this, *infra*, p. 105.

LETTER XVI.—*To Capt. Francis Bacon.* Mentioned previously. See on
p. 20.

P. 43.] *slain by Ravillac.* See on p. 47.
Town and City are distinguished by the fact that the latter is the seat of a
Bishopric. But as applied to Paris, a difference of locality is meant. *Cf.*
Evelyn, 24 Dec. 1643. "The City is divided into 3 parts whereof the Towne
is greatest. The City lyes between it and the University, in form of an
island." *Cf.* F. Moryson, *Itinerary*, 1617, i. 157.
Crot of Paris. *Cf. Forreine Travell*, "the hudge and durty." *Germ. Diet*, 63.
great Philosopher. I have not been able to trace this.
vagina populorum. Mr. Bradley has referred me to Jordanes (Jornandes)
where I find (*Getica*, ed. Mommsen, iv. 25,) "Scandza insula quasi officina
gentium velut vagina nationum."

P. 44.] *Louvre*, the present building was begun 1539.
Italian Mile, either the modern Roman mile of 1628 yds. or the Tuscan of
1808. Moryson, *l.c.* i. 294, gives the various European miles.
where the English resort. In his *Forrein Travell* J. H. recommends keeping
away from English abroad for the same reason. He advises instead,
devotions to a *Divota* or Nun. Perhaps he was thinking of the heroine of
the worsted stockings, *supra*, p. 40.

LETTER XVII.—*Richard Altham.* See on I. i.
P. 45.] *Filous*, rogues. A word used by Butler, and *cf. Nicholas Papers*, 75.
Chevalier du Guet, mentioned later on, p. 98, but in a passage derived from a
work of fiction where the names are expressly said to be fictitious.
Jack White. The reader may select from the J. Whites given in Evelyn, 211
(Chandos ed.); Edwards, *Raleigh*, i. 60; Forster, *Elliot*, ii. 475, and P.
Warwick, *Memoirs*, 255.
Pont Neuf, described, together with the statue, by Evelyn, 24 Dec. 1643.
Henry the Great, the work of John of Bologna.
Florentine Horse. The materials were sent by Cosmo II. from Florence.
beat the Hoof. *Cf.* the slang expression "pad the hoof."

P. 46.] *Plush Cloak.* Perhaps a cloak lined with plush as that mentioned by
Pepys, Oct. 28, 1664.
Luines, Charles d'Albert, Duc de Luynes (1578-1621), Captain of the Louvre
1616, Peer of France 1619.
Vacandary. See *supra* on p. 40.

LETTER XVIII.—*To Sir James Crofts.* See on I. i. 4, p. 22.

P. 47.] *Sir Herbert Crofts* or Croft († 1622), a grandson of Sir James Croft,
the Controller of Q. Elizabeth's household. He was converted to Roman
Catholicism

Catholicism in 1617 (Mr. Lee's note on Herbert of Cherbury, 135). He died at Douay, 1622 (D.N.B.).
The King of France with forty thousand men. Halliwell in his *Nursery Rhymes and Tales*, p. 3, adopts this statement of Howell's. It is, however, called "Old Tarlton's Song," which would place its composition before 1588, long before the death of Henry IV. in 1610.
Ravillac, a Lay-Jesuit. This well-known event occurred as told here on 14 May 1610.

P. 48.] *Henry II.* was wounded by Count de Montgommeri at a tournament at Paris 29 June 1559, and died on the 10 July following.
Henry III., assassinated by Jacques Clément, 1589.

P. 49.] *Duke of Bouillon,* Henri de la Tour d'Auvergne (1555-1623). He was well known in England, where he had been as Ambassador. He is the "Fox of Ardennes" in H.'s *Dodona's Grove.*
Cardinal of Perron, Jacques Davy Duperron (1556-1618).

P. 50.] *Count of Soissons,* Charles de Bourbon (1556-1612); the same story is told *infra* p. 564.

LETTER XIX.—*To my Brother.* See on I. i. 5, p. 25.

P. 51.] *Signior Conchino,* Concino Concini, created Marquis d'Ancre 1613, assassinated 24 April 1617. The story is also told in Howell's *Lustra Ludovici.* 37-9 ; *Germ. Diet,* 63.
Prince of Condè, Henri II. de Bourbon (1588-1646) was imprisoned in the Bastile 1 Sept. 1616, and not liberated till 20 Oct. 1619.

P. 52.] *retire to Blois,* 3 May 1617.
His Wife, Leonora Galegai, was executed 8 July 1617.
Picture in Virgin-wax, it was supposed that by witchcraft wounds inflicted on an image could be transferred by sympathy to the person they represent.
8 Sept. 1620. The murder of Concini is spoken of as more recent than three years. For reasons for antedating Howell's residence, see Introd. p. xxviii.

P. 53.] LETTER XX.—*To my Cousin, W. Vaughan,* of the "Vaughans of Cors y Gedol," of whom an elaborate account in 4 *Arch. Camb.* vi. pp. 1-16, where Howell's cousin is mentioned pp. 11, 12. They were connected with the Bacons and the Gages, *ib.* 273. He took his degree in 1609, Clark (*Reg.* iii.). H.'s Cousinship consisted in having a sister married to a cousin of Vaughan's. See Pedigree.
Lower Britons speak no language but our Welsh. It was colonised by emigrants from Britain in the fourth century.
Armorica. Howell's suggestion is that this has the same root as Morgan, and he is so far justified by Littré, who derives Armorica from *ar* on and *mor* (*cf. mare*) sea, but see next note.
Pelagius, said to be a Latinisation (?) of Morgan, which is said by a folk-etymology to mean "marine."

P. 54.] *Hoell the Great,* Hywel Dda († c. 950), whose laws were the first code compiled for the Welsh. The Howells claimed descent from him, according to James, *infra,* but without justification. See the Pedigree.

LETTER XXI.—*Sir John North, Kt.* of the Bath, 3 Nov. 1616 (*Metcalfe,* p. 168). He was appointed Gentleman Usher of the Privy Chamber. He brought the news of the failure of Raleigh's expedition (Nichol's *Progresses of of Jas. I.*, iii. 483). He was younger son of the eldest son of Roger Lord North of Guildford (Nichols, *ib.*, 222 *n.*).

P. 55.] LETTER XXII.—*Mr. Tho. Porter*, brother of Endymion Porter. He died Dec. 1655, and was buried at St. Andrew's, Holborn (Malcolm, *Lond. Red.* ii. 218). He seems to have been in the navy.
I met here, in imagination, it would seem, as Porter is included among the friends in England.

P. 56.] *Duke of Ossuna.* See on I. iii. 37, p. 208. The same anecdote is told in *Parthen*, 31, and is perhaps derived from *Don Quixote* (C.H.F.).
Camillo, Mazalao. Italian workmen at the Glass House in Broad Street. The latter is mentioned p. 65.
with you. From this it would seem that Porter had some connection with the Glass House.
Ship behind Exchange. Also mentioned on p. 75. Pepys was merry there till late at night on Sept. 6, 1661.

P. 57.] LETTER XXIII.—*Sir Jas. Crofts.* See on p. 22.
Barcelona. Cf. Defoe's account in *Capt. Carleton*, c. iii. *ad fin.*
Bandoleros, the Spanish equivalent of Banditti.
Monserrat, said to be so called from its shape, *Mons Serratus:* it is full of hermitages. *Cf.* Ford's elaborate and florid account in the *Handbook to Spain*, pp. 495–8.
Herds. Read Herbs as in ED. PR.

P. 58.] *Diogenes' Tree.* Referred to again p. 373. See Stanley, *Hist. Phil.* ed. 1655, vii. 22, who quotes Stob. *Ser.* 55.
Hoping to meet your Letter. Here again we have one of the natural touches occurring through the Letters, which either vouch for their authenticity or argue great art on the part of H. in concocting them.

LETTER XXIV.—*Dr. F. Mansel.* See on p. 21.

P. 59.] *O blessed Clime.* H. makes the same remark, *For. Tr.* 75. Readers will remember Charles II.'s boast that in the English climate men may work out of doors more days of the year than in any other : it was probably drawn from this statement here.
Morviedre, now Murviedro (*i.e. muri veteres*), was a Greek city established in Spain long before the Carthaginian supremacy.
Hanibal, the siege, is described by Sil. Ital., i. 271.
Many monuments. These were destroyed by Suchet's soldiers during the Peninsular War. Ford, *l.c.*, 455.

P. 60.] LETTER XXV.—*Christopher Jones*, a college chum of H.'s. See Clark, *Reg.* ii. 298, iii. 306.
Barillia. Salsola soda. "The salt of glass-wort (called in England Barillia)." *Phil. Trans.* xlii. 71, quoted *New Eng. Dict.*

P. 61.] LETTER XXVI.—*Sir John North.* See on I. i. 21, p. 55.
Marcia, should be "Murcia," as in ED. PR.
Andria Dorea (Doria), the liberator of Genoa, 1468–1560. The anecdote is quoted from Howell by T. Forde, *Apophthegms*, 28.
Algier Men of War. The pirates swept the West Mediterranean from about 1616. See note in Forster, *Grand Remons*, 228.

P. 62.] *Bannier at Algier.* See Lane-Poole, *Barbary Corsairs*, c. xvi.
Scylla.

Scylla. *Cf.* Sandys, *Travels,* 193.
Phare. *Cf.* Sandys, *l. c.* It is probable H. used Sandys.
Malamocco, visited by Sandys, *Travels,* p. 1, F. Moryson, *Itin.* i. 75 (" the hauen of Venice "), and by Coryat, *Crudities,* i. 200.
pratic, the word is still used for quarantine. *Cf.* Card. Newman's *Letters,* i. 423.

P. 63.] LETTER XXVII.—*Dr. Howell.* See on I. i.
twenty-one hours. Italian clocks used to be divided into 24 divisions, and strike continuously from midnight to midnight, as was recently recommended by the Astronomical Conference at Washington. A few English clock-makers adopted the custom for a time.
Virgin City. "This untainted Virgin," says Coryat, *Crudities,* ii. 75, and *cf.* Wordsworth's Sonnet.
Infames Scopulos. Hor. *Odes,* i. 3, 20.

P. 64.] *Corinth, now Ragusa.* This is a mistake of Howell's. *Cf.* 3 *N. and Q.* vii. 179.
As stutterers use. On this curious idea see 7 *N. and Q.,* xii. 589, and 8, i. 113.
Non cuivis. Hor. *Epist.* i. 17, 36.
Zacones, should be *Lacones* (misprint in ED. PR.). See *infra,* p. 467. The statement is derived from Sandys, *Travels,* 63.

P. 65.] LETTER XXVIII.—*Sir Robert Mansell,* one of the best known admirals of James I.'s reign (*cf.* Lardner's *Brit. Admirals*), and is frequently mentioned in the memoirs of the time (Herbert of Cherbury, 26, and in Weldon, ii. 6 ; Forster, *Eliot,* i. 469 *n.* ; Gardiner, iv. 10, &c. ; Nich. *pass.*). His relations with Howell, see on I. i., and for his connection with Venetian glass, *cf.* Hondoy, *Les Verreries,* pp. cxxviii.-xl. This letter is quoted entire by W. W. Mansel, *Family of Mansel,* p. 75.
Miotti and Mazalao, mentioned previously. See note on pp. 37, 65. The family of Miotti were distinguished in the history of glass-making. *Cf.* Hondoy, *l.c.* p. xci., and Nesbitt, *Descr. Cat.* cxx.
Symns, mentioned later, pp. 67, 79.
Sir Henry Wotton, the celebrated ambassador who lied abroad for the sake of his country (1568-1639). *Cf.* Herbert of Cherbury, ed. Lee, 150, 231, 265.
your late marriage with Anne, daughter of Sir John Roper. Sir Robert's first wife was a sister of Bacon, who refers to him as " my brother " in a letter, Spedding, *Life* vii. 320.
Arsenal of Venice. H. refers to this in *For. Tr.* 71, and *S.P.Q.V.* 5, 35, 65, also in *Therologia,* 68, 91.

P. 66.] *Duke of Ossuna* (Ossone), 1579-26 Sept. 1624, the Viceroy of Naples who refused to establish the Inquisition there ; for a full account of him, see *infra,* p. 201. Another account is given by Howell in his *Parthenopæia,* p. 31.
Murano, still celebrated for the excellence of its glass. See also *Harl. Misc.,* v. 68, Evelyn.
Greek told me in Sicily. The only mention of Howell's having landed in Sicily ; one of the "natural touches" which tell for the authenticity of the Letters, or for that of the present one.
Camels' Dung. This piece of information H. almost certainly got from Sandys, *Travels,* 98 ; he certainly used the book.
your Consaorman. A query was made of this in 1 *N. and Q.* xi. 475. It is passed over in the *New Eng. Dict.,* and I can only suggest some confusion with *consorte* or partner.

P. 67.]

P. 67.] LETTER XXIX.—*Brother.*   See on I. i. 5, p. 25.
Symns, mentioned before, p. 65.
admit no poison. This property was generally attributed to glass or crystal, and was often made use of as a test of suspicious beverage. It has, of course, no foundation in fact.
P. 68.] *Lasses and Glasses.*   H. uses this jingle again, *S.P.Q.V.* 38, 39.

LETTER XXX.—*Richard Altham.*   See on I. i.
O dulcior illo. Ovid, *Tristia,* V. iv. 30. For *Mille* in next line read "Melle" as in ED. PR.
P. 69.] *High Beauty.* H. refers to this *For. Tr.* 40, *Londin,* 387, *S.P.Q.V.* 37.
Streets of Paris. Their foulness has already been referred to, *supra,* p. 43.
League of Cambray, between the Pope, the Emperor, France and Spain against Venice, 10 Dec. 1508.
P. 70.] *Bishopsgate Street.* See note on p. 34.

LETTER XXXI.—*Dr. Fr. Mansell.*   See on p. 21.
Hoellus: this and the title *Epistolæ Ho-Elianæ* are sufficient to indicate the pronunciation of Howell's name, which disregards the "w" altogether.
Which Marriage. Evelyn saw it in June 1645. *Cf.* also Sandy's *Travels,* p. 2. Byron refers to this marriage of the Doge with the Adriatic in his *Childe Harold,* iv. :—

> " The spouseless Adriatic mourns her lord,
> And, annual marriage now no more renew'd,
> The Bucentaur lies rotting unrestored,
> Neglected garment of her widowhood."

F. Donno published a long heroic poem, *Lo Sponzalitio del Mare,* just as H. was in Venice.
Galeass, a compromise between rowing galley and sailing galleon. See Lane-Poole, *Barbary Corsairs, pass.* and plates, p. 69 and 227.
Bucentoro. See the quotation from Byron, *supra.* The origin of the name seems to be uncertain according to the Oxford Dictionary. It is generally connected with the figure-head of the vessel.
P. 71.] *that famous Ship at Athens,* which went yearly to Crete in memory of the Minotaur and Theseus' escape. Plato, *Phædo,* 58A.
Hereford School. See Fisher's poem, *infra,* p. 689.
Lambskin Hood in Oxford, as a Bachelor of Arts, who, in full dress, wears such a hood with his gown.
Cælum non animam. Hor. *Epist.* II. xi. 27.
P. 72.] *Microcosm.* See Prof. Mayor's interesting note on microcosm in *Ferrar's Life,* pp. 239-40. Van Helmont's *Paradoxal Discourses concerning the macrocosm and microcosm* was published Lond. 1685. There is also a dissertation of Elert, *De homine Microcosmo,* Leipzig, 1709. Purchas' *Microcosmus,* 1627, is based on the idea to the extent of 818 pp.

P. 73.] LETTER XXXII.—*Richard Altham.*   See on p. 33.
Bezoar, sometimes called *Snakestone,* and regarded as a powerful antidote; it was really taken from a Persian wild goat. Yule, *Hobson-Jobson,* s.v., and *cf.* Benfey, *Panschat.* 1, § 71.
potable gold, also a powerful antidote in the mediæval pharmacopœia. Forde talks of changing "*aurum palpabile* into *aurum potabile,*" *Fam. Lett.* 49. On its use Mr. Firth refers to Dr. F. Anthony, *Apology of . . . aurum potabile,* 1616, and Dr. John Cotta, *Cotta contra Antoninum.* There was also an answer by Gwynne, *Aurum non aurum,* 1617 (Lowndes).

P. 74.]

P. 74.] LETTER XXXIII.—*Sir John North.* See on p. 54. The present is nothing more than a model letter. (It is called " A Letter of Gratitude " in the original index.) It is unlikely that H. would have sent so merely formal a letter without saying where he was, &c. But perhaps this part of the letter was excised to avoid repetition.

LETTER XXXIV.—*Dan Caldwall.* See on p. 27.

all the other nine, the spheres of the sun and moon, the six planets, and the fixed stars in the Ptolemaic system. See note on p. 26.

tenth of June. If the post from Venice to London took twenty days, it is hard to see how Howell could have acknowledged on 29th June a letter dated 10th in London.

P. 75.] *Ship Tavern,* mentioned previously, p. 56, see note there.

Treasury of St. Mark. H. refers to this again in his *S.P.Q.V.* 37.

P. 76.] 29 *July* 1621. The date of the month is inconsistent with H.'s statement of the time the post took from Venice to London.

LETTER XXXV.—*Sir James Crofts.* See note on p. 22.

Lord Ambassador Wotton's, referred to before, p. 65. One of Isaac Walton's *Lives* is devoted to him. He was ambassador at Venice 1604, 1616, and 1620.

P. 77.] *Sclavonia.* In Speed's map of Italia in his *Prospect of the most famous Parts of the World,* 1626, he places Sclavonia E. by N. of Venice. It was really the tract of country between the rivers Slav and Drau. H. mentions it, *For. Tr.* 57.

Battle of Lepanto, the ancient Naupactus. Don John of Austria defeated the Turks there in 1571.

there are in all sixty. Coryat, *Crudities,* i. 212, says seventy-two. Moryson, *l.c.,* i. 76, agrees with H.

P. 78.] *Grand Cairo.* H. has a description of "the gran Cayr" in the Appendix to his *For. Trav.,* ed. Arber, p. 86. See also Webbe's *Travels,* pp. 21-6.

LETTER XXXVI.—*Robert Brown.* Evelyn's father-in-law was so called, also a person named in Warwick's *Memoirs,* p. 282.

P. 79.] *Master Web.* This may be Edward Webbe, Master Gunner, afterwards Chief Master Gunner of France, whose interesting *Travels,* 1590, have been edited by Prof. Arber. He would be about sixty-six at this time.

Cousin Brown. It is impossible to identify so common a name.

Randal Symns, there was a Kent family of this name. Mentioned *supra,* 65, 67.

Ship Lion was engaged in the fight against the Spanish Armada. Froude, xii. 378, 403, but the name was a common one.

famous Hexastic, given also in Howell's *S.P.Q.V.,* in the Proem. He possibly got it from Coryat, *Crudities,* i. 179 (1726 reprint).

P. 80.] *Sannazaro* (1458-1530), author of *De Partu Virginis.*

hundred Zecchins. Coryat, *l.c.,* says "a hundred crownes." He adds, "I would to God my friend Mr. Beniamin Johnson were so well rewarded for his Poems." Zecchens = sequins.

Sir Hugh Middleton was H.'s countryman in the sense of being a Denbighshire man (1555-1631). He was knighted 1613. See note on p. 427.

Ware River, now called the New River. H. refers to this, *For. Trav.* 73, and in his *Londinopolis.*

Mr. Leat, a cousin of R. Altham's (p. 156). See on p. 154.

LETTER XXXVII.—*Captain Thomas Porter,* mentioned in *Poroysland Coll.* xx. 132, among the "Captaines that goeth for Algiers."

30,000

30,000 *times* seems impossible, 500 a minute.

P. 81.] *Another Passage.* This anecdote was taken from Howell by T. Forde in his *Apophthegms*, 1660, p. 87.

that disease, syphilis, which each nation desires to credit to foreigners, the English calling it the French disease, the French the Neapolitan, and so- on. Its origin is obscure, but is generally attributed to America. Traces of it, however, are said to be found in the bones of the cave men (Boyd Dawkins, *Cave Hunting*), and it has been conjectured that the leprosy of the Hebrews was only its secondary symptoms. H. makes it a French invention in *Germ. Diet.*, 59. *Cf.* Creighton, *Epidemics*, i. 73.

LETTER XXXVIII.—*Sir William St. John*, mentioned in Edwards, *Raleigh*, i. 562; Nichols, *Prog. James I.*, ii. 418, iii. 772.

Antenor's Tomb. Evelyn gives the inscription on it, p. 166 (Chandos ed.),. and so does F. Moryson, *Itin.* i. 72.

P. 82.] *three Million of Souls.* Hume discusses this census in his Essay on the Populousness of Ancient Cities.

Herriot. H. makes another reference to this *Parth.* Proem. A heriot is, of· course, the best moveable left at a tenant's death which can be chosen and seized by the landlord.

P. 83.] *Charles III.* should be Charles the Fifth, as in ED. PR.

Mark of distinction, a quoit-shaped ring of different coloured cloth stitched on to the outer garment. On the whole subject, with illustrations, see article on *La Roue des Juifs* in *Rev. des Etudes Juives*, t. xiii.

Vespasian's Amphitheatre, the Colosseum.

P. 84.] *Pius V.* (1504-72). H.'s gossip is quite incongruous with the account· given of him as an ascetic in Ranke, *Popes*, iv. § 7.

Statues at Belveder. The celebrated Apollo Belvedere ; but the Laocoon was also in the Belvedere Gardens, as Evelyn informs us, 18 Jan. 1645.

Duilius, C., the admiral in the great naval fight with the Carthaginians near the Lipari Islands. The inscription celebrating it was dug out of the ground in the sixteenth century, but doubts have been raised as to its· genuineness. Niebuhr, *Hist. of Rome*, iii. 529 ; *cf. Lectures*, i. 118. Howell got it from Brerewood, *Inquiries*, 1614, p. 44, who gives it as here. (See on pp. 384, 459.

P. 85.] *Columna Restrata*, so in ED. PR. Should, of course, be *Rostrata*, with. reference to the "beaks and prows" of the vessels.

St. Austin. "Augustinus fertur tria videre cupiise; nimirum Christum in carne, Paulum in cathedra, Romam in flore." Freigius, quoted by Prof. Mayor in note on *Lives of Ferrar*, p. 191. Prof. Mayor also compares the passage from Howell.

P. 86.] LETTER XXXIX.—*Sir T. H. Knight*, probably Sir Thomas Hawkins,. to whom there are other letters. See on p. 403.

Courtesans. Evelyn places their number at 30,000, 6 Feb. 1645.

P. 87.] *Tarantola*, the dance of those bitten by the spider so-called, is pro- bably meant by H., but why he mixes it up with manna I cannot conceive. Perhaps they were: the two specialties of Naples that his correspondent would be likely to be interested in.

P. 88.] LETTER XL.—*Christopher Jones.* See on p. 60.

thirty odd months. So on p. 99 he speaks of having been away "almost three years."

P. 89.]

P. 89.] *Agnomination*, clearly equivalent to alliteration. H. alludes to this again, *For. Tr.* 48. Rice in his Welsh grammar, Lond. 1592, pp. 277-83, deals with the similarity of Italian and Welsh with regard to alliteration in poetry (I owe this to Prof. Rhys).

Tewgris, todyrris. Prof. Rhys has kindly given me the following text and version :— *Tewgrys tô dyrys ty'r 'deryn gwyllt* = The thick shroud, the tangled thatch of the wild bird's house, &c.

Donne, O danno. In *For. Tr., l.c.,* H. gives another example, *Vlisse, ô lasso, &c.* Both passages are from a long Italian poem quoted in Rice's Welsh Grammar, p. 277, with which H. was acquainted, as we know from p. 460, where see.

My Tutor, Master Moor Fortune. Perhaps the same as the one mentioned in R. Smyth's *Obituary* (Camd. Soc.), p. 13. " 1637, May 17, More Fortune, bayliff of St. Martin's, died."

Sir Charles Williams. He was not knighted till 10th April 1621 (Metcalfe, p. 178), *i.e.* after the date of this letter, if genuine, though not after the date added in second edition. Sir Charles was a relation of Sir Trevor whom H. claims as uncle (Harl. MS. 4181, f. 281).

P. 90.] LETTER XLI.—*Sir J. C.,* probably Sir James Crofts. See on p. 22.

P. 91.] *the subtillest.* H. gives them the same character in his *For. Trav.* 41, "when a Jew meeteth with a Genoway, he puts his fingers in his eyes, fearing to be over-reached by him."

St. George's Mount, overlooking Genoa.

P. 92.] *Snik and Snee.* Du. tool and knife.

Winds the Penny, we say now "turn a penny," and speak of the "nimble ninepence."

P. 93.] LETTER XLII.—*Capt. Francis Bacon.* See on p. 36. He was related to the Vaughans with whom the Howells' were connected. See note on p. 53.

Padua the Learned. In his *S.P.Q.V.,* p. 55, Howell gives the original. "Venetia richa, Padoua dotta, Bologna grassa, Roma pomposa, Napoli odorifera e Gentile, Genoa di Superpia altiera piomba, Florenza bella, Grande Milano." He got it from Moryson, *l.c.,* iii. 50. *Cf.* too *Germ. Diet,* p. 22.

Duke of Feria. He is mentioned by Evelyn (Chandos ed.), 182. See also Gard. vii. 348, and D.N.B. s.v. Feria.

Dormer, a life of *Jane Dormer, Duchess of Feria,* by P. Clifford, appeared as recently as 1887.

P. 94.] *the Dome,* the world-famous Milan Cathedral, begun in 1385.

Citadel of Antwerp. See on p. 38.

Nova Palma, also referred to in *For. Tr.* 43.

Genius of the Nation. H. gives a somewhat similar characterisation in *Germ. Diet.* Moryson's *Itinerary,* 1617, III. i., c. iii. is devoted to a comparison of the nations of Europe. *Cf.* also Defoe's account in *Memoirs of Cavalier.* ed. Bohn, 23.

P. 95.] *greatest embracers of pleasure.* H. uses the same phrase of the Italians in *For. Tr.* 41.

LETTER XLIII.—*Sir J. H.* Probably a misprint for Sir T. H., Sir Thomas Hawkins, on whom see pp. 86 and 403.

Mr. Lewis. There is a Lewis mentioned in Spedding, *Life,* vii. 30, as patentee of berths from Wales, who may have been H.'s friend or related to him.

P. 97.]

P. 97.] *Twelve in the hundred.* Adam Smith, ed. Nicholson, p. 38, mentions that between 1720-60 it fluctuated from 2 to 5 per cent.
LETTER XLIV.—*Mr. Tho. Bowyer.* See on p. 28. He died 8 Feb. 1659 in London according to Wood, *Athenæ.* There is a Dr. Bowyer mentioned in the Fairfax correspondence, ii. 37.
Calvin's Time, his influence at Genoa is referred to, p. 516.
Strange Accident. The earliest form of this story I can find is in Poggio's *Facetiæ.* Mr. King has traced it in Bayle, *Dict.,* s.v. Buridan, Salan's *Invisible World,* No. xxxvi., and Crowe, *France,* i. 353. H. got it from Rosset, *XVIII. Histoires tragiques,* Paris 1609, whence also he took the story of Coucy Castle on p. 323.

SECTION II.

Consisting of twenty-five letters relating the events of two years, 1620-22, during which Howell "coached" the young Savages, one of whom was after-wards Earl Rivers, and then travelled in France and Holland with young R. Altham.

P. 99.] **LETTER I.**—*To my Father.* See on p. 19.
Almost three years. See also *For. Tr.* 63, where the grand tour is said to take three years and four months, and *ibid.* p. 87, forty months.
Dr. Harvey, the great discoverer of the theory of the circulation. Mr. Bennett suggests that Howell might have met him at Padua, where Harvey had been studying. This cannot be, as Harvey took his degree there in 1602.
M. Cadenet, brother of Luynes (138, 150). His coming is dated by D'Ewes, *Autob.* i. 164, 29 Dec. 1620. *Cf.* Gard. iii. 589, and Herbert, *Autob.* ed. Lee, 225 *n.* II. gives anecdotes of him, *Lustra Ludov.* 36, and *Finetti,* 67, 193.

P. 100.] *Tall Men.* There is the same anecdote in the *Apophthegms* of Bacon, who was probably therefore not above 5 ft. 6 in. himself. H. gives the story again, *Germ. Diet.* 30, and it is quoted by T. Forde, *Apophthegms,* p. 88.

P. 100.] **LETTER II.**—*Rich. Altham.* See on p. 33.
Female long'd, alluding to the superstition (or fact?) that women when *enceinte,* take capricious and violent longing for things they see, and must not be thwarted.
three hours' riding from Norberry, where this is addressed. See on p. 101.

LETTER III.—*D. Caldwall, Esq.* See on p. 27.
at Battersay. Cf. Morant, *Essex,* ii. 219, where it is stated that he was the son of Lawrence Caldwall of Battersey.

P. 101.] **LETTER IV.**—*Sir James Crofts.* See on p. 22.
Norberry. Probably Norberry Park, co. Surrey, afterwards the residence of the Lockes mentioned so frequently by Mad. D'Arblay.
Lord Darcy. Thomas Darcy (†1640) was created Lord Darcy 8 Oct. 1613, and Viscount Colchester 5 July 1621, and Earl Rivers 4 Nov. 1626. *Cf.* E. C., *Complete Peerage,* iii. 22, and *cf.* Morant, *Essex,* ii. p. 458.
St. Osith, in Essex on the sea : the estate here referred to was originally a monastery, Chiche St. Osyths, which was given to Cromwell at the Dis-solution, and then came to the Darcys (Morant, *l.c.,* i. 28, 140, ii. 396, 397, 457).

Council

Council of Prague. H. means the Bohemian Estates assembled at Prague.
Palsgrave was elected King, 16 Aug. 1619 (Gard. iii. 309).
Par negotio. H. was fond of this phrase ; he uses it in his letter to Clarendon,
p. 668.

P. 102.] *Dr. Hall,* afterwards Bishop of Norwich, the well-known poet and
satirist (1574-1656). He had only recently returned from the Council of
Dort. See on p. 149, and *cf. D.N.B.,* s.v.
Duke of Bavaria, the Elector Maximilian the Great.
Sudden Battel. Frederick was dining with the English ambassadors at the
time, so little was an attack expected (Gard. iii. 383 and *n.*). The battle
was known in London, 24th Nov. 1620 (C.H.F.).
a whole twelve month, 5 Sept. 1619-29 Oct. 1620.
Castrein. See Mrs. Green, *Princesses,* v. 350 ; " Custrin, a princely residence
forty-eight miles from Berlin."

P. 103.] LETTER V.—*Dr. Fr. Mansell.* See on p. 21.
a running Academy. The same phrase is used *Germ. Diet,* 7.
Sir Robert Mansel. See on p. 65. He was absent as commander against the
Algiers pirates, Oct. 1620-June 1621 (Southey-Bell, *Brit. Admirals,* v.
60-63, after Purchas, *Pilgr.* 885-6).
Sir John Ayres. For a curious incident between Sir John and Lady Ayres
and Herbert of Cherbury, see the latter's *Autobiography,* ed. Lee, pp. 129-
38, 141. Sir John Eyre (as he is also called) was ambassador to Con-
stantinople, 1616-21. See also on p. 141.
Resignation. Dr. Mansell became Principal, 3 July 1620, and resigned in
May 1621 in favour of Sir Eubule Thelwall (Wood, *Colleges,* 577, and
Lloyd, *Mem.* 540).
North Wales Men. This is a point in favour of H.'s birth-place being in
South Wales, but does not decide between Abernant and Bryn, since both
Carmarthenshire and Brecon are South.
Landloper, Dutch for vagabond, *Landlooper.* Scott uses the word in the
Antiquary : "But what will come of the *landleuper ?*" Is it possible that
this can be the origin of the seamen's "landlubber"?

P. 104.] LETTER VI.—*Sir Eubule Theloall* was a Denbighshire man, B.A.
both of Cambridge and Oxford, and a great benefactor to Jesus College
(Wood, *Colleges,* 574, 577).
Fellow of your new Foundation. Prof. Rhys has found evidence of Howell's
election as Fellow in Jesus College books (see Doc. xl.). The new foundation refers to the Charter which Sir Eubule obtained on June 1, 1622
(Wood, *l.c.,* 574). The main object of this was to permit the College to have
only half the old foundations, viz., eight fellows and scholars instead of
sixteen.
id. Mart 1621. Obviously wrong in the month, as the charter was dated
1 June 1622, and H. refers to it, 15 Mar. 1621-2. In fact the whole Letter
is misplaced, as H. was elected during his second visit to Spain in 1623.

P. 105.] LETTER VII.—*To my Father.* See on p. 19.
I am to go travel with them. He did not after all (*infra,* p. 111),'so that this
seems like a natural touch vouching for the authenticity of this letter. But
see at end.
Sir James Crofts. See on p. 22.
Long-Melford, four miles N. of Sudbury. The Hall was an old seat of the
Savages, and was plundered during the Civil Wars.
St. Osith in Essex. See on p. 101.

Lora

Lord Savage. Sir Thomas Savage, who had married Lord Darcy's daughter and heiress. Sir Thomas became Viscount Savage in 1626, and was therefore only Sir Thomas at the presumptive date of this letter.
Lord Darcy. See on p. 101.
Q. Anne is lately dead. March 2, 1619 (Gard. iii. 294. Law, *l.c.* ii. 86).
Denmark House. Somerset House, for some time named after Anne of Denmark. A mistake; the death took place at Hampton Court. E. Law, *Hampton Court,* vol. ii., devotes c. vii. to her death.
last fearful comet, another reference *infra,* 576. Gardiner notices it, iii. 295, and refers to Corbet, *Poet. Epistle.*
one Piero. Nichols, *Prog. Jas. I.,* iii. 548 *seq.* The Herbert Papers, No. cxci., contain an "Inventory of the Things found in the two Trunks of Piere Hugon, 8 Oct. 1619" (*Powysl. Coll.* xx. 247). Law, *l.c.* p. 83, calls him Pira or Pierrot.
" Goody Palsgrave." *Cf.* Coke Papers (Hist. MS. Com.), i. 64, *Jas. I.,* ii. 252. Lloyd was censured for saying, "What has become of your goodman Palsgrave?" D'Ewes, *Autob.* ii. 189. *Cf.* Campbell, *Chief Justices,* i. 366.
Secretary Winwood. Sir Ralph (1565–1617). He was dead at this time, but H. does not necessarily refer to him as living.
Cautionary Towns. See on p. 36.
Sir John Walter was one of Shropshire's worthies (Fuller, ed. Nicholls, ii. 259) and a benefactor of Jesus College, which may account for H.'s acquaintance with him. Fuller says of him, "When a *Pleader,* eminent ; when a *Judge,* more eminent ; when *no Judge,* most eminent," because he resisted benevolences and lost his place thereby. He died in 1630.
Master J. Lloyd. There is a Lloyd mentioned in Herbert's *Autob.,* ed. Lee, p. 8, who may possibly be the man referred to.

P. 106.] 28 *Mar.* 1618. Under the old dating this would correspond to 1619, and is therefore a suitable enough date. But the slip about Denmark House is suspicious, as well as the reference to Sir Thomas as Lord Savage. And H. could not have been in England so early as the spring of 1619.

LETTER VIII.—*Dan Caldwall.* See on p. 27.

P. 107.] *Bon Christian Pear,* still grown under the name of "Bon Chrétien." The name is thus one of the rare examples of a foreign name Anglicised and then reverting to the foreign form.
Bergamot, a variety of the pear. "The best perrie is made of . . . Bergamot," says Markham, *Country Farm,* 417.
Muscadel. This is properly the name of the raisin ; the vine from which it is grown is technically known as "Muscat of Alexandria."
Mr. Daniel. There is a Daniel mentioned in Winwood, *Mem.* iii. 367.
House of Long Melford, near Sudbury in Suffolk.
Manor of Sheriff, properly Shreves or Sherwaies in Lexden Hundred, co. Essex. See Morant, *Essex,* i. 220.

LETTER IX.—*Robert Brown.* See on p. 78.
Sir Robert Mansel being now, up to June 1621. See *supra,* on p. 103.
hogling. A misprint for *bogling.*

P. 108.] *back stratagem.* "He crossed the river below Coblentz . . . suddenly wheeling round, he recrossed the line" (Gard. iii. 368).
Take Oppenheim, Sept. 4, 1620. Kreutznach and Alzey had already capitulated (Gard. iii. 369). There is no evidence of his appearing before Oppenheim previously. A good account of the capture of Oppenheim is given by Defoe, *Memoirs of Cavalier,* c. v., probably derived from some more trustworthy source.

Marquis

Marquis of Anspack or Ansbach, a marquisate generally associated with that of Bayreuth. At this time both principalities were held by Joachim of Brandenburg, who granted that of Ansbach to his son Earnest, the person here meant.

Spinola's (1569–1630). General-in-Chief of the Spanish army in the Netherlands from 1604. Referred to Nicholls, *Prog. Jas. 1.*, iii. 805.

an Ass laden. A saying of Philip of Macedon, quoted Cic. *ad Att.* i. 16. *Cf.* Hor., *Carm.* III. xvi. 13.

Sir Horace Vere (1565–1635) spent a great part of his life on the Continent, helped to defend Ostend when Spinola attacked it 1604, and had been governor of the Brill. Frequently mentioned in Herbert of Cherbury, *Autobiography*, ed. Lee, xvi. 21, 113, 117, 146. A saying of his at the Palatine Council of War given by Forde, *Apophth.* 24. An account of him in Markham's *Fighting Veres*, 1888 (C.H.F.).

Sir Arthur Chichester (†1625) had been Lord-Deputy of Ireland. Mentioned Nich. iii. 1, Fairf. iii. 39.

P. 109.] *Middle Isle* [aisle] *of Pauls*, *i.e.*, of Old St. Paul's. This was a favourite lounge, as we know from the polite literature of the time.

Cheapside. A favourite resort of H.'s, as we know from other references, p. 265.

LETTER X.—*R. Altham.* See on p. 33.

5th of this present. H. had waited long to answer if the letter was really written on the 30th.

Polldavie Ware, also "polderay," the coarse bagging stuff used for sacks. So the dictionaries (Nares, Whitney); but would "ware" be used of such things?

Lady Savage, Elizabeth, daughter of Lord Darcy, and wife of Sir Thomas Savage, who was to have succeeded his father-in-law in his title. See *supra*, on p. 105.

Earl Rivers, is a premature title, as Viscount Colchester was only promoted to that title in 1626.

Hilary Term begins on Jan. 23, so that the letter, if authentic, would be written about the end of the year.

P. 110.] LETTER XI.—*Algier Voyage.* Sir R. Mansel's fleet returned in June 1621. See the reference on p. 103.

Hoggies. Hadjis who had performed the pilgrimage to Mecca.

Maribots, now spelt "marabout"; the monks of Islam.

Countryman Ward, his achievements among the Barbary Corsairs have been recounted by Gardiner, iii. 65, 66. There are contemporary pamphlets on his exploits, see Lowndes, s. v. Barker and *News* (II. K.). *Cf. Germ. Diet*, 36, and Nicholls, ii. 158.

Danskey the Butterbag Hollander should be Dansker, Gard. *l.c.*, or Simeon Danser, according to Stanley Poole, *Barbary Corsairs*, 226. Butterbag (also "Butterbox") is a slang term for a Dutchman, containing some allusion to his proverbial corpulence.

P. 111.] *One in the hundred.* This may be regarded as a kind of insurance against pirates, though the tax seems to have been not to save their own ships, but to pay for destroying those of the Corsairs.

Colchester Oysters have been celebrated from Roman times.

Lord Colchester. Lord Darcy was made Viscount Colchester, 5th July 1621, which would agree with the date of this letter.

green finn'd are supposed to be a special delicacy. Prof. Ray Lancaster has traced

traced the origin of the colour to the chemical composition of the banks in France whence they are derived.

LETTER XII.—*To my Father.* See on p. 19.

P. **112.**] *Baron Altham, son.* Richard, frequently mentioned. See on p. 33, and Index.

My Brother, afterwards the Bishop of Bristol. See on p. 25.

Prince Palsgrave arrived at the Hague in April 1621 (Gard. *Pref.* to vol. iv., where he discusses the authenticity of this letter).

the old D. of Bavaria's Uncle. "Whatever that may mean," says Prof. Gardiner; I will not rush in where he fears to tread.

Arch sewer, corresponding to the Germ. *Erztruchfess,* a title held by the Electors Palatine till 1623. (I owe this interesting point to the courtesy of Mr. H. Bradley.)

Count Mansfelt begun to get a great name in Germany in the spring of 1622 (Gard. *l.c.,* and *cf.* iv. 195).

Halverstade (Halberstadt), the Duke of Brunswick was Frederick Ulrich, the last of his line.

Sir Arthur Chichester. See on p. 108. He returned from Germany at the end of 1622 according to Gard., *l.c.,* who has certainly selected a very glaring example.

Sir Horace Vere. See on p. 108.

My Lord of Buckingham. He was only Earl of Buckingham till 1623, when he was made Duke.

Master of the horse. He was elected to this office in 1616.

High Admiral of England. But he had been appointed to this office in 1616.

Treasurer Cranfield (1575-1645) afterwards Earl of Middlesex, one of Bacon's chief opponents, and distinguished for his economies in the king's household. See also Gard. iv. 233.

formerly a Merchant. He was the proverbial apprentice who marries his master's daughter (and heiress).

19 *Mar.* 1622, *i.e.* 1623. Prof. Gardiner, in the Pref. to his fourth volume, points out the many discrepancies in this letter which, professing to give the news of the day, wobbles about between 1619 and 1623.

P. **113.**] LETTER XIII.—*Sir John Smith.* See on p. 17, the opening letter of the second edition.

Trevere or Vere, on the Island of Walcheren, north of Flushing.

365 *Children.* This legend is found located at Landona (Loosduenen) in Brereton *Travels* (Chet. Soc.), p. 35 (C.H.F.). Evelyn also refers to it under date 1 Sept. 1641.

P. **114.**] *Mr. Altham.* Richard, with whom H. was travelling. See above, Letter XII., p. 111.

Sir John Franklin, mentioned in Nicholls, *Prog. Jas. I.,* iii. 24, as being knighted, 2 Oct. 1614.

at the Hill. Tower Hill, where Sir T. Savage seems to have resided, p. 132.

Mr. Scil's the stationer in Fleet Street. See Bibl. List No. 39. *Cf.* Arber, *Stat. Reg.* iii. 684 *c.*

LETTER XIV.—*Lord Viscount Colchester,* previously Lord Darcy. See on p. 105. This is one of the points of accuracy about title referred to in Introduction, p. lxxviii.

P. **115.**] *Came, saw, and overcame.* A reference, of course, to Cæsar's *veni, vidi, vici.* But the translation is somewhat peculiar, and is the same as that used in *As You Like It,* v. 2, and 2 *Hen. IV.,* iv. 3, whence H. may have derived it. Shakespeare was favourite reading of Charles I.

chang'd his coat. Seemingly an early use of this somewhat slang expression, but

but in reality H. is using it quite literally with reference to Spinola's change of uniform.
Imperial Ban. H. gives some account of this in his *Disc.* 45, also *infra*, 298.
Duke of Bavaria. This seems a reference to the change of Electorate in 1623 (Gard. iv. Pref.).

LETTER XV.—With this should be compared Fynes Moryson's elaborate survey (in his *Itinerary*, 1617, Bk. iii.), and Evelyn or Feltham's satiric *Character of the Low Countries*, 1660. (This latter has been erroneously attributed to Howell.)

P. 116.] *Unweildy Woman.* The Duchess Margaret, natural daughter of Charles V. Part II. of Motley's *Rise of the Dutch Republic* deals with her Administration, 1559–67. Why H. calls her "unweildy" I know not. She was masculine in appearance, and wore a moustache. That she was liable to gout is a point in favour of H.'s epithet (Motley, *l.c.*, i. 230).
Golden Fleece, is a Burgundian Order, having been founded by Philip III., Duke of Burgundy, in 1429.

P. 117.] *Egmond*, Lamoral, Count of Egmont, 1522-1568, the earliest leader against the Spaniards in the Netherlands ; now best known perhaps as the title-hero of Goethe's drama.
Horn, Philip Montmorency, Count of, executed with Egmont, 1568, for opposing the Spaniards. He was himself a Protestant.
Bloetrad. Dutch "Bloody Council." *Cf.* Howell's *Patricius*, p. 7.
Duke of Alva. Ferdinando Alvarez de Toledo, Duke of Alva (1508-83), the celebrated Governor of the Netherlands.
Cousin Pacecio, Pachicho or Paceotti, an Italian engineer and architect of the Antwerp citadel, but not related in any way to Alva, nor was Alva the cause of his death, as he was put to death during an *émeute* at Flushing (Motley, ii. 361).
Don Luys de Requiluis, properly Requesens y Cuñega, who succeeded Alva in 1573.
Pacification of Ghent, the Congress of Ghent in 1576.

P. 118] *Don John of Austria* (1546-78), the conqueror of Lepanto, was Governor of the Netherlands for the last two years of his life. His life has been exhaustively treated in the masterly monograph of Sir W. Stirling-Maxwell.

P. 119.] *Earl of Leicester.* His adventures in the Netherlands are told at length in Motley, *United Netherlands*, vol. i.
Flushing and Brill. See *supra*, p. 36, and Motley, *l.c.*, i. 301, 342. Sir Philip Sidney was the first governor of Flushing.
Count Maurice. See on p. 124.

P. 120.] *twelve years*, 1609-21, the Twelve Years' Truce with Spain which intervened between the struggle for Dutch Independence and the Thirty Years' War.
dispensed with himself from payment. Cf. Weiss, *L'Espagne sous Philippe II.* (C.II.F.).
Goletta, the port of Tunis. See Stirling-Maxwell *Don John*, ii. 9.
A State of Holland.
A Province of Flanders, now Belgium.

P. 122.] *Antwerp.* See *supra*, p. 38, and *cf. For. Tr.* 71.
Gresham was King's Agent at Antwerp from 1552 onwards.

P. 123.] *Amsterdam. Cf.* the elaborate comparison at end of *Londinopolis* and *supra*, pp. 25, 29.

P. 124.] *Baluc.* There is no Dutch word similar to this, which must there-fore stand for "bailiff," the Dutch for which is *Schout*, which is ingeniously Englished by H. as *scout*. Brereton, *Travels* (Chet. Soc.), p. 9, says " Baylie or Scout, *id est*, High Sheriff."
Vroetschoppens. Town Councillors; the word is now spelt *Vroedschap.* Brereton, l. c., p. 8, calls them "Vornscapp or aldermen."
Prince Maurice (1564-1625), son of William the Silent, whom he succeeded as Stadtholder.

P. 125.] *Busses,* the vessels used in the herring-fishing. There is a tract called *Britain's Buss* in Prof. Arber's *English Garner*, vol. iii. 621 *seq.*

P. 126.] *Eight Quarts.* H. repeats this in his *Germ. Diet,* 19, but raises the quantity to twelve quarts (three galls.).

P. 127.] *Trevere.* See on p. 113.
Scots Trade. Even after the Union of the two crowns the Scots trade was quite independent of the English. *Cf.* Seeley, *Expansion of England*, pt. I., c. vii. p. 131.
Jews in Rome. See *supra,* p. 2.
Outward Mark. See *supra,* note on p. 84. Evelyn gives a curious account, 6th May 1645.
Waggons. On this see a passage in Vaughan, *Protectorate of Oliver Cromwell,* ii. 468 (C.H.F.).
Mariner's compass, invented by Chinese, was passed on to Europe by the Arabs, long before the Dutch came into prominence (*Cf.* Klaproth's *Lettre à M. Humboldt*) ; even the thirty-two points are early, and are mentioned by Chaucer in his *Astrolabe.*

P. 128.] *Walloon.* See on p. 474.

P. 129.] LETTER XVI.—*Mr. Hugh Penry*, probably some relation of J. Penry the Brownist, executed 1593 (see p. 579). He was Vicar of Dyfynog, according to the family pedigree of the Howells. For his descendants see Jones, *Brecon,* i. p. 662. He died in 1637, if H.'s date (*infra,* 339) is to be trusted. He was elected Fellow of Jesus at the same time as H. (see Doc. xl.).

P. 130.] LETTER XVII.—*Dr. Howell.* See on p. 25.
Anne. See preceding letter.
Mansfelt. See on p. 112 a further reference to his defeat, p. 163.
Ambassadors. They were the laughing-stock of the Continent, says Forster, *Eliot,* i. 96 (referring to Howell).
Sir Richard Weston, afterwards Lord Treasurer. On him see Gard., *Span. Match,* i. 336, where he is mentioned with reference to the embassy here referred to. He was one of the *"pioneers of British Agriculture."* Pro-thero, p. 32.
Sir Edward Conway. See on p. 240.
Lord Carlisle, "honest camel's face," as Charles I.'s sister called him. Forster, *Eliot,* ii. 194, 2nd ed. We shall meet him again at Paris, p. 215, and Madrid, p. 171.
Sir Arthur Chichester. See on p. 108.
Lord Digby (1580-1652), afterwards Earl of Bristol. H. became well ac-quainted with him later on at Madrid, so much so, indeed, that Bucking-ham refused to help him on because he was so "digbyfied," p. 239.

P. 131.] *to Winter,* rather early in June. See next note.
10 *June,* 1622. This does not agree with the statement just made that they were going to winter in Paris.

LETTER

LETTER XVIII.—*Dr. Tho. Pritchard.* See on p. 31.
Worcester House in the Strand, the house of the Marquis of Worcester of the "Century of Inventions."
Pont de Cé. H. gives an account of the battle in his *Lust. Lud.* 49 under the date 1620.

P. 132.] *Inns of Court,* Gray's Inn. See on p. 33.

LETTER XIX.—*Sir Tho. Savage,* 2nd Baronet, afterwards created Viscount Savage, 1626, and was to have succeeded his father-in-law as Earl Rivers, but predeceased him. H. was for a time tutor to his two sons. *Cf.* Ellis, i. 262 ; Nichols, iii. 348 *n.*
Rochel. H. gives a tolerably full account of the quarrel between Louis XIII. and the Reformers in his *Lust. Lud.* p. 52 *seq.*

P. 133.] *Celestines.* In *Lustra Lud.* p. 52. H. says 200,000 by the Pope, 200,000 by the College of Cardinals, and 200,000 by the French clergy.

P. 134.] *that's under France,* part of Navarre being in Spain.
they of the Religion, i.e., of the Reformed religion. This phrase occurs frequently in H., *infra,* 150, 225, and *For. Trav.,* ed. Arber, 46.
Cardinal of Guise. Louis III. of Lorraine (1575-1621). No account of the quarrel is given in *Lust. Lud.,* which seems to prove that H. did not utilise that book, then in process of making, to fill out the *Letters.*

P. 135.] LETTER XX.—*D. Caldwall.* See on p. 27.
River Sequana. Latin name of the Seine.
Lewis of Poissy. This story is taken from H. by T. Forde, *Apophthegms,* 89.
Table book. Tablets. See Earle, *Microcosmography,* ed. Bliss, p. 315.
as I did once at Rouen. See *supra,* p. 40.
Whitest kidskin were thus better in England than in France at this time. The glovers of England were not incorporated till 1638.

P. 136.] LETTER XXI.—*Phlebotomy.* Harvey's discovery gave a new impetus to bloodletting ; Riolan and Botal declared it a panacea, and were followed by Willis. *Cf.* Dechambre, *Dict. enc. des sciences medicales,* s. v. Saignée.

P. 137.] *two Columns.* With reference to the doctrine of the four elements : the body made of earth and nourished by air is supported by fire and water.

LETTER XXII.—*Sir Tho. Savage.* See on p. 132.

P. 138.] *D. of Luynes.* See on p. 46. He was made Constable of France 2 Ap. 1621. *Cf.* the account in *Lust. Lud.* 55 of his interview with Herbert of Cherbury.
Cadenet. See on p. 99.

P. 139.] *Valtolin,* the Spanish Governor of Milan, had seized the valley of Valtelline, near Grisons, Dec. 1620. Gard., *Sp. Match,* i. 389. Valtelin is the canton of Switzerland nearest Austria.
15 *Dec.* 1622, at least eighteen months post-dated.

LETTER XXIII.—*Sir John North.* See on p. 54.

P. 140.] *Anne de Arque.* A curious form for Joan of Arc.
Vacandary. See on p. 40. Digby sent him off from Madrid to Flanders about 2nd Feb. 1622 (Rec. Off. S. P. For. Spain, Bundle 60).

P. 141.]

P. 141.] LETTER XXIV.—*Sir Jas. Crofts.* See on 22.
Epernon. See on 131.

P. 142.] LETTER XXV.—*Cousin, Mr. Will Martin.* Perhaps the W. Martin
mentioned in Nichol's *Prog. Jas. I.,* iii. 366.
Intelligencer, writer of news.   H. was himself destined to have peculiar
practice in this kind of letter-writing.

P. 143.] *Ragged Staff,* used as a metaphor for Spain elsewhere, pp. 297, 436.
The reference is probably, as Mr. Bradley suggests, to the cognisance or
emblem of St. James of Campostello, the patron saint of Spain.   H. uses
the expression for Spain throughout his *Dendrologia.*
la pomme du pin. The most renowned literary inn of Paris, at the corner of
the Pont Notre Dame. It is mentioned by Villon, Rousseau, Regnier,
Boileau, Dumas (*Trois Mousq.*), and Ste. Beuve, who calls it "la veritable
taverne litteraire." *Cf.* De Ris, *Les ensignes de Paris,* p. 15, and F. Michel,
Histoire des Hotels, ii. 303 (I owe the latter reference to M. Paul Meyer).

SECTION III.

This section contains the letters relating to the Spanish Match and Prince
Charles' visit to Madrid, Feb. 17–5 Oct. 1623. They are seemingly less
"cooked" than the others. Some of the originals appear to have been in the
possession of the late Earl of Westmoreland (*Hist. MSS. Com.* X. iv. 55).

P. 144.] LETTER I.—*Lord of Arundel* and Surrey (1592–1646), was Earl
Marshal of England, 29 Aug. 1621.
Sir Henry Montague, raised to the Barony of Montagu of Boughton in 1621,
but H. is referring to him as Judge. The same anecdote is told in Bacon's
Apophthegms, xxi. D'Ewes, i. 160, says he gave £20,000 for the post.
Lord Cranfield, afterwards Earl of Middlesex, 16th Sept. 1622, so that there
is a scrupulous accuracy about his title.

P. 145.] *Kinswoman.*   Ann Brett (C.H.F.).

LETTER II.—*Mr. John Savage,* afterwards Earl Rivers, and formerly H.'s
pupil. See on p. 235.
the same lodgings. This seems a touch of nature vouching for the authenticity
of the present letter. H. is referring to the tour with Altham.

P. 146.] *Inglese Italionato.* This saying seems to have been first quoted by
R. Ascham in a passage of his *Schoolmaster* quoted at length in the intro-
duction to my edition of Painter's *Palace of Pleasure. Cf.* also Vernon Lee,
Euphorion.
my Lord your grandfather.   Lord Darcy, see on p. 101.
Brawn in collars.   A receipe "*to collar a pig,*" is given in W. C. Hazlitt,
Old Books on Cookery, 105.
Mr. Thomas Savage.   John's brother, and likewise a former pupil of H.'s.
Mr. Bold, probably a member of the Lancashire family, Bolds of Bold Hall,
and the governor or travelling tutor of the young Savages, a post which H.
had declined.   He was made Fellow of Jesus, see p. 697.

P. 147.] LETTER III.—*Sir James Crofts.* See on p. 22.
Sir Richard Weston. See p. 130 *n.*
called them his Ambassadors.   "Bring stools for the ambassadors" were his
words, Dec. 11, 1621. Gard., *Sp. Match,* ii. 140. Wilson makes James
say, "Here are twelve kings come to me."
Sir Edward Coke, the celebrated opponent of Bacon. He was imprisoned
on the present occasion. He is the "Eirenurch" of H.'s *Dodona's Grove.*
on

on the point of Dissolution, a protest on liberty of speech for the Commons. Gard., *l.c.*, 149. The Protest was on Dec. 18, 1621 ; the Dissolution on Jan. 6, 1622.
Lord Digby. See on p. 130. He was despatched to Spain about March 24, 1622. Gard., *Sp. Match*, ii. 216 *n*.

P. 148.] *Lady Hatton*, grand-daughter of Burghley. An account of the wrongs she suffered at the hands of her second husband, Coke, is given in the Pref. to *S.P.* for 1634.
her Husband Coke, with whom she had quarrelled about the Hatton estate. Gard., *l.c.*, i. 93.
Lord of Colchester. See on p. 114.

LETTER IV.—*Brother Mr. Hugh Penry.* See on p. 129.

P. 149.] *Synod of Dort* lasted from 13 Nov. 1618 to 29 May 1619. Hale's letters from the Synod are given at the end of his *Golden Remains* (C.H.F.).
Lord Bishop of Llandaff. Bishop Field, H.'s friend, on whom see on p. 230.
Balcanquell (or qual), Dr. Walter; his letters from the Synod are also contained in Hale's *Remains, ad fin.*
Arminius. See on p. 32.
Vorstius (1569-1622). One of whose theological tracts was burnt by order of James I. He is frequently mentioned in the memoirs of the time (D'Ewes, 82 ; Sir D. Carleton, *Letters pass.;* Earle, *Microc.* 103. Cf. Forster, *Grand Rem.* 107).
Dole in Lorrain, between Dijon and Geneva. It belonged to Spain at the time, and till conquered by Louis XIV. The Jesuit's palace is still one of the sights.
16 *Apr.* 1622, flagrantly misdated ; the return from the Synod could not have been later than June 1619.

LETTER V.—*Lord Viscount of Colchester*, Lord Darcy. See on p. 101. He was raised to the title of Viscount Colchester in 1621 : H.'s accuracy about titles is striking.

P. 150.] *Venetian Gazette*, practically the first newspaper in Europe. It was so called after the coin paid for it, and this received its name from Gaza in Palestine.
Mansfelt hath been beaten at Wimpfen, April 26, 1622, after which he retreated into Alsace. Gard., *l.c.*, ii. 197.
Berghen-op-Zoom, besieged in Aug. 1622. The siege is mentioned by Herbert, *Autob.*, 21, and described in dispatches of Sir D. Carleton's in Sir T. Roe's *Negotiations*, 1740 ; Letters, l. lix.
Cardinal of Guise. See on p. 134.
Lord Hays. Query Baron Hay of Sawley, created 1615, but he became Viscount Doncaster in 1618, and Earl of Carlisle 1622, when this letter is supposed to be written. H. calls him Lord Hayes (after Earl of Carlisle) in *Lust. Lud.*, p. 34.
Sir Edward Herbert of Cherbury. His clashings with Luynes are told at length by H. in his *Lustra Ludovici*, p. 57. Letters to him, pp. 352, 427.
the greatest Favourite. See a similar description of him on p. 138 *n*.

P. 151.] LETTER VI.—*Turky Company*, also called Levant Company, founded by Elizabeth 1579.
Sir Robert Napper, or Napier. For letter to him, see I. iii. 34, p. 205, *infra*.
Captain Leat. See on p. 154.
Sir Charles Cornwallis. Was knighted 11th May 1603 (Metcalfe, 141). There is a letter to his lady, *infra*, p. 422.

P. 152.]

P. 152.] *Sir Paul Pindar.* See on p. 543.
Mr. Walsingham Gresly. See on p. 204.

P. 153.] LETTER VII.—*Sir T. Savage.* See on p. 132.
Digby. See on p. 130. He was despatched to Spain Mar. 24, 1622. See on p. 147.
Abbot, Archb. of Canterbury (1562–1633), see D.N.B. This homicide happened 24 July 1622, and was taken advantage of by his enemies to humiliate him. *Cf.* D'Ewes, *Autob.* i. 201 ; and Ellis. 3 *Orig. Lett.* iv. 183.
Sir Henry Martin. Cf. Nicholls, *Prog. Jas. I.,* i. 135 *n.*
Guilford (Guildford), where the almshouses still exist, for I have seen them.

P. 154.] 9 *Nov.* 1622. Abbot's homicide in July could not have been known in March before Digby set out.

LETTER VIII.—*Capt. Nick. Leat.* A full account of him appears in A. Brown's *Genesis of the U.S.,* in the biographical Appendix of the second vol. (C.H.F.). He is mentioned in both Stow and Malcolm's Histories of London (H. K.).
Wounding the Sergeants. This looks like an authentic touch.

P. 155.] LETTER IX.—*Arthur Hopton,* died 1649. See Skelton's *Oxfords.,* Evelyn (Chandos), 200, 485, Nichols, iii. 877.
a very comely lady. This description is quoted in *Somer Tracts,* ii. 536 *n.*
big lipp'd. Grammont has much to say on the big lips of the Emperor Leopold (C.H.F.). *Cf.* Burton, *Anatomie,* I. ii. 1, § 6, " The Austrian lip and those Indians' flat noses are propagated " (*i.e.,* are hereditary).
Austrian Family of Bourbons. The Bourbon lip is celebrated, and is mentioned by Carlyle about Marie Antoinette.
Sixteen. " Had now entered on her seventeenth year," says Gard., *Sp. M.,* ii. 273.
Don Carlos. Not the Carlos of the play, who died in 1568. This one was the king's brother. His death is mentioned *infra,* p. 286.

P. 156.] LETTER X.—*Capt. Leat.* See on p. 154.
Mr. Simon Digby. Frequently mentioned in the memoirs of the time (Sir D. Carleton, *Letters,* ed. 1780, p. 402 ; *S.P.,* p. 520 ; *Jas. I.,* ii. 354 ; Jesse, i. 333). He was a great traveller ; we hear of him in H.'s letters at Madrid, Vienna, Moscow, and Constantinople. Digby records his arrival at Madrid " Vpon the thirtyeth day of January here arrived my Cosen Simon Digbie," 2nd Feb. 1622 (Rec. Off. S.P. For. Spain, Bundle 60).
Olivares (1587–1645) was chief minister of Philip IV. from 1621. H. gives an account of him in *Parthenopæia,* 41. The " Chonandra " of H.'s *Dodona's Grove.*
Junta Committee. The Junta later referred to was the Junta of Theologians appointed to settle certain theological points in the *Spanish Match.*

P. 157.] LETTER XI.—*Viscount Colchester.* See on p. 114.
Mr. George Gage had been sent to Rome to watch the negotiations (= " Don Jorge Gaze " of Francisco de Jesus, ed. Gardiner, C.S. 33) ; he took Madrid on his way from England to Rome, *ib.* 44, about Sept. 17, 1622. He occurs frequently (Rushw., i. 23, 66, 121 ; *Jas. I.,* ii. 219, 323, 341, 414 ; [H.K.] *Letters* (C.S.), 129 ; Spedding, vii. 429, 431 ; Gard., *Sp. M.* ii. 119, 236, 283.

taking

taking of Ormus from the Portuguese by Shah Abbas, assisted by the English fleet, 22 Apr. 1622. It is referred to in Herbert, *Travels*, 46 ; *cf.* Gard., v. 237. Digby refers to it in his letter from Madrid, Jan. 12–22, 1622–23 (Rec. Off. S.P. For. Spain, Bundle 60).

P. **158.**] *Duke of Lerma* had been dismissed from the post of first minister in 1618. H. has many anecdotes of him, *infra*, 162, 184 ; repeated in *Parthen.*, 82, 90.
Duke of Uzeda. Mentioned Nicholls, iii. 868, as "Ozeta."

P. **159.**] 3 *Feb.* 1622, *i.e.*, 1623, at least five months too late.

LETTER XII.—The beginning of this letter is a very fair abstract of the actual letter sent by James by Porter, and given in *Cabala*, 1st ed. 1651, p. 238, 2nd ed. 1663, p. 259. H. must therefore have seen it at Madrid.
Master Endymion Porter arrived Nov. 1, 1622. Gard., *Sp. M.* 268 ; on him see 535 *n*.
Heidelberg taken, 9 Sept. 1622. Gard., *ib.*, ii. 247.
Postil. As a matter of fact it forms part of the body of the letter.

P. **160.**] *sub regimine Matris.* "His Majesty will oblige himself privately that they shall be brought up *sub regimine matris* . . . until the age of nine years." From letter of Calvert in F. de Jesus, ed. Gardiner, App. p. 338, where the actual article of the treaty is given.
first of September. James' letter was dated Oct. 3, 1622. But see next letter, from which it appears that old Howell's letter was enclosed in one of Sir James Croft's, dated Oct. 2.
23 *Feb.* 1622[–23]. Again too late.

P. **161.**] LETTER XIII.—*Sir Jas. Crofts.* See on p. 22.
2d of October, utterly incongruous with the date at end of letter.
Dispatches from Rome. These had come with Gage from Rome to England, Aug. 25. Gard., *Sp. M.* ii. 237–9.
express from Rome, a reference to Gage. See p. 157.
Mr. Endymion Porter. Gard. iv. 364–411, c. xlii., deals with "The Mission of Endymion Porter."
the two points. §§ 13, 14 of the Marriage Treaty (F. de Jesus, 333) deal with the jurisdiction of the ecclesiastical superior, § 22 about the tutelage of the children (*ib.*, 338 and *n*).

P. **162.**] *Don Rodrigo Calderon.* A "Relation of the death of Don. R. C." appeared in London 1622. He appears in literature, in *Gil Blas*, and in Southey's *Doctor* (II. K.). *Cf. Cabala*, i. 208.
12 *March*, obviously post-dated from the reference to Oct. in the body of the letter.

LETTER XIV.—*Sir Francis Cottington* (1574–1651), afterwards Lord Cotting-ton, held the position of Secretary to Prince Charles at this time, but was not created a baronet till Feb. 16, 1623. Gard., *l.c.*, ii. 302.

P. **163.**] *Surprizal of Ormus.* See *supra*, p. 157.
now Earl of Bristol. He was created Sept. 15, 1622.
brought him over his patent. How could that be, since Gondomar was recalled in May (Gard., *l.c.*, ii. 220) ?
Victory at Fleurus, near Breda, on Aug. 18 (Gard., *l.c.*, ii. 227).
Capt. Leat. See on p. 154.

P. **164.**]

P. 164.] LETTER XV.—*Sir Tho. Savage.* See on p. 132.
on Friday last. March 7, 1623, Gard., *l.c.,* ii. 305; this was a Friday (F. de Jesus, p. 202). Wotton, *Life of Buckingham,* p. 89, says "Wednesday fifth of March."
Mr. Thomas Smith, the name under which Buckingham travelled.
Sir Francis Cottington. The "Sir" was now justified. See on p. 162.
Mr. Porter. He and Cottington had been outridden by the others. Ellis, 1 *Orig. Lett.* iii. 134.

P. 165.] *Sir Lewis Dives.* See on p. 428, where there is a letter to him.
till the king passed by. Same account in F. de Jesus, p. 205; a different one by Meade, *cf.* Ellis; *l.c.,* 137. *Cf.* Nichols, iii. 820, who quotes H.
The King himself. Meade reports the same, Ellis, *l.c.,* 135. Gardiner does not mention it.
Sir Walter Ashton (Aston). Frequently mentioned : Herbert, *Autob.* 232–3; Straff. *Lett.* ii. 149; Fuller, *Worthies,* ii. 315–6; Nichols, *Prog. Jas. I.,* i. 225 *n.* See D.N.B.
Prado. Still the favourite resort of the Madrid *beau monde.*
27 March 1623. This is a week too late N.S., more than a fortnight O.S., which H. would naturally use.

P. 166.] LETTER XVI.—*Sir Eubule Theolall.* See on p. 104.
Mons. Gramond. "The Count de Gramont at Bayonne took an exquisite notion of their persons . . . yet he let them continently pass." Wotton, *l.c.,* 89.

P. 167.] LETTER XVII.—*To Capt. Leat.* See on p. 154.
ship Amity. A previous reference to this, p. 156.
releasement of Prisoners. "The prisons were all opened." 1 Ellis *Orig. Lett.* iii. 143.

P. 168.] LETTER XVIII.—*Captain Tho. Porter.* See on p. 55.
For outward usage. This passage is quoted in the *Somers Tracts,* ed. Scott, iv. 540, at the end of the reprint of De la Parma's *Relation of the Royal Festivities at Madrid,* 1623.
Lope de Vega, the celebrated dramatist (1562–1635). I cannot find any trace of this epigram elsewhere, though Gard. v. 18, mentions his participation in the festivities : translated it runs—

"Charles Stuart am I,
Love has guided me far,
To Spanish heaven I come
To see Maria, my star."

P. 169. *Not long since.* H. is the only authority for this interesting episode, except a reference to it by the Venetian Envoy to the Doge. Gard., *l.c.,* 346*n.* He dates it June 3/13.
cousin Archy Armstrong, James I.'s Court Fool (see Mr. Lee's elaborate life in D.N.B.) F. de Jesus takes note of his existence at Madrid (ed. Gardiner, p. 252).

P. 170.] *Archy answered.* The same anecdote is given in *Parthen.* 27.

LETTER XIX. *Cousin Tho. Gwin at Trecastle.* His genealogy is given in T. Jones' *Brecon,* pp. 622 *seq.;* a brother, Rowland, is mentioned, *infra,* p. 216. T. Gwyn married a daughter of Sir D. Williams. (Jones, *l.c.*)

P. 171.]

P. 171.] *Mr. Vaughan of the Golden Grove.* Sir W. Vaughan (1577-1640), author of *The Golden Grove*, an allegorical poem in three books, 1600. See also 4 *Arch. Camb.* xii, 274.
Sir John Vaughan the Judge (1608-74). *Cf.* Spedding, *Life*, vii. 405. The *Golden Grove* was dedicated to him.
Lord Carlisle. See on p. 130.
Lord of Holland. See on p. 116.
Lord of Denbigh. An incident connected with him is mentioned on p. 175.
P. 172.] *Duke of Buckingham.* He had been raised to the Dukedom in May 1623. His arrogant conduct to Olivares had much to do with breaking off the Spanish Match.
Mr. Washington, probably one of the Bucks family, is said to have summoned Ballard (Gard. *Sp. Match,* ii. 395).
Ballard, an English Priest, a Jesuit, an Oxford man (Wood, *Fasti*), *cf. Jas. I.,* i. 453, ii. 255, 295; Nichols, iii. 1026; Gard. v. 102. F. de Jesus (Cam. Soc.), 249.
Sir Edmond Varney. His interference in this affair is told, after H., in the *Verney Papers* (C.S.), 112-3. It created a bad impression at the time in Spain as a warrant how Roman Catholics would be treated in England.
P. 173.] *Ballads and Pasquils.* Chief among these was *Vox Populi,* reprinted in the *Phœnix Britannicus.*
Fopperies and Plays. One by Middleton, *A Game at Chesse,* in which Gondomar is the Black Knight. Middleton was imprisoned for it.
Frankindale. Frankenthal, the siege of which was broken up by Tilby, 24 Nov. 1622. It was sequestered under treaty 19 Mar. 1623.
London-Wall. Perhaps a reference to the Althams, who lived near there. See on p. 36.
Tower-Hill. Sir Thos. Savage. See on p. 132.
LETTER XXI.—*Lord Viscount Colchester.* See on p. 114.
Walsingham Gresley. See on p. 204.
and House. A line has been accidentally omitted here. Should be "and touching the Constitutions and Orders of the Contratation House of the West Indies," &c. The Contratation House is mentioned by H., *For. Trav.,* 40, where he also mentions that "its Constitution is the greatest Mystery of the Spanish Government." See an account in Prescott, *Chas. V.,* ii. 569; also Croker, *Bassompierre,* 14. Hakluyt, iii. last page.
P. 174.] *Junta.* Frequently mentioned in F. de Jesus as the Giunta (Committee) of Theologians. It was summoned to determine on what terms Philip could take the oath, *ib.* 233. See also on p. 156.
Bishop of Segovia. I cannot find any reference to this incident in the authorities.
the foot with goads. Known as *Banderilleros.* These bull-fights were probably of the kind known as *Reales,* by high-born amateurs on valuable horses, instead of by professional toreadors on blindfolded knackers. This passage is quoted in Nichol's *Progresses of Jas. I.,* to illustrate a contemporary pamphlet describing the bullfights.
P. 175.] *Taking a pipe of Tobacco.* This incident does not appear in any of the ordinary authorities.
LETTER XXII.—*Sir Jas. Crofts.* See on p. 22.
From Turkey a letter this week. Seemingly a year *post eventum.*
Sultan Osman, the Grand Turk. Othman II. (1610-1622).
P. 176.] *late ill success.* His repulse by the Poles at Choczin, Oct. 1621.
Beglerbeg. A title corresponding to Marquis, according to Herbert, *Travels,* 171; literally "Lord of Lords," according to the same authority, *l.c.* 129.
                                                                    P. 177.]

P. 177.] *Mustapha I.* Othman succeeded him 26 Feb. 1618, but he was reinstated in 1622, as here related.

P. 178.] *capi-Aga.* Aga is "the next under a Bassa" (Pasha), says Sir K. Digby : Hakluyt ii. 293, gives "Capi-aga, High Porter."

P. 179.] *cauph houses,* also spelt *cauphe,* p. 452. On the introduction of coffee into England, see note on p. 662.
mufti, spelt *mufiti* in *For. Tr.,* 85 : "The Mufiti who is their chiefest Bishop."
Sir Tho. Roe (†1644), referred to, Herbert, *Autob.* 25 and *n.* ; Fairfax, i. 322 ; B. Jonson, *Works,* Epigr. cxxiii. His correspondence while at Constantinople has been published. A letter from him on this very subject is quoted in Nimmo's *British Letter-Writers.*

P. 180.] *Mr. Camden.* His *Annals of Elizabeth* is referred to here.

LETTER XXIII.—*Sir T. Savage.* See on p. 132.

P. 181.] *Pope Gregory was dead.* Gregory XV. died 8 July 1623.
Pope Urban VIII. succeeded 6 Aug. 1623. His election is referred to in *F. de Jesus,* p. 251.
Proxy. This was actually made out in the names of the King and the Infante Carlos. Gard., *Sp. M.* ii. 406.

P. 182.] LETTER XXIV.—*Capt. Nich. Leat.* See on p. 154.
his brother. Sir James Altham, i.e., his half-brother. See on p. 34.
Wagers 30 *to* 1. Bristol wagered a ring worth £1000 that Charles would spend the Christmas of 1623 in Madrid. Gard., *Sp. M.,* ii. 406.

P. 183.] LETTER XXV.—*Sir Jas. Crofts.* See on p. 22.
Escurial. For a description see p. 207, and *cf. For. Tr.* 71.

P. 184.] *Dizen me.* Sp.—"They tell me you are dying of grief; as for me, I fear my years more than my enemies."
Sir Sackvil Trever. On him see Nichol's *Prog. James I.,* i. 440 *n.*

LETTER XXVI.—*To my Brother.* See on p. 25.
Mr. Wadsworth, author of *The English Spanish Pilgrime,* 1629, and often mentioned as a Jesuit in the memoirs of the time (Nichols, *Prog. Jas. I.,* iii. 734 ; D'Israeli, *Chas. I.,* i. 36; Walton's *Lives,* 143). Howell denounced his son later as a spy. See p. 649.
Father Boniface. The Infanta certainly did take English lessons (Gard., *Sp. M.* ii. 417).
Sir Walter Ashton. See on p. 165, and *infra,* p. 190.

P. 185.] *Mr. Clerk* brought a letter from Charles delaying the marriage by proxy, even if the dispensation should come from Rome (Gard., v. 121 *n.*). Charles complained of Clerk for having no power over his arm. Clarend., *Hist.* i. § 141. He is also mentioned, Spedding, *Life,* vii. 425 ; Gard., vi. 160.
St. Mark, i.e., of course, Venice.
embrace a cloud, a reference to the legend of Ixion.
Sir John Franklin. See on p. 114.
Sir John Smith, to whom the first letter of the *Epistolæ,* 2nd edition, is directed.
at the Hill and Dale. Tower Hill, see p. 132 ; but what Dale ?

P. 186.] Letter XXVII.—*Sir John North.* See on p. 54.
Mr. Clerk. See on p. 185. In the Conway Papers at the Record Office it is
mentioned that Clerk arrived from Spain 26th July, and was dispatched
thither again, 10th August.

P. 187.] *Mr. Killegree* arrived with despatches, Nov. 26, only three days before
the wedding was to have taken place by proxy. Killigree was the well-
known Sir R. Killigrew; on him see p. 500.
watched velvet, should be *watchet* as in Ed. Pr.

P. 188.] *contratation-house.* See on p. 173.
Lord Paget. The first Baron, Sir W. Paget, K.G., created in Edward VI.'s
reign.
25 Aug. 1623. As Killigrew arrived at the end of November this date is too
early.

P. 189.] Letter XXVIII.—*Lord Clifford.* Henry Clifford, son of the Earl
of Cumberland, was not summoned as a Baron till 3 Car. I., so that the title
is premature.
took a ring, mentioned by Gard., *Sp. M.,* ii. 458. This occurred Jan. 28,
1623.
Feather beds, a very early instance of tarring and feathering. A still earlier
one in Archer, *Crusade of Richard I.*

P. 190.] Letter XXIX.—*Sir John North.* See on p. 55.
Mr. Vaughan, H.'s "cousin," see on p. 219. Sir John Vaughan (? his father)
was also at Madrid, p. 171 and *n.*
Lord Aston was only Sir Walter at this time. See Gard.
Marquis of Inojosa. For this accusation of the Spanish Ambassador against
Buckingham in the spring of 1624, see Gard. v. 188, 207, 226, 228, 244,
268. H. refers to it in other works : *Parthen.* 37, 193 ; *Finetti,* 193, 243.
Nichols, iii. 972, quotes H.'s as the best account.

P. 191.] *Lord Conway.* See on p. 240.
26 Aug. 1623. Inojosa's accusation was made in April 1624 (Gard., v. 226).

P. 192.] Letter XXX.—Sir Kenelm Digby (1603-1665), philosopher,
traveller, and inventor of the "sympathetic powder ;" see Mr. Lee in D.N.B.
Three Souls. The usual Aristotelian view.
Trigonus in Tetragono. Lit. "a triangle in a quadrangle," but in all probability a reference to the three souls of man inclosed in the four elements of
his body.
Ex traduce. Probably a reminiscence of Prudentius, *Apoth.,* 983, according
to Dr. Gow. But H. would probably know Sir Kenelm Digby's Annotations on the *Religio Medici,* 1642, one of whose sections is "Soul not *ex
traduce.*" *Cf.* also H.'s *Therologia,* 140-1.

P. 193.] *Mr. Thomas Cary,* related to Sir R. Cary, to whom H. has a letter,
infra, p. 574. Probably the Tom Ca. of pp. 403, 627, where see.
snatch'd from you. This is a natural touch which seems to vouch for the
authenticity of the present letter.

P. 194.] Letter XXXI.—*Cousin Mr. J. Price.* There is a Price referred to
in Herbert's *Autob.,* ed. Lee, p. 95, who may have been H.'s "cousin :"
there are other letters to him, pp. 378, 404, 411. The cousinship probably
consisted in the fact that H.'s sister Rebecca married Mr. John Price of
Richardston, our present Price's father (see Pedigree).

one

one late audience, that in which the Earl had to postpone the marriage by proxy on Nov. 26, 1623.

P. 195.] LETTER XXXII.—*Viscount Colchester.* See on p. 114.
short survey, possibly derived from Wadsworth's, which appeared in 1630.
P. 196.] *Don Julian.* W. S. Landor made a fine drama out of this subject.
P. 197.] *Biscayners have much analogy.* H. says much the same, *For. Tr.*, 50 ; *cf. infra*, p. 473.
Inquisitors. One of the chief works of the Inquisition was the inquiry into *Limpieza de sangre, i.e.*, purity of descent.
The King. *Cf.* Don Quixote, II. c. xlviii., "as good a gentleman as the king himself, for he was a mountaineer."
Chico. Bobadil, the last king of Granada, was so-called.

P. 198.] *the first proffer.* The story being that Columbus came over to England to offer to go to the Indies by the west route on behalf of England.
Sun shines. Curious to see the phrase now used of the Queen's dominions used of the Spanish monarch's, as here and in *Therologia*, 83.

P. 199.] *Village of Madrid, i.e.*, not a city because not the seat of a bishopric. The choice of Madrid for a court residence has had disastrous results for Spain.
15,000 *students.* Ford says only 5000 in the sixteenth century (*Handbook*, s. v.)

P. 200.] *Spanish Legend.* I have never come across this anywhere but in H.
Lurks. Borrow, in his *Bible in Spain*, has several mysterious references to traces of secret Jews he had found in the Peninsula. Borrow was very imaginative.

P. 201.] *Goatish race.* A punning reference to the descent of the Spanish nobility from the Visigoths.
Primera. For an account of this game see Brand, *Pop. Ant.*, ed. Ellis, ii. 266 ; also Earle, *Microsm.*, ed. Bliss, pp. 35-7.

P. 202.] *All the cards.* Spanish cards have still "Real Fabrica" on them. *Cf.* Willshire, *Descr. Cot. Play-Cards in Brit. Mus.* 102.

P. 203.] *A compleat woman.* From Moryson, *Itin.* iii. 49.

P. 204.] 1 *Feb.* 1623, *i.e.*, 1624, which might be a not unsuitable date.

LETTER XXXIII.—*Mr. Walsingham 'Gresley*, frequently referred to : Nichols, iii. 896, 902 ; *Jas. II.*, ii. 321, 444 ; Gard., v. g. On his name see Nichols' *Herald*, viii. 221. His capture by Algerian pirates is mentioned *supra*, 152, 162. He died 1633, ætat. 48 (Nichols, *l.c.*).
Sir Ferdinando Cary, was not knighted till 6th Feb. 1629 (Metcalfe, 196), so that this is another case of premature title.
Our Friends in Bishopsgate Street, the Althams. See note on p. 38.

P. 205.] LETTER XXXIV.—*Sir Robert Napier.* Referred to already, 151, as being connected with the "Vineyard" affair. Aubrey has a long account of him, *Misc.*, 90, 159-61. A life of him in Anthony à Wood.
Letters of Mart, i.e., threats that English privateers would harass Spanish trade if satisfaction were not made for the loss of the "Vineyard."

P. 206.] LETTER XXXV.—*Mr. A. S.* I have no suggestion to make as to the identity of A. S.
Couvrez-feu Bell. The old folk-etymology for curfew.
Besamanos. Sp. "Kiss the hands," salutations.

P. 207.] LETTER XXXVI.—*Sir T. S.* Probably Sir Thomas Savage, who lived on Tower Hill, *supra*, p. 132.

Escurial.

Escurial. II. refers to this as one of the wonders of the world in *For. Tr.* p. 71.
St. Quintin. Where French were defeated by the Spaniards, 1557.
Vault called the Pantheon. The kings of Spain are still buried there.

P. 208.] LETTER XXXVII.—*Viscount Col*[chester]. See on p. 114.
Duke of Ossuna or Ossone (1579-26, Sept. 1624). Viceroy of Sicily, 1610;
  Viceroy of Naples, 1616-20 ; recalled because he refused to establish the
  Inquisition in Naples. § xiv. of H.'s *Parthenopœia*, is "Of the Duke of
  Orsuna," at the end of which is a list of the accusations brought against
  him by the Neapolitans, including those mentioned on the next page.

P. 209.] *witty passage* is repeated in Mr. W. C. Hazlitt's *Jests.*
Tutele of the Jesuits. The same story is told in *The Italian anatomised by an
  English Chirurgeon,* 1660, p. 25 (C.II.F.)

P. 210.] 13 Mar. 1623, *i.e.*, 1624. Hardly, if the Duke died 26 Sept. 1624.

LETTER XXXVIII.—*Simon Digby.* See on p. 156.
Crytology. Misprint for Cryptology of ED. PR.
A. Gellius. *Noct. Att.* lib. xvii., c. ix. "De notis litterarum quæ in C.
  Cæsaris epistolis reperiuntur deque aliis clandestinis litteris."

LETTER XXXIX.—*Sir Jas. Crofts.* See on p. 22.
His Majesty's Jewels. Among the *S. P.* there is one dated 1 Nov. 1624.
  "Note of jewels lately brought from Spain." In Ellis' *Orig. Lett.* are many
  references to them. *Cf.*, too, *Archæologia*, xxi. 148-57 ; and Nichols, *l.c.*,
  iii. 832-3.

P. 211.] *Mr. Wiches.* Afterwards Sir Peter Wych. See on p. 254.
Alforjas, Sp. saddlebags or portmanteau.
Sir Tho. Fairfax, probably the grandfather of the general.
Lodging Void, this is a natural touch that seems to vouch for the authenticity
  of the present letter, especially when combined with the reference at the
  beginning to the gentleman who was to carry it to London.
6 *Sept.* 1624. Judging from the reference in the *S. P.*, this seems a suitable
  month for the journey. But see the reference to the death of Ossuna, *i.e.*,
  26 Sept. on p. 208 ; and to Charles' fall on p. 212.

SECTION IV.

  This section contains an account of H.'s search for employment on his
return from Spain. At last he gets comfortably settled at York.

P. 212.] *Prince's Jewels.* See on p. 210.
Capt. Love. Mentioned *Powysl. Coll.* xx. 132 ; Masson, *Life,* ii. 519. In
  Conway Papers, 1623 (Rec. Off. S.P. For. Spain, Bundle 60), under date
  April 25th, I came across the entry "Capt. Love went in ye Antelope."
fall off a Horse occurred Oct. 1623. Nichols, iii. 848.
Treaties both of Match and Palatinate. The former, the agreement as to the
  Spanish Match, is given at the end of F. de Jesus' treatise, ed. Gardiner for
  Camd. Soc.
chain of pearl. "A goodly roape of pearles," James wrote to his "sweete
  Boyes," Nich. iii. 833.
good business of it. He was to have made £3000. See *supra,* p. 193.

P. 213.] LETTER II.—*R. Brown.* See on p. 78.
Field in Sicily, another reference to H.'s being in Sicily. See *supra,* p. 62.

P. 214.] *Blackfriars,* the theatre in which Shakespeare had a share: it had
  been built by Burbage.

                                                                    Cock

Cock Pit. Pepys often refers to new plays produced here. It was in Drury Lane, and was likewise termed the Phœnix.

LETTER III.—*Viscount Colchester.* See on p. 114.
Venetian Gazette. See on p. 150.
Count Mansfelt was "brought to lodge in St. James's, in rooms near the Palace," *S. P.* 19 Apr. 1624, "in the very chamber intended for the Infanta," *ib.* 24 Apr. *Cf.* Gard. v. 265. He sailed for Boulogne before April 30, 1624.

P. 215.] *Hollander.* The Dutch had captured Pernambuco. D'Ewes, *Autob.* ii. 3; a further reference to this *infra*, p. 258.
scandalous information. See *supra*, p. 190. Inojosa was ultimately released and freed from the charge of bringing false accusation against Buckingham. (Gard. v. 268).
5 Feb. 1624, *i.e.*, 1625, nearly a year too late. But on any showing H. was in Spain when Mansfeld was in London.

P. 216.] LETTER IV.—*Mr. Rowland Gwin*, a brother of Thomas Gwyn of Trecastle, on whom see p. 170. It is difficult to understand H. making up a letter of this kind or the other two following unless he had them in hand.

LETTER V.—*Thomas Jones*, perhaps a relation of H.'s college chum, Christopher Jones, for whom see p. 60.
Cillibub or syllabub, a concoction of crushed apples and cream, if I remember right.

LETTER VI.— *To D. C.* David Caldwall. See on p. 27.

LETTER VII.—*Father.* See on p. 19. This letter is given by Scoones *English Letters*, No. lv. p. 73.
Thomas Gwin of Trecastle. See p. 170.
Sunday fortnight. "27 March [1625], about noone King James died and King Charles was instantly proclaimed at Theobalds and the same afternoone at London," Conway's *Letter Bk.* *Cf.* D'Ewes, *Autob.* i. 163. Laud was preaching that Sunday at Whitehall (Nich. lii. 1034; Masson *Life*, i. 321). *Sir Edw. Zouch* died in 1634, *Strafford Letters*, i. 265.

P. 217.] *Countess of Buckingham*, the Duke's mother. Much suspicion was aroused by her action in this matter. See Gard. Among others D. G. Eglisham wrote a pamphlet, *Prodromus Vindictæ in Ducem Bvckinghami pro virulenta cæde Regis Iacobi*, 1626 (C.H.F.), the English version of which, *The Fore-Runner of Revenge*, is thought by Wotton to have led to Felton's deed: it is given in *Somers Tracts*, edit. Scott, v. 437 *seq.* The suspicions were referred to by Elliot in his attack on Buckingham. *Cf.* Hutchinson, *Life*, ed. Firth, i. 119 *n.*
Sister without a Country, the "Queen of Hearts," the Princess Elizabeth, whose husband the Palsgrave had lost the Palatinate. All this, however, sounds like a *ratiocinium post eventum*.

P. 218.] *The Plague* broke out in June 1625. Its ravages are frequently mentioned, *Lives of Ferrar*, 23, 220 ; D'Ewes' *Autob.* i. 275–8 ; P. Warwick, 11 ; Spedding, *Life of Bacon*, vii. 530 *seq.;* Sir T. Roe, *Neg.* 459 ; *Court of Chas. I.*, i. 32; Gard. *England under Buckingham*, ii. 189, 222 ; Forster, *Eliot*, i. 214, 221, 227, 254, &c. A full account in Creighton, *Hist. of Epidemics in England*, vol. i.
at the Cape of Good Hope. A favourite phrase of H.'s. See Suppt., p. 259.
Brother

Brother and Sisters at the Bryn. Probably Cefn-Bryn, co. Brecknock. This is a point in favour of II.'s being a Brecknockshire man. But the reference may be equally to Bryn-a-Minin, co. Carmarthen, where one of II.'s brothers, Howel Howel, lived. See *S.P.*, 3 Sept. 1640.

LETTER VIII.—*De Prichard.* See on p. 31.
(*ne gry quidem*). Properly "ne γρὺ quidem," "not worth a grain." The expression is taken from Plautus.
Lord Chancellor Bacon died 9 April 1626 (Spedding, *Life*, vii. 551).

P. 219.] *Pitiful letter to K. James*, doubtless that given in Spedding, *Life*, vii. 382-6, which does conclude with the words quoted by Howell, "Help . . . study to live." This letter was published in *Cabala*, 1654 ; *Baconiana*, 1674; and in Sir Toby Matthew's *Collection* (Spedding, *l.c.*, p. 381); but was never actually delivered.
last Lord Chancellor. Sounds like a *vaticinium post eventum* ; up to 1645 the seal was used by the Lord Keeper or was in commission, but there was no actual Lord High Chancellor till Clarendon at the Restoration (Haydn, *Dignities*, 104).
6 Jan. 1625, *i.e.*, 1626. Inconsistent with the reference to Bacon's death.

LETTER IX.—*Mr. T. V.* Thomas Vaughan referred to in Herbert's *Autob.*, ed. Lee, p. 28 and *n.* Cf. with this letter the one on marriage prefixed to the *Lexicon Tetragl.*, and reprinted in Suppt., p. 665.
Socrates. This story is also given in Gower, *Conf. Amantis*, III. ii. 1. It is repeated again, *infra*, 568.

P. 220.] *C. B.*, probably *Coke*, whose quarrels with Lady Hatton are referred to above, p. 148, and *Bacon*, who was grievously offended with his Lady at the end of his life, Wilson, p. 159 ; Spedding, *Life*, vii. 539.
Stroud our cook. The same story is told again in the same words, *infra*, p. 568.
English Proverb. Cf. W. C. Hazlitt, *Proverbs*, 385.

P. 221.] LETTER X.—*Lord Clifford.* Henry, son of the fourth Earl of Cumberland (Nicolas, *Hist. Peerage*, 113). See on p. 189.
From Holland, where he had been to negotiate an alliance against Spain. He returned Dec. 1625. Gard. v. 37.
Prince Frederick Henry, a youth of much promise. Mrs. Green, *Princesses*, v. 469.
Insland Slough. Should be "Inland Lough," as in ED. PR.
Bank of Money. For this see the classic treatment of Adam Smith, *Wealth of Nations*.

P. 222.] *Vessel turned over.* Came in contact with another boat (Green, *l.c.*). "Jan. 14, 1629, Newes brought of the Palsegrave's eldest soon drowned in Herleem Meer in Holland" (R. Smyth, *Obituary*, Cam. Soc., p. 4).
A sad destiny! He died on Jan. 17, 1629 (Green, *l.c.*), three years after the supposed date of this letter.
The Match with Henrietta Maria. She was already married by June 13, 1625.
Coshionet. See note on this word, 5 N. & Q. viii. 118 ; it is a diminutive of "cushion," and is actually spelt "cushionet" in *Lust. Ludov.* 66, where this story is given. Cf. *Poet. Misc.* (Percy Soc.), p. 7, and *Harl. Misc.* viii. 399.
Cardinal de Richlieu. He had been made Cardinal in Sept. 1622.
He died on the journey in 1625.

Bunnol.

Bunnol, sic. in ED. PR., should be Bommel in Guelderland. See Rimbault in *Overbury's Works*, p. 311.

P. 223.] *Mountauban*, unsuccessfully besieged by Louis XIII. 17 Aug.–17 Nov. 1621.
Mr. Ellis Hicks. A fuller discussion of this action of Hicks is given *infra*, 614–6. .
Parliament. The summonses were issued by Williams on Dec. 16, 1625. Gard. v. 37. D'Ewes, *Autob.* i. 275, gives 11th July as the date.
some employment. On his own showing he had been doing nothing since the return from Spain till the end of the year 1625, about eighteen months.
The Plague. See *supra*, p. 218. From Dec. 16, 1624, to Dec. 15, 1625, the Bill of Mortality for London was 54,265, of which 35,417 was from the plague (*S. P.* 15 Dec. 1625).
25 *Feb.* 1625, *i.e.*, 1626. There is a wretched jumble here of events of the beginning of 1625 (French Match), the end of 1625 (Buckingham from Holland), and the beginning of 1629 ! (drowning of Prince Frederick).

LETTER XI.—*Rich. Altham.* See on p. 33.

P. 225.] LETTER XII.—*Lord of Carlingford at ¡Golden Grove.* Sir John Vaughan of the Golden Grove, co. Carmarthen, created an Irish Peer 18 Jas I., and Earl of Carberry by Charles I. See *supra*, p. 171.
28 *May*, 1625 ; this is thus dated in ED. PR. This must be N.S., as in the body of the letter reference is made to the marriage (by proxy) taking place on the 11th of this month, which was 1 May (Gard., *Engl.* i. 175).
Queen Margaret of Valois, who was Roman Catholic at the time of her marriage with the Protestant Henry of Navarre.
King of France. The full treaty of marriage in 18 clauses is given by H. in *Lust. Lud.*, 64–6, and by Croker, *Bassompierre*, Append. II., dated 10th Nov. 1625.

P. 226.] *Family.* This is a technical word meaning "household." See p. 234.
eighth Alliance. H. afterwards wrote an account of all the Royal Marriages. See Bibl. List, No. 63, *Royal Matches.* He gives a list of the eight between France and England in *Lust. Lud.* 67. They were Chas. I. (900) and Louis XII. of France, and Hen. III. and V., Ed. I. and II., Rich. II., and Chas. I. of England.

LETTER XIII.—*Sir Thomas Sa.* Sir Thomas Savage. See on p. 132.

P. 227.] *Monsieur.* The story is told with more circumstances in *Lust. Lud.* 73.
deep Plot. H. refers to this in the *Lust. Lud.* 73, but adds—" But I beleeve this was a groundlesse surmise."

LETTER XIV.—*Marchioness of Winchester*, daughter of Sir Thomas Savage, who doubtless recommended H. to her. She is mentioned Nichol's *Prog. Jas. I.*, i. 189 *n.* She was honoured by an epitaph composed by Milton, as well as with one by Ben Jonson (Masson, *Life*, i. 211). Collins, *Peerage*, ed. Brydges, ii. 380, quotes Howell's encomium of her.

P. 228.] LETTER XV.—*Lord Clifford.* See on p. 189.

Town

II. 3 A

Town of Breda, on May 26 (5 Jun.) 1625. Gard., *Engl. under Buck.* i. 186.
Lord of Southampton, Henry Wriothesley, to whom Shakespeare dedicated
    the first heir of his invention : he died in 1624.
Earl Henry of Oxford, died 1626 according to Nicholas, *Hist. Peerage,* 370.
    He is mentioned Nicholl's *Progr. Jas. I.,* ii. xii. *n.,* iii. 947 *n.*
Grave Maurice's, Prince of Orange (1667-1625), who caused John of
    Barneveldt to be executed : he died at the Hague 23 April 1625.

P. 229.] *Grave Henry,* generally known as Frederick Henry, who ruled
    1625-47.
Sir Edward Vere was killed at the siege of Bois-le-Duc, 1629, Markham,
    Fighting Veres, p. 438 (C.H.F.).
Sir Charles Morgan, mentioned in Herbert, *Autob.,* ed. Lee, pp. 143 and
    330. He was afterwards sent to the assistance of Christian IV. of
    Denmark.
19 *March* 1625. At least three months too early for a reference to the fall
    of Breda.

P. 230.] LETTER XVI.—*Mr. R. Sc.,* probably one of the Scroops, related to
    the Earl of Sunderland.
Second Arrow. *Cf.* Longfellow's song, " I sent an arrow into the air."

LETTER XVII.—*Dr. Field, Bishop of Landaff.* Theophilus Field (†1636),
    Bishop of Llandaff 1619, translated to St. David's 12 July 1627, and to
    Henford 1635. (Wood, *Athenæ ;* Nicholas, *Hist. Peer.*).
Mr. Jonathan Field, probably a relative of the Bishop's. H. has a letter to
    Mr. E. Field, *infra,* p. 585.
Wimbledon's Fleet, which had unsuccessfully attacked Cadiz : it started for
    home 16 Nov. 1625. (Gard., *Eng. under Buck.* i. 324.) Wimbledon's
    own account of the expedition was published in 1626.

P. 231.] *Ships without Gallies.* In contrast with the Spanish Armada, where
    there were both.
High-Admiral, i.e., Buckingham himself. See p. 233.
St. Mary Port, in Cadiz Bay, Gard. vi. 15.
Cales, i.e., Cadiz.
Council of War. See Gard., *l.c.,* i. 325.
Mercurius Gallobelgicus. Practically the first newspaper. The files from
    1588 to 1594 were published at Cologne in 1598. *Cf.* Overbury, *Works,* ed.
    Rimbault, p. 101, and note p. 294.
Capt. Love. Sir Thomas, mentioned by Masson, *Life of Milton,* ii. 519,
    Powysl. Coll. xx. 132, Gard. vi. 14, and frequently in the *S.P.,* 1625-6.
Fort of Puntall. *Cf.* Gard. vi. 20.

P. 232.] *Lord de la Ware's,* the fourth Baron, ob. 1628.
Lord of St. David's. Laud, who was elected 1621, and translated to Bath and
    Wells 18 Sept. 1626. Field succeeded him in the last, 12 July 1627.
20 *Nov.* 1626. Here, again, we have two incongruous dates in the same
    letter. Wimbledon's fleet returned in the winter of 1625, Laud was trans-
    lated to Bath and Wells in Sept. 1626. It is true H. speaks only of the
    rumour about the translation.

LETTER XVIII.—*Lord D. of Buckingham,* the celebrated favourite of Jas. I.
    and Chas. I. For a description of his death see *infra,* p. 253.
fortunate should be *infortunate* as in ED. PR.

P. 233.] *last was boistrous.* Charles's first Parliament.
                                                              P. 234.]

P. 234.] *Mansion house and Family*, the latter used here, as on pp. 184, 226, for an established household.   D'Ewes uses the word for the Queen's servants, *Autob.* ii. 171-2.
late unfortunate Earl.   Essex, of course.

LETTER XIX.—*Sir J. S.*   Probably the Sir John Smith of the first letter of the collection.

P. 235.]·LETTER XX.—*Earl R.*, probably Earl Rivers.   The Viscount Colchester was created Earl Rivers 4 Nov. 1626.   See on p. 101.   But see next letter.
Count Mansfelt is in Paris.   He died in Bosnia in Nov. 1626, after having been defeated by Wallenstein at Dessau in the April of that year.

P. 236.] *Bethlem Gabor*, should be Bethlen, Prince of Transylvania, Prince Rupert's godfather (Warburton, i. 32).   He is frequently referred to in Sir T. Roe's *Negotiations*, 1740 (*cf.* D'Ewes, *Autob.* i. 144; Croker, *Bass.* 50; Rushw., ii. 29; *James I.*, ii. 434; Sir D. Carleton, *Dispatches, pass.*).
Sir Ch. Morgan was commander at Breda, *supra*, p. 229; on him see Herbert, *Autob.*, ed. Lee, p. 143 and *n.*, and 330.   "They should have numbered 6000 men, but their commander, Sir Chas. Morgan, reported on April [7, 1626], that only 2472 answered to their names."   Gard., *l.c.*, ii. 124.
adjourn'd to Oxford till 1st Aug. 1625.   Gard., *l.c.*, i. 231.
clashing, referring apparently to the reciprocal charges of high treason between the two nobles, brought before the House of Peers in April–May, 1626 (Gard., *l.c.*, ii. 42-6).   See also Fairfax, *Letters*, i. 42-7.
putting his Majesty, really of conspiring with Gondomar to get Charles to Spain.   (Gard., *Eng. under Buck.* ii. 44).
Lord Conway.   See Gard., *l.c.*
15 Mar. 1626.   Here again we have a curious mixture of dates.   A reference to Sir Chas. Morgan and to the quarrels of Bristol and Buckingham refer to the spring of 1626 ; the adjournment of Parliament to Oxford was for the August of the preceding year.

LETTER XXI.—Lord Viscount C.   Probably Colchester ; but see preceding letter, *ad init.*
Sir John North.   See on p. 54.

P. 237.] *a very splendid Equipage.*   "On the 14th of May [O.S. 1625] Buckingham arrived in Paris.   To the world in general he seemed to have set his soul on displaying his handsome person and his jewelled attire at the court festivities."   Gard., *l.c.*, i. 180.   Prof. Gardiner discredits the story of his having purposely lost precious stones from his costumes as he danced.

LETTER XXII.—*Mr. Hugh Penry.*   See on p. 129.
jealous, should be *jealousies* as in ED. PR.

P. 238.] *big-lipp'd.*   See note on 155.
Canterbury.   Both D'Ewes, i. 271, and P. Warwick, 6, give the same information : a touch like this could scarcely be introduced long *post eventum.*
Dyvinnock in Brecon, a point in favour of H. being a Brecknock man ; but see *Introd.* p. xxiii.

LETTER

LETTER XXIII.—*Uncle Sir Sackville Trevor*, mentioned previously, 184. He is mentioned, Nicholl's *Prog. Jas. I.*, i. 440 *n.* How he was H.'s uncle is unknown to me, though he was certainly of Welsh descent, being included in the Welsh pedigrees contained in Harl. MS. 4181, f. 281. He married one of the Savages.

Sir John Elliot. This incident is referred to in Forster's *Life*, 2nd ed., i. 260. It was while the chairman was reading that Black Rod appeared. June 1625.

P. 239.] *D. of Buckingham.* The High Speech is given in Gard., *Hist.* vi. 103–7 ; Forster, *Life*,[2] i. 324–30. It was delivered May 10, 1626. *My Lord Keeper Williams* parted with the seal 25 Oct. 1626. *Sir Thomas Coventry* (1578-1640) ; he had been Recorder of London and Solicitor-General. His succeeding Williams is mentioned by D'Ewes, *Autob.* i. 280. *Cf. Fairfax Papers*, i. 23.

the Sickness. See *supra*, p. 218.

Oxford, 6 Aug. 1626. "The letter," says Forster, *Life of Elliot*,[2] i. 260 *n.*, "is an evident compilation from one or two letters of widely different dates, and the main incident refers rather to the second parliament, dissolved in June 1626, than to this Oxford parliament closed in August 1625."

LETTER XXIV.—*too much Digbified, i.e.,* too much in favour of the Earl of Bristol, Buckingham's great opponent. Several letters to him are in the present collection, see p. 277.

Mr. Secretary Conway. See on p. 240.

moving agent, a polite term for a spy, as can be seen from the third particular, mentioned in the succeeding letter.

P. 240.] *The Sickness.* The highest number noted by Sir S. D'Ewes in his *Autob.* is 4463 in the week Aug. 11-18, 1625.

Sir John Walter, referred to also on p. 105 as counsel for H.'s father. He had been Attorney-General, and became afterwards Chief Baron (Gard. vii. 112.)

LETTER XXV.—*Lord Conway* (ob. 1630) was created Viscount Killutagh 15 Mar 1626, and Viscount Conway 26 June 1627 (D.N.B.).

P. 241.] *the danger.* This shows the nature of the employment, which must have been practically that of spy.

I am a Cadet. Compare H.'s account of himself, p. 373, at top.

£100 a Quarter. In *For. Tr.* 26, H. calculates the minimum personal expenses of a traveller at £300 per annum, besides £50 for each servant. His charge could not be considered exorbitant.

8 Sept. 1626. At this time Lord Conway was Viscount Killutagh. See note above.

LETTER XXVI.—*Dr. Howell.* See on p. 25.

Lord Conway demurr'd. See preceding letter.

P. 242.] *Lord Scroop, Lord President of the North,* afterwards Earl of Sunderland. See p. 251.

Worcester house, where Dr. Prichard was (see *supra*, p. 131), who probably recommended H.

Your house in Horsley. West Horsley, co. Surrey, of which Dr. Howell was rector.

Cashier'd this week, on July 31, O.S. 1626 (Gard., *l.c.*, ii. 90-2). It is frequently mentioned in the Memoirs, D'Ewes' *Autob.* ii. 189, *Lustra Lud.* 75-6.

Croker's

Croker's *Bassompierre*, p. 1. Roe's *Negot.*, Letters cdiii. cdiv. Whitelock
Mem. 8. E. Law, *Hampton Court*, II. c. ix., "Dismissal of French suite."
Sir Thomas Edmonds. Mentioned in Herbert's *Autob.* 106, 208. *Cf.*
Nichols, i. 156 *n.* ; Fairfax, i. 184.
Master Montague. Gardiner says Carleton was sent beforehand to mollify the
French King's wrath.

P. 243.] LETTER XXVII.—*Lord S.* can scarcely be Lord Scroop, as *he* would
know of H.'s going to York. Perhaps it is meant for Viscount Savage.
Sir Charles Morgan. See *supra*, p. 229.
Stoad, now Stade. It was surrendered April 27, 1628 (Gard., *l.c.*, ii. 269).
A reference to it in Sir T. Roe's *Negotiations*, 731.
Tilly pursueth his victory. Probably that over Christian IV. of Denmark at
Lutter, 17 Aug. 1626. The news reached England 12 Sept. (Gard., *l.c.*, ii.
94).
Privy Seals for Loan monies. An established method of raising money, but
it raised great objections (Gard., *l.c.*, ii. 98, 105).

P. 244.] LETTER XXVIII.—*R. L.*, probably Richard Leat. See p. 248.
J. Harris. Perhaps related to the T. Harris of p. 644.

P. 246.] *en querpo*, in doublet and breeches without cloak. Scott uses the
expression in *Fortunes of Nigel*, and *cf.* Ferrar's *Lives*, 197, and Prof.
Mayor's note.
Sir John Ayres. This incident is mentioned in Sir T. Roe's *Negotiations*,
i. 54.
Chequins=sequins. Coryat, *Crudities*, ii. 21, gives a full account of this coin.

SECTION V.

This deals with H.'s sojourn at York, his election as M.P., and his wanderings while he held his post at York. It ranges between the years 1626 and
May 1629.

P. 247.] LETTER I.—*Dan Caldwall from York.* See on p. 27.
Smug the Smith. "The Merry Jests of Smugge the Smythe and Mine Host
of the George" is the title of a seventeenth century jest book given by
Lowndes s.v. *Jests.* It does not follow that Smug was an imaginary person,
no more than Tarlton, Scoggin, or Peele, under whose names jest books
were published. See also Hazlitt, *Handbook*, s.v. Brewer.
Still-yard or steelyard, in Upper Thames St., the home of the Hanseatic
League in London. See Pauli's *Pictures from Old England ;* F. Martin,
Hist. of Lloyd, c. 1.

P. 248.] LETTER II.—*Mr. Richard Leat*, doubtless a relation of Captain
Leat, on whom see p. 154.
Sir Arthur Ingram. See on p. 268.
the Sydonian Merchant, J. Bruckhurst. Probably Edmund Brockhurst of
Oriel, who matriculated 1610, the same year as H. (Forster *Alumni Oxon.*
i. 185). But why Sydonian I know not.
Lord Weston. See on p. 130. He became Lord Treasurer in 1628, and
afterwards became Earl of Portland.
Treasurers of all tenses. Manchester, mentioned above as Sir H. Montagu ;
Middlesex, (Cranfield), and Marlborough, (Sir James Ley), all three earls.
Marlborough. See Life in Campbell, *Chief Justices*, i. 362-9. He was "the
old

old man eloquent " of Milton's Sonnet to his daughter. If he was as "eloquent" as he was "unstained in gold and fee," he must have been tongue-tied.
Venetian Gazetta. See *supra*, p. 150.

P. 249.] LETTER III.—*Sir Ed. Sa.* Savage, one of H.'s old pupils, and son of Earl Rivers. He was knighted in 1625.
at Bordeaux. See Gard. vi. 147.
Writs issued out for a Parliament. The third of Charles's reign.
made choice of me. See note on next letter.
Master Christopher Wandesford, frequently mentioned in the early part of Strafford's *Letters;* also in Forster, *Elliot,* i. 289, &c. He got a seat for Thirsk. Forster, *l.c.*, i. 423. He was an adherent of Wentworth's.
that would not conform to Loan monies. See *supra*, 243. H. was one of the court party for whom Loan monies were causing trouble.
2 *March* 1627. *Cf.* date given to next letter. As a matter of fact H. was returned 11 Mar. 1627-8 (*Names of Members of Parl.* i. 479).

P. 250.] LETTER IV.—*Town of Richmond,* co. York. Forster attributes H.'s success against Wandesford as due to the influence of Scrope. *Elliot,* ii. 422.
Sir Talbot Bows, mentioned Nichol's *Prog. Jas. I.,* iii. 275 *n.* He was of Streatham, co. Durham.
Colleague. H. and Bows were elected 11 March 1628 (see *Names,* &c.).
24 *Mar.* 1627. Nearly a fortnight after the election.

LETTER V.—*Lord Clifford* at *Knaresborough.* See p. 189 *n.*
Isle of Ree or Rhé, on the Breton coast. The Philobiblion Society have printed Lord Herbert of Cherbury's account of the Expedition, which started 27 June and returned Nov. 1627. Evelyn mentions the return, p. 225 (Chandos ed.).

P. 251.] *Lord of Newport.* Referred to in Herbert, *Autob.* 19 *n.*, 164 *n.* Montjoy Blount was Baron Montjoy in 1627, the time of the expedition to Rhé. He was created Earl of Newport, 3rd August 1628.
Sir Charles Rich, is included in a "list of those going to the Palatinate," *Powysl. Coll.* xx. 132 ; frequently mentioned in *S.P.* 1627-8.
Sir John Heydon. In Sir D. Carleton's *State Papers,* 1627, p. 252, he is called Sir *W.* Heydon, and it is stated that he was drowned at Rhé. *Cf.* Gard. vi. 274.
Sir Jo. Burrowes. For an account of his part in the expedition see Rushworth, i. 463, Forster Eliot, ii. 63-70, and D'Ewes' *Autob.* i. 366, who gives his date of death as 26 Sept. 1627. His last words are given by T. Forde, *Apophthegms,* p. 24.
Sir John Blundel. Is this a slip for Sir George Blundell, mentioned frequently in *S.P.* 1627-8 ?
Sir Alex. Bret. See Nichol's *Prog. Jas. I.,* i. 164, iii. 1067. Evelyn (Chandos ed.), 384, and Gard. vi. 198.

LETTER VI.—*Earl of Sunderland.* Emanuel Scrope, 11th Baron Scrope of Bolton, was created Earl of Sunderland 19th June 1627 ; he died 1630.
Earl of Denbigh, mentioned previously, 171. He returned from an unsuccessful attempt to relieve Rochelle May 27, 1628. Gard., *l.c.,* ii. 272.

stupendous

stupendous works. Prof. Gardiner doubts whether Blake or Nelson would have tried to destroy them (Gard., *l.c.*).

P. 252.] *five subsidies granted.* " In order to make the medicine more palatable to Charles the resolution for the five subsidies was at last reported to the House." Gard., *l.c.*, 251.
Petition of Right, c. xviii. of Gardiner's *England under Buckingham* is devoted to this. It was assented to by the King June 7, 1628.

LETTER VII.—*Countess of Sunderland.* Referred to Nichol's *Prog.* iii. 453. She was sister to the Earl of Rutland and aunt of the Duchess of Buckingham, his daughter. This letter is quoted by Scoones, *Eng. Lett.*, No. lvii. p. 75, and in Nimmo's *British Letter Writers,* p. 315.
D. of Buckingham was slain on Aug. 23, O.S. 1628. There is another contemporary account in 1 Ellis, iii. 261, which agrees mainly with H. See also D'Ewes, *Autob.* i. 381-5; Warwick, 32-3; Fairfax, *Papers,* i. 142-3; and Gard., vi. 349-59.
Lord of Rutland. Francis Manners, succeeded his brother 1612, died 1632.

P. 253.] *Saturday,* 23 Aug. O.S. 1628, was on a Saturday, a detail which says much for the authenticity of this letter.
Mons. Soubize. Fairfax, i. 144, refers to his presence at the murder. For a moment it was thought that he had committed the murder. Gard., *l.c.*, li. 337. He is frequently mentioned (Nichols, iii. 767, Croker, *Bassompierre,* 57, Forster, *Elliot,* i. 343-5 *n.*).
Col. Fryer. Sir Thomas. He was a short man, and it was while Buckingham was stooping to speak to him that Felton aimed the fatal blow.

P. 254.] *Dutchess.* Niece of the Countess to whom H. is writing. Gardiner also gives this detail, *l.c.*
the word "where is the villain?" was mistaken by Felton for "where is Felton?"
Jack Stamford was the Duke's servant. Sanderson, *Reign of Chas. I.,* p. 140 (C.H.F.). A certain Capt. Stamford was hanged in 1629. Straff. *Letters,* i. 51.
Mr. Nicholas, the Secretary, afterwards Sir Edward. See on p. 354.
Capt. Mince, probably Capt. John Menres, or Mince, frequently mentioned in *S.P.* 1628-9.
Capt. Chas. Price. One of H.'s correspondents and relations. See on p. 410.
5 Aug. Really written, according to H.'s account, on Monday, Aug. 25, 1628.

LETTER VIII.—*Sir Peter Wichts* [Wych] is mentioned in Sir T. Roe, *Negociations,* 73, 822 (a letter by him); also in Clarendon, ii. 396; Mayor, *Ferrar,* 397, 342; Spedding, *Life,* vi. 177; and Wood, *Athenæ.* A life in Collins's *Baronetage,* iv. 220-1. His death is referred to later, 423. H. knew him in Spain and helped him to bring home Prince Charles' jewels, *supra,* 230.
third time. One only knows of Wimbledon's and this of Lindsey's. Perhaps H. is counting the Expedition to the Isle of Rhé.
Lord of Lindsey. See on p. 583.

P. 255.] *Whelps,* in navigation, are pieces of wood for holding cables (Philip's *New World, s.v.*), but evidently here used in the sense of small ships called the Lion's Whelps, and known as first whelp, second whelp, &c. They are defined as pinnaces, *S.P.*, 1628-9, pp. 3, 103 (C.H.F.).

to

to build Paul's. Mentioned again, 617. , *Cf.* P. Warwick, 82-3 ; and Evelyn's *Life of Laud*, p. 504.
Lord of Newport. See on p. 251.
all the colours. Evelyn notices this (Chandos ed.), p. 44.
Rochel hath yielded, Oct. 28. The King, Louis XIII., entered in triumph Nov. 1, 1628.
Nunca vi, &c. ''There was never so bad a peace that was not better than the best war.''

P. 256.] LETTER IX.—*Mr. St. Geon at Christ Church*, mentioned in Campbell, *Chief Just.*; also 1 *N. and Q.* vii. 520. Another letter to him 326, from which it appears that he turned Roman Catholic.
Quæ, la vel Hipps. Dr. Venn has kindly made a search for me for this technical term among the old logics, but without success. H. insists on the advantages of Logic, *For. Tr.* 16.
Concoction and Agglutination, the former clearly answers to digestion, but agglutination or adhesion is probably what we now term assimilation.
teneri should be *tenere* as in ED. PR.

P. 257.] *Multiplicity of Authors.* Bacon's advice on study may be compared with this in his fiftieth Essay. H. recommends Books for the choyce ones in his *For. Tr.* 22.

LETTER X.—*Sir Sackvil Trevor, Knight.* See on p. 238.
sea-chest of glasses. Probably a box with divisions to hold glasses securely at sea.
Holy Spirit. S.P. Jan. 31, 1629. ''On the taking of the St. Esprit, petitioner was by Sir Sackville Trevor put in as purser.'' *Cf. Harl. Misc.* v. 108.

P. 258.] *Preserv'd from drowning.* The Prince's barge was being swept out to sea, when Sir Sackville in the ''Defiance'' threw out ropes which were seized by the crew, and Charles passed the night on the ''Defiance.'' Gard., *Sp. M.* ii. 413. *Cf.* ref. in Masson, *Life*, i. 466, ''The Prince's Escape at St. Andero.''
Todos los santos. Pernambuco was captured by the Dutch 1629.
26 of Octob. 1625, should be 1627, as in second edition.

LETTER XI.—*Capt. Tho. B.* Probably T. Bowyer, for whom see p. 97.
1st of March. It took a long time if this letter was written on the 1st of August, as the date added to the second edition states.
Sir Richard Scot, mentioned in Spedding, *Life*, vii. 255, 256.

P. 259.] *Swearing.* Mr. Besant, *French Humourists*, has some remarks on French cursing. There is also a *Cursory History of Swearing* (Paul, Trübner, & Co.).
a King. Cf. the quatrain given by Brantome, by which each French King is known by his favourite oath—
　　Quand le '' Pasque Dieu '' décéda, [Louis XI.]
　　'' Par le jour Dieu '' luy succéda, [Chas. VIII.]
　　'' Le Diable M'emporte '' s'en tint près, [Louis XII.]
　　'' Foys de Gentilhomme '' vint après. [Francis I.]
an Italian. I have been told the same story as having happened in London at the beginning of this century.

P. 260.]

P. 260.] *Lady Southwell's.* See Hasted's *Hist. of Kent.* (H. K.) I cannot find it ; Blomfield, *Norfolk* x. 275, mentions the marriage of Sir T. Southwell (†1648) with Margaret Fuller.
hundred Thousand Sacraments. Can this have any reference to the celebrated " Potztausend " ?
Death. "Morbleu," the well-known euphemism for "Mort de Dieu."
five wounds, probably a reference to "Zounds."

P. 262.] *O Heaven Chrystalline,* the *primum mobile.*

P. 263.] *Tom Young,* perhaps the one whose initials formed part of the well-known SmecTYmnuus. A letter to him later, p. 371.
1 *Aug.* Perfectly incongruous with the reference to March 1st in the body of the letter.

LETTER XII.—*Will Austin* (1587-1634) of Lincoln's Inn and Southwark. His works were published posthumously (D.N.B.).
Passion of Christ. If this was published at all, it must have been in his " Meditations," 1635.
Bankside to Paul's-Churchyard. Austin resided at Southwark, Stow-Strype, ii. 15. Paul's Churchyard was the Paternoster Row of the period. The phrase is therefore equivalent to " from privacy to publication."

P. 264.] LETTER XIII.—*Sir J. S.,* scarcely J. Smith, who was a Kentishman. A Sir John Savill is mentioned, *supra,* p. 269. This may be he, but the name is not given in the Table prefixed to ED. PR. (Doc. xxxix.)
The best News. Peace was looming in January 1629 (Gard. vii. *ad fin.*).
Harwich Men, your Neighbours, who had probably been troubled by the depredations of the Dunkirkers, of whom we hear much about this time.

P. 265.] LETTER XIV.—*Father.* See on p. 19.
Mr. Hawes, a mercer in Cheapside, probably son of Sir James Hawes, Lord Mayor of London, 1574.
Thomas Howell, mentioned in Strype's Stow, v. 58, as one of the benefactors of Draper's Hall, who gave more than £500 to it. He left " 12,000 dukats to buy 400 dukats of rent yearly " with which to dower " 4 maydens of my lynnage." See T. Falconer, *The charity of Thomas Howell established for the benefit of his Monmouthshire kinsfolk and others,* A.D. 1540, Lond. 1860. The pamphlet refers to H. and complains that the charity is mismanaged. If the donor was a Monmouth man he was not likely to be akin to the Howels of Pencaerau.

P. 266.] LETTER XV.—*Dr. Howell.* See on p. 25.
Sir Arthur Manwaring, mentioned D'Ewes' *Autob.* i. 87 ; Spedding, Life, vii. 256 ; Nicholls, i. 205.
Keeping of your Act, for his degree of D.D. presumably. This was usually by holding a public disputation to show competency. Where the stag came in I am unable to guess, nor is any hint given in Wordsworth, *University Life.*
Other Spanish. Bologna was at this time within the Spanish dominions. Charles V. was there crowned Emperor, 1529.
Living hard by Henly, called Hambledon, at the S.W. corner of Bucks, between Henley and Gt. Marlow. We find him at H., 499.
Dr. Pilkinton, perhaps the one mentioned Nichol's *Prog.* i. 172.
Dr. Domlaw, not mentioned in the *Athenæ.* Perhaps the Dr. Dorislaw afterwards murdered by the royalists abroad as a regicide (Wood, *Athenæ,* iii. 666.

P. 267.]

P. 267.] *Dr. Mansell.* See on p. 21.
Mr. Watkins. Richard, of Ch. Ch. (Wood, *Athenæ*, iii. 945).
Mr. Madocks, given in Clark, *Reg.* ii. 326, 337, but as of Jesus.
Mr. Napier. Afterwards Sir Richard, originally of Wadham and then of All Souls, an eminent physician. *Cf.* Wood, *Fasti,* ii. 47.

LETTER XVI.—*Mr. Ben Johnson,* the well-known poet, whose name is generally spelt without *h*. Howell was one of the Tribe of Ben. See Introduction.
your Fox, i.e., Volpone, produced 1607.
Catilin, produced 1611.
Epigrams were not published till 1640, unless in his *Workes,* 1631.
Magnetick Lady. This was Jonson's last play but one, and was produced in 1632 (Masson, *Life.* i. 398).
Est Deus in Nobis. Ovid, *Fasti,* vi. 5.
Dr. Davies's Welsh Grammar, i.e., Antiquæ Linguæ Britannicæ nunc communiter dictæ Cambro-Britannicæ. . . . Rudimenta, Lond. 1621 ; there is a poem by H. on this book, infra, 277.
Vulcan. A reference to the fire in which many of Jonson's MSS. were burned.

P. 268.] LETTER XVII.—*Sir Arthur Ingram,* frequently mentioned (*Jas. I.,* i. 262-367 ; Nichol's *Prog.* ii. 288 *n.* ; Strafford *Letters,* i. 6, &c. ; Spedding, *Life,* vii. *pass.* ; Fairf. i. 277, ii. 311 ; Pepys (Chand.), 137, 240).
Temple Newsam, near Leeds, where Darnley was born. The house was built by Sir A. Ingram, and is now one of the seats of the Marquis of Hertford.
Lord President, i.e., the Earl of Sunderland, who was his patron at the time.
Dr. Napier. See on p. 267.

LETTER XVIII.—*R.S.* It is difficult to understand why H. inserted this letter except as a model of an Epistle Expostulatory. There was another letter to R.Sc., *supra,* 230, which we conjectured to be written to a Scrope.

P. 269.] LETTER XIX.—*Countess of Sunderland.* See on p. 252.
my Lord, i.e., the Earl of Sunderland, Lord President of the North.
Napier's. See on preceding page and p. 267.
Dr. Mayern. Sir Theodore, born at Geneva 1573, died at Chelsea 1655. His case books, giving the medical history of the most distinguished persons of the time, are still in the British Museum.
Wickham, East W. in Kent, near Woolwich.
Atkinson. An account of him is given in Munk, *Surgeons,* i. 87-8.
D. Lopez, a Spanish crypto-Jew, Elizabeth's physician, who was executed for attempting to murder her. Supposed to be the original of Shylock. See Mr. Lee's paper in *Gentleman's Mag.* Feb. 1880.
Sir Jo. Saville, frequently mentioned in the Strafford *Letters,* i. 2, 3, 4, 11, 12, &c. He was of Howley, co. York ("their countryman"). He was created a peer 21 July 1628. *Cf.* Herbert, *Autob.,* 29 *n.*
White Staff generally indicates the Lord Chamberlain, but Saville did not hold this office, being only high-steward of the royal honour of Pontefract, and afterwards Controller of the Household (Burke, *Extinct Peer.* 467.)
Lord Weston. See on p. 130.
Lord Cottington. See on p. 162.
Swedes under Gustavus Adolphus, but he did not embark for Germany till June 1630.

My

My Lady Scroop, or Scrope, wife of Thomas, tenth Baron Scrope of Bolton, who died 1609.
Sir Posthumus Hobby. On him see Pref. to *Fortesque Papers* (C.S.), also 1 *N. and Q.* vii. 626, and for the name Halliwell, *Dict.* s.v.
Biggin-Farm. This seems a local touch that is scarcely likely to have been inserted afterwards.
Sir Will Alford, referred to, Nichol's *Prog. Jas. I.,* i. 118 *n.*
Sir Tho. Wentworth, afterwards the Earl of Strafford. See on p. 279. His defection from the popular cause is treated by Forster, *Elliot,* Bk. ix. c. v., under date of 23 May 1628.
Mr. Wansford. See on p. 249 : he was a satellite of Wentworth's. Forster, *Eliot²,* ii. 66.
Lady Scroop. Philadelphia, daughter of Henry Carey, Lord Hunsdon, married Lord Scrope of Bolton, father of the Earl of Sunderland.
P. 270.] 5 *Aug.* 1629. This does not chime in with the reference to *Sir* John Savile or to the date of the defection of Wentworth.

LETTER XXI.—*Dr. H. W.* From the "Table" of ED. PR. we learn that this is Dr. H. Wicham, perhaps Wickham.
Female Promises. Cf. Balthasar Gracian, *Oraculo Manual,* § 202.
Mr. B. Chaworth, a relation probably of George Viscount Chaworth.
Lady Robinson. This does not imply a double marriage of the lady, since Mrs. was applied to single ladies.

P. 272.] LETTER XXII.—*Mr. Tho. M.* There is a letter to Mr. T. More,. 541, and to Mr. T. Morgan, 556. The latter is also mentioned, p. 88.

P. 274.] LETTER XXIII.—*Countess of Sunderland at Langar.* "Here [at Langar, Notts] was an ancient house, now re-edified by Hen. Lo. Scroope," whose monument is there (Brayley and Britton, *Beauties,* 225).
Bolton Castle, at West Bolton, co. York, whence the Scropes take their title of "Scropes of Bolton."
Lord Carleton. He was now "Lord," but II. seems to apply this term to Baronets and Knights as well. Sir Dudley Carleton was ultimately Clerk of Council (*infra,* 667), and is frequently mentioned in the memoirs of the time (e.g. Herbert, *Autob.,* 151–61 ; Forster, *Eliot,* i. 556 ; Mayor's *Ferrar,* 16, 189).
Wanless Park. Not in the Gazetteers.
Rabbi Castle, sic in ED. PR. Should be Raby Castle, co. Durham, but this was purchased by Sir Henry Vane, *temp.* Jas. I., and is still in the hands of his descendants (Brayley and Britton, *Beauties,* v. 232 ; Collins, *Peerage,* iv. 505).
Lord of Wentworth was made Lord Deputy 3 July 1633.

P. 275.] *Lord of Pembroke.* Philip, Earl of P., who afterwards went over to the Parliamentarians, and was addressed, in consequence, by H. in a scathing letter (Bibl. List, No. 20).
Sir David Fowler, sic in ED. PR., should probably be Fowles (C.II.F.). A full account of the quarrel and of Sir D. Foulis' character, by Wentworth himself, is given in a letter dated York, 24 Sept. 1632, in the App. to *Handb. Dyce and Forster Coll.* p. 95.
Attorney's place in York. See the two letters exchanged between Sunderland and Wentworth in Supplement dated Dec. 15, 1628, and May 5, 1629.

John

John Lister. Formerly M.P. for Hull. Forster, *Elliot,* i. 429. He is mentioned Spedding, *Life,* vii. 258.
Ratcliff, mentioned in II.'s own letter to Wentworth, *infra,* p. 650.
Dutchess your Niece, the Duchess of Buckingham. See *supra,* on p. 254.
York House, in the Strand, where Bacon was born. At his death it was
borrowed by the Duke of Buckingham from Matthews, Archbishop of York,
whose official residence it was—theoretically. It is called "Jorschaux" in
Croker, *Bassompierre,* 25.
1 *July* 1629, inconsistent with the reference to Wentworth as Lord Deputy of
Ireland, 1633, and to the quarrel between him and Fowlis. On the other
hand Mr. Ratcliff became Sir George in July 1633, a touch confirming the
authenticity of the present letter.

LETTER XXIV.—D. C. D. Caldwell. See *supra,* p. 107.
House in Essex, at Shreves or Sheriff.
Jack T. Toldervy mentioned, *supra,* 28. He is mentioned in Hasted, *Kent ;*
and from the Harl. Soc., *Visitation of Essex,* turns out to be Caldwell's
brother-in-law.
Will die in a Butt. This prophecy turned out false as Toldervy turned
Quaker and wrote a conversionist pamphlet as late as 1656 (H. K.).

P. 276.] LETTER XXV.—*Sir Thomas Lake.* H. K. gives the following refer-
ences : Wood, *Ath.* and *Fasti ; Jas. I.,* i. 216 ; Lysons, *Environs ;* Bayley.
Tower of London ; D'Israeli, *Misc.,* 338 ; Jesse, i. 72–5 ; Croker, *Bass,*
85–9 ; Add Nichols, ii. 264 *n.* Another letter to him, p. 499.
Martial's. Lib. x. cp. 47, the fine description of a happy life.
Sir Kenelm Digby. See on 191.

LETTER XXVI.—*Ben Johnson.* See on. p. 267.
Dr. Davies's British Grammar. See on p. 267.
The Rabbies pass my reach. In other words, II. does not know Hebrew.
Clenard. Nicholas (1495–1542). His *Institutiones linguæ Græcæ,* 1530, was
the standard text-book of Greek Grammar of the time.

P. 277.] *for Irish.* Scarcely M. Clery's *Lexicon Hibernicum,* Louvain, 1643,
which is too late. Perhaps the *Ratio legendi Hibernicam* of 1571, given by
Watt under Subject with a wrong reference under authors.
Bascuence. Basque.
Catarac. Caractacus, shortened and changed for exigencies of rhyme.
Lucius. The proto-Christian King, on whom see p. 387.

LETTER XXVIII.—*Earl of Bristol* (1580–1677). Buckingham's opponent
(D.N.B), frequently mentioned by II. The Sophronio of his *Dodona's Grove.*
See Index.
Sherborn-Castle, co. Dorset (Brayley and Britton, *Beauties,* iv. 493). It had
belonged to Raleigh, and was given to Sir J. Digby by Jas. I. for £10,000.
Cf. Edwards, *Raleigh,* i. 469–80.
Lord Cottington. See on 162. He was sent to Spain in the autumn of 1629,
and signed the treaty of peace with that power, 5 Nov. 1630. He was not
raised to the peerage till 10 July 1631 (D.N.B.).
old business of the "Vineyard," see *supra,* 151.

P. 278.] *Peace with the Dane,* June 7, 1629 (Gindely, *Thirty Years' War,* i.
445).
Gustavus King of Swethland. Gustavus Adolphus of Sweden.
Taken Mecklenburgh in 1630. Gustavus summoned Capt. Hume to "Mickle
Bury land" (*S.P.* 1629–31, p. 431).

Don

Don Carlos Coloma, mentioned also in *For. Tr.* 60. He is mentioned as having arrived, *S.P.* Dec. 22, 1629. See also *supra*, pp. 190, 255. 20th *May* 1629, inconsistent with Cottington's title and the capture of Mecklenburgh.

LETTER XXVIII.—*J. P.* John Price, for whom see p. 194. He is not in Metcalfe's *Book of Knights*.

P. 279.] LETTER XXIX.—*Viscount Wentworth.* He was created Viscount, 10 Dec. 1628.
Pignerol. H. gives an account of its capture and the importance of it, *Lustra Ludov.* 93-4 ; *sub anno*, 1630.

P. 280.] LETTER XXX.—*Sir Kenelm Digby.* See on p. 191.
Happy return from the Levant. He landed at Woolwich, 2 Feb. 1629. His "Journal of the Scanderoon Voyage" has been published by the Camden Society.
Bay of Scanderoon, i.e., Alexandria, see *infra*, 442. Digby fought the French and Venetian vessels in the harbour. A reference in Aubrey, *Lives*, ii. 238 ; also in H.'s *S.P.Q.V.* 167.

P. 281.] *our Aleppo Merchants.* Digby had to retire "because his presence in the Levant jeopardised the position of the English merchants at Aleppo and elsewhere," D.N.B., s.v. p. 61*b*.

LETTER XXXI.—*Sir Peter Wicht.* See on p. 254.
Master Simon Digby. See on p. 210.
First of June, i.e., 1629, for the letter is dated 1 Jan. 1629, *i.e.*, 1630, but six months is rather long for the delivery of a letter even from Constantinople.
Sir Tho. Edmonds. See on p. 242. He is mentioned by Herbert, *Autob.* 106, 206 ; Nichols, *Prog.* i. 156 *n.* and *pass.;* Fairfax, i. 184 ; also in Granger, Lloyd, and the *Strafford Letters.*
Mr. Burlemach, the chief financial agent of the period, and frequently mentioned as such (Spedding, *Life*, vii. 49 ; Carleton, *Letters*, 17, 435 ; Roe, *Negot.* Lett. lxi., lxii. (from B.) ; Forster, *Eliot*, i. 470, 471 *n.*, ii. 97 *n.* ; Herbert, *Autob.* 188 *n.; Powysl. Coll.* xx. 139).
Chateauneuf, mentioned frequently in *S.P.* 1629-32 from Sept. 25, 1629, onwards.
Lord Treasurer Weston. See on p. 130. He became Earl of Portland in 1633, so that H. is accurate in his title. His eldest son Jerome, afterwards second Earl, did marry Lady Frances Stuart, the Duke of Lenox's daughter.

P. 282.] *Bishop Laud of London*, since 1628.
his Persian Expedition. Bagdad was taken by Murad IV. 25 Dec. 1638.

LETTER XXXII.—*Sir Tho. Wentworth.* We had him as Viscount, *supra*, 279.
Attorney's Place. A reference to this, *supra*, 275, and in Supplement, from which the date would be between Sept. 1628 and May 1629.
Lord of Sunderland, further references to his illness, *supra*, pp. 268-9.

P. 283.] *Bever Castle, i.e.*, Belvoir Castle, co. Leicester, the home of the Manners.
Mr. Haws of Cheapside, on whom see p. 265.
Capt. Philips. There is a Philips named in Spedding, *Life*, vii. 542.

Lady

Lady Carlisle, the reigning beauty at Charles's court about this time. *Cf.* Forster, *Five Members,* 133-9; P. Warwick, 224; Lilly, *Life,* 234. It was
she who warned the five members. Dorothy Osborne calls her "extraordinary," *Letters,* 171, and her editor, Mr. Parry, explains the epithet by
a characterisation, *ibid.,* 167.

LETTER XXXIII.—*Lord Cottington.* See on p. 162. He went as ambassador to Spain in the autumn of 1629.
Harry Davies. Mentioned in the *Strafford Letters,* ii. 285, as a kind of
courier or king's messenger.
Correo Santo. Sp. lit. "sacred courier," but his exact functions I cannot
ascertain. Probably king's messenger to Rome.

P. 284.] *old business* of the "Vineyard," *supra,* 151.
the Swedes, under Gustavus Adolphus at latter end of 1630.
Sir Kenelm Digby. See on p. 191. He landed in England after his Scan-
deroon voyage, 2nd Feb. 1628.
Mr. Goring, afterwards Sir George Goring, the Cavalier officer (*cf.* Wilson,
104; Weldon, 92; Gard. iii. 218; Croker, *Bass.* 48; Clar. ii. 417; Fairf.
i. 263 *n.*).
Mr. Jermin, referred to Gard. vii. 218, 333; letters by him, Warburton,
Rupert, i. 502-3.
Duels, on the frequency of duelling at this period Herbert of Cherbury's
Autobiography affords abundant proof. See also a proposal of Bacon in
Spedding, vi. 108-10; and a paper of Carlyle's, *Miscell.* ii. 213-37, "A
Fragment about Duels."
Mrs. Baker. There is a Mrs. Baker mentioned in *S. P.* for 1639. She was
probably related to Baker, the Duke of Buckingham's servant (Nichol's
Prog., iii. 1033).
Sir Arthur Ingram. See on p. 268.
1 *March* 1630. This conflicts with the account given by Sir K. Digby of the
same duel in which H. was wounded and, as Digby alleges, cured by his
"sympathetic powder." See Suppt. Doc. xxii. and notes, in which I show
that H.'s account is the more probable—for once.

LETTER XXXIV.—*Viscount Rocksavage, i.e.,* Sir Thomas Savage that was,
for whom see p. 132. He was created Viscount Savage of Rock Savage,
6 Nov. 1626. This accuracy about titles is one of the points in favour of
the authenticity of some of the Letters. See Introd. p. lxxviii.

P. 285.] LETTER XXXV.—*Earl of Bristol.* See on p. 160.
battel of Leipsick, in which Gustavus defeated Tilly, 7 Sept. 1631.
Sir Tho. Roe (1580-1644), whom the Queen of Hearts and Bohemia addressed
as "Honest Tom," previously ambassador to Constantinople; he negotiated
the peace between Sweden and Poland, 1629.
near Augsburg, at Rain on the Lech, 5 April 1632: he died within three
weeks after, so had little use for a wooden leg.
at Munchen. He entered this 17 May 1632.
at Mentz, now Metz.

P. 286.] *Sir Henry Vane* (1509-1654) the Elder, at this time ambassador
extraordinary to the Kings of Denmark, Sweden, and the Princes of Germany (*S.P.* 1631-3).
Sir Robert Anstruther, a well-known diplomatist of the time (Spedding, *Life,*
vii. 81; Fairf. i. 256). He was sent to Ratisbon, June 1630 (Gard. vii.
173), and to Vienna, March 1631 (*l.c.* 178).

brother

brother Don Carlos is lately dead, in 1632, aged 26. See *supra*, p. 155, 182.
23 April, 1630. This is antedated a year, if the reference to the Battle of Leipsic and Anstruther's Vienna mission was in original.

LETTER XXXVI.—*Lady Cor.* Probably Lady Cornwallis, to whom a later letter is addressed, see p. 312.
marinate. Mr. W. C. Hazlitt in his work on *Books of Cookery*, p. 101, gives a recipe, "To marinade a Leg of Lamb." They still marinade pilchards in Cornwall, Mr. Sketchley tells me.
P. **287.**] *ollia.* "To make an Olio Pye" is the title of a recipe quoted by Mr. Hazlitt, *l.c.* 109-10.
common sense, now called by psychologists the organic sense.
after the mode. Probably the kind of beef *à la mode* known in French cookery as *Bœuf à la mode à la Paysanne*. See Marin, *Dons de Comus*, Paris, 1758, t. i. p. 197, "mettez . . . un peu de lard maigre au fond."

LETTER XXXIV.—*Mr. E. D.* Another letter to the same, 308, connects him with Bury [St. Edmunds], and suggests that he was one of the Drury family. *T. B.* Can this be Tom Bowyer, frequently mentioned in these *Letters?* See Index.
such a place. This vague phrase cannot have been in an original letter.
Caligula's Horse named Incitatus. Suetonius only says he was *intended* for the Consulate ("consulatum quoque destinasse traditur").

P. **288.**] LETTER XXXVIII.—*Earl of Leicester.* Robert Sydney (†1677), created Earl 1618 ; for a Latin account of his embassy written by J. H., see Supplement.
Lord Weston. See on p. 130.
late death of the Lady Sophia, Queen Anne's mother.
Baynards-Castle, on the banks of the Thames, just below St. Paul's. At the time it was the home of the Earl of Pembroke. One of the unpublished letters of the Earl of Leicester relating to his embassy is dated thence (Rec. Off. S. P. For. Denmark, No. 9, dated 9th Aug. 1632).
Secretary in this Ambassage. His account of the Embassy, written in the capacity of Secretary or "Orator," is given in the Appendix.

P. **289.**] LETTER XXXIX.—*Alderman Moulson.* Sir Thomas, mentioned Nichol's *Prog.* iii. 597 ; Fairf. i. 89. He was Lord Mayor of London for part of 1633 and for 1634. Stow, v. 153.
Merchant Adventurers. Were incorporated by Elizabeth, 1564. They were practically what we now call importers.
the Staple. Referred to *supra*, 243.

LETTER XL.—To *Alderman Clethero.* Sir Christopher. He was M.P. for City. Forster, *Eliot*, ii. 100, mentioned Fairf. i. 89. He was Lord Mayor in 1636.
Mr. Skinner. Perhaps Milton's friend to whom one of the Sonnets is addressed.

LETTER XLI.—*Earl of Leicester.* See on p. 288. His instructions for the embassy are given in the *Sydney Papers*, ii. 374.
Petworth, co. Sussex, the old seat of the Percies.
Sir John Pennington, one of the most distinguished admirals of the time
mentioned

mentioned in Edwards' *Raleigh*, i. 600, 649, ii. 353, 372 ; Fairf. i. 20–21. According to *S.P.* there was a dispute between him and Capt. Plumligh as to who should carry Leicester. *S.P.* June 4, 1632.

P. 290.] *at Margate.* "Margett" in ED. PR., as in all contemporary documents.
Mr. Burlamach. See on 281.
Sir Paul Pindar. See on 543, where there is a letter to him.
25th of July. From the official record it will be seen that it began from as early a date as Dec. 8. 1631.
Luckstadt, Gluckstadt, spelt Luxtoad by Pennington in his Log.

LETTER XLII.—*Lord Mohun.* John, 2nd Baron, *ob.* 1644.
12th August. By the date at end it took him over a fortnight to answer.
unseasonable, a subtle dramatic touch which seems to vouch for the authenticity of this letter.
It was founded first. As a matter of fact, it took its rise with the persecution of the Albigenses, 1203, and was hence introduced into Spain, 1248.
P. 291.] *Whosoever was found.* II. may have got this from an old pamphlet : *A discovery and playne declaration of sundry subtile practices of the Holy Inquisition of Spain,* 1568, or more likely from his own knowledge.
brangling, branling, ED. PR. Both forms are used, and imply the same as their original, the French *branler*, "to totter." II. was fond of the word, and the quotations in the Oxford Dict. are mainly from him.

P. 292.] *an Act of Faith.* Port. *Auto da fé.*
Chaperon, a small cape, the original use of the word ; the later application is of this century. Skeat, *Etym. Dict.* s.v.

SECTION VI.

And last of Book I., originally published in 1645. This therefore contains a record of the fourteen years 1632–45, *i.e.,* nearly as long a period as the remaining five sections. It is chiefly occupied with the Embassy to Denmark in the autumn of 1632 ; for this I have given a contemporary account of Howell's and Admiral Pennington's Log (See Docs. iv., xxiii.–vii.). The remainder of the Section is taken up with II.'s wanderings through the United Kingdom, and his seizure and imprisonment in the Fleet.

P. 293.] LETTER I.—*To P. W.* Philip (afterwards Sir Philip) Warwick, 1608–93. He is frequently mentioned both by Pepys and Evelyn, and Fairf. i. 81, ii. 160, 309 *n.* His *Memoirs* are of some value, and have been translated into French. There is a life of him in *Biog. Univ.*
Sir John Penington. See on p. 289.
Margets, the ordinary spelling of the time.
Monday, 17 Sept. 1632. See Pennington's Log.
Rensburg, in Schleswig-Holstein. See next page.
Richsadgt, should be Richsdagh, as in ED. PR.; it is Danish for Parliament. *Cf.* Germ. *Reichstag.*
Mr. Burlamach. See on p. 281.
Mr. Avery. There is a letter from him to the Earl of Leicester on this very occasion in the *Sydney Papers,* ii. 373–4.

find

find out Wallestein. He attacked him at Nuremberg at the end of Aug. 1632.
Mr. Railton. William, mentioned in *Straf. Lett.* i. 310, 348 (C.H.F.), "a very honest, able man."

P. 294.] LETTER II.—*Viscount S.* Savage probably, see on p. 132.
Orator. "Jacobo Howell Oratore" is the heading of H.'s Latin account.
Secretary Naunton, Sir Robert (1563-1635), author of the *Fragmenta Regalia.* Cf. Herbert, *Autob.*, pp. 337, 348.
I made another, referred to in H.'s Latin account, p. 652.
Pr. Frederick. He succeeded his father in 1648, the king elect having predeceased the king.

P. 295.] *Husem in Ditzmarsh,* now called Husum, about twenty-two miles west of Schleswig and on the sea.
thirty five healths, the carouse in Hamlet, Act i. sc. 3, is obviously recalled by this toasting of the King of Denmark. T. Forde has some interesting remarks on the origin of toasts in his *Fam. Letters,* p. 49.
Gothorp Castle, in Schleswig, also referred to in the Latin account, *infra,* 652.
I made a speech, not referred to in Latin account.
Rensburgh, now Rendsburg, on the borders of Schleswig and Holstein.
Sir Robert Anstruther. See on p. 286.
9 *Oct. 1632.* A tolerably likely date, and the contents are sufficiently attested by the Latin account.

LETTER III. *Earl R.* Rivers probably.
Hans, or Hansiatick League. The best English account of this is Miss Zimmern's *Hansa Towns,* in the "Story of the Nations" Series.

P. 297.] *Staplers and Merchant-Adventurers,* the former was incorporated as early as 1319, the latter as late as 1564.

P. 298.] *Easterlings,* from whom we get the expression sterling.
Monopolists. These had been declared illegal in England at the end of the preceding reign after a fierce controversy.

P. 300.] *Alderman Cockeins.* For a full account of his proposals, see Gard. ii. 386; *cf.* also *supra,* p. 36; and Spedding, *Life,* vi. 283.

LETTER IV.—*Capt. J. Smith,* a Capt. John Smyth was discharged of his captaincy of Gravesend, 27 Mar. 1632 (*S.P.* under date).
Mr. James Crofts, son of Sir James, on whom see 22; he had been up at Oxford in H.'s time (Clark, *Reg.* ii. 39).

P. 301.] *they resemble the English.* Howell makes the same remark in his *For. Travel,* ed. Arber, 48; *cf.* also a passage quoted from Worsae in 2 *N. and Q.,* iii. 489, also *Germ. Diet.*
English nation came first. This is, of course, now a commonplace of English history; *cf.* the opening passage of Green's *Short History.*
Island call'd Angles. H. probably refers to the district of Holstein known as *Angeln;* H. again draws attention to the fact, *infra,* p. 461.

P. 302.] LETTER V.—*Earl of Br.,* i.e., Bristol, on whom see 160. This letter again goes over the ground covered by the Latin account in the Supplement and in Letter II. *supra.*

P. 304.]

II.   3 B

P. 304.] *Pass by the Hague.* As a matter of fact he sent Crofts instead, *supra,* p. 300.
would engage his honour. This fine action is likewise quoted in H.'s treatise on Ambassadors, at the end of his *Precedency of Kings.*
Husem, a reference to this in the Latin account, p. 652. See also on p. 294.
our King's Aunt, his mother's sister.
Stode where Lesley was Governor. Stade, see p. 243. On Lesley see Warburton, *Rupert,* i. 169 ; and Carlyle, *Cromwell,* i. 344.

P. 305.] *Broomsbottle.* Brunsbüttel. See Pennington's Log, Sept. 18.

LETTER VI.—*Dr. Howell, House in Horsley,* co. Surrey, where he was vicar, *supra,* 25.
fall of the K. of Sweden, 6/16 Nov. 1632. They learnt it about the 26th (? O.S.).
One Jerbire. Mr. C. H. Firth suggests this is a misprint (of the ED. PR.) for Dalbier, who is mentioned (*Court Chas. I.,* ii. 202) as having brought the news.
slain at Lutzen. For other contemporary accounts see *Court Chas. I.,* ii. 202 ; *Straff. Lett.* i. 80.

P. 306.] *whose Anagram is Augustus,* counting the *v* as *u.*
Marquis Hamilton (1606–49). See Gard. vii. 174 ; Warwick, *Mem.* 110–8 ; also in Burnet's *Life* (C.H.F.).
Mr. Mouschamp. There is a Sir T. Mouschamp mentioned, Nichols, i. 469 ; and Sir. W. iii. 299.

LETTER VII.—*Dr. Field.* See on p. 230.
Father's death. It is a question whether H. would have acted a lie about such an event as the death of his father.

P. 307.] LETTER VIII.—*Earl of Leicester.* See on p. 289.
Mr. Secretary Coke. Sir J. Coke, Secretary to the Admiralty, whose valuable papers are now being calendared by the Hist. MSS. Commission. (D.N.B. and Warwick, *Memoir,* 153).
an Account of the whole Legation. This is now at the Bodleian and is printed in the Supplement, pp. 651–3.
Mr. Alderman Clethero. See on p. 289.
the same day. That is scarcely likely, for, from Pennington's Log, we know Leicester embarked on Nov. 21, and even if that was N.S., it is improbable that it took five days from Hamburg to Brunsbüttel.
Prince Palatine, died at Mentz, 29 Nov. 1632. See also *Straff. Lett.* i. 80.

P. 308.] *this Pope Lutherano,* Urban VIII. See *supra,* 237. He suppressed the order of female Jesuits about this time, which may account for the name.

LETTER IX.—*Mr. E. D.* See on 287.
at Bury St. Edmunds, co. Suffolk.
St. Dunstans in the west. Strafford was baptised there.

P. 309.] *John Oxenham.* Readers will remember the effective use made of this superstition by Kingsley in the first chapter of his *Westward Ho!* An account is given in *Gent. Mag.,* Jan. 1794, of the last appearance of the bird (*Cf.* 2 *N. and Q.* iii. 212).

Town

Town hard by Exeter. Kingsley also makes John Oxenham in his story a Devonian.

LETTER X.—*W.B.*, possibly W. Blois, the only W.B. among H.'s correspondents. See p. 494.

P. 310.] LETTER XI.—Sir Arthur Ingram. See on p. 268.
New Attorney General. Noy, on whom see p. 319.
Judge Richardson, afterwards Chief Justice. *Cf.* Campbell, *Chief. Just.* i.
Tax called Ship money. The first design appears to be a suggestion of Sir T. Coke, *S.P.* 1634-5, p. 100. This was about June 1634. But see a curious note of Evelyn's in his *Observations on a late History of Chas. I.*, 1656, p. 120-1.
from Bullen, i.e., Boulogne.

P. 311.] *Lord of Holland.* See on 171.
House at Kensington. The well-known Holland House, which came to him by his wife, Miss Cope.

LETTER XII.—*Wentworth.* See on p. 269.
Queen-Mother. See *Lustra Lud.* 99, sub anno 1631.
Monsieur. H. tells the story, *Lustra,* 103, sub anno 1632.
1 of April, 1633. This letter would seem to be misdated and misplaced.

P. 312.] LETTER XIII.—*Lady Cornwallis.* See 286. Elizabeth, widow of Sir Frederick Cornwallis.
Christmas-day, scarcely "now near approaching" if we could trust the date, 3 Feb. 1633 [-4].

LETTER XIV.—Lord Clifford at Knaresborough.

P. 313.] *the Jews.* A similar account in Bk. II., Letter viii. *infra,* p. 383, *seq.* The present was utilised by H. in his introduction to Josippon (Bibl. List, No. 40). He got his information from Sandys, *Travels,* 109-116, and Blount, *Voyage.*
first Christian Country, not precisely correct. The expedition from England was in 1290, and Philip Augustus expelled them from France from 1182 to 1198.
France in 1301. *Spain* in 1492. *Portugal* in 1511.
Brokers and Lombardeers. See on this M. Loeb, *Le juif de légende et le juif de l'histoire.* H. got the notion from Sandys, *l.c.*, p. 115.

P. 314.] *Benjamin's Tribe.* I cannot say how H. got this idea.
Tribe of Judah, whence the name of Jew.
settled in Portugal, whither they were driven from Spain in 1492.
Alchoran. The first English translation of this, by Alex. Ross, appeared in 1642. But there was an account of "Alcaron" published by Wynkyn de Worde.
fulsome scent. On this Sir T. Browne has a chapter in his *Vulgar Errors.* See also George Eliot, *Dan. Deronda,* c. xlii.

P. 315.] *misterious Cabai.* The Cabbala mystical doctrine, chiefly founded on the Sohar, a mystical commentary on Genesis, attributed to a Rabbi of the second, but really composed by one of the twelfth century. H.'s
account

account of it was probably taken from H. Blount, *Voyage*, 3rd ed. 1638, pp. 117 *seq.*
the Africans, the ordinary Rabbinic Jews, who in Howell's days had their chief seat in Africa, owing to the expulsion from Spain in 1492.
the second, a reference to the Karaites, who reject the Talmud or traditional interpretation of Scripture.
Samaritans, of whom a few are still extant at Shechem. They are the only Jews who still actually sacrifice the Paschal Lamb.

P. 316.] *drink no wine.* This is some error : strictly orthodox Jews do not drink wine unless made under their own supervision, but there is no such thing as Dispensation in Judaism.
kind of cupboard, called the Ark, and representing rather the Holy of Holies than the Tabernacle.
Jehovah is pronounced, a mistake. "Jehovah" is a fabricated word with the vowels of *Adonay* and the consonants of the Tetragrammaton, the true pronunciation of which is now lost.
Linen-Cope. Still used and called a *Talith.* H. got the expression from Sandys, *l.c.*
lower creation. H. probably gets this entirely erroneous idea from Blount's *Travels.*

P. 317.] LETTER XV.—*Mr. Philip Warwick.* See on p. 293.
Swedes at Nordlinghen. The Archduke Ferdinand defeated the Swedes 6 Sept. 1634.
Monsieur's Marriage, given by H. in *Lustra*, p. 106, sub anno 1633.
Love call'd Platonick Love. There is a letter of Clarendon's to Lady Dalkeith on the subject, under date 1647 (C.H.F.) Davenant wrote a Tragœcomedy entitled *The Platonick Lovers*, 1636. H. refers the invention to Marguerite de Valois in his *Lust. Lud.* p. 26, with her celebrated aphorism, "Voulez vous cesser d'aymer ? Possedez la chose aymée."

P. 318.] LETTER XVI.—*Mr. H. P.* Penry, for whom see 129.
1st of September scarcely agrees with date at end.
murmuring against the Ship-money. This took shape in the autumn of 1634.
Noy, the Attorney-General. See on 319 ; and *cf. Strafford Papers*, i. 242, 262.
a Scotchman. "One Capt. *Lashly* hath got a Patent to collect the Penalty the Statute imposeth on Swearers." Howell to the Lord Deputy, 30 July 1635, *Straff. Lett.* i. 446.
1 Aug. 1633, obviously inconsistent with the reference to Ship-money.

P. 319.] LETTER XVI.—*Viscount Savage, Long Melford.* See on p. 284.
Attorney-General Noy (1577-16 Aug. 1634). He devised the writ of ship-money, though Finch is thought to have suggested the idea. See on p. 318.
Tunbridge. Noy died at Brentford, according to Lysons, *Environs of London*, ii. 28.
Edoardo, to whom there is a letter, *infra*, p. 329. He died in a duel, so that his father's presentiment was justified, D. Gilbert, *Hist. Cornwall*, iii. 156.

. 320.] *William Noy, I moil in Law.* H. was very fond of these Anagrams. See Index, *sub voce.*
Judge Jones (1566-1640), was one of the five judges who declared against Hampden (Foss, vi. 340), and it was he that tried Felton. Forster, *Elliot*, ii. 373.

LETTER XVIII.—*Countess of Sunderland.* See on p. 252.

Lord Deputy Strafford.   This was with reference to the Attorney's place at York, *supra*, p. 275.
Nephew Princes.   Charles and Rupert, the sons of the Palsgrave.
Prince Robert, known to us as Rupert.   He is called Robert in his brother and mother's Disclaimer of him in 1642, *Somers Tracts*, iv. 498.   It was contemplated sending him to Madagascar.   Warburton, *Rupert*, i. 59. See also King's Pamphlet in Brit. Mus. (240-16, K. 1636).
Capt. Bond.   A Mr. Secretary Bond is mentioned in Spedding, *Life*, vi. 148 ; others, Nichol's *Prog. Jas. I.*, i. 547, iii. 986.

P. **321.**] LETTER XIX.—*Earl of Leicester.*   See on 289.
flying Journey.   No other record of this can be found.   There is a letter of Mainwaring to Windebank from Orleans.   *S.P.* Feb. 16, 1633.
Secretary Windebank.   Sir Francis was appointed to succeed Cottington in June 1632.   For Life see *Biog. Brit.*, and further reference in Clar. Gard. 1 *N. and Q.* iii. 373 (H.K.) ;   Carlyle, *Crom.* i. 110.
Montmorency, Henry II., Duke of (1595-1632), joined Monsieur's conspiracy, was defeated by Schomberg and executed at Toulouse 30 Oct. 1632.   H. repeats all he says here in *Lustra*, 105.
Infant Cardinal.   H. tells this incident about Monsieur under date 1634, *Lustra Lud.* 106.

P. **322.**] *Sir Robert Pye*, auditor of receipts at the Exchequer, frequently mentioned in *S.P.* for 1631-33.   *Cf.* Whitelocke, *Mem.* 693, 696.
Lord of Lindsey.   Robert Bertie, created Earl of Lindsey 1626, was son of Baron Willoughby de Eresby, who had gone to Denmark as Ambassador in 1582.

P. **323.**] *compleat Diary*, that was preserved in the Bodleian and reprinted in this edition, p. 651 *seq.*
your own late Legation to Denmark.

LETTER XX.—*Mr. Ben Johnson.*   See on p. 267.
a choice story.   For the variants of this well-known tale (one in Boccaccio) see my edition of Painter, *Palace of Pleasure*, I. tale lviii.   H. simply took it from Rosset., *XVIII. Histoires tragiques*, Paris, 1609, and his statement as to hearing it is but a white one.

P. **324.**] *Musæum*, the celebrated Tribe of Ben who acknowledged his literary dictatorship.   They met chiefly at the Old Devil Tavern, near Temple Bar, where Jonson's *Leges Conviviales* were inscribed.
Sir Inigo Jones, the celebrated architect (1573-1652), whom B. Jonson satirised as Vitruvius Hoop in *The Tale of the Tub* in 1633.   P. Cunningham gives a full account of the quarrel in his *Life of Inigo Jones* for the (old) Shake-speare Soc.

LETTER XXI.—*Capt. Tho. Porter.*   See on p. 55.
your brother Endymion, for whom see p. 535.

P. **325.**] LETTER XXII.—*Capt. Saintgeon.*   Oliver, as the "Table" of ED. PR. informs us, a brother of William St. John, *supra*, 256, and probably son of Sir William, *supra*, 81.   Not to be confounded with Chief Justice Oliver St. John, "the dark lanthorn man" (Campbell, *Chief Justices*, c. xiii.), but probably the one mentioned by Campbell in a footnote, p. 449, as having been called to the Bar in 1638.

Peter

Peter van Heyn. Pieter Hein (1570-1629) captured the Plata fleet, 9 Sept. 1628 (Gard. vi. 374), and died in battle 20 Aug. 1629, so that this letter is much misplaced, if authentic. Brereton saw the monument to him at Delft (*Travels*, p. 23).

LETTER XXIII.—*Viscount S.* Savage, see on p. 132.
from Scotland. Charles visited Scotland and was crowned there, 18 Jan. 1633.

P. 326.] *D. of Bavaria.* H. refers to this in one of his letters to Strafford under date of 30 July 1635. *Straff. Lett.* i. 446.
young Lady Elizabeth, eldest daughter of the "Queen of Hearts." The wooing of the Polish King Uladislaus extended from 1632 to 1637, and is told by Mrs. Green, *Princesses,* v. 542-7; *cf.* Sanderson, *Charles I.,* p. 213. The Polish embassy arrived in England about June 1636.

LETTER XXIV.—*Mr. Will. Saintgeon at St. Omer,* where there was a celebrated Jesuit College. Permits to travel generally contained the proviso that the traveller would not visit Rome or St. Omer, *supra,* p. 22. On W. St. John, see p. 256.
at the course you take of being converted to Roman Catholicism.

P. 327.] *your Father,* probably Sir W. St. John, on whom see 81.

LETTER XXV.—*Lord Deputy* Strafford, see p. 229.
Earl of Arundel, his return is mentioned, Gard. viii. 202.

P. 328.] *French King hath taken Nancy* on Sept. 30, 1633.
Viscount Savage is lately dead, in 1635, see 132.
Father-in-law. Earl Rivers. See 132.

LETTER XXVI.—*Mistress C.* Dan Caldwell's widow.
dear Friend your Husband. Dan Caldwell: he died 13 Nov. 1634. See Morant, *Essex,* i. 220, ii. 219; and *supra,* p. 27. There is an elegy on him in II.'s *Poems,* p. 98.

P. 329.] LETTER XXVII.—*Mr. James Howard.* Probably the dramatist who wrote two comedies in which Nell Gwyn appeared and was seen by Pepys (D.N.B.).
Banished Virgin. This work was published by H. Moseley, H.'s publisher, in folio, "The History of the Banished Virgin, a Romance, translated by I. H." It does not occur in Watts, Lowndes, Allibone, or the Dyce or Bliss libraries.
Every read "very" as in ED. PR.
Eromena, "For Love and revenge," translated by J. Hayward of Gray's Inn, Lond., fol. 1632, with commendatory lines by H. (Bliss on Wood, iii. col. 752).

LETTER XXVIII.—*Edward Noy.* See Wood, *Athenæ,* ii. 583 and 7, *N. and Q.* vi. 297 (C.H.F.). Sir J. Maclean, *Trigg Manor,* ii. 119.
Ambassador Aston. Sir Walter, see 165, 190. H. himself refers to his starting for Spain about 30 July 1635 in *Straff. Letters,* i. 446.
dirty Town of Paris. See *supra,* p. 43 for the same description.

P. 330.] LETTER XXIX.—*Sir Peter Wichs,* should be *Wicks* as in ED. PR., see on p. 254, where the name is spelt Wichts.

                                                            Sir

Sir Chas. Morgan. See on p. 229.
Lengua. Lemgo according to Warburton, *Rupert*, i. 83–91, who gives an account of the battle practically in agreement with H.

P. 331.] *Prince Robert, My Lord Craven* was captured, 1638. Sanderson, *Chas. I.*, 220, (C.H.F.); Warburton, *l.c.* i. 90.
Brisac. Alt-Breisach in Baden, besieged and taken by Duke Bernhard of Saxe-Weimar, Aug.–19 Dec. 1638.

LETTER XXX.—*Sir Sackvil C.* Crow, ambassador to Constantinople and afterwards Treasurer of the Navy. On his wooing of the Widow Bennet see *Proceedings in Kent* (C.S.), xv. (C.H.F.); *Court Chas. I.*, i. 437. See also Forster, *Eliot*, ii. 344, 349; *Nicholas Papers*, 78; *Straff. Lett.* pass.
excellent a Lady. Mary, daughter of Sir Geo. Manners and sister of the eighth Earl of Rutland (Collins-Bridges *Peerage*, i. 447).
Warfurzee. See *Strafford Letters* (C.H.F.).

P. 332.] *Walstein.* Known now as Wallenstein (1583–1634), or properly Waldstein; an account of his death is given in *Strafford Papers*, i. 216.
Col. Butler, said to be Devereux in Warburton, *Rupert*, i. 90, but H. is confirmed by the *Strafford Letters, l.c.*; and by Gindely, *Thirty Years' War*, ii. 186.

LETTER XXXI.—*Dr. Duppa.* Brian Duppa (1589–1662), Dean of Christ Church, Oxford, and Bishop of Chichester, 29 May 1638, Salisbury, 1641, Winchester, 1660. Mentioned both by Evelyn and Pepys. *Cf.* Ferrar, *Lives*, 136.
Mr. Ben Johnson died 6 Aug. N.S. 1637.
Johnsonus Virbius appeared in 1638 about the beginning of March. See Cunningham's note to the smaller edition of *B. J.* iii. 496, where *Jonsonus* is reprinted, where H.'s poem appears twelfth, on p. 507.
Sir Thomas Hawkins, who also contributed a poem, the third, to *Jonsonus.*

P. 333.] *Light* read Life as in ED. PR.
1st May 1636, obviously about two years too early. Besides this, the address is suspicious, as Duppa cannot have been Bishop of Chichester when getting together the laudatory poems in honour of Jonson. The preface of *Jonsonus* is signed E. P., *i.e.*, Endymion Porter.

P. 333.] LETTER XXXII.—*Sir Ed. B.* Mr. Firth suggests that the sentiments of the letter were inspired by Browne's *Religio Medici*, which appeared in an unauthorised form in 1642. I confess I cannot see the resemblance.

P. 334.] *custom in Poland.* This was used in the great speech of Eliot's, 26th Jan. 1629 (Forster, *Eliot*, ii. 416), which Howell, who sat in that Parliament, may have heard.

P. 335.] *Cinque-Ports are open.* The five senses. The same *équivoque* is employed by H. in his *For. Trav.*, ed. Arber, 12.
quietus est. This the technical term for a receipt in full (hence our "quits") in the old Latin Treasury accounts, which were often by tally, *i.e.*, notched pieces of wood split in two.

P. 336.] *every day in the week in a several Language,* Welsh, English, French, Italian, Spanish, Latin, Greek probably.
motion of the tenth Sphere. *Cf. Batman vppon Bartholome*, Lib. VIII. c. vi.
P. 337.]

P. 337.] *a Brownist's.* See on p. 29.

LETTER XXXIII.—*Simon Digby, Moscow.* See p. 210, and *cf. Straff. Letters,* i. 439. He went to Moscow as a Consul at the cost of the Muscovy merchants (*Straff. Lett.* 435).
Mr. Pickhurst, otherwise unknown, so far as I can ascertain.
Bishop Lord-Treasurer, Juxon, Bishop of London, who was Treasurer for a short time in 1636.
Metropolitan at Lambeth. Laud.

P. 338.] *The Sovereign of the Sea.* This vessel is referred to by Evelyn in his *Diary* several times (Chand.), 24, 563. A poem about her is quoted in Hist. MSS. Com. X. iv. 21. H. makes a further reference to Edgar in *Discourses,* 32.
one whole year's ship-money. D'Ewes, *Autob.,* ii. 129, reckoned this at £320,000, four times as much as H., who estimates it elsewhere at 2½ subsidies (*infra,* p. 657); Warwick has £236,000, *l.c.,* 57.
Ranulphus Cestrensis, i.e., Ralph Higden of Chester whose *Polychronicon* was the favourite *Weltgeschichte* of the Middle Ages in England. Holinshed i. 339 (reprint 1807), makes it a fleet of 1600.
four Kings. Holinshed's accounts vary between 6 and 8 (i. 205, 694).
Sophy of Persia, whom we now call the Shah. Herbert in his *Travels,* 129, which H. read, has a similar account of his titles.

P. 339.] LETTER XXXIV.—*Dr. Tho. Prichard.* See on 31.
Scale, there is probably some pun implied here on the name of the "fatal individual." But H. is possibly only using *scale* in its Latin sense of ladder.
who got the Persian Empire. This seems like a reference to Darius Hystaspes, but differs from the account in Herod. iii. 84.
the Bath, the place we now simply call Bath.
Brecknock, another point in favour of making H. a Brecknockshire man.
Sister Penry. H.'s sister Anne, who married Hugh Penry, who is mentioned *supra,* 129.
thirteen Shires, including Anglesey (F. Moryson, *Itin.* iii. 143).

LETTER XXXV.—*Sir Kenelm Digby.* See on p. 191.
divers Baths abroad, also discussed in *Germ. Diet,* 36.

P. 340.] *Vierbio* read Viterbio as in ED. PR.
Dr. Jordan. Dr. E., whose *Discourse of Natural Baths* appeared in 1631.

P. 341.] *agent spirit and patient matter,* a piece of Aristotelian metaphysics with reference to the νοῦς ποιητικός.
Motion is the fountain of heat. Seemingly an anticipation of Prof. Tyndall's *Heat as a Mode of Motion,* but in reality it is quite scholastic and unscientific, the motion being between spirit and matter!

LETTER XXXVI.—*Sir Ed. Savage at Tower-Hill,* brother of Sir Thomas, to whom so many letters are addressed. See on p. 249.

P. 342.] *Mr. James Dillon,* probably related to the Lord Dillon who is one of the signatories in *Straff. Letters,* ii. 346, at Dublin in 1639.
brother Payn. Probably the J. Payne of Nichols, *Prog. Jas. I.,* ii. 145, 650; brother=brother-in-law.

Sir

Sir Paul Davis. Clerk of the (Irish) Council of State. He became Principal Secretary of State in 1661 (Haydn, *Dignities,* 445).
Sir Will Usher, brother of the Archbishop.
succeed Sir William Usher. As a matter of fact, H. ultimately got an appointment for a similar post to the English Council of State.

LETTER XXXVII.—*Dr. Usher* or Ussher (1580–1656). Archbishop of Armagh, and author of the received Chronology of the Scriptures put in the margin of ordinary Bibles. (*Cf.* Herbert, *Autob.* 198 ; Fairf. iii. 150, and an interesting description of him, Brereton, *Travels,* 139.)
Your learned Work. Eccl. Brit. Primordia was published in 1639 according.

P. 343.] *Cardinal Barberino,* or Barberini, was an authority on English affairs. Forster, *Five Members,* 225 *n.* H. translated a letter to him (Bibl. List, Nos. 19, 24).
Works of Fastidus. The *De Vita Christiana,* previously included among St. Augustine's works, was vindicated for Fastidius by Holstenius, who published an edition in 1636, three years before the date of this letter.
a strange passage. The story fills four folio pages of Kuster's edition of Suidas ii. 115–9, but is obviously a mere fable derived probably from some lost apocryphal Gospel.
Queen is deliver'd of a Dauphin, afterwards Louis XIV., on 16 Sept. 1638, nearly twenty-three years after the marriage of Louis XIII. and Anne of Austria, 25 Oct. 1615. The distance between the two dates gave rise to certain suspicions. See Michelet.

P. 344.] *Mar.* 1639. The Dauphin's birth in September would be rather stale news in the following March, yet Usher's *Primordia* bears the date 1639, which would convict this letter of being "cooked" at least, if not of being fabricated.

LETTER XXXVIII.—*Lord Clifford.* See on p. 189. This letter is quoted in Nimmo's *British Letter Writers,* p. 22, probably on account of its Scotch interest. H. was not exactly a Scotophile, witness his *Description of Scotland* (Bibl. List, No. 32).
Palermo in Sicily, another reference showing that H. landed in Sicily during his grand tour. See *supra,* 113.
National Assembly. The General Assembly met at Glasgow, 21 Nov. 1638, the Parliament in Edinburgh, 15 May 1639.
Lord Traquair. Sir John Stuart (†1659), created Earl of Traquair 22 June 1638, was Lord Treasurer-Deputy of Scotland.
Our Lord of Canterbury. Archbishop Laud, of course.
black Dog. The same anecdote in *XII. Treat.* (C.H.F.).

P. 345.] *Shoe-maker.* This story is repeated in Sir Roger L'Estrange, *Fables,* No. 494.
Edinburgh, 1639, probably about June. H. had probably been sent by Wentworth in connection with the formation of .the Army of the North, which fills the latter portion of the *Strafford Letters.*

LETTER XXXIX.—*Sir K. Digby.* See on p. 191.
fancy of Trees. H.'s first book, *Dendrologia or Dodona's Grove,* a political allegory (see Bibl. List, No. 1), published in 1640.
Seralio, so in ED. PR. spelt *Seraglio,* p. 513.

P. 346.] LETTER XL.—*Sir Sackvill Crow.* See on 331.
naval Fight beginning 7 Sept. 1639, described in Sanderson, 279 (C.H.F.).
in the Downs. The Spaniards were driven under the Dover coast, and afterwards twenty-three were sunk in the Downs. *Cf.* Sanderson, *l.c.*, and add
Warwick, *Memoirs*, 105, 130.

P. 347.] *Sir John Penington.* See on 289.
Oquendo. Cf. Whitelocke, *Memorials,* f. 31.
Nardic, probably misprint or mistake of ED. PR. for Mardyke (C.H.F.).

P. 348.] 114 *Sail*, "near a hundred sail," says Sanderson, 280.
Brother Edward, previously mentioned, *supra*, p. 265.

LETTER XLI.—*Sir J. M.* May possibly be Sir T. Middleton, brother to Sir
Hugh, who went in deeply for alchemy.
'tis costly. H. brings the same objection against "chymistry" by which he
means alchemy, in his *For. Tr.*, ed. Arber, p. 80. *Cf.* too *Germ. Diet*,
p. 20.
Sixtus Quintus (1521–90), the Pope who excommunicated Elizabeth. Her
nickname for him refers to the throws at dice. The book presented was,
according to Mr. R. Steele, J. A. Augurellus *Chrysopoeia*, 1517. The Pope
was Leo X., not Sixtus (Tiraboschi, *ap. Biog. Univ.*, s. v. Augurello).
Magistery. The full command over the secrets of nature. See on p. 435,
and the whole letter II., 42, which is full of alchemical expressions.

P. 349.] LETTER XLII.—*Simon Digby.* See on 210.
Catalonia, submitted to France in 1640. H. discusses the causes in his *Lustra*,
128.
King of Portugal. Duke of Braganza was proclaimed John IV. 1 Dec. 1640.
Bean-cake King, another name for the Lord of Misrule and similar mock
royalties. Brand-Ellis, *Antiquities*, i. 275.

P. 350.] *this Breach.* The Solemn League and Covenant.
The Ship Swan. Mentioned as trading with Lucar. *S.P.*, Sept. 1634, p. 221.

P. 351.] *Sir K. D.* Kenelm Digby. See on 191.
John Pennant. Taken from *Relation of a serpent found in the left ventricle of
the heart of John Pennant*, printed in 1636 and republished in *Somers
Tracts*, ed. Scott, v. 558 (C.H.F.).
In the Air. A similar account is given in App. H. to Nugent's *Hampden*
(C.H.F.), from a contemporary pamphlet, *A Great Wonder in Heaven*, 1642.

P. 352.] *outrag'd in his house. Cf.* Evelyn, *Life of Laud.*, p. 425 (Monday,
11th May 1640).
Capt. Mahun, or rather Lieut. Will. Mohun. *Cal. State Papers*, 1640
(C.H.F.).

LETTER XLIV.—*Lord Herbert of Cherbury* (1581–1648), philosopher and
adventurer (D.B.N.)
Dodona's Grove couch'd in French, by M. Bardouin, according to Sir K. Digby.
See Supplement, No. xxii.
Academie des beaux Esprits, the French Academy, founded by Richelieu 1635.
Howell gives it the same name. *German Diet*, 44 ; a further reference, p.
510.
Cardinal at Ruelle. Readers of the standard French history of this period,
Les Trois Mousquetaires, might mistake the Cardinal mentioned here for
Mazarin. Howell, however, again refers to the interview in the Dedicatory
Epistle to *Lust. Lud.*

P. 353.]

P. 353.] *Caga-fuego.* "A Spanish word signifying Shitefire" (Phillips, *World of Words*), or, as we say now, Spitfire. One of the Spanish ships captured by Drake was called *Cacafuego.*
De veritate was published in Paris 1624, so it was somewhat late for the Paris wits to have discovered its beauties.

LETTER XLV.—*Mrs. Eliz. Altham* (†1662), third daughter of Baron Altham of the Exchequer. She married three times, like her father (Foss, *Judges*, vi. 50–1). This letter is quoted by Scoone's *Eng. Lett.*, No. lix. p. 79.
Lord Robert Digby, her second husband (Collins-Brydges, *Peerage*, vi. 376), died June 6, 1642, which should fix the date of this letter.
Baron your Father. For whose life see Fors. *Judges* vi. and D.N.B.
Sir James, her half-brother. See on p. 34. His death, in 1623, is mentioned *supra*, 182.
Master Richard Altham. H.'s friend and companion on the grand tour. See *supra*, p. 33, and Index.
Sir Francis Astley, her first husband, a Kt. of Hill Morton, co. Warwick.
1 *Aug.* 1624. The year is right, but the condolence would be rather stale in August. This letter is so full of references to the Altham family, that its allusions will be best elucidated by the following genealogy :—

BARON JAMES ALTHAM.

=(1) Margaret Skinner   =(2) Mary Stagers   =(3) Helen Hyde

Sir James   Richard   Dr. =1st Earl of Anglesea.   Dr. =2nd Earl of Carberry.   ELIZABETH
=(1) Sir Fr. Astley
=(2) Robert Lord Digby
=(3) Sir Robert Bernard

P. 354.] LETTER XLVI.—*Sir P. M.* Sir Philip Mainwaring, as we learn from the "Table" of ED. PR.
Sir Edw. Nicholas, succeeded Windebanke as Principal Secretary of State in 1641 (Haydn, *Dign.* 171).
Clerkship of the Council. H. gives an account of these assurances in the Enclosure to his Petition to be confirmed as Clerk to Chas. II. (Suppl. No. xvii. p. 666).
Duke of Espernon. The same anecdote is told *Lustra Lud.* 123, where it is remarked that he was over 100 years old.
de la Valette. Told in *Lustra Lud.* under the year 1638, *l.c.*, 122. *Cf. S.P.* Oct. 21, 1638, "The Duke de la Valette, fled out of France, is landed privately in Cornwall."

P. 355.] *E. of Leicester* did succeed Strafford in 1641, but he never went over to Ireland.
7 *Sept.* 1641. This would serve for the change in the Lord Lieutenancy, but the De la Valette incident must then have been introduced.

LETTER XLVII.—*Earl of B*[ristol]. See on p. 160. This letter was No. lv. in ED. PR.
seiz'd on all my papers. This was evidently the object of the capture, the hope of finding material incriminating to the Royalist cause.

P. 356.] *the Committee* appointed to examine Delinquents or Recusants.
some papers of mine. Probably relating to his secret missions to Ireland, Scotland, and France.

Mr.

Mr. Corbet was the usual agent in such matters, being the chairman of the notorious Committee for examination which dealt so sharply with Lilburne and others. See Masson, *Life of Milton*, ii. 517, *S.P. pass.* Miles Corbet was one of the regicides, and executed as such after the Restoration (see Biography in D.N.B.).

report to the House. The result seems to have been the definite order for his committal, entered in the Commons Journal 14 Nov. 1642. *Cf.* Introd. p. xlii.

20 *Nov.* 1643. The year is obviously wrong, and if H. could make a mistake on such a point, it is useless to expect anything like accuracy on points affecting him less deeply.

LETTER XLVIII.—*Sir Brevis Thelwall.* Should be Sir Bevis, as in the Table of ED. PR. A brother of Sir Eubule. See on 104. This letter was No. liv. in ED. PR.

Peter House in London. The chapel in the Tower is called *St. Peter ad vincula.*

2 *Aug.* 1643. H. forgets that he had fixed upon November for the date of his imprisonment. It is perhaps worth remarking that Lovelace's *To Althœa in prison*, in which occurs the celebrated "Stone walls do not a prison make," appeared in his *Lucasta*, published in 1649.

P. 357.] LETTER XLIX.—*Mr. E. P.* Endymion Porter. See p. 535. This was Letter No. xlvii. in ED. PR., and the following letters are two less in enumeration till the end of this part.

old fellows. Such kidnappers were called "spirits" a little later, *S.P.* 1661-8, Pref. p. xxviii. (C.H.F.)

miraculous passage in Hamelin. It is doubtful whether Browning got his *Pied Piper* from H. here, or from Verstegan's "Restitution of Decayed Intelligence" (whence probably H. got it), or from Wanley's *Wonders of the Little World.* See the elaborate list of occurrences of the legend in Dr. Furnivall's *Browning Bibliography.* This letter is quoted by Dr. Furnivall, also in Nimmo's *British Letter Writers*, p. 23. It is referred to in the *Spectator*, No. 5, which may be derived from H.

P. 358.] *in that Town they date their bills. Cf.* Browning.
They made a decree that lawyers never
Should think their records duly dated
—unless there was a reference to the date, 22 July 1376.
story is engraven. Cf. again Browning,
They wrote the story on a column.

LETTER L.—*Lord G. D.* George Digby, eldest son of the Earl of Bristol, who succeeded him as second Earl. He died 1676.

sayings in Seneca. I cannot find them in *Senecœ et Syri Sententiœ*, ed. E. Swedenborg.

P. 359.] *A Tale of an Ape in Paris.* Did Swift get his adventure of Gulliver in Brobingnag from this? In some of the apocryphal lives of Cromwell a similar tale is told of his youth (C.H.F.).

Adrian IV. Pope 1154-9. I cannot trace this saying.

P. 360.] LETTER LI.—*Sir Alex. R.* Sir Alexander Ratcliff, as the "Table" of ED. PR. informs us.

P. 361.] *Iliacos intra muros.* Hor. *Ep.* I. ii. 16.

LETTER LII.—*Mr. John Batty*, or Battie. See Wood, *Athenœ*, ed. Bliss, iii. 752. This letter was prefixed to Batty's book.

The

The Merchant's Remonstrance, not mentioned by Lowndes or Watt, according to Bliss, *Athenæ*, iii. col. 752, it was published in 1648, *i.e.*, three years after the first book of H.'s letters—which is absurd.

P. 362.] *Walls of this Kingdom.* Perhaps the earliest reference to England's fleet of Themistocles' saying about Athens' wooden walls.

P. 363.] LETTER LIII.—*Mr. E. P.* Endymion Porter. See p. 535.
Pope Urban VIII. is dead, on 29 July 1644. His Italian poems were published 1640, his Latin ones, from which H. quotes, in 1642.
no Pope yet arrived. Pio Nono broke the record in this respect.
Cardinal Pamfilio. Giovanni Battista Panfili (1574-1655).
Innocent X. succeeded Urban, 15 Sept. 1644.

P. 364.] *Sir Kenelm Digby* was sent to Rome by the English Catholic Committee sitting in Paris in 1645 (D.N.B. s. v. p. 63ᵃ).
Covert Baron. Law term signifying "covered by the protection of her husband," "baron" being old legal for "husband." *Cf.* 5 *N. and Q.* vii. 148, 211.

P. 365.] LETTER LIV.—*Lord Bishop of London.* William Juxon, 1582-1663, afterwards Archbishop of Canterbury, became Bishop of Hereford in 1633, and was translated to London the same year. He was present at Charles I.'s execution.
White Staff, the mark of the Treasurer, which office Juxon had held for the year 1636 (Haydn, *Dignities*, 108).
Marq. Pawlet. H. probably means W. Paulet, Marquis of Winchester, Lord Treasurer, 1551-8.

P. 366.] *by being a Willow*, a reference of course to the fable of the *Oak and Reed.*

LETTER LV.—*Sir E. S.* Probably Sir Ed. Savage, see on p. 249.
Dutch word. H. probably means the German.

LETTER LVI.—*Tho. Ham*[mon], as we have it in the "Table" in ED. PR.

P. 368.] LETTER LVII.—*Phil. Warwick.* See on p. 293.

P. 369.] *these thirty months, i.e.*, about April 1645, would be thirty months from Nov. 1642.
Los Pattuecos. H. gives practically the same account in *For. Tr.* 51.
Cabin upon the upper Deck, this is probably to be taken literally as a room on the upper floor.
Master Hopkins, there is a letter to him later, 521, where see.
3 Nov. 1645. The first edition received the "Imprimatur Nat. Brent June 9, 1645," which makes the reference to thirty months having elapsed rather sailing close to the wind.

P. 370] LETTER LVIII.—*Sir Ed. Sa*[vage]. See on 249.
thirty one months would be May 1645, sailing again very close to the month of publication fixed by the censor's imprimatur. See on 369.

quadrat

quadrat solid wise men. The Laureate's "four square" suggests itself, the reference is ultimately Platonic. "Quadratus" is used for "strong" in Suetonius, *Vesp.* 20 (Dr. Gow).
involve in his own virtue. Hor. *Carm.* iii. 29, 54.
fractus illabatur orbis. Hor. *Od. III.* iii. 7.

P. 371.] *Lycanthropy,* the learned word for the condition of the wehrwolf.
1 *Dec.* 1644. Does not agree with the reference to thirty-one months of imprisonment.

LETTER LIX.—*Mr. E. P.* Endymion Porter. See on p. 535.
Leuantanse los muladeres, Sp. "The muleteers go up and the walls go down."
2 *Jan.* 1644, *i.e.,* 1645.

LETTER LX.—*Tho. Young.* Probably Milton's friend (Mason, *Life,* i. 32-7, 172-3; ii. 533). See on p. 263. Comp. with this letter the one above to Vaughan, p. 219, and that in the Supplement.
past the Meridian, I should say so: H. was about fifty-two at the time of writing.

P. 372.] *a huge Hill situated South-East,* has been taken to refer to the Bryn, but may be somewhere near Abernant. See Introd. p. xxiii.

P. 373.] *Cadet.* His brother Thomas was older than he, and likewise his brother Howell, but he had at least two younger (*supra,* p. 265).
Ground upon Parnassus. Can scarcely be a reference to *Dodona's Grove* in prose. Refers perhaps to the *Vote* (B.L. No. 3), and to miscellaneous verses scattered about.
divers children. The Bibliographical List gives 13 numbers before the first edition of the *Letters* is reached.
French. The French translation of the *Dendrologia* (B. L. No. 2).
Latin. H. may refer to his feats during the Danish embassy; otherwise nothing is known of any Latin work of his at this date.
Italian. H. translated from the Italian *St. Paul's late Progress* (B. L. No. 13).
English. B. L. Nos. 1, 3-12.
speech it was of the Cynick, quoted again, *supra,* p. 58, where see.
modern physician. An undoubted reference to Sir Thomas Browne's *Religio Medici* (*cf.* "his own religion") Pt. II. § ix. "I could be content that we might procreate like trees, without conjunction."
Paracelsus. Bombast (1493-1541), Prof. of Natural Philosophy at Basle, professed to be able to make *homunculi,* if not men. See also Browne, *Rel. Med.* i. § 36, whence H. got the idea. Dr. Greenhill refers to Paracelsus' *Opera,* vi. p. 201, ed. Frankf.

P. 374.] *nine long lustres, i.e.,* 45 years: I should think so, as H. was 52 at the time.

BOOK II.

This was published in 1647 as a "New Volume of Familiar Letters." See Bibliog. List, No. 21. It was dedicated to James, Duke of York, afterwards James II. The advertisement of the printer (see Supplt. II., No. xxxi., p. 682) declares that the letters were taken from those previously retained when H.'s papers were seized. See Introduction, p. lxxix.

P. 375.] LETTER I.—*Master Tho. Adams*, afterwards Lord Mayor of London, (*cf.* Pepys 501, *Letters* (Cam. Soc.), *pass.* Gard. x. 29).

LETTER II.—*Mr. B. J.* Ben Jonson.
P. 376.] *Anser, Apis, Vitulus,* similar reference on p. 556.
A Royal Architect. Inigo Jones, of course.
F. B. Short for "Father Ben."
Mr. Jones. Inigo Jones. See a reference to this quarrel, p. 324 and notes.
P. 377.] *Copies of the Satire. The Tale of a Tub,* first published 1633.
Lost some ground at Court. See P. Cunningham's account in his *Life of I. Jones* (O. Shaks. Soc.).
3 July 1635 should have been 1633.

LETTER III.—*D. C.* Daniel Caldwell. See on p. 27.
C. Mor. Obviously from what follows a Christopher Mor, but neither Lowndes nor Allibone know of such an English author.
Kit, short for Christopher. Surely H. is not referring to Kit Marlowe, died 1593.

P. 378.] *Alchoran.* The first English translation of this appeared in 1646 (C.H.F.). This might seem to imply pre-dating of this letter; but see next note.
black Bean. Taken from the same statement in Sandys, *Travels* (1615), p. 41. I cannot trace any ground for the statement in Mahomedan tradition.

LETTER IV.—*T. D.,* probably the Tom D. referred to in the letter to Dr Prichard, *infra,* 382.
First, Strongest, and Wisest. Adam, Samson, and Solomon.

P. 379.] *nature of woman. Cf.* H.'s equally ungallant account in *Therologia,* 59.
One Hair of a Woman. Possibly the source, certainly a parallel, of Pope's "And woman draws us with a single hair." *Rape of Lock,* ii. 28.

P. 380.] LETTER V.—*G. G.* George Gage, a travelling agent frequently mentioned in the memoirs of the time (Rushw., i. 23, 66, 131; *Court Jas. I.,* ii. 219, 323, 341, 414. (H. K.) add Bacon, *Letters,* vii. 429, 431; Cam. Soc., *Letters,* 129).
R. Grosthed, the well-known Bishop of Lincoln, 1175-1253. H. is probably referring to his celebrated letter to Innocent IV. Ep. cxxviii. of Luard's edition in the Rolls series. References to Lucifer occur there, pp. 434, 435.

P. 381.] *Lady Elizabeth Cary,* mentioned Nichols' *Progr. Jas. I.,* ii. 674 *n.* There is a letter to Lady Mary Cary, *infra,* 598.

Mr.

Mr. Hoskins. Preface to Gard., ii. 249; Nichols, *l.c.*, i., xix. *n.*, 128, iii. 5; perhaps also in *Court Jas. I.*, i. 390.

P. 382.] LETTER VI.—*Dr. T. P*[richard]. See on p. 31.
T. D., probably the same to whom the letter is addressed, *supra*, 378.

P. 383.] LETTER VII.—*T. B.* Cannot well be Tom Bowyer, who was a captain.

LETTER VIII.—*Dr. B.* This gentleman, one suspects, was an ancestor of Mrs. Harris, known to Mrs. Gamp. There could have been no reason for concealing his name. However, there is a reference to a Dr. B. on p. 640. Mr. Firth suggests that H. wanted to leave the impression that he was in correspondence with Dr. (Sir) Thomas Browne.
Gresham College. The earlier meetings of the Royal Society were held here.

P. 384.] *Judaism. Cf.* with this the letter above to Lord Clifford (I. vi. 14), p. 312 *seq.* Mr. Firth points out that this and the succeeding letters were adaptations of Brerewood, *Enquiries touching the Divinity of Languages and Religions,* 1614.

P. 385.] *Phœnician,* referring to Sanchoniathan, who impressed Dr. Primrose so much.
Josephus saith, only that they remain in the land of Syria "to this day," *Ant.* I. ii. *ad fin.;* he says, however, that he had seen the pillar of salt of Lot's wife (*ib.* c. xi.). Howell perhaps confuses the two.
Cabal. See on p. 315.
Three Sects. See on p. 315.
Cacams, lit. "wise." H. got the word, as most of his information about the Jews, from Sandys, *Travel,* 114: a query was asked on the word, 5 *N. and Q.* vii. 148.
Amurath gave Mendez the Jew. See Graetz, *Gesch. der Juden. Cf.* Harl. MS. 471, Nos. 65–71, also *Jew. Quart. Rev.* ii. 293. H. gets the information from Brerewood, p. 92, who quotes "Boter. Relat. p. 3, l. 2, de Giudei."

P. 386.] *Dominions of England.* Mr. L. Wolf has shown that there were always a number of Jews in England between the expulsion in 1290 and the return under Cromwell. See his paper in *Anglo-Jewish Exhibition Papers,* 1888. One of these, Dr. Lopez, is referred to by H., p. 269.
Brokers. Sandys refers to this function of the seventeenth-century Jew, *Travels,* 6th ed., 115.
Tribes. See on this p. 314 note.
other ten. Strictly speaking nine, but Joseph's sons, Manasseh and Ephraim, are reckoned as two tribes. The lost Ten Tribes have been located every-where, literally from China to Peru.
run their course. The River Sambation, which plays a large part in the legend of the Ten Tribes.
whence they expect. This location of the Messiah is derived from Sandys, 114.

P. 387.] LETTER IX.—*Dr. B.* See on p. 383.
K. Lucius. His correspondence with Eleutherius, Bishop of Rome (c. 167 A.D.), is referred to in Beda, *Hist. Eccl.* i. 4. Mrs. Hutchinson refers to the legend, *Life,* ed. Firth, i. 8 and *n.*

Proto-

Proto-Christian King. Lappenburg is inclined to believe in the authenticity of Lucius (*Eng. under Anglo-Saxons,* i. 48). H. uses the expression again, *Germ. Diet.* 36.
Aóostles. A reference probably to Joseph of Arimathea and his bringing the Holy Grail hither.

P. 388.] *Habassin.* Sandys uses the same name for the Abyssinians, *Travels,* 133, whence H. may have got his information, as with so much of his Oriental lore. H. refers to circumcision among them in *For. Tr.* 57.

P. 389.] *Habassia.* See *supra* on p. 388.
Observingst Travellers, possibly Sandys and Moryson (*Itin.* i. 233), whose travels were much used by H., as we have seen.

P. 390.] *In Asia Russia.* Poland and Lithuania made such a large bite out of European Russia, that it is not strange to find the remainder included in Asia.
Zocotora, i.e. Socotra. On the history of Christianity in that island see Yule, *Marco Polo,* ii. 400; and *cf.* Herbert, 25. The passage is from Brerewood, *l.c.* p. 73, "But on the E. side of *Afrique,* excepting only *Zocotora,* there is no Christian isle." B. quotes "Paul. Vinet. l. 3, c. 38," *i.e.* Marco Polo.
Quinsay in China, the old capital, and in Marco Polo's time the most populous city on earth. See plan in Yule's edition, vol. ii. p. 194; and *cf.* also Herbert, *Travels,* 137.
Chingis or Genghis Khan, the great Tartar conqueror, 1163-1227.
K. of Tenduck. H. is very nearly right about Prester John, so far as the latest researches, *e.g.,* of Zarncke and Col. Yule, go. He may have got the view from Herbert, *Travels,* and *cf.* H.'s *For. Tr.,* edit. Arber, p. 57.
Scaliger would have it. H. got this from Brerewood, *l.c.* p. 74, who quotes in margin, "Scaliger *De Emend. Temp.* Annot. in comput. Æthiop."

P. 391.] *Castilia del oro,* "otherwise termed *Nuebo Reino,*" says Brerewood, *l.c.* 77, whence H. got his erudition.

LETTER X.—*Dr. B.* See on p. 383. Again from Brerewood.

P. 392.] *no Jew is capable.* This piece of information is derived from Sandys, *Travels,* 42 : "No Jew can turn Turk till he first turn Christian, they forcing him to eat Hogesflesh and calling him *Abdulla,* which signifieth son of a Christian; who, after two or three days abjuring Christ, is made a *Mahometan.*"
Alfange, a mistake for *Alfaqi.* See 5 *N. and Q.* vii. 148, 516.

P. 393.] *the Persian,* who is of the Shiite sect.
Cambaia. A survival of this kingdom occurs in the Gulf of Cambay, or it may refer to Camboia, near Siam, the country whence *Gamboge* comes. See Yule, *Hobson-Jobson,* s. v. Camboia. (Add Herbert, *Travels,* 42.)
Bengula. This form for Bengal was the usual one in H.'s day. It occurs in Herbert, *Travels,* 200.

P. 394.] *Ports of Banda,* from Brerewood *l.c.* p. 85.
eight wives. This is twice too much. Brerewood *l.c.,* p. 85, only says "many wives" but otherwise gives the same account of the spread of Islam as H.

P. 395.] *in the Alcoran.* This depends on what is meant by Angelical Joys.
LETTER

LETTER XI.—*Dr. B.*   See on p. 383.   Again from Brerewood's *Inquiries.*

P. 396.] *Corelia.*   H. got this straight from Brerewood, who says *l.c.* p. 67, " But toward the North Lappia, Scriefinia, Bearmia, Corelia, and the North part of Finmark (all of which together pass commonly under the name of *Lapland*)."

Biarmia, also known as Permia, that part of Russia to the east of the White Sea.

Scrifinnia.   See passage from Brerewood quoted above.

Finmark, not Finland, for H. refers rather to Lapland.   Finmark is the extreme north province of Norway.

Kingdom of Congo.   See Pigafetta's *Kingdom of Congo*, translated by Hutchinson, 1881, showing how much of modern knowledge about Congo was possessed by the Portuguese in the sixteenth century.   *Cf.* Brerewood, *l.c.* 69, " Congo and Angola, which, An. 1491, beganne first to receive Christianity."

Cingapura = Singapore.

P. 397.] *Morduits.*   The Mordvins, a Turanian tribe in Russia : on their folklore see J. Abercromby in *Folk-Lore Journal*, vii., and *Folk-Lore*, i.   Brerewood refers to them *l.c.* 91, as "both baptised like Christians and circumcised like Mahometans."

Cardi.   Coords or Kurds, as it is variously written ; they are referred to as Coords, *supra*, 176, Brerewood.

Druci.   The Druses in Lebanon.

Kerns.   I can find no confirmation of this very interesting and curious fact.

P. 398.] *India.*   The view that all knowledge comes from India is shared by many nowadays.   The same history of human knowledge is given again by H., *For. Tr.* 14 ; also *Poems*, p. 29, "On the Progress of Learning."   H. got the view probably from Herbert, *Travels*, 1634, p. 36.

Brachmans.   This form of Brahmin comes from the Greek through the Latin.   It is used also in Herbert, *Travels*, 36.   (Add to Yule's exx. *Hobson-Jobson*, s. v.)

Hermes Trismegistus.   Quoted again, 533, 631.

33rd Century from the Creation, *i.e.*, 7th, 6th, and 5th centuries B.C.   H. naturally follows the chronology of his friend Usher.

one of his letters.   Now recognised as a fabrication : the passage H. quotes would be a sufficient proof of this.

Secretaries of Nature.   H. uses this fine expression again, *Theologia*, 55.

P. 399.] *We read that the Gauls.*   In Cæsar, *B. G.* vi. 13.

The Altar.   Acts xvii. 23.

P. 400.] *Southern Clime.*   In all old maps there is a continuous belt of land round the Southern Pole which was called Terra Australis, and from this imaginary cap of land Australia gets its name.

P. 401.] *requested the fifth part.*   H. says the tenth,' *infra*, p. 516.

P. 402.] LETTER XII.—*T. W.*   The only suggestion I can offer as to the identity of T. W. is that he was one of the Wroths of Petherton Park of Castle.   *Cf.* p. 519 and pp. 495, 536.

P. 403.] *an Italian.*   *Cf.* the similar characterisation, *supra*, 95.

The French.   *Cf. supra*, 96, and F. Moryson, *Itin.* III. i. 3.

Foy farewell banquet.

LETTER XIII.—*Sir Tho. Hawk*[ins], author of *Unhappy Prosperitie*, 1632, and translator of Horace, 1635.
B. J. There is no doubt that these initials refer to Ben Jonson. There are letters to him in this collection, pp. 267, 322, 376, and H. wrote a poem in *Jonsonus Virbius*. Masson, *Life*, i. 393, quotes this description from H. *T. Ca.* Perhaps T. Carew, one of the "Tribe of Ben." There is a letter to T. C. in Book IV., *infra*, p. 627, but this cannot well be Carew, who died 1639, *ætat.* 50. Carew was of the Herbert set. *Cf.* Herbert, *Autob.*, ed. Lee, xxvii. 170 *n.* T. Cary is another and more likely candidate for identification. See on p. 627.
forbid self-commendation. Aristotle, *Eth. Nic.*

P. **404.**] *Jamque opus.* Ovid, *Metam.*, xv. 871.
Exegi monumentum. Hor. *Odes*, III. xxx. 1.
O fortunatam. The line is known from Juvenal, x. 122, from Cicero's lost poem " De meis Temporibus."

LETTER XIV.—*J. P.*, probably J. Price, H.'s nephew. See on p. 194.
Gravesend. See note on p. 22.

P. **405.**] *Hoghen-Moghen.* The regular phrase for "Dutchies." See *Hudibras*, ii. 115. It is used in the S. P. for 1645, p. 520. Scott uses it under the form "Hogan-Mogan" in *Peveril of Peak*, c. xxii.

LETTER XV.—*Capt. B.* The only Captain B. with whom H. is elsewhere in correspondence is Capt. Bowyer. But the terms here are more distant than in those addressed to him, *e.g.* 97.

P. **406.**] LETTER XVI.—*Thomas W.* See on p. 402.
Dr. H. King's Poems. H. King (1592-1669), afterwards Bishop of Chichester. His poems were published in 1657, and must have been seen by H. in MS. He was of the Tribe of Ben and contributed to *Jonsonius Virbius.*
Mrs. A. K., obviously the Mrs. Ann King of the poem. "Mistress" was applied to maiden ladies, as here.

P. **407.**] *F. C.* Perhaps the F. Coll. of Letter XXVI., *infra*, p. 418.
Platonick Love. See on p. 317, and add that there are three poems on the subject in Herbert of Cherbury's *Poems*, ed. Collins.
T. Man, perhaps one of the Mansels. He is obviously the T. M. of p. 520.

LETTER XVII.—*Lord C.*, perhaps Lord Carlingford (see on p. 225), or perhaps Lord Carlisle (see on p. 130).
Two sayings. Both given by T. Forde, *Apophthegms*, 28, from H.
My Lords, stay a little. Given in Bacon's Essay *On Dispatch.* In his *Apophthegms*, No. 76, it is attributed to Sir Amyas Paulet.

P. **408.**] *the Spaniard.* "Spaniards have been noted to be of small dispatch," says Bacon, *l. c.*

P. **409.**] *Quodam cum strepitu*, this is at the side in ED. PR. The reference is to Pliny, *Nat. Hist.* xvi. 18, 30, § 74. The mulberry was only introduced into England in 1607, according to Mr. W. C. Hazlitt, *Cookery*, 149.

LETTER XVIII.—*Sir J. Brown*, mentioned in Herbert, *Autobiography*, ed. Lee, pp. 28, 81 *n.*

Catalonia.

Catalonia. See on p. 349, from which it appears that the date of this letter is suitable enough.

P. 410.] LETTER XIX.—*Capt. C. Price,* brother of J. Price and nephew of Howell. He is mentioned in Forster, *Five Members,* 338; Elliot, i. 425; Herbert, *Autob.,* ed. Lee, p. 186. He was killed at Maidstone (*Fairfax Papers,* iii. 33). He was "cousin" to H., either as related to the Price who married H.'s sister Rebecca, or the Ap-Rice who espoused his sister Roberta. See Pedigree.
Fortify nor fiftify. This anecdote is quoted by T. Forde, *Apophthegms,* p. 28.

P. 411.] LETTER XX.—*Cousin J. P.* See on pp. 194 and 378.

P. 412.] *answer a Letter.* A different account of Italian civility in this regard is given by Sir H. Yule in the Preface to his *Marco Polo.*
Anatomy-Lecture. Evelyn actually saw dissections at a private lecture. *Diary,* 11 Apl. 1649.
Ployden, meaning Plowden. See *supra* on p. 33.

LETTER XXI.—*Nephew J. P.* Evidently the same as the preceding, viz., John Price.

P. 413.] *swallow of them,* perhaps a reminiscence of Bacon's advice about study, which H. quotes in *For. Trav.* 22.

LETTER XXII.—*Sir Tho. Haw*[kins]. See on p. 86.

P. 414.] LETTER XXIII.—*Lady Elizabeth Digby.* See on p. 353.

P. 415.] *left Ventricle.* H. was a friend of Harvey (see 623), and may have been acquainted with his views on the circulation of the blood, in which the left ventricle of the heart plays so important a part.

LETTER XXIV.—*Sir J. B.,* probably the Sir J. Brown of II. 18, p. 409.

P. 416.] *Q. Zenobia.* H. again refers to this unsavoury topic, 567. Montaigne also refers to it.
Roman Empress. Probably Messalina is referred to.

P. 417.] LETTER XXV.—*P. W.* Philip Warwick. See *supra,* p. 293.
Baucis. Ovid, *Metam.* viii. 631 *seq.*
Super omnia. Ibid., 677-8.
Two Treasurers. Probably Marlborough and Portland. See on p. 248.

P. 418.] LETTER XXVI.—*F. Coll.* Probably identical with the F. C. of 407, but otherwise unknown to me.
Courtesans. See *supra,* pp. 86, 209.
Vesuvius, erupted in 1631 (Phillips, *Vesuvius,* 47), so that the date of this letter seems concocted.
Near the Terceras, i.e., the Azores, but there are all kinds of fables about islands in the Atlantic. *Cf.* J. Winsor, *Hist. of America,* i., 46-57.

P. 419.]

P. 419.] LETTER XXVII.—*T. Lucy*, one of the Herbert set, and mentioned frequently in the *Autobiography*, ed. Lee, pp. 107–111, 127, 272.
Husbands get. This kind of "action at a distance" is referred to in *Therologia*, 88.
Weapon Salves. A reference to the celebrated "powder of sympathy" of Sir Kenelm Digby, first tried on H. (See Supplement II., No. xxii.), and *cf. Therologia*, 133 ; Butler, *Hudibras*, I. ii. 228–40 ; Scott, *Lady of the Lake*, vi. 262, Note IV., and 2 *N. and Q.*, iii. 315. Dryden used the idea and the name "weapon salves" in the first two scenes of the fifth act of his perversion of the *Tempest. Cf.* Pettigrew, *Medical Superst.*, last essay on Sympathetic Cures, pp. 157–67.
Fish more salacious. Falstaff does not think so, 2 Henry IV., iv. 3, "Making many fish-meals . . . they get wenches." According to Jewish medieval folklore (*Rokeach*, § 394), a bridegroom should eat fish on the second day after marriage. The Friday fish diet of Jews is somehow connected with the superstition, yet the Catholic Church connects fish-diet and continence. *Cf.* Badham, *Fish Tattle*, 76.
Lady Miller. The wife either of Sir Robert (Nichols, i. 218 *n.*) or of Sir John (*l.c.*, iii. 524). A Captain Miller is mentioned later, 627.

P. 420.] *Chrystal glasses.* See on p. 66.
Mithridate. An aromatic electuary supposed to contain the celebrated antidote to poisons invented by Mithridates. *Cf.* Littré *sub. voce.*
T. T. No identification suggests itself to me.

LETTER XXVIII.—*T. Jackson.* Too common a name to identify with any certainty, but probably a relative of Jackson, Bishop of London, to whom H. dedicated the Latin version of his *England's Tears* (see Bibl. List, No. 37).
Lambeth-House. Laud.

P. 421.] *Suarez' Works.* F. Suarez (1548–1617), known in England by his *Defensio catholicæ fidei contra anglicanæ sectæ errores*, burnt by the common hangman in 1613.

LETTER XXIX.—*Sir Edw. Sa*[vage]. See on p. 249. His death is referred to *infra*, p. 602.
Grunnius' Testament. An imaginary will of a pig, given in Topsell, *History of Four-footed Beasts*, 663 (C.H.F.). A query on the subject occurs 3 *N. and Q.*, vii. 179.

P. 422.] *Lord of Cherberry.* Herbert, a friend and correspondent of H.'s, and author of an important philosophical work *De Veritate.*
Sir K. Digby. Sir Kenelm was a philosopher as philosophers went in those days, *i.e.* a natural philosopher.
Lord G. D. Probably Lord George Digby. See p. 358.
Mistress A. K. Ann King, Bishop King's daughter, mentioned *supra*, 406.
Lady Core. In ed. II. this is *Cor*, with a space left white. Probably Lady Cornwallis. See on 286.
Rabelais, spelt *Rablais* in Ed. II. Ladies scarcely study French to get access to Rabelais nowadays.
Sir Lewis Dives. See on p. 428.
Endymion Porter. See on 535.
three Sisters. H. mentions Mrs. Gwin and Mrs. Roberta Price (Ap Rice) and his niece Banister in his will, *infra*, p. 668. The third sister was Rebecca Howell, thrice married. See Pedigree.

Cousins

Cousins their Children. This use of cousin for nephew occurs frequently. Some of these cousins have been already addressed, *e.g.* the Prices.
Sir H. F. Possibly Sir Harry Vane the younger, whose name is often spelt with an F. See the elaborate *Life*, by J. K. Hosmer, 1886.
this Motto is actually placed on his monument in the Temple Church.

P. 423.] LETTER XXX.—*Lady Wichts*, widow of Sir P. Wichts, or Wych, on whom see p. 254.
Master Controuler, of the Household. See Wood, *Athenæ*, s.v., iv. 489.

P. 424.] *Ambassador at the Port*, in which capacity II. addresses him above, p. 254.

LETTER XXXI.—*E. S., Counsellor.* E. Seys is the only Counsellor with these initials in Foss' *Judges* for the Commonwealth period, vi. 415.

P. 425.] LETTER XXXII.—*R. B*[rownrigg], though one of the same name occurs at the end of this letter, probably a relative. The name is given in the Table of ED. PR.; he was a Counsellor of Law; married Mary Bloss (? Blois) of Belstead; lived at Rishanger, and died at Beseley, 1669. Page *Suffolk*, p. 484.
multiplying glass. Microscope invented by Jansen about 1590.

P. 426.] *R. Brownrigg.* Probably a relative of the addressee, and of Bishop Brownrigg of Exeter, on whom see Wood, *Athenæ*.

LETTER XXXIII.—*Capt. C. Price*, a nephew of H.'s. See on p. 410.
bring it o'er the helm, a technical term in alchemy for distilling out of the retort over into the alembic (Mr. R. R. Steele).
resurrection to mortified vegetables. Paracelsus claimed to burn a plant to ashes, and then revive it. Cf. *Kel. Med.* i. § 47, and Wilkins' note. Sir II. Power, in writing to Browne (Wilkins, i. 358), calls it "the reindividualling of an incinerated plant."
green Lyon and Dragon, terms applied to the sublimation of the salts of mercury. One of Ashmole's treatises in his *Theatr. chem. Anglicanum* is *The Hunting of the greene Lyon.*
Powder of Projection. The powder which, by removing the imperfections of the baser metals, would project them into the nobler.

P. 427.] *Cardigan silver Mines.* These have again been worked quite recently. Sir Hugh Middleton made his fortune out of them and lost it on the New River. He exhausted the mines, which accounts for the failure of II.'s friends. Cf. Hunt, *Brit. Mining*, 152, who quotes Waller, *Account of Cardigan Mines.*

LETTER XXXIV.—*Lord of Cherberry.* Herbert of Cherbury. See on p. 352.

P. 428.] LETTER XXXV.—*R. Br*[ownrigg]. See on p. 425.

LETTER XXXVI.—*Sir L. D*[ives], a full biography of whom appears in *Gent. Mag.*, July–Dec. 1819. He is mentioned in Evelyn, the Strafford *Letters*, and Bayley's *Tower* (II. K.). Add *Gard.* x. 192; *Nich.* iii. 604, 820. The passage in Evelyn (6 Sept. 1651) gives an interesting account of his escape before execution. Life in D.N.B., s.v. Dyve.
Lewis XIII. H. refers to his work *Lustra Ludovici* (see Bibl. List, No. 16), which appeared in 1646, which agrees with the date at the end of this letter.

P. 429.]

P. 429.] *Sir J. St*[rangways], who was in the Tower at this time (Bayley, *Hist. of Tower*, 574), and was a brother-in-law of Sir L. Dives (Gardiner), and was captured together with him at the surrender of Sherborne Castle in 1645 (Hutchin's *Dorset*, iv. 273).
Sir H. V. Probably Sir Harry Vane. See on p. 422.

LETTER XXXVII.—*R. B*[rownrigg]. See on p. 425.
Master Bloys. See on p. 494 (Brownrigg married a sister of his).

LETTER XXXVIII.—*G. C.* Possibly one of the Carys, with whom H. was in close relation, or possibly a misprint for G. G., George Gage, p. 380.

P. 430.] *Legend of Conanus*, which occurs in Godfrey of Monmouth, and thence gets into the Lives of the Saints through Baronius, or so it appears from Butler, *Lives of Saints*, s. v. Ursula, Oct. 21.
Ursula. The 11,000 is supposed to be a folk-etymology of Onidesima, one of the companions of St. Ursula.
Colen. This form is used by Coryat, *Crudities*, iii. 1. *Cf.* Germ. *Köln*.

P. 431.] LETTER XXXIX.—*End. Por.* Endymion Porter. See p. 535.
of the late King her Brother. Louis XIII., brother of Q. Henrietta Maria. H. refers to his *Lustra Ludovici* (Bibl. List, No. 16).

P. 432.] *Aviso's* Sp. News.
L'Sperance, i.e., "*L'Espérance*," the motto of the Order of the Thistle in France, established by the Duke of Bourbon in 1370, and hence adopted by the Bourbon family. *Cf.* Dielitz, *Wahl-und Denksprüche*, 1884, p. 88.

LETTER XL.—*J. H*[all]. John Hall of Durham, not to be confused with Bishop Joseph Hall, the satirist. Probably the same mentioned in Worthington's *Diary*, 7, 10, 15, 17. See also on p. 492.
Essays. Hall's *Horæ Vacivæ, or Essays and some occasional considerations*, published in 1646.

P. 433.] LETTER XLI.—*my B*[rother], *the L*[ord] *B*[ishop] *of B*[ristol].
makes his approach. See the same expression p. 429. Probably a reference to Charles I.'s being brought south after being sold at Newcastle, Jan. 1647.

P. 434.] LETTER XLII.—*Sir L. Dives.* See on p. 428. This letter, Mr. Steele assures me, is full of correct alchemical phraseology.
refine the dross and feculency. This was the object of the alchemists, the prevailing view being that all metals were gold, with more or less of "leprosy," which could only be cleared away by fire.
Chymist calls it. Paracelsus, who compares the "leprosy" of the baser metals to original sin, only to be removed by purgatorial fire.
Perillus Bull. Perillus was the statuary who made the brazen bull for Phalaris, and was the first victim offered up in it (*Gesta Romanorum*, No. 48).
in ventre equino, i.e., in horse dung used to produce slow distillation.
antequam corvus. An expression used, Mr. Steele tells me, by E. P. Philalethes (*i.e.*, Geo. Starkey).
five times, i.e. 750 days, or a little over two years. This is incongruous with later statement of 55 months, *i.e.*, 4½ years.
distillation, sublimation, &c. *Cf.* Ripley's *Twelve Gates of Alchemy* in Ashmole, *Theatr. chem. Anglic.*

P. 435.] *Magistery.* Another name for the philosopher's stone, according to Meyer, *Hist. of Chemistry*, 40, but see on p. 348.

Treacle

Treacle of this Viper, i.e., a *theriacal* antidote against the θῆρ, *i.e.*, the serpent. Treacle was originally an electuary made of pounded vipers, used as an homœopathic antidote against snake poison. According to Littre (s.v. *theriaque*) it was invented by Nero's court physician. Our treacle is merely the syrup or mother liquid in which the antitode was taken.
23 *Feb.* 1645, should be 1647, on the face of the statements in the body of the letter.

LETTER XLIII.—*Lord R*[ivers], probably.
Catholick King, of Spain.
a fatal year, 1646.
lost Dunkirk, to Condé on Oct. 12, 1646.

P. 437.] *Chapines.* D'Ewes mentions that these were worn by Spanish ladies, *Autob.* ii. 448 ; Coryat, that they were used by Venetian courtesans, *Crud.* ii. 36. Evelyn describes them as "high-heeled shoes particularly affected by these proud dames," and adds that "courtesans or the citizens must not wear *choppines.*" Titian's "Venetian lady dyeing her hair" has laid aside her *chapines.*
Sister to a King of France. Isabella of France, married to Philip IV. in 1615.
common Enemy of Christendom, the Grand Turk.
setting upon Candy, but they took it in 1645, a year earlier than the fatal year, 1646.
the Peace . . . at Munster, known as the Peace of Westphalia, which closed the Thirty Years' War, and was signed Oct. 24, 1648, which makes the date at the end of this letter absurd, and the references to the taking of Dunkirk incongruous. The letter must at least have been "cooked."

P. 438.] LETTER XLIV.—*E. O.* There is no E. O. among the Counsel of Jas. I.'s or Chas. I.'s reign given in Foss' *Judges.* Perhaps Privy Councillor is implied, and the reference may be to Mr. (afterwards Sir) Edward Osborne, mentioned in the *Strafford Letters,* i. 264, 281.
Dr. Pritchard. See on p. 31.

P. 439.] LETTER XLV.—*J. W.* Query J. Wilson, to whom a letter p. 603, where see.
Mouse in lieu of a Mountain. A reference to *Parturiunt montes.*

LETTER XLVI.—*Tho. H*[ammon], according to the Table in ED. PR. See on p. 367. From the tone of this letter it is scarcely possible that T. H. can be identified with T. Hammond the Regicide, for whom see Wood, *Athenæ,* iii. 499, and D.N.B.

P. 440.] LETTER XLVII.—*S. B.,* probably identical with [the Sam. Bon[nel] of a later letter. See p. 637.
Baudius, Dominic, of Leyden (1561-1613).

P. 441.] *she was a Princess. Cf.* Green's elaborate character in his *Short History.*

P. 442.] LETTER XLVIII.—*Dr. D. Featly* (Fairclough) (1582-1645), full life in Wood, *Athenæ,* iii. 156-69 (*cf.* also Masson's *Life of Milton,* ii. 518; Forster, *Eliot,* ii. 332 *n.* ; Worthington, *Diary,* 74).

your

your Answer, possibly Featly's *Answer to a Popish challenge touching the true Church,* 1644, but I think it likely that H. is referring to Featly's *Dippers Dipt,* 1645, which contained an answer to Milton's *Doctrine of Divorce.* See Masson, *Life,* iii. 311–12 and *n.*
futilous Pamphlet. If the suggestion in the preceding note be correct, this would refer to Milton's *Doctrine of Divorce,* or to the *Tetrachordon,* in which Milton replies to Featly (Masson, *l.c.*). Milton would then be the "sterquilinous Rascal" and "Triobolary Pasquiller" of this letter. It must be remembered that his *Poems* first appeared in 1645, published by H. Moseley, who was also H.'s publisher.
tressis agaso, "threepenny groom," Pers. v. 76.
Prurigo scripturientium. Sir H. Wotton was the author of this saying, and desired it to be engraved on his tombstone.

LETTER XLIX.—*Capt. T. L*[eat]. See on p. 154.

P. **443.**] *Dr. Burton,* brother of the *Anatomy* Burton, and historian of Leicestershire.
Master Davies, probably J. Davies, mentioned as a Counsel *temp.* Chas. Foss, *Judges,* vi. 234.

LETTER L.—*Sir S. C*[row]. See on p. 33. The letter is quoted by Scoones, *Eng. Lett.,* No. lviii. p. 76, and in Nimmo's *Brit. Letter-Writers,* p. 314. *going abroad.* Going out, as we say.

P. **444.**] *our Aristotle.* This does occur in the Stagirite ; so Dr. Gow thinks the reference is to some English philosopher (Bacon ? Hobbes ?)

P. **445.**] *recarnified. Cf.* "All those creatures are but the herbs of the field digested into flesh in them, or more remotely carnified in ourselves." Browne, *Rel. Med.* I. xxxvii. (C. H. F.).
nearer approach. Something of the same feeling as appears in Hood's "I remember, I remember the fir trees tall and high."
rambling meditations. Mr. Firth suggests that they are an imitation of the *Religio Medici,* and there is certainly a Brownesque tone about the language. Yet some of the most curious words "Animalillios," "Ephemerans," &c., do not occur in Browne, nor do the sentiments exactly. At best, this imitation of Browne would only make the date inappropriate, not necessarily disprove the authenticity of the letter.

P.**446.**] LETTER LI.—*Serjeant D.* The only Sergeant D.'s for the whole period, 1603-60, mentioned in Foss as of Lincoln's Inn is J. Denham, 1609, R. Diggs and J. Dany, both 1623 (Foss, vi. 29). But the letter is only a formal or model one, and may have been merely written to fill space.

LETTER LII.—*Lady M. A.* Possibly one of the Althams, but the points of reference are too slight for sure identification.

P. **448.**] LETTER LIII.—*W. P.,* should be P. W. as in ED. PR., and then can be identified with Sir Philip Warwick, on whom see 293.

P. **449.**] *my dear Phil*[ip Warwick], clinching the identification.
The Vote. There was another poem of H.'s with this name published separately (Bibl. List, No. 3), and with the Letters, *supra,* p. 5.

P. 450.]

P. 450.] LETTER LIV.—*Lord Cliff*[ord]. See on p. 189.

discourse of Wines, possibly in imitation of John Taylor's *Drinke and welcome, or the famous Historie of the most part of Drinkes in use now in the Kingdomes of Gt. Britain and Ireland,* 1637. I cannot ascertain where H. got his knowledge about Eastern drinks from.

Italian vineyard-man. The same saying is quoted from Howell by T. Forde, *Apophthegms,* 28.

P. 451.] *Metheglin,* Welsh, *Medd y glyn. Cf.* W. C. Hazlitt, *Cookery,* 64, 204, for old recipes for making it.

Usquebagh, or whisky, of which it is the earliest form. See Mew and Ashton, *Drinks,* 1892, p. 146, for a recipe of *Usquibath or Irish Aqua Vitæ* in 1602, Moryson, *Itin.* iii. 163, spells it *Vsqueboagh.*

Sir John Oldcastle, as the original of Falstaff; and in Brewer's tract.

Smug the Smith. See on p. 247.

it perished with them, an interesting legend how the last Pict kept the secret is told in Chambers's *Pop. Rhymes of Scotland.*

P. 452.] *drink call'd Cauphe.* See on pp. 179, 662. Sandys, *Travels,* 51, gives an account of coffee as an Eastern drink entirely. Sir H. Yule has some interesting quotations as usual, s.v. Coffee.

Tripe full of Pelaw. Cf. "Pillaw (Rice sod with fat of Mutton)," Sandys, *Travels,* p. 57. H. uses Sandys frequently.

Narsingha. See Yule, *sub voce.*

P. 453.] *Drink called Banque,* known now as *Bang.* See Yule's discussion of the word in *Hobson-Jobson,* s. v. *Bang.*

holy kind of liquor. Can this be a reference to tea?

Nubila promissi. Ovid, *Fasti,* iii. 322.

Legitimation of a child. The same test is given in H.'s *German Dict,* p. 73.

P. 454.] *Magnais* is the name of the Mexican *agave,* so that H. has made a mistake here, or has misunderstood his original. *Cf.* Hehn, *Culturpflanzen.*

in Egypt. Herodotus mentions a kind of brew used by the Egyptians.

Pindar's words. Pyth. i. 1.

Martial's. Ep. XI. xi. 1, for "torcumata" read "torcumata," as in ED. PR.

P. 455.] *which is the great Continent of America.* All that we call North America was not reckoned, beside the conquests of Cortes and Pizarro.

Mobbi. made from the *batata* or sweet potato. *Cf. Cavaliers and Roundheads in Barbadoes,* 1883, p. 44 (quotation supplied by Mr. H. Bradley).

Tents. A kind of wine still used; the term used to be applied to what was called Cape wine. Probably, Mr. Bradley suggests, from *vino tinto.*

Portugal affords. This shows that the days of Port were still to come.

P. 456.] *Bachrag.* Bacharach on the Rhine. See also *Germ. Dict,* 18. It is also referred to in Butler, *Hudibras,* ii. 18.

P. 457.] *Psalts,* a misprint for Pfalts=Germ. *Pfalz,* the Palatinate. The Palgrave is the equivalent for the Germ. *Pfalzgraf.*

P. 459.] *Ut, Re, Mi.* The musical notes. These are generally traced from Guido's Leonines to St. John, beginning "*Ut* queant laxis *Re*sonare fibris."

LETTER LV.—*Earl R*[ivers]. This and the succeeding letters are a series of discourses on the chief languages of the world, derived from Brerewood, ch. ii.–ix.

P. 460.] *Dr. David Rice,* not given in Lowndes or Watt. Prof. Rhys informs me that the reference is to *Cambrobrytannicæ Cymraecæve Lingæ Institutiones*

tiones a Joaane David Rhæso, Lond. 1592, with which H. was acquainted as he quotes from it *supra*, p. 89.
fourteen, enumerated later, 476.
Armorican. Breton ; the philological identity is also referred to, *For. Trav.* 48. See also Selden's note on Drayton, *Polyolbion*, ed. 1622, p. 132.

P. 461.] *learned'st of that nation.* Probably Archbishop Usher, with whom H. had some acquaintance.
some navigators. It was mentioned first in Lloyd's *Cambria*, 1584, and thence in Hakluyt, iii. p. 1.
Welsh Epitaph, given in Herbert, *Travels*, p. 216 *seq.*, and thence *infra*, p. 608, where see.
Pengwyn. This example is quoted by Drayton (? Selden), *Polyolbion*, ix., ed. 1622, p. 148, also by Herbert, *l.c.*, *Cf.* too, Butler, *Hudibras*, 1. ii. 83, 84.

So horses they affirm to be
Mere engines made by Geometry,
And were invented first from engins,
As *Indian Britains* were from *Penguins.*

Madoc, the hero of Southey's poem. On his reputed discovery of America see J. Winsor, *History of America*, i. pp. 109-11.

P. 462.] *Purely British*, referring to the monkish legend which represents her father as a British or Caledonian king.

LETTER LVI.—*Earl R*[ivers], as on p. 459.

P. 463.] *as also in Persia.* This anticipation of the identity of the Indo-European languages H. got from Herbert, *Travels*, p. 171 *seq.*, and refers to again in *For. Tr.* 57, where he attributes the view that German was spoken in Paradise to Goropius Becanus. *Cf.* too, *Germ. Diet*, p. 64.
Sclavonic languages. All this from Brerewood, ch. viii. "Of the language of the Slavonique, Turkishe, and Asiaticke tongues."

P. 464.] *Alexander the Great.* II. took this from Fynes Moryson, *Itinerary*, 1617, i. 15.

P. 465.] LETTER LVII.—*Earl R*[ivers], as before. This letter is from Brerewood, ch. iii. "Of the decaying of the Greeke tongue."
Mithridates, King of Pontus, is said to have known twenty-five (not twenty-two) languages (Justin, xxxvii. 2). Moryson makes the same mistake, i. 22, and handed it on to H. On his antidote to poisons see *supra*, on p. 419.

P. 467.] *Lacocones*, probably a misprint of ED. PR. for Lacones. A similar reference, *supra*, 64, under the name of Zacones. The information comes from Sandys, p. 63.

P. 468.] LETTER LVIII.—*Earl R*[ivers], as before. From Brerewood, ch. iv. "Of the ancient of the Roman tongue."
Fifty mile compass. So Evelyn.

P. 471.] LETTER LIX.—*Earl R*[ivers], as before. This is again from Brerewood, ch. v. "Of the beginning of the Italian, French, and Spanish languages."

P. 472.] *Hetruscan*, similarly spelt in *For. Tr.* 53.
Mesapian, like the Etruscan, now an unknown tongue. H. gets this piece of erudition from Brerewood, p. 45.

P. 473.].

P. 473.] *Bascucnes.* The Basque ; II. refers to it again in *For. Tr.* 50. See also *supra,* p. 197.

P. 474.] *Island tied to France.* True, but scarcely within the quaternary period.
Cæsar and Tacitus say nothing so strong, according to Dr. Gow, Cæsar, *B. G.* v. 14, of the Cantii, " neque multum a Gallica consuetudine differunt ;" and Tacitus (*Agric.* xi.), "proximi Gallis et similes sunt."
Walloon, the language of French Flanders.

P. 475.] *call'd Franco.* The *lingua franca* of the East. H. refers to this in his *For. Tr.* pp. 45, 52.

LETTER LX.—*Earl R*[ivers], as before. Derived from Brerewood, ch. ix. "Of the Syriacke and Hebrewe tongues."
thirteen. It was fourteen before, *supra,* p. 460.

P. 476.] *Jazygian.* H. probably means Lithuanian, but the Jazyges were a Sarmatian stock who settled in Wallachia, and afterwards in the south, not north, of Hungary.
Cauchian. The Czech, a Slavonic language.

P. 477.] *Arabic.* This was probably taken from Herbert, *Travels,* 43-5. H. was acquainted with the book. See *infra* on p. 608.
language of Paradise. Cf. Max Müller, *Science of Language,* i. 145-50, for this belief and the curious vagaries to which it led.

P. 478.] *in this language.* Not accurate, as the Talmudic dialect is Chaldaic.
Rabbi Jonathan, the supposed author of the Targum or Chaldaic paraphrase of the Prophets.
Rabbi Onkelos or Aquilas, the author of the Targum on the Pentateuch. H. speaks of him and R. Jonathan as different from the Targum, which shows his ignorance, or rather second-hand knowledge, from Brerewood, p. 63.
Thus we see. This passage was put into italics by some accident of printing ; it is in ordinary type in ED. PR.

P. 479.] LETTER LXI.—*Car. Ra.* Carew Raleigh, Raleigh's eldest son. The whole of this letter is quoted in *Somers Tracts,* ii. 456-7, at the end of the reprint of Carew Raleigh's *A brief Relation,* 1661.
one Letter, I. i. 4, *supra,* 22 *seq.,* which deals with Raleigh's voyage to Guiana.
Historiseth. A reference, of course, to Raleigh's *History of the World.*
that Declaration, given in Harl. Misc. vol. iii. *A Declaration of the Carnage of Sir W. R. . . . and of the true motives which occasioned his Majestie to proceed in doing justice on him,* 1618.

P. 480.] *that Apology.* "For his voyage in Guiana," published in 1650 in R.'s *Judicious and Select Essays,* pp. 1, 69.
Sir R. Baker in his " Historical Collections," which appeared in 1641, and ultimately formed his *Chronicle of England.* See pp. 437-8 of ed. 1670.
Capt. Kemys, called Capt. Remish in the earliest letter, p. 24, see note.

P. 483.] *printed Relation.* Probably the Declaration mentioned *supra,* on p. 479.
faithless cunning Kt. Sir Lewis Stukeley, generally known at the time as Sir Judas Stukeley, who took money to assist Raleigh to escape after his return from

from Guiana, and then was the means of his being taken. He was convicted of clipping coin, and died at Lundy, as H. mentions. There is an *Apologia* by him in *Somers Tracts*, ii. 444.

P. 484.] *Mr. Nat. Carpenter*, a Devonshire divine (1588-1635), one of the early opponents of Scholasticism. The quotation in the text is probably from his *Geographie Delineated*, 1625.
Cadet. See on p. 373.

P. 485.] LETTER LXII.—*T. V*[aughan] probably, on whom see 219.

P. 486.] *horrid Profaneness*, such as that used by Hugh Peters or Peter Smart in their sermons and addresses. Even Milton is an instance of the general low level of controversist language at this period.
shops open. This struck Evelyn also, who notices it on several occasions (Chandos ed.), 224, 226, 254. On Christmas 1657 he was actually arrested for keeping Christmas.
Earl of Kildare. H. gives the same anecdote, *Patricius*, p. 13.
Excise, established by the House of Commons Jan.–Apr. 1644. See a later reference, p. 492.

P. 487.] *Kentish Knight.* Mr. Firth suggests that this is Sir E. Dering, a full account of whom appears in the Preface to *Proceedings in Kent* (Cam. Soc.), ed. Bruce. He died in 1644, and was certainly a trimmer or apostate, and he died of an imposthume (Bruce, *Pref.* p. 23).
A Pamphlet. Two appeared by Sir E. Dering in 1644, the presumable date of this letter, *A Declaration* and *A Discourse on Sacrifice.* Neither refer to H. so far as I can see.
William Ro. There is a letter to W. Roberts, *infra*, p. 606.
Tale of the Gallego. T. Forde gives this in his *Apophthegms*, 28, no doubt taking it from the *Epist. Hoel.*
Sir J. Brown. There are letters to him pp. 409, 415. He is no relation to the well-known doctor, who was not knighted till after the Restoration.

P. 488.] *squares.* The only meaning which suits the context is the application to bodices with square opening in front, used here for the ladies generally.

LETTER LXIII.—*His Majesty at Oxon.* Chas. I. was at Oxford, off and on, Oct. 26, 1643—Apr. 26, 1646. This letter is at once a defence to the king against any charge of lukewarm loyalty, and a hint to the Parliamentarians that H. was not too obtrusively royalist.
Foreign Minister. Mr Frith suggests this is Harcourt.

P. 489.] *reflecting on the Times.* A reference to H.'s *Parables reflecting on the Times.* Published in 1643 (see Bibl. List, No. 6).

LETTER LXIV.—*E. Benlowes*, a rather well-known writer of the time. See Mr. Bullen's account in *D. N. B.*, his genealogy in *Essex Visit.* (Harl. Soc.), i. 347, his residence in Morant. Mr. Wheatley refers to him in his book on *Anagrams. Cf.* 1 *N and Q.* iii. 287. Evelyn met him on 31 Aug. 1654. H. wrote a commendatory poem on his chief work, *Theophila.*
Aristæus, the supposed author of a fictitious letter giving an account of the origin of the Septuagist version of the Old Test.
Table of Proportions, properly a mathematical figure. *Cf.* Gow, *Hist. Greek Math.* pp. 73, 74, but used here for the instrument used in constructing the figure. As Josephus tells the story (*Ant. Jud.* xii. 2), the king desired to
have

have tables five times as large as those of the Temple (*cf.* the description of the table, Joseph. *l.c.*, § 9).
Table of Poems, probably B.'s *Lusus Poeticus Poetis*, 1635.

P. 490.] *purple Island*, of Phineas Fletcher, an allegorical poem, published 1633; it was dedicated to Benlowes.
Apollo himself. Fletcher, who was Rector of Hilgay, co. Norfolk, where he died, c. 1660.

LETTER LXV.—*Lady A. Smith*, probably related to Sir J. Smith of Leeds Castle, to whom Letter I. i. 1. is addressed. See note on p. 17.

P. 491.] LETTER LXVI.—*G. Stone.* Perhaps related to the R. Stone of D'Ewes, *Autob.* ii. 139.
Irish. " Now t' Irish or Back-Gammoners we come," *The Complete Gamester*, 1680, poem explaining frontispiece. The game, a sort of back-gammon, is explained, *ibid.*, p. 109. A good deal of discussion has gone on of recent years in *N. and Q.* on "Irish." See No. of 12 March 1892.
Glaucus with Diomedes in Iliad vi.

P. 492.] *Carates*, should be *caratts*, as in ED. PR.

LETTER LXVII.—*J. J.* Perhaps Joseph Jane, author of *Ikon Aklastos*, 1651, one of the answers to Milton's *Iconoclastes*. But it is possible that the initials are misprinted and should be " J. H." *i.e.* John Hall, for whom see on p. 432. Hall published in 1648, *i.e.* the year after the publication of this part of the *Epist. Ho-El.*, "Sparkles of Divine Love " (Lowndes).
Sparkles of Piety. *Cf.* title of Hall's book in preceding note. It would still be in MS. when Book II. of *Epist. Ho-El.* was published in 1647.

P. 493.] LETTER LXVIII.—*Capt. W. Bridges.* Perhaps he that afterwards became Col. Bridges and Governor of Warwick Castle. *Cf. S.P.*, June 1660 (p. 81). He was a Kentish man from the reference to Maidstone over page. The present letter is supposed to be written in Madrid in 1622, and is certainly full of Spanish lore.
burnt down. Riots took place in Feb. 1647. See Rushworth, vii. 792 (C.II.F.).

P. 494.] *war makes thieves.* Quoted by W. C. Hazlitt, *Eng. Prov.* 495. The statistics of crimes of violence in Germany went up alarmingly after the Franco-Prussian War.
Judge Rives, probably E. Reeve, Justice of Common Pleas, who died 27 March 1697 (Foss, vi. 357–8).
Cousin Fortescue. This should give the clue to both Bridges and his cousin.

LETTER LXIX.—*W. B.* W. Blois. The third of that name who married Cicely, daughter of Sir Thos. Wingfield, and died in 1673. Page, *Suffolk*, p. 53.
Grundesburgh, in Carlford Hundred, S.E. Suffolk.

P. 495.] *my trees.* A reference to H.'s *Vocal Forest.*
Jewel of our times. Observe how cunningly H. here and on p. 484 repeats and publishes compliments paid him by others.

LETTER LXX.—*J. W.*, probably John Wroth, mentioned in Table of the second edition, having been added to that of ED. PR. See on p. 536.
P. 496.]

P. 496.] LETTER LXXI.—*Capt. T. P[orter].* See p. 55. This professes to be a letter of early date, 1622.
Mr. Gresley. See on p. 204.
speak with hands only. The first book on the deaf and dumb language with fingers appeared at Madrid, 1620, by J. P. Bonet. It has just been translated into English, 1891. Sir Kenelm Digby interested Charles I. in the subject when at Madrid (*A Relation*, quoted D.N.B.).

P. 498.] *black Plush. Cf. supra*, p. 46.
To-Maria-Mas, literally I will take (*tomaria*) more (*mas*). H. probably learnt much from a Divota himself. See on p. 44.

P. 499.] LETTER LXXII.—*Sir T. Luke*, should be Lake (misprint of ED. PR.). *Cf.* 3 *N. and Q.* vii. 116. See on p. 276. This letter was written on his marriage, or professes to be.
your wife. Mary, daughter of Sir W. Ruther, Lord Mayor of London (Wood, *Fasti*, i. 261), but H. could not have been old enough at his marriage.
Lord George of Rutland, the eighth earl, who did not succeed till 1632.
Hambledon. H. had bought the advowson of a living there. See p. 266.
my voyage to the Baltic Sea. This can only be the embassy to Denmark, 1632.
1 *May* 1629. Antedated three years if the voyage is the embassy.

P. 500.] LETTER LXXIII.—*R. K.*, probably R. Killigrew, father of the dramatist, mentioned *supra*, 187. *Cf.* Ellis, i. 144; Grammont, 402; *James I.*, ii. 174, 391, 394, 441 (H.K.); add Gard. v. 429.
Dr. Baskervil. Is this the same as the Baskervil mentioned by Nicholls, i. 537 *n.*?
to go into the dark. Cf. Bacon's Essay on Death, *ad init.* "Men feare Death as children feare to goe in the darke."

P. 501.] LETTER LXXIV.—*Sir R. Gr.*, either Sir R. Grosvenor (*Nich.* iii. 753 *n.*), the ancestor of the prese nt Duke of Westminster, or Sir R. Granville, or more probably still Sir R. Gr osvenor the second baronet, who succeeded the first in 1644 and died 1664.
Maundy Thursday, *i.e.* day preceding Good Friday,'which would be 15 April in 1647.

P. 502.] *King being* Christian. A reference to the legend of K. Lucius, *supra*, pp. 277, 387.

P. 503.] 30 *April* 1647. More than a fortnight after Maundy Thursday. H. seems incorrigible about dates.

LETTER LXXV.—*R. Howard*, probably a relative of J. Howard, to whom there is a letter, *supra*, 329.
T. P. Can this inconsiderate friend be the Tom Porter who is elsewhere so cordially treated by H.
comic Poet. Terence, *Eun.* I. ii. 25, " Plenus rimarum sum ; hae atque illae perfluo."

P. 504.] LETTER LXXVI.—*E. P.* Endymion Porter, on whom see 535.
achaques. Sp. ailments. *Cf.* Strafford, *Lett.* i. 206, 225, 263.
Mestizos. Spanish, half-breeds.

P. 505,

P. 505.] *now Scot-free,* Dec. 21, 1646, when the agreement for the Scotch
army to retire was signed.   See Carlyle, *Cromwell,* Letter xlii.
four and twenty Seas, or Sees.   A reference to the disestablishment of the
Episcopacy and the passing of the Presbyterian Platform.   See Carlyle,
Cromwell, Letters xliii. xliv.
aurum Tolosanum.   Treasure taken from Toulouse by Q. Servilius Calpio,
B.C. 106, who subsequently suffered a severe defeat, supposed to be on
account of the sacrilege.   Gellius, iii. 9 (I owe this piece of information to
Dr. Gow).
Aerians.   See on p. 607.
one of the prime precepts, given to his brother Sir George Wentworth to convey to his son (Rushworth, viii. 760).   The exact expression was " Moth
and Canker."

P. 506.] *multitude of Witches.*   A further reference to this, *infra,* 548.   The
account of witchcraft best known is that of M. Hopkins, *The Discovery of
Witches,* 1647.
button their doublets outwards.   Cf. G. Allen, *Falling in Love, &c.,* Essay ii.
on Right-handedness, where he notices the same difference between men
and women (in England).   II. mentions the distinction, *For. Tr.* 31.
Nine worthies.   Joshua, David, Judas Maccabeus ; Hector, Alexander, Julius
Cæsar ; Arthur, Charlemaine, and Godfrey of Bouillon.

P. 507.] LETTER LXXVII.—*Sir K. D[*igby].   See on p. 191.
Landloper.   Cf. *Supra,* p. 103, where I have suggested that this is the source
of our expression "landlubber"?   II. uses the same expression in his *For.
Tr.* 67.
little world.   The microcosm of one's own consciousness, *cf.* note on p. 72,
and add title of Wanley's *Wonders of the Little World.*
wisest of Pagan Philosophers.   Seemingly a reference to Solon, but the geo-
metrical reference seems to apply to Plato.

P. 509.] LETTER LXXVIII.—*Sir K. D*[igby], as before.
That Poem, probably the *Vote* published Cal. Jan. 1642-3.   Cf. text, pp. 5-12.

P. 510.] ADVERTISEMENT.   This was attached to ED. PR., and shows II. a
pioneer in rational orthography.   His suggestions were not uniformly
adopted in his own text, such is the force of trade custom.
Academy of wits.   The French Academy founded in 1635.

BOOK III.

Published in the Second Edition, 1650, " with an addition of a third Volume
of new Letters," and a Dedication to the Earl of Dorset.

P. 511.] LETTER I.—*E. of Dorset,* Edward Sackville, 8th Earl, ob. 1652.   An
elegy on him, *infra,* p. 642.
Dr. S. Turner.   Mentioned in Forster, *Elliot,* i. 478 *n.,* 498-9 ; and Evelyn
(Chandos), 495.
a new tract.   Senault's *L'usage des passions.*   II. probably refers to the translation by the Earl of Monmouth, 1649 : this was published by Moseley.
                                                                        P. 512.]

P. 512.] *St. Mark bears up* against the Turks, who had attacked Candia.
those of Naples increase. A reference to the revolt of Masaniello, of which
H. translated an Italian account.
Emperor of Ethiopia, i.e. Abyssinia.
Quinzey. See on p. 390, and *cf.* Herbert, *Travels*, 131.

P. 513.] *Emperor of Muscovia.* Alexis, who ruled from 1645 to 1676; he was
Peter the Great's grandfather.
Common Fruiterer, Masaniello who headed a successful revolt in 1647. See
H.'s account (Bibl. List, No. 37, 42).
Frederick, afterwards Frederick III., who succeeded to the throne in 1648.

P. 514.] LETTER II.—*En. P.* Endymion Porter. See on p. 535.
Demicasters. Hats, it would seem, from the reference to beavers; but Fair-
holt in his glossary gives it as a short cloak.
Charenton. Evelyn visited one on the Marne 6 Jan. 1644.

P. 515.] *Points. Cf.* Fairholt's *Picture of an English Antique* in his *Costume
in England*, 248.
Bishops' Lawnsleeves. Dr. Owen, Ch. Ch. Ox., wore "Spanish leather boots
with large lawn tops." Fairholt, 251.
Boots and Shoes. Perhaps a reference to the large tops of boots, with "many
dozen of points at the knees" (Fairholt, *l.c.*).
Not a cross. An allusion to the iconoclasm of the Puritans, who threw down
all crosses, including Q. Eleanor's, which Evelyn saw 2 May 1643.

LETTER III.—*W.* B[lois]. See on p. 309.

P. 516.] *Hoties.* Greek, the "becauses" of things.
Old Greek words. Milton's "And new Presbyter is but old priest writ large."
Buchanan (1506-82), poet, historian, and James I.'s tutor.

P. 517.] LETTER IV.—*Sir J. S.*, one of the Royalist *emigrés.* Cannot be the
Sir J. S. of I. i. 1, who died 1632. See on p. 17. Perhaps Sir T. Sackville.
See on p. 599.
panem Dominum. With the latter noun in apposition implies transubstantia-
tion which *panem Domini* equally explicitly rejects.
Cleopatra's Pearl which she dissolved in vinegar.

P. 519.] *Præ quo quisquiliæ cætera*, "compared with which all else is rubbish."

LETTER V.—*T. W.*, probably Wroth. See on p. 402.
P. Castle. Probably a mistake for P[etherton] Park, the residence of Thos.
Wroth. See Wood, *Athenæ*, iii. 514. He translated Virgil.
that monster. H. wrote an account of a similar (? the same) monster under
the title *Strange news from Scotland* (Bibl. List, No. 22).

P . 520.] *Mr. T. M.* Probably T. Man, to whom there is a reference, p. 407,
in a letter also to T. W. Unless both letters are authentic, this is a very
artful coincidence on the part of H.

LETTER VI.—*William Blois.* See on 494.
Nephew. How he was H.'s nephew I have been unable to ascertain.
five years. This would fix the date of this letter at 1647-8.

N.

II.   3 D

N. Brownrigg.   N. probably stands for Nephew, as Brownrigg's name was Roger.

P. 521.] LETTER VIL.—*Henry Hopkins,* is mentioned as being in the Fleet, 369.
'tis good for many things.   Kingsley probably got his well-known encomium, put in the mouth of Sebastian Yeo in *Westward Ho*, from this passage ; he knew and used the *Epist. Hoel.*   See *supra*, 309.   *Cf.* Herbert, *Autob.* 210, and generally the catena of passages collected by Prof. Arber in his edition of James I.'s *Counterblaste.*

P. 522.] *who told me.*   The same case is related, *supra*, pp. 282–3.
taken backward.   *Cf.* letter to Judge Rumsey, *infra*, p. 663.
petty conclusion.   This story is told by Oldys in the Life prefixed to Raleigh's *History of the World*, p. xxxii., and is quoted by Prof. Arber in James I.'s *Counterblaste*, p. 88, who also gives H.'s account.
smutchin, i.e. snuff.   Snuff is taken with a quill by Mr. Henderson in Mr. Stevenson's *Kidnapped*, p. 156.

P. 523.] *Dr. Thorius' "Pætologia."*   See Wood, *Athenæ*, ed. Bliss, ii. 379. The exact title of the book was *Hymnus Tabaci sive de Poeto Libri II.*, Lond. 1627.   An English translation by P. Hansted appeared in 1651. *Pætum* = Petun, the Brazilian name for tobacco.   *Cf.* Arber, *l.c.*, 93.

LETTER VIII.—*Lord of D*[orset].   Edward Sackville the eighth Earl, died 1652.   This letter is mainly an essay on Learning.

P. 524.] *Grosthead.*   See on p. 381.

P. 525.] *Another great philosopher.*   A mistake of H.'s : it was, of course, Archimedes himself of whom the story is told.   Both points are told of Archimedes in Burton, *Anatomie*, I. ii. 3, § 15, the section dealing with "Study a Cause" of Melancholy, which H. may have had in his mind. *conclusum est*, told by Burton, *l.c.*, but his authority is "Fulgosus, l. 8, c. 7."

P. 527.] *Dr. Gwyn.*   Probably P. Gwyn, mentioned as a counsel *temp.* Chas. I. in Foss, vi. 235.
Judge Finch.   Lord Finch of Fordwich, 1584–1660, had the reputation of carrying through the measure of ship-money (Foss, *Judges*, vi. 310–317). He was the successful wooer of the Widow Bennet, beloved also by Sir E. Dering and Sir Sackville Crow (see Bruce's amusing Pref. to *Proceedings in Kent*).
Phormio before Hannibal.   See on p. 626.

P. 528.] LETTER IX.—*Doctor J. D.*   Dr. I. Day according to the Table of the second edition, to which it was added.
Powder of Projection.   See on p. 426.
Lunary World.   Bishop Wilkins' *Discovery of a New World . . . another inhabitable world in the Moon*, had appeared in 1638, and doubtless inspired this discourse.

P. 529.] *Bishop's name.*   St. Fergil, Bishop of Salzburg, an Irishman who wrote on the rotundity of the earth.   Pope Zachary did not exactly ex-communicate him, but threatened to disfrock him if he held there were men on the other side (Dict. Christ. Biog., s.v. Virgilius).

wisest

wisest of men. Solomon, but I cannot find the reference, which is probably from the Apocrypha.
one day certifieth. Probably meant as a quotation from Ps. xix. 2, in the Prayer-book version, "One day telleth another and one night certifieth another."

P. 530.] *the old world.* *Cf.* "Antiquitas sæcli juventus mundi," Bacon.
first of whom. This is a mistake of H.'s, confounding Pythagoras with Socrates. It occurs *infra* 598, 637, and in *For. Trav.* 14.
middle age. This is putting Plutarch much too late : can H. have confounded him with Petrarch?

P. 531.] *Artificial Prospective.* Galileo applied his telescope to the moon first in 1610. Milton's fine lines on "the spotty globe" refer to this, *Par. Lost.* *Cf.* also *Lust. Lud.* 107.

P. 532.] *Old opinion* among the Gnostics and Neo Platonists, who were followed by the Cabbalists. The whole of Arabic philosophy is dominated by the conception which was taken from them by the mediæval Jewish philosophers. *Cf.* Stöckl, *Gesch. d. Phil. im Mittelalter.*

P. 533.] *yours touching Copernicus* and his geocentric views. *Cf.* note on p. 26.

P. 534.] LETTER X.—*Lady E. D.* Possibly Lady Digby, to whom there are other letters, 353, 414.

LETTER XI.—*R. B.* Might be the R. Baron of the Table; it could also be R. Brown or R. Brownrigg, but is probably a brother Richard of the W. Blois at Grundesburgh, 494, since H. addresses him likewise as Nephew.

P. 535.] LETTER XII.—*En. P.* Endymion Porter. It should be remembered that Digby and Porter, and the whole *entourage* of the Queen at Paris, were Catholics, or nearly so. Endymion Porter, who has accompanied us throughout the *Epist. Hoel.,* is one of the most striking persons of the time. *Cf.* Fairf. ii. 396, iii. 30; Nichols, iii. *pass.* ; Evelyn (Chandos ed.), 200; *Jonsonus Virbius.* H. K. adds Croker, *Bass.* 69; 2 Ellis, iii. 314; *Strafford Letters, Jas. I.,* Sir John Suckling, and Davenant. There is a fine portrait of him by Dobson in the National Gallery.

P. 536.] LETTER XIII.—*John Wroth.* See *supra,* 499. Ben Jonson wrote a poem on his mother, Lady Wroth.
Petherton Park, near Petherton, co. Somerset.
Spartam nactus. Cic. *ad Att.* iv. 6, the translation of a fragment from Euripides' *Telephus.*

P. 537.] *Your great Uncle.* Probably Sir Roger Wroth the founder of the family. See Collinson, *Somerset,* iii. 68.

LETTER XIV.—*W. B*[lois]. See on 494.
Nephew. The exact relationship here implied is difficult to ascertain ; later on in the letter II. uses " nephew" as the English of *nepos.*

P. 538.] *quarters now.* "In Whitehall, in St. James'," &c. Dec. 2, 1648. Carlyle, *l.c.,* i. 345, on Letter lxxxv. "Pride's Purge" followed soon after.
Insurance

Insurance of ships. See *supra* on 350.
10 *of Dec.* 1647, should be 1648.

LETTER XV.—*Sir K. D*[igby].

P. 539.] *Lycanthropy*, the condition of being a were-wolf.
Isle of Wight, from which the King was taken to Hurst Castle, Nov. 28, 1648.
Carlyle, *l.c.* *Cf.* the chronogram in Bibl. List No. 28.
first propositions, query those of the Oxford Negotiations in 1643?
5 *May* 1647, pre-dated eighteen months.

LETTER XVI.—*W. Blois*, probably the father of the W. Blois, whom H.
addresses as nephew.
Suffolk, Grunesburgh.
17*th current.* How can that be when the letter is dated May 7?

P. 540.] *Scots routed*, at the battle of Preston, Aug. 17, 1648. See Carlyle on
Letters lxiii.-vi.
Hamilton's Design. The Duke of Hamilton, who led the Scots into England
and at Preston.
7 *May.* In obvious disagreement with the statement in the body of the letter
about the 17th current.

LETTER XVII.—*R. Baron.* Mentioned by Pepys, p. 48 (Chandos ed.).
Cyprian Academy. Full title given in W. C. Hazlitt's *Handbook.* It appeared in 1648.

P. 541.] *Spaniard.* Anne of Austria, Queen Regent.
Italian. Mazarin, at this time at the height of his power.
Marquis of Ancre. See *supra*, p. 39.
Nephew. H. seems to shine in the character of uncle.

LETTER XVIII.—*Tho. More.* Perhaps the crazy person whose character is
given by Wood, *Athenæ*, iv. 179. He died 1685.
Uncle. What, again!

P. 542.] LETTER XIX.—*W. B.* Blois. See on p. 494.
full of horses during the predominance of the Puritans. *Cf.* Evelyn, *Letter* of
18 Dec. 1648.

P. 543.] LETTER XX. Sir Paul Pindar, diplomatist, ob. 1650, just after the
publication of this division of the *Ep. Hoel.* H. K. gives references for
him to Malcolm's *London ;* Rapin. ii. 380 ; Granger, *Stratford Letters ;*
Court of Jas. I. and Lowndes. Add *Fairfax Letters*, iii. 131.
St. Paul's Progress." See Bibl. List, No. 16. It was published in 1645,
and had this and the following letter prefixed.
" *Christ's Passion.*" *Christus Patiens.* A sacred tragedy translated into
English by G. Sandys, 1640.
25 *Mar.* 1646. As the book to which this was prefixed was published in 1645,
the date is added without thought.

                                                              P. 544.]

P. 544.] LETTER XXI.—*Sir Paul Neale*, or Neile, mentioned in Wood, *Athen.* iii. 902, 903 ; North, *Exam.* 60; *Strafford Letters*, i. 516; Evelyn (Chand.), 275 ; *Hudibras*, II. iii. (he is supposed to be the original of Sidrophel), Nich. iii. 272 ; Fairf. i. 281, ii. 398. Evelyn, 8 May 1656, calls him "famous for his optic glasses." *as I spake elsewhere. Supra*, 440.

P. 545.] *begins but now in Law.* The legal year begins on Mar. 25, as all know to their cost who have to deal with dates O. S., which require double dating between Jan. 1 and Mar. 25.

LETTER XXII.—*Dr. W. Turner*, mentioned in Wood, *Athen. pass. ;* Forster, *Eliot*, i. 478, 498-9 ; Nich. iii. 120 ; Evelyn (Chandos ed.), 495. Probably related to Dr. S. Turner of p. 511 *supra.*
Pengruns. This is a reference to Lilly's Prophecy of a White King (C. H. F.). Lilly published *A Collection of the Prophecies Concerning these Times*, 1645, and in the previous year *England's prophetical Merlin*, to which H. here refers. There is a further reference to these prophecies in H.'s *Bella Scot-Anglica, ad fin.* Lilly got himself into trouble later on by a too accurate prediction of the Great Fire, *cf.* Ball, *Math. Recreat.* 1892, p. 184.
"*Balaam's Ass.*" "A Vision of Balaam's Ass," by Peter Hay, appeared 1616, according to Watt. Hence the reference to "hay" in the poem. According to Mr. Firth it is a reference to the Earl of Carlisle.
Mr. Williams. He was hanged, drawn, and quartered, for writing the "Vision of Balaam's Ass " (Nichols, *Prog. Jas. I.*, iii. 537, who gives full title).

P. 547.] LETTER XXIII.—*Sir Edward Spencer*, son of Robert, Lord Spencer, of Wormleighton.
near Branceford, Boston Manor at Brentford, which came into his possession on his marriage with Lady Reade in 1625 (Lysons, *Environs of London*, ii. 45, 555.
Manuscript you lent me of Dæmonology. Possibly Dr. N. Horne's *Dæmonologie and Theologie*, which appeared in 1650.

P. 548.] *Johannes ad oppositum.* See 3 *N. and Q.* vii. 114. The phrase occurs in the *Zurich Letters*, Grindal to Foxe (Parker Soc.), p. 233 (H.K.). From a later account *N. and Q., l.c.*, p. 187, it appears to be merely a Latin translation of "Jack on both sides," meaning a turn-coat.
to deny there are witches. See on this subject Lecky, *Hist. of Rationalism*, i. 46-138. Howell may be thinking of Montaigne, III. iii.
holy Codex. Exod. xxii. 18 ; Deut. xviii. 10.

P. 549.] *Marchioness of D'Ancre.* See *supra*, 51.
execution of Nostredamus (1503-66). He died at Satow, 1566, and was not executed. His *Centuries* were translated into English.
St. Paul for a Witch. Cf. Acts xxviii. 5.
to buy and sell winds. Cf. Scott, *The Pirate.*
Olaus Magnus. Lit. III. c. xiv., "De magica arte Erici Ventosi Pilei."

P. 550.] *Plutarch. De Defectu Orac.* c. 17.
Pan is dead. Cf. Mrs. Browning's poem. Sir T. Browne has the story in *Vulgar Errors*, vii. 12, and (wrongly) in his *Letter to a Friend*, § 2. Howell got it, as much else, from Sandys, *Voyage*, p. 9.
Lieut. Jaquette. See *supra*, 98.
P. 551.] *three hundred Witches.* They were six hundred shortly before. See *supra*, p. 506.

P. 552.] LETTER XXIV.—*Sir Will. Boswell.* Can this be Bacon's executor?
Spedding,

Spedding, *Life*, vii. 539, 552, *cf.* also Worthington, *Diary*, 60, 68, 82 ; *Jas. I.*, ii. 268 ; Ellis, i. 195, and *D. N. B.* s. v.
That black Tragedy. The execution of Chas. I.
let blood in the Basilical Vein. This does not seem to imply any great emotion on the part of H. The "Index" or Table of Contents refers to this letter as follows, "England cured of the King's Evil."
Mr. Jacob Boeue. Perhaps an ancestor of the W. Boevey whose widow is supposed to be the perverse widow of the *Spectator*, No. 113. See Morley's note *ad loc.*

LETTER XXV.—*Mr. W. B*[lois]. See on p. 494.

P. 553.] LETTER XXVI.—*R. A'*[illigrew], probably as on p. 100. The sentiments of the letter do H. great credit, but had been anticipated by the catholicity of the *Religio Medici.*
Themistius. A philosopher and orator of the fourth century A.D. H. knows of him from Suidas, see next note.

P. 554.] *Praetor of Byzantium*, for Prefect of Byzantime, a post which Suidas erroneously confers upon him (Suidas, ed. Kuster, s.v., Smith *Dict. Class. Biog.* s.v.).

BOOK IV.

P. 555.] This appeared in 1655 (Bibliog. List. No. 49). The letters contained in it are more theoretical and less historical than in the preceding books.

LETTER I.—*Sir James Crofts.* It is somewhat doubtful whether this can be the Sir James of Book I., on whom see p. 22.
Lempster, now Leominster, co. Hereford.

P. 556.] *Anser, Apis, Vitulus,* referred to *supra*, 376.

LETTER II.—*T. Morgan.* See on pp. 427, 520. There is a Morgan mentioned in the Fairfax correspondence.
Doctor Dale. Valentine Dale, D.C.L., ob. 1589 (*Dict. Nat. Biog.* s.v., which quotes the Hebrew anecdote from H.).
Brennus. H. makes the same unfounded statement as to B.'s nationality, *Discourse*, 5. Prof. Rhys writes that the Welsh word *Brenhin*, "a king," was probably the cause of this erroneous idea, which is little more than a folk-etymology.

P. 558.] LETTER III.—*Lady E. D*[igby], a sister of R. Altham.
grows at the foot. A further reference to Howell's personal acquaintance with Sicily. *Cf. supra*, on p. 63.

LETTER IV.—*Marquis of Hartford.* William Seymour, 11th Earl and first Marquis. He became Duke of Somerset at the Restoration.

P. 559.] *knee-timber.* A term in shipbuilding for a piece of wood naturally bent at an angle and used for brace and tye.
Sir P[ercy] *Herbert,* in his *Certain Conceptions or Considerations,* 1652. Gard. ix. 270, refers to him.
holy Anchorite. This well-known story has been traced to the East, among others, by M. Gaston Paris, *La Poesie au Moyen Age,* p. 151 *seq.* In England it is well known through Parnell's poem, probably derived from the *Spectator,* No. 237, which took it either from Howell here, or from J. Lacke's *Boke of Wisdome,* 1565 (see *Cens. Lit.* vi. 233), from whom Herbert may have got it.

P. 563.] LETTER V.—*Richard Baker,* probably a son of Sir R. Baker of Chronicle fame. He wrote commendatory verses to the Earl of Monmouth's translation of Bentivoglio's *Wars of Flanders* (Wood, *Athen.* iii. 516 *n.*).
morning spittle kills Dragons. On this superstition see Brand-Ellis, *Pop. Antiq.* iii. 141. It is mentioned by Browne, *Vulgar Errors.*
Ramirams, a mistake (of ED. PR.) for Ramadams, the great fast of the Mahomedan year.
Beirams. Sandys refers to this fast (*Travels,* 93) as the "little Beyram."
dawn in the morning. A mistake, if a reference to the day of Atonement, which is a strict fast from eve to eve.

P. 564.] *Henry the Great.* The same anecdote is told *supra,* p. 50.

P. 565.] LETTER VI.—*R. Manwayring.* Probably related to the Sir Arthur M. of p. 266, or to the Sir Philip M., to whom a letter is addressed, p. 354. Perhaps a son of Roger Manwaring Bishop of St. David's, on whom see Wood, *Athen.* iv. 810.

P. 566.] LETTER VII.—*Sir Edward Spencer.* See on p. 547.
opinion truly befitting a Jew. See on p. 316.

P. 567.] *an Empress in Rome.* H. refers to this before, p. 416.
Zenobia. Cf. supra, 416.
Queen in England. Eleanor, wife of Edward I., according to the legend.
Artimesia. The same example in *Germ. Diet,* p. 2.

P. 568.] *B. and C.* Bacon and Coke, see *supra,* p. 220.
Xantippe. A similar story of her in Gower, *Confess.* III. iii. 1.
Strowd's Wife. The same anecdote, *supra,* 220, where see.
ride upon Coltstaves, or cuckolds. See Brand, *Pop. Antiq.,* and *cf.* 1 *N. and Q.* xi. 475.

P. 569.] *eight wives.* A mistake, repeated *supra.*
poor shallow-brain'd Puppy. There can be no doubt Milton is meant here, on account of his books on Divorce, *Tetrachordon,* &c., in 1645. H.'s friend Featley was one of Milton's opponents.
toting-horn or tooting-horn, but there is obviously some reference to cuckoldom.
secure their body. Possibly a reference to the barbarous belts used in the early middle ages, which ensured chastity during a husband's absence. One used to be exhibited at St. Cloud that had been worn by one of the Merovingian queens.
cornu ferit. H. was probably thinking of Horace, *Sat.* I. iv. 34, *fænum habet in cornu.*

P. 572.]

P. 572.] LETTER VIII.—*T. V*[aughan]. See on p. 219.
Mrs. E. B. Did Vaughan have aspirations after the wife of Benlowes, on whom see 489. But "Mrs." does not necessarily imply a married woman at this period.

P. 573.] LETTER IX.—*Sir R. Williams.* Can scarcely be the Sir Roger Williams of Elizabeth's time unless this is a very early letter.
Recorder Fleetwood, mentioned in Foss, *Judges*, vi. 36.

P. 574.] *Tom Waters, Mr. Watts.* Scarcely sufficient to identify either of these gentlemen, though the same names appear in *S.P.* for 1631.

LETTER X.—*Sir R. Cary.* Mentioned Forster, *Grand Remonstrance*, 99 ; Nicholls, iii. 804 *n.*, and *pass.*
once a year. A reference to the proverb "Christmas comes but once a year," which must accordingly have been current in H.'s day. *Cf.* Hazlitt, *Proverbs,*[2] 99.

P. 575.] LETTER XI.—*J. Sutton*, probably a relative of Lord Lexington. This letter was printed as an introduction to a translation of Sandoval's *History of Spain.*
Mr. Wad[sworth]. See on p. 184.

P. 576.] *As Cicero hath it,* "Nescire autem quid, antea quam natus sis, acciderit id semper esse puerum." Cic. *Orator*, c. xxxiv. § 120. As H. quotes from memory he probably got it from his friend Archb. Usher, with whom the reading of this sentence was the turning point of his life (*Biog. Brit.* s.v.), and thus, indirectly, the cause of the dates in the Authorised Version of the Bible.
Murat, known as Amurath. An account of his accession is given in Sir T. Roe, *Negociations*, Letter clvi.
Blazing star in Virgo, referred to as presaging Q. Anne's death, *supra*, p. 105.

P. 577.] *Mr. Simon Digby.* See on p. 210.
15 Jan. A truncated date, which may account for absence of dates in other letters, H. having put his pen through them all.

P. 578.] LETTER XII.—*Marquis of Dorchester*, previously known to us as Sir Dudley Carleton. See on pp. 274, 487. For another characterisation of Elizabeth see *supra*, p. 441.

P. 579.] *Stubbs and Page.* The former had his hand chopped off for publishing *A Gaping Gulf* against Elizabeth's match with Anjou. Page was the publisher of the pamphlet (Froude, xi. 161).
Sir John Heywood, also known as Sir J. Hayward. The condemned book was a history of Henry IV., dedicated to Essex. One of Bacon's *Apophthegms* is about him. *Cf.* Nicholls, *Prog. Jas. I.*, iii. 582.
Penry, Hugh. One of the early Puritans, and connected with the Marprelate Controversy. See Arber, *Introd. to Marprelate Controversy.*
Alured. See Rushw. i. 91 (C.H.F.) ; Forster, *Eliot*, ii. 256 ; Spedding, *Life*, vii. 110.
quit Havre-de-Grace, which was retaken by the French in 1563.

P. 580.] *Hans, Jocky, or John Calvin.* Lutherans, Huguenots (?), or Calvinists or Puritans generally.

P. 581.] LETTER XIII.—*R. Floyd.* Probably the Rice Floyd who matriculated at Oriel in 1610 (Clark, *Reg.* iii.).
Uncle J[ames], *i.e.* cannot well be Howell himself.

P. 582.]

P. 582.] LETTER XIV.—*R. Jones*, author of *The British Gem*, an abstract of the Bible in Welsh verse, Lond. 1652, 12mo, to which this letter of H. was prefixed (Wood, iii. 344).
Maternal tongue. Welsh of course. Eight years later H. published a collection of Welsh proverbs at the end of his *Lexicon Tetraglotton.*

LETTER XV.—*J. S*[utton]. See on p. 575.
Duke of Espernon, Jean de la Foix. Neither Burnet nor the Brit. Mus. Cat. have anything by him of a philosophical cast.
Privatio. All matter before being provided with form is deprived of it: therefore this deprivation of form (Privatio, στέρησις) is a universal principle of all matter. So argued the scholastics, and for so arguing were laughed at by Descartes and the Port Royalists.

P. 583.] LETTER XVI.—*Earl of Lindsey*, 2nd Earl of, ob. 1666. The information contained in this letter could have been got by H. from J. Marwood, *Law of Forest*, 1590 (C. H. F.).
Ricot, now Rycote, co. Oxford ; Q. Elizabeth was once prisoner there.
Grimsthorpe, co. Lincoln, four miles from Corby. H. is probably referring to Grimsthorpe Castle, near the hamlet.
Battel of Keinton, or Edgehill. As a matter of fact, the battle was fought nearer Keinton than Edgehill (see map in Gardiner, *Civil War*, i.).
Vocal Forest. The second title of the *Dendrologia.*

P. 584.] *Forest, Chase, Park.* Buckingham was Warden of the Royal Parks, Chases, and Forests. Arber, *Eng. Garner*, iii. H. gives a list of the various royal forests, &c., in his *Precedency of Kings*, 72-3. *Cf.* too Oldys, 546.
Swanmote Court. To be held in a Forest thrice a year by the Verderers, according to the charter of the Forest. Derived from "Swain," according to Cowel, *Interpreter*, s.v.
Liber Rufus. Now being edited by Mr. H. Hall of the Record Office.
great Meadow. Runnymede.

P. 585.] LETTER XVII.—*Mr. E. Field*, son of Bp. Field, on whom see 230. *one of Aristotle*, also referred to *Germ. Diet*, 53.

P. 586.] *great country.* Lord Mansfield's celebrated judgment was thus clearly judge-made law.
Bodin. A quotation from his *De Republica.*
Three Queen-Mothers, Catharine de Medici, Marie de Medici, and Anne of Austria.

LETTER XVIII.—*Dowager Countess of Sunderland.* See on 252.
Venice Looking-glass, "or a letter written by Card. Barberini." Published under that title by H. in 1648. See Bibl. List, No. 24.

P. 587.] LETTER XIX.—*Earl of Clare.* John Holles twelfth Earl, died 1665. This letter was prefixed to H.'s edition of Cotgrave's French and English Dictionary, 1650. (Bibl. List., No. 34.)
come frequently. Cæsar B. G. vi. 13. On Cæsar and Tacitus' statements, see *supra* on p. 474.
the county was called Wallia. This is wrong according to Prof. Rhys, Wales, Walloon, and Welschland (for Italy) are etymologically connected, being all

all Teutonic expressions for "stranger," but they are not connected with Gallia, though possibly with the Volcæ, an extensive tribe of early Gauls.

P. 589.] *tied to Gallia.* See *supra,* p. 780.
Pausanias saith. The geographer, but I doubt if H. got his knowledge first-hand. Prof. Rhys has looked up the passage for me, Book x. c. 19, and reports it accurate. " Howell is quite right ; the Welsh word is *march,* which is our poetry word for a ' horse ' and our every-day word for a ' stallion.' "
pure British. H.'s examples are unfortunate—*airain* from *æs, havre* from Teut. *hafen, putaine* is common Romance, *prou* is an interjection.
Baragouin may possibly be Celtic, but is not French but recognised to be Breton.

P. 590.] *Emblema.* The story is in Suetonius, *Tiberius,* 71, but Howell has confused it, as the Emperor objected to the word ἔμβλημα in a decree of the Senate.
Monopolium. Tiberius apologised for using the word. Suetonius, *l.c.,* (Dr. Gow). ·

P. 592.] *Gentlewoman.* Marie de France, on whom see my *Æsop,* i., where the same lines are quoted in Moll's text. H. got them doubtless from Pasquiere's *Reserches de la langue française,* ed. 1643, p. 675.
Geoffrey de Villardouin, the historian of the fifth Crusade (1167-1213).
Maratre, Paratre, Filatre, merely *mère, père, fils,* with the termination *-aster* instead of the prefix *belle* or *beau.*
crank is used for merry, but the meaning "bent" will cover both derivatives.
cocu, pleiger, Abry. H. is fairly correct about these.

P. 594.] *Beffroy.* Littré knows nothing of this etymology of H.'s, but derives it from Germ. *Berg-fried.*
Lupi illum. Virg. *Ecl.* ix. 54. cf. Browne, *Vulg. Errors,* III. c. vii.
Anglois. Littré confirms H. and gives an example from Marot.

P. 595.] *true sense.* Quite imaginary. It is the past participle of *honnir,* derived from Germ. *höhnen,* to mock (Littré). The proper spelling is *honni.*
bewray'd is used in this sense in Florio's *Montaigne,* ed. Morley.

P. 596.] *Mareshal.* It is just possible that the word may come from the Celtic word for horse, *march,* mentioned by H. above, see on p. 589, and Prof. Rhys' remarks there.
Majesty. Littré quotes " Votre Majesté " being used of a dean as late as the fourteenth century.
divers Dialects. A fairly accurate and full account.
Symmachus. Q. Aurelius (fl. 382), almost the last pagan Pontifex of Rome.

P. 597.] LETTER XX.—*Dr. Weames.* Only known to me as the father of Miss Weames.

P. 598.] *Mrs. A. W[eames],* who published *A Continuation of Sir P. Sidney's Arcadia* in 1651.

LETTER XXI.—*Lady M. Cary.* Referred to, Nichols, i. 173, 177. This letter is quoted in full, Nimmo's *British Letter Writers,* p. 315.

P. 599.]

**P. 599.] LETTER XXII.—*Lord Bishop of Ro*[chester], John Warner, who held the See from 1637 to 1666.
Si fractus illabatur orbis. Hor. Od.
Sir J. Sackvil. A relation of the Earl of Dorset.

**P. 600.] LETTER XXIII.—*Sir W. Mason.* Was knighted 28 March 1645 (Metcalfe).
Second part, which appeared in 1644 (Bibl. Hist., ed. 11).

**P. 601.] *Cardonian.* " Cardonia, Scotland, so-called from 'Cardonas, a thistle.'" Key to *Dodona's Grove.*
Classican, not given in the Key.
Druina. " England, from a Greek word which signifieth an 'Oke.'" Key to *Dodona's Grove.*
Basilean, member of the King's party.
Arborical, a reference, of course, to the allegory in which trees are the characters. H. had a Biblical precedent in Jotham's fable, Jud. ix.
Vatinius, Publius, a creature of Julius Cæsar's, against whom there is a speech of Cicero's extant.

**P. 602.] LETTER XXIV.—*Countess Rivers*, wife of Viscount Savage, was created Countess Rivers for life, 21 April 1641. She died in 1650.

**P. 603.] 2 *Feb.* A discrepancy with the date of the following letter.

LETTER XXV.—*John Lord Sa*[vage], grandson of Lord Rivers, and one of H.'s old pupils. This must have been written on the death of Earl Rivers in 1639.
10 *Dec.* Scarcely agrees with date of preceding letter.

LETTER XXVI.—*J. Wilson*, possibly the I. W. of previous letters *supra*, pp. 439, 495, if so he would be of Gray's Inn. The reference, however, to " your Town " shows that he was not a Londoner at anyrate at the time of H.'s writing. This letter is quoted in Nimmo's *British Letter Writers*, p. 22.

**P. 604.] LETTER XXVII.—*Sir E. S*[pencer], as on p. 547, where see.

**P. 605.] *Poet-Laureat Skelton.* John Skelton (1460–1529), Poet Laureat to Henry VIII., whose *Workes*, ed. 1568, H. had been clearly seeking for on behalf of Sir E. Spencer.
skulking in Duck-lane, now Duke Street, West Smithfield, probably, from H.'s reference, a kind of Holywell Street of the period, where second-hand books could be picked up. *Cf.* Pepys, 13th April 1668, " To Duck-lane, and there kissed bookseller's wife and bought *Legend.*"
Salve plus decies. Printed on the reverse of the title-page of Skelton's *Workes*, ed. 1568. See Dyce's edition, i. 177.

LETTER XXVIII.—*R. Davis.* Clearly married to some female relative of H., and so another cousin ! Can scarcely be R. Davies of Gwysaney, co. Flint (1616–66), who defended Gwysaney against Parliamentarians.
Helvetian, probably identical with the long German mile = 5·743 Eng. miles.

P. 606.]

P. 606.] *Lemster's Ore.* Drayton says in his *Polyolbion*, Song vii.—

" Where lives the man so dull, on Britain's farthest shore,
To whom did never sound the name of Lemster Ore?"

and goes on to explain that it rivals the silkworm's web for smallness. It was merely a cant phrase for the wool of Leominster, Lempter, or Lemster, co. Hereford. Defoe also used the phrase, Mr. Firth informs me.
art of making cheese. This is confirmed to some extent by the fact that the word itself is derived from the Latin ; but it is doubtful whether the Welsh *caws* is not independent.

LETTER XXIX.—*W. Roberts.* Another letter to him, 487. Perhaps to be identified with the W. Roberts who afterwards became Bishop of Bangor.

P. 607.] *Aerians.* So named after Aerius of the fourth century, who denied the superiority of bishops over presbyters, &c. Neander *Ch. Hist.* iii. 461-3. *Chrysostom* held at one time views very similar, (*Hom. ix. on Tim.*). *Epiphanius.* Panar. hær. xv. the chief authority on Aerius.

P. 608.] LETTER XXX.—*Howel Gwyn.* Probably a brother of T. and R. Gwin, to whom H. writes, *supra*, pp. 170, 216.
Herbert's Travels, p. 216, where the Welsh and English are given. Prof. Rhys informs me that the English version is very free, and the Welsh text very impure.
many authors. In the Pref. to his Welsh Proverbs H. refers to Hakluyt, who briefly notices the tradition, iii. p. 1.
creek called Gyndwor. Herbert, *l. c.*

P. 609.] *Bertrane d'Argentre* (1519-90), author of *Histoire de Bretagne*, whence the ensuing information is taken. Hoel V. was Duke of Bretagne, 1066.

LETTER XXXI.—*W. Price.* Probably related to C. and J. Price, H.'s cousins, to whom there are several letters.

P. 611.] LETTER XXXII.—*Sir K. D[igby].*
Thirty years servant. H. met Sir Kenelm first in Spain, 1623.

LETTER XXXIII.—*R. Lee.* Probably related to H.'s landlord lawyer Lee in Fetter Lane. See on p. 664.
Deeds are men. Cf. *supra*, on p. 270.

P. 613.] LETTER XXXIV.—*Sir J. Tho[mas]* probably, but the name is not in Metcalfe's *Book of Knights*.
late History. A. Wilson, *History of England, being the Life and Death of King James the First.* Lond., 1653.

P. 614.] 1621. H.'s letter professing to relate the circumstance, as a contemporary witness, is dated 1625 (*supra*, p. 223). The real date is June 1624 (*Fairfax Corr.* i. p. liii.).
Peregrin Fairfax. An account of his death, drawn up by his brother, Sir Ferdinando, is given in the *Fairfax Correspondence*, i. pp. liii.-vi.

P. 615.] *Tho. Webb.* Probably a son of E. Webbe, chief master-gunner of France ; he was the great friend of P. Fairfax's, and a letter from him on this affair is in the *Fairfax Corr.* liv.

Mr.

Mr. Hicks, was a scrivener's son (*Fairfax Corr. l.c.*), and became a knight. H. refers to him and this exploit in *Lust. Lud.* 58, as " *Mr.* (now *Sir*) Ellis Hicks."
Died of a fever. A mistake ; he died of his wounds at Montauban, *Fairfax Corr.* i. p. lii.

P. 616.] *Sir Ferdinando Fairfax.* Brother of Peregrine, and frequently mentioned (*e.g.* Gard. x. 200).

LETTER XXXV.—*Mr. Lewis.* Perhaps a relation of the Lewis who succoured H. at Lyons, *supra*, p. 95.

P. 617.] *poor Paul's.* See *supra*, 255.
touching Judaism. Mr. L. Wolf has shown that there existed in London a congregation of crypto-Jews long before Manasseh ben Israel thought of coming over. See his *Resettlement of the Jews in England*, 1888.
P. 618.] *Sir T. Williams.* Sir Trevor, mentioned by Carlyle, *Crom.* ii. 7–8.

LETTER XXXVI.—*J. Anderson.* Probably a relative of Sir H. Anderson who was dismissed the Long Parl. for royalism, Carlyle's *List of Members* in Cromwell, vol. iii.
Roman Church. These sentiments do H. honour, but Mr. Firth thinks they are but an echo of the *Religio Medici.*

P. 619.] *Uniformity.* Mr. Kepling's Mulvaney claims this for his church, that wherever he may die the same service will be said over him.

P. 622.] *Malignants.* A term that arose in connection with the Grand Remonstrance (C.H.F.). *Cf.* the long discussion on the term in T. Forde, *Fam. Lett.* pp. 22–5, and Prynne *infra*, p. 680.

P. 623.] LETTER XXXVII.—*Dr. Harvey* (1578–1658), the great discoverer of the true theory of the circulation of the blood (D. N. B.).
St. Lawrence Poultney, where Harvey then resided, perhaps to be near Gresham Cottage.
Dodona's Grove, which appeared 1640, the second part in 1650 (B. L. No. 35).

P. 624.] LETTER XXXVIII.—*R. Bowyer*, a relation of the T. Bowyer of old days, perhaps the Dr. Bowyer of *Fairfax Corr.* ii. 37.
new Act. Scobel, *Acts*, p. 236, 1653, c. vi. It was passed by Barebones' Parliament. See Masson, *Milton* (C.H.F.). Dorothy Osborne has a reference to it in her *Letters*, p. 147. The Act was expunged from the Statute Book at the Restoration : there is a draft of it in *Somers Tracts.* St. John C. J. thus married his daughter (Campbell i. 477). Burton gives the debates on it, *Diary* ii. 38, 39, 44, 67–74, 75, 77, 337, 338.

P. 625.] *Barebone's shop.* The celebrated Praise-God Barebones, whose leather shop was in Fleet Street, at the corner of Fetter Lane (Gard. x. 105), and therefore near Howell's own lodgings. See on p. 664.

LETTER XXXIX.—*J. B.* Probably James Bonnell, to whom H. presented a copy of his *Londinopolis*, with an inscription "For his very worthy friend, Mr. James Bonnell, 5 Nonas Junii 1657" (*Welshmam*, May 2, 1891). There is a letter to his father, Sam. Bonnell *infra*, p. 637.

P. 626.]

P. 626.] *Phormio*, a Peripatetic of Ephesus, only known from this story as told by Cicero (*De Orat.* ii. 18). Hannibal's opinion of him was that he was the greatest old blockhead he had ever seen! The story is referred to *supra*, 527.

P. 627.] LETTER XL.—*Major Walker.* He was not one of the Majors-General of whom there is a list in Carlyle, *Cromwell.* Probably a relative of Sir E. Walker, to whom a letter in Supplement, *infra*, p. 664. *Gildas saith.* H. gets this from Usher. *Primordia*, 442. *Capt. Miller.* Perhaps a relation of Lady Miller, *supra*, p. 419.

LETTER XLI.—*T. C.* Query T. Carew, who is referred to as meeting H. at supper at Ben Jonson's (*supra*, p. 403). This letter is quoted by J. Taylor, *Eccentric Letters*, 1824, p. 57. If authentic and addressed to Carew, it must have been in H.'s hands since before 1639, when Carew died. It might also be T. Carey, brother of the Earl of Monmouth, whom H. mentions *supra*, 193; Wood says (*Fasti*, i. 352) he turned out "a most ingenious poet." He died in 1648, so this identification implies a long period (seven years) between the writing and the publication of this letter. *Metheglin.* See on 451.

P. 628.] LETTER XLII.—*Sir E. S*[pencer]. See on p. 547.

P. 629.] LETTER XLIII.—*Lady Sibylla Brown.* Probably wife of Sir J. Brown, to whom there are also letters, pp. 409, 415. *Sherborn.* Probably the Lodge, as the Castle had been taken in 1645 and demolished. *Casaubon* Isaac (1559–1614), well known in England where he died. *Urganda.* A fairy who appears in the *Amadis de Gaul.* *Lady of the Lake.* Vivien is so-called in the *Morte D'Arthur.*

P. 630.] *The Sibyl.* H. could have got his erudition from the Paris edition of the *Oracula Sibyllina*, the introduction to which gives the properties of the traditional Sibylls, but he merely transcribes what is contained in Sandys, *Travels*, pp. 221–3. He used Sandys very much in making up his *Letters.*

P. 633.] *Enoch Evans*, of Shadwell, pa. Chenne, co. Shropshire, was a matricide and fratricide, and this was attributed by some (*e.g.*, Studley in *Looking Glass of Schism*, 1634) to his Dissent; by others (*e.g.*, R. More in *True Relation of the Murders*) to insanity. The murders are referred to by Brereton, *Travels* (Chet. Soc.), p. 187. Evans' confession is contained in *S.P.*, 15 Aug. 1633. *Marquis of Montrose* (1613–50), was hanged at Edinburgh. H. conveniently forgets the hanging, drawing, and quartering of the English law.

P. 634.] *young King.* Charles II.

LETTER XLIV.—*Sir L. D*[ives]. See p. 428.

P. 635.] *Jett should draw.* Solinus and Priscian noticed the electrical attraction of gagates (jet) found in Britain. Attention had been directed anew to the fact by Gilbert, the founder of electricity. *Cf.* Guillemin, *Electricity and Magnetism*, 139 n.

Sympathetic

Sympathetic powders, or weapon salves. See on p. 419.
German Diet. H.'s book of that name, published in 1653 (B. L., No. 43).
T. B., query T. Bowyer.
History of Naples. H.'s *Parthenopœa* appeared 1654 (B. L., No. 48).

LETTER XLV.—*Sir E. S*[pencer]. See on p. 547.

P. 637.] *Microcosm.* See on p. 72.
Pythagoras. The same confusion with Socrates, see on p. 530. There is
nothing to this effect in Stanley's *Hist. of Philosophy,* part i. of which deals
with Pythagoras, and may have been read by H. as it appeared in 1655 and
was published by Moseley, H.'s publisher..

LETTER XLVI.—*Sam. Bon*[nel]. "A wealthy man and stout royalist,"
says D.N.B. s.v. Bonnel, James. He had been in Italy, at Leghorn and
Genoa, hence his knowledge of Italian.

P. 638.] *Italian Manuscripts.* Giraffi's account of Masaniello's insurrection,
which H. translated (B. L., Nos. 37, 42).

LETTER XLVII.—*W. Sands.* In *S.P.* 1661-2, there is a petition of a W.
Sandys, who may be the same.
Power and Wealth. A remarkable testimony of the influence of Cromwell
abroad.
the sword. H. had written on "the Sway of the Sword" (Bibl. List No. 603).

P. 639.] *Don Rodrigo.* Referred to previously, p. 196.

LETTER XLVIII.—*E. of S*[underland]. See on p. 251.
Pope sick. Innocent X., who died 1655, the year of publication of Part iv. of
the *Letters.*
Donna Olympia Maldalchina, sister-in-law of the Pope. On her influence
with him, see Ranke, *Popes,* ii. 323 *seq.*

P. 640.] *Dr. B.* Can this be the Dr. B. of the four letters on religion,
supra, pp. 383 *seq.*
Huomo de tre Pele. Curiously enough Bismarck was always a *huomo de tre
pele* for the German caricaturists of his late years, but his three hairs were
on his scalp.
Lustra Ludovici. H.'s Annals of the reign of Louis XIII., which appeared
in 1646 (B. L., No. 16); no second edition ever made its appearance.
Survey of Venice. H.'s *S.P.Q.V.* "a Survey of the Signoire of Venice," 1651
(Bibl. List No. 38).

P. 641.] LETTER XLIX.—*Earl Rivers.* Probably T. Savage, the sixth Earl
to come to the title in 1654.
Gallery of Ladies. "The Gallery of Heroique Woemen" by John Pawlet,
Marq. of Winchester (ob. 1673). He was married to Lady Jane Savage,
one of H.'s old pupils (*supra,* p. 227). Aubrey came across a copy of the
"Gallery" and wrote about it to Wood (*Athenæ,* iii. 1005 and *n.*).

P. 642.] *Elegy.* Printed separately under the curious title *Ah ! Ha ! Thalamus,
Tumulus* (Bibl. List, No. 45).
E. of Dorset. See *supra* on p. 511.

P. 644.]

P. 644.] LETTER L.—*T. Harris.* Probably a relative or (even owing to a misprint) identical with the J. Harris of 244. This one was evidently an old friend who had met H. "abroad under many Meridians."

P. 645.] *Sympathetic Powder* of Sir Kenelm Digby. It was first tried on H. See Suppt. II. No. xxii. and on p. 419.
Zaphyrian Salt. I have not met with this name for it.
Dr. Highmore. Nathaniel, M.D. (1613–85) one of the earliest English students of embryology and author of a *History of Generation*, 1651, in which he discusses the powder of sympathy (D.N.B.).

P. 647.] *Doxological Chronogram.* See J. Hilton, *Chronograms*, 1882, p. 10. Mr. Hilton remarks that H. "gives a very bad excuse for a very bad chronogram." The MDLLLLCCVVVVVII. of the inscription make up exactly 1927. *Cf.* the chronogram in title-page of H.'s *Winter's Dreame* (Bibl. List, No. 28).

SUPPLEMENTS.

It will be sufficient, in the annotations on the documents contained in these Supplements, if the points in which they illustrate the *Letters* are touched upon to the exclusion of others. In many cases even these are obvious, and nothing need be said.

P. 649.] DOCUMENT I.—*Lord Conway.* See on p. 240. H. must have begun to act as "intelligencer" or spy when this letter was written.
Sr. Charles Cornwallyes. See on p. 151. H. was acquainted later with Lady C.
James Wadesworth. Referred to *supra*, p. 184.

P. 650.] Doc. II.—*Earl of Sunderland.* See on p. 251.

Doc. III.—*Mr. Radcliff*, after Sir George, being knighted by Strafford at Dublin 25 July 1633 (*cf.* life in Lloyd, *State Worthies*, pp. 148 seq., and Evelyn, 5 Oct. 1649). This confirms H.'s statement on p. 275, that he had sold his reversion to Radcliff.

P. 651.] Doc. IV.—*Legatio.* H. himself refers to this document in his letter to Lord Leicester, *supra*, p. 322 : "a compleat Diary of your own late Legation."
6° *Decembris.* H. says 25th July, *supra*, 290. Is it possible that the further extension was a later grant?
P. Burlemachi. See on p. 281.
Roffam, Rochester.
Margetts. The ordinary spelling of Margate. See Pennington's Log in Suppt. II.
Convertina. See the correspondence between H. and Pennington in Suppt. II. The *Convertine* had been to Guinea with Raleigh, *cf. supra*, p. 24.

P. 652.] *Princeps Fredericus* afterwards succeeded his father as Frederick III. *orationem.* An exactly similar account is given by H. on p. 294.
paginis subsequentibus. This referred to the remainder of the diary and accounts in the Bodleian MS. There are also several papers in Latin in H.'s handwriting at the Record Office (State Papers, Foreign, Denmark Bundle 9).

P. 653.] *Robertum Anstruther*, · See on p. 286.

Doc.

Doc. V.—*Sir F. Windebank.* See on p. 321. Here we have a specimen of H.'s talents as intelligencer.
taken Leipsic. Captured by the Imperialists August 1633. News travelled quickly, to judge by the date of this letter.

P. **654.**] *Alderman Freemans,* was Lord Mayor of London. *Cf.* Stow, *Strype,* v. 153.
2 *English ships,* the *Hector* and the *William and Ralph* (*S.P.,* 23 Aug. 1633). *Lo: denbigh.* See on p. 151.
ye great Mogor. See note on p. 7.
28 *Aug.* From the reference in *S.P.* above it would seem that part at least of H.'s news was five days stale.

P. **655.**] Doc. VI.—*Dr. T. Howell,* afterwards the Bishop. See on p. 25. *humble servant.* Very much so. The whole letter is a revelation of a subservient sneak. No wonder he got on compared with his volatile brother. *Walbrooke.* Dr. H. was Rector of St. Stephen's, Walbrook.

P. **656.**] Doc. VII.—*Lord Deputy.* Strafford, among whose correspondence this, with some ten others of the same kind from H., occurs (Straff. *Letters,* i. 376, 410, 422, 429, 437, 445, 461, 474, 488, 503, 516, 522, ranging from 5 March 1634 to 15 March 1635.) The other letters to Strafford *supra* 311, 327 are very much in the same scrappy style.
Prince Palatine. This is referred to in the *Letters, supra,* p. 320.
Sir John Pennington. See on p. 289. He was an old friend of H.'s.
Match with Poland, between the King of Poland and Prince Palatine's sister. See on p. 326.
Ban and Arriere Ban, i.e. the feudal militia and reserve.

P. **657.**] *Lord Savage.* Formerly Sir Thomas, and H.'s very good friend.
The business, referred to before in Straff. *Letters,* i. 337.

Doc. VIII.—*Appointment.* This confirmation of H.'s claim to rank as one of the Clerks of Privy Council I owe to the courtesy of Sir C. Lenox Peel, who kindly permitted me to search the Minutes of the Privy Council.
Clerk of Council in Extraordinary. See H.'s own account later, p. 667, "the case truly stated."

P. **658.**] Doc. IX.—*Sir J. C.* Probably Sir James Crofts, to whom so many of the letters are addressed. See on p. 22.

P. **659.**] Doc. X.—*lyeth at the Cape of Good Hope.* A favourite expression of H.'s. See on p. 218.
Benoni. A reference to Gen. xxxvii. 18.

Doc. XI.—*James Duke of York,* afterwards James II. He was about fourteen years old at the time.
five and fifty months. This would bring us back to October 1642, near enough for such an inaccurate person as H.

P. **660.**] Doc. XII.—*John Selden,* the great scholar (1584-1654). This letter

letter probably accompanied the book, now in the Bodleian, the inscription on which is given in Suppt. II. No. xxxii. It is dated 1652.
Ignorance beyond Barbarism. P. Fisher uses this expression in his encomium on H. ("Testimonia" *supra*, p. xv.) which makes it probable that it was put in his mouth by H. himself.

P. **661.**] Doc. XIII.—*Authorities of Mr. Selden.* This accounts for the preceding letter to Selden, which was more business-like than appears on the surface.
if the State. H. was thus evidently prepared to serve under the Common-wealth. In fact his translation of the case of Anthony Ascham was done for the Council of State (See Bibl. List, No. 26).

Doc. XIV.—*Judge Rumsey,* was an old college chum of H.'s. See Introd., p. xxvi.

P. **662.**] *Instrument in Munster.* The peace of Westphalia. See on p. 437.
Coffee. Of the introduction of coffee into England there are many accounts, two by Anthony à Wood, *Life,* ed. Bliss, 1848, pp. 48, 60 ("This year [1650] Jacob, a Jew, opened a coffey-house," "Cirques Jobson [1654], Jew and Jacobite, sold coffey in Oxon"). One by Evelyn, *Diary,* ed. Forster i. 10 ("one Nathaniel Conopios out of Greece . . . was the first I ever saw drink coffee [1637]"); another in Anderson's *Hist. of Commerce,* 1652 ("Mr. Edwards' Greek servant Pasqua"), and still another in Aubrey's account of Sir H. Blount ("first coffee house was set up by Bowman, coachman to Mr. Hodges, in or about the year 1652"), *cf.* 1 *N. and Q.* i. 26, 139, 314.
Shastres, or holy wisdom of the Hindoos, the four Shastras or sacred books. *Cf.* Yule, *Hobson-Jobson,* s. v.

P. **663.**] *worthy gentleman, Mr. Mudiford* afterward Sir James : he thus makes the sixth claimant for the honour. Mr. Lecky has some interesting pages on the important social influence of the introduction of hot drinks into W. Europe, *Hist. Ration.* ii. 336 seq.
Concerning Tobacco. Cf. supra p. 521.

P. **664.**] Doc. XV.—*Sir Edward Walker* (d. 1677), had been Secretary at War to Charles I., and accompanied Charles II. in exile.
late Dissolution, by Monk.
Monk professeth. This must have been just on the eve of the declaration in favour of Charles II.
stylo loci. "Year X. of the Republic," which such an ardent Royalist as H. cannot bring himself to use.
Mr. Lee, whose widow is mentioned by H. in his will.
Pye Inn, i.e. Magpie Inn in Fetter Lane on right hand side near Holborn.

P. **665.**] Doc. XVI.—*Many a Shrew. Cf.* with this whole letter the one at the end of Bk. I.
Horse in Smithfield. From F. Moryson, *Itin.* III. ii. 53.
one hair of a woman. Cf. supra p. 378.

P. **667.**] Doc. XVII.—*Court was at York.* Not true ; the event occurred just a couple of days after the raising of the King's standard at Nottingham.

P. **668.**] *Sir Tho. Mewtis,* who had been Bacon's secretary.
Sir R. Brown. Scarcely the R. B. of the *Letters.* See on p. 78.

Doc.

Doc. XIX.—*Lord Clarendon.* The great Edward Hyde.

P. 669.] *Great Dictionary.* The *Lexicon Tetraglotton. dedicated to the King.* The dedicated copy is now in the British Museum.

Doc. XXI.— *Will.* Drawn up a few weeks before death.
Parish of St. Andrews. Probably near the Pye Inn, as six years before.
large black Marble. Still extant in the triforium of the Temple Church. See the cut of it in Introd. p. xlix.
Howel Howel. H.'s eldest brother mentioned in *S.P.*, 3 Sep. 1640, as escheator of co. Carmarthen, and dating from Brin-a-Minin, probably the Bryn mentioned *supra*, p. 218.
Elizabeth Banister. Daughter of the Bishop and wife of James Bannister. See Pedigree.
Arthur Howell. Another son of the Bishop.

P. 670.] *Latin Epitaph.* Reproduced in the cut, Introd. p. xlix.
Roberta Ap-rice. I take this to be different from the Rebecca Howell who married John Price.
Nephew George. Son of the Bishop.
Thirty pounds in a white bag. A touch of nature in the weary man of letters, who thinks of his monument more than of aught else.
Henry Howell. Also a son of Bishop T. Howell, who wrote the letter contained above No. vi. p. 655. Yet the chief names mentioned in the Will, including that of the executor, are those of the Bishop's children. James was a better Christian than his brother.

P. 673.] Doc. XXII.—This Discourse was published both in French and in English during H.'s lifetime, which to some extent vouches for the authenticity of the anecdote. Where and when to place the incident is more difficult. See Introd., p. xxxv.
Monsieur Baudoin (1588–1650), a very voluminous translator from classical and modern languages.
at Court. This settles that the incident could not have been in Spain, as Mr. Lee suggests (D.N.B. *s.v.* Howell), and likewise that it could not have been in King James's reign, as I once thought. This fixes the date between 1625 and 1628.
fighting a duel. There can be little doubt that Digby is referring to the same duel mentioned by Howell, *supra*, p. 284. Now this occurred when Cottington was in Spain as Ambassador after Buckingham's death, 1629 *seq.*, and Sir Kenelm only returned from his Scanderoon voyage February 2, 1629. Hence it is impossible that Buckingham could have been concerned in this first use of the sympathetic powder. For once H. is a superior authority.

P. 674.] *Powder of vitriol.* Digby's specific seems to have been nothing more: one can quite understand his only using it on wounds from a distance.

P. 675.] Doc. XXIII.—*Secretary Nicholas.* See on p. 354.
Capt. Pennington. See on p. 289 and two following letters.
Convertine. See the Latin account, *supra*, p. 651.
Whelps. See on p. 255.

                                                                        Doc.

Doc. XXIV.—*Capt. Pennington.* See on p. 289.
Elsinore, i.e., the intention was to go right round to the Sound and travel to Copenhagen. The next letter declares a change of intention, and the voyage is only as far as Hamburg.

Doc. XXV.—*Capt. Pennington.* See on p. 289.
Hamborough, now spelt Hamburg.

Doc. XXVI.—*Capt. Pennington.* As before.
reason of the flatts. Pennington had probably reported that he could not lie off Tilbury comfortably.
my last except one. Probably a letter explaining the change from Yarmouth to Tilbury as the chosen port of embarkation.

Doc. XXVII.—*Admiral Pennington's Log.* Inserted here as confirming in every particular the details given by H. of his voyage to Hamburg and back. The Embassy to Denmark is the point in which we can check H. most completely, and on the whole he comes out triumphant.
Broomsbottle. Brunsbüttel, just at the mouth of the Elbe, on the right-hand bank, and therefore belonging to Denmark before the loss of Schleswig-Holstein.
Luxtoad. Gluckstadt, farther down the Elbe, still on the right-hand bank, and half way between Brunsbüttel and Hamburg.

P. 679.] Doc. XXVIII.—*Sir John Coke,* Secretary of State. His papers, now in the possession of Earl Cowper, have been calendared by the Hist. MSS. Com.
Sir J. North. See on p. 54.
manuscript of mine. Probably the *Dodona's Grove,* which is certainly "a historical discourse couched under a disguise." A quotation from it given in *Some Sober Inspections* (B. L., No. 59) is dated 1638.

P. 680.] Doc. XXIX.—*be discharged.* The contrast between the fate of the two Howells is carried throughout the story of their lives.
Pleasure of the House. This cannot have been for debt, as Wood hints; there must have been some political motive at the root of it all.

Doc. XXX.—*Prynne* (1600-1669), one of the typical figures of the period, author of *Histriomastix* and a hundred other violent tirades. He roars against H. as mildly as any sucking dove.
Malignants. The term really arose during the time of the Grand Remonstrance.

P. 681.] *who had the perusal.* Probably Corbet. See on p. 356.
been in army, at Edgehill, according to Prynne. See next page.

P. 682.] *suppressed at the Press.* This is a new and rather important fact, as showing the weight attributed to H.'s utterances by the Parliamentarians.

Doc. XXXI.—*The Stationer.* Inserted as confirming my views as to the origin of the Letters. See Introd. p. lxxix.
Moseley, on him see Introd. p. xliii.

                                                                    Doc.

Doc. XXXII.—*Dedication.* This settles the dates of the two documents in Suppt. I., Nos. xii., xiii., as written in 1652.

Doc. XXXIII.—*Contemporary Notices.* Rather scanty, I fear, but there was no *Athenæum* in H.'s days. For a kind of continuance as regards the Letters, see the *Testimonia*, pp. xv.–xx.

P. 683.] *Sir W. Dugdale*, the great antiquary (1605–86). *Sir R. L'Estrange.* See on next page.

P. 684.] *Ye Rose*, probably at the corner of Thanet Place with a garden (Wheatley-Cunningham, iii. 172; Larwood, *Signboards*, 126). *F. Williams.* Perhaps a relative of Sir R. Williams, to whom there is a letter, p. 573.

Doc. XXXIV.—*L'Estrange*, Sir Roger (1616–1704), one of the earliest of English journalists, was Censor of the Press at this time. He was a reader of H.'s letters, and uses one of his anecdotes in his omnium gatherum of an *Æsop.* See *supra*, p. 345. *if he that wrote.* L'Estrange himself wrote the *Caveat.*

P. 685.] *wears a title.* "Some Sober Inspections." *another miserable paper.* The "Inspections."

Doc. XXXV.—*R. Loveday*, translator of Calprenede's romance "Cleopatra." *Mr. H.* I judge this to be Howell by the reference to Cotgrave, which he edited (B. L., No. 34).

P. 686.] *M.* Moseley, Howell's publisher. See Doc. xxxi.

Doc. XXXVI.—*T. Forde* (fl. 1660), author of various things, from plays to characters, which are enumerated in Mr. Lee's Life in D.N.B. s.v. His *Lusus Fortunæ* has a Latin poem signed J. H., which may be by Howell, as Mr. Lee suggests, but see next note. Forde makes much use of the *Epist. Hoel.* in his *Apophthegems*, bound up with the *Fam. Lett.* *J. H.* There are other letters in the same collection to J. H. on pp. 66, 69, 79; but the two former are to another than our hero, being addressed "honest Jack," and written in quite another strain. The letter to J. H. on p. 79 is to Howell.

Doc. XXXVII.—*Generall.* The title adopted was Historiographer Royal. *Artist this way.* This gives H.'s ideal as an historian (if Dr. Murray will allow me to use the heavy article).

P. 688.] *Sir H. Wootton.* See on p. 65. He was never historiographer, but Thoms' *Book of the Court*, p. 340, asserts that Henry VII.'s poet laureate was also historiographer royal. H.'s epitaph reads "primus in Anglia."

Doc. XXXVIII.—*Payne Fisher*, poet laureate to Cromwell. I fancy that he had little to do with these verses, which were probably Howell's own. *Mariduvensi.* This should settle the birthplace question in favour of Abernant, co. Carmarthen (Maridunum in Latin). *Montaccola.* This should give the name of H.'s birthplace: unfortunately it is unknown

unknown to Record searchers (it is not included, *e.g.*, in C. T. Martin, *Record Interpreter* list of Latin names of British localities) Mr. Martin suggests that the name must begin with *Pen*. It is equally likely to be *Bryn* which is also a hill or mount.

P. 689.] *Harlœus.* Referred to at our p. 19 as "a learned (tho' lashing) master."
Flacci. See on H.'s classical attainments, Introd. p. xxvi. It is likely that H. has made a "howler" here, and refers to the Æneid as "Flacci epos."
Sphistœo. Curious Latin for "Sophister." See on p. 34.
Socium. See Doc. xl.

P. 690.] *cognovit Iber.* A reference to the earlier Spanish voyage.
Borealis, the residence in York 1626-8.
Orator, the Danish Embassy.
Siculi. A further reference to the landing in Sicily. See on pp. 62, 63.
ter refers to three sessions, not three Parliaments.

P. 691.] *Vocales.* Here begins a selected list of H.'s works ingeniously characterised ; the footnotes of the original will give the clue.

P. 694.] *P. Piscator, i.e.,* Payne Fisher. See on p. 688.

Doc. XXXIX.—TABLE, *i.e.* list of persons to whom the letters are addressed. The list is by no means complete and may be supplemented by the names printed in Clarendon in the Index. They serve, however, very frequently to identify names only given by initials in the text. Names in brackets were added in the second edition, 1650.

P. 696.] Doc. XL.—HOWELL'S ELECTION. I owe this interesting confirmation of Howell's claim to be a Fellow of Jesus, to the present Vice-Principal of Jesus, through the kind intervention of Prof. Rhys. The curious point comes out that there were two James Howells elected on that day and that H. Penry, H.'s brother-in-law, was also elected at the same time.

QUERIES.

[It would, of course, be misleading to suggest that the following are the only points left unsettled in the preceding annotations. They merely represent those which, according to my plan, I should have liked to have found something about, but have failed. Lists of more elementary difficulties, all solved in the present edition, were given in *N. and Q.* xi. 475; 3 vii. 179; 5 vii. 148, xi. 407. But those were merely "pass" exams.]

1. What were the names indicated by the following initials— A. S. (206), E. D. (287), Sir E. B. (333), T. D. (378), F. C. (407), T. T. (420), Lady M. A. (448), T. C. (627)?

2. Who were the following, and where are they mentioned in contemporary records—Father Boniface (184), J. Harris (244), Mr. Gilpin (298), Mr. Pickhurst (337), C. Mor (377), W. Pawly (421), J. Meredith, Hodge Powell (427), Mr. Watts, T. Waters (573), Major Walker (627)?

3. Explain the meaning and etymology of the following words— *Gazull* (60), *consaorman* (66), *Quæ la vel Hipps* (256), *Otraqua, Tampoy, Chiffi, Mingol* (453, 454), *Yef.* (455)?

4. What great philosopher called mankind a "Molehill of ants" (43), and who wished to be blind to think the better (444)?

5. What Duke of Milan was poisoned by letter (73)?

6. Where were the Rammakins (36), Wanless Park (274)?

7. What King of Persia was elected for seeing the sun rise first (339)?

8. Where does Seneca say *Nihil est infelicius, &c.* (358), and *Nullum est majus malum, &c. (ib.)*?

9. Who were the authors of the following—*Quod divinitus contingit, &c.* (613), *Proh superi! quantum mortalia, &c.* (617), *Distinguas inter tempora, &c.* (619)?

10. Whence did Howell obtain his learning about drinks (II. lv. p. 453 *seq.*), and his alchemical knowledge (434)?

11. What was Lady Southwell's news from Utopia (260)?

12. When and why was Howell sent to Orleans (321) and Ruelle (352)?

INDEX.

—+—

NOMINUM, LOCORUM, RERUM, VERBORUM.

NAMES in **Clarendon** type refer to persons to whom Howell's *Letters* are addressed. Items in *italics* are rare, obsolete, peculiar or early uses of words: short explanations are added (in brackets) when necessary. Words in square brackets refer to matters only referred to, not given, in the text, or occur only in the Introduction and Notes. Where fuller information is given in the notes an italic *n* is added to the number of the page in the text. Numbers in square brackets refer to statements in the Supplements, pp. 649–98.

Aaron's Tribe, Jew of, 29*n*.
A., Lady M., 446*n*.
Abbot, Archbishop, accidental homicide by, 153*n*.
Abdula (Mahommedan term for Christian), 392*n*.
Abraham's Oak seen by Josephus, 385*n*.
abroad, going, 443*n*.
Abyssinians, *see* Habassins.
Academy, French, 352*n*, 510*n*.
accostable (sociable), 403.
achaques, 504.
a clock (o'clock), 164.
Acquests (conquests), 506.
Act (for degree) kept by presenting stag, 266*n*.
Act of faith (*auto da fé*), 292.
Action at a distance, 419.
Adam, Master Th., letter to, 375*n*.
Adamites, 384, 607.
Admiral, Lord High, Buckingham appointed, 112*n*; recommended to resign, 233.
Adrian IV., Pope, saying of, 359*n*, 527.
Adriatic, Doge marries the, 70*n*.
adulted (mature), 334.
adust (dry), 571.
adventitious, 472.
Adversity tries friendship, 366.
Aerians, 505, 607*n*.
Aetna described, 8, 63; flowers on, 558.

Affidavit about domicile, 280.
African Jews, 315*n*, 385; languages, 476.
After-birth alive, 114.
Aga, Capi, 178.
Agaric (mushroom), a remedy for phlegm [662*n*].
Agent, moving, in Italy, J. H. offered post of, 239; salary, 241*n*.
Agisters (royal forester), 584.
Agglutination, 256.
Agnomination (alliteration) common to Tuscan & Welsh, 89*n*.
Air, influence of, on glass making, 66; men seen in, 351*n*; regions of, 443.
Alcala, strange occurrence at, 205.
Alcoran, 314*n*, 378*n*, 392*n*, 477, 607; sole guide to Mahometans, 392; allows eight wives, 569*n*.
Ale, medical virtues of, 137, 451.
Aleppo merchants, 281*n*; pigeons sent from, to Alexandria, 442.
Alexander the Great, charter to the Slavs, 464.
Alexandria called Scanderoon, 442; pigeons sent to, 442.
Alfange (alfaqi ?), 392*n*.
Alford, Sir W., 269*n*.
Alforjas, 211*n*.
Algier, pirates capture Spanish ships, 61; capture Mr. Gresley, 152; Capt. Porter returns from, 110; English slaves at, released, 280.
Alguazil (Spanish watchman), 200.

809

St. George's Mount at Geneva, 91.
St. James' Monastery, Prince Charles
visits.
St. James', Mansfelt at, 214.
St. John, Sir W., letter to, 81*n*.
St. John's, Cambridge, J. Hall at,
432.
St. John's, Oxford, J. P. at, 412.
St. John's Pool, Oxford, 412*n*.
St. Lawrence, Poultry, 623*n*.
St. L., Madame, anecdote of, 379.
St. Louis, anecdote of, 96; born at
Poissy, 135.
St. Malo, English dogs at, 54.
St. Mark, Treasury of, 74.
St. Martin's Lane, J. H. at, [650].
St. Mary Port, 231*n*.
St. Oen, Church of, at Rouen, 41*n*.
St. Omer, J. H. not to visit, 22; W.
St. Geon at, 326.
St. Osith, Lord Darcy and Sir Jas.
Crofts at, 22*n*, 101, 105, 147; seat of
Earl Rivers, 109*n*.
St. Paul's, London, 542*n*. *See* Paul's,
St.
"St. Paul's Progress," 543, 544.
St. Quintin, battle of, 207*n*.
St. Thomas plundered by Raleigh,
24*n*, 482.
Salamanca, 16,000 students at, 199*n*.
Salary of moving agent, 241.
Salic Law, 586.
Salisbury, Earl of, saying of, 372.
Sallet, 90.
[Salmasius, xcviii.
Saloniche, churches at, 389.
Salt used as ballast, 350.
Salutiferous, [662].
Samaritans a Jewish sect, 315*n*, 385.
[Sambation, River, in India, 386*n*.
Sambenito, 292.
Samogitia, 396.
Sands, W., letter to, 638.
[Sandys, used by J. H., 62*n*, 66*n*,
385*n*, 452*n*, 467*n*.
Sanguine, 10*n*.
Sannazaro, Latin poem on Venice by,
79*n*; gets 100 zecchins a line, 80*n*.
Santon, 177.
Santo Thoma, 24*n*.
Sapphics by J. H., 70.
Sardinia, Viceroy of, seizes "Vine-
yard," 151; suit against, 154, 162,
167, 277, 284.
Satan, Tabernacle of, 486.
Sattin, 89.
Savage, Lady, 109*n*.

Savage, Lady Jane, letter to, 227*n*.
See Winchester, Marchioness of.
Savage, Lord, 105*n*; his sons, 145; a
Roman Catholic, 111.
Savage, Mr. John, letters to, 145*n*,
603. *See* Rivers, Earl.
Savage, Mr. Thomas, 146.
Savage, Sir Edward, letters to, 249*n*,
341, 366, 370; at Tower Hill, 341;
death of, 602*n*.
Savage, Sir Thomas, 105*n*, letters to,
132*n*, 137, 153, 164, 180, 207, 226.
See Rock Savage, Viscount.
Savage, Viscount, death of, 328,
[657].
Save-all, 599.
Savill, Sir John, 269*n*., 599.
Savoy, policy of Duke of, 94; claim
to Geneva, 97.
Saxen Weymar, success of, 331.
Sayings, 61, 90, 95, 119, 120, 128,
179, 305, 321, 347, 359, 407, 409,
410, 527, 621.
Sc., Mr. R., at York, letter to, 230*n*.
Scale (ladder), 58, 339*n*, 410.
Scaliger's views on Prester John, 390;
on lust, 570.
Scanderoon, name of Alexandria,
280*n*, 442.
Scarlet Island, 490.
Scholar, useless, 525, 526.
School-language, 22*n*, 422, 472.
Sciatica, [661].
Scientificallest, 530.
Scil, Mr., the stationer, 114*n*.
Sciolist, 610.
Sclavonia, 77*n*.
[Scoones, Mr. W. B., his opinion of
the letters, xix.
Scot, Sir Richard, 258*n*.
Scot free, 505*n*.
Scotick, 462.
"Scotland, People of," by J. H.,
lvi., xc.; recent notice, lvi.*n*.
Scots, Pasquil on, at Rome, 89; trade,
127*n*; soldiers of fortune return
from Sweden, 326; defeated, 540*n*.
[Scott, Sir W., uses Letters, cii.*n*, 24*n*.
Scout, 124*n*.
Scriffinia, 396*n*.
Scroop, Dowager-Lady, ill, 270*n*;
buried at Hunsdon, 274.
Scroop, Lady, 269*n*. *See* Sunderland,
Countess of.
Scroop, Lord, 242; letter to, 251.
See Sunderland, Earl of.
Scrue, 502, 574.

www.ingramcontent.com/pod-product-compliance
Lightning Source LLC
Chambersburg PA
CBHW052341110726
47901CB00005B/1313